A LIFE IN THE HILLS

Katharine Stewart was born in 1914 in Reading. Following the Second World War and after a spell running a hotel in Edinburgh she moved with her husband, Sam Stewart, and daughter Hilda, to the croft at Abriachan near Loch Ness, where she began her writing career with *A Croft in the Hills*. For many years she wrote a weekly column, *On the Croft* and *Country Diary*, for the *Scotsman*, as well as several other books on Highland life including those collected in this *Omnibus*. Later she trained as a teacher before, on the death of her husband, becoming the local postmistress at Abriachan. She died in 2013 and is survived by her daughter, Hilda.

A LIFE IN THE HILLS

The Katharine Stewart Omnibus

BIRLINN

This combined edition first published in 2018 by
Birlinn Ltd
West Newington House
10 Newington Road
Edinburgh
EH9 1QS
www.birlinn.co.uk

A Croft in the Hills was first published in 1960 by Oliver and Boyd
New editions published by Melven Press in 1979,
by Mercat Press in 1991 and by Birlinn Ltd in 2012
Text © Katharine Stewart 1960, 1979 and 2012
Illustrations copyright © Anne Shortreed 1960

A Garden in the Hills was first published in 1995 by Mercat Press
A new edition was published in 2012 by Birlinn Ltd
Text © Katharine Stewart 1995, 2012
Illustrations © Anne Shortreed 1995

A School in the Hills was first published in 1996 by Mercat Press
Text © Katharine Stewart 1996

The Post in the Hills was first published in 1997 by Mercat Press
Text © Katharine Stewart 1997

ISBN: 978 1 78027 507 9

British Library Cataloguing-in-Publication Data
A catalogue record for this book is available from the British
Library

Set in Bembo at Birlinn

Printed and bound in the UK by Clays Ltd, Elcograf S.p.A.

CONTENTS

A CROFT IN THE HILLS

A Garden in the Hills

A School in the Hills

THE POST IN THE HILLS

A CROFT IN THE HILLS

TO MY FAMILY

'All of you with little children . . . take them somehow into the country among green grass and yellow wheat—among trees—by hills and streams, if you wish their highest education, that of the heart and the soul, to be completed.'

Richard Jefferies

INTRODUCTION
to the First Edition

WHY, you may ask, record the simple fact that three people took to the hills and lived quiet lives under a wide sky, among the rock and heather, working with the crops and beasts they could manage to raise there, in order to feed and clothe themselves. There is certainly little room for dramatic highlights in this story of ours. But we heard the singing and we found the gold. And I believe that each small stand taken against the shrill wind of disenchantment which is blowing across the world has more positive human value than many of the assertions being made by science today.

Science says: 'Here is a stone. It weighs so much. It measures so much. It is so-and-so many years old.' But a man needs to discover that the stone is strong, so that he can stand on it, and cool, so that he can lay his head against it: that it is beautiful and can be fashioned as an ornament, or hard and can be built into his home.

How does he make these discoveries? With his own eyes, his own wits, his own imagination. His assessment of the stone includes a measuring of his own stature. And as his hand passes over the firm surface his brain is alert, his imagination lit. He is alive.

If the human being is to hold to his identity, he must, somehow or other, keep on making his own discoveries. The tragedy of today is that it is becoming increasingly difficult for him to do so. He is even in danger of becoming a back number, for the powers that would govern his life have found that the machine is, for competitive purposes, so much more efficient and reliable than he is.

When you have lived for a few years in the bare uplands, where life has been precarious from the start, you learn, first, not to panic. Then you are ready to love wholeheartedly what need no longer be feared. You become so deeply involved in the true drama of cherishing life itself that mere attitudes and the pursuit of possessions are discarded as absurd. You discover that under snow there is bread, the secret bread, that sustains.

Panic gone, you can plot a course with steady hand and eye. And, after all, human steadfastness is the only ultimate weapon fit to guarantee survival in a real sense.

That is why I thought it worthwhile to record the process by which three small human beings, completely re-enchanted with their world, found the strength to walk without fear among the astonishing beauty of its wilderness.

I should like to thank Mrs. Anne Shortreed for capturing so delightfully, in line, the spirit of life in the uplands. And my special thanks go to Mr. Neil Gunn, who gave the book his blessing.

KATHARINE STEWART

FOREWORD
to the First Edition
by
NEIL M. GUNN

The typescript of this adventure story reached me out of the blue—or very nearly, for the croft is about a thousand feet above Loch Ness: marginal land, hill-top farming, where on a February morning the blue may be vibrant with lark song or obscured by a snow blizzard. This is the oldest of all Highland adventures and will be the last. It is heartening and heart-breaking. Why do people go on thinking they can make a living out of a hill croft? In particular, what drives strangers, not bred in crofting traditions, to make the attempt? This is the story of such an attempt, with all the questions answered, and it is told so well that I find it absorbing.

For the author and her husband see everything with new eyes. They meet their problems as they arise, and they arise daily. Their capacity for work is all but inexhaustible. If I hesitate to use the word heroic it is because there are no heroics in this human record; only day-to-day doings, the facts of life, but, again, facts that spread over into many dimensions, the extra dimensions that give the book its unusual quality, its brightness and its wisdom. For the attitude to life is positive; it somehow contrives to survive the frustrations; and that today is rare. Often, too, this is seen in coloured threads running through the main texture, as in the growing up of their child to school age and her responses to the myriad influences of the natural scene; or in the spontaneous help given by, and to, neighbours at difficult or critical times—the old communal warmth that survives the hazards, or is there because of them.

I commend this book to all those who are interested in such things and may have sometimes wondered if there is any meaning in the ancient notion of 'a way of life'.

FOREWORD
to the Second Edition
by
EONA MACNICOL

It is a great honour for me to be asked to introduce this reprint of *A Croft in the Hills*. The book gave me great delight when first it appeared, I treasure my copy; and I am happy that now many more readers may enjoy it too.

I am myself of the old stock of Abriachan, the place which the author chose for her brave venture into crofting life, I have therefore the keener interest in it. But I know that through this book, and through the Folk Museum with which she has more recently been associated, Katharine Stewart has illuminated the crofting life not only of Abriachan but of the Highlands of Scotland.

CHAPTER I
DIVINE DISCONTENT

WE had both, since our earliest days, found it difficult to live in a city. Every free half-day or week-end, every summer holiday, had found us making for the nearest patch of country, anywhere where we could breathe and smell the earth and see the sky in great stretches, instead of in tiny squares between the huddled roof-tops.

I shall always remember walking down Oxford Street, during a war-time rush-hour, and finding myself nearly losing my footing among the crowd, because my mind's eye was fixed on the rim of a steel-blue Highland loch, and I was smelling the scent of the bog-myrtle and hearing the weird, lonely cry of a drifting curlew. Jim, at that time, used to stand, during the brief spells of leisure his exacting job afforded, gazing through the huge, plate-glass windows of his place of work and seeing, beyond the racketing crowd, an oasis very like the one I had wandered into.

Later, we managed to make some sort of a compromise. We lived on the edge of the country and he went off to work at an unearthly hour of the morning, clad in the respectable black coat and hat of the city worker and shod with large, hobnailed boots (which he changed on arrival), for the two-mile walk to the bus. In the evenings I would go to meet him and in still weather I would hear the ring of the hobnails on the road long before he came in sight.

We had a garden; we had trees and the sky in stretches; we grew vegetables; we kept bees and hens and ducks. But the journeys to and from work were exhausting, though Jim would never admit it, and compromises are never really satisfactory. We were chafing against the tether.

Then Jim's work took him to a small town in the north of Scotland. That was the end; city life is bad enough but small-town life is far worse.

In a city one has, at least, the feeling that there are thousands of kindred spirits about, if one only knew them, folk just as dissatisfied as oneself with the mechanics of living, who know that it is not enough to have acquired some little skill or other, which will enable one to make enough money to buy shelter and clothing and food, so that one may continue to employ one's skill so as to be able to go on buying shelter and clothing and food, and so on... *ad infinitum*. In a city there is at least a spark of the divine discontent, an only half-submerged longing to catch a glimpse of the larger design, but in a small town everyone seems so glad of the boundary wall.

By this time our small daughter, Helen, was growing into a sturdy youngster. As I wandered hand in hand with her, back from the shops and along the row of trim villas to our home, I found my mind straying, as it had done years before in London, to some imagined remoteness.

I pictured Helen splashing in a hill-burn in summer, rolling like a young Sheltie in the snow in winter, racing the wind on the moor, gazing at birds and minute creatures among the grasses. 'Sheer nonsense!' a small, nagging voice would hiss in my ear. 'A child needs all the amenities of town life—a good school and lessons in music and dancing, and all the other benefits civilisation has to offer. Without them she'll only grow into a hopeless misfit.' But... would she? Wouldn't it be better for her to have at least a glimpse of the roots of things, not allow her to accept life as she would a shining parcel neatly wrapped in cellophane? Wouldn't close contact with natural things give her a perspective and a poise she would never lose? I firmly believed it would.

Jim worked long hours; sometimes it was late evening before he reached home, and he would have to leave again in the morning without getting more than a glimpse of Helen. We both knew that it was only half a life we were living.

We had bought, very cheaply, because it was in an appalling state of neglect, a house in a good residential district of the town. We had done it up and found that light paintwork everywhere and the installation of electricity and some additional plumbing transformed it into quite a pleasant place. We tackled the wilderness of a garden and cleared a plot for vegetables. There would be room to keep some hens and even a goat, we decided. We would be able to unearth the beehives we had brought from our southern garden and there were some derelict stable buildings where we thought we could perhaps grow mushrooms.

But there might be objections from the authorities. We still felt hemmed in, particularly as we knew that all our outdoor activities were discreetly observed from behind impeccable net curtains by our distinctly circumspect neighbours! There was no doubt about it, we were getting restless again.

We began to scan the columns of various newspapers, under jobs, houses, houses, jobs. Could we get some sort of a joint post which would allow us to live in open country with security? We made one or two abortive attempts in this direction, and also inspected several smallholdings on the outskirts of the town.

Then we saw it—an advertisement for a seven-roomed house, in a place with an excitingly unfamiliar name, with forty acres of arable land and an outrun on the moor, for the comparatively small sum of five hundred pounds. We got out the map, found the spot and repeated the name out loud, looking wonderingly at each other. Music was sounding in our ears.

Instantly, our minds were made up. It was within quite easy reach; we must see it, just see it, at least.

On Jim's next free day we got out our old van, packed a picnic, opened the map and set off. Through Inverness we went, and along the shore of Loch Ness, to a point about half-way to Drumnadrochit. There, a small road branched off from the main one. There was no sign-post, just this rough-shod track, pointing skywards. 'This is it!' We beamed at each other and put the van sharply at the rise.

We climbed slowly, changing gear every few yards, one eye on the panorama spread out below us, the other on what might emerge round the next blind corner ahead. After about a mile of this tortuous mounting we found ourselves on more or less level ground. Hills rose steeply on either side. There were small fields carved out of the encroaching heather. Croft houses were dotted here and there and there was a school, a tiny post-office and a telephone kiosk.

We made inquiries and found we had another mile or so to go. We came within sight of a small loch, lapping the foot of a shapely hill. It was remarkably like the Oxford Street oasis.

We branched right at this point and the landscape opened out into great distances. Another half-mile and we left the van at the roadside and took, as directed, the footpath through a patch of felled woodland. Then, at last, the roof and chimneys of a dwelling came into view. We stopped at the stile and took a long look at it.

Four-square and very solid it stood, facing just to the east of south, its walls of rough granite and whinstone, its roof of fine blue slate. Beyond it was the steading and in front a line of rowan trees, sure protection against evil spirits, according to Highland lore. A patch of rough grass all round the house was enclosed by a stout netted fence and on either side of the door was a small flower bed.

Round the house and steading was the arable ground and beyond that the moor, rising to the hill-land and to farther and farther hills against the horizon.

It was May and the warmth of the sun was bringing out the scent of the first heath flowers. A small, soft wind out of the west blew on our hands and faces, a bee hummed through the springing grass at our feet. The flanks of the farthest hills were swathed in blue mist.

We saw the good lady of the house. She pointed out the boundaries and we talked of the various possibilities of obtaining a piped water supply. The only well was a good hundred and fifty yards away, and below the level of the house. But she had had a diviner out and her son had started to dig for water at a spot indicated by him, within a stone's throw of the house. We gazed hopefully into this chasm and agreed that it would be all to the good if water could be found there.

The house was in an excellent state of repair; over the lintel was carved the date 1911. We learnt later that the house was actually built in 1910, but as the mason found it easier to make a 1 than a 0 he engraved the date as 1911! We also learnt later that in former times practically every crofter had a trade at his finger-tips, which he practised along with the working of his croft. This house, like nearly all those in the district, had been slated by the man who was to become our nearest, and very dear, neighbour.

Downstairs were two good-sized rooms, one stone-floored, the other with a new floor of wood. The stone-floored room had originally been the kitchen, but as the cooking was now done in a built-on scullery the range had been removed, the original wide hearth restored and a most attractive chimney-piece of rough, local stone built round it. Off this room was a small bedroom and a door leading to the substantial scullery. Upstairs were two good bedrooms and a box-room with a skylight.

Our experience with our town house had taught us what points to look for in examining property. The walls and wood-work were shabby but the structure was sound and weather-proof. It was the sort of house you could start to live in right away.

The steading was of the usual Highland design—a long, low building divided into three parts—byre, stable and barn—with thick stone walls and a roof of corrugated iron, and like the house it was in excellent repair. Beyond it were the ruins of the 'black house' (a small stone cottage, thatched with heather, its walls blackened with peat-reek), which had been the original dwelling on the holding. Opposite the steading, in the shelter of four giant rowans, was a small wooden hen-house.

The fields had been cultivated only spasmodically over the last years, but they had a healthy slope to them, and we knew that it was possible to obtain grants and subsidies for ploughing-up and fertilising such marginal land as this. Only a small area in the one level part of the arable ground was really damp and choked with rushes. We reckoned that a good clearing-out and a repairing of drains would help there. The rough grazing gave promise of a good summer bite for sheep and hardy cattle.

The fencing was patchy, to say the least of it, but we had already noticed on our way through the felled woodland the quantity of quite sound wood that was lying about. Some of it would surely be fit to make into fencing posts, and we knew of an excellent scrap-yard in Inverness where wire could often be picked up very cheaply.

The access road for vehicles was shared by our two immediate neighbours to the east. (In Scotland, as nearly all the glens run roughly east and west, one always goes 'east', or goes 'west', when visiting neighbours.) We could see that deliveries of heavy goods would have to be made during the drier months, as the road surface was distinctly soft, but it seemed to have a reasonably hard bottom and livestock could be loaded at a fank at the side of the main road.

The only thing that did really worry us a little was the lack of shelter. The woodland, which had formerly broken the force of the wind from all the southerly points of the compass, had been felled during and after the war. The view from the scullery window at the back was superb, but there seemed to be little but the heady air between us and Ben Wyvis which lay, like a great, dozing hound, away to the north.

But it was May-time and one of May's most glorious efforts in the way of a day—warm and sweet-scented and domed with milky blue. It is difficult on such a day really to visualise the storm and stress of winter.

We walked to the limit of the little property and stood looking down the strath. Several small, white croft houses stood on either side of the burn flowing down its centre. The fields adjoining them looked tidy and well-cultivated. Plumes of smoke rose from squat chimneys. Here and there were the ruins of former houses, where one holding had been incorporated into another. There was, on the whole, a feeling of quiet snugness about the prospect. It seemed incredible that we were standing nearly a thousand feet above sea-level.

Probably an upland area such as this would never have been settled at all had it not been for the clearances of the eighteenth and nineteenth centuries. One certainly shudders to think of the labour that must have gone into the wresting of the small fields from the bog and heather. The dry-stone dykes remain as memorials to those who heaved the mighty stones out of the plough's way and made the crops sheep- and cattle-proof.

The crofters' tenacity and innate gift for husbandry had resulted in their being able to maintain their families in health in these surroundings. Could we, who had so little experience, reasonably hope to do the same? We had health and strength and a tremendous appetite for this kind of life; we each had close links with the soil. There were Government schemes of assistance undreamt-of by the older generation of crofters and we could realise a certain amount of capital. We were braced and eager to take the leap.

With Helen staggering ahead of us, a bunch of small, bright heath flowers in her hand, we made our way back to the house. I think the lady in possession must have read her fate in our faces. She gave us tea and we told her, as sops to our conscience, that we would think it over and let her know our decision in a day or two.

Quietly and methodically she told us that there was a postal delivery every day, that an all-purpose van called every Wednesday and another on Saturday, but that, as it was often the early hours of Sunday before this latter one arrived, she preferred to deal with the Wednesday one. Small parcels of meat and fish, she said, could be sent through the post.

We made a mental note of all the information she gave us, thanked her and walked slowly back to the road. We *did* have a look at another place on the way home, but it was quite out of the question, twice the price and very inaccessible and, as the French have it, it 'said nothing to us'.

The house on the hill was already making its voice heard. All the way back in the van we listened in silence to what it had to say. It was a supremely honest little place. It hid nothing from us. Its fields had been neglected, its access road was little more than a track, its water supply was altogether unhandy. In winter it was liable to be cut off by impenetrable snow-drifts. But—it offered a challenge. We had enough imagination to visualise its possibilities and most of its impossibilities. Experience had taught us that the worst hardly ever happens, and if it does, it can usually be turned into a best.

Our minds were seething with positive plans. All traces of discontent, however divine, had vanished utterly.

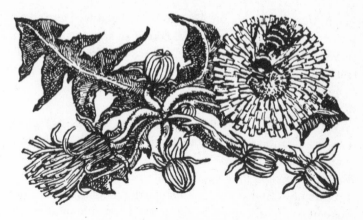

THE HOUSE ON THE HILL

Within a week the deed of purchase of the house and land was signed and sealed by us. Occupation was 'to be arranged'. This meant that the seller would be leaving very shortly and that we should take over in the autumn.

Immediately we set about selling our own house. We knew this would not be difficult as it was now classed as a 'desirable residence' and was much sought after, occupying, as it did, a most favoured site in a most favoured neighbourhood. The angels had been on our side after all. Like fools we had rushed to buy it, only wondering by what stroke of luck we had managed to get it so cheaply and easily. Not until after the sale was concluded did we hear the gruesome rumour that the roof was afflicted with dry rot. For several days we were haunted by this nightmare, till a thorough investigation by the builder called in to do the repairs assured us that the rumour was completely ill-founded. There were traces of the activity of woodworm in some of the cupboards but of dry rot there was no sign. So we were able to dispose of our house with the greatest ease and at a considerable profit.

Meantime, we besieged the local offices of the Department of Agriculture and loaded ourselves with pamphlets concerning

15

grants, subsidies and so on. We discovered that we were eligible for a grant of fifty per cent of the cost of an approved scheme of water installation for the house and steading of the croft; that some of the land would qualify for the ploughing-up grant of five pounds an acre and that we could get help with the buying of lime and fertilisers.

We then called at the North of Scotland College of Agriculture, in Inverness, and were told that their expert would come out to take a sample of the soil in the various fields, for analysis, so that the amount of lime needed could be accurately determined, and that he would draw up a complete cropping and stocking programme for us, all this without any sort of fee. Another expert, a lady (later on referred to affectionately as the 'hen wife'), would come to give us advice on all matters relating to poultry-keeping.

Everyone was most friendly and helpful and charming. Helen would sit on my knee during the various interviews and would almost invariably end up with a peppermint to suck or find herself carried off to the typists' room, to be beguiled with bangs on the typewriter, when business was not too pressing! All in all, we felt surrounded by a solid wall of encouragement and goodwill.

Once a week we set off early, to spend a long day at the croft. We cleared rubbish from the outbuildings and repaired the garden fence; we prospected for wells and picnicked on the moor, or in the empty living-room if it was wet. We made the acquaintance of our nearest neighbours and began to get the feel of the place.

About this time, a piece of land to the west of our croft came on the market. It had been bought some years previously by an Inverness man, who meant to run Highland cattle on it. His plans had fallen through and he wanted to dispose of the land. As it would give us some sixty additional acres of good rough grazing, we decided to make an offer for it. So, for ninety pounds, it became ours.

The seller wished, however, to retain the mineral rights. This intrigued us. We made inquiries and discovered that when digging a drain he had come on several deposits of blue clay. He had had an expert from London up to examine these and had been told that they might be of commercial value, but only if found in sufficient quantity to justify excavation. Later on we turned up quite a lot of this blue clay when ploughing our own ground. We sent a specimen to the Geological Department of the Edinburgh Museum and the opinion we received on it tallied with that of the London expert. We are still hoping we may find a use for it some day.

In the meantime this addition to our croft land has provided us, in addition to the grand grazing, with a supply of first-class peat—the black, well-seasoned stuff which cuts into hard, stiff blocks and gives a much hotter fire than the brown, crumbly variety.

Another find on this newly acquired land was the 'golden' well, so called because of the brilliant marsh-marigolds which grow in the boggy ground all round it. This had always been a death-trap for sheep and other animals. On a hungry spring day, irresistibly attracted by the fresh, green growth, they would plunge into the bog for a bite and get engulfed. During our second summer, after we had lost a ewe lamb in this way, Jim cut a channel for the spring overflow and the ground round about is now quite hard and dry. Could a scheme be devised there is enough water in this source to provide a piped supply for all the crofts lower down the strath.

Our search for water near the house had become almost an obsession. We grudged the expense of laying a long pipe-track from the existing well, even though we should have to bear only half of it ourselves. Some further digging in the hole already begun revealed nothing, not even a trickle. We got in touch with another diviner and watched, goggle-eyed with fascination, while the stick jigged and cavorted in his hands. It seemed there was water here, there and everywhere. At last he selected a spot above the level of the house, whence a supply could gravitate easily to a downstairs tank. Our hopes ran high. The digging started but, after three days' heavy work, all that we came on was a thin, muddy trickle which would not pass the analyst's test.

We decided to seek Government approval for a scheme to install a pump at the existing well, which would raise the water to the level of the house. A sample of this water was found to be quite satisfactory and the Department of Agriculture agreed to give us a grant of fifty per cent of the cost of the work.

As the profit on the sale of our town house had been a substantial one, we decided to have some plumbing installed at the croft and to wire the house for electricity. We had been assured that a main supply from the Hydro-Electric Scheme would be available within the next few years. In the meantime the wiring could be connected to a cheap, wind-driven dynamo to provide us with light though not with power.

We looked on this expense as an investment. It would increase the value of the property and it would pay dividends in other ways. Spared the drudgery of incessant water-carrying, we should have more time and energy to give to productive work and I should be able to get quickly through my household chores and be free to take a proper share in the outdoor jobs. The electric wiring we intended to extend to the steading, in part of which we were going to keep hens, on the deep-litter system, with a light to encourage winter egg-production.

It was difficult to find men to tackle the work on the house. Jim was still busy at his job and had only a very limited amount of time and the place was too difficult of access for men to come out daily from Inverness.

Finally we accepted the quite moderate estimates of some young tradesmen, just setting up in business, who would live on the job if we would provide them with the necessaries for camping in the empty house. We gladly agreed and they took up all the bedding, pots, pans, crockery and so on, we could spare, in a lorry, on the day of their preliminary investigation.

There were the usual delays, for material was still difficult to come by. Mid-October came, the time we could spend at the croft grew shorter as the days drew in, and still the main work had not been begun. We were afraid the frosts would set in before the pipe-track was dug.

Jim packed up his job and we decided to move by the first of November. Then the men really got busy. On our last weekly visit we found the place reverberating with hammer-blows and cheerful whistling and shouting and clanking.

The day of our arrival came at last. The removal people had sent too small a van with the result that two journeys had to be made. We had to spend an extra night in town, as it was too late to make the trip ourselves that day.

Next morning, when we reached our destination, we were greeted by the sight of half our worldly goods standing stacked at the roadside. Furniture, books, pictures, pots and pans stood there, looking forlorn in the chill, grey light.

We had arranged with a neighbour to ferry our belongings from the road to the house on his tractor-trailer, as the van could not manage to make the journey to the house with the access road in its wintry state. Luckily this neighbour had had the good sense to cart all the bedding and really perishable stuff along to the house the day before, and the night had been fine, so no irreparable damage was done.

We changed into gum-boots and started right away to rescue the most precious books, as the sky was clouding and rain threatening. At once we were overwhelmed with goodwill. The tractor came lurching into view and strong arms soon had another load secured. Our eastward neighbour appeared at her door as we passed and offered to take charge of Helen for the day, so that we could get on with the work as quickly as possible. They were already firm friends, she and Helen, and we gladly agreed. On arrival at the house we found a roaring fire in the kitchen, more cheery faces and a welcome brew of tea.

All day the tractor plied back and forth with load after load of goods and chattels. There was hammering and singing and mud and plaster everywhere, but by tea-time we had everything under cover and the beds made up, so we fetched Helen from our kindly neighbour. The men brought pail after pail of water from the well and we all ate an enormous meal of ham and eggs. I even managed to give Helen her tub, as usual, before carrying her through the 'burach' to the safe oasis of her bed. Then we lit a fire in the great hearth in the living-room and sat round it, all six of us, till our eyelids drooped.

Those were happy days as, slowly, our house began to take shape. The men were up at six and had a fire in the kitchen for me to cook breakfast. After dark they worked on by the light of oil-lamps so as to get done and, as they put it, 'out of our road'. Secretly, I think they were missing the pub and the cinema of their little home town. Certainly their singing and whistling grew more light-hearted and obstreperous as they kept up their spirits till the time came for their release. But they were good sorts and did their best in what were, for them, difficult and unusual conditions.

We celebrated Helen's third birthday with a cake I had made weeks before. Our black Labrador presented us with a litter of pedigreed pups. At last the men completed the plumbing and wiring and departed with cheerful waves and 'rather-you-than-me' expressions on their faces.

Then Peter, a young friend of ours who was waiting to start a new job, came to help Jim dig the trench for the water pipe. For nearly three weeks they dug, pausing only for meals and fly cups of tea. Sometimes they would be lost to view in the mist, and only the ring of the pick and the scrape of the shovel told us they were still hard at it. But the job was accomplished, though we were still to wait a long time before the water would flow from the tap.

Meantime, I was clearing rubble from around the outside of the house and making a gravel path to the door so that some, at least, of the mud would not be brought inside on the soles of our boots. I got to know the ways of my new oven and I carried water, and more water!

At last, towards the beginning of December, when the house was more or less straight and Peter had departed, with a twinge of regret, I think, that he had to go back to the city treadmill, we felt we were really settled in. That first evening on our own I went out after dark to get some washing-water from the butt by the back door. I stood, kettle in hand, staring at the sky beyond Ben Wyvis. Great pale beams were moving, like searchlights, across the whole northern section of the heavens. I called to Jim and he stood with me, gazing at these incredibly beautiful northern lights. Then we fetched Helen, wrapped her in a big coat, and held her in our arms, while we all three watched the spectacle. Jim and I felt very small and very humble but young Helen gurgled with delight. At once we joined in her response: this was her inheritance, she had recognised it at once. It was the first of the joys she was to discover in and around the house on the hill.

CHAPTER III

WINTER AND ROUGH WEATHER

As though to put us through a lovers' test our small domain soon took on its most forbidding aspect. We were hardly into December when the first snow came whirling out of the south-west. We woke one morning to find the doors and windows plastered, as though some giant had hurled a vast white pudding at the house.

The first essential was to keep warm. Luckily, we had already got a good stock of logs sawn and split and there were some peats in the barn, left over from the year before, so we could be fairly lavish with fires.

Normally we relied on the kitchen stove for warmth in the daytime and only lit a fire in the living-room in the evening, when we had leisure to sit at it, before bed. But we kept a blaze going in the living-room all that day and, last thing at night, we carried shovelfuls of red embers to the bedroom grate. We put Helen's cot in our room and unearthed all the spare blankets and so spent quite a snug night.

By next morning the road was blocked with snow-drifts, and it was the day the grocer's van was due. Over a steaming cup of morning tea I mentally reviewed the contents of the larder. It was not very promising; we had been caught unawares. Having as yet no sources of supply of our own, we were certainly not equipped to ride out a storm.

The first thing to do was to get water. The pump was not yet connected and, if this weather were to continue, it looked as though the chances of our having water in the tap before spring-time would be fairly remote. Jim took a pail and a shovel and went to dig out the well. Then we thawed out the tap on the water-butt and filled a big crock with washing-water. While I prepared a meal with our last tin of meat, Helen, in snow-suit and gum-boots, went out to revel in her first snow and Jim knocked up a sledge.

In the early afternoon we set off, with Helen perched on the sledge, in search of eggs from a neighbour, half a mile down the road. It was heavy going but we returned home in triumph with all the eggs intact. The sky was pure, deep blue and there was a sparkling silence everywhere. Our little house looked more snug and secure than ever in its winter setting and we felt the bonds that linked us to it grow perceptibly stronger.

Jim brought in more logs while I made an enormous dish of scrambled eggs and then we shut the door reluctantly on the stars and drew the supper-table close to the fire.

All that month winter fretted at us. There was little we could do outside but repair fences between the storms, but we carried several fallen tree-trunks down on our shoulders and cut them with a cross-cut saw. On the fine days we would work away at the chopping and splitting till the sky faded to mauve and clear shades of green and gold came up about the setting sun. Every morning, when I opened the door, I would find two out-wintered Shetland ponies waiting patiently for their bite of bread. They belonged to a distant neighbour and one day we had taken pity on them and given them some crusts. So every morning, till the spring grass came, they would be there to greet us at the door.

In the evenings we made plans and discussed endlessly the absorbing topics of sheep and cattle, hens and pigs, fertilisers and farm-machinery and crops. This 'shop' never grows stale. It has an inexhaustible fascination, perhaps because one has the assurance that one is dealing with fundamentals, perhaps because one knows that there's always the unpredictable lurking in the background ready to upset the best-laid schemes, perhaps just because it relates to things one instinctively loves. We began to long for the days to lengthen and the air to soften so that we could start putting our plans into operation.

On Christmas morning the plumber arrived to try once more to connect the pump. He had walked the two miles from the bus and was quite tired out when he reached us and amazed at the wintry conditions in our hills. In Inverness, he said, there had been promise of a reasonably mild day and he had had hopes of getting the job done. We have now come to accept this sort of thing. We leave home on a bitter winter's morning and find spring, with a flush of green in the trees, at Loch Ness-side. It's not the distance of two miles that does it but the rise of close on a thousand feet. There was little he could do, the plumber decided, so he shared our Christmas dinner and set off again to walk to the bus. At dusk we lit the candles on our little Christmas tree and played games with Helen till bed-time.

There was a party for all the children of the district in the village hall, to which we took Helen. We met her future teacher and a dozen or so lively youngsters. There were games and songs and a piper and there was tea and cakes and oranges and sweets. It was a simple little festivity but a very happy one. Everyone asked kindly how we were faring. 'It can be fearful wild here in the winter', they said, almost apologising for the climate in their hills. 'We like it', we said, and they looked at us out of their clear, shrewd eyes and I think they almost believed us. We began to feel that we nearly belonged.

On New Year's Eve we sat by the fire talking, as usual, and when midnight came we filled our glasses and slipped upstairs and pledged each other over Helen's sleeping head. We went down again and got out the black bun and some extra glasses and put fresh logs on the fire. We thought it more than likely we should have a neighbour for a first-foot. Distance would not daunt the people of Abriachan, we were sure, and the night was fine.

We sat till two o'clock, getting drowsier and drowsier. No one came and we went to bed. At about three-thirty we were dragged from the depths of sleep by what sounded like an aeroplane crashed outside the front door. We fumbled our way into heavy coats and staggered out, to find three neighbours clambering off a tractor. There was much handshaking and back-slapping. We poked the fire into a blaze and drank a toast. Later we helped them to remount and stood at the door, watching the tractor lurch off on its way to the next port of call. How the two passengers managed to keep their precarious balance, draped over the rear mudguards, will remain for ever a mystery. But we were immensely cheered by their visit and went back to bed and slept till the middle of the morning.

During the first days of the new year we made many pleasant visits to neighbours. Some we had called on before, but there was one whose house we had never been in. He lived, with his brother and his cousin, in a high fold of the hills to the south-west. Several other families had lived up there at one time, but now only the ruins of their little dwellings are left. Finlay's place, however, had been completely modernised under the Hill Farming Scheme, and there, in the little house nestled in the shelter of the rock, we found a most heartening welcome. We were given tea before a fine red fire and were shown, with quiet pride, the bathroom, the new scullery with its gleaming sink and hot and cold taps, the enamelled cooking stove, the bright paintwork everywhere.

Later we were told how Finlay's forebears had been evicted from a place in a fertile glen and had started all over again in this green upland, first building themselves a rough house of stone and thatch, then clearing little fields from the heather. We were also told how the men who now live there had laboured, as boys, before and after school, to make the road which carries cattle-floats these days up to their snug farmstead. We began to understand how it was that the Highlander made such a splendid pioneer in Canada and New Zealand.

Towards the end of January the wind at last got back to its normal westerly quarter and the air became soft and damp again. The plumber returned and our shining new taps at last began to function. It was thrilling to see the water actually flow from them—it was bright green in colour, but somehow that only added to the delight. After a time the piping settled down till there was only a faint tinge of green about the water and it had no ill effect on our stomachs.

The mild spell, unbelievably, continued. There was almost a warmth in the sun and the midges were dancing. Encouraged by this overture we took a spade to the garden plot. It had been neglected for years, but it had a dry-stone wall protecting it from the north and east and we could see its possibilities. In a couple of days we had the turf skimmed off and our spades bit delightedly into the good, black earth.

We began to get very impatient to start the real work of the place. The first essential, we knew, for the growing of crops, was sound fencing. Every afternoon we went up to the old woodland, selected pieces of timber suitable for making into fencing posts and carried them down on our shoulders. We pointed the ends and stuck them to soak in a pail of creosote.

But we realised that it would take weeks to make all that were needed. Our land marched for almost half a mile with Forestry Commission land. This Forestry land was unfenced, pending replanting, and sheep from various airts were roaming over it and finding their way into our fields. On our next trip to Inverness Jim went to see the Forestry people and asked when they meant to fence. To our astonishment and great satisfaction they said that although they did not intend to plant immediately they would put forward the fencing and make a start at it in the early summer. This news cheered us greatly; it really did look as though things were going our way.

We bought a tractor and a single plough. The tractor had a small bogey attachment and during the long weeks we waited for the ground to dry out for ploughing we found this extremely useful for all sorts of carting work. We were able to fetch wood in large quantities, both for fuel and for fencing posts, and load after load of stones for patching the road.

February brought another blizzard and the road was blocked again, but this time we had the larder well stocked. We were learning! By the end of the month the larks were singing. There is perhaps nothing in hill-life so thrilling as the sight and sound of the first returning lark. You go out, on a still February morning, your footsteps ringing on the hard cobbles of the yard. Suddenly, something makes you stop in your tracks and look up. Against the pale blue sky you see two, maybe three, or even four, small brown specks tossing madly in the air. As you look, one detaches itself from the rest, rises in a series of ecstatic leaps and comes slowly down again, its song rippling from its tiny throat. How something so small can let loose such a volume of sound is what amazes you. Soon the others join it and then the whole sky rings with music.

'The larks are singing!' Each year we make the announcement to one another. The words are sober enough, but what they convey, it is almost impossible to express. It means that our hills and moors are again fit places for new life, for song and work and laughter, all the things we cling to so passionately, in the name of living. Each year, the rising of the larks has meant a little more to us, as we emerge from one more winter to greet the new season.

After the larks come the peewits. They usually arrive at dusk, and far into the darkening we hear their wild crying. Next morning we go out eagerly to watch them flashing and swooping over the bare, brown fields. Each day after that we listen for the curlews and, when we see them gliding over the moor in the evening light and catch the sound of their call, which seems to come from some other very far-off place, we know that spring is really with us.

By mid-March the upper field in front of the house was ready for ploughing. It was to be sown to oats. The bigger field, below the house, was to carry a crop of oats, undersown with grass, and we were to grow two acres of turnips and half an acre of potatoes. Later on we would put more under grass. We were to work on a five-year rotation.

On this still March morning we could feel the warmth of the sun on our hands and faces. Not only to see the sun, but to feel its warmth, that was what gave a lift to the day! Jim hitched the plough to the tractor and began slowly turning over the sward. I stood watching the work from the door and as soon as the household chores were finished I went out to dig the garden. Helen scampered between field and garden, calling encouragement to each of us. It was a morning none of us will forget.

Of course, winter had not finished with us. The very next day, the wind shifted unaccountably to the east and sleet began to fall. Jim finished ploughing the top field, completely unperturbed by the weather, and in the afternoon he made a start at the lower field. We knew that there were patches of bog here and though we had scythed the rushes and given the drain a preliminary clearing the ground was still treacherous. As dusk was falling the tractor stuck and no amount of manoeuvring would get her clear. We went along to our nearest tractor-owning neighbour, who came willingly to the rescue. It was then that we got our first inkling of what good-neighbourliness can mean in lonely places. Since that day, we have borrowed and lent everything from a loaf of bread to a broody hen and have exchanged services of every kind, from a hand at the dipping to the rescue of a snow-bound truck. We are all faced with the same fundamental problems and we have learnt how utterly dependent we are upon one another in dealing with them.

CHAPTER IV

CUCKOO-SNOW

WE were soon well in the grip of spring fever. In the lengthening evenings we would take a pleasure stroll round the fields after supper, for to stay indoors had become positively irksome. We acquired our first stock—a dozen laying hens, which we bought from a neighbour. We settled them in the stable, in a litter of peat-moss and straw, and began to keep a tally of eggs laid.

About this time it came to our ears that the croft immediately to our east was likely to come up for sale. The man who had bought it, a few years previously, was trying to run it in the time he could spare from another full-time job and it had become a burden to him. There were about fifteen acres of well-fenced arable ground, some more rough grazing, and the croft carried the right to graze sheep on the open hill on the other side of the road, a right shared by four other places in the neighbourhood. There was an excellent steading, with a brand-new corrugated iron roof, and a small wooden bungalow adjoining it, in place of the ruined dwelling house.

We were tempted to acquire this place as it would give a reasonably good access road to our land. Our own very indifferent road came through part of this holding and in the past, we learned, there had been a certain amount of dispute about rights of way and the upkeep of communal gates and fences. We could grow our first crops in the well-fenced fields, thus giving ourselves time to do the other fencing more or less at leisure. We could winter cattle in the steading and keep the one near home for the house-cow and the hens in deep litter. The proposition was certainly attractive—could we scrape the bottom of the barrel? We had still our basic stock to buy.

For several days we looked at the thing from all angles. Then, over a cup of tea at the kitchen fire, on a blustery, wet afternoon, we discussed it with J. F., the owner of the croft. We could have it lock, stock and barrel, he said, it was proving too irksome for him, with his other commitments. The lock we knew about; of barrel there was no sign! But we agreed to examine the stock. This consisted of one cross cow, in milk (she was brown and horned and had a touch of Guernsey about her, her owner said. This was later borne out by the quality of the cream she produced), and four stirks, all hardy crosses, two score sheep, a couple of goats, two dozen hens, a dozen khaki-Campbell ducks and—Charlie, a straw-coloured Highland pony of uncertain age. There was also a cart, a set of harrows, a mower, a turnip-chopper, barn tools, all things we should need and have to spend precious time looking for in the second-hand market. Here they were on the spot. Finally we did a deal and the signing of one more scrap of paper satisfied our land hunger at last.

The animals were in poor shape and we got them cheaply enough. They had had a lean winter of it, but we knew a summer's grazing could work wonders—and so it proved. We were able to sell the stirks in the autumn for more than twice the amount we paid for them. But in the meantime our immediate problem was to find something to put in their bellies, until such time as the natural herbage had grown sufficiently to satisfy their appetites.

Here, again, our neighbours came to the rescue. Willie Maclean, from over the burn, sent word that we could come at any time to fetch a load of turnips. He was getting on in years and would not be putting down another crop. He had been ill the previous autumn and had only been able to gather in enough turnips to do his one remaining cow. The rest were lying in small covered heaps in the field, and we were welcome to help ourselves to them. We gladly accepted the offer and went round with Charlie and the cart. On our departure we were told 'that was an awful wee load' and we were to 'be sure and come back for another'. As we were about to set off with the second load, we were bidden to come again for some corn sheaves, for 'the horse would be the better of a feed of oats'. On our return next day Sadie, the young girl of the house, was there to help fill the cart with sweet-smelling sheaves and to give a hand to secure the load with stack-rope. We threshed the sheaves in the old-fashioned way, by beating them with a stick, and it warmed our hearts that evening to see the cattle-beasts munching bundles of good oat-straw and chopped turnip and to watch Charlie devouring half a pailful of corn.

We installed Daisy, the cow, in the home byre and cut rushes with a sickle to make her a clean bed. I washed her udder with soap and water and brushed the accumulation of caked mud off her flanks. The College vet. took a sample of her milk for testing and it was declared free of T.B. bacilli. She was a nice quiet milker and we drank quantities of milk from that time on.

We now found ourselves struggling to overtake the rush of spring work. Loads of lime and fertiliser had arrived and were waiting to be spread, there was dung to be carted out to the potato ground, there was still some ploughing to do. We decided we should need some help for a week or two so we asked our good friend the post if he knew of anyone who might be available. There were two brothers, he said, young lads who were often available for odd work. It sounded hopeful.

Next morning Jim went off to see them and a few days later, on a Friday, they turned up for work. They went hard at it all day, carting out lime, while Jim was harrowing with the tractor.

On the Saturday they worked with us till evening and we began to feel we were really getting ahead. On Sunday we went for a walk down to Loch Ness-side, in celebration, and found the trees showing a flush of green and the first primroses in flower.

We bought fifty day-old cockerels for fattening and ordered a hundred growing pullets to be delivered in June; these were to be our winter layers.

We now found that the routine work of milking, attending to the poultry and feeding the stirks took up a lot of time, but we managed to keep abreast of the field work and at last, towards the third week in April, we were ready to make our first sowing of corn. The weather had been blustery and uncertain for several days but we felt we couldn't delay any longer. We sowed in the time-honoured way, from a canvas tray slung round the neck. It was satisfying to see Jim pacing up and down, his arms moving rhythmically, the yellow seed-corn falling in a fine arc on to the brown earth. Helen and I were standing, hand-in-hand, at the edge of the field watching him when, over the hill to the east, a great black cloud came sailing. The wind rose suddenly and a moment later snow began to fall. Helen and I had to run for shelter but Jim went calmly on with the sowing. We stood at the kitchen window watching him till he was almost lost to view among the whirling flakes. It seemed to me that there was something symbolic about making one's first sowing in a snow-storm. There must be a riddle in it somewhere, I thought, but I couldn't find the answer.

The black cloud soon passed over and the sky to the west cleared to a limpid green. As I opened the door to Jim we heard the cuckoo call quite distinctly, three times, from the birches on the edge of the woodland. We looked at each other and smiled, A moment later Billy came in, knocking the snow from his boots. 'It's the cuckoo-snow', he said, in his most matter-of-fact voice, and he began calmly washing his hands. We knew then what it was to be bred in these hills. It meant that you took in your stride whatever came, without panic or jubilation: that you foresaw the worst and so were quietly thankful for the best.

The cuckoo sang in the snow-storm; the seed was sown. We sat down hungrily to our hot supper.

That was indeed a topsy-turvy spring. No sooner was the sowing of the corn completed than the rain came down in torrents. We stood at the kitchen window in the grey evening light and watched it carving wide runnels in the sloping fields. It looked as though every scrap of seed would be washed clean out of the ground.

The garden plot was now securely fenced and I limed it and put in two dozen cabbage plants. I surveyed the neat rows with some satisfaction, but I had forgotten about the agility of goats. One evening, one of them sailed blithely over the fence and in ten minutes demolished every scrap of young cabbage plant!

We lost almost half the cockerels when a gale blew out the brooder lamp one night. The robber goat died, not from a surfeit of young cabbage, but as a result of the lean winter she had had. We had hoped to use her as a supplementary milk supply, to tide us over the cow's dry period, before calving. But she was a trial, anyway, and as full of tricks as a box of monkeys. It took two to milk her, one to hold her steady and the other to coax the milk into the pail. Daisy the cow, on the other hand, was so quiet and placid that you could milk her in mid-field, without even tethering her.

'April is the cruellest month', I would murmur sometimes, as I watched the sleet lashing the bare ground and saw the thin, dispirited cattle-beasts stand shivering in the lee of the steading walls. But I knew it was only a question of biding our time, of getting used to disappointments and losses. I spent the worst days catching up on arrears of housework, while Jim made fencing posts in the shelter of the barn. We were cheered, too, by visits from neighbours and Helen had many happy games with the children from Woodend and young Bertha, from over the burn. We had first made the acquaintance of this lively, yellow-haired small girl when she had been sent over, one day at the end of winter, with a bottle of milk for Helen, from Willie Maclean's newly calved cow. She had been boarded out with the Macleans since an early age and was one of the many children they had brought up along with their own daughter.

Practically every croft house has one or more of these foster-children and we have seen several grow from little thin-faced waifs into burly youngsters. Their up-bringing is supervised by officials from the city of their birth (in most cases it is Glasgow), who pay them regular visits and provide them with clothing and pocket money. In most cases they are regarded as sons and daughters of the house and they come back, once they are launched into the world, to spend their holidays, or bring their own families to visit in the only real home they have known. In the Macleans' house at this time there was Bertha, aged ten, Billy, twelve and Sadie, eighteen, and they were a happy, lively trio of whom we were to see a lot.

Willie Maclean himself ('Beelack', as the affectionate Gaelic diminutive of his name was pronounced) was a man of the old Highland type, well-read, with an inquiring mind and a genuine courtesy of manner. In his younger days he had been a great piper. His brother was a well-known doctor in Glasgow. His kindly wife would always meet us on the doorstep with the greeting, 'Come away in' and we could be sure of good talk over a cup of tea at her fireside. As we left, her 'haste ye back!' would ring in our ears, as we made our way over the little bridge and along the track through the heather to our home. At night we would see the yellow glow of the light in her kitchen window and in the morning we would watch the smoke rising in a thin blue plume from her chimney and we found it immensely cheering to know we had these hill-folk for friends. They would anticipate our needs before we were fully aware of them ourselves. Many a time Bertha has come flying across the moor with a drench for the cow, because we had mentioned that she was off her feed, or a broody hen to mother some chicks whose own parent had abandoned them.

At last May brought more genial weather. The rush of work was over and we dispensed with the boys' help. Jim borrowed a ridge-plough and ridged the potato field and we spent a couple of days planting potatoes. It is back-breaking work, tramping up and down the drills, bent double, dropping the potatoes into place. But the weather was wonderful and we made a picnic of it. I spread a rug on the grass verge at the top of the field, on which Helen sprawled with her dolls. Every now and again she would seize a small pail of potatoes and thrust a dozen or so tubers solemnly into the ground, then scamper back to the rug and instruct each doll in turn in the art of potato-planting. At mid-day we stretched out on the rug beside her and ate sandwiches and drank flasks of tea. Overhead, the sky was a pale, milky blue and the air rang with lark song. We were glad to be alive and to be doing exactly what we were doing.

With the potatoes safely in the ground there was a lull till turnip-sowing time. We spent most of this gathering fuel from the felled woodland. The Forestry fence was going up rapidly and we wanted to lay in a stock of wood for winter before this useful source of supply was shut off. So, once again, we made a picnic of it and spent several whole days carting loads of wood to a dump on our own ground.

For the turnip-sowing we sought the good offices of Charlie. This was the first field work we had done with him and he at once proved his worth. With the bite of good grass he was now getting he had improved tremendously and was looking almost sleek. No one knew exactly how old he was, but one neighbour reported having seen him working on a croft some miles away nearly thirty years before. But he was by now a firm family friend and we preferred to ignore all rumours about his probable age. He toiled up and down the turnip drills and, quite literally, never put a foot wrong. He was as patient with us novices as an indulgent father, and we found an affection for him which was to grow steadily over the years.

On the first fine, windless day, we sowed the grass seed. It is so light and feathery that even a gentle breeze will scatter it in the wrong direction. We gave the fields a good rolling and felt that at last we could relax a little. There was still much to do, but the pressure had eased.

On the last Saturday in June, when the sun was blazing from a deep blue sky, we packed a picnic and made for Loch Laide. It's less than a mile from our home and it's the perfect place for relaxation; summer or winter, we never tire of walking by its shore. This June day we lay on our backs in the heather, watching a curlew glide round the shoulder of the hill, uttering its long, drowsy call. Then we plunged into the smooth, dark water and Helen splashed in the shallows of the little beach. We made a fire of roots and twigs to boil our kettle; and we walked home deeply refreshed and ready to tackle whatever might come next.

CHAPTER V
FIRST HARVEST

With the crops safely in the ground and the cattle and sheep finding a succulent bite in the clean, natural grazing, we had time to take stock of our position and to analyse rather more closely our aims, both long-term and immediate. Our farming, even bolstered as it was by Government subsidies, could never be more than subsistence farming: we were fully aware of that. As a business proposition its appeal was absolutely nil, but, of course, we had never looked at it—in fact, we had never looked at anything—strictly in that light. As a way of life it had endless fascination and reward—the smallest thing could give us a glow of satisfaction. To see the green flush of corn shoots, or of turnip seedlings in ground that had yielded nothing for years, was an obvious thrill. But there were also the small delights of watching a drain flow freely after it had been cleared of silt, of driving the horse and cart along a road made passable with new patchings of stone, of seeing the sheeps' foraging among the new-sown grass thwarted by a stout fence, hung on the posts we had made in the dark, winter days. Every way we looked there was a reward and a new challenge springing up behind it, something to give us a small, encouraging pat on the back and to spur us on before we had time to smirk.

Perhaps one of the greatest satisfactions of our life was the knowledge that we were in this thing together, as a family, as a unit. There was no seeing father off every morning, to struggle with his own remote set of problems, while mother and child coped with theirs at home. There were no watertight compartments. When it was time to hoe the turnips we all set off to the field together and worked side by side all day, Helen, too, wielding a diminutive hoe among the seedlings. At supper-time Jim stoked the fire and, when we'd eaten, we tackled the day's accumulation of dirty dishes together and it took only a few minutes to smooth the well-aired beds before we slipped between the sheets!

Good food we had in abundance: not for us was the policy of selling every available egg to the van and buying doubtful commodities in their place. It was surely better, we felt, to have a huge, golden-shelled egg on your breakfast plate and health in your eye, than cash accumulating in the tin box. Likewise with milk—though there, of course, there was no question of any being sold—the best was for ourselves. The rich, yellow cream we would churn into butter, after setting aside the jugfuls for porridge and tea. Any surplus would be fed to the growing chickens. Later on we hoped to rear a baconer for our own use and some table poultry.

When the garden really came into production we meant to have a good supply of all the hardy vegetables and fruit. An evening stroll with the gun would often yield a couple of young rabbits for the pot. Very good they were in those days, and now, although the crops are certainly better off without them, we do miss the meals they gave us.

In fact, our aim was to be as far as possible self-sufficient in the way of food and to cut down other living costs to a minimum. The fuel problem, for instance, we hoped would take care of itself, with the limitless supplies of peat and dead wood that were to hand. As for clothes, they had only to be serviceable, not decorative, so that hard-wearing stuff such as corduroy and denim and leather, which would survive for years, was our chief rig. In Helen's case, of course, we had to allow for growth, which was rapid. But, by buying things several sizes too big and taking in ample reefs and tucks, even these were made to last. Corduroy slacks, which began voluminous and ankle-length, she could still wear several years later, almost skin-tight and reaching not much below her knees, and still be in the fashion! Only on footwear were we all extremely hard, and gum-boots and leather shoes have had to be renewed at alarmingly frequent intervals.

The surplus eggs were already beginning to bring us in a useful supply of ready cash, and in an extremely handy way. Every Thursday we left a boxful at the gate for collection by the van from the packing-station and the following Thursday we found an envelope containing the pounds, shillings and pence and a note explaining exactly how many eggs were first-grade, second-grade, cracked or 'rejects'—so that we knew where we were and what we could count on in this department. The grocer's van was calling regularly every week and the money from the previous week's eggs usually met his bill for bread, tea, sugar, butcher-meat and oddments.

In other ways, too, we meant to be self-sufficient. We had to rely on our own resources for mental stimulus. We had hundreds of books, accumulated over the years, and we had come to treat them with a new respect during the evenings of our first winter in the hills. We had always read a lot and loved music. But to read a book in a half-circle of firelight, with the feet-deep snow outside cutting off all possible interruption, to hear on the wireless a symphony of Sibelius above the shrieking of a north-east gale, is to experience these things in the raw. I shall always remember rereading *Wuthering Heights* in these conditions and entering, as it were, barefoot, into Emily Brontë's world.

The last thing we wanted to do was to run away from life. We were all too well aware of what went on in the wider world and we listened as avidly as the next household to B.B.C. news bulletins and talks on current affairs. We could get a paper delivered to the door on the afternoon of its day of publication. But we did firmly and passionately believe that close contact with natural things was the only means of getting the savour of balanced living. It was the deeper world we wanted to explore, not the wider.

On the croft we could work hard all day, feel the sun on our hands or the rain on our faces, come in to eat food fresh from the ground and still have time to stand on the doorstep in the evening light, to watch the birds gliding in the shadowed air, engaged in their own lives, and to see the stars come out, and to wonder.

We were fully aware of the fact that man had prefabricated a ghastly doom for himself. Nuclear weapons could destroy cities, could wipe out the records of a whole civilisation, and that was bad enough. But that they could also destroy the earth upon which, ultimately, all depended, that was the final horror, we felt. To devote all one's energy to working for the banning of the use of nuclear power as a weapon, was that the only reasonable thing to do with one's life, we sometimes wondered. But negative purposes have never a deep appeal. Surely the only appropriate gesture to make in the face of enormity is a positive one, however small. We could cultivate our portion of earth. It was little more than wilderness, lying exposed to every kind of blasting weather, but it was earth, and earth responds. Learn to understand it a little, work along the rhythm of it and it will repay you in ways beyond your reckoning.

Soon we saw a thick green sheen come over the cornfields and the potatoes began to push through in crowded rows. The garden plot, which had been so well limed and manured, was producing lettuces of real succulence and flavour.

The stirks were coming on amazingly well on the natural grazing and were scarcely recognisable as the lean, shivering creatures we had bought only two or three months before. Our aim was to sell them profitably in the autumn and buy in a couple of good calving heifers, from which we would build up a small herd of four or five breeding cows. There were two licensed Aberdeen-Angus bulls in the district, for service. The sheep also we meant to sell at a profitable time and with the proceeds buy a score or so of well-bred, black-faced ewes or gimmers, to form the nucleus of a breeding flock which we could increase to about a hundred.

We meant to keep a hundred and possibly, later on, two hundred pullets in deep litter and to rear a few pigs if feeding permitted. Our plan was to slough off all the rag-tail stock by the autumn and start afresh then. And so it worked out.

The first item in the new stock we had to acquire almost at once—a hundred five-week-old pullets, which were to come into lay about the end of September. We put them into two rearing houses in a field near the house and let them run on good clean grass. All went well until the weather broke but then the trouble started. Almost every morning we would bring in two or three sodden chicks and dry them out in boxes by the stove. As they grew bigger they began to crush each other on cold nights and we would retrieve one or two small suffocated bodies from the pile in each corner of the hen-house. We tried every device to keep them from crowding, but to no purpose. They were obstinate little devils and seemingly had entered into a vast, grisly suicide pact. By the time they developed some sort of sense we had lost at least twenty of them, and even then our patience nearly gave out, as we dodged each other round the henhouses each evening at dusk, chasing the elusive little rascals in to bed. The two or three ex-broody hens, who were complacently rearing ducklings in the next field, looked on at these manoeuvres with a faintly derisive twinkle in their elderly eyes. Don't you know there is no substitute for mother, even foster-mother, love, they seemed to say!

We had no hay crop to worry about that first summer, and once the turnips were hoed and the potatoes ridged we turned the attack once more to the ever-recurring problem of fencing. Our southern flank was now very adequately protected by a first-class Forestry Commission fence. To the north and east we were moderately well defended but our western approaches were badly in need of safeguard. We had a frontage here of three or four hundred yards along the roadside and the fence was practically non-existent. So, one Saturday, we loaded the trailer with posts and wire, packed a picnic basket and set off for what we called 'the west end'.

We had had a spell of very dry weather and the water was coming into the storage tank in the house in only the smallest of trickles so we had to use it very sparingly indeed. At the 'west end' there is a burn which never dries up. It has its source in the hill and its water is clear amber and lies in pools, where the small trout flash. Remembering this burn, and the cool delight of it, I packed a bundle of washing and a bar of soap among the fencing material and, while Jim dug holes for the strainers, I did the family wash in a pool of golden water. I hung it to bleach on the dwarf alder bushes, while Helen splashed about and floated twig boats in the pool. We made a fire to boil our tea kettle and afterwards I helped to stretch wire for Jim. We bumped home happily in the trailer, Helen and I each clutching a bundle of clean linen, Jim whistling softly with satisfaction at the thought of a job well begun.

We spent several more days working at that fence. Strangers passing along the road in cars, seeing our picnic fire and Helen gallivanting in her sun-suit, mistook us for holiday-makers and gave us an encouraging wave. We waved back enthusiastically for we did almost feel we were on holiday. I say almost, because even the most fascinating of holidays had never given us quite as satisfying a feel as most of our working days gave us. To know you were achieving something real, in the best company in the world, with the sun warm on your hands and all the wild things you loved—bird, hill, flower, sky—surrounding you, was deeply pleasurable. Of course, we hammered our thumbs, we dropped staples at crucial moments in the rushes, we tore our legs on pieces of barbed wire, but that was just the pepper and salt. When the last stob was in and the last wire tightened, we waded in the burn with Helen and sat on the bank watching a heron flap his lonely way up to the lochan in the hill beyond Rhivoulich.

By the third week in September the corn was ripe. This is a reasonably early date for these heights—the previous autumn we had seen stooks still lying out in November. And the crop was really one to be proud of. We had had a very heavy thunderstorm in August which had laid part of the oats in one field, where the yield was particularly heavy. But, on the whole, it was a good, standing crop. On the twenty-fourth of the month Jim began cutting 'roads' for the binder, that is, cutting a border around the edge of each field with a scythe to allow the binder to work freely without damaging any of the corn. I followed in his wake, tying the swathes into bundles with a stalk and setting them up in stooks.

We hadn't been long on the job when we saw Willie Maclean making his way slowly across the burn and up through the heather to join us. He was leaning heavily on his stick and he looked tired and a little shaky, but his face lit with pleasure as he picked up a sheaf and shook it by his ear. 'It rattles!' He beamed at us through his glasses, 'It's fine when you hear it rattle!' He looked over the small golden field appraisingly. 'It's a grand crop you have there', he said, and we felt a small glow of pride. To hear a neighbour praise a crop or a beast always brings a small thrill of pleasure to their owner. Hill people are not given to expressing enthusiasms, but when they do, in their own quiet, well-worn phrases, you know you can believe what they say.

In a couple of days the corn was cut and then began the laborious process of stooking. Everyone was busy at the same time, with their own crop, so that it was impossible to exchange help. But the weather remained magnificent until the last afternoon. It was a Saturday and we began to panic just a little as we saw the sky clouding and felt the first small drops of rain. We had to get the field in stook before dark so we worked on steadily, stopping only for a snatched cup of tea and then, at about half-past four, we saw a pair of legs swinging over the fence at the top of the field. Their owner gave no sign that he'd seen us working away at the bottom, but simply began stooking his way in our direction. Only when we were within earshot did he greet us with 'Aye, aye, you'll be wanting to get done before the rain'. It was our friend Bill (pronounced Beel) the post. He'd finished his letter-round, his own well-nursed crop was already in the stook and he'd arrived exactly at the right time to give us the lift we needed.

For several weeks the crop stayed out in the stook. Then one afternoon, Alec, an easterly neighbour, and his two boys arrived, unannounced, in the field. He stood looking round the crop. 'It would be as well in the rick, I think', he said, as he pulled a handful of grain from the nearest stook and straightaway he and the boys began stacking the sheaves into a small circle. A short while later Willie Maclean appeared, with Billy and Bertha in his wake, and the nine of us worked with gusto.

It was a perfect October evening. The sky was glowing red and the air was pungent, with a hint of frost. When the enormous yellow moon came looming over the arc of the hill, I went up to the house with Helen and Bertha and we stoked the fire, to set the kettle boiling, and made toast and a panful of fried eggs.

On the next two evenings this band of neighbours worked with us, till all three cornfields were decked with small, sturdy ricks. 'It'll be safe enough now, whatever', they said, as they bade us good night. They had quietly watched our progress through the year and had taken, I think, a modest, communal pride in our first harvest. They just wanted to be sure we should secure it, knowing as they did from their long experience what tricks the weather was capable of. We marvelled at their undemonstrative good-neighbourliness, and we blessed them for it.

Later on we had a couple of days' hired help to make the big stacks, from which the corn would be threshed. The last few ricks had small caps of snow on them before they were at last brought in. When the stacks were completed, on the last day of October, we knew what had gone into the fashioning of them—the work, the anxiety, sunshine, storm, good fellowship—the whole of our new life was symbolised in those five rugged cones, standing stark against the crackling stars.

Yes, it was the last day of October when we put aside our pitchforks, and we'd hardly had time to eat supper and warm our stiff, calloused fingers at the fire, when there was a loud knock at the door and into the kitchen marched the oddest-looking collection of creatures we'd ever seen. Their faces were completely masked in old bits of black stocking, or white calico. On their heads they wore scooped-out turnips, battered hats or turbanned scarves. The remaining parts of their persons were swathed in garments that defy description; one wore a horse-hair tail. We'd almost forgotten —it was Hallowe'en, and these were the guisers. After various attempts to guess their identity had failed, we offered them apples and sweets, which they had the utmost difficulty in eating, as their mouths and even their hands were muffled in disguise. However, an ill-suppressed giggle finally revealed the identity of one or two of them and they were persuaded to sing a song for a sixpence before they disappeared into the night.

The stacks became so much a part of the landscape that we were quite sorry to see the arrival of the threshing-mill and to have to undertake the slow dismantling of them. However, there was compensation in watching the plump, burnished grain pouring out of the hoppers into the sacks and to note that there was an astonishing amount of first-grade stuff among it. We would take a sample in a grimy palm and gloat over it, like a miser with his gold.

Our corn had been sown in a snow-storm and it was to see another before it was finally gathered in. When the job was three-quarters done the snow began to fall in soft, feathery flakes. It was not wetting stuff and did not deter the squad. But next day, when Billy came to help us finish off the straw-stack, it was blowing a blizzard and most of the chaff, which I had looked forward to gathering for the deep-litter house, was soaked. However, the grain was got safely under cover and Jim and Billy battled away with the stack of straw and secured it with weighted ropes. Next day, the seed-merchant's lorry came to collect the surplus grain and we received a substantial cheque.

Billy worked with us for several days, clearing up the aftermath of the threshing, and we decided to get him to stay on for a bit at a weekly wage. We had the potatoes to riddle and the turnips to lift and we foresaw winter catching up with us before this work was done, if we had no help. A bothy was fitted up for Billy in the bungalow and he had food with us in the house.

We borrowed a mechanical riddle and sorted the potatoes into ware, seed and chat. We found we had several tons surplus to our own needs, which we sold at once rather than risk having them deteriorate in the pit.

We sold the sheep and the stot stirks, keeping the two heifer stirks, one black and one blue-grey, which had improved sufficiently to warrant retaining, and bought thirty-five magnificent black-faced ewes and a ram, the sort of beasts any sheep-man would be proud to own.

Finlay, from up the hill, had given us a collie pup, Bess, and the place began to echo with shouts and whistling, as we started to train her to the shepherding. She was so anxious for work that she would be for ever rounding up whatever came in sight— hen, pullet, duck, cow, or anything else.

We were well into winter by the time the last of the turnips was lifted and pitted. The pullets were snug in their deep-litter house, the cow and the heifers were warmly bedded in straw, Charlie was crunching oats in his stable. With our first harvest secured, we could face the coming months with a reasonable measure of confidence.

CHAPTER VI
CEILIDHS

Two days after Christmas, the day of the little children's party we had planned, the ram died. He had been ailing for a week or so and we had done our best in the way of dosing, but to no purpose. As I looked up from my sandwich-cutting, at the kitchen window, I saw Billy making his way slowly up through the rushes in the lower field, carrying the bedraggled hulk of the once majestic creature on his shoulders. It was a sad moment, but luckily we hadn't time to brood. Jim and Billy performed the brief funeral rites, while I brought out the jellies and cream.

Eight youngsters from the three neighbouring crofts arrived at dusk, their faces gleaming with cleanliness and anticipation, and we had a very lively party indeed, Billy joining in with surprising gusto. The children taught us their own enchanting singing games, which have since become our favourites—'The wind and the wind and the wind blows high' and 'We are all maidens' and 'In and out the dusty bluebells' and many others with sweet, nostalgic cadences. Party-making is easy when you have unlimited quantities of eggs and cream, one of the little self-sown conifers (which need thinning, anyway) for a tree and a handful of unspoilt youngsters, eager for enjoyment. Each year we have a small gathering of children in the house at Christmas.

Soon after Hallowe'en we start planning it and long after it's over it's still a subject of chuckling reminiscence.

The smallest social occasion has a savour to it here. Some neighbours we may only see twice, or at most three times, in a year. They live, perhaps, only a mile or so away, but in the summer they're busy with their crops and in the winter snow or storm may prevent them venturing far at night. So, when we do meet, it's a small celebration in itself. First comes the firm handshake, as we congratulate each other tacitly on the fact that we are still in the land of the living. Then come the comments on the state of the weather and on the condition of crops and beasts, leading to the climax of the interview—the exchanging of any real tit-bits of news, the spicier the better! Finally, over a cup of tea, or a dram, if it is a really special occasion, a mellow, reminiscent mood settles on the company. This is when Jim and I hold our breath and wait for the old stories to come out for an airing in the fireside glow. We hear of an old bachelor who lived in the remains of a once-model croft house and would tether his cow to the foot of his bed to keep her from straying at night: of Mary, who had the second sight, and could see, on a winter evening's walk, the funeral procession of those who were soon to die: of the old widow who had the evil eye and could bring about the death of a favourite beast, or wish ill-luck on a whole family. These were all men and women who had lived hard lives, had been a law unto themselves and had left their legend lurking among the tumbled stones which had been home to them.

We never pass one of these pathetic ruins but we visualise the children scampering about the doorways. Many of them died young, as the headstones in the burial ground testify, but most of those who survived left their mark in other parts, in Canada or New Zealand. The depression in agriculture after the First World War was the immediate cause of many of these upland holdings being abandoned, but probably it would have come about in any case. With the improvement in communications, the standard of life was changing: the community was no longer isolated. The young people could get to town at the cost of a two-mile walk to the bus, instead of having to wait for the odd occasion, when they would go on foot, or on the steamer on Loch Ness. Once in town they would fall under the spell of the shop-window. A small holding could not stand the strain of providing cash for bought commodities. When the old diet of milk, meal, potatoes, eggs and a barrel of salt herring, carted from the west, was no longer considered adequate, holdings had to be enlarged or other means of subsistence found. Whether the children are healthier now, with the addition of tea and wrapped bread and sweetstuff to their menu, is perhaps a moot point. Certainly, preventive and remedial health measures save them from the epidemics which carried off many youngsters in the old days. These epidemics, when they did occur, hit them exceptionally hard, reared, as they were, in isolation from germs, and so lacking natural immunity. Labour-saving devices do spare the women, and the men, a lot of killing drudgery. But how far the real quality of human health and happiness has been improved would be difficult to say. To look at the serene faces and hardy frames of some of the older generation is to make one doubtful of using the word 'improve' at all. One neighbour it is always a special delight to meet is a grandmother of close on eighty who lives, now, alone in her croft house. She has reared a large family and has known every kind of trouble and grief. Yet there is always a smile on her face, to challenge the wrinkles; and she thinks nothing of walking miles, straight across country, fording burns and climbing fences, to visit relatives of a younger generation who may be sick.

Finlay, who guided us in all our affairs with sheep, on hearing that the ram had died, immediately gave us one of his on loan till the end of the tupping season. So our fear that some of the ewes might not bear lambs was allayed.

The year came to an end with a storm of alarming fury. The scullery window was blown right out. One of the henhouses (mercifully devoid of hens) was scattered in bits across the field. But, miraculously, the straw-stack stood intact: we blessed the day we had battened it down with weighted ropes. After battling with the elements in the kitchen, doing my indoor chores in gum-boots and balaclava, I developed a heavy cold and we spent our Hogmanay dozing over a huge fire, myself well drugged with aspirin.

New Year started auspiciously for me, with Jim and Helen bringing me tea and toast to bed, and immediately all sneezing and snuffling were at an end! In the afternoon we walked out across the moor in the still, glittering cold and came home to a dinner of roast duck.

Then the ceilidhs began. Since the previous Hogmanay our neighbours had become friends and a good year's work had established a firm bond among us. We knew our way about. To us there is no place on earth so comforting as a croft kitchen on a winter night. As you approach the glow of the lighted window, the smell of the peat-reek comes at you in a waft of welcome, pungent and homely. On reaching the threshold you brush the snow from your boots with the small besom provided for the purpose. Then the door opens and you're bidden, with an outstretched hand, to 'come away in'. Inside, the flames are licking round the up-ended peats, there's the hiss of the pressure lamp and the ticking of a huge, old clock. The pattern is the same everywhere. It hardly varies, yet it never fails to delight. We're a little company gathered in sheltering walls that huddle against the vastness of the night and of the cold. We're supremely glad to have warmth and calm and relaxation.

The men stretch their legs and slowly stuff their pipes. The women move quietly about, placing the kettle, the tea-caddy, the cups in strategic positions. The children sit, bright-eyed, on the settle, hoping bed-time will be overlooked: at New Year, it usually is. The kettle is not brought to the boil till the men have had their dram, the women their glass of port and the children their fruit wine, to wash down the raisin-cake and shortbread. Tongues are loosened at this time of year and throats well moistened. You can almost forget the wireless in the corner by the window, the weekly paper stuffed under the chair cushions, and expect the ceilidh to resume its old character. You almost wait for the song and the story to come floating out of the shadowy corners of the room, but of course they don't. The stories are reminiscences, fascinating in themselves and never wearisome, however often they are repeated. They're founded on fact and they haven't the wild sweep and gusto of the old, imagined tales. The song, too, has died. There is no longer even the cheerful scrape of a fiddle, though here and there a young lad will produce a tune from an accordion 'box'.

We spent many evenings at neighbouring firesides that New Year. Helen enjoyed them as much as we did and was indulged with sweets and oranges, and walked home across the moor at midnight without a stumble, scorning to be carried.

The days were not arduous, for there was little we could do but feed the horse, the cattle and the hens, look over the sheep and split logs for the fire. Jim and Billy did, however, get ahead with the fencing, whenever the weather allowed, and made several gates. I tackled the accumulation of mending and took advantage of the well-banked state of the fire to do some large bakings.

On the worst days, when all outdoor work was at a standstill and it was too cold even to work in the barn for more than an hour or two together, we all turned our attention to improving the living arrangements in the house. All through the previous year we had used only the ground-floor rooms, for warmth in the winter and for convenience in the summer.

Now, however, we began to explore the possibilities of the upper regions. I scrubbed out the two bedrooms and the men shouldered the beds and furniture up the narrow stairway. The walls and paintwork were shabby in the extreme, but decorating would have to wait until the better weather came. The rooms were clean and we installed an oil-stove in each, which we would light an hour or so before bed-time each night.

Then we made the spare downstairs room into a second sitting-room, where we could relax, or so we hoped! The living-room had a felt-and-linoleum covering over the stone and we could go in there gum-booted, dogs at our heels, without fear of doing damage. The new sitting-room we planned as a sort of inner refuge, snugly carpeted, its walls lined with the books and pictures we had at last extricated from the boxes in the cupboard. Outdoor foot-gear and dogs were to be strictly prohibited. We foresaw long Sunday afternoons spent in the comfort of this oasis, but actually it didn't turn out that way. Sunday afternoons were usually spent attending to lambing ewes, chasing cattle out of the crops or catching up on domestic work, and the room itself had often to be converted into sleeping quarters for a benighted contractor. But still, we did enjoy brief moments in it and the knowledge that it was there was a satisfaction in itself. We began to feel we had got past the stage of the initial assault and were beginning to dig in for the campaign.

It was not a hard winter and by mid-February the larks were singing. Soon, we began to sense the slow tilting of the earth towards the sun and then a rash of activity broke out. Dung was carted to the fields, the vegetable plot was enlarged and dug, houses were got ready for the new batches of chickens.

We got wind of activities on other fronts. The hill-road down to Loch Ness-side was being widened and resurfaced, the worst of the bends rounded and a fine new bridge built, to replace the rickety one over the burn that cascaded down from Loch Laide. It was said that when this work was completed, the bus company would seriously consider putting on a weekly service to Inverness.

There were rumours of various new enterprises starting up in the district. A nursery garden, at the foot of the hill, where tomatoes were grown in soil heated by electricity generated by local water-power, was already well established. Now, we learnt, another 'in-comer' was to cultivate the sheltered slopes immediately above this garden for the production of soft fruit: another was setting up a small dairy farm and yet another was going in for mink. The place was buzzing with reports of the activities of the 'tomato-man', the 'strawberry-man', the 'mink-man' and the 'dairyman'. All these concerns were sited in the comparatively sheltered district overlooking Loch Ness. Each time we passed that way on our journey to town we would watch, goggle-eyed, for signs of the progress of these fascinating enterprises. We began to feel, with our adoption of more or less traditional methods, distinctly back numbers. Still, our oats had impressed even the seed-merchant the previous autumn and our ewes were in grand shape. Perhaps there was something to be said for a quiet merging into the landscape.

The scheme for the testing of cattle came into operation at this time. We had ours tested and found, to our dismay, that Daisy and one of the heifers were reactors. Daisy's milk had been declared free of bacilli and she appeared to be in radiant health, but she didn't make the grade, so she and the heifer had to be despatched to the market at once. We bought in a good cross cow, brown, with a white star on her forehead, which we christened Hope, in token of our feeling towards her, and a sleek, demure, quite enchanting little cross-Shorthorn heifer, which we could only call Pet. The name exactly fitted her.

The byre had a thorough cleansing and disinfecting and whitewashing before these new beasts were installed in it and we hoped our little herd could now be established without further skirmishings. A cow, particularly a house-cow, is so much a part of the family that one hates to have to exchange her for another. We had just got to know all Daisy's little whims and quirks, knew what blandishments she particularly appreciated and how to humour her and to cope with her occasional moods. Now we should have to start all over again with Hope. She was to calve in a few weeks' time and was slow on the move and quite placid; she proved an excellent milker and we soon came to have a real affection for her. A cow certainly responds to kindness. I soon discovered that Hope would let down her milk most willingly to music—'Lilli Marlene' was her favourite tune. As soon as I began to intone it, to a slow rather melancholy rhythm, I would glance along her back and see her ears twitch and a dreamy look come into the one eye visible to me. Then the milk would spurt steadily into the pail and I knew all was well.

The pace of spring was now increasing rapidly. Each evening at dusk we would see the gleam of fires, as the heather was burnt to make room for new growth. In the distance we could see the small black specks of figures silhouetted against the glow. With sticks and switches they were keeping the flames under control. The boys of the neighbourhood took a sort of primitive delight in assisting at these firing operations, and it did seem as though the purifying flames were really laying the ghost of winter in the hills.

With the approach of the lambing season there was another ghost to be laid—that of the threatening, elusive fox. A drive was organised and all guns mobilised. One cold Saturday afternoon Jim and Billy set off, with the others, to search the crags and thickets round the Red Rock. They swarmed up precipices and slid down scree, but never a fox did they bag. However, a gesture had been made and some good sport enjoyed. Communal activity always acts as a tonic—the men came home with a gleam in their eyes and a chuckle in their throats.

The ploughing was easier that year, for Jim and Billy could take turns at it, and all the field work went quite smoothly. But we were coming to a crucial point in our enterprise. Our capital was all laid out in the land and stock and it would be some time before either could give us a substantial return. Could we hold on and keep the place going till that time arrived? Were we justified in paying Billy a wage, small though it was? As Jim crawled up and down the field on the tractor, as I gathered pailfuls of stones from the garden plot, with Helen making mud pies in her own corner, these questions were nagging away at our minds.

Finally, we went to see our man of business in Inverness. He is at all times most helpful and understanding, and a problem shared is usually half-way to being solved. The banker, too, was co-operative. All bankers have a spine-chilling effect on us, but I think the small country-town banker who, in many cases, is of farming stock himself, is perhaps the one representative of the order who does come within our understanding. Our particular banker has enjoyed several days shooting grouse and hares over our acres and looks positively human in rough tweeds with a gun under his arm.

Finally, we decided that we could cope with the situation and that Billy could be kept on for the time being at any rate. The pullets were showing a profit and at this peak time of egg production we would be cleaning eggs till midnight, while listening to a radio play. The ducks, too, were laying again. The sun had a warmth to it, coltsfoot was blazing along the sheltered bank of the burn, the peewits were tossing and flashing over the fields, the wild geese had gone off, honking their way gaily into the white north sky. It was a time of promise after all.

Hope presented us with a tidy little black bull-calf, one morning at seven. Two days later the first of the lambs was born. Each morning after that we would look out first thing to see how many new white specks had appeared on the moor overnight. Helen was the quickest at spotting them and she kept the tally. Each evening we would walk right round the flock, watching for any ewe that needed help; but they were wonderful mothers and we only lost one lamb. Billy quickly skinned it and draped the small, fleecy coat over the body of a lamb which had lost its mother. The bereft ewe, after an astonished nosing, adopted it as her own. We had some anxious moments, for there are so many creatures ready to make a meal of a new-born lamb—the fox, the buzzard, the killer dog. The weather itself can be cruel. Driving rain is one of their worst enemies. But we were lucky, for the weather though cold was mostly dry, and the lambs got safely on their feet and began to thrive.

One Sunday in mid-April, when everything was more or less under control, we left Billy in charge and set off for Loch Ness-side. The primroses were in flower on the wooded slopes, the birds were singing their heads off in the leafing trees. The water was blue and glittered in the sunlight. It was a morning out of time and we each had a foot in Eden.

CHAPTER VII
THE PIGLETS ARRIVE

By the end of April the place was swarming with young things. Hope's calf was let out of the byre and went charging round the field like some fantastic clockwork creature. Home-hatched ducklings were weaving through the rushes, in a long, golden line. Tiny yellow balls of chickens were scattered over the short, bright grass. Lambs, startlingly white, as though freshly laundered in a favoured brand of detergent, were bouncing about in the heather and making wild dashes across the fields. Then the goat made a contribution to this nursery world, in the shape of a tiny brown kid. It was the most fascinating baby creature of them all. Faun-like, yet quite fearless, with bright, intelligent eyes, it would stand poised on a pinnacle of stone, gazing quizzically at everything, then suddenly leap and cavort in the air, for the sheer joy of using its limbs. Helen would watch its antics for hours on end, completely under its spell.

Meanwhile we had, thanks to our banker, added a further twenty gimmers to our sheep stock and put a fresh batch of five-week-old pullets in the rearing-houses.

We certainly had our hands full, but it was a real delight to be working among all these young things. We didn't find the long hours a burden. I think the spring air, the fresh, plain food and the deep, trance-like sleep we fell into at night kept us going. This sort of life generates its own energy, it imposes its rhythm and if you respond to it you can keep up a steady pace. There is none of the rushing and jolting, interspersed with blank spaces of boredom, which wastes so much vital force in an artificial way of living. It has its own routine, of course, but within that routine there is always something fresh cropping up to hold the interest and to challenge initiative powers. One is conscious of keeping all the faculties in trim—brain, brawn, imagination and understanding are all constantly in play. One is on one's toes, yet relaxed.

There was now only one thing needed to complete our happiness—a pig! Could we woo the banker to the point of allowing our overdraft the generosity to embrace one little porker, we wondered. It appeared we could. Anyhow, Jim went to Dingwall market one beautiful May morning and came home with, not one pig but four small, squirming bundles of sacking in the back of the van, and a triumphant twinkle in his eye. As we loosed each bundle its contents turned out to be a plump, dapper little porker, which scampered round the pen then stood four-square in front of us, on its neat, pink trotters, looking at us out of unwinking eyes, brashly demanding sustenance.

We had to like the little beggars. They were impudent, yet fetching and they grew at an alarming rate. We had skim milk for them and potatoes, to which we added protein, and they found a lot of nourishment in the ground itself. In fact, we had always wanted a pig or two, not only because the market was good and they could give a quick return, but also because of their value as cultivators. Jim had fixed up a shelter for them from sheets of corrugated iron, lined with straw, encased in wire-netting. This he had placed in an enclosure on a piece of rough ground, full of couch grass and heather. The whole thing, shelter and enclosure, was movable. Our idea was for them to bull-doze and fertilise, bit by bit, this piece of ground, which could then provide first-class grazing for sheep and cattle. The piglets soon got the idea and the morning after their arrival their little pink snouts were black with burrowing in the peaty soil. Whatever it was in the way of vitamins and minerals they got out of the heather roots and the ground, I don't know, but they certainly did thrive. There was no lolling about in a clean, concrete sty for them, they worked for their living and they liked it. The exercise in the confined space certainly didn't prevent them putting on good, healthy flesh.

Neighbours came from far and wide to cast an eye over them, prod them with sticks, scratch their backs and murmur 'porky, porky!' into their appreciative ears. A pig does love to be flattered, and the neighbours would say, as they lit their pipes and shook their heads slowly from side to side, 'grand pigs, grand pigs…' in a ruminative, almost wistful way. In the old days, when weaners were to be had for half a crown, every croft had its pig, tenderly reared in a small, dark sty: in November it would be stuck and salted. Mrs. Maclean had given me the recipe for the brine mixture and told me tales of the great feastings they had always had with their Christmas ham. However, these particular little pigs were to go to market, and go they did a couple of months later, when they fetched more than double their purchase price and we bought six more with the proceeds.

That month we had a real heat wave. Warm, dry weather is so much the exception to the rule here that we tend to welcome it with open arms, and to revel in it unthinkingly. The heat shimmers over the moor, the hills are shrouded in blue haze, the scent of the small flowers is honey-sweet and lulling. Helen scampers around, in the briefest of sun-suits, and in no time at all is burned gipsy brown. But a heat wave brings its problems.

We hadn't had much snow that winter, the springs were running low and to our dismay we found that there was not enough of a flow to drive the pump at the well. The storage tank in the house was empty and we began a frantic search for an additional supply. We wished the golden well were not so far away, it would have solved all our problems. Neighbours, sympathetic as always to our troubles, told us of several spots where they remembered water rising long ago. We followed their directions and eventually came on the old 'horse well', where our predecessors had always watered the horses. It looked promising. Jim and Billy cleared the rushes, dug down to the source of it and laid a pipe, to connect the flow with that from our existing source. It was not strong enough to make much difference immediately, but we were confident that it would help after a good spell of rain. In the meantime, we had to carry water for drinking and cooking in pails, every morning and evening, while for washing we still had some in the big butt at the back door. When that was done I carried the clothes down to the near burn and laundered them there. It was very pleasant on a burning hot day. I would lay the linen on a flat stone and rub it clean, then rinse it in the clear flow. Now and again, an astonished trout would flash through the washing pool: a frog would give me an incredulous stare before bounding to the safety of a cool, green hollow in the bank. When my back began to ache I would stretch out on the grass and watch Helen splashing in her own pool upstream.

Dinner would be a picnic eaten on the doorstep that day, and I would make up for it by producing ham omelette and a cool salad at supper-time. I am thankful that eggs agree with us all and that they can be made into an almost endless variety of dishes. An egg and a lettuce, bread, butter and milk—I think we could all live on those for ever!

One evening, after a blazing day, which had left us really limp, we noticed the sky clouding at sunset. Helen was asleep upstairs, the chickens and ducklings had all gone to roost. Everything was very still and quiet and we were sitting in the cool of the living-room, looking through the papers, when I felt my ears twitch. I listened intently: it was the sound we had been waiting weeks to hear—the patter of rain on the tin roof of the scullery. We jumped up and looked out. The branches of the rowans were stirring, a breeze was rising and the rain was hissing on the parched ground. I think no sailor on a waterless raft in mid-Pacific ever greeted a thunder-plump as deliriously as we did!

In a remarkably short time the water-butt was overflowing. As we couldn't bear to see this water going to waste, I struggled into gum-boots, mackintosh and sou'-wester and put every available pail, basin and bath, in turn, under the overflow spout. Jim quickly bored a hole in the scullery window-frame, inserted a length of rubber tubing in the top of the butt, passed it through the hole and into the sink. To see the sink filling with this lovely, soft rain-water sent me nearly crazy with delight. We rushed in and out carrying pails, till we were soaked to the skin, our eyes bright in our gleaming faces. The supply of water we accumulated that night lasted us until the weather resumed its normal dampness.

We had a really grand crop of potatoes that year, at the cost of a deal of labour and anxiety. The field they were in had borne such an exceptionally heavy growth of corn the year before that the weeds had been well smothered. It had been ploughed each way, in the spring, so that the tilth was as fine as one could wish. We had borrowed a ridge plough to open the drills. The planting had been heavy work, but with three and a half of us on the job we had managed it fairly quickly. Then came the closing of the drills, a tricky operation with a tractor. The implement being in one's rear, it is the easiest thing in the world to knock the tubers out of place when covering them, with the result that they are liable to come up unevenly spaced, or through the side of the drills, or even in the spaces between the drills. Many people prefer to use a horse-plough to close the drills as, by this method, you can see exactly where you are and have greater control of your implement. However, Jim was determined to use the tractor and, at bottom, we applauded his courage, but our hearts were in our mouths as we watched the great, shining blades scattering the nicely placed tubers in all directions.

After completing the first few drills, Jim got into the way of the work and the crop certainly seemed to be covered, Next day we went up and down the field with hoes, pushing an odd tuber here and there into place. Then other things claimed our attention and we had to leave the potatoes to their fate.

Soon we began to cast an anxious eye over the field. Sure enough, the dark green, crinkled shoots were coming through the ground in the most unexpected places. The field, which had hitherto had the beautiful symmetry of a chessboard, now began to look like something that had come out in a rash.

We refused to be dismayed. Each armed with a hoe, we worked up and down the field, pushing and scraping, until we had virtually transformed each drill into a space, and vice versa. The effect was slightly irregular, of course, but when the plants came to maturity the leafiness of them hid the waywardness of their ranks and they were a noble sight. The heavy hoeing had killed every would-be weed at birth and the potatoes had it all their own way throughout the summer.

The turnips, too, were good that year, though by the time we finished singling them we felt we'd been born with a hoe in our hands. Smack, pull, smack, pull we went, day after day, along the interminable drills. We saw turnip seedlings sprouting in our dreams and wished the cows were not so desperately fond of the things. It was only the thought of being able to dump a pailful of succulent slivers under the nose of a stalled beast on a winter morning that kept us going. A turnip is indeed a handy thing to have about the place in winter: it gives a savour to the family soup pot; the hens love to peck away at one, when the snugness of their deep-litter house begins to pall and they're longing for a little diversion; and the sheep will gladly polish off any still left in the field, in the hungry gap of early spring.

We managed to keep the garden fairly clear of marauders that summer, though every time I went up to get a lettuce or an apronful of peas, I dreaded what I might find in the way of damage done overnight. The black-faced sheep has all the instincts of a mountaineer and is quite able to scale, or barge through, an ordinary wire fence. Cows have elasticated necks, with an amazing reach, and a distinct fondness for flower-heads of all kinds. Anything growing on the other side of a fence has an irresistible attraction for them. I sometimes wonder what they secretly made of the taste of the luscious-looking nasturtium leaves they devoured. Then there were all the other garden enemies—the goat, rabbits and moles and hares. Even the chickens were most unhelpful; in the early part of the season, when they were on free range, they would fly over the fence and scratch up the new-sown seed in a kind of demented frenzy.

One morning, I found Charlie, the horse, standing with a rather shamefaced, bewildered look in his eyes, in the midst of the trampled cabbages. It transpired that the children had left the gate open the evening before, Charlie had wandered in, the gate had blown to and he couldn't get out again. It was surprising, really, the small amount of damage he had actually done. I think he'd had a conscience about it! Anyhow, he seemed glad enough to be released from his enforced captivity among the vegetables.

It was a minor miracle that even one carrot should survive in the face of all these hazards. Our appreciation of the perilous journey which each bit of greenstuff or root had endured, before it reached the dish, gave an added savour to our meals.

All in all, that was a good year for the garden. The currant bushes, which a neighbour had given us, began to bear fruit. Mint, parsley and chives were all flourishing, along with carrots, parsnips, radish, peas, beans, chicory, beetroot, spinach and all the usual greens. There were even a few knobbly cauliflowers. In his few spare moments, Jim had made a glass-house on a framework of scrap picked up at the Inverness yard. I had high hopes of producing tomatoes in this and I did put a dozen plants in home-made compost in margarine boxes. But they took too long to ripen, in the meagre heat, and only developed some rather tight, pale balls of fruit, which I made into chutney. However, I found the glass-house an excellent place for bringing on flower seedlings, and subsequently it was put to other uses. It served as a brooder-house for day-old chicks and it once saved the lives of some weakly piglets. One year it grew a vegetable marrow and it now produces strawberries and mushrooms and gives us some most welcome out-of-season lettuce. It has done much to add spice to our lives and it has become quite a landmark. Sun and moonlight glisten on its roof, making it wink cheerfully across the landscape.

In a small enclosure off the garden Jim had placed our much-travelled beehives and he liked to talk bees with anyone who was interested. Every croft had its hive or two, but there were no real enthusiasts in the district. However, word soon got round that Jim was bee-minded and he travelled miles to collect swarms. The real bee-man is born, not made, either you have a feeling for the little creatures, or you haven't. Jim undoubtedly has; he works away quite unconcerned among them, scorning hats, veils and other protective apparatus. There is only a short clover season here, but the heather is right on the bees' doorstep and they were soon revelling in it and laying up another small harvest for us.

Our cattle all passed another tuberculin test, but Hope suddenly became alarmingly ill. On entering the byre one morning for the milking, she lay down in her stall and refused to move. Her stomach was swollen like a balloon and she was groaning in a most distressing way. We thought she had probably overeaten herself in the lush summer grass, and was blown. If that were the case, the only remedy, we knew, was the drastic one of plunging a sharp instrument into her side, to release the accumulation of gases—and we knew it had to be done at once, if she was to be saved. We looked at one another, wondering who would have the courage to perform the operation. Then, by great good luck, we happened to notice the vet's car drawing up at Willie Maclean's; he was on his testing round. Billy was despatched with an urgent message and, within a quarter of an hour, the vet was examining Hope. She was not, he said, blown, the swelling, apparently, was in the wrong place for that. With a mighty, combined effort we got her to her feet and he gave her a drench and told us to keep her in the byre, with her forelegs higher than her rear. We obeyed instructions and she slowly recovered, but she had very little milk for some time after that.

We were thankful disaster had been averted. The loss of a cow, on a small place such as ours, can be a very serious matter indeed. The result of this mysterious affliction was that Hope failed to come into season at the appropriate time. It is most important on a bleak, hill farm to have the calves born about April or May, so that cow and calf get the benefit of the good weather. To this end, the cows must be served in early or mid-summer. With some beasts you can detect at once the restlessness which means that they are, in local parlance, 'wanting away'. Immediately, you sling on the rope halter and allow yourself to be dragged the up-hill mile to the bull's domain. If you're lucky, the one trip will suffice, if not, you may have to accompany the wayward lady twice, or even thrice, on her nuptial journey.

With other beasts it is sometimes extremely difficult to detect the signs: they may occur only at night, when the household is asleep. You're lucky, then, if a kindly farmer will allow your cow or heifer to run with his bull for a lengthy period, to ensure satisfaction.

That summer, Hope had not the slightest desire to gallivant. In the end, in desperation, we had to get the vet to give her an injection, which had the desired effect of making her head post-haste bull-wards. We have since spent many anxious hours trying to anticipate the moods of various members of our small herd and have often wished that artificial insemination were not such a skilled and costly business.

On the rare occasions when we had leisure to lean on a gate, in those early summer days, we couldn't help feeling a certain sense of achievement. The cattle and sheep were thriving, the pigs were rootling and putting on weight. The lambs were all safely inoculated and bid fair to become winners. The hens and ducks were still laying hard and the new pullets were making good progress. They were white Leghorn, crossed with light Sussex, and as trim and elegant as ballerinas. The potato and turnip crops were lush and green. There was a ripple through the young grass and the oats were showing a milky sheen. There was much to consolidate, much to improve, but we felt we had at least passed a couple of milestones on our road.

CHAPTER VIII
FIVE YEARS A-GROWING

On a hill croft, once the turnips are singled and the potatoes ridged, there is a lull until hay harvest. On the low ground, the hay is usually ready soon after the turnips are done, and the lull is between hay and corn harvests. With us, getting in the hay is generally a very anxious and long-drawn-out affair, which may well go on till it overlaps the cutting of the corn, so that we're very glad of a respite before the grass is ready.

With most hill-people this respite takes the form of an expedition to the nearest moss to cut peat. A bus-man's holiday, if you like, for the work is hard. Still, days at the peats do have a feel of jollity about them. For one thing, they mean a change of scene, as some people have to go several miles to find suitable ground. Then it's work all can share and very often men, women and children from several crofts will join forces, the men to do the cutting, the women and children to stack the peats to dry. Food will be taken and a fire lit from old, dry heather roots, to boil the dinner kettle. There is always much leg-pulling and wise-cracking— communal work always goes with a swing.

Later in the year another expedition will be made, when the small heaps of peats will be built into larger ones. It is rather like making stocks into ricks. Then in the autumn the whole lot will be carted home and built into a stack near the house door. It's a harvest that hasn't much worry attached to it. Even if the weather is so bad that the peats never really dry out, they will still burn reasonably well. There is also a definite sense of satisfaction in making oneself independent of the coal-merchant. We should have liked to have cut peats that summer, but there was still a lot of pioneering work to be done in the way of fencing and draining and this had to have priority.

Peat-cutting apart, July is a less strenuous month than some and so it is the most suitable time to hold agricultural shows. The second Friday in July is the day of the traditional Wool Fair in Inverness. It is still called the Wool Fair, although no wool is sold at it now. Wool has its own Marketing Board these days and one has to abide by the rules and regulations in the selling of one's crop. But Wool Fair day still retains its atmosphere of holiday. It has become a horse show and sale and everyone who can possibly spare a day goes to the market place to see the sights, to meet friends and have a dram.

We had heard that it was still sometimes possible to pick up a Shetland pony for a fiver and we went in hopes of getting one for Helen. But evidently something had happened to either the supply or the demand or both, for the Shelties all reached nearer the twenty-pound mark that year. However, it was a delight to see the magnificent beasts that were put through the ring. A superb Clydesdale was withdrawn at close on a hundred pounds. One admired the spirit of his owner. He certainly looked worth an untold amount, with his arched neck, his burnished coat and his huge, powerful limbs. All working animals have a dignity about them that no beast kept for pleasure or sport ever achieves. They may have lost their wild, native pride, but at least they never fawn or whimper. They demand respect and they get it from the men who work with them and know their value.

The next day we had a visit from a dealer, who practically insisted on buying Charlie from us. We had the greatest difficulty in making him accept our firm refusal. Charlie was one of us, we said, even supposing he never did another day's work, as long as there was a bite for us there would be a bite for Charlie. Eventually we pacified the dealer with a cup of tea and saw him off the premises. He gave us a half-pitying look as he climbed into his magnificent car. From the corner of my eye, I could see Charlie kicking up his heels with joyful derision, in the lush pasture down by the burn, and I could have sworn he knew exactly what had been going on. From that day on, our attachment grew stronger than ever to our wise, old, tawny-coated Charles.

Finlay came one evening, with his cousin Tom and a lad from a neighbouring farm, to clip the sheep. Jim and Billy had made a fank of wooden palings, and we had the sheep safely penned before our helpers arrived. We went indoors, with satisfied grins on our faces, to snatch a quick cup of tea before the operation began. But we'd evidently underestimated the strength of mother-love. The ewes, separated from their lambs, which were bellowing pathetically round the outside of the fank, made one wild stampede, completely ignoring the admonitory snaps of young Bess, whom we had left on guard, and broke through the rails. Within seconds the whole flock was scattered and all our gathering was to do over again. Luckily, the squad arrived soon after this disaster. They had two experienced dogs with them and between us we soon had the situation under control. It's a fascinating thing to watch a good dog and a good sheep-man penning the last few obstinate members of a flock. Not a hint of force is used, but the eyes of man and dog never leave the bewildered beasts. From the side of his mouth the man now and then utters a brief command. With stick outstretched he points; then, with a sort of uncanny mesmerism, man and dog impose their united will on the sheep. They lurch into the fold, the gate clicks to. We relax and breathe more freely.

All evening the men worked away at the sheep with concentrated energy. There was only the sound of the clicking shears and of an occasional scuffle with an unruly beast. Now and then, Tom would crack a quiet joke and Billy would curse the midges. Helen and I went out to help carry the fleeces into the barn, then I put her to bed—and still the clipping went on. At last, at ten o'clock, it was done: the last sheep staggered to her feet and went lolloping off to join her offspring. A freshly shorn sheep is perhaps the most pitiful-looking object in the world. Bereft of its fine, shaggy coat, her outline is anything but imposing. Where, one wonders, is the fine, arrogant beast which stamped defiance when a dog came too near her lamb, only a month or two ago? Surely this ungainly body, swaying off on its spindly, bandy shanks, can't be hers? But it is; her lamb finds her as alluring as ever and is soon trotting happily at her side.

The men were glad of their ham and eggs that night and we all relaxed, bare brown elbows on the table, till the last tints of the sunset had faded from the sky.

Later, we packed the fleeces into the huge bags supplied by the wool-broker in Leith and carted them to the road-end, to await collection by the float. The first harvest of the year was secured.

Still the grass was not ready for cutting. I made up my mind, while there was time to spare, to tackle the re-decoration of the house, so I started with the bedrooms. They had been distempered, walls and ceilings, one in blue and one in pink, but the distemper was flaking. All I had to do, I thought, as I donned an old overall and tied my head up in a scarf, was to scrape this distemper off and apply a coat of cream wall-paint in its place. I took a scraper and began on the ceiling of the blue room. I soon found that the removal of the blue distemper revealed a layer of off-white beneath, and of some indeterminate shade of green beneath that. But, having made a start, I had to go on and I scraped till my arm and shoulder were almost burnt up with aching and my neck had developed a permanent crick. Helen, determined to take part in whatever was going on, scraped away laboriously at small sections of wall and practically removed the plaster right down to the hard stone!

I could only spend a limited amount of time at the work, for the cow and the hens and the garden, which were my particular provinces, had to be attended to and large meals cooked thrice daily. Gradually something began to emerge from the welter upstairs. A pleasant smell of fresh paint was wafted about the house and at last I was able to show some result for my labours. It was amazing, the impression of light and space and airiness the light cream paint-work gave to the bedrooms. When the floor-boards were restained and the grates painted black, we felt we had at any rate two really presentable rooms. That meant that the rest of the house had to be tackled, for the shabbiness of it was all the more apparent. I developed quite a passion for decorating and it was very satisfactory to see the transformation that could be achieved. I did the landing and staircase walls and worked my way down to the living-rooms. There I had to do some preliminary plastering-up and I felt quite a professional as I daubed away with plaster and trowel. We left the kitchen to the last, chose a fine day, carted everything movable out on to the grass and went at it together, for the kitchen can never be out of action for long. The effect of the light paint there was quite dazzling, for hitherto the wood-work had been a most depressing drab brown. Finally, I painted the front door and the window-frames a rich blue, which gave a welcoming gleam to the house.

While these absorbing operations had been going on in the house, the grass had been quietly and steadily ripening. One warm, still morning, Jim hitched the mower to the tractor and, with Billy perched precariously on the swaying seat, guiding the blades, moved slowly along the edge of the field. I couldn't be expected to concentrate on cooking stew and apple-pie that day, even in my dazzling kitchen. Every few minutes I would be poking my head outside to get a sniff of the new-cut grass. Helen was trotting round in the wake of the mower, gathering flowers and shouting encouragement to the men. There was a feeling of excitement about. Miraculously, for that first hay harvest of ours, the weather held. One calm, blue day followed another and there was just enough stir in the air to dry the crop satisfactorily. We borrowed Bill-the-post's horse-rake and Charlie plodded up and down gathering the grass into win-drows. We turned it and made it into small ricks and hardly a drop of rain came to interrupt the work. Grass, cut at the right moment, quickly made and dried by sun and wind, has a high protein content, whereas the stuff that's been sodden and turned over and over again, and only dried at last into a stiff, dark tangle, has little feeding value and will only serve to fill a void in a beast's belly. In subsequent years we've wrestled with hay till, near the point of exhaustion, we've sworn we'd never bother to cut the crop again. We've hung it on the fences, like washing, to dry, we've seen the ricks collapse into a black, treacly mess, we've had every kind of hay disaster, but that first crop was really a pleasure to handle.

Jim decided not to make the precious hay into stacks, but to store it under cover along at the far steading. There was no proper loft, but he made ceilings in byre, stable and barn by stretching wire-netting from wall to wall below the rafters. Then he stuffed the hay into the spaces between ceiling and roof. Billy looked doubtfully on this operation. It was certainly an innovation, but it worked. The hay kept perfectly through the winter, except in one portion where the snow blew through an ill-fitting skylight, and the insulation kept the building warm. For feeding purposes it couldn't have been handier. All one had to do was to take a fork and tumble the hay down on to the hungry beasts below.

The only interruption to our days of haymaking that summer came not from the weather but from the four porkers on the heath. They were by this time massive creatures, with strong wills of their own and highly developed bumps of curiosity. They would stand on their hind legs, snouts resting on the rail of their enclosure, scanning the alluring horizon. The combined pressure was usually too much for the fence, sturdy as it was. There would be a crack and a clatter, and a tally-ho from Helen, 'the pigs are out!' We would drop whatever implement we were holding and rush to head the four great hulks off from the cornfield. Sometimes they would be too quick for us and would go crashing into the corn, making four separate runways through the beautiful up-standing stalks. Now and again they would pause and turn to leer at us out of their mischievous, unblinking eyes. I believe they thoroughly enjoyed those chases and indulged in them for sheer devilment. We found them exasperating and exhausting, so much so that we decided the only thing to do was to pack the porkers off to market. They strongly resisted our combined efforts to load them on the float. The driver lost his temper, the lovely summer morning air was defiled with raucous shouts and we made several picturesque additions to our growing vocabulary of the vernacular! But at last we waved them off and at the end of the day they covered themselves with glory by fetching quite spectacular prices at the market. Jim was so elated that he bought six more youngsters at once. We worked late that night, preparing a clean place for them on the heather.

We also sold the goats and have not since then had any more truck with the capricious tribe, for we found them more bother than they were worth. Tethered, they are a constant worry. They have to be continually moved to fresh ground and one is tormented by the thought that that muffled groan one caught, when upstairs making the beds, was one of them strangling herself. One rushes down and out, only to find it is a ewe which has temporarily mislaid her lamb. On free range goats are horribly destructive. In theory of course they rid the place of thistles and other noxious weeds, but in practice, when they're not in the garden selecting the most succulent of the greens, they're having a nibble at the bark of a beloved tree. Trees are so scarce and so precious here and we only have the one thin line of rowans to remind us that trees really do exist. The goats gnawed the bark off several, thus slowly killing them. I found the goats far more difficult to milk than any newly calved heifer. It always took two of us to do the job—one to hold and the other to extract the milk, and at the end of this tedious business there would only be a couple of pints, at most, at the bottom of the pail. We had heard the story of the wonderful nanny, who lived on practically nothing, came into the scullery of her own accord, morning and evening, to yield ungrudgingly her quota of creamy fluid and was so devoted to the family that she couldn't bear to be left alone and even had to be taken out in the car for a Sunday run! No doubt this story was true, but the goat concerned must have been an exceptional lady. The idea of a goat is fascinating in the extreme, but the reality may be quite otherwise.

I think Helen was sorry to see ours go, but Jim and I couldn't bring ourselves to shed a tear. Helen was rapidly developing a personality. Rising five, she had become, as we imagined she would, remarkably independent and adaptable. Birth and death she accepted as she did sun, snow and the sprouting of the seed in her garden plot. Death, I think, sometimes caught her on the raw, particularly when it came unexpectedly, say, to an adored yellow ball of a chicken, but then another birth would come along and the shadow would be gone. She loved to bring Hope in for the milking and it was amusing to watch the tiny figure in blue dungarees, brandishing a hazel-wand and making the appropriate noises, while the great, brown hulk of the cow came swaying up the field and lurched into the open byre. She showed great concern for all the animals' welfare and would spend hours trying to restore a strayed lamb to its mother. She could hear and see with astonishing acuteness; it was a quiet world she lived in and any sound which came to disturb the quietness had to be interpreted at once. Bess had only to set up a barking, from her vantage point at the end of the steading, and Helen would come rushing in with the news. 'It's Feely (Finlay), Mummy, I see him coming along the heather with Tom. P'raps they want to borrow the mower.' It was more than likely that that was indeed the explanation for the hubbub. Once, it happened that I was the first to glimpse a loaded lorry coming down the hill road to the back of us. 'There's a load of straw for someone', I said, gazing at the vehicle, which looked like a child's toy, crawling down the slope. 'Not straw, Mummy, it's hay that's in it', Helen said, in a matter-of-fact tone. I looked again but, for the life of me, I couldn't have distinguished the greenish-yellow of hay from the golden-yellow of straw at that distance. To Helen, it came quite naturally.

She took an intense interest in the weather, understanding instinctively the effect it had on all our lives. The stars had a deep fascination for her. They are her bright lights. This fascination has grown, over the years, and her present ambition is to become an astronomer. Jim and I have exhausted our stock of knowledge of the subject and have imparted all the legends we know, too. We've given her two star-books and she often drags us out, on a glittering cold night, to identify planets and look for shooting stars. We wouldn't have it otherwise; we gladly suffer frozen toes and a crick in the neck so that she may revel in the blaze of the night sky. She is a great stickler for accuracy, and I'm certain that at the back of the statistics she's catching the steady gleam of poetry.

During that summer she began to get 'itchy feet'. She could already manage a hill walk of three or four miles, with us. Now she showed definite signs of wanting to go off occasionally on her own. Sometimes it would be to Woodend she'd go, sometimes over to the Macleans, where young Bertha was always ready for a game. We'd watch her progress from wherever we were working, see the small figure bouncing from tussock to tussock across the moor-ground, watch it disappear behind the raised bank at the burn-side and emerge seconds later on the other side of the water-splash. She was always sure of her welcome in the little house, where Mrs. Maclean would have a drink of milk for her, or lemonade, if the day was warm, and a pancake off the girdle and a sweetie for the way home.

She was big for her age, strong and independent, yet she was still not much more than a baby. Every day, after dinner and after supper, I used to take her on my knee and read her a story, from a book with large print and plenty of pictures. One day I suddenly realised that she was growing up. It was wet and I was mixing a cake in the kitchen. Helen was sitting quietly in the living-room. All at once she came to my side, dumped an open book in the midst of the floury mess on the table and began, quite calmly, to read to me. The words were simple and mostly of one syllable, but she hardly hesitated. I just held my breath and listened. It seemed like a minor miracle to me. To her, it was the simplest thing in the world, quite obviously. Since that day she has gone on reading steadily and our only difficulty now is to keep her supplied with books.

Helen found the wireless a great delight during that last pre-school year and she would caper round the kitchen to 'Music and Movement', tap with the poker to 'Time and Tune', and sing at the top of her voice with William Appleby. She even listened, enthralled, to the adventures with prehistoric monsters in 'How Things Began' and insisted on having 'Science and the Community' turned on full blast, though what she made of it none of us were sure!

She was never bored—every day brought something different to do. Times of celebration, such as Christmas, Hallowe'en and birthdays, were eagerly looked forward to and prepared for.

'How lonely she must be!' several of our friends said, at various times. They no doubt had a picture in their minds of one small girl surrounded by acres and acres of solitude and quiet. From the cosiness of suburbia, where there are iced lollies round the corner, shop-windows full of glittering toys, and a bus to take hordes of good children to the Saturday morning film show, this vision must have been something to turn from with a shudder.

Alone she undoubtedly is, in the sense that each one of us is alone, to the end of time. But she has learnt to face that aloneness from the start, she has grown up with it, so that she knows it's not a fearful thing. It will never become a bogy, to be dodged, but is already a companion she can walk with hand in hand. She has always had to do the last bit of the road from school on her own, along the track through the heather. Sometimes, if the day is really bad, we have hurried to meet her, for she still seems such a minute scrap of humanity, set against the vastnesses of hill and sky. But not once have we found her in the least disconcerted by snow, gale or thunder. She plods along, with a twinkle in her eye, taking whatever comes.

All in all, by the end of that second summer, we felt that our plan for Helen was working out better than we hoped.

CHAPTER IX
AN IMPROMPTU HOLIDAY

THE combination of hay-harvesting (comparatively easy though this had been) and house-painting, interspersed with pig-chasing left us, we had to admit, a little jaded, and the really big task of the year—the harvesting of the corn—was still to come. Everything was under control; the potatoes were in full bloom, the new pigs still at the amenable stage, the pullets settled in their deep-litter. Suddenly, simultaneously into our two minds, leapt the idea that a little holiday, just a long week-end, would be wonderful! We still had Billy. We might not have him another year, but for the moment we had him. We had never had the slightest qualm about leaving him in full charge when we had had to be away for a whole day at the market. He was as honest as daylight and well used to looking after himself.

Surely we could leave him to cope for the week-end? we asked ourselves. It was really more of a statement than a query and within twenty-four hours our minds were made up.

There is never any wondering with us what form a brief holiday shall take. We simply bundle ourselves, some bedding and some food into the old van and are off. That is half the joy of it, really, the knowledge that you can, within a matter of minutes, almost (though not quite!) as birds take wing, be on your way. There is no wearisome planning and contriving and agonising over expense. The van is there, we have to eat wherever we are, and a few gallons of petrol can't break the bank.

We decided to leave on the Friday and to be back by the following Tuesday afternoon. I unearthed the two inflatable rubber mattresses, an old cot mattress of Helen's and the warm sleeping-bags. I packed three biscuit tins with food, filled an egg-box, gathered an assortment of plates, cups, knives and forks, bathing suits, old rubber shoes, extra garments, the bivouac, a book or two and the camera, into a kit-bag, and we were ready for the road.

Where to go is never any problem; the west is in our blood and we simply gravitate towards it, as the birds migrate with the sun. Billy was most helpful and quite entered into the spirit of the thing. He even gave the van a clean-up and stuck a bit of canvas over a leaky portion of the roof, then he filled an extra can with petrol and stood by to give us rather a wondering farewell wave. Perhaps he doubted whether he'd ever see us all alive again.

It was drizzling, and certainly rather chilly, as we crawled up the 'overside'. We turned our heads at the top of the rise and glanced back at our little fields of ripening corn and potatoes and roots. The sheep and cattle looked small, defenceless dots in the distance. We felt a little guilty about leaving these well-loved tyrants of ours, even for a few days, but—'Ach, everything will be all right without us', we said, to ease our minds, and we chugged slowly north and west.

We went through Beauly, Muir of Ord and Garve—pleasant places all of them, but just a little tame. Then we swung on to the moor road and we knew we were really on our way. There was a grey mist over the hills and the burn was foaming amber after the rain. With every mile the authentic smell of the west came at us more strongly—there s nothing like it anywhere. It's made of the scent of wet heather and sea-tangle and mist and hill-air and it always goes straight to our heads. We opened the windows wider and poked our noses out, to get a delighted sniff. Helen clutched Duchess round the neck and began groping for her spade and pail.

We cruised along the side of Loch Broom into Ullapool, passed the last straggle of the village and looked for a turning to the sea. We knew we simply had to get our hands into sea-water that day. Another mile or so and we were bumping along a deep-rutted track towards a small lighthouse. Right at the point we came to a halt on a rise of bright green sward. Straight ahead lay the Summer Isles; the water between was gleaming in the pale, evening sunlight. We sat a moment looking and listening to the slapping of the small waves on the pebble beach. Then Helen, already shoeless, made straight down to the water's edge and we followed, strolling at leisure, as though there were all the time in the world for everything—the west had already imposed its rhythm on us.

From the contemporary point of view, the average west coaster is a failure: he has no ambition, no drive. Because he has no desire to be for ever 'bettering' himself, he is considered lazy and feckless. True, in former times many people from the west went to America and Canada, where some of their descendants have made names for themselves; we hear of the few, but of the many there is no record. It is not always realised that those emigrations were, in most cases, enforced by the ruthless, alien landlords, who emerged after the real clan system had broken down. The men were driven to the boats, the women and children were carried aboard, and the songs which drifted back across the water as the boats put out were laments, bitter, hopeless laments. Many a settler would sit, years afterwards, looking across the 'waste of seas' and in his dreams 'behold the Hebrides'. He had no natural desire to leave his native coast—why should he? Times might have been bad, but they might be bad anywhere. At least, as long as he was not interfered with, the west coaster need never have starved. Even if the crops failed utterly, he could get his fish from the sea and his bit of game from the hill. The seaweed itself made a tasty dish, full of iodine and health-giving minerals. And he had his horizon; he could see things in the light of infinity, which is the only way to get a true perspective. Why should he want to exchange all this, for a mad rush after money? What could money buy that wouldn't bring him envy and discontent, an aching head and ulcers in his stomach? The west coaster will leave it to others to achieve brilliance as politicians and administrators. He'll also leave it to others to become spivs or invent the nuclear bomb. Give him three rooms to house his family, a few acres and a boat and he's the happiest man on earth. He still believes in happiness.

These thoughts were in our minds, as we looked back across Loch Broom and saw the tiny fields sloping down to the water's edge. Every inch of ground was cultivated; the small patches of corn and potatoes and roots were bright and flourishing. The natural manuring of the beasts, plus the application of seaweed and shell sand, has resulted in a high degree of fertility in the crofting ground. The Cheviot sheep that were grazing right down to the water's edge looked remarkably fit and strong. Hay-making was in full swing and every available pair of hands was busy hanging the grass on tripods to dry.

When Helen had dabbled to her heart's content in the clear, green water, we looked for a spring, gathered driftwood and built a fireplace. Soon, ham and eggs and tomatoes were sizzling in the pan and we ate a leisurely meal, washed down with hot, delicious tea, and stretched ourselves on the turf in relaxation. Sun, moon and stars were to be our timepieces for the next few days. Our watch was not reliable, anyway, and we wanted to discard all sense of urgency. There was no cow to be milked, there were no pigs or hens to feed, no eggs to collect, no weeds to watch for—there was nothing to hinder our entry into time-lessness. And that is surely as near as we'll ever get to a glimpse of the infinite, this side of Styx.

When Helen began to yawn I unrolled her mattress and placed it across the two front seats of the van. Jim collapsed the other seats, to make the back part flat, and we blew up the rubber mattresses and laid them lengthwise there. Duchess was accommodated in the bivouac, along with the stores.

Helen was asleep in a couple of minutes. Slowly, we washed and dried the dishes and made ourselves another brew of tea, while the sunset colours faded from the sky and little flashes of light began to wink out from the far headlands. We were loath to sleep. Why, at any rate in summer, did people bother to live in houses? we wondered, and we found again the contradictions in ourselves. We loved our own small house, every stick and stone of it. We loved the bonds that held us to the work of cultivation, and we knew every corner of each of our fields. To see them in good heart gave us the deepest kind of delight. To watch something edible, anything, even a lettuce, grow, where nothing but weeds had grown before, was the most satisfying thing we knew. Yet here we were, completely happy as nomads! We had unearthed an even deeper level of existence.

Jim tells me that the Stewarts have always been quite content among the tinkers and I, a Stewart by adoption, would be happy to join forces with them. After the '45 Rebellion, many of them were obliged, like others of the resistance movement of the time, to take to the hills, and their descendants to this day find it difficult to conform. Every summer some of them pitch their small, brown tents on the edge of our moor and make tin pans for us, in exchange for our discarded scraps of clothing and shoe-leather. Their brown faces are lean and wrinkled, but their eyes are bright, and we've heard them in the evenings scraping away at a fiddle for the fun of the thing, with no one in miles to throw them a sixpence. They're not exactly useful members of society, perhaps, but they keep their own particular brand of integrity while many a County Councillor has lost his, somewhere on the way. Who knows?—they may make a better death on a bundle of heather under the stars than he will on his sprung, quilted bed.

In the morning we were all awake early and we lay, snug in our sleeping-bags, watching the fishing fleet sail into Loch

Broom. The sea was a dazzling glitter of blue and gold. The sky was a vast, crystal dome. It was a morning of ceremonial splendour. The normal climate of the west is damp and sunless, maybe, but, funnily enough, on nearly every occasion when we've been there, we've come on these splendid, colourful days.

After breakfast we went down to the beach and dabbled in the water. Helen had a dip and we looked for agates among the pebbles. It wouldn't have surprised us that morning if we'd discovered gold! We gathered more driftwood and watched the gulls gliding over the sea, and the day slipped away over our heads.

We got into our sleeping-bags quite early in the evening and lay watching the sunset, till we could almost identify ourselves with each shred of cloud about the sky, each gleam of light, each shaft of colour. All the petty aches and worries that ruffled the surface of our daily working lives were smoothed away, as we made contact with these remote, unearthly things. They were with us all the time at home, but there we viewed them differently. When we looked at the sky, it was usually to try to foresee what kind of weather was in store—rain to swell the root crops or sun to ripen the grain. Now, we could see the sky as sky, a law unto itself, not necessarily something which would further our own small ends. Moments of detachment and reassessment are vivifying. One such moment, if it is sufficiently intense, may leave an impression on the mind that will withstand a lifetime of living. The universe is not a cosy place specifically designed to suit human needs. If everyone could grasp that fact afresh every morning, perhaps we should spend less time thinking up ways to exterminate one another. We should be grateful, as the tinker is, for a blink of sun to warm our bones in summer and the friendliness of a rock cave to shelter us from snow; we should be in touch again.

Sunday we spent wandering along the cliff-top to the next bay. St. Martin's Isle lay green and deserted in the middle of it. Saints had a liking for islands and I can see the point. It's sometimes difficult to remain sufficiently an island unto oneself, but to live on one perpetually does seem rather like dodging the issue. The difficult thing is to stay in touch on the land mass. There are many more saints than those recorded in the annals of holiness.

Helen skipped ahead of us on the springy turf. She was a small, lithe slip of humanity, all right, yet she was part of the blue morning, the curving wave, the gliding sea-bird, the withdrawn sky. The sight of her made us feel clumsy and awkward, with our loads of living pressing on our shoulders.

We made for the beach and let the clear water swirl about our ankles. We found beautiful fluted, moulded shells, smooth coloured pebbles, swathes of glittering sea-weed. We gulped down lungfuls of ozone. The world was one vast morning, brimful of light, and we understood why the Gael has for his promised land 'TIR NAN OG', the land of youth.

As we came back within sight of our camp, in the late afternoon, three large, brown cows looked at us with startled eyes and went lurching off across the sward. What had they made of our intrusion into their domain? we wondered. A moment later we knew the answer—they had certainly made the best of it. The pan that I had left filled with scrubbed potatoes, ready for our evening meal, had been overturned and its contents had completely disappeared. A cow does love a tattie! And so do we, when we're ravenous, after a long day in the air. There was nothing for it but to fetch water and scrub another lot of potatoes for supper. Within the hour, we were sitting cross-legged round the fire, eating mashed potatoes and poached eggs and drinking gipsy tea. There was magic in the air, the pure and simple magic of being alive and in touch with the moment.

Next day we decided to make for Gruinard Bay and spend our last night there, before pushing home. I remembered it from some twenty years before, as an enchanted place, where the green water came foaming over dazzling white sand. It had been to me then a 'faery-land forlorn'. There was a wide sweep of turf, I remembered, where we could make our camp.

We went round by Dundonnell and the shore of Little Loch Broom and we passed an alarming number of notices announcing 'Teas' and 'Bed and Breakfast', outside croft houses, which looked hardly big enough to accommodate their owners, let alone stray visitors. I took a look at the map, though there could be no question but that we were on the right road. Then the cars began, and the caravans, and the droves of cyclists. Twenty years before it had been an event to meet one crofter on the road, driving his cow or his sheep to pasture.

As we came round the last bend, into the sweep of the bay, we had to draw sharply into the side of the road, for a large sports car nearly had us ditched. The green sward was dotted with cars, caravans and tents of every description. In the one clear space some youths were kicking a football about. At the roadside stood a large receptacle, clearly labelled 'Refuse'. If it had served its purpose one could have forgiven it for being there, but the refuse was all too obviously littered here, there and everywhere, on the sand, the grass, the road.

When my dismay had subsided a little, I began to appreciate that it was an excellent thing that others had discovered this place. One should, of course, never hug a haven to oneself. I saw the fat, brown babies staggering about the caravans, the mothers lying with their toes in the sand. It was good that they should be there, but in my shared paradise I'd make a law that everyone must bury their rubbish, under penalty of expulsion.

It was getting late as we drew into the only secluded spot we could find, at the far end of the bay, beside a burn. Helen sped across the sand and into the water. She was in Abraham's bosom still, and saw only what she wanted to see. The water was as clear, the sand as soft as it had ever been.

We had supper early, for mist was coming in from the sea, and crept into our sleeping-bags. Then the midges began! We swatted and slapped at them then tried to smoke them out. We covered ourselves in lotion and buried ourselves completely under the covers. Nothing was any good; we lay scratching and tossing through the small hours. At last, at about five o'clock, we could stand it no longer so we dragged on our clothes, flung everything into the van and made off.

We crawled up the long, steep rise to the next headland, where a delicious breeze met us. We stopped and let it play round our hot, aching limbs. Only then, in the lovely early sunlight, did we really examine the damage we had suffered. Our faces, arms and legs were covered with lumps and blisters of a most fantastic size—it would have been funny if it hadn't been so infuriatingly irritating. We daubed ourselves with lotion again and as we were doing so, a shepherd passed by with his dogs at heel. 'Aye, it's a fine morning', he said, and he couldn't quite manage to hide the astonishment in his eyes as he saw us doctoring ourselves at the roadside so early in the morning. He would never have dreamt of commenting on it, of course, and after we'd agreed about the fineness of the weather we had a talk with him about the progress of his lambs and other shepherding matters. We could picture his wife enjoying the little tit-bit of news he would relate to her that evening over his supper!

We made a fire, boiled our kettle and cooked our bacon in the lovely breeze on the headland. Our spirits rose, as our blisters subsided, and we began to look about us with calm eyes again. By mid-morning we were at Gairloch and we had to stop for half an hour there to let Helen have a last scamper on the sand. Then we took the road along the side of Loch Maree to Kinlochewe, thence to Garve and our own territory. All the way, with our backs to the west, we were wishing we could turn about at the next bend. But that's the way a holiday should end; we'd caught it on the wing and we knew it would be with us for good.

Billy met us with his usual, cheerful grin, and we saw at once that all was well. We went the round of the animals and cast a loving eye over the fields. Then, as it was wet, we made a fire in the hearth and sat quietly at it, content to be hugged by our own four walls again.

CHAPTER X
'GRAND LAMBS!'

A<small>FTER</small> that holiday jaunt of ours we found we had, from time to time, to indulge our urge to wander. We spent several long afternoons gathering brambles at Loch Ness-side. I think they must be the most succulent brambles in the world, those that grow with their roots in the water. The loch-side is the ideal place for a gipsy meal: there's driftwood for a fire and natural shelter in the tangled undergrowth should it rain. An expedition down there never fails to yield treasure. In spring, there are primroses, willow catkins and violets; in summer, bluebells and wild strawberries; in winter, holly berries. Autumn, of course, is the most fruitful season. There are sloes with a bloom on them like that on hot-house grapes, and brilliant haws and rowan-berries. Under the trees grow many kinds of fungoids, including the bright red, white-spotted, fairy-tale variety. I often wish I could be sure which were the edible ones, so that we could put them in our stew, as the French do. The brambles we make into jelly and jam and also, by simply steeping them in sugar, into wine, which looks, and even tastes, very like port. The rowan-berries from our own trees we always make into wine. I have sometimes made jelly from them, but even with the addition of apple it's rather bitter as a tea-time spread, and really only popular as a relish with meat. The wine is child's play to make. You simply pour boiling water over the berries, add a small piece of root ginger and let them steep for ten days. Then—bottle! After a year or so maturing, this wine is really good, pale amber in colour and with quite a kick in it. A friend of ours was once given a glass of it and asked to identify his drink. He took a sip, rolled it round his mouth, smacked his lips and solemnly pronounced: 'Liqueur whisky!' For a moment, I thought he was pulling my leg. When I saw that he wasn't I felt quite gratified! I thought of the skirmishings that went on in these hills years ago over the distilling of whisky. I remembered the subterfuges and the heartbreak that the illicit business involved, the kegs which had to be thrown into the loch when the excisemen appeared on the horizon, the searchings that went on for years, though the precious stuff was never recovered. Yet here was I, openly making my brew, with no kind of apparatus at all, gaily bypassing all kinds of tariffs and restrictions and offering a sup to all and sundry. There is something to be said for living on one's hump. It would be a pity if the easy world-wide exchange of produce, which lines many a middle-man's pockets, should make us completely overlook the resources that are to hand. In the press-button age, when a minimum of effort for a maximum return is the slogan for living, what will be the spur to enterprise? The creative efforts of the few will leave the many gaping, incapable of wonder, blank-eyed with boredom. In these conditions, war might well appear a relief to the unending tedium. The thwarted child will revel in destruction; it's a means of drawing attention to his plight, if nothing else. Give a boy a mountain to climb and he'll forget all about wanting to kick his neighbour on the shins. He'll be only too thankful the other fellow is there, hanging on to the other end of the rope to steady him.

In our own life we had to plan for a scrap of leisure. We found it was comparatively simple, if no emergency cropped up, to organise Sunday into a day of relaxation. The animals would be fed a little later than usual, and by eleven o'clock all the necessary work would be done. Then six hours would lie before us, to be used as we liked. If we had had a heavy week at field-work, we were sometimes more or less obliged to divide this spell into two watches, during which one of us would stretch out upstairs, with a book, while the other indulged in some quiet ploy with Helen. Then we would relieve each other with a cup of tea at half-time. But most often, at any rate in summer and autumn, we would put an apple and a scone in our pockets and make off into the hills.

The more closely we lived with the hills the more compelling we found them. Away from them, we were never quite happy and a day in town had no real charm for us. Once our immediate business was done we would wander round, look into shop-windows, buy a weekly paper, have a cup of coffee, think to ourselves, 'This is a change, a relaxation, I'm enjoying this'. But we knew quite well we weren't, really. The moment of delight would come when we reached the top of the road again and saw the outline of the hills and smelt the tang of the high air.

On these Sunday expeditions we would get right into the folds of the hills. One of our best-loved places was the shore of a small, nameless lochan, half-way to Glen Urquhart. We would sit there on a calm day listening to the stillness. Helen loved this game. She would crouch, 'frozen', like a young hare, her eyes round, ears on the stretch, waiting to catch sights and sounds. We would watch a puff of wind rippling through the rushes and across the face of the water. A strange shape would come flapping across the sky towards us. 'A heron!' one of us would whisper and we'd watch the gaunt, grey form wing slowly closer and settle at last on the far edge of the lochan. We would lose it among the sedge, then find it again, and watch it laboriously probing the mud.

We would examine the mosses at our feet, peer into the heart of the tiny flowerets they sported, watch, fascinated, the scurrying of insects through the grasses. Most of these forms of life we couldn't put a name to: we knew nothing, really, of their ways, but the thing to do was to stay absolutely still and let them speak for themselves.

On the way back Helen would scamper ahead, leaping from tussock to tussock and as we neared our home ground we'd sing and tell each other stories and earnestly discuss what we'd most like for supper.

September is always an anxious month in these heights. Even though the hay is safely out of the way, as it usually is by then, there is always the fear that the corn will not be ready for cutting before the evenings close in. By that time the potatoes are ripe and the two harvests overlap; then there is one hectic scramble to get everything done in the short days, before the snow comes. That September the weather was extremely mixed. We would have all plans ready to make a start at the corn, when the wind would suddenly veer to the west and down would come the small rain. There would be nothing for it then but to stump off to the barn to do some tidying-up, or repair tools and implements. There is a quiet satisfaction in doing these jobs on a winter afternoon when there's nothing much else that needs doing, anyway. But to have to do them with your mind elsewhere and half an eye on the weather, knowing that the passing of each day is going to make the main business of the year trickier than ever, is frustrating in the extreme. As you sit in the barn, making stack-rope into coils, the beating of the rain on the iron roof sounds unnecessarily loud and even mocking.

That particular September we had every variety of unwelcome weather—rain, hail, thunder, the whole bag of tricks. At last, in the third week of the month, Jim made a start at cutting roads for the binder. Then we had to wait our turn for the 'binder-man'. At that time the Government tractor-service, a war-time innovation, was still operating. All the small places, which couldn't afford to carry a complete set of implements, were utterly dependent on it. It has since been abandoned and is sorely missed. Private contractors have taken over the work, but they charge much higher rates and are not so reliable. Many of them use inferior implements, which are liable to break down and hold the work up at crucial moments. We had, or could borrow, enough implements to cope with most operations ourselves, but for cutting the corn and threshing it we relied on the Government service.

It was the first of October before the binder at last came clanking its way into the cornfield, and that was the day the lambs were to be sold. Alec had helped Jim to pen them in the fank at the roadside. Finlay passed by on his way to the market and he cast an appreciative eye over the lambs and thrust knowing fingers into the wool on their well-padded flanks. 'Grand lambs', he said 'they'll top the sale, I'm thinking!' We smiled with pleasure. They were certainly good lambs, but as for topping the sale, well, there was surely a touch of poetic licence about that pronouncement! Yet hill-men don't usually exaggerate or risk judgement unless they are pretty sure of their ground, I reflected. However, I had no time to ponder the matter. I waved the float good-bye and immediately set to work, stooking in the wake of the binder. Helen helped too, and we staggered up and down with armfuls of sheaves, till it was time to boil die tatties for the binder-man's dinner.

By mid-afternoon we had a good row of stooks standing. Jim would be pleased that we'd managed not to let the sheaves accumulate, I thought. The rain began to come down in sheets, but still we kept on stooking, till I saw the old brown van nosing its way down the side-road towards us. Then, dripping wet, but happy, we made across the field to greet Jim. He thrust a grinning face through the open window. 'Finlay was right. The lambs did top the sale. Ninety-one shillings a-piece!' He stepped out into the rain and we gazed at each other, still hardly believing in our luck.

Then we all made for the shelter of the kitchen and celebrated with hot tea and scones at the fire. In those days, ninety-one shillings was a sale record. It is still a substantial price for a lamb straight from its hill grazing, not stuffed with fodder in a lowland park. We received congratulations from far and wide. On our next trip to town, Jim bought me a Stewart tartan jacket as a memento of the occasion. While the extravagant fit was on, I bought two rose bushes, one for each side of the front door.

Most of October the weather was even worse than it had been in September, but about the middle of the month we managed to snatch two or three days to make stacks. The three youngsters from across the burn came to help and we split into two teams, one with the tractor and trailer, the other with Charlie and the cart, and in this way we managed to rush the corn into the stack. We put in an order at once for the threshing-mill, for we were not sure about the keeping quality of the grain.

Meanwhile, the potatoes were ready for lifting, but the ground was far too soft to bear the weight of a tractor for the job. We dug several drills with graips. It was a back-breaking process, and we could see nothing for it but to leave half the crop in the ground till the spring. It has been done sometimes, with surprisingly little damage to the crop. At the beginning of November we borrowed a digger from some friends on the low-ground, whose crop was snugly pitted. We set to work hopefully with the tractor, but after half an hour or so the whole outfit got bogged. We tramped up and down, caked with mud from head to foot, groping for potatoes in the sodden ground. What fun potato-lifting can be on a sunny autumn afternoon, when the tubers come bobbing to the surface, as if by magic, in the wake of the spinner, and you scramble for them like children scrambling for a flung handful of pennies, and have time to sit on your up-turned pail for a moment's rest before the tractor comes round again! But that floundering in the quagmire was sheer misery.

Then everything took a turn. One morning, in the middle of November, when there was a hint of an Indian summer in the pale sunshine and the light, drying wind, we saw a little cavalcade approaching from the east. There was a white horse drawing a cart piled high with gear, a man and three boys. It was Alec with all the male members of his household come to lift our tatties with the horse and plough. It was the unexpectedness of this neighbourly gesture that really lifted our hearts. With a nod of greeting, Alec made straight for the field and hitched the plough to the horse. There are certainly times when the horse comes into his own, and this was one of them. It was heavy going, but by dusk we had a good few bags filled and carted to the pit.

Next day Alec came back with his boys and in the afternoon the threshing-mill arrived with a squad of eighteen helpers. Sadie came over to help me and never have I been so glad to greet her. It is always difficult to cater for a threshing squad. The day of their arrival is uncertain and hardly ever coincides with the visit of the grocer's van. You lay in a stock of butcher meat and do a huge baking for the day you expect them. They are sure to be held up at another place, and with the best will in the world your small family cannot eat its way through the joint and the mounds of scone and cake, and half of it has to go to the dogs. Then, on the day the mill does arrive, you have only tinned stuff and stale baking to fall back on, and your shame is great! However, this day, with Sadie's help, we managed to produce a compromise of a meal and the men were so hungry that they praised it quite wholeheartedly.

There is always a thrill of excitement about a threshing. The huge, unwieldy, yellow-painted mill has all the glamour and mystery of a piece of circus equipment. The steady humming of the mechanism suggests power without end, and the way the grain pours out in separate streams, one for each quality, seems like sheer magic to the uninitiated. The men tend the monster with steady, rhythmic movements of the arms, their faces set in serious lines of concentration. You can tell at once that machine-minding does not come naturally to them and there is a hint of the schoolboy's awe in their expressions. But when the tea-kettle and the baskets of scones appear and the noise of the mill subsides for a few minutes, they relax and gladly crack a joke in the returning calm.

Alec gave us still another day of generous help, while the weather held. Then the rain closed in again and we had to leave the last quarter of the field to chance. December came and frost and snow. We lifted several cart-loads of turnips and dumped them in an improvised shed. The fields were still wonderfully green, that is the one advantage of the late hill-season. The hungry gap comes all right at the end of the winter, when it seems as though spring is going to miss us altogether: but the back-end of the year can produce quite a tasty bite. However, once turnips are on the menu, the cattle go crazy for them. Life becomes one long round of carting, chopping and feeding turnips. Every beast about the place was partial to them, even the pigs, and fortunately we had a grand crop of them that year. They were so heavy that it was as much as I could do to carry two, swinging by their green tops, in each hand, from the field to the hen-house.

Our second lot of porkers were slower to fatten than the first had been, and they were developing rather unevenly. We put them under cover, along at the far steading, and stuffed them with potato stew. When we judged one of them was at last ready for market, we loaded him, after a terrifying tussle, into the back of the van, as it was not worth going to the expense of hiring a float for one pig. That was an epic journey, as Jim recounted it to me later. He had as front-seat companion a town friend, Mr. S., who was on his way to catch a train at Inverness. He was glad of the lift, but a little doubtful of his rear travelling companion. He himself was in his best rig, and spruced up for the occasion, whereas the pig was, to say the least of it, decidedly odoriferous! However, as long as they made up their minds to ignore each other, Jim thought he could manage to get them each to their destination. But a pig is an inquisitive creature. They had barely reached the main road when this one of ours, at a sudden jolt, broke loose from his moorings and thrust a grimy, inquiring snout against the back of Mr. S.'s shining collar. The unfortunate human passenger had, on Jim's instructions, to spend the rest of the trip scratching a bristly back with his soft, white fingers and murmuring 'porky, porky!' into a grubby ear, much to the delight of the pig and of the crowd of small boys, who peered incredulously into the van when it was held up at the first set of traffic lights.

That autumn we decided to avail ourselves of the services of a Government-owned ram, instead of buying one of our own.

'The Board', as the Department of Agriculture for Scotland is still called in these parts, undertakes to supply the crofter with one or more rams, according to his need, during the tupping season from November to January. One crofter in the district sends in a note of local requirements and arranges the distribution and subsequent collection of the rams. They are magnificent beasts and ensure a crop of high-quality lambs. The crofter pays four pounds for his ram, of which one pound is refunded if the animal returns intact from his tour of duty.

Only comparatively few crofts here have sufficient grazing to carry a flock of breeding ewes, but practically everyone takes in sheep from other parts for wintering. Some undertake to supply them with turnips, and make a higher charge for their boarders, others simply provide grazing on the outrun and the wintry in-bye fields. Others again find it profitable to buy in a score or so of Cheviot lambs once the harvest is secured, feed them on turnips and a little crushed oats and sell them before ploughing-time. As well as bringing in a cash return, the wintered sheep contribute to the well-being of the croft, by treading and manuring the ground. With their predatory habits they are a worry where fencing is anything but reliable, and are the cause of a good deal of heart-burning between neighbours, but their coming is part of the scheme of things and has to be tholed.

With the arrival of the tups and the winterings, we know that winter is really closing down on us. We've seen the great gaggles of wild geese come honking out of the cold north sky and watched them disappear into the evening haze, round the shoulder of the hill, and we've felt a little comforted to think that to these hardy creatures our bleakness is a refuge, that there are winter regions infinitely more desolate than ours. We've seen the fieldfares strip the last of the berries from the bare branches of the rowans and we're glad now of the cheerful company of the chaffinch flocks about the barn door.

There is, in spite of everything, a sort of cosiness about winter, a drawing-together of man and beast, in shared mistrust of the elements. The byre is an inviting place at dusk on a cold December day. It is filled with the sweet scent of dry grass and clover and of the breath of healthy cattle-beasts. The cows rattle their chains and turn their heads inquiringly, as we stagger in with armfuls of straw and hay and pailfuls of turnips. The hens 'sing', as they scratch contentedly away at the dry litter in their brightly lit quarters. Charlie comes to the doorstep, morning and evening, and stands rattling the door-knob till we give him his 'white drink', a pailful of water, with the chill off it, and a handful of oatmeal scattered in.

It's in winter that we realise fully how interdependent we all are. Also we have the satisfaction of seeing the result of our summer work in the fields. Perhaps only on a very small farm such as ours, where practically everything is produced for immediate home consumption, can these results be so startlingly apparent. We can almost identify each turnip we place in the slicer. As we throw a log on the fire, we sometimes pause to gaze at the flames licking it and murmur: 'That's a bit of the dead birch we had such a job to get over the fence.'

Life on a large farm can be almost as much a matter of mechanics as life in a factory or office. On a croft there is the intimacy and warmth of immediate contact with the fundamentals, and there is wholeness. What chance has the factory worker, who stands all day at his bench making an infinitesimal part of some giant machine, or the city typist who taps out another's words in triplicate, of acquiring wisdom or judgement, the capacity to see things in the round. Even the leisure of these unfortunate people is drained away in evenings spent gaping at the cinema or television screen. The penny-in-the-slot machine churns out the daily requirements of living. It can be quite pleasant to jog along with the blinkers on: those who still like to see the beginnings and the ends of things are considered uncomfortable finnicks.

To wrestle with things in the raw is a craving of every healthy human being. The height of happiness to a child is to scramble up a tree, to plowter through mud, to find shelter in a rock.

The more scratched and torn and filthy he gets in the process, the wider his grin of delight when he staggers home. Deprived of this natural outlet, a city boy will find satisfaction in breaking windows, in slashing cinema seats or other boys' noses. If the immediate matter of making his living were one where a man could use the whole of himself—his strength, his wits and his imagination, the problem of how to fill his leisure would not arise, and he would be too preoccupied to spend more than the odd day thinking up ways to exterminate his fellows. His culture would not be imported in canisters from the other side of the world; he would make it himself, from a brain and a heart kept bright and taut with satisfactory living. It may be fascinating to have a picture of life among the peasants of Andalusia flashed to one's fireside, but how much more fascinating it would be to feel a song of one's own dancing on one's own lips out of the joy of one's own doings.

A natural life has its own tensions, its own moments of fulfilment and disaster, out of which art can leap unfettered, as a man tries passionately to record his glimpse of the pattern. For those who are not artists, there is the satisfaction of craft. I've seen it in the face of the man who selects a hazel branch from the thicket by the loch-side and slowly fashions it into a crook. In his strong, stubby fingers, the living wood is shaped and smoothed into an object that's not only vitally necessary to his daily work, but is beautiful into the bargain. He has made dozens of these crooks, yet no two are alike, each has its own individual feel in the hand.

Of course we can't put the clock back. We've got to go on from noon. At noon our inventions lie about us, glittering in the light like new-made toys. Where will we get the wisdom to lay hands on the wonders and to discard the monstrosities among them?

CHAPTER XI
THE BIG GALE

About the middle of December occurred one of those minor miracles, which are apt to be left out of a normally well-reasoned forecast of events, and which we have learnt to accept as tokens of beneficence. After a spell of snow, which had blocked the road and held up the grocer's van again, we suddenly emerged one morning into a day of blue and gold, with sunshine enough to set the midges dancing. We could hardly believe in it, yet we had to admit the evidence of our senses.

Our one thought was—the potatoes! As soon as the routine jobs were done, we made a final assault on the potato field. The frost had hardened the ground sufficiently to allow the digger to get a bite, and yet had not been severe enough to damage the tubers. In two days stolen from spring, we got the remaining drills lifted, and so our epic struggle with the potato crop ended in victory.

We needed every tattie we could lay hands on, for the pigs were consuming them in ever increasing quantities, and we sold none that year. Jim's ambition was to invest in a couple

96

of in-pig gilts, in the spring, after all the porkers were sold. He had pig-fever badly. Small fortunes were being made in the pig-trade and we needed cash to build up the overall soundness of the place. Though it was a fickle business, liable to ups and downs unheard-of in the steady sheep and beef-cattle trade, we hoped we could catch it at an opportune moment.

Meanwhile, we lost Billy but we knew this was bound to happen sooner or later. He went to take up what had always been his main interest—the tending of sheep. We missed seeing him about the place. There was an elemental quality in him, a simplicity, a generosity, that was quite disarming.

'Little' Billy, from over the burn, who was gleefully approaching the end of his schooldays, began to spend every minute he could spare from home chores giving us a hand. He would work away all Saturday afternoon at whatever job Jim was busy at. After supper, he would play reel tunes on his mouth organ, while Helen cavorted about the kitchen. Those were happy evenings.

We passed the shortest day, confident in the knowledge that we were adequately prepared for winter. The whole of the year's effort is really directed towards this end. If the work has gone well, it results in a real snugness, with everything battened down and stores of food, fodder and fuel lying to hand, so that winter can be not only endured but positively enjoyed. If things have gone badly—a crop has failed or not been properly secured—then winter is a time of nagging anxiety, and sometimes the margin between the two states can be very narrow indeed.

By living thus, near to the bones of things, the simplest bounty can be a delight. It never fails to astonish me that the hens can lay eggs by the huge, golden dozen, while the snow is lying feet deep round their house and the wind is driving it through the minute crevices below the roof. True, we have worked all season to achieve this end: we've hatched eggs, or bought chicks at the appropriate time, we've spent hours liming and turning the litter of peat-moss, chaff and straw that warms the hens' feet, we've grown corn and potatoes to feed them, we've given them a light to simulate spring. Yet still it remains a marvel that the eggs are produced so ungrudgingly in the dark, bitter days. Similarly with the cow, the wonder is that the pail still brims with milk, though clover is only a memory wafted from an armful of hay.

The least co-operative of the animals were the pigs. Their job was to put on weight, and that is a thing no beast can be expected to do in a hurry, on a hill-top farm, in winter. However, we eventually shipped them, one by one, to market and though they didn't do as spectacularly well as their predecessors, they fetched quite satisfactory prices.

Christmas, as always, we made into a small oasis of light and relaxation. It's surprising that, in a part of the world as near the midnight sun as northern Scotland, there is no midwinter celebration like that held in Sweden, called the 'Festival of Light', when the youngest girl in the family, wearing a crown of candles, carries a light into every room in the house, shedding a beam into the darkest corners. Light is precious; it's fitting that there should be ceremonial in honour of the basic things. In the Catholic west, they still set a candle in the window on Christmas Eve to show the Child the way, but in the Calvinist north and east, Christmas passes almost unsaluted. However, I think our recognition of the Festival touched off a spring in the young people of the district. We returned home from a shopping expedition late one evening, hurried in at the front door and hastily changed into gum-boots and old coats before struggling out with torches to do the feeding round. I opened the back door and into my arms fell a mysterious object, dark, prickly and aromatic. A beam from the kitchen light struck it and I saw that it was shining with frost crystals. It was a Christmas tree, decked by nature! Tied to its trunk with a wisp of straw was a scrap of paper scrawled over with five words: 'Here is a tree. Billy'. It was the sheer unexpectedness of the gift that made the moment! We felt a glow in us, in spite of the numbness of our fingers, as we tossed hay and corn to the stalled beasts that evening.

Helen helped to decorate the tree that year. We dug up the tin of rowan-berries we had buried in the ground in autumn, and found they were as fresh and shining as the day they were picked. We collected fir branches and trails of ivy from the wood; and we had roast duck and apple sauce for our Christmas dinner. Then we gathered all the children about us and played games of magic by the fire.

Winter doesn't seem long when you have Christmas to prepare for and enjoy and New Year following close on its heels, with ceilidhs that go on till well into January. By the twelfth of the new month—date of the 'old' New Year, which is still kept in mind by the older generation here—there is 'an hour on the day', they say. It's a precious hour, for it means that you can do just that little extra bit of work outside before coming in for the night. You can repair a fence, or make a gate, or go after a strayed ewe, and indulge in a grin of satisfaction as you knock the snow from your boots and move the kettle on to the hot part of the stove.

'Whatever do you do with your evenings up there?' friends have asked us on several occasions, with an almost perceptible shudder in their voices. We sometimes wonder what we did with our evenings when we lived a town life; we just can't remember. Here, every one of them is memorable. To begin with, it is a joy to have achieved evening. We've been, say, sawing logs all afternoon, till the light has faded from mauve to green behind the hills. We've crunched our way about the yard feeding the animals, and we've come in with the pail of milk, the basket of eggs, the sack of fuel. We're pleasantly tired, and glad of shelter, and we've had a good hot meal, and tucked Helen into bed. Now there are books to hand, there may be some music we want to hear on the wireless, or a play. There is the diary to write, and a letter or two, and there are things to mend, events to be discussed, plans to be made.

Sometimes the door will open and in will come a neighbour without knocking. The absence of a knock is a sign that we're accepted as friends, and it always delights us. The evenings are never long enough: our pet vice is to sit gazing into the fire hours after we should be in bed. Are we hopelessly unambitious, anti-social even? Is there something lacking in us that we are content with the company of one another, a few neighbours, the beasts which depend on us and the slowly swinging stars? I don't know. But I do know that it is very satisfactory to be content to find the family unit, the neighbourly unit, the man-and-beast unit fitting securely into the pattern of hill and field and sky. Dr. Johnson himself, who surely ranks among the sophisticates, once said: 'To be happy at home *is* the ultimate result of all ambition.'

With the turning of the year, we began to prepare for the big event in Helen's life—school. She was five years old and could already read and write and do simple sums. She had a naturally inquiring mind and was as eager to learn as a collie pup to chase sheep. The Abriachan school was quite accessible, only about a mile down the road from our gate. But at that time it had only six pupils, all but one of whom were boys. There was not much prospect of happy companionship for her there. To send her to the girls' school in Inverness as a weekly boarder was financially impossible. Besides, we both have strong feelings about boarding schools; they seem to create their own rather artificial, even unhealthy, climate. Youngsters reared in them often find difficulty later on in adjusting themselves to the extremes of temperature in the world outside. We would rather that ours grew hardy and resistant from the start, with a background of family and farm life to keep her on an even keel.

The children from the Maclean household had all been to Glen Convinth school, which was about two miles away, on the Beauly road. One day, towards the end of January, we decided to walk over to see the headmaster of this school. Helen came with us, and we took exactly the road she would have to take—the path through the heather and across the burn to the Macleans' house, the short cut up the grassy slope and over the stile to the road, along the rise to the eleven-hundred-feet level and down the steep plunge to the wooded strath at the foot of Glen Convinth.

It was a brilliant day. The smoke from the few croft houses was rising straight into the still air. The Strathfarrar hills lay in a soft, blue haze. We reached the little grey-stone school, with its two high-windowed schoolrooms, and the Dominie's house adjoining. We noticed his neat garden, the apple-trees and the row of beehives. It was a pleasant place. I remembered the forbidding corridors and bare, windswept playgrounds of town schools and was glad Helen was to be spared those. Here there were two classrooms with a small lobby between. The huge branches of an oak were tapping the window panes. There was a grass patch edged with flowers for the children to run on. Behind the school building was a small, modern cook-house, where the midday meal was prepared.

We stood together, in the lobby, listening to the murmur of voices from the two rooms. Then we tapped on the door of the infants' room and a small lady, with a mother's face, came out to greet us. We told her we should like Helen to come to her school. She smiled, and went to fetch her husband from the senior room. He was tall, and looked a scholar. He wore a suit of rough Harris tweed, and when he opened his mouth out came the music of the western speech. We could feel at once the kindliness and warmth and humour of the isle-folk, and we knew Helen could not be in better hands than these. Having heard so much from town friends about the difficulty of getting a child into a school, we asked him somewhat diffidently if it would be all right to send Helen to him. Perhaps we were breaking some regulation, should she have gone to Abriachan school, which was nearer? He simply asked Helen her name, shook her hand and said: 'You come to school tomorrow, Helen.' And that was that.

We walked home in a happy mood. Through the half-open door of the infants' room we had glimpsed a row of small girls with fresh faces and old-fashioned ringlets. We thought of the fun Helen would have, the new games, the small, whispered confidences. We called in at the Macleans on our way home; they were delighted to hear that Helen was to go to Glen Convinth, and made plans for Bertha to meet her every morning at the burn and shepherd her to school. In the evening she was to wait for the bus which brought the scholars from the Junior Secondary school at Tomnacross to within half a mile of the stile and Bertha would see her safely to the burn again. In her ever kindly way Mrs. Maclean made everything seem simple and serene, and we felt confident as we sipped our tea at her fireside.

Two days later Bertha came over with a book from the school library for Helen. It was a kindly gesture on the Dominie's part and it gave Helen a taste for reading which has developed at an alarming rate over the years. We decided that she should start school as soon as the days began to stretch and the weather to soften a little.

January had been promising: we had had days when we'd been tempted to make a start at the ploughing. The bright air made it seem as though one small leap would land us in April—but we should have known better. On the last day of the month we were wakened early by the sound of a fierce north wind roaring up under the slates. We felt the whole house shake and give, like a ship in an Atlantic gale. We went down and peered out of the living-room window. Snow was being driven horizontally across the fields by a wind which must have been near to hurricane force.

Jim managed to open the back door and it took the two of us to shut it after him. He staggered out to see to the animals in the steading. I tried to light the fire in the kitchen stove, but I found that the force of the wind was so great that there was no suction in the chimney and the smoke billowed back into the room. So I lit the living-room fire and boiled a kettle and made toast there.

Jim came in, the breath completely knocked out of him on the short journey from the steading. One of the three giant rowans was up by the roots, he said, and the roof was off the henhouse, where we kept a small overflow of poultry. Sheets of corrugated iron were scattered over the near field and the cows' backs were powdered with fine snow, driven through minute cracks in the byre wall. Otherwise everything was all right!

We carried the woebegone hens bodily down to the byre and gave them a feed of corn. In the comparative warmth and shelter they soon revived and strutted happily among the cows' legs. Two of their mates were frozen stiff on the perches in the roofless house and we had to put them in the larder.

The rest of the day we spent huddled at the living-room fire, listening to the roar of the wind and the groaning of the house-beams, between trips to the steading. The deep-litter hens were completely unperturbed; they actually laid a record number of eggs that day. But Hope, the house-cow, didn't care at all for her coating of snow. We hastily stuffed every crevice in the byre wall with bits of sacking and wisps of straw. In the evening I stood, in complete outdoor rig, frying ham and eggs on a spirit-lamp in the ice-box of a kitchen, waiting for the crashing of the stove pipe on the iron roof.

Next day we heard on the wireless of the damage that the storm had done. Square miles of timber had been uprooted, square miles of coast flooded and scores of people made homeless. We had come off comparatively lightly in our little stone house on the bare hilltop.

By Monday evening everything was calm in the pale sunshine. We went the round of the sheep; they were all quite placidly grazing. We sawed some limbs off the fallen tree. Rowan logs burn well wet or dry, and we had a particularly bright fire that evening, but it was sad to see the flames licking the bark of this friendly old giant. On our next trip to town we saw hundreds more like him lying prone about the fields, their roots exposed, their huge crowns flattened against the earth. It was only then that we realised fully that it was indeed a hurricane we had survived. Being right in the centre of it, with immediate, practical problems to solve, we had not been aware at the time of the ferocity of the force let loose about our heads.

The terror of this day soon faded from our minds and we began to plan the spring campaign. We should have to tackle it on our own this year, as there was no source of casual labour in the district. Then it struck us—might there not be a student, somewhere in the city of Edinburgh, who would be glad to spend a few weeks working on a Highland croft, in the spring of the year, for his keep and pocket money? We had heard of various schemes whereby young people were sent to help on the small crofts in the west. They undertook such jobs as draining, peat-cutting and harvesting on a voluntary basis, in return for their keep. But they went, as a rule, to very small places which might fail utterly without help on account of the age or infirmity of their occupiers. Our place was not quite in that category! Still, we thought, we might apply privately for a student.

One night, when the wind was roaring about the house again, and the logs were hissing on the hearth and spring work seemed a hundred years away, we sat with a writing-pad between us and drew up a letter to the Secretary of the Students' Representative Council in Edinburgh. Between the sheltered quadrangle of the University and our few acres crouched against the hills a great gulf was certainly fixed. Would any student care to venture into these unknown wilds? we wondered.

We wrote a brief description of the place, the stock it carried and the work that was to be done. We offered to pay the rail fare and one pound a week pocket money to anyone who would live with us, as one of the family, and work from eight in the morning till about four in the afternoon. After that, his time was to be his own. He could do some reading, go out with the gun, or follow his fancy. If we had been students, we reflected, we should have jumped at the chance. We imagined there must still be a good few young men about the dusty classrooms who would be glad to give their lungs an airing and pit their wits against a fresh set of problems. We made no bones about it—the work would be hard, the food plain, and of streamlined entertainment there would be absolutely none.

With some misgiving we thought of a thin and pimply youth trying vainly to work out the intricacies of fitting Charlie to his harness, by a process of logical deduction, whereas the one thing needful, as a rule, is a bent nail, a length of stack rope or a kind word in his ear. Worse still, we thought, would be the embryo mathematician who would work out on squared paper the exact number of eggs we should be getting from each pullet if she were to justify her existence, bearing in mind the cost of feed, our own labour, overheads, etc. We might feel compelled to cull a quarter of our flock and, heaven knew, they might well come up to scratch yet if given a few weeks' grace! There are some things better left in the lap of the gods if each living hour is to keep its shine. And that was exactly where we left the procuring of our student help. If he were not a misfit, much mutual good might come of his stay. The Easter vacation, from mid-March to mid-April, should coincide, weather permitting, with our big rush of spring work. We posted our letter in hope and went on riding out the winter.

CHAPTER XII

SHINING MORNING FACE

THE larks were rising and falling in a blue, windless sky on the day Helen and I set off for Glen Convinth school. Lessons began at ten, so we left the house just after nine. Helen had her small, brown satchel on her back—it contained only a biscuit and an apple, but it looked quite impressive.

Bertha met us at the burn and we walked gaily. As we approached the school, three small girls came running to meet us. I recognised the bright faces and ringlets I had glimpsed through the open door a few weeks before. They were sisters, Bertha said. That was clear, for they were as like one another as three chickens. They immediately took charge of Helen, in a charming, motherly way, and she had vanished into the schoolroom before I'd even had time to say good-bye to her.

It had been arranged that I was to wait in the house where Mrs. Maclean's daughter lived, a stone's throw from the school, until the eleven o'clock play, when Helen and Bertha would come down to see me and report progress, before I set off for home. I was given tea and entertained with kindly talk. But still I couldn't help remembering my own unhappy beginnings in the schoolroom, and wondering how Helen was reacting to her strange surroundings. I needn't have worried. At eleven o'clock, the two youngsters came rushing up the garden path and into the little parlour. Their eyes were bright and Bertha was as excited as an elder sister, as she proudly announced that Helen had got all her sums right!

Helen herself was quite overwhelmed by the attention of the motherly small girls and the thrill of all the new ploys she had embarked on.

At dusk we watched for the two small figures coming down the grassy slope. It had been a long day for a five-year-old, but when Helen came into the lamplight in the kitchen her cheeks were glowing and her eyes round as she recounted, in a few breathless snatches, the doings of the day.

Her schooldays had got off to a good start. She began to make progress at once, for her innate wish to learn was recognised and fostered. Her teacher, who had reared and taught four fine children of her own, knew instinctively the approach to make to a young, fresh mind.

The little classroom had none of the streamlined equipment deemed essential to the schooling of the modern infant. There were no glittering devices to allure young minds and make it seem that learning is some kind of glorified game. But there was something no large, impersonal classroom could achieve—the comfort of a relaxed atmosphere. The teacher didn't have to spend precious energy acting as a policewoman all the time. With only a handful of children confronting her, she found it comparatively easy to keep order, and she could give of her best to the actual job of teaching. Each child was known as an individual. His background was understood and thus his shortcomings could be accounted for and efforts to overcome them directed along the lines most likely to lead to success.

There was a homely feeling of security about the classroom itself. On bleak winter days the children found it a real refuge. Wet coats and boots were put to dry by the glowing stove, which was opened up for a few minutes to allow small, numb fingers to be rubbed in the warmth before lessons began. There were nice, friendly little customs; a new child had an older one to 'mother' her, to see that she put her things to dry, to accompany her on trips outside, to see that she washed her hands before dinner and that she made a good meal.

During the half-hour that Helen had to spend waiting for the bus, in the afternoon, while Bertha was still at her lessons in the 'big room', her teacher took her into the house and gave her tea and cake. On arrival at Mrs. Maclean's, she was again fortified with a hot drink and biscuits in winter, or lemonade in summer, so that the journey didn't seem wearisome or long. In fact, it was one gay adventure. Sometimes, after a day of torrential rain, the burn, which had been quite easily crossed in the morning, would be impassable by evening. Then Bertha would accompany Helen along to the road, over the bridge there and in through the gate at the 'west end'. We would hear the laughter rising above the roaring of the burn and we would see the torches weaving patterns in the dusk and we would go to meet the pair of them. Our own torch would reveal a couple of gleaming, laughing faces and we'd never catch a whimper of distress. Bertha would turn about for home and I would shepherd Helen into the kitchen, strip off her wet things and make her sit at the fire in her dressing-gown till she'd swallowed a cup of hot, sweet tea.

On spring evenings they'd dally all the way home, swinging their skipping ropes and stopping to examine the progress of the clutch of meadow-pipit's eggs in the tiny, neat nest in the bank by the well, or to watch the peewit fledgelings scurrying through the rushes, in their anxious mother's wake.

The following year, when Bertha had gone on to the Junior Secondary school, we would take it in turns to walk Helen to school in the mornings. For the return journey she still had Bertha's company from the school bus. We used to beguile the journey with the telling of a serial story, each of us, including Helen, taking it in turn to add our chapter. Jim usually managed to leave the protagonists in some fantastic predicament, from which I had to extricate them before Helen took over.

In these small country schools the children receive a thorough grounding in the basic disciplines, at a time when their minds can grasp first principles with amazing ease. This is important in an age when glamour seems to be invading even the infant classroom, and to 'have fun' seems to be the end of existence for too many youngsters. The healthy young imagination doesn't need much titillating, but the growing mind does need discipline. There are regular periods for drawing and singing, needlework and knitting for the girls, and handwork for the boys, but the main emphasis is on plain learning. In a very short time Helen was coming home, bristling with information in the fields of grammar, history and geography. 'Surely', we said, 'you're not doing that!' as we racked our brains to answer some question regarding the use of personal pronouns, or the place of embarkation of the Pilgrim Fathers. 'No', was the reply, 'but class four is.' We heard later from Bertha that Helen, when she had finished the task set her by the teacher, would sit wide-eyed and wide-eared, 'listening-in' to the lessons being given, in the same room, to another class.

These little schools are well supervised by the authorities. Inspectors pay them regular visits and a good standard is maintained. Most of the teachers and inspectors are people of Highland origin and have all the Highlander's respect for learning. There is nothing slap-dash about their attitude to letters. Doctor and dentist also pay regular visits. The nurse, who comes on a monthly tour of inspection, gets to know the children well. Medical examination holds no terror for them, as it has always been part of their routine.

The Education Authority is wisely keeping open the country schools, even when the number of pupils falls to as low as half a dozen. To transport the children to a bigger school, or even to a town school, would he comparatively simple. But once embark on that scheme and the depopulation of the remoter areas is assured. Up here, the boys would be happy as larks, tough, clear-eyed and skilled in country ploys, brought up to hard work, but getting an immense amount of fun out of a game of shinty, an afternoon's sledging, a day at the fox-drive. Come across them in town, and you find them lolling round Woolworth's, eating a bag of chips for their dinner, ogling a bunch of giggling girls, conforming to the inevitable pattern. They're soon ashamed of their old skills. To know how to thatch a rick, to snare a rabbit, to guddle trout has become for them the mark of the uncouth. Their one ambition is to 'come up on the pools', or find some other way to get rich quickly. Very soon, there's little to distinguish them from the town-bred youth of all the world.

It is a sad fact that in some of the remoter areas sheep flocks are disappearing, though there is greater need than ever of good, home-produced mutton and wool, because men cannot be found to undertake the shepherding. The skilled shepherd gets a good wage, a good house, good perquisites, everything necessary for a healthy, satisfying life, but he and his wife and family must be willing to live at a distance from the shops, the pub and the cinema. Apparently that is too much to ask of young people who have once had a taste of these things. So the 'Situations Vacant' column remains a long one, under the heading 'Agriculture', and only occasionally does one find a *cri du coeur* in the 'Situations Wanted'—'Young man wishes work on estate or farm. Remote area preferred.' Perhaps it is the voice crying in the urban wilderness, remembering the lost gods of hill and moor and sky.

There is no doubt that it is the willingness, or otherwise, of the female partner to embark on a lonely life, which can encourage or discourage a young man in the pursuit of a country career. A wise Education Authority has foreseen this, and in the Junior Secondary schools in the Highlands every effort is made to encourage the girls to be self-reliant and to take a pride in the old home crafts of cooking, laundering, needlework and childcare. There are several institutions, actually in the Highlands, where young women can be trained as instructresses in these crafts, without having to go near an urban centre.

Scotland is not a country of great natural resources. Her contribution to the world is all the greater because of that bare fact. Her contribution lies in the character of her people, which has been tempered in the struggle to make the most of what resources the land can yield. A man will easily grow fat when the ripe fruit falls into his mouth as he lies in the shade of the tree. But when he has to plough the soil a few inches deep on a rocky hill-side before his little crop of oats will blossom, if blossom is the word, then he'll have to grow tough and skilled and resilient, or perish—and the Scot has no notion to perish. He loves his rocky hillside with the fierce passion of a man for a woman who will not easily yield.

Scotland today is becoming more and more industrialised. The Scots character, after a generation or two, is swallowed up in the standardisation imposed by an urban way of life. The remote areas remain the breeding-ground of the country's most precious asset —character. Only there can the Scot remain completely true to himself, for that is where he is rooted. Other countries, other parts, have exploited his abilities for long enough. When he comes home, in his dapper suit, his Stetson and his rimless glasses, to grasp his brother's rough hand again, he is looking for something. His pockets may be brimful, but he has learnt, in his canny way, that money imposes its own tyranny. He is no longer independent in the old, satisfying way.

Why is it that the influx of exiled Scots, come to take another look at the country of their origin, grows steadily greater every year? It's because, at bottom, every Scot recognises the validity of the old human virtues. You can't fob him off with make-believe. He doesn't live easily in a climate of success, he must have something to get his teeth into. He was always happiest ploughing his few inches on the rock, or sailing his boat smack into the wind. He'll work all the hours there are, tending his own few acres and his stock, but give him an assured job and he's the worst clockwatcher in the world.

We have a neighbour, thin as a wraith and crippled with old wounds. It is a greater miracle each year how he gets his crop gathered and a fresh one down in spring. But he must be working about his fields, or there would be no cheery twinkle in his eye, no witty word of greeting as he meets us on the road. When he mangled his hand in his barn mill, he would walk the two miles to the bus to go into town for daily treatment as an out-patient rather than spend a week in hospital, as the doctors recommended. He had his beasts to see to, and his independence to preserve. It will be a bad day for the world when toughness like his has been destroyed by the palliatives of a welfare state. The best way to keep alive is to be constantly at grips with one's universe.

One evening in early March we were sitting quietly at the fire when Billy burst into the kitchen, wide-eyed, a little scared-looking. 'The hill's on fire', he announced, 'we were afraid the van might get it!' We rushed to the window on the other side of the house; the whole of the southern sky was glowing orange. The Macleans, whose house faces the hill, had evidently been watching the advance of the flames and had sent Billy to warn us. We flung on our coats and boots and made for the spot where the van was standing. True enough, the flames were within a few yards of it and, though the road lay between, the rising wind might easily carry a spark across the narrow safety belt. We moved the van as far as possible out of harm's way and began beating out the flames along the roadside, but within minutes the thing was hopelessly out of control. We could only stand listening to the terrifying roar and crackle and hope that the wind would die before morning.

After an hour or so of fruitless efforts to control even the burning of the rushes at the roadside, we went back to the house. From the upper windows we could see the full extent of the fearsome blaze. By morning it had died down considerably, but was still burning here and there. Luckily the sheep were out of harm's way and the fencing on the eastern boundary had escaped damage. It was a warning to us for future heather-burning operations of our own. Once again we were thankful for the Macleans' vigilance and goodwill.

The smell of heather burning and the sight of plovers swooping over the fields, in the cold, afternoon light, make the reality of an upland spring. We've seen small tokens of a change in things from mid-February, perhaps—a softening in the light that pours down the hill-side from the peak of the noonday sun, the sudden, un-looked-for blooming of a daisy or a coltsfoot in a sheltered hollow by the burn. But the burning of the old heather and the wild agitation of the returning birds mean that things are really happening—space is being sought for new life and growth.

The first new arrivals in our own spring season came in small cardboard boxes from hundreds of miles away—a batch of day-old chickens all the way from Dumfriesshire. Train and bus had brought them to the foot of the hill, the post's motor-bike pillion conveyed them to our door. When we opened the boxes on the kitchen table, it seemed a miracle that these small, yellow, chirping atoms had safely and cheerfully survived such a journey on the day of their birth. We installed them, with two brooder lamps, in the glasshouse and they throve wonderfully well; we lost only three out of a batch of one hundred.

We presented a broody hen with a dozen day-old Aylesbury ducklings. She took to them at once, and they to her. They grew so fast that, within days, she had difficulty in keeping them covered. Finally she gave up the attempt and would strut after them, with much exasperated clucking, as they waddled off, in a determined line, to seek their own kind of fortune among the damp rushes. A few weeks later we took them in a crate to the butcher. They went to grace the tables of the more expensive Inverness hotels. They were lovable, comical things and we missed the sight of them about the place. I doubt if we shall ever acquire the complete detachment of the man who makes rearing for the market his business.

CHAPTER XIII
'GAUDEAMUS IGITUR'

WE had one reply to our request for a student to help during the Easter vacation. One, out of all the hundreds who must have seen the small notice pinned on the board in the University quadrangle, had had the courage to take at least a tentative step towards our fastness! He was a veterinary student, which sounded promising, John by name. We answered his letter hopefully, and it was arranged that he would come in the middle of March.

No sooner was this plan fixed than we heard from an Arts student, Henry, who sounded very enthusiastic. We hated to turn him down; perhaps two students would be better than one, we thought. They would keep each other company and that might make for a happy atmosphere. Besides, one never knew, the first one might fall by the way. So we offered to engage Henry as well as John. However, we received no acknowledgement of our letter to Henry, so we concluded he would not be coming.

As the day of John's arrival drew near, I managed, between thrice-daily trips to the chickens and bouts of liming and

114

digging the garden plot, to get a room ready for him. It was bare enough, but it had the elements of simple comfort. We guessed that a young man who would venture, in mid-March, to a spot one thousand feet above sea-level would not be too fussy.

The day we were expecting John, a wire came saying that Henry was due at Inverness station the following afternoon! That was a hectic day by any standard. We had been over to say good-bye to Willie Maclean, who was going into hospital. We were behind with the work, and I had a baking to do for the extra mouth we were expecting, and now it seemed we had to expect two after all.

Still, the evenings were lengthening. After tea, we harnessed Charlie and brought a spare bed along from the bungalow. Bertha came over to give a hand—Mrs. Maclean must have guessed we had a crisis on hand. We set the mattress and blankets to air, we collected odds and ends of furnishings from all over the house, and, by the time Jim returned from the station with John, Henry's room was ready and I was able to welcome our guest with a calm which quite belied the storm that had been raging all day.

We took to John at once. He wore corduroys and carried his gear in a rucksack. He was tall and quiet and looked as though he wouldn't easily be defeated. He confessed right away that he'd never worked with a horse, but said he could drive a car and was sure he could manage the tractor.

Next day we went to meet the three-thirty-four train. After unsuccessfully accosting several young men, who looked as if they might have come north for a working holiday, we finally ran Henry to earth at the very end of the stream of passengers. He was dark, twinkling and dapper and he was struggling with a heavy suitcase. A more complete contrast to John could not be imagined; Henry hardly ever stopped talking or laughing. But after a day or two the five of us settled into a pleasant enough routine.

The weather was superb. After dispelling the morning mist the sun rose, day after day, into a sky of sheer, summer blue.

The larks were singing, the peewits flashing, the curlews gliding over the moor. I think John quietly revelled in the freshness and Henry, who was a good deal older and had knocked a bit about the world, couldn't help feeling a touch of the magic. John soon learnt to harness and drive Charlie; he took to the field-work at once. In a battered old tweed hat and jacket he'd stride about the place, taking things calmly, as a countryman does. Henry, on the other hand, couldn't quite adjust himself to the tempo of the land, and he always managed to look dapper. He'd make the most extraordinary noises of encouragement to Charlie, as though they were both something out of a circus. But Henry was certainly anxious to be helpful. One very stormy day he offered to feed the hens for me. I gladly accepted and gave him the pail of mash. But my heart nearly stood still as I heard the terrified flutterings and squawkings issuing from the hen-house. Henry's imitation of a mother-hen was enough, had he only known it, to put any self-respecting pullet off the lay for several days!

Helen enjoyed the boys' stay immensely. After supper, Henry would set her problems in arithmetic, or do a drawing for her, or make wonderful models out of plasticine.

The boys could certainly work. They spread cartfuls of lime and manure; they scythed rushes; they helped to dip the sheep. And they were ready to deal with any emergency. After the first ten days or so of superb, unbelievable spring weather, we had two or three days of real storm. The water came swirling off the slope of the moor and began to seep into the glass-house, where the chickens were. The boys set to with spades and deepened the trench round the glass-house before the chickens were engulfed. They enjoyed this battle with the elements. We could hardly dissuade Henry, after that, from digging drains; so great was his enthusiasm that he drew up a plan for draining the whole moor. We had to explain that, much as we should have liked to embark on some such scheme, we had to submit to the pressure of other work. When you're running a small place on your own, you hardly ever manage to catch up with the bare essentials, let alone undertake the more grandiose projects—it's always a case of 'next year' for the big things. So Henry had to be dragged from his draining to spread muck on the potato ground.

I was kept hard at work, during those spring weeks, coping with the boys' appetites. Well I remembered how we had been perpetually hungry in our first months in the hills. After a day or two working in the keen air, there was a gleam in the boys' eyes as they came into the kitchen at meal times. Henry would quite openly sniff the warm smell coming from the oven and rub his hands with satisfaction as he sat down. John would just murmur, 'That Irish stew's good. Funny... I'd never look at it in the canteen, but here...' I knew what that 'here' meant. The vitalising effect of satisfying work in the high air was working its spell. As I heaped John's plate, I glanced at his face. The pale, rather haunted look of the student had gone, I noticed, and there was a hint of the countryman's weathered confidence about his features. Perhaps our scheme *was* having the two-way effect we had hoped for.

The boys were to have one day in the week completely free. On their first holiday they both went to Inverness. But after that they put sandwiches in their pockets and had a long day in the hills. In their free time, after five o'clock, they never once opened a text-book; but they climbed the near hills, they went over the moor with the gun, they called on various families in the district and were made welcome in Highland style.

John, as a veterinary student, was naturally interested chiefly in the animals. I think he was genuinely sorry that his spell with us would be over before lambing started. I'm sure he would have settled quite happily, at any time, into a hill-man's life. Henry, on the other hand, never quite accepted his sense of isolation. He was inclined to want to post letters, send wires, or make telephone calls at all sorts of odd moments. He had the townsman's attitude to living arrangements. Milk came out of a bottle, water out of a tap, and that was that. It never occurred to him to wonder how it was that water did, in fact, come out of a tap, in this wilderness. The result was that he would let the water run while shaving, till the cistern was emptied and the household threatened with drought until it had time to fill up again. Poor Henry! He couldn't quite understand the maledictions that descended on his good-natured head! Perhaps only those who've carried water in pails, dragged logs from the wood and sawn them, can fully appreciate the value of the simple necessities—water and fire.

Towards the end of the month, John had a shot at ploughing the field we were to bring into cultivation that year. The boys had scythed the rushes that were choking it, they'd removed several large boulders, and now it was ready for ploughing. John did very well. We called the field 'John's field' and we sowed it later with oats and grass seed. When John came to see us, several years later, he cast a reminiscent eye over it. It had obviously been quite often in his thoughts. The day the boys were due to leave, John's father and sister arrived to fetch him. They had come north by car, for a long weekend, and were picking him up on their way home. We were all out finishing off a job in the yard when they arrived. It was a typical spring day of sudden squalls and gleams of sunlight. Mr. S., getting no answer to his knock at the door, rounded the gable of the house, clutched his hat as a gust of wind nearly carried it off, caught sight of us and roared, 'You don't really *live* here, do you?'

I'm afraid that is the reaction of quite a lot of chance visitors to our small domain. By the time they have found the place on the map (large-scale), been directed by several neighbours, with varying degrees of explicitness, have drawn the car into the side of the narrow road, taken the path through the heather, climbed the stile and pushed open the garden gate (which is always so well barricaded against marauding cattle, that it's sometimes easier to climb the fence, anyway), there is generally an expression of blank dismay on their faces. We have come to know it well, but we have our defences ready. A chair drawn up to a blazing fire, a cup of steaming tea and a plateful of well-buttered scones will usually work wonders in winter or spring.

In summer or autumn, a dish of fruit and cream and a stroll out on to the moor will generally do the trick.

Perhaps the most enthusiastic visitors we have ever had were two young Norwegians, man and wife. They stayed a week with us in very stormy weather, one October, and they loved every moment of their stay. It was just like home, they said. The only thing that surprised them was that we allowed the sheep to roam the hills all winter. In Norway they have to be brought into shelter and hand-fed for months. Some of the most 'marginal' of our land would be considered, they said, quite first-class in parts of Norway, where soil is so precious, and the fields have actually to be built before anything can be grown. The deep-litter system of poultry-keeping intrigued them greatly.

The very day after the boys' departure, the lambs began to arrive. There was half a gale blowing as we staggered round the moor, looking for the tiny white specks. Over the following days, it rained, it snowed, it blew, and the lambs kept on appearing. We wished John were there to help. Mercifully, no mishap occurred, though it was the kind of pitiless, harsh weather that is very hard on a new-born lamb.

Towards the end of April we decided to sell 'Red Mary', the cross-Highland cow. She had always been a bit of a terror. Having bigger and better horns than any of the other cows, she had become a bully, and her athletic powers had increased over the years. She could jump, if not over the moon, at least over the highest fence we could manage to erect. Any fence she didn't feel like jumping she would persistently lean against at a weak spot until it gave way, when she would step elegantly over, inviting the other cows, with a toss of her head, to follow. We felt we couldn't put up with her tricks for another growing season. Already, the year before, Jim had had to take to sleeping with his bed jammed against the window, so that he could look out at first light to see what marauders were in the crops. Many a morning he had gone out in pyjamas and gum-boots, to drive Red Mary out of the springing corn.

It was a bitter morning of snow, and blowing hard, when Jim went to take Red Mary to the fank to await the cattle float. I decided to keep Helen at home, for the moor road looked most uninviting. Jim had been gone a full hour and I was plodding round the yard, seeing to the hens, wondering when the float would arrive, when I saw Alec and a Forestry man coming down the path from the stile. 'Have you a ladder?' Alec asked. 'Why, yes, I think so.' One is never surprised at being asked for anything up here, but I did find the ladder puzzling, and Alec's manner was a little strange.

'It's Jim', he went on, 'He's not bad, really, but... the heifer dragged him, he...' My heart began to jump.

'The heifer dragged him...' That wretched Red Mary! He'd had her on the rope, she'd been determined to break free, Jim had been equally determined that she wouldn't. He'd held on firmly and she'd dragged him for yards along the road. I stopped trying to picture what might have happened and found a short ladder. I took a rug and followed the men to where Jim was lying at the roadside. No bones were broken, but he was sick and his face was the most ghastly shade of green, with a mauve tinge round the mouth. Alec and the Forestry man carried him to the house on the improvised stretcher. We pulled off his boots and lifted him into bed, then I smothered him with blankets and hot-water bottles. I persuaded him to drink a cup of sweet, hot tea and we left him to lie quiet.

Alec promised to see to all the cows for me. Nellie, our easterly neighbour, came to offer to take charge of Helen if I wanted to go for the doctor, but Jim wouldn't hear of this. Duncan went the lambing round. As ever, we felt surrounded with goodwill. I got a fire going and slipped in to see Jim every half-hour. He was sleeping peacefully and I was thankful to see that his face was its normal colour. By tea-time he was sitting up, eating a boiled egg. I could hardly persuade him to stay in bed until the following morning. 'That darned heifer', he muttered, at regular intervals. She was, alas, still with us, for the snow had deterred the float from coming. As I looked out into the dusk, I could see her doing her best to resist Alec's efforts to get her into the byre for the night.

April had been, as it most often is, a cruel month, though March had been so lovely. But we managed to get the corn and the grass-seed sown. Come what may, seed-time and harvest are always somehow or other achieved. I think it will always remain a bit of a miracle to us that this is so, perhaps because we were not actually born to face the odds of hill-top farming. To the native hill-man it is just in the nature of things that there should be endless difficulties to overcome. If everything went smoothly, he would be inclined to suspect a catch. To us, the wonder is that the stacks still rise against the skyline each autumn, though it may be November before the last ones appear, that the beasts thrive, the little chimneys have each their plume of smoke and the men and women smile a welcome, inevitably, in the doorways.

Towards the beginning of May, when the weather was beginning to relent, we heard disquieting news from over the burn. Willie Maclean was home from hospital and his wife was hoping he would soon be able to get a breath of the soft air. What he needed was to sit on the seat at the gable of the little house and feel the sun warm on his face and hands, she said. But Willie couldn't pick up strength to walk that far; he could only sit in his room and talk in quiet snatches and make plans for his wife and his household. He had got very thin and weak. The doctor could do nothing for him, and one Sunday night he slipped away.

The minister held a service in the house on the Tuesday evening; on the Wednesday was the funeral. Jim was asked to help at the graveside. We were deeply touched by this gesture and we were proud to think we had been his friends. The children and young people of his and of his daughter's house spent the day of the funeral with Helen and me. From the window we heard the cadences of the Gaelic hymns rising and falling in the still air. We watched the long procession of men following Willie to his rest. It is sad when a man like Willie goes, for there are none to take his place. Willie could work his fields, talk of history and poetry in the Gaelic and the English idioms, slate a roof, play the pipes, and keep a secure home for his family. He was a man deeply rooted, complete in himself. Men don't seem to grow to that wholeness now.

When the last of the potatoes were in and the garden planted, and while we were waiting for a little rain to moisten the ground before sowing the turnip seed, I started the spring cleaning. It was the first really big one I had tackled, for hitherto the house had nearly always been in some state of upheaval and thorough cleaning had been done piecemeal, as each room came into use. Now, however, we were more or less settled, our living had fallen into a pattern. Most modern housewives would shudder at the amount of sheer brute force needed for a croft cleaning—there are no shortcuts.

Jim gave me a hand to carry the upholstered chairs and the carpets out on to the grass, where I beat them till the dust flew away in clouds. I washed the blankets and draped them on the bushes in the sun. Curtains and paintwork keep very clean in the hills, for there is no grime to encrust them. Only the living-room and the kitchen really needed much in the way of hard scrubbing. Oil-lamps certainly make ceilings black. Kitchens which are used for every conceivable purpose—and may have to be converted at a moment's notice into hospitals for sick lambs and chickens, or (on occasions, when the outside boiler breaks down) into cookhouses for pigs—can do with any amount of cleaning. But I really enjoyed this hard work. After the long, dark winter, when damp seeps into the corners, it's good to be able to set doors and windows wide and to feel the warm, scented air flowing through the house.

The Highland crofter-wife takes a great pride in freshening her house every May-time. The fabric of her dwelling may not be all that could be desired. In many cases the rooms are unlined, just 'plastered on the hard', but she makes tremendous efforts to keep the place neat and cosy, against appalling odds. She has no water laid on, her fire is an open range, her light an oil-lamp or a candle. Yet every spring she repapers one or more rooms, she distempers her kitchen ceiling, she paints her doors and window-frames. As long as she keeps a gay flag flying there will still be life in the hills. She is well aware of all the devices of the day for making the housewife's lot an easier one. Has not her daughter, who's married to a townsman, a pressure-cooker and a washing-machine? She doesn't hanker miserably for these things, any more than her daughter might hanker for a trip to the moon. But the wise crofter is the one who, on getting a good price for his stirks at the autumn sales, brings home a boiling-ring run on bottled gas, or a pressurised oil-heater for the bedroom. These things do help.

Every croft house has its small flower patch by the door. It is difficult enough some years, goodness knows, to get even the crops to grow, and a little kail for the soup-pot. But it is only an abandoned dwelling that hasn't its little bush of roses:

'...the little white rose of Scotland
That smells sharp and sweet—and breaks the heart',

its few pansies or marigolds, to greet the sun. Summer must be made the most of, must be received with at least a touch of ceremonial. That is why the croft-wife thumps her mats and hangs them in the sweet air with such glad enthusiasm. Her life still keeps time with the natural swing of the universe. In a centrally heated, hygienically contrived flat, equipped with every labour-saving device, there is no real need of a special turn-out in spring. No doubt it is at all times in almost immaculate state, and spring-cleaning has become little more than an accepted custom. For the small house in the hills, it's as though it were putting out fresh leaf and bud, as the heather does in May.

CHAPTER XIV
A DINNER OF HERBS

THE sixteenth of June was a red-letter day in the life of the community. It was the day our bus service to Inverness was started. Once a week, on Tuesday (market day), the small, red-and-yellow bus was to come nosing its way up the long, twisting hill to a point just above the school, where it would turn and await its passengers. The Caiplich folk had a mile or more to walk before joining it, and some would harness up the pony and 'machine' for this part of the journey. The bus went off at eight-thirty in the morning and left Inverness again at three in the afternoon. Later, the time of departure was put on to ten-fifteen, so as to give the women-folk time to get the morning work done. It was impossible, at any rate in winter, to get the cow milked, the hens fed, the children off to school, dinner put ready for those left behind, and oneself changed by eight-fifteen, or earlier. So now we leave in a state of composure at the back of ten and are home again at six-thirty.

These are changed days, indeed, for the women who remember having to be at the pier at Loch Ness-side at eight in the morning, or else having to jolt all the twelve miles behind a tired pony: and for the men who remember walking home on market night, sometimes through chest-high drifts of snow, when they'd come across old friends and had missed the steamer!

There are people still not past middle-age who tell of mothers and aunts walking to Inverness with a great basket of eggs on their arm, which they would sell in order to buy scraps of comfort for their families. Now, the egg-van passes every gate weekly and leaves his price in a neat envelope. Of course, fifty years ago the croft produced practically all the simple necessities of hard living. The oats were ground at the mill, which still stands today, and were made into brose, porridge and bannocks. The cow gave milk, butter and crowdie, the fields potatoes and turnips, the garden patch kail and cabbage. The rabbit made a tasty, nourishing stew. Whisky itself, the water of life, was made locally by those with skill and daring! In autumn the men from several neighbouring crofts would set off with the horse and cart to fetch a barrel of salt herring from the west—and a fine holiday jaunt they made of it! There was a lot of honest-to-goodness happiness about in those days. Those who could afford to do so would pickle a sheep or a pig for winter eating. Each district had its own shoemaker and sometimes its own tailor. These would often give of their skill in return for a service or a load of peats from the hill. In a countryside where practically every family bears the same surname, it is essential to have some distinguishing mark and the old trade names come in handy. This is Fraser country. We can easily tell which Fraser we are talking about, for one will be 'the tailor', one 'the shoemaker', one 'the mason', or else it will be the name of his place we shall use—Rinudin, or Corry-foyness, or Ladycairn. A money economy has taken the place of the old self-sufficiency. The crofter now sells all he can for cash, even his surplus potatoes and a few bags of oats; and spending facilities are not lacking. In addition to the grocer's weekly visit, we have a call a week from the Cooperative travelling shop and two from an Inverness butcher. But the old communal independence and self-reliance are still strong. The exchange of goods and services between neighbours is looked on as part of the natural scheme of living.

The handling of money still comes awkwardly to gnarled fingers and the older Highland mind still assesses things in terms of their actual value in the fostering of life. A load of peats will warm his house; tatties, eggs and milk will feed the bairns; a stack of corn will keep cattle, horse and hens in good heart for many a winter week; whereas money just seems to slip away, leaving no trace.

The crofter still doesn't quite believe in the Welfare State. He's glad enough of his pension, of course, when it comes, and of the doctor's services, should they be needed. But he has always had his own welfare assured by his own community. Should he fall sick, he knows that his neighbour will see to his cattle and his crops as though they were his own. Should his wife be ill, his neighbour's wife will come morning and evening to look after his household.

He would always rather be aloof from outside interference, and is even a little wary of it, however well it may be meant. And who can blame him? In the past, Government measures have done him little good. In fact, the reverse has most often been the case. After the breakdown of the clan system, which had its measure of security, and the arrival of the moneyed, absentee landlord, who sanctioned evictions of a most barbarous nature, the crofter felt lost and bewildered. Is it any wonder, when his roof was burnt about his head and he and his family were 'compensated' with a strip of shelterless bogland? The old feeling of resentment against an alien authority dies hard. Human dignity, when ambushed, takes many a queer twist but, thanks be, it is the last thing to perish in the hills. The authorities find the crofter hard to regiment, he exasperates officialdom, but his sheer doggedness has carried him through. At last, with the passing of the Crofters' Act of 1955 and the establishment of the new Commission, with a man of imagination born of crofting stock at its head, the crofter is beginning to feel his way back to a real status.

In an over-industrialised world where all sorts of artificial supplies clamour to create artificial demands, the validity of the crofter's way of life may be in doubt. Has any man the right to go on quietly cultivating his small fields, rearing his beasts, meeting most of his own needs, and thriving into the bargain? Is he not a bit of an anachronism? How can he be catered for in a world where the cash nexus is supreme? Ought he not to be cutting out his neighbour, sharpening his wits, striving to capture new markets, making money surplus to his requirements, so that he can buy the television sets, the labour-saving gadgets, the patent medicines which every man alive is supposed to need so urgently? In the name of progress, what is he doing, all alone on his plot of wilderness? He's simply minding his own business, working his own hours, keeping a clear head and a stomach free of ulcers, that's all. And, heaven knows, that is a major achievement for an industrial slave, be he machine-minder or company director these days. A country suffering from the effects of a top-heavy economic regime, now looks to the crofter to produce one extra carcass of beef and mutton, one extra box of eggs, so that his place in the scheme of things may be justified.

As the summer wore on we began to wish, more fervently than we had ever wished for anything, that we had been born to crofting ways. Our notion of what was essential for a good working life was still affected by our urban background. We had never been really 'up against it', as the crofter has, most of the time. We had spent nothing on luxuries, but when we needed an implement we bought it instead of making do with a substitute. The tractor, though it had done much useful pioneering work in our early days, we now found was a continual drain on our resources. The cost of running it was out of proportion to the benefits it bestowed. We should have done better to have made use of the Government tractor service for the big operations and relied on the horse for light work. We had never imagined we could have become as adept as we actually had in managing Charlie and the horse-drawn implements.

We decided to sell most of our mechanical contraptions and with the proceeds from them increase our stock. The sheep were beginning to show a return. They produce two crops a year—wool and lambs, but we hadn't room for more than we were carrying. Cattle are slow to give a return; they are two or three years a-growing and nine months a-breeding and a hard winter can so easily set them back. Our fattening pigs had done well and had given Jim a definite leaning towards a piggery. We had a sound spare barn along at the far steading. A good sow can produce two litters of up to a dozen piglets a year, and the market was good. So it came about that on the fourteenth of July three Large White in-pig gilts were delivered to us by float.

They were magnificent creatures. Alec came along to see them the following day. He stood, slowly shaking his head and murmuring, 'What pigs, what pigs! I never saw the like!' Neither had we. They were so pink and white and massive and self-assured, the very cream of the pig aristocracy. We felt we ought to apologise to them for the bareness of their new surroundings, for the quality of the feeding we had to offer. To scratch their backs and murmur 'porky, porky!' into their pink, transparent ears seemed like sacrilege.

A week after their arrival, one of them produced seven piglets. A few days later, another had a litter of fourteen, two of which died at birth, and then the third produced a small litter of five. Every spare moment found us leaning over the side of the pens, gazing at these twenty-four small, squirming youngsters. A lot depended on them. We had had to buy in some expensive feeding to keep their mothers in good trim, and we were over-drawn at the bank to the limit the banker could allow. If the pigs could bring us in a quick return, which would carry us on till the sheep and cattle really began to show a substantial profit, our vital corner would be turned. We were in our tricky year, and at the trickiest part of it. Spending money was short, as the hens were in their seasonal decline and the new pullets would not be in production for another two or three months. We cut down expenses to the bone, literally to the bone! Instead of buying a small pot roast, or stewing mutton, I went hunting for the beefiest-looking bones at the butcher's and made potfuls of good soup with the tender garden vegetables. Milk could be turned into an endless variety of dishes, and eggs and cheese gave us most of our solid protein.

The pigs made a lot of work, for their quarters had to be cleaned out daily and the potatoes that eked out their expensive rations had to be boiled. But they and their offspring throve. After a few weeks, we moved them out into home-made arks on the heather, and it was rewarding to see them revelling in the sun and air. Slowly we began to gain confidence in the pig plan. Billy had left school and was spending nearly all his time helping us. We decided to put the thing on a business footing by paying him a small weekly wage, which we managed to squeeze, somehow, out of the housekeeping money. He certainly justified his keep, for he worked the same hours as we did ourselves. It was sometimes difficult to persuade him to go home. Even on Sunday mornings, he would come over to feed the pigs, so that Jim could take it easier. After breakfast he would potter about, or go for a sheep that had strayed, or tinker with implements in the barn. In his own young, only half-articulate way he was quietly yet stubbornly determined to make a life on his own terms.

The grass was cut by the man from 'the Board' that year. The weather was very mixed and we had a lot of heartbreak before the hay was made. It had to be turned and turned again, hung on the fences to dry and left out in small coils in the fields for weeks. But what nearly broke our backs, as well as our hearts, was the turnip crop. The field was one of the worst on the place, it had only had a scant harrowing in spring, owing to pressure of other work, and the tilth was not nearly fine enough. Through lack of moisture the seed had taken a long time to germinate and the weeds, which, apparently, nothing will deter, had shot ahead of the tiny seedlings. By the time these were ready for singling, they were engulfed in a mass of flourishing vegetation of every obnoxious kind. We slashed and battered at the drills, till every muscle in our bodies was stiff and aching. At the end of it all, we had about half a crop to show for our labours. I think the punishment I should choose for my worst enemy would be a few weeks singling turnips in a field strewn with sods and boulders, and with weeds leering maliciously from every drill!

The nightmare of the hay and turnips was hardly over, when it was time to cut the corn. Jim and Billy had only just time to make the roads before the Board tractor came chugging into the field. No sooner was the cutting done than the rain came down in torrents. There are few jobs as depressing as setting wet sheaves in stook. No protective clothing can keep you really dry; the rain pours off your coat, seeps down the back of your neck and into your boots. As you lift the sheaves, the water runs up your sleeves and soaks you to the elbow. That was altogether a depressing harvest.

We began to cast about for ways and means of making a little ready cash. There were quite a few grouse about, on our ground, but we never had time to go after them with the gun. We had heard fascinating tales of how the crofters used to leave a few stooks out in the field, long after harvest, and set them with snares, to catch the grouse. The town butcher relied on the 'parcels' smuggled in to him, along with an old boiling fowl from the back of the crofter's cart. We soon learnt to make the nooses of fine wire and to fix them on the stooks and every morning we would go out early to look for our catch. We got about a dozen birds in this way and took them hopefully to the butcher, on our next trip to town, but he gave us very little for them. No doubt many moors are commercialised now, and the shops are well stocked. We were only sorry we had not put the carcasses into our own oven.

The lambs were a poorer lot that year and didn't look as though they would make more than moderate prices. We knew that we couldn't expect things to go our way all the time, but we would have given a lot for a lift during those anxious weeks. We had come to have a liking for life in the hills that amounted almost to a passion and the thought of having to abandon it was intolerable. We must, we resolved, find some way of getting round our difficulties.

In mid-September a new arrival came along to take our minds off our worries. A new face about the place always cheers one up. The livestock marketing people, who had helped us over the buying of the gilts, agreed to let us have a boar, on the 'never-never', that is, we put a small sum down and undertook to pay the rest of the purchase price when the piglets were sold. These arrangements are disarmingly simple when entered into. With a few nods and smiles and flourishes of the pen, the bargain was made and McFlannel was among us.

There was no other name we could have given him. He was a good deal smaller than his intendeds and hadn't a trace of pomposity about him. He was quite unspoilt, cheerful and anxious to please. We housed him in an ark, in a field of his own, where he settled quite contentedly. He made overtures through the fence to a few inquiring sheep and he had no objection to the hens joining him in his feed of slops. He was altogether a much more lovable creature than the haughty, pampered members of his harem. They, however, did agree to consort with him at the appropriate time and thus, we hoped, another generation of piglets was assured.

Meanwhile, things were not going too well in the pig trade and prices were falling. It certainly began to look as though we had entered the field too late, as there had been over-production and a glut was threatening. About the middle of October we decided to sell one piglet to test the market. He was a nice, compact little fellow, obviously off well-bred stock, and we felt quite proud of him when we saw him in his market pen and compared him with others on offer. He fetched ten pounds. It was quite a good price, in the state the market was in and, a fortnight later, we got another lot of piglets ready for sale.

The float was late in coming to fetch them; that is the price one has to pay for living in the remoter areas. The float-hirers always leave the difficult places to the last. They would rather avoid them altogether, if they could, and they all have an aversion to loading pigs. The result was that our lot did not reach the market until the sale was almost over. They looked wretched, having been cooped up for hours, and they made very disappointing prices. We decided to take the remaining pigs in individually in the van, but by this time there was a real landslide in prices. The day we took one on our own demand was exceptionally slow, and we brought him home again rather than let him go for a song.

Then, about a week before Christmas, poor old McFlannel fell ill. The male of any species is never anything like as tough as the female. We laid him on a stretcher of planks and carried him, inch by inch, to a warm place in a corner of the byre, where we made him a deep bed of straw and then sent for the vet. He diagnosed pneumonia. Next day, McFlannel died. Billy was nearer to tears than I have ever seen him; I think he had a real affection for McFlannel. We buried him with heavy hearts. His widows looked flourishing enough, but we took extra care of them, just in case. A lot depended on their bringing forth McFlannel's offspring safely, in the New Year.

CHAPTER XV
WE WEAR THE GREEN WILLOW

ONE day early in January Jim, Billy and I were clearing mud
from the yard. The weather had been mild and the accumulation of squelch was such that one was liable to leave a gum-boot
behind in it on one's journey to the steading. Charlie stood
patiently, while we filled the cart over and over again with the
heavy, gluey muck. There can be a touch of magic in a winter
afternoon, but that particular one hadn't a glimmer about it.
The sky was overcast. The pigs and pullets looked dejectedly
out from the mesh doors of their dwellings. We were spattered
with mud from head to foot, our backs and arms were aching,
and still the wretched stuff never seemed to get any less. Yet
the strange thing was we were perfectly happy. I caught Jim's
eye: suddenly, for no reason that we could think of, we found
ourselves chuckling!

In a flash it came to me—might not people who were forced
to spend their working hours between walls like to hear about
what went on in a hill-top croft, of how it was possible to get
an immense amount of fun and satisfaction out of lifting loads
of mud into a cart, even though your boots were leaking and

you knew there was not enough in the kitty to buy another pair? Would they like to know about the way light could stream down a blue hillside on a spring noon, how a lark could suddenly leap into a pale, washed sky after a night of storm and make the air ring with song, of how it was possible to get by every sort of difficulty as long as there was this knowledge that you were all in it together, this solidarity with rock and sun and bird? I believed they would.

The next afternoon when everything, including ourselves, was fed and I had a couple of hours to spare before going to meet Helen at the burn, I sat down at the kitchen table and wrote a short piece about the stillness of January in the hills, about the satisfaction of keeping the animals tended and biding one's time till the earth swung round to the sun again, about the small thrill of seeing the child of the house come safely home into the lamplight each evening, her cheeks glowing with the frosty air. The writing came easily, for I was talking about the things our days were made of. I had always liked writing, though I had only had an odd story or two published many years before. Luckily, I still had my old typewriter.

The next evening I typed my sketch, attached a snapshot of the croft and sent it to the editor of a Glasgow paper. In Glasgow, I thought, there must be many Highland exiles, who might like to read about the life they had once known at first hand. The typescript was back within the week, with a polite letter from the editor explaining about shortage of space and so on.

I posted it to the editor of the *Weekly Scotsman*. A few days later, back came the large return envelope I had enclosed. I took it from the post and had my usual chat with him about the weather and the doings of the day. I opened the other communications he had brought—a couple of bills, a circular and a Government form. I picked up the 'reject' envelope and was about to toss it on to the dresser with the others, when it struck me that it was surprisingly thin. I held it up to the light. There was certainly no typescript inside. I tore it open and drew out a single sheet of paper. It was a letter from the editor, thanking me warmly for the article and the photograph, which he proposed to use in his next issue, and indicating that he would like me to send one every month, for a trial period! I opened the door and called to Jim. He came into the kitchen and took the letter in his muddy fingers and we looked at each other with disbelieving eyes.

Before the end of the month the article appeared, along with the picture of our house. I have gone on writing these little articles ever since, and I have found each one a pleasure to do. They have brought us friends from places as far apart as Texas and Australia.

The kindly welcome given to my effort by the editor of the *Weekly Scotsman* I found most heartening. Every spare moment—afternoons in stormy weather, evenings when the day was spent working outside—I gave to writing. I wrote a longer piece about remote living and sent it to the B.B.C. To my astonishment it was accepted: I could hardly believe in my luck. We celebrated with a family Burns Supper and sat round the kitchen fire, with platefuls of haggis and mashed potatoes and turnips on our knees. Jim read bits of 'Tam o' Shanter', Helen sang 'My love is like a red, red rose' and we pledged the immortal memory in glasses of rowan wine.

That small mid-winter cheer did us good, but the worry of our financial position still kept nagging away at us. It was becoming clear that the pigs were going to turn out a liability rather than an asset. We thought of selling the bungalow, with its steading and fields, and concentrating on producing eggs intensively, to carry us through till the sheep and cattle really began to show a profit. But the demand for small places had fallen away, and a decrease in our securities would mean a lessening of our overdraft at the bank. There were already signs of a tightening-up of credit facilities. Ready money was also extremely short, for the pullets which had started to lay so promisingly were slackening off.

In mid-February we sold the last of the porkers. The price they fetched was not reassuring. Two of the sows produced quite good litters of ten a-piece, but the third sow was, as we had feared, not in-pig and we had to sell her empty. We decided to put the youngsters off as weaners. By the time they were ready for the market, prices had slumped so alarmingly that we could see nothing for it but to go out of the pig business as quickly as possible. We sold the whole lot, along with their mothers, and just managed to repay the market people their advance.

It was now obvious that we should have to find an additional source of income quite soon. My writing would not be enough to bridge the gap. It was an uncertain business. I had had several short stories, on which we had pinned hopes, returned. We put an advertisement in a Glasgow paper, announcing that we would welcome a small family to share our life during the summer months. We emphasised the fact that we should like children, for this was just the place for them to run wild, and Helen was highly delighted at the prospect of having playmates in the house. But, of course, the success of this scheme was problematical. Jim decided that he would have to take on a job, once the crops were sown. Many a crofter has done this before him and there are several round about who go away to work as ghillies during the shooting season, returning in time for their late harvest. In some parts there is Forestry work available most of the year, but here, at that time, there was none. Jim would have to work in Inverness, getting home when he could, and I would carry the place on with Billy's help.

In April the man from the Board came to do the ploughing. Billy harrowed the ground with Charlie and they did very well together. We had some hectic weeks putting everything in order before Jim went off. There was the corn and grass-seed to sow, the lambs had to be dressed and inoculated, the seed potatoes prepared. Somehow or other we managed to accomplish it all. The weather was not helpful; we had one of the worst rainstorms we had ever known. One day the burn rose in a couple of hours to the size of a river, and Helen had to be kept at home till it subsided.

Then on the sixth of May we saw Jim off on the Inverness bus. It seemed very strange without him. Billy worked hard and cheerfully, but for me there was a blankness about the days. We had always shared every job, from spreading muck on the fields to wiping eggs for the van. When you work as a team the job swings along however hard or monotonous it may be. Now the rhythm had gone out of everything, and I knew Jim would be hating every moment of every day in town. Gradually, however, we adapted ourselves to our new circumstances. We each had plenty to do and the knowledge that we were fighting to save our way of life kept us going.

The sheep were causing us a lot of bother; they had got a bite of spring grass in a neighbour's grazing and were for ever breaking through to indulge their appetites, and every morning Billy had to go to fetch some of them home. Most of his days were spent mending weak portions of the fence. I took Helen to school on the carrier of my old bicycle, so as to save time on the return journey. I would leave the bicycle in the shelter of a ruined croft house near the road, to avoid having to haul it over the moor and across the burn.

Jim came home once a week. His first two days at home he spent furiously fencing with Billy. The sheep were becoming a menace. One night they raided the newly planted garden and ate a hundred cabbage and kail plants. A man who leased some grazing land adjoining ours began to complain bitterly about their depredations. Jim worried about the situation, knowing that he would have to be away some time. The banker was calling for a reduction of our overdraft, so the sheep had to be sold. We knew that this meant that the croft would never provide us with more than half a living, but the fact had to be faced.

Alec and Billy came to gather the flock and separate them into their categories—ewes with lambs at foot, and gimmers. Jim got a lift home on the evening before the sale. We shut the gimmers into a field and put the sheep with lambs into the enclosed space round the house. All night we heard them moving restlessly around. At six o'clock we were out taking a last look over them then we all went in to the market. Jim stood watching the sheep in their pens, but I couldn't bring myself to see them sold; that was a hard day.

But things had to go on. On Jim's next day at home a neighbour came, with his tractor, to open the potato drills. We planted the potatoes in the wake of the tractor and the drills were closed the same evening. Later on, this same neighbour came to prepare the turnip ground and Billy sowed the seed with Charlie.

I had to resort to all sorts of devices to get certain jobs done. There was the wringing of hens' necks, for instance. That was a thing I had never been able to do and Billy, curiously enough, would rather not attempt it either. When I had half a dozen birds to sell to the butcher, I had to put the poor creatures in a pen and ask the post to do the necessary, when his own work was done. He was always ready to help in any emergency and he took this quite as a matter of course.

Then there was the business of taking the cows to the bull. With our particular cows, who all had wills of their own, this had always meant that two people must accompany them—one to hold them on the rope, the other to open and shut gates. I therefore went, as a necessary part of the bridal party, as far as the last gate, where I waited discreetly, before resuming my duties on the return journey.

Billy spent much time, that June, cutting peats. It is hard work, skimming off the turf and cutting the blocks out of the bank. Two or three times a week I would go along in the afternoon to help him, setting the chunks in small heaps to dry. Later on we made the small heaps into bigger ones. Sometimes Sadie would come over for an hour or two and the time would pass quickly, in company. On a Saturday Helen and Bertha would join us; then the peats would fly, and the sweat would pour off Billy's face, as he struggled with all the feminine competition. There's always an element of holiday in days at the peats; it's hard work, but it's different. You're working away from your usual haunts and the air is sweet on the moor in June. On the way home we would paddle in the burn and gather handfuls of bog-cotton and huge, yellow 'butter-balls' to decorate the kitchen table.

Helen came home for the holidays with a first prize for class-work and a passionate resolve to become a teacher! Each fascinating thing she learnt had to be imparted urgently to anyone within earshot. The walking to and from school had made her hardy and resilient. Some of the questions she began to ask showed that her mind was clear as a bell. A child brought up out of the reach of the multifarious distractions of town life keeps a keen, uncluttered perception. She doesn't have the adult world thrust at her in all its distorted forms, from the cinema screen, the advertisement hoarding, or the chance over-heard conversation of strangers. She grows into it naturally and accepts its responsibilities as she does her food. If she wants an egg for her breakfast, she knows that the hens must be fed and cared for first. She realises that the enjoyment of a glass of milk involves fetching the cow from her grazing, seeing that she's comfortable and helping to scald the pail and basin. Even the boiling of a kettle means the gathering of good kindling sticks, and she soon learns which make the best burning. She sees life whole because she has begun by discovering its roots.

That summer we got wind of a development which was to affect the lives of almost every one of us. A meeting was called in the village hall and an official of the Hydro-Electric Board announced that the power line would be coming our way in the near future. He explained very patiently all the working of the scheme, the outlay involved, the cost of consumption and the help that could be given in the purchase of equipment. The talk at neighbourly ceilidhs over the next months was alive with comment on the plan, and practically everyone was determined to scrape the bottom of the barrel, so as to share in the benefits of electricity. For ourselves only a minimum of expense would be involved, as the house was already wired for light, and we should only need to have power plugs installed.

One amusing story went the rounds. It concerned an old countryman in the south who went to stay a night with a daughter whose house had lately been equipped with electricity. 'Well, Sandy, how did you like the electric light?' he was asked, on his return home. 'Ach', he said, 'I canna' be daein' wi' it. Kept me wakened a' nicht. It's in a bottle and ye canna' blaw it oot!'

Within a few days of the meeting, the surveyors were out on the moor and the Hydro Board's small, white van was scurrying up and down the hill road, visiting every croft. The officials were all most courteous and patient as they answered our eager questions and explained exactly where the poles were to be erected. The surveyors were scrupulously careful to avoid the arable ground. All being well, they said, we should be connected up within the year.

Ours is a bleak, forgotten sweep of upland, barely snatched from wilderness, but in the short time we have been here, we have seen it take a leap of a hundred years. A good road now links us with our market, we have a bus service and as many van deliveries of goods as we could wish for, and now—electricity. This is progress in the real sense. To equip people in their millions to mind machines and then to cater for their leisure with the provision of such hectic delights as will allow them to bear their daily boredom without complaint is not necessarily progress. To provide basic facilities for those still engaged with the earth is a thing worth doing.

CHAPTER XVI
A STORMY CHRISTMAS

TWO small families made arrangements to spend their fortnight's summer holiday with us—one in the second half of July, the other in the first half of August. Each party consisted of a small girl and boy and their parents. We were confident that they would fit into the scheme of things, for they would not have chosen a small, unknown place in the Highlands for a holiday if they had been difficult to please.

Their coming involved a good deal of turn-about in the house. We made three rooms ready for their use and fitted up the living-room and the spare room off it as our camping quarters. They used the front door, and thus their part of the house was quite self-contained and they could come and go as they liked without disturbing us at our labours in the kitchen.

Ten days before their arrival, Hope obligingly calved, so that we were able to greet them with brimming jugs of cream and mounds of fresh butter. The hens were laying well and the garden was stocked with greenstuff. The foundations of good, simple meals were to hand, but I had forgotten that people living near to shops are accustomed to variety in their diet. I had to rush up and down to the gate to catch every available van in an effort to avoid monotony.

Each family had a car and they were co-operative and always willing to fetch fish and extra meat when they went off for the day. The children asked nothing better than to be left to play about with Helen in the sand-pit, climb the rowans, explore the burn, bring in Hope for the milking, help Billy cart peats home from the moor. They had all the natural child's zest for imaginative play and Billy excelled himself as host. He let them lead Charlie and ride on his back, and in the evenings they all sat in the straw in the empty byre and had shots on Billy's latest acquisition—his accordion. That was a month of hard work, but it was rewarding—our visitors became friends, with whom it was a pleasure to keep in touch.

While the house was full I had to put all thought of doing any writing aside, but as soon as we settled back into our routine I got busy again. I had had several articles about Highland and crofting life published in Scottish monthly papers, and had entered a story, of the woman's magazine type, for a competition advertised in a daily newspaper. This had been solely in the somewhat forlorn hope of making a little needed money. The prize was, I think, a hundred pounds. I hadn't really expected my story to win anything, and it didn't: it came back. But, instead of the usual rejection slip there was a polite letter expressing regret that my effort had not won a prize, admiration for the writing and confidence that, if I could 'get on to the right lines', I should be able to make a success of magazine story-writing. I was doubtful about this as I was mainly interested in writing about things I understood and loved. I was not at all sure that I understood or loved 'love' in the sense accepted by the women's magazines!

I went on writing about the hills and the men and women who grow among them—the tough, obstinate, shrewd, kindly folk, who grumble one minute and chuckle the next. They haven't a shred of glamour to them, but they are real, and there are not many of them left. Already the members of the younger generation who still work in the hills are acquiring the mass-produced responses of the day; the impact of the wireless and the daily paper is slowly steamrollering them into the accepted mould. I wanted to record those whose individualities have not yet vanished, but of course it was not the way to make money.

One afternoon I was sitting at the window, writing about the reaction of an elderly crofter's widow to the coming of the electricity. I looked up, as a movement by the stile caught my eye. A tall man, wearing kilt and bonnet, was coming towards the house. In his wake was another man and behind him two women. I watched the little company approaching and saw the expressions of slight bewilderment, which no stranger manages to hide, on nearing us. Then the dogs set up a furious barking and I hurried out to greet the arrivals.

The kilted man introduced himself as the writer of the letter encouraging me to do stories for his paper. No one less like one's conception of an editor of 'pulp' could be imagined. He and all his party at once took a delighted interest in our place. They took photographs of Charlie, they inspected a new-born calf, they watched for Helen coming home across the moor.

They had come north, they explained, for a long weekend and thought they would like to look me up on their way home. We talked a little about writing matters and had a cup of tea, then I saw them off in their stream-lined car. I did write several 'love' stories after that, and an odd one or two were published, but I think this kindly editor knew as well as I did that I was not likely really to get 'on to the right lines'.

That September we had a displenish sale in our midst. It was a fine autumn day; the sunlight lay in long, pale beams across the flowering heather. It was a day for looking forward, for sniffing the earth-scent and planning next year's work. But about the croft there was only the drab confusion of buying and selling and 'flitting'. Crockery, books, pictures, all the odds and ends that had gone to make a home, stood in forlorn heaps, on top of dressers and tables. I bought a couple of peat-knives for a shilling, but I can't say I felt particularly proud of my bargain. It was as though a whole way of life were being put under the hammer and 'going … going… gone!'

The place was bought by an active couple who turned it into a poultry farm. Practically every place in Abriachan was by that time occupied by an in-comer. In addition to the 'tomato-man', the 'strawberry-man' and the 'mink-man', there was now the 'poultry-man', and the gamekeeper's croft had been taken by a lady who kept Dexter cows and guinea-fowl and hens which laid golden-brown eggs. She was bred to country ways and it was always a delight to drop into her house for a chat and the loan of a book or a paper. Her never-failing welcome did much to help me over my spells of loneliness, when I wore the green willow for Jim.

Jim came home in time for the corn harvest at the beginning of October, and we had to rush it in between spells of storm. The potato crop was only a small one and we lifted it with the graip, taking it in turn to dig and pick. Then we went hard at the lifting of the turnips as we had to secure them before the arrival of the sheep we were to winter, for Jim had decided he would have to work away from home for another spell, in order to strengthen our financial position.

Billy would be leaving us as soon as harvesting operations were over as the Welfare people considered, quite rightly, that it was time he was embarking on a definite career. We said good-bye to him at the beginning of December and he went to work on a big dairy farm near Beauly. He had done well by us as he had always been willing to tackle anything—from taking Helen to school to painting the gable beams of the house—he had been happy with us, I think. We liked to see him laugh— and to listen to the tunes he got out of his accordion. Whenever he went to town he brought back a piece of chocolate for Jim, because he knew he liked it, and he always remembered our birthdays with a small gift shyly pushed along the kitchen table. He was growing into a big, burly fellow and he had the makings of a man of sound heart.

A few days before Christmas Jim went off to work. I took the Glen Convinth bus to town, to do the last of the Christmas shopping. The shops were warm and glittering and full of excited people, jostling one another to secure their tokens of goodwill. I felt very lonely and bewildered among the crowd so I made my purchases as quickly as possible, drank a hurried cup of tea and made for the early bus. I was thinking of our small, storm-tossed home and longing to be back in it, with Helen safe beside me. It had been blowing a gale when I left in the morning; Heaven only knew what damage might have been done in the interval. Also there would be no Jim to meet me at the gate, to take the parcels from my aching fingers, to tell me all was well, the animals were seen to, and there was a good fire in the kitchen. That was his normal welcome when I returned from a shopping expedition, but this time I would have to manage everything alone.

We picked Helen up at the schoolhouse door. As she and I emerged from the bus ten minutes later, at the crossroads, a gust of wind caught us and literally sent us spinning on our way. I don't think I've ever felt anything like the force of the gale that was blowing that night. It was from the north and it came at us like a wave of solid matter pressing on our backs. Helen was tossed ahead of me. Only my superior weight, and the weight of the bags I was carrying, kept me more firmly anchored to the road. To climb the stile, a thing normally accomplished quite automatically, became a precarious operation. It was touch and go whether we landed on the other side upright or prone in the heather.

Reaching the Macleans' house at last, we staggered into the warmth and light of their kitchen, gasping for breath. Bertha had just recovered from measles and Mrs. Maclean was not too well, but they had seen us coming from the little back window, and they had tea ready for us and a plate of pancakes. The hot drink and their kindly concern put heart into us for the last lap of the journey.

We left most of our parcels with them for collection next day and, with the loan of a stick and a torch, set off to cross the burn and make our way up the moor path. As we neared the house I sensed that something was missing. I peered about in the gloom and saw that another of our giant rowans was lying prone, its roots streaming in the wind, like pennons. We reached the back doorstep and nearly stumbled over the huge, galvanised water-butt, which had been blown clean off its brick foundation. I pushed open the door and we burst thankfully into the calm of the kitchen.

There were many jobs to be done, but the first essential was warmth. I lit a candle (the windmill batteries had perished in the frosts of the previous winter and we hadn't renewed them, as the electricity was on its way), and soon had a fire going and the kettle on the spirit-stove. Then I lit the lamp and settled Helen at the fire, with a cup of cocoa and a book, while I went to see to the animals. The hens had long since gone to roost, but their crops would be well filled, for they had hoppers of mash and had only to help themselves whenever they felt peckish. I groped for the eggs by torchlight and made my way to the byre. The cows had been in all day and were ravenous and they turned their heads towards me expectantly, as I hung the storm-lantern on the hook in the roof-beam. I was thankful that hay and corn sheaves were to hand, in the false roofs Jim had made, and had only to reach up with a fork and tumble the sweet-smelling stuff down into the beasts' fodder-racks. Then I had to fetch pail after pail of water, to satisfy their great winter thirsts. Each time I staggered out to fill another pail at the byre butt I wondered if I would be blown into the next parish before I could get back with it!

I came in at last for the night and found Helen curled content-edly in her chair. She was to prove a most steadfast companion during the weeks and months we were to be alone on the croft. She never minded in the least being left by herself in the house, while I saw to the animals or went up to the gate to fetch the grocery box. Very often she accompanied me about these jobs, but many times it was too wild for her to be out. Then she would stay quite happily on her own, even after dark or during a severe thunderstorm.

Darkness, thunder, gale have never held the slightest terror for her. To grope one's way home on a pitch-black night, when the torch battery has failed, she considers fun. I've seen her stand at the window watching delightedly for the next lightning flash and counting the seconds till the great, satisfying crash of the thunder came. She seems to sense that these wild, natural outbursts are only rather spectacular phenomena, which have nothing to do with her inner composure.

By the following morning the gale had lessened and I let the cows out for an airing and a drink and had a look over the sheep. I had just done the feeding round that evening when the wind began to rise again. It was coming in sudden squalls, straight out of the north, and it now had an edge to it—it seemed as though there was nothing between us and Iceland. The grocer's van came late that night; the force of the wind was such that it blew me round in a complete circle as I came down from the gate with the box of groceries clutched in my arms. I was a little worried, for the following day was the day of the Christmas concert at Helen's school. She was to take part in two little performances—one she had been practising for some time and one she had taken over just a few days before, when another child went down with measles. Luckily, she herself had got her measles over at the age of eighteen months! In the evening there was to be a party for all the children of the district in the Abriachan schoolroom and somehow or other I had to get Helen to both these festivities.

I lay awake that night listening to the wind tearing at the house and making the beams rock. I slipped down early in the morning and peered out into the gloom: snow was whirling out of the bitterly cold wind. I lit two candles and we had our breakfast crouched by the living-room fire. I left Helen in the warmth, while I went to feed the horse and the cows and hens. Then we had to face our two-mile walk into the teeth of the storm.

I tucked Helen's skirt into a pair of old breeches and made her wear two coats and a scarf wound round her balaclava so that only her eyes were showing. By the time we reached the Macleans we were already plastered from head to foot with driven snow. We found Mrs. Maclean far from well and I promised to telephone the doctor from the kiosk by the school. We struggled on, heads down, along the exposed stretch of road and down the long hillside to the comparative shelter of the glen where the school lay. I left Helen in the cheerfully warm, excited atmosphere of a small schoolroom on closing-day, rang up the doctor and made the return journey comparatively easily, sailing along before the wind.

It was after mid-day when I reached home again and I was so hungry that it hurt! I cooked a chop on the spirit-stove and made a big jug of coffee. Then I fed and watered all the animals liberally as this feed would have to last them until the following morning. I changed, reluctantly but dutifully, into a tidy outfit, swathed myself in coats again, and set off once, more to the school.

The little performance went off beautifully and Helen said her pieces without a hitch. Afterwards we drank tea and ate cream buns and sang carols with the children. The room was an oasis of warmth and light and colour. It seemed scarcely possible that a storm was still howling outside—but howling it was!

I knew it would be madness to attempt the long journey home and then the extra mile to Abriachan, on our own, in the blackness. So I rang up the school bus driver, who runs a car for private hire, and asked him if he would take us round. He was a little doubtful whether he'd manage to get up the hill, as it was very slippery, but said he would try. He's a great, burly fellow, always laughing and game for anything. His own bus, which he runs into town twice a week, is something of an institution. He stops at each regular passenger's gate or road-end, with a friendly toot of his horn, in the morning, and in the evening will go out of his way to put everyone down as near their door as possible, should the weather be bad. He does messages of every imaginable kind, from posting a letter to handing in a sewing-machine for repair and will load his bus with anything from bags of cement to tomato-plants and day-old chicks, in season. For everyone he has a cheery word of greeting, and should a housewife overspend herself and have nothing left for her fare he'll soothe her with kindly laughter and say, 'Ach, I'll get it again'. Small wonder, then, that such a man took us safely up and round by the loch, though his headlights and wind-screen were almost obscured by driven snow.

The Abriachan schoolroom was another oasis, a positive wonderland to come upon on such a night. A huge fire was blazing in the open hearth and a Christmas tree stood, glittering in a corner. Nearly all the children turned up, in spite of the storm, and it was a delight to watch their small, numbed faces opening like flowers in the light and warmth.

That was a memorable party; we played the Grand Old Duke of York and Blind Man's Buff and all the other well-tried games; we sang carols and Gaelic songs and we ate hot pies and iced cakes and drank scalding tea. There was a tinkling of bells outside, a huge knocking on the door and Santa Claus came in with a toy for each delighted child.

We were loath to button ourselves into our coats for the walk home, but to our astonishment we found ourselves emerging into a still, crystal world. The wind had dropped, the sky was gleaming with stars, the hills seemed enormous and remote, under their covering of shadowed white, as we walked home briskly and happily over the crisp snow. Helen sat drowsily content in the candle- and fire-light. I carried her to bed and we both slept till the bellowing of hungry cows woke us in the morning.

CHAPTER XVII

THE STILL CENTRE

JIM came home for a brief spell on New Year's Eve, but we were both too tired to stay up all evening. We went early to bed, after setting the alarm-clock for just before midnight. When it rang, we got up, poked the kitchen fire into a blaze and drank a toast in our dressing-gowns. Jim went out to fire the traditional shot from the gun, to warn the evil spirits away, and we crept back under the blankets. He had to go off again later that day. Helen took his comings and goings very calmly. She loved his company, for he could enter completely into her world. He could tell her the most fascinating stories, he could invent games out of nothing at all and he could set her the sort of problems she loved to work out in arithmetic or geography. Geography was her special passion. 'Could an elephant', Jim would ask solemnly, 'walk from Paris to the Cape of Good Hope, without getting his feet wet?' Helen would screw up her eyes, while she visualised the map, then rush to the atlas to confirm the route she had planned. The two of them were endlessly happy together, yet after Jim had gone Helen settled quite calmly again.

For myself, I was too busy ever to feel that acute loneliness I had known sometimes, years before, when I lived among a city crowd. Sometimes, during the day, when I was alone and there was a deep winter silence everywhere, I found myself having quite earnest conversations with Hope, the cow, or with Charlie or the hens. This might have led a chance visitor to assume that I was a bit queer in the head! But I firmly believe that these creatures like the sound of the human voice, when it is not raised in anger. Hope certainly lets down her milk better after a friendly chat and the hens 'sing' delightedly when you enter their quarters uttering a stream of nonsensical remarks.

Only once, while Jim was away, did I get a bit of a scare. I was sitting by the kitchen fire knitting a sock, late one evening, when I heard heavy footsteps coming round the gable of the house. There was a scraping on the doorstep and the knob of the door was rattled. I thought—could it be Jim come home unexpectedly? He came whenever he could, even if only for a few hours, but he always gave a shout outside so that I should know who it was. My heart jumping a little, I got up and slid back the bolt on the door. I opened it and found myself peering into the long, yellow face of Charlie, the horse. Dear old Charlie! He liked to slip out of his stable whenever the door was not quite securely fastened. I stroked his nose and he stood, half in the kitchen, half out, while I filled a pail with water and scattered oatmeal in it. He drank it gratefully and I backed him out again and heard him wander off into the near field. Many times after that he came along for a late snack, and it was comforting to hear him pacing steadily round the house at night, like a policeman on the beat.

On the fifth of January came the day Helen had to start school again. We had decided that she would have to leave Glen Convinth and go to Abriachan school. Now that I was on my own, I was finding it impossible to walk with her the two miles every morning. It was usually eleven o'clock before I got back and then every job about the place had to be started almost from scratch and finished before darkness came down at half-past three.

Helen accepted this arrangement calmly enough. Her new teacher, Miss Fraser, received her with kindness and understanding and after a day or two she settled into her fresh surroundings. Miss Fraser, who was born and brought up in the district, had herself been a pupil at the school where she was now in charge. She had seen its roll diminish from over a hundred to a mere handful, but she and her sister, Miss Kate, who cooked delicious dinners for the scholars, kept smiling faces and went briskly about their work. They always made us most welcome in the schoolhouse and they understood our interest in the district. If only So-and-so were living, they would say, he would have been able to tell you so much about the place.

No local history or guide-book contains more than a passing reference to Abriachan, but the older people with the lively minds, such as our neighbour Mrs. Maclean, could make the place come to life for us. The chance visitor here, looking up towards Rhivoulich, will see only a little stone house falling into decay in its hollow on the hillside, and the bright green growth on land that had once been tended. To our eyes, thanks to Mrs. Maclean, it is the place where a cherished neighbour had her first child, when the doctor rode over on horseback, in the falling snow, from the next glen.

Likewise, the tumble of stones on the near slope to the west is the place where the good wife baked a whole boll of meal in preparation for a wedding in the family, and the festivities went on for a full week.

On the hillside, beyond our march, we can visualise the small drama that took place one day in the colourful time of the last occupant of the croft there. He was a man of many skills and one of them was the making of a dram. One day word reached him that the excisemen were on their rounds. It was winter, snow had been falling, and only that morning he'd been up the hill for a drop from the hidden 'still' to keep the cold out. The imprint of his boots had left a clear trail on the shining white ground.

So he calmly borrowed a score of sheep from a neighbour and drove them up and down the hill, and round and round his dwelling, till every tell-tale footprint was obliterated. And the secret of the whereabouts of his still went with him to the grave.

Bottles and jars of the stuff were easily enough hidden in the house itself, favourite places being in the mattress of a relative put hastily to bed and said to be at the point of death, or behind the voluminous skirts of an invalid granny who couldn't be persuaded to rise from her chair.

When we watch the two burns foaming along the edges of Mrs. Maclean's east field, after a night of heavy rain, we remember how this piece of ground got its strange name 'The Island of the Cheeses'. After a downpour the field, with a burn on either side of it, does indeed become an island and, one day of exceptionally heavy spate, the cheeses that the women had made up in the shieling by Rhivoulich were carried down the burn and landed on this green patch.

On our own ground we often come on small, neat piles of broken stones and we can picture the man who worked away at them and had them ready to sell to the roadmakers, when death overtook him. This is an old land. Stone Age implements are found in the bogs and traces of very ancient habitation can be seen on the hill slopes. In spite of hydro-electricity, the telephone and the weekly bus, the links with the past are strong, and they make the present so much less shadowy and unreal.

At the foot of the hill, on the shore of Loch Ness, lies the font-like stone, its hollow always brimming with water, said to have been used by Columba for baptising the faithful. And what of the monster, that link with a very remote past? Had they ever seen it? we asked several neighbours during our early days here. Well, no, they hadn't, but they knew others who had, and seeing, we gathered, is not the only way of believing. There were so many unaccountable things in the world, anyway, that a loch monster was not such a great source of wonder after all.

The nearest we ourselves have come to seeing the monster is to have caught the reflection of its appearance in the wide, bright eyes of Sadie and Bertha. One summer evening we came on them pushing their bicycles up the hill. They had been riding along the loch shore when they came unexpectedly on a sight of the beast, cruising quietly along, quite near the bank. One or two cars stopped, they said, and a small group of people watched until the creature disappeared below the surface. It had a face like a Cheviot sheep's, Sadie said, and a sinuous, black body. Since that evening we feel we are practically one of the band of 'seers'.

Near our own march fence runs the road which the women of Glen Urquhart took to meet their men coming home from Culloden. A neighbour once found a shoe, of the type worn by the soldiers at the time of the '45, preserved in the peat, near this road. We like to think it was lost by a Redcoat in too hot pursuit of a fleet Highlander and to imagine him having to give up the chase and limp back to camp.

Among the scattered birches on the hill slope, where Helen likes to play at Jacobites and Redcoats with some of her friends, is a stone memorial to a forgotten clan chief, who died in a forgotten skirmish. On a neighbouring estate are several modest memorials, consisting of a Gaelic inscription let into a piece of natural stone. The laird responsible, a historian by inclination, wisely considered it important to record, not necessarily that a battle occurred at a certain spot but such things as the simple fact that this was the place where the shoemaker lived and worked, that even this small green field had a name.

Then there are the intangible legacies from the past. A neighbour of ours, young and active and full of fun, will still look anxiously at a heron, bird of ill-omen, flapping his way from the hill, lest he should pass too near her place. And a man is remembered who, in his youth, had to walk thirty miles in a day without speaking to anyone he might meet, to visit the only person who could cure him of the evil spell which had been cast upon him for spite.

Fear, along with its fantasies, lingers in the corners of the Highland mind, but it is a fear of the unknowable and an altogether healthier thing than fear of the calculable horrors of concentration camp, or nuclear warfare. You can live with a fear of the unknowable. It does get at the root of the thing for, at bottom, it's an honest enough acknowledgment of the existence of the mystery of evil. Once acknowledge the existence of the mystery and its manifestations, however horrible, can be seen in some sort of perspective. And it works the other way, too. Time and again, when we've been near defeat, wondering at the narrowness of the girdle which keeps happiness intact, we've been aware of a sort of hovering of friendly wings about our roof.

One snowy morning I was trudging about the steading, with armfuls of straw, when I saw a figure coming slowly down from the stile, a suitcase clutched in either hand. It was Jim! I dropped the straw and hurried to meet him. He had got several weeks' leave, before taking on a new job in spring. It had come about suddenly and he hadn't been able to warn us, even by a telephone message to the Post Office. It was better that way, the surprise was a delight in itself.

He had had to walk the two miles up the hill, from the bus, carrying his cases and was nearly exhausted. I cooked him a dish of ham and eggs and we sat talking away the rest of the morning. Then he changed into his old corduroys and dungarees and was soon tramping about the place as though he had never been away.

Jim was back just in time. The following morning we awoke to the now familiar sound of a northerly gale tearing under the roof slates. A storm of blizzard proportion battered at us all day. We struggled out three times to see to the animals. The rest of the day we spent huddled at the living-room fire, swathed in woollen garments, heating panfuls of broth and making tea and cocoa. Helen loved those days of storm, when we were marooned together cosily, in the firelight, with the world whirling madly outside the window-panes. Jim taught us to play cribbage and we went early to bed, with nearly all our clothes on and hot-water bottles stuffed down our jerseys.

We were wakened in the dead of night by the sound of water dripping on the stairs and got up to investigate. The water was pouring steadily through the ceiling at various points. Evidently the oil-lamp which we kept burning by the cistern had not provided enough heat to prevent the pipes from freezing. The overflow pipe was blocked and the water was escaping where it could.

We tried to turn on the taps in the scullery to relieve the pressure, but they were frozen, too. Next moment the water began coming through on to our beds. We lit lamps and candles, we moved the beds on to dry spots, we put every available pail and basin at strategic points to catch the drips. Every now and again a drip would stop, only to start up again somewhere else.

By this time every step on the staircase was coated with ice and going up and down in the dark was a tricky and dangerous business. We got a kettle boiling. Jim at last managed to thaw out one of the scullery taps and the drippings slowly ceased. Since that night we have always left one tap slightly on in frosty weather.

Next morning the wind had shifted to the south-west and was blowing the snow into great drifts along the road. The food van was already a couple of days overdue and we were running short of bread. I was reluctant to ask for the loan of a loaf from a neighbour, for I knew that everyone would be as short as we were ourselves. Bread is a thing one is apt to take very much for granted, total lack of it seems a calamity. That evening I baked what I hoped would turn out to be a loaf in a cake-tin. It was edible, that was all! It certainly hadn't the authentic texture or flavour of bread, but we enjoyed thick slices of it spread with butter and home-made jam.

Next day the sky was a radiant blue and the icicles along the steading roof dazzled our eyes. We went to look over the sheep and found them in surprisingly good shape. They were patiently scraping away at the snow to get a bite of heather or a mouthful of rush-tops. We filled our lungs with the cold, still air and forgot our small needs and worries. We had a sound roof to shelter us, peat and wood for warmth, milk, eggs and potatoes in plenty to keep us fed. Health and strength we knew to be the enormous benefits they really are. We were free to open our minds and let the stark beauty of hill and moor and sky strike into us.

It was like a morning before time began to tick, before life started its endless nagging. We were isolated, apart, and face-to-face with a brand-new, yet age-old, world. There was a whole, strange, unknown patterning in the crystals on a frozen blade of grass. Under the ice the water lay black and deep and remote, keeping its own counsel. This was primeval water, heedless of its function to minister to human needs. A dog barked from a croft a mile away and the silence was cracked from end to end. We made our way happily back to the job of keeping life astir, tingling with the rare refreshment that seeps from the springs of things.

As soon as the snow-plough had opened the road, John Maclean, to whom our wintering sheep belonged, came to take his flock away. They were grazing in a rushy hollow, some distance from the road. We tried to drive them slowly the half-mile to the gate, but they could scarcely move. The frozen snow had formed into heavy balls on their fleeces so there was nothing for it but to leave them where they were till they thawed out. We carried bundles of hay to them and gave them as many turnips as we could spare. Two or three days later the thaw came and they quickly recovered their normal agility.

The drains couldn't carry all the sudden rush of water and a flood rose in the byre. The water swirled alarmingly round the cows' hooves and we had to lodge some of them temporarily in the stable. Then by degrees everything settled down. The food van came and we had a meal of steak and onions and fresh bread.

By the end of the month the first larks were singing. It had seemed scarcely possible that a bird would ever sing over our fields again, yet here they were, as determined as ever to enchant us! But it was only a brief overture, for in mid-February a second blizzard struck us. It was of far greater intensity than the January one. We woke in an unusual darkness. The windows were plastered with frozen snow. We opened the door and peered out at the fantastic shapes that had risen about us during the night. Between the house and the steading there was a drift five feet deep, and the snow was already packed hard as cement.

We ate a hot breakfast, then we muffled ourselves in the heaviest clothing we could find and cut a way through to the byre. As I sat down to milk the cow the young blackbird, which had taken up its abode in the steading since the previous storm, flew down from a beam below the roof and perched on a bundle of straw near me. His bright eyes darted swift glances in my direction. As soon as the milk began to spurt into the pail he set up a tiny, inward warbling. It was one of the sweetest sounds I have ever heard. From that day on, he would greet me every morning. He was shy and shadowy yet infinitely companionable and I missed him when spring came.

Later in the morning we hacked a way to the turnip pit. The turnips were sound, under their thick cover of turf and snow, and the cows ate them greedily. The post didn't come that day. We were not surprised, for the drifts on the road were chest-high, and we knew that had there been any urgent communication for us he would have got through, though it took him till well into the night. The vanman, too, we knew would have made every effort to reach us, but it was obviously impossible. The storms always came on, or near, van-day, when supplies were at their lowest and though we had laid in an emergency ration since the last blizzard it wouldn't last a week.

In former times the crofts and farms always stocked up for the winter, so that they were independent of outside provisioning from October to April. A barrel or two of salt herring would supplement the home-produced oatmeal and potatoes; milk and eggs, of course, were in daily supply. Dry groceries were bought in bulk, when the lambs or stirks were sold. But today life is lived on a weekly basis and the vans go everywhere, now that there are roads that they can negotiate. Eggs are produced in greater quantities, we sell them weekly and buy our groceries weekly. When a breakdown in communications occurs, following the natural calamity of storm, we have to face a certain amount of hardship, but it is a lively experience trying to make the most one can of one's own resources.

We certainly never came anywhere near suffering real hunger. Life is sweeter near the bone. We would come in, glowing from our exertions in the snow, to eat vegetable soup and huge, floury potatoes, with a relish. Afterwards we would stretch out in our chairs by the fire, to listen to the evening news bulletin on the wireless. It was strange to hear the smooth, remote voice breaking into the stillness of the kitchen, telling of the things we had been battling with all day: we are not used to hitting the headlines. We heard of crofts isolated for days, supplies running low, telephone lines down. Well, we can do without the telephone for a while! Should there be a real emergency, sickness or accident, we know that neighbours would hack a way through any drift to get help. There are still sledges handy, there is even an old horse-drawn snow-plough on a nearby croft and there is real satisfaction in putting one's independence to the test.

What worried us, during that second blizzard, was the fact that our supply of oat-straw for the cows was running short. We had had to feed them liberally, from the turn of the year, in order to keep up their body heat, and had known that we might be faced with a shortage, for our last harvest had not been good. We had meant to buy in a load of fodder about the middle of February, but we knew that it would be some time before even a tractor could reach us. With every road in the north impassable, it might be weeks before the hard-pressed snow-plough team would come our way.

Once again Mrs. Maclean came to our rescue. She had an ample supply of fodder, she said, for her one cow. We were welcome to take as many bundles of straw as would tide us over till the road was opened. So every day we went back and forth to her barn, crossing the burn quite easily on the packed ice, each carrying two or three bundles of straw roped to our backs. It was exhausting work but it saved the cows' lives. As soon as the road was opened we got a trailer-load of straw from a farm a mile away. The tractor couldn't get into the steading, so the load had to be left at the roadside, whence we carried the whole half-ton of it down to the barn, on our backs. When spring eventually came it felt strange, indeed, to walk anywhere without an enormous burden strapped on our shoulders.

All the rest of that month we had storms, big and small. Sheep on the hill-grazing had to be dug out of drifts. We lived a hand-to-mouth life, but we kept fit and forgot what a normally planned existence was like. By the beginning of March the larks were singing again, and the black ground began to show in great, gaping patches about the fields. We looked at them curiously, for it was so many weeks since we'd seen anything but whiteness surrounding us.

An elderly neighbour died that month. The road was still closed to wheeled traffic, as it was impossible to shift the hard-packed snow by ordinary means. Jim went with the others, to help carry the coffin to the point the snow-plough had reached. In days gone by the coffins were always shouldered by neighbours, over the hill-track, to the burial ground in the next glen. The old funeral paths are still clearly visible and the cairns, where the bearers stopped for a rest, still stand. How comforting it must have been to know that one would be carried on friendly shoulders, through the sweet air, not trundled in a stuffy hearse!

By that time the grocer's van was managing to reach a point about a mile from our gate and from there we carried our goods, or pulled them on a sledge. Just before we ran out of paraffin the road was finally cleared. We swarmed eagerly into the van and laid hands on all the things we needed.

The evenings were lengthening and the moor came alive again, with peewits, snipe and curlew in possession. Slowly we discarded our heavy garments and let the soft air play about our bare heads and arms bare to the elbow. We gathered a handful of earth and let it trickle through our fingers, marvelling that it was actually warm to the touch, and dry and friable. We had witnessed one more silent miracle.

CHAPTER XVIII
THE WAY AHEAD

THAT was not to be a fully realised spring, for us. The snow was still lying on the high tops when the ploughs were set to work on neighbouring places. Horses and tractors were moving steadily up and down the small, steep fields everywhere all day and far into the darkening. But for us there was not to be a full seed-time. Reluctantly, we had had to devise a new scheme for living. We would graze sheep throughout the year and cattle during the summer months. We would buy in feeding stuff for the hens, and keep only as many as would show a profit on this basis. Our aim was to supply our essential needs—milk, eggs, potatoes, vegetables and fuel—from our own resources and to obtain cash for our further requirements from Jim's spells away at work, from the rent for the wintering and from what I could earn by writing. We had sold the van and had cut our wants down to a minimum. This shedding of the load of possessions and needs gave us a renewed sense of freedom. The van had been useful, certainly, but it had brought its own set of problems. Many a time it had refused to start, or had broken down at some crucial point on the journey home. We now found that it was the easiest thing in the world to walk to the bus when we had business abroad. There would be a layer of worry less, on the surface of our minds, and we'd have more time to watch the slow, high circling of the buzzards over the moor, and to chat with a neighbour at his field-side as we passed down the road on foot. With life being lived at its simplest level, we discovered a fresh savour in the smallest things. A fried egg, mashed turnip and a floury potato, on one's plate, was a meal to look forward to. To stretch one's fingers to a blaze of logs, during the hour before bed, was a happy occasion. Shelter, basic food and warmth, our small place would always give us. Then the mere fact of being together, the three of us, was a constant source of celebration. Further separations were inevitable, but we learnt to keep the thought of them out of sight and to live delightedly in the present. We had achieved perspective and who can fail to do that who has the sun to make him sing, the rock under his feet, the stars waiting, each night, to be wondered at?

We lost Charlie that spring. He had come through the winter in surprisingly good shape. Then one warm day, when the grass was beginning to come to a flush, he wandered into a bog and got himself caught. We tried to pull him out with ropes, but it was impossible and he had to be destroyed. It was a sore blow, but it was better for him that he should go that way rather than linger into sickness or disability. He died enjoying the freedom that he throve on and we buried him where he fell.

Summer came, a summer of real heat and brilliance. Jim was at work and I spent a lot of time writing. When Helen's holidays began, she and I practically lived out of doors. Housework came almost to a standstill. After several weeks of drought, the water system broke down, for the flow was not strong enough to work the pump. We had to fetch our drinking water in pails from the spring, and we relied on the store in the rain-water butts for other purposes. We wore the simplest clothing, which could be washed out in a minimum of water, in a pool in the burn. We ate lettuces and eggs and hardly ever lit a fire.

In the mornings we worked in the garden, and nearly every afternoon we went to the loch for a dip, as Helen loved the water and was fast learning to swim. We were both burnt gipsy-brown by the sun. We spent several days helping to pick fruit for the 'strawberry-man' and I made enormous quantities of jam. I did my writing in the cool of the evening, after Helen was in bed, and I sold several articles and sketches of Highland life to Scottish papers.

In the autumn the Hydro-Electric Scheme began to push its nose our way; jeeps and lorries careered through bog and heather, performing fantastic feats of transportation. In an incredibly short space of time a long line of poles sprang up, its straight, geometric design striking a strange note in a landscape of curves and hollows. But we quickly got used to the spectacle. The men on the job were an odd collection of types and nationalities. We boiled their dinner-kettles for them and took them into shelter on the worst days of storm. Later we stood open-mouthed to watch them swarming up the poles with climbing-irons. At last, in mid-December, we were 'lit up'. Most of the crofts in the strath were participating in the Scheme. It was cheering to see the lights flash on and off in the evening. Occasionally someone would forget to switch off a light at bed-time, and next day Sandy or Duncan would be hugely chaffed about the late hours he kept! Those who had electric fires or cookers were able to keep secret the hour at which they started the daily round, for it was no longer possible to tell, by the rising of the thin plume of smoke from the chimney-head, when the mistress had set her porridge-pot to boil!

It is, perhaps, in the winter mornings rather than the evenings that we most relish the comfort of the 'electricity'. To be able to slip from bed and flood the room with light and warmth at the flick of a couple of switches is little short of a miracle to those who have had all their lives to grope for matches in the early dark and to struggle with damp kindling sticks and paraffin oil. And to have a kettle that boils before you even have time to set out the cups and fill the teapot is certainly better than a trip to the moon. This is the sort of progress the down-to-earth Highlander really appreciates. He is still sceptical about most of the contraptions which the townsman considers essential, but something which will help him with his own fundamentals, that he is quick to prize.

That winter I began taking Helen to the village hall, on Saturday afternoons, for a lesson in the rudiments of music on the piano. We would make an expedition of it, walking over the hill on the fine days, and finishing up with a fireside chat with a neighbour before the return home. One afternoon we met the post as we reached the road. He handed me several letters, among them was one of my own familiar, self-addressed, large envelopes. 'A reject', I thought, 'I'll take a look and get it over'. I slit the seal hurriedly, meaning to forget the disappointment in the joy of the frosty, sparkling afternoon. To my astonishment, I drew out a brief, polite letter from a B.B.C. producer, which stated simply that he liked the story I had sent him, that he would use it as a Morning Story on a date in January, and that it would be read by the actor, James McKechnie.

He read the story with exactly the right emphasis and understanding, and that was the beginning of a happy collaboration. 'Why don't you write a play?' some of our friends suggested. But that I don't think I could do. I'm content for the moment that a glimpse of the Highland way of life should be borne from time to time on the back of this voice from nowhere. The truth about the Highland people is not in drama, but in the small, daily acts of living, in the long, slow rhythms which shape their lives. The spotlight is not for them. It is fitting, to my mind, that they should be 'on the air' in the morning, in the calm daylight of reality.

That Christmas I received several letters from people in far-off places—in Australia, America and the other side of Canada—who had read the little articles I had done for Scottish papers about life on the croft. I found these more heartening than the cheques the work brought me. They were mostly from Highland Scots who had emigrated and who still called themselves 'exiles'. They were proof that economic prosperity can still leave a gap in the mind and in the heart. I read lately in the paper that in the United States, among that section of the community which is satiated with the good things of life, it is quite common practice for people to take a 'happiness' pill, when they want to revive themselves, before a party. It is not surprising that thoughtful people everywhere are beginning to wonder where progress is leading us all. We can rush round half the globe, now, in a matter of weeks, provided we have a pocketful of pills to keep us in trim. Or we can sit at home and peer at the antics of the other half reflected on a tiny screen. Yet how much wiser are we at the end of the day?

There is the moon, you'll say, there is outer space. Now that we know so much about the world we live in, is it not up to us to concentrate all our energy on probing into these farther regions? But—do we really know so much about this world we've glimpsed, maybe, at second-hand? It still takes a man with a seeing eye a whole lifetime really to know the few acres he lives on.

Friends of ours, who know something of the practical difficulties we have had to overcome in the years we have spent in the hills, sometimes wonder how it is that we look so fit and are obviously so happy in what must seem to them extremely precarious circumstances. I think it is because we've learnt to set our lives to the old rhythm, we've learnt a little of the old wisdom. Men and women everywhere are burning their brains out in the gigantic effort to change the face of things, but there is, in fact, a point of submission. The small man, whose work is governed by the movement of sun and wind, of star and cloud, knows this, and so is set free. It is the marvelling eye which sees the flower pushing through the sod, beside the food-crop, and the roughened hand reaches down to gather it. Grace before meat has a meaning to folk who have nursed their potato plants to fruition and tended the cow till she yields milk abundantly. The songs that are still sung in the west all celebrate some human fundamental—birth, love, marriage, death, harvest, home-coming. Where there is no superfluity of trappings, people get the whole savour of living, and the savour so delights them that they must make a song on it.

In these hills we are still too near to 'civilising' influences. The town is only twelve miles off and we can go there every week if we will on a bus which now passes our gate. The younger people are gradually adopting contemporary habits of speech and dress. They no longer think long thoughts, or assess things in terms of human values. The members of the older generation, who were as individual as the numbered pines on the hillside, are dying out. Already some we knew in our first years here are becoming a legend. Willie Maclean has gone, and Johnny F., and now Willie Fraser and Neil, the retired schoolmaster, and John Maclean, who wintered sheep with us. Men such as these were shrewd, and could be tough and obstinate when circumstances pressed hard on them. But they held their heads high, as members of an old race do, and their everyday speech had the far-sounding echo of poetry. Why was this? It was because they were conscious of playing a real part in the fostering of life, and the things they spoke of were real things, closely observed, as the poet, the 'seer', observes them. These people had the manners and breeding of natural aristocrats. To boast, to show curiosity or surprise, to admit to poverty, was a thing they abhorred. You could be sure of a welcome in their house at any hour of the day, however busy, and you were never allowed to go without your taste of whatever their cupboard held.

Why is it that we go so gladly to visit an old lady who has lived all her life across the burn from us? It's because we know that she'll draw us in by the hand to a seat at her fire, her eyes alight with welcome: that we shall talk of the way the larks are singing, or the corn yellowing, or of the good thing it is that the hens are back on the lay. When we talk of the weather, we shall not dismiss it as some vague nuisance in the background of our lives. We shall speak feelingly of the May frost, for it blighted the young potato crop, on which we depend so utterly. We shall congratulate ourselves on the heat in the autumn sun, which encouraged a late green bite for the cow. We know that our old lady will chuckle, as she sets the kettle simmering and patiently teaches us a Gaelic phrase ('There are some things you can't get *the feel* of, in the English!'). We know that we can sun ourselves in her warm, well-mannered geniality, that when she says 'Haste ye back!' she will mean it from the heart. She is genuinely, closely, in touch with life.

We are glad that Helen is spending her formative years under a wide sky, near to the roots and bones of things. I think, wherever she may go in later life, her yardstick will remain here. Whatever doesn't measure up to the standard of the hills she will instinctively reject. She'll need the sky's space, the cleanness of snow, the invigoration of winds blowing off the moor, the coolness of loch water and the warmth of a high-riding sun to keep her world in perspective. Already she can look and listen, and that is more than halfway to understanding. Touching will come later and then, perhaps, she will be ready to make her own contribution to things.

A child engaged in watching a chicken emerge from an egg will not bother to raise her head to watch the antics of the latest jet-aircraft in the sky. She takes aerobatics for granted. They are mostly a matter of mathematics, and can be understood. There is nuclear fission but that, too, is understandable, though the threat of its misused effects, dimly grasped from the reading of a newspaper column, is something she recoils from in dread. The real wonder is close at hand, close, yet infinitely remote, lovable, inexplicable, and thus an endless fascination.

As for living, making the most of the space between the mysteries fore and aft of her, I think the gift for that is in her hands. She loves to run out barefoot on a summer morning, to warm herself at the fire on a frosty night, to climb trees, to make things out of discarded scraps, to lie on her stomach in the grass doing nothing, but utterly absorbed in being. She's found her identity, she's in tune.

And what of our two adult selves? We've learnt this much— to work with unending patience, and to work with the rhythm of the unfathomable, never against it; to recognise the point of submission without qualm or bickering; and to make a small ceremonial about the simple acts of living. Moving this way, we can feel the light and warmth that is at the core of things fall, like a blessing, on our faces and hands.

END PIECE

IT is nearly twenty years since I set down this account of our life on the croft in the hills above Loch Ness, yet each day's doing is as bright in my mind's eye as if it happened yesterday. I am thankful that we had the immense good fortune to live for even a few years among the members of that small community which has now all but vanished. Linking hands with them, setting our lives to the rhythm of theirs, we were conscious of reaching far back into the folds of time. The signs of continuity were everywhere. The shieling huts of ninety years ago were made to the same pattern and of the very stones of those of the people of four thousand years before. Flints were picked up and used as pipe-lighters. The fields carved from the heather were not much bigger than those hacked out by the farmers who settled in the age of bronze. The sun was still the dominant factor in life. How could it be otherwise when survival depended on ripened crops and fattened beasts? The feel of veneration was still there, though the rituals of worship were long overlaid by those of Christian belief.

Now, during the last ten years or so, change has almost over-whelmed us. The green slopes of the high strath of Caiplich are nearly all deeply scarred and planted with conifers. Some of the surviving older people can hardly pass that way for sorrow. Land that was originally cleared, thousands of years ago, for food crops and has been added to slowly, over the generations, and drained and walled, this good land has reverted to timber. Some is owned and neglected by absent proprietors. A field which I look at every day from my window was taken out with the spade by a man whose grandson tells me the children had to take him by the hand to his work in the morning and lead him home at night, when his eyesight was failing. It is still green, this hard-won field, but unworked, and the heather is creeping back.

But our own old place is still an oasis. And it has been added unto. Several of its heather slopes have been drained and ploughed and brought into cultivation. Cheering, too, is the sight of the two well-worked crofts beside the little loch, with their quota of black cattle in the fields and hens strutting round the midden. Two resident proprietors of some of the highest ground are wisely allowing the old fields to be worked again and the rotational grazing of cattle and sheep is slowly building up fertility.

I suppose we are all, in varying degrees, subservient to technology now and the small green upland places are not much more than breathing and stamping grounds for those fully engaged in it. Yet there is a steadily growing demand, especially by young people, for a stretch of earth, a small, plain house, some place where a simple lifestyle can be followed. Where will they turn to when every inch is covered in holiday homes or commercial forests?

But this story of ours is no lament. It's rather a giving of thanks. And I am still, in the way life moves, very fortunate. I have only to cross the threshold to find myself walking on moss and in heather, through scattered pines and over rock, to the ridge where time stops still. Right round the horizon are the unchanging outlines of the hills. I can stoop to gather a palmful of spring water and turn to watch snow-bunting on the wing.

I am still aware of blessing. I live in the old school-house that used to seem a mansion and, from the front porch, I work what some say is the smallest Post Office in Scotland. I must use the singular pronoun for Jim, now, walks the fields of Tir nan Og. A stone of hill-top granite stands in a quiet corner of Kilianan and bears his name. His sayings are in many minds and the way into that croft of ours is still known as 'Stewart's gate'. Helen, after studying and travelling Europe-wide, never lost touch with the homeland and lives with her husband and family on a small farm only twenty miles away. She milks the Jersey for the children and is as proud of a well-doing calf and a row of sturdy cabbages as ever we were with our lambs and turnips on the croft.

I have only a garden now, but it produces all the fresh food I need, and to spare, and is a habitat for bees and chickens and a goat. What is missing is the sense of community, the sharing of glad things and setbacks by people engaged in a common way of life. So, in a sense, this story of ours is a tale of other times, almost a glimpse of legend. To us it was the reality of our lives.

A GARDEN IN THE HILLS

FOREWORD
BY
NAOMI MITCHISON

A garden is always pulling one like a three-year old grandchild wanting to get away and do something that the grown-ups don't want him to do. Things you put in carefully just decide not to grow. Or else something you almost throw away produces a flower that takes your breath away with its beauty. What you see from a book may show things as they are in a garden, or it may only show you things that someone—the gardener—chooses to let you see. When you read this book you must decide how real is the picture that goes into your mind's eyes. I think this book will help you to see things as they are, their problems and difficulties, but also the special beauty of a garden in a difficult place, the excitement when everything goes well. In a book like this the happiness, the flowers and the people go on and on for as long as you read it.

Naomi Mitchison

Dedication

To my family, who share my love of gardens and the hills

Weeds... the ever-recurring problem

In the Beginning . . .

God Almighty first planted a Garden. And indeed, it is the purest of Human Pleasures. It is the greatest Refreshment to the Spirits of Man.

Francis Bacon

When the three of us—my husband, my daughter and I—came to live in the old schoolhouse at Abriachan we had just, reluctantly, had to give up working our croft a little further up the hill. Before long, therefore, we had the three-quarters of an acre of school garden made into a mini-croft with chickens, a goat and honey bees, as well as many kinds of vegetables and flowers.

It had been hard going, as the ground had been neglected since the closure of the school some years previously. But we worked away, clearing drains, mending fences and dykes. We planted a plum tree to companion the old apple-bearer and brought in fantail pigeons to delight the eye. Soon we were able to see a pattern emerging and to relax a little.

My husband was postmaster, working from a tiny office in the front porch, and I was teaching in Inverness. As his health was beginning to fail, though he would never give in, I took early retirement to be at home full time, but sadly, a few years later, he died. By that time, our daughter was married, with a growing family, and living on a farm some twenty miles away.

I carried on the work of the Post Office. Now, left on my own, I found the garden my source of joy. Since that first garden was planted 'east in Eden', so many have blossomed, in so many different ways, and have been at the heart of so many peoples' lives. Thousands of years ago, in Arabia, South America and elsewhere, men scraped over some ground, drove off marauding animals, made a hole with a stick and dibbled in some seed.

Since then we have seen such miracles as the Hanging Gardens of Babylon, Tudor Knot Gardens, Versailles, Sissinghurst,

Giverny, Pitmedden, Inverewe, and beloved plots such as the one tended by the mother of Laurie Lee.

To me, my garden has given me the chance to consider many things. For instance, there's the mystery of growth—how that tiny acorn can become that massive oak; that small, brown bulb develop into that dazzling flower. Sometimes I wonder whether this whole planet of ours is capable of growth, of change, of evolution. Of course, I am not a scientist, but science itself now acknowledges, I believe, that there are, perhaps, things it does not fully comprehend.

By recording some of the days spent in and around this garden, I may, I hope, be able to share it with people, unknown to me, who love gardens and the hills and with those, too, who may not have the blessing of a garden of their own.

My friend Anne Shortreed who captured so happily, in line, the spirit of the place, died a few years ago. She came often to see me. She loved the garden and the hills surrounding it. Naomi Mitchison, whose appreciation I cherished, she too is no longer with us.

But life is here. My daughter and her husband and family, with their combined youth and strength and love of plants, have made a most beautiful garden, full of colour and greenery, out of these beginnings. It will give joy for many years to come.

I should like to thank Tom Johnstone of the Mercat Press for his ever sympathetic handling of the text and I am grateful to Highland Regional Council for permission to quote from the Log Book of Abriachan School.

OCTOBER

October 19th

'The snow-birds are here!' That's a form of neighbourly greeting, the first acknowledged signal that winter has really arrived in these uplands. This year the snow-birds—the fieldfares and redwings—are having a feast, for the rowans are loaded with berries. The old trees at the top of the garden are alive with the flutter of wings and the delighted chatter of hungry birds. A long flight they've had of it from their northern homes and we're glad to make them welcome, reminding ourselves that they're fleeing from winters colder than ours.

The geese came in some weeks ago, and are still coming, some stopping in nearby firths, some making for estuaries further south. It's always thrilling to hear their wild voices and to stand in amazement, staring at the brilliant formation of their flight.

Through the window it's a delight to watch the antics of our own small garden birds—blue-tits, coal-tits, great tits, siskins, chaffinches—as they chase from one nut container to another. A robin looks on angrily, frustrated by his lack of acrobatic skill. A couple of wrens, who sometimes seek shelter in the house, and a tree-creeper or two, along with the blackbirds and thrushes, make up our winter company, now that the summer birds have gone. A flock of long-tailed tits sometimes flits through the garden on its way to the plantation up the road, where the bullfinches dazzle the dark pines.

As everything settles into winter retreat, we miss the company of butterflies and bumble-bees. This has been the year of the butterfly. In early summer the small blue and the Scotch argus came out in the welcome warmth, then white cabbage and tortoiseshell were everywhere, orange-tip on the wayside flowers and, in late September, four red admirals on the marguerites, so unafraid one could have reached out a hand to touch them. One memorable summer, painted ladies appeared among the herbs.

The honey bees are snug now in their winter cluster. Walking up to check the hive, on the well-trodden path through the stand of willowherb which makes their summer paradise, one comes back, covered in white fluff, to tackle the last of the garden harvests—the late potato crop. The shaws are blackened by early frost, but the tubers come up safe and sound, dry and handsome, with a lift of the big garden fork. They're a joy on the plate, as they crumble and melt in the mouth, almost before there's time to savour the taste! The peas and beans have cropped well. Carrots and beetroot gave more meagre returns. The onions are small but well ripened and good keepers. Leeks and turnips are always a great stand-by and are the making of many a pot of broth. The kale crop looks ready to survive the winter through. This year I sowed some extra seed to supply a neighbour whose plants always get decimated by rabbits.

October 23rd

Waking to find a scattering of snow above the tree-line on the hill, I think 'time to gather the apples'. The day turns brilliant, blue and gold and windless, and just to gaze at the apples—some red, some green, tinged with yellow—against the deep blue of the sky is a moment of delight. They come crisply from their stalks, the ones within reach. A good shake of the higher branches and soon the biggest and brightest are lying on the mossy turf. The old tree—it must be nearly a centenarian—is still putting out new shoots. I think it's a happy old tree. The scholars would scramble over the garden wall, when the master was having his dinner, to pillage the forbidden fruit. Though it looked so attractive it had a bitter taste, being meant for pies and jelly. The discarded cores must have given many a night-time meal to playground rodents of many kinds.

The plums are not so plentiful this year. The tree must have been having a year off, though the blossom was beautiful. But wild fruit is everywhere. The rowan berries we make into jelly, a bitter jelly, even when mixed with crab-apple juice, but good

a boletus or two to cook in a little oil

as a relish. Our great favourite is rowan wine. We simply steep the berries in boiling water, with a small piece of whole ginger, let it stand for ten days, strain, and add sugar, a pound to a pint. Then, after three weeks, or when fermentation has ceased, you have a drink of a colour to delight the eye and which possesses, so they say, the secret of eternal youth. I drink a glass at supper-time each day!

On the wooded slopes down towards the big loch there are brambles, rose-hips, haws, sloes, fruit enough to fill a store-cupboard for the longest winter. And this has been the year of the mushroom, as well as the butterfly. I think the early warmth in May and June, followed by plenty of moisture, may well have done the trick. Fungi are everywhere. I keep to the three I'm sure of—boletus, field white and chanterelle. This year I've tried drying the last two, with some success. At the moment I can gather supper from the roadside—a boletus or two to cook in a little oil, perhaps with an egg, and a cupful of brambles to eat with a dash of yoghourt or cream.

There are hazel nuts in plenty, too, for protein. They do well in the grinder, then mixed with onion and oatmeal to make 'hazelburgers'. I often think that at this time of 'Okto-berfest' one could survive quite happily on natural produce. Time is needed, of course, to gather in the harvests and to prepare them for keeping, with sugar or vinegar or salt. We're lucky, indeed, to find so much almost on our doorstep, or within easy reach.

October 25th

A glorious blue sky and time for a day off from harvesting and preserving garden or natural produce. So—into the hills above the tree-line, past the russet and gold of larch and birch and, warily, into the domain of the red deer. The stag's roar reminds us to keep our distance, as we watch him, through the field-glasses, lording it over his placid hinds. The roar is echoed from across the hill, a rival stag appears, there is the clash of antlers.

It's thrilling to watch and hear this annual ritual, which ensures the survival of the fitter hero and so of the fit herd. We stay a while, then retreat, before we're mistaken for possible rivals of another ilk. Homeward bound, we stop at the river to watch for leaping salmon. Sure enough, a huge fish jumps, leaving a widening circular ripple on the smooth, black water. This shatters the reflections of the golden trees, then subsides till another fish emerges. It's good to know that all this roaring and leaping means that another generation of these marvellous species is assured.

On our own territory there's another stop to be made—at the small hill loch up the road. It's mostly covered in thin ice this day, but over by the rushes there are patches of melt and there, upending or sailing majestically, their necks proud and straight, four whooper swans, dazzling white in the dark water, have stopped overnight. Another sure sign of winter, this, but a happy sign. We hope others will come and that they'll stay for a while, keeping company with other winter visitors—goldeneye, goosander, pochard, little grebe, along with tufted duck and mallard.

October 31st

Back to work again! Gertrude Jekyll, I remember from her writings, was a great believer in hard work, so she must lead the way. A walk up the bedraggled garden reveals a massive tidying-up operation is waiting. But the wind's in the east, with scutters of sleety rain numbing the fingers. This is when you long for a greenhouse, preferably a heated one. The small one I bought second-hand, some years ago, for a few pounds, has, alas, not survived the gales. In it tomatoes ripened, along with peppers and even a cucumber or two. But one can make do in other ways. One year a crop of mushrooms appeared mysteriously in some compost in the garden shed. And I've grown marigolds, sweet william and pinks in trays on a sunny bedroom windowsill.

So with thoughts firmly fixed on next year's bounty, I set about gathering burnable dead growth to add to the pile already lying dry under a plastic cover. Dried stalks of willowherb and docken, withered raspberry canes, wind-blown branches of birch, pine and rowan, the garden trees, all make excellent ash to scatter on the strawberry bed. I can almost feel the sweet succulence of the first fruits of next June.

At dusk the bonfire rushes into light, defying cold and sleet and roaring a welcome to the guisers. In twos and threes they come, in the strangest assortment of garments, some with painted faces shining weirdly in the firelight, some carrying traditional turnip lanterns. A song or poem or a dance for apples and nuts makes a great celebration, as the evil spirits are banished for another year. Better than any firework display is the light of colours—red, yellow, blue, green—in the heart of the fire and the swoop of flame and spark into the black sky. And there's the warmth for numbed fingers and the prospect of tatties baked in the embers later on. Far into the night the glow lingers, till we cover it with earth for fear of a rising wind. Under the ash will be one spot of really weed-free ground, we reflect.

Weeds . . . the ever-recurring problem, that's the one we shall have to get down to again next day. The persisters—docken, sorrel, bishopweed, creeping buttercup—will be carted by the barrow-load to the compost heap. Smaller growth—shepherd's purse, chickweed et al, will be dug in with the lime or organic fertiliser.

NOVEMBER

November 4th

A sudden blast of cold air from the east and hoar-frost transforms the picture from the window. The trees stand motionless in a dazzle of white, as though decked out for Christmas. The grasses are tall still, and strong enough to carry their own small crowns of crystal. And over this whole amazing scene the sky is an arch of deepest blues.

It's a day to be out, to forget indoor chores, to put every available scrap on the bird-table and to don scarves, gloves, thick stockings and balaclavas. The garden ground gives the ring of iron to the spade. There's no chance of digging up a carrot for the soup-pot. It's not even a day for a bonfire. The pile of debris set aside for burning is stiff with rime.

So it's down the road to the woodland while there's warmth in the unclouded sun. Rose-hips are still bright on the bushes, each one capped in white. And the darker red of berries on the old hawthorn glows bright in the wayside hedge. What of the sloes, I wonder, as I turn off to follow the track through the wood. A touch of frost improves most berries, but this freeze-up may be just too hard. The rowan berries were few this year and the meagre crop had gone to beleagured birds.

The path is slippery with frosted leaves. I search in vain for a few fallen hazel nuts. There will be time to gather them yet. In older times the women would walk barefoot the ten miles to the town, carrying baskets of nuts to sell for Hallowe'en. This is deserted woodland, with its own feel of enchantment and intrigue. Big hazel trees, blown down in gales, lie across the way. This is where a neighbour and his brother used to gather the wood to make superb walking sticks. Delicately tapered, with a curved and polished handle, they are a joy to finger and to use. I treasure mine.

Walking on, stepping over fallen trunks, stooping under branches, I reach the outcrops of rock under the high banks. Here, in little hidden bothies with a camouflage of heather, the illicit brew was distilled. Some was sold to meet the ever-increasing cost of rents. The elixir was renowned. Excisemen would sail up and down the big loch, looking for tell-tale signs of fires, but the distillers knew of a smokeless fuel—the juniper. Bribes were offered for information, but to accept would be unthinkable, unless the information were misleading and the money could be used to buy new equipment!

I wander on, taking a short cut down the wooded slope towards the big loch. Enormous oaks grow here, dwarfing the birch and hazel. Druids must surely have found it a place to offer sacrifice, perhaps to teach the young, to heal the sick. It is certain that on the sheltered ground below, where the great burn cascades into the loch, Columba's followers made a settlement when the saint was on a mission to Inverness. His 'font' stone is there, a huge slab of bedrock with a hole in the middle, which, mysteriously, is always filled with water, though there is no apparent source. Within living memory the women would come to give their babies a surreptitious lick of this water, though the minister had baptised them officially in church. There are still signs of early occupation here—marked stones and grave slabs—and a preaching site is recorded in the eighteenth century. The monks were skilled agriculturalists, growing food crops and healing herbs, so it is appropriate that this is where our local Nursery Garden is, on the site of the monks' garden of 1,300 years ago.

The big loch steams when the frost is hard. The water level is strangely low. This has been a sunless summer, but the rainfall can't have been as great as it seemed. Rocks show up stark and black, especially the big one, once used as a look-out post for the steamer coming. Legend has it that it was thrown across the loch by a witch on the other side to avenge a quarrel. As the sun dips behind the hill, I make my way back by the road, refreshed by a foray into what seemed like another age.

When the thaw comes there will be jobs in plenty. Leaves, leaves, leaves are everywhere. We curse the clutter of them in rhones and 'valleys' on the roof, but we're glad to gather them, to make nourishment for generations of growth to come. The trees discard them graciously, leaving branches bare and fragile, outlined in delicate shades of mauve and orange. Some leaves, not twisted by frost or wind, I gather for their shapes and colours—red, yellow, brown. In my hand I have an ivy leaf, dried but still green, pale green, with gold veining. Tall grasses, with rushes from the loch shore, myrtle and heather shoots, all from the moor, dried, bring the beloved outdoors into the house for the winter.

November 8th

A glorious day. Very often we get this bounty in November, an out-of-season day of still-warm sun and brilliant sky. Spring is always late and often disappointing, but autumn makes amends with these bright surprises.

The grass is still green, though the bracken's golden. It's a time to leave spade, rake, hoe and barrow in the shed and take a jaunt up the road. Coming quietly on the loch, round the edge of the trees, we check that the swans are still there. Once, on a day such as this, we chanced on a rare surprise. The air was still, with a touch of frost. The water was calm, yet there was a sound of splashing. We looked back along the tree-lined shore. A family of otters was having a marvellous game together, totally unaware of any intruding eyes. We sat to watch as the heads bobbed, the tails thrashed to the tune of happy grunts and squeaks. Then, as though exhausted, the two adults and the two young quietly submerged and swam away to their resting place among the rushes.

Today there is no sign of otters, but the swans are superb as they come gliding towards us, heads held high on long, straight necks. They seem as tame as the curved-neck swans of picture post-card fame. But, looking at them, we remember the hazardous flight they've made from the ice-floes of the north. Here, they'll gather strength for the flight back in spring to rear their young in the brief arctic summer.

A heron rises laboriously from the small island and flaps his way, with slow wing-beats, into the rushes on the far shore. He knows all the likely spots for a feed.

We make our way back through the pines on the shore. The needles are inches deep underfoot. We gather them in handfuls. Well-rotted as they are, would they make a mulch to keep some of those weeds at bay? Would they be too acid? We'll be back another day with a bag and give it a try.

Reaching the road again we find other treasures that must be fetched. Contractors have been at work gouging out great ditches at either side, revealing layers of peat, quite irresistible for making compost of John Innes type, along with saltless sand the builders have left behind at a housing project. Everywhere there are stones for rockeries or raised beds, most beautiful chunks of rose-red granite and shiny whinstone. Further along are small deposits of abandoned grit and gravel, fine and large, ideal for mulching rock plants or making plantings on scree.

So, planning to return on a real recycling trip another day, we reach home at dusk.

With twigs as kindlers and a couple of logs from the old pine that fell to a gale last winter the fire is soon blazing. And there's toast with a spread of last summer's honey and a huge cup of tea. Thus energised and thinking of the treasures of the roadside, I sit down to write a reasonable letter to the Council asking them, please, not to send the mower up next year to trim the wayside verges. A neighbouring council, I hear, is very progressive in this respect. We hope ours may take heed. The wild flowers must be allowed to come again. The early ones—primrose, wood-sorrel, violets—are safe enough, growing well in from the verge. Those at risk are the summer ones, in par-ticular lady's smock, the cuckoo-flower, beloved of orange-tip and other butterflies.

November 12th

We're back to more normal weather now, with days closing in long before tea-time, skies of several different shades of grey and a hint of sleet in the rain. Soon we shall begin to count the weeks to the shortest day, as if counting had the miraculous power to make the time go more quickly. But no one can tamper with time. It must have its own way.

Meanwhile, the most boring jobs begin to loom. The out-house across the back yard hasn't been turned out for years. Taking a deep breath, putting on thick boots and gloves and pocketing a torch, I venture in. There is a strange mixture of smells—of damp sacking, perished rubber, turpentine—some quite impossible to identify. I shine a light into the far corners. Some stones have fallen from the wall where ivy had encroached under the eaves. There is broken glass on the cobbled floor. I gather the stones and lay them ready for replacement with cement later on. The ivy has now been cut back. It would gladly rampage everywhere, even through the smallest cracks round the window of a disused room.

Then bags and pails and boxes are filled with broken jars kept for vast jam-making times, discarded bottles meant for summer wines, old paint brushes, worn and petrified, broken hand-tools, rusted and paper-thin, half-empty tins of paint, long since solidified. There is a box of odds and ends of things which might have come in useful—scraps of metal, leather straps, reels of wire. I discard most of them, hoping that there might be a recycling agency somewhere . . . Then it's a great pushing of barrow-loads of the packaged rubbish to a point where it can be taken to the big dump ten miles away. There, I'm thankful to say, it will be placed in appropriate sections for further disposal.

Another day is needed to complete this uninspiring work. Occasionally I come on something with a whiff of nostalgia about it. Wasn't that the hand-fork I used to disentangle the overgrown rockery all those years ago? It has lost its handle and I bought a strong one made in China some time since, so it must go to the graveyard—or, hopefully, the place of resurrection—of half-broken tools. That rusted heugh, hidden in the far corner, as I turn it this way and that it brings back so clearly the days spent hacking a way through the rank growth round the apple trees, when I used to wish for a machete in my Christmas stocking!

Cracked plastic flower-pots are the most depressing objects. One imagines them staying in their cracked or broken state for all eternity. Broken clay pots can have a useful further life, providing drainage for future plantings.

When at last enough floor space has been cleared for a sweep with the hard broom to reveal the cobbles again, I retreat for a coffee break. Then, grasping the comfort of the warm mug in both hands, I look round at the emerging order. Those floats and a tangled piece of fishing-net brought back from an island holiday years ago bring an instant vision of ice-green water and shining pebbles on a clear white beach. They can't be discarded. I can think of no actual use for them, but they are there, in their own right, themselves.

There are other things like that—parts of a bee-hive, recalling summer days when I had eight colonies busy working the flowers, a Victorian water-can bought at a garden sale, marvellous in operation, but so heavy it sapped one's strength on warm evenings. These are things I shall still give space to, now that the real rubbish is cleared away.

Tea-time brings tiredness, but a sense of relief, a tedious but necessary task having been disposed of. I linger a short while by the fire, then feel impatient for some breaths of air to banish the dust of the debris. Perhaps a short walk up the road? I put on a thick jacket and scarf and step outside. The sky has cleared, cleared to a strange luminosity. I reach the gate and look to the north, beyond the trees. Great shafts of light are moving, fading, re-appearing, across the whole of the northern sky. I turn and look to the west, the south, the east. The whole arc is now lit by moving beams of coloured light, coloured pale green and blue and gold. It's a glory and must be shared. I go in and ring neighbours who might be sitting, unaware, at the fire. Voices and footsteps are heard. 'The lights! Aren't they magnificent?' 'They are!' 'Are the children up? They must see the lights'. No man-made spectacle could come within a mile of this. We wander till the lights begin to fade and the 'merry dancers', as they are called, begin to slow. Then it's in to stoke the fire and to let the wonder sink in. They say it means a change in the weather when the lights are bright. No one can remember ever seeing them as bright as tonight, so what kind of weather will surprise us, we wonder.

There are books and papers to hand and . . . catalogues! A catalogue of flowers, not vegetables but summer flowers, that's reading that will match the mood, I decide. Just to look at them is real delight, now that colour photography has reached such perfection. Hollyhocks—this year I must get some hollyhocks to grow against the wall at the back of the border. Pyrethrum, delphinium, canterbury bells, all my favourite flowers are here. I turn page after page, then go slowly up to bed to drift into a marvellous sleep, with the lights still reflected on the ceiling.

November 20th

Thoughts of summer may make many a happy evening dream, but reality comes in the morning, with tales of six cars stuck on the hill road, in an early frost that caught the gritters unawares. And then—snow. So work in the garden has to be minimal.

The first snowfall makes it possible to check what marauders may be up there among the winter greens—the kale and broccoli and spinach. Sure enough, the unmistakable pattern of the hare's footprints is there, also signs that the local pheasant has been on his rounds. Later in the winter even leek-tips will be eaten by the very hungry. Luckily, I'm spared the ravages of the rabbit, though some years ago I had to resort to desperate measures, covering each cabbage plant with a plastic pot to keep it safe. Neighbours not far away still have the problem, now that myxomatosis seems to have disappeared. In older times, roe-deer must have been a menace, as there are vestiges of a stretch of wire-netting above the four-foot wall. But I have only once seen a roe here, when a hind appeared outside the window, quietly grazing on the green. Keeping well hidden, I watched her move off and leap gracefully over the wall and into the scatter of pines on the hill beyond.

What I would dearly like as a garden resident is a hedgehog. I have tried. One evening, walking home at dusk, I spotted a small creature ambling quietly up the road ahead. I couldn't believe it—a hedgehog! He seemed just waiting to be picked up in the newspaper I happened to be carrying! I managed to open the door with one hand and groped about for a big cardboard box. In this, with a saucerful of cat-food, my hedgehog spent a peaceful night. Next morning I carried the box up to the top of the garden, laid it on its side, open to the wilderness, with another saucerful of food nearby. But I never saw my lodger again.

Another time, in October, a neighbour brought me a hedgehog he had found on a road miles away. A box again and a dish of cat-food and, as it was near hibernating time, I put him in a deep bed of straw in the shed. But, sadly, he did not survive. I'm still hoping one small, trusting, prickly creature may yet come up the garden path, like what he finds and stay around.

November 25th

This is Thanksgiving Day in America, thanksgiving for the early immigrants' first harvest. The Canadians celebrate theirs more than a month earlier, on October 11th. There are probably many reasons for this—climatic, social, possibly religious. But I wonder whether the fact that so many of the early Canadian settlers were of Scottish highland origin had anything to do with it. Certainly those that survived the horrors of the voyage out must have been hardy and resilient. Some were, of course, bitter at having to leave their homeland, some were ambitious and eager to make a new life. They were all used to tackling hard

Down the wooded slope
towards the big loch

physical tasks and to enduring days of numbing cold and near starvation. They could also savour a time of achievement. Their first harvest home must have been a great thing to celebrate.

I see them, at least in their early state, when they were prospering well enough in their original homeland, as our first conservationists. Alexander Carmichael, in his book *Carmina Gadelica*, a collection of traditional Celtic lore, tells us:

> A young man was consecrated before he went out to hunt. Oil was put on his head, a bow was placed in his hand and he was required to stand with bare feet on the bare grassless ground. Many conditions were imposed on the young man, which he was required to observe throughout life. He was not to take life wantonly. He was not to kill a bird sitting, nor a beast lying down, and he was not to kill the mother of a brood, nor the mother of a suckling. It was at all times permissible and laudable to destroy certain clearly defined birds and beasts of prey and evil reptiles, with their young.

In the 'Hunting Blessing' there are these lines:

> Thou shalt not eat fallen fish or fallen flesh,
> Nor one bird that thy hand shall not bring down,
> Be thou thankful for the one,
> Though nine should be swimming.

Hunting was not a sport then, but a means of surviving, for the hunter and the hunted. Simple rules kept greed and impetuosity at bay. The people were always aware that there was a power in the world far greater than themselves. It was a power which could be invoked for blessing on every aspect of their lives. So from the rekindling of the fire in the morning to the smooring of the fire at night there was a blessing asked for every one of the day's activities—milking, herding, sowing, reaping, clipping, weaving, fishing, rowing—everything, they felt, would prosper if blessed. Perhaps it was this sense of working along with the powers-that-be that helped them to win through, even in the most adverse conditions, in their new homes in the New World.

My own Thanksgiving Day would have been somewhere between the Canadian and the American one this year. One day about the middle of October I could have gloated a little as I made the first really big pot of autumn broth with leeks, onions, carrots, swede, beans, parsley and sage, all home grown, with a little imported barley for bulk, followed by a panful of tatties cooked till they crumble, eaten with a pat of butter and cheese, and apple and bramble purée, made from the few apples my old tree produced this year and a chance picking of scarce brambles made on an outing to a favoured spot.

That was a memorable meal and it has been repeated many times, with a different pudding, perhaps one made with the strawberries my neighbour kindly kept for me in her freezer. She also kept for me, last year, some cowslip seed, as I was told it liked to be frozen. I duly planted it in a pot of compost when the time came and waited. The waiting was long. Now, at last, I see some tiny plants, recognisable as minute cowslips, are emerging. I'm leaving them to face some more cold and hope that, in spring, they'll really grow. They're very scarce in these parts. I've seen them flower in only one place—the railway embankment on the route south. Railway embankments do host many lovely plants. This one sports marguerites, corn marigolds, flax, comfrey and many more. They must have been there since the days of steam and soot.

I'm told that plants are thriving along the big motorways now, along with wildlife of various kinds. This sounds like some sort of a pact between man and nature. The nearest main road here is certainly no motorway, but it's bordered with flowers from April to October—primroses, daffodils in masses, then foxglove and marguerites, with honeysuckle climbing the trees, wild roses and woodland strawberries on the banks and, of course, all the heathers in season. In autumn, the trees put on their own display.

Wildlife mostly keeps its distance, for it has plenty of other living space, but roe deer and hedgehog do venture onto the tarmac and get killed. Pine marten and foxes are tempted by the picnickers' remains.

Thinking of these things helps to get the shortest days on their way. Daylight from 7.30 in the morning to 4 in the afternoon is little enough when the chores seem to take longer each day. Clearing snow, sweeping leaves and twigs after a gale, gathering kindling, fetching coal, arranging the unavoidable shopping trip, all these things take up energy and time which one longs to spend creatively. But nature has a time of hibernation. We must give in graciously and take to keeping warm and replete.

DECEMBER

December 1st

To celebrate the first day of the last month of the year the 'power' is off. Machinery of all kinds has to have its days for overhaul and replacing spare parts. We know that and are forewarned, though sometimes we wonder why it has to be done in times of gale, frost, snow, whatever the winter may be throwing at us.

For those of us who remember pre-power days the loss of the 'electric' for a day or two is not a great hardship. Sometimes I think of the Tilley lamp with a whiff of nostalgia. Once it was primed and pumped it made such a comforting hiss and gave a real feel of warmth, as well as shedding soft light on table, book or bed. Candles were always at the ready, as they are today. I'm up sharp this morning, in balaclava and woollen coat, to get the fire going and to set a kettle on the picnic stove.

At other times we are left in the dark without warning, though experience has taught us to anticipate trouble when the gale is from the north-west or the snow is lying heavy on trees and cables. I remember the time when the power-line was being set up. How the men accomplished it, in weather of every kind, is a story of heroic proportions. Erecting giant poles in remotest moorland, climbing them to fix the cables, ferrying in material—I'll never know how they managed to achieve these feats of skill and endurance. Several times we had a worker in to thaw out frozen fingers and to down a hot drink.

When the power was finally installed the celebrations were legendary. The only drawback was that once an elderly neighbour had acquired an electric heater for her kitchen there was no smoke signal from her chimney in the morning to let us know she was up and well.

One funny story went the rounds. A grandfather who wasn't going to bother putting in the electric at his time of life, went to stay for a few days at his son's home, as was his wont, to recuperate after flu. His son's wife put on the heater to warm up his room and the lamp beside his bed. In the morning he was up early. 'How are you today, granda?' he was asked. 'Ach, I was wakened a' night . . . The candle's in a bottle and ye canna' blaw it oot!'

The men who are called out these days to repair the power lines on black nights of snow and gale are as heroic as their predecessors who set them up. We really have little to grumble about as we sit up late beside a glowing fire, reading by the light of the candle we can 'blaw oot' if we wish.

Listening to the wind in the trees and to the sound of driven snow battering the window panes is a great refreshment to the spirit, making one realise, as our ancestors did, that there are forces we shall never control, that we must learn to live with them. A little humility is quite comforting.

Of course, there are problems for people with lives dominated by technology. Deprived of power, machinery breaks down. Freezers and fridges disgorge their uneatable contents, the T.V. screen is blank, the telephone dumb. Clothes must be washed by hand, as long as the water runs free. Tropical fish may perish in their tanks. There's also the question of transport. With side-roads sheeted in ice and the main road blocked by drifting snow, cars sit aimlessly in yards or garages. I'm glad I can go happily on foot to visit neighbours within my radius. I'm glad, too, that I have never lost the habit of stocking the cupboard in early winter with oatmeal, flour, lentils, tea, coffee, sugar, dried milk and tins of beans and peas. My back kitchen is as good as a freezer when the wind's in the north, so that cheese and margarine keep the length of several storms. I do the cooking wearing mitts and balaclava!

This is when you re-discover the pleasure of listening to the radio. Mine is battery-operated and portable so that it's always on hand for listening to news bulletins and weather forecasts. On candle-lit evenings it's quite a treat to tune in to great music, a poetry reading, a play or, perhaps, a repeat of one of those marvellous old comedy series 'The Goon Show' or 'Round the Horne'.

I'm glad to hear that radio is being re-discovered anyway, storms or no storm. It's a medium which spurs creativity, as reading does, when images spring alive in the listener's mind.

Being snow-bound for a spell, cut off from the busier world that one is aware of, out there, humming with activity, can certainly be a blessing, giving pause, a healthy pause. Should something unforeseen occur—a serious illness or accident—then recourse could be had to technology of a life-giving kind—a radio help-call link summoning the services of snow-plough, ambulance, or, should conditions allow, helicopter. We need never feel forsaken.

December 15th

More early snow today and a very heavy fall, the branches of pines and cypresses weighed down alarmingly. The school mini-bus couldn't cope with conditions on the hill, so the four-wheel drivers got into action, ferrying children and messages. Phone-lines are intact, but soon the electric power goes off, when a tree collapses onto an installation several miles away.

Fire-glow and candle-light are better than anything the 'electric' can provide, after a day coping with frost and snow-drifts. But cooking on a spirit-stove is limited in scope. This year, however, a kind neighbour who has a solid-fuel cooker provided the most wonderful surprise—a hot meal brought by torchlight and on foot!

With the thaw came branches brought down by the weight of wet snow, a slate or two off the roof and rhones displaced, the usual battle-scars. Nothing could be done in the garden, of course, but my thought was for the bees. Normally, I don't feed them till after new year, but the summer had not been a good one for honey and they might well be short. I made up a feed of icing-sugar, mixed with hot water to the consistency of putty. This they love. On lifting the lid of the hive I found a mouse, or mice, had been having a happy time, nesting in the warm covers and no doubt feasting on honey. I slipped my offering on to the top of the brood-frames and for my reward got a very painful sting on the eyelid. At least this meant the bees were alive and kicking! I tidied up the mess and went back for a trap for the marauders.

The snow was melting fast. Pausing near the door, blinking from my sting, I noticed a small winter marvel—buds, tight-curled, on the white lilac near the door. With this reassurance giving a lift to the whole day, it's in to the fire again, curtains drawn against darkness and cold, to dream up gardens of the mind.

Here's one! Through an archway of yellow roses there's a stretch of grass, herbaceous plants flanking it, in curves of glorious colour. Further on, to the right, along a stone-flagged path, herbs grow, in shapely plots. Then there are the rows of vegetables, tidy in season, the soft fruits and the old trees of apple and plum and beyond these again, the corner of a wilder-ness, where the bees suck willowherb and thyme and there's a small stone seat under the rowan. Not that there's anyone sitting there, least of all one's self, for sitting is a rare pastime in a garden, even an imagined one. On those few afternoons when it's too hot, shall we say, for weeding, in the garden of reality, it's usually a question, not of sitting, but of stretching out on the grass, face well covered in midge lotion, gazing at the bloom on the little cherry tree and the blue arch of the sky above and breathing in the scent of honeysuckle and clover. But there are many short strolls to be taken, shutting one's eyes to weeds and faded flower-heads and revelling only in the living shapes and colours. I always reckon it's summer when I can carry breakfast tea and toast out to the garden, sip and crunch by the hawthorn hedge and throw crumbs to the fledgling blackbirds. The wait for mornings such as those seems interminable. But gardens must rest. That's what this one is doing now. Roots are snug, well below the reach of frost. Above ground there's the dazzle of frozen grasses and the delicate outlines of bare bush and tree.

And, as I bend to look closely, there, under the window, is the first thrust of hellebore, the Christmas rose, the flower itself resting on the bare ground. It's almost incredible how anything can work its way up through the cold earth, to the winter light, in these short days. But then a garden is an incredible, living thing. And it's an integral part of the house that it surrounds. Coming in from a short winter walk to the welcome shelter of the old rooms you find signs of the garden everywhere. By the window there's the potted geranium, brought in to bide its time till spring. From a bowl of dried herbs on the table the scent of summer rises. You stretch your fingers to the fire and watch the flames curl round that bit of birch you had to cut from the old tree after the autumn gales. A cup of tea—and you wonder—raspberry jam or heather honey on the toast? Both are familiars of the garden. Everything is known.

While roots are resting and light hours are short, then is the time to think about the actual garden, as well as those of the mind, to think, to plan and to remember. Remembering, first, means an outreach beyond the scope of present memory to things recorded more than a century ago. This garden is roughly a quarter of an acre, carved from a heather slope. The house sits squarely facing south, fronted by flat ground. Behind it there is a gentle rise, to the contour of the hill and the protection of a four-foot wall of natural stone. The window makes a good hide to watch whatever may appear—a red squirrel in the ivy, rabbits and hares sitting up on the grass to wash behind their ears, the cock pheasant abandoning his stately gait to try desperately to balance on the bird table, siskins and great tits doing gymnastics on the bags of nuts hanging just beyond the glass and birds of many kinds in their season. Butterflies and moths, too, fly close by in fearless animation.

All this, and more, was here over a hundred years ago, when the site was levelled for the building of a school and schoolhouse. The first master to live here, Mr Maclean, must have had a job wrestling with the natural ground. Even today the wild growth takes every chance to reappear. Clumps of heather and rushes will surface among the tattie drills, clover swarms into the strawberry bed and willowherb makes a protective curtain around the bee-hives. As long as it's kept in place, it's more than welcome there as a valued source of nectar and a most attractive backdrop to some rather stolid rows of neeps and kale.

Successive schoolmasters must have done what they could. In the Inspector's Report of 22nd February 1909, when Mr Campbell was in charge, it is stated that 'For the further development of the Nature Study, Practical School Gardening is to be introduced forthwith.' And so it was, by April 9th.

On June 20th 1912 we read that 'The Garden was inspected by Andrew T. Fowlie of the College of Agriculture.' There were problems. On May 11th 1923 the entry records 'As sheep are constantly breaking into the garden work has been stopped till the walls are rendered sheep-proof.' I know exactly what he meant. More than sixty years later the sheep, the more agile variety, are still sometimes managing to leap over the wall, where the superimposed netting has given way. That can mean goodbye to all the summer lettuce and the winter greens, not to mention the precious flowering plants and all the work that went into producing them.

On 7th November of that same year the Log Book records that 'The school garden has unfortunately had to be placed in the lowest grade as, for want of a fence, the plants and vegetables were devoured by sheep.' Some ten years later, on June 14th 1934, 'The school was visited by a Mr Black, organiser of agriculture for the county. He gave a lesson on agriculture in Scotland, crops and stock, and inspected the school garden.' His verdict is not recorded.

At the end of the following year Mr Neil, the teacher, retired and Mr Denoon, a keen gardener, was appointed. In October 1936 the Log Book records that 'The garden here is in course of reconstruction. Plans have been carefully made and the results are looked forward to with great interest and confidence.'

The Inspector's Report for 1937 to 1938 records 'The Head Master and his pupils deserve great credit for the improvement

a Victorian water-can,
bought at a garden sale

effected in the layout of the school garden. The results in the horticultural side enhance considerably the amenities of the school.'

On June 30th 1938 'Colonel Baillie (of Dochfour) visited the School, signed the registers and had a look round the school buildings and garden. He is giving a prize for the best kept plot and is sending his gardener to examine said plots after the summer vacation with a view to judging the best.' This was encouragement indeed. The next Inspector's Report (16th August 1938) records that 'The Head Master here has transformed a poor, neglected garden into something very pleasing and deserves very great credit. With the help of the pupils the following improvements have been carried out: flower plots, herbaceous border, lawn, rockery, crazy paving, hedges, rustic fence with roses, all carefully planned and neatly executed. The productive side is also included and the educational aspect kept in view.'

During the war, as part of the 'dig for victory' campaign, the lawn was made into a potato patch. In 1941 lectures were given on bee-keeping and by the following year there were hives to be inspected in the garden. Mr Denoon also kept chickens and goats in a bid for self-sufficiency. In close on ten years he had created what was almost a smallholding and a very attractive one. But the school roll had fallen to 45 and thereafter was to decrease steadily until, in 1958, only two small girls remained and the school was forced to close. Subsequently several short-term tenants of the schoolhouse came and went, so not much was done to the garden. When we arrived, wild raspberries, willowherb and sweet cicely had largely taken over. To bees and butterflies and to many kinds of birds, this was paradise! For us, it held all the thrill of uncharted territory. Every day a fresh discovery was made. Even now, I come on surprises each summer.

As the top growth was cut down the outlines of the old plots began to emerge, terraced to follow the upward slope of the ground. We borrowed a rotavator and decided to clear half the area the first year. When digging began we came on stone drains. The cost in work hours involved in laying them must have been tremendous. Realising how essential they were we tried to protect them, though subsequent work has, unfortunately, caused damage in places.

Digging revealed many other interesting things—worn-out toys, pieces of pottery, a pile of school slates from a dump against the top wall, evidently discarded when jotters came in—and, most interesting of all, several 'scrapers' dating from prehistoric times. An archaeologist friend told us some years ago that the garden was plainly on the site of a bronze or iron age settlement. Just over one wall is a hut-circle which we long to have excavated some day. Meanwhile, I often imagine my predecessors here looking on the same outline of hills, the same scoop of the burn in the hollow, listening to the same sounds of lark and owl, the bark of deer and many more long gone—the howl of wolf, maybe the growl of bear. The heather would have been their late summer delight, making drinks of tea or ale, thatching for their roofs and kindling for their fires. Sometimes I envy them the simplicity of their lives, though the hardships must have been great. They didn't have a Christmas to celebrate, but they knew all about the winter solstice and they must have been happy to see the bright berries on the holly, as we do today.

Christmas preparations here still hold the magic of earlier times. The holly and the ivy grow just outside the door. The tree is a small spruce with roots which I dig up every year from the garden and replant later. It thrives on this treatment and each Christmas sports a slight fresh green top shoot.

Welcome neighbourly home-produced gifts circulate—shortbread, honey, eggs, hand-painted cards, wax candles, plants and the most beautiful arrangements of dried flowers. Brightly wrapped packets of tea for pensioners are handed in, with a greeting and a smile, by members of the Community Council. The local school makes up hampers for a few lucky senior citizens. And the children practise their carols in preparation for their evening round, even remembering those favoured by different households.

After Christmas there's the ceilidh, with much music—clarsach, accordion, fiddle and pipes—and song and dance. And, with the past not having quite caught up with us, we have the bonus of keeping Christmas going till Twelfth Night and the date of 'old' Christmas!

JANUARY

January 2nd

The diary is silent on the first day of the year. Good resolutions are buzzing in the head, along with memories of new years long gone and of the one just celebrated. In older times the head of the house would open the door to let the old year out and the new year in, then he would step outside to fire a shot at any evil spirits that might be lurking about. Shots from other places would be echoing. Then, armed with a bottle and a lump of peat for luck, it was time to set off to first-foot the nearest neighbour.

Nowadays we meet in the house of our oldest neighbour for Hogmanay, drink a toast as midnight strikes and then it's singing, in Gaelic by our host and by some of us trying valiantly to follow, in English by others, and a dram by the glowing fire for each succeeding visitor, till the room is so warm that pullovers are discarded and tea is made to revive flagging energies. Neighbours who may not meet often, leading very separate lives these days, each having their sphere of work, they cherish this chance to meet and engage in communal enjoyment. The intimacy of shared song is very special, as eyes and smiles meet, each voice with its own pitch and intonation, carrying the singer's memories and meanings. Parting is reluctant, even in the early hours. But home means a deep and dreamless sleep, more refreshing than longer time spent in a half-waking state.

Day-time visitors arrive as the black bun comes out and there's still a half-bottle of something in the cupboard. This is a day when people largely dependent on motorised transport—car, quad-bike, tractor, van—find their legs again and go walking, with children running, not strapped to car seats, and dogs let off the lead when the sheep are safely by-passed. Summer plans are discussed on long walks up the forestry roads, plans for garden development, for summer holidays, for sorting out the ever-growing accumulation of books and papers, so that chairs are uncluttered and visitors can take their ease! Thoughts of the shed clearance are inspiring. Perhaps Oxfam could benefit. One and every project seems possible of achievement as the new year swings in.

With the light fading and when the day's visitors have gone I feel a sudden hunger for a good bowl of freshly-made soup, to chase away the taste of rich, sweet cake and wine. In the vegetable rack are carrots, onions, turnip, the 'keepers' of the harvest. Taking the small fork I go out into the dusk to prise up some leeks. The ground does not resist. There is even a feel of freshness about it, as though it might be turning in its winter sleep, at the touch of the new year. There is parsley, lemon-scented thyme, balm and sage in the sheltered containers by the window. I add barley and a few lentils and soon a great potful of broth is simmering happily on the stove.

Later, sipping my bowlful, with a big heel of brown bread, I think of that bare, brown ground outside and resolve to make a start at forking in the compost next morning, while the going looks good.

Sure enough, in the morning the going is good and, to my amazement, as I step outside, I'm greeted by the sound of birds giving voice, softly, happily, in the hawthorn hedge. I stop in my tracks to listen. Was I mistaken? No, I hear them again. Could this be my reward for feeding them regularly through the hungry days? It must be the slightest increase in the length of daylight, which they, with their hyper-sensitivity, can detect. If the people in high places had sensitivity to match that of the natural world our lives might be better lived.

I put out more seeds and nuts and a ball of fat to keep our song-birds in good heart and voice and plunge the big fork into the compost-heap. There's plenty of good nourishment there. I spread barrow-loads on the bare ground for next spring's salad crop. A flight of long-tailed tits flutters by overhead. They are too shy to come to the bird-table, but they seem fit and lively on whatever sustenance they can find.

January 12th

With the 'new' New Year well and truly brought in, we remember that today is the day of the 'old' New Year. An elderly neighbour used to say that by this date there was 'an hour on the day'. Sure enough there is the feeling that this old planet may just be tilting its face towards the sun. As I watch the great dazzling winter orb travel slowly along the ridge of hill opposite my window it seems to me it disappears just a little further to the west. The tree-covered slope below is in its winter glory. The Forestry Commission wisely left the 'natural generation' untouched. Now there are wedges of dark green conifer between the stands of birch—skeletal and mauve—with a border of russet larch. The colours are incredible. I've asked an artist friend to paint it for me.

On this 'old' New Year's day the second snowfall of the winter keeps us from work outside, but watching the whirling flakes and the ever-lengthening icicles along the eaves you remember the blessings of winter. Roots will be lying snug under the insulating cover and the frost will be killing off unwelcome pests. Siskins venture out of cover to join the tits at the nuts hanging by the widow. Fox and pine marten risk daylight robbery in a neighbour's poultry run. All life has a hunger to be satisfied.

That night the wind moans out of the north-west and by morning the whole world has changed shape. Trees are bowed down, the tips of their branches touching the ground. The boundaries of field and road have disappeared under great mounds of snow. Everywhere there are sculpted patterns of indescribable beauty.

By noon the wind slackens and we have to get out. The usual signs of garden visitor are there—the tracks of hare and mouse, bird-prints, too. We can't grudge anything to any creature on such a day. All that protrude are the tips of giant kale. There's a deep pile of snow on the roof of the hive, but that will keep the bees cosy. Then it's a walk up the road, kicking steps all the way, looking at the blue light in the hole made by the stick, marvelling at the snow-shapes and watching as their contours slowly change with the guiding pressure of the wind. It's a living landscape. We're in, we feel, at the fashioning of a new world.

With the early fading light the wind falls away, the sky clears to reveal a dazzling sunset. The frost will be a killer. Of course, we don't grow tender plants up here—we're 700 feet up—and everything is well acclimatised. My worry is the water-pipes! One year the pipe carrying water from the spring far up in the hills froze outside. I had to resort to breaking the ice on a nearby burn and filling pails. This went on for nearly a week, with much time and energy consumption. Now I have bales of hay, covered in plastic, at strategic points outside and lagging of many kinds, including old nylons, inside. So, it's in to the fire and a routine check of lagging. Then—supper. There's leek and carrot soup to hand for a warm starter. Then the oven goes on to heat up the kitchen and I slip in two big tatties in their coats, a big onion and a huge apple, stuffed with honey and sultanas. And I'll wash that down with a glass of rowan wine!

I often think we miss a lot by ignoring or discarding the natural growth that surrounds us. The original hill folk of this upland area had the reputation of enjoying long and active lives. Nowadays incomers have deepfreezes and easy access to the supermarkets in the town. How their health and strength and longevity will compare with that of their predecessors has yet to be seen. But the wild plants are there, in their hundreds, to be had for the picking and choosing, fresh in spring and summer and preserved dried, pickled or fermented—for autumn and winter.

We're lucky enough to miss out on chemical spraying. The little fields have gone, mostly, to sheep grazing, the foresters are wary of our drinking springs and those of us with gardens grow organically. So . . . to the hills, the background of all our lives. Hills mean heather and heather is food for sheep, deer, hares, grouse, all the life of the hills, and for many insects and honey bees. In older times it had many uses besides—for thatching, rope-making, the making of baskets, brooms and scrubbers and for bedding and fuel. For humans, the flowers were used as a brew—a hot infusion or an ale. In the far ancient times the Picts made a drink of young shoots of heather, mixed with thistle and honey. The invading Romans were said to be envious of the strength of their Pictish enemy and to have tried, in vain, to discover the recipe for the drink that seemed to give them almost miraculous power. Nearer our own day, Robert Burns is said to have enjoyed heather tea, made by infusing three or four sprigs of dried flower heads to a pint of water. Robert Louis Stevenson had a poem on heather ale:

> From the bonny bells of heather
> They brewed a drink lang syne
> Was sweeter far than honey
> Was stronger far than wine.

Now, down from the hills and to the garden—and the weeds. But what is a weed? The Oxford English Dictionary says it is 'A wild herb springing where it is not wanted.' But mine are not unwanted, not totally. The butterflies and bees would agree. Mine include nettles, docken, bishopweed, thistles, willowherb, chickweed, sorrel, dandelion, silverweed, tansy and many more, a rich source of vitamins and minerals. Feverfew and sweet cicely thrive like weeds and have to be continually cut back and plantlings given away to friends and neighbours. Taking each one:

Nettles:
It is said they were introduced into Britain by the Romans, who couldn't live without them! They are full of iron. Pick them young, wearing gloves! Cut them down later on for a second growth. Cook them like spinach or make them into a delicious soup, with a little onion and a thickening of milk, with butter and flour or oatmeal. They can also be made into wine or beer.

They make a valuable addition to the compost heap and I have a friend who rubs them on rheumaticky knees to relieve pain! In older times the fibres were used to make cloth and dyes.

Docken:
Unlikely as it seems, these can be stuffed, as the Greeks stuff vine leaves. Use young leaves and stuff them with rice, onion, egg, herbs.

Bishopweed:
This was probably also introduced by the Romans and once cultivated as a pot herb. It was said to be good for gout and was grown at inns and monasteries. It can be cooked like spinach.

Willowherb:
The young shoots can be used as a substitute for asparagus! Cook the leaves fresh as a green vegetable or use them dried as a herbal tea.

Chickweed:
This plant is rich in iron and copper. It was once sold in bunches, like watercress, at markets. Use it like cress in sandwiches or in salads, plus the flowers. It also makes a delicious cream of chickweed soup.

Dandelion:
A beloved plant which brightens the spring of the year and delights the bees. Use the young leaves in salads or in soup. The flowers make wine or tea (four tablespoonsful to a pint of water). The roots, cleaned, dried, ground and roasted make an excellent substitute for coffee.

Sorrel:
This is a plant, a member of the docken family, which loves my damp, acid ground. It is much prized in France. The leaves give a sharp, lemon flavour to salads and the soup is really superb.

Take 1 lb. sorrel leaves, 4 oz. butter, 4 cloves of garlic, 2 pints of water, 2 oz. of flour, $^1/_2$ pint of cream, salt and pepper. Enjoy it chilled in summer or hot in winter.

Silverweed:
Known as 'one of the seven breads of the Gael'. It was cultivated at one time in the highlands and much used before the introduction of the potato. The root was ground into flour for baking.

Going beyond the garden walls again and taking a summer or an autumn walk along the hill tracks or down the path into the wood bordering the big loch (Loch Ness) we find, and we smell, three aromatic herbs. First, wild thyme growing in the short turf, wild mint among the grasses and wild garlic in the damp hollows by the burn. The mauve-blue flowers of the thyme, when dried, make a drink on a winter day that brings all summer back. Mint and garlic I use sparingly to give savour to soup or vegetables. Wild comfrey grows here, too. The dried leaves make a healthy infusion (2 teaspoonfuls to a pint) and, soaked, they produce a valuable fertiliser, being full of potash. In older times the root was grated and used as a plaster, whence the old name for the plant 'bone-setter'.

Meandering, now, up the road to the little loch on a summer's day, a swim in the cool water in mind, we come on the summer flowers which I asked the council verge-cutter to avoid. We use them, of course, very sparingly and only when they are flowering in profusion as these three do:

Meadowsweet:
An infusion of the flowers is an excellent cure for headaches, the dried leaves are good for flavouring and, of course, there is the sparkling 'champagne'.

Lady's Bedstraw:
The flowers make a honey-flavoured tea.

Clover:
Both red and white make a pleasant infusion.

Near the water's edge, among the dwarf alder and willow, there are stands of wild raspberries for refreshment and on the moor ground, further on, are blaeberries to stain the mouth and fingers and to take home for pies and jellies. Later, there will be mountain cranberries to gather for sauce.

Autumn is, of course, the real harvest time. That's when a walk down through the wild woods of oak, hazel, birch, rowan and pine that fringe the big loch will reap rewards. First, we come on the roadside rose bushes with their clusters of shiny red hips, so lovely just to look at and full of vitamin C. A little further down there are hedges of blackthorn with the berries just coming to their purple bloom. Very bitter they are, but good for a winter drink and, of course, to add to a bottle of gin. The rowan berries glisten in the sun, a glorious sight when the sky above is blue. They make a good, slightly bitter jelly and, of course, a very acceptable wine. Juniper grows in some profusion in the clearings. At one time the berries were exported from the area to Holland, for the making of gin. Nowadays they are used to flavour boiled potatoes or cabbage and they do add a piquancy to many dishes.

There are elderberries, too, for wine, and haws, but the most succulent crop is the bramble one. Some bushes grow with their feet right in the shallows of the loch and when we've gathered them and tasted them, to our delight, we can walk over the beautiful, rounded pebbles on the shore and wonder what creatures may be living under the water. At a winter teatime spreading the jelly on a scone, all the feel of the autumn gathering-day comes back to mind.

Retracing our steps and keeping our eyes on the ground we find hazel-nuts. Sadly, there are fewer squirrels nowadays, so this means plenty of nuts among the fallen leaves. They are said to contain more protein, fat and carbohydrate than eggs. They can be roasted, salted, and put into the blender with a little butter, to make a nutritious spread, or, of course, they can be eaten raw, as can the other ground-cover we come on in the moss among the birches—chanterelles. They are a delight to look at, with their delicate, fluted, saffron-coloured underlay, and to smell, with their apricot scent, and to taste. Better still, cook them gently in butter when you get home. Then there are boletus, which make excellent soup, white field-mushrooms, puff balls and many more. They can be dried or frozen and made into memorable winter meals.

We who have access to all these natural foods in a relatively pollution-free area, are, of course, the lucky ones. Friends from central Europe, over on holiday, were amazed at what we neglect or despise. Boris, from the Czech Republic, would come home from a walk up the nearest hill with a rucksack bulging with dead wood for the late summer fire and a hatful of berries and, to me, unidentifiable fungi, most of which I wouldn't dare to eat on my own but which he would turn into an unforgettable supper dish—which we all survived!

Here are four possible menus:

Spring
Nettle soup   *Rowan Wine*
Mushroom omelette
Salad (dandelion, chickweed, willowherb shoots)
Raspberry compote
Dandelion coffee or herbal tea

Summer
Sorrel soup (hot or cold)   *Dandelion Wine*
Stuffed dockens
Ground elder (hot) or salad
Strawberries and cream *or*
Blaeberries and cream
Dandelion coffee or herbal tea

Autumn

Mushroom soup *Meadowsweet Wine*
Hazelnut purée on toast (with rowan jelly)
Brambles and cream
Dandelion coffee or herbal tea

Winter

Potato soup *Elderberry Wine*
Hazelnut roast (with rowan jelly)
Dandelion roots (stewed)
Blaeberry pie
Dandelion coffee or herbal tea

January 18th

A winter aconite, flowering through the snow! True, it's in a sheltered spot, close by the front door, but its flowering seems a miracle, nevertheless. I take a close look at the small bed under the window. Sure enough, the Christmas rose is not to be outdone. The darling bud is lying there, tight closed, on the white ground, ready to open when the cold eases.

This is not the weather for garden work, apart from checking fences, but in the short, bright afternoons there's time to walk and look and plan. Every year I try to take in another small piece of overgrown ground, a little patch to be sown to kale or sorrel, something for the winter soup-pot or the spring salad. This is a garden on the wild side, and the wild would so soon take over. There's still plenty of wilderness round the edges, where wildlife is more than welcome, but the plots must be harnessed, not allowed to bolt. This year I plan to clear what looks like a most unpromising few square yards in the lee of a leggy hedge of cotoneaster and where the roots of willow and rowan lie. Rhubarb, given by a neighbour years ago when we first brought the garden back into cultivation, planted with a good dressing of dung, is doing well nearby and apple mint is thriving. So I reckon a good pile of manure and compost should make this small piece of desert

But gardens must rest.....

bloom, once the weeds are out. We're lucky in having supplies of manure to hand—farmyard stuff just up the road and horse dung down the way. These do bring in weed seeds, particularly chickweed, but a handful of that is delicious, eaten like cress in a tea-break sandwich, and the rest goes onto the compost.

I must have one of the biggest compost heaps in the country. In fact, I have three or four, but I'm afraid I don't organise them methodically. Some of them sprout a variety of weeds. Spectacular nettles for the butterflies are allowed to thrive and subsequently put back in again. From time to time I excavate the bottom layer and dig out loads of good black loam from well below the reach of noxious seeds or roots.

Over the years I've learned to live with my weeds. For some I've even acquired a degree of tolerance. Nettles do make that delicious soup and bishopweed (ground elder) really does eat like spinach. My most persistent and invasive plant (I don't want to call it a weed) is sweet cicely. I think it must have been introduced at one time as a useful herb. Certainly the flower can be used as a sweetener when stewing rhubarb or other tart fruit. And there's the clerical connection, too. I believe the monks, in former times, used it to make liqueur. I wish I had the recipe! It rampages here. I used to try to dig it up, but the roots grow impossibly deep. Children use the stems as aniseed-flavoured pea-shooters. I give small plantlets to friends, with dire warnings about keeping it in check.

Another plant which appears regularly in spring is feverfew. I lifted one some years ago from the abandoned garden of a former croft house up the road. The mistress there, I was told, 'grew many herbs'. I think she must have been one of the lost generation who knew what herbs could do. I now give plants of feverfew to friends who suffer from migraine and they consider it beneficial. A few leaves eaten straight from the plant do bring relief. And the small, daisy-like flowers are very attractive.

Dandelions I allow to flourish, even in the strawberry bed, as they are an early attraction to bees, butterflies and other insect life. I even planted two rows of them, near the hives.

The main delight for the bees, of course, in later summer, is the willowherb. It is allowed to form a great swathe, almost engulfing the hives. One year, a swarm landed on a sturdy plant, bowing it almost to the ground. That was one swarm easily collected and put back safely in a hive.

Another bee crop which I planted some years ago is clover. I cleared a patch not far from the hives, bought good agricultural seed and sowed it. Now, it is rampant! But it's easily shifted where it's invasive and it nourishes the ground. It has taken over the grassy paths between the plots. Walking there is almost like walking on a chamomile lawn!

The one weed I do heartily dislike, which has put in an appearance only over the last two years, is the horse-tail. This really unpleasant-looking little 'soldier' is the bane of my life, as it marches on, invading a little more territory each year. And it has perniciously inextricable roots! It's not a plant I'd care to talk to. The language might become unseemly. I can imagine, though, having quite pleasant conversations with the willowherb, if I could make myself heard above the buzzing of the bees!

January 25th

'As the day lengthens, the cold strengthens'. These old sayings invariably ring true. Something has happened, lately, to the direction of our wind-flow. The prevailing westerlies, reasonably mild and bringing welcome soft rain, have been swinging to the north and even to the north-east or south-east. One day I'd like to consult a meteorologist. We, whose lives are so closely linked to weather conditions, really need such a consultation, as we sometimes need one with a medical doctor. The television weather-men rarely get their suns, clouds and arrows quite right for our particular area. Sometimes I feel like shouting back at them when they somewhat smugly predict mild air for us and wintry conditions further south, when we are lying under six inches of snow and goodness what is happening in the Pennines!

Wearing clothes almost too heavy for active service I step out into the cold. The snow has gone for the time being, but the ground is sodden. Great heavy clumps stand up in weird shapes, sculpted by the frost. Leaves and shoots of winter greens have been chewed off by hungry hares. Branches and twigs lie in unusual places, scattered by those alien gales. The compost heaps have been ravaged. Undigested scraps of kitchen waste— tea-bags, egg-shells, onion skins—clutter the path. It's a scene of desolation. Will anything ever grow again? I have to remind myself that roots and seeds are lying snug, below the reach of frost, or warmly blanketed by snow.

There will be time yet to doctor that leached earth, to scatter compost and a sweetening of lime. I think of the islands in spring, when the winter gales have driven the white shell sand onto the coastal grass and this precious ground, the machair, is suddenly a carpet of flowers.

I can expect no such miracle, of course, but nevertheless, in a sheltered corner, near the west wall, I come on a tiny primula, blooming quietly to itself. That atom of reassurance is enough to make the day. And the day is lengthening now, by a good hour. I wander round, checking the bee-hive for signs of marauding mice, piling fallen branches, raking leaves, till the light fades at five o'clock.

Indoor chores become unbearably tedious when one is impatient to get on the move outside. I remember a farmer friend who kept Sunday as a day of rest, yet couldn't bring himself to sit at the fire, but would be out roaming the fields, planning the season's work, looking over the sheep. If he dropped in to a neighbour's house the talk would be always of the weather, then the state of the crops and beasts, before a grumble or two about the government, national or local. There's never a question of boredom when it's a struggle to survive. The weather can be a common enemy or blessing. Every morning means a step into the unknown, the largely unpredictable.

Feeling as restless as our farmer friend, I go in to make a phone call to another farmer, one who lives nearby. Could I get a load of manure, please, perhaps while the ground is hard, so that the trailer won't stick. He agrees, quite happily. The byres are needing a good muck-out. I remember how crofting neighbours used to have strong doubts about the 'artificials', promoted by the agriculturalists all those years ago. Long gone are the days when the house thatch, well impregnated with peat-reek, would be ploughed into the fields, along with the saturated straw, bracken or other bedding material from stable or byre. In the islands, of course, seaweed gave great fertility. 'Artificials' may produce quick results, on a big scale, but in the long term the earth needs to be cherished, not force-fed. As long as human greed dictates policy we shall have those obscene mountains and lakes we all know about, and an increasingly impoverished earth. Thinking of these things I get out the box of seed-tags and clean them, ready for this year's labelling. One small positive gesture can dispel a cloud of doubt.

In the evening, sitting at the fire, I eat supper of mashed neeps and tatties, with a mealy pudding (haggis is not for me) and drink a small toast to Rabbie. He had a kinship with animals and flowers, with the whole earth, which so many have lost. His 'Red, red rose' is surely the greatest love song of all time.

FEBRUARY

February 1st

This is the festival of St Bride. Her name is the christianised version of the name of the Celtic goddess of spring—Brighid, the modern equivalent being Bridget. The time of Brighid was a celebration of the first signs of returning light and life, after the darkest of the winter was past, a time of creative impulse and energy.

Bride of Kildare was an Irish saint who founded a nunnery in Ireland and was the patron saint of many people, including milkmaids. I gave her name to my white Sanaan goat, she of the golden eyes and the elegant, capering legs. She came into milk about the time of Bride's day, giving always an adequate supply, on a diet largely composed of natural herbage.

This year Bride's day dawns unbelievably bright. A step outside and there's the sweet smell of fresh earth. You draw in great gulps of air, scrutinising the sky. Is it too bright, too early? Streaks of pink cloud are stretching from the east, round towards the south-east. The west is faintly blue. Or is it grey? No, it's bluish. That's a good portent, for the weather is in thrall to the west.

I take an early walk round the edges of the garden. Buds are swelling on the flowering currant. Catkins on the willow are beginning to shine. Finches are chattering in the hawthorn hedge. High overhead a pair of buzzards is circling happily. Life everywhere is bursting to emerge.

I go in reluctantly for a quick breakfast, standing at the window, keeping a weather eye on this special day. It still looks promising. The light from the east is golden now as the sun climbs confidently into a clear sky. To the west the blue is deeper. This looks like a superb Candlemas eve . . .

The phone rings.

'It looks like a good day. What about a walk this afternoon?'

'The very thing.'

'Good. See you at the road-end about one.'

There is never any doubt about which road-end is meant. We can take our pick of walks from this particular spot—along the peat-road onto the hill above the tree-line, where the old peat-workings are filled with water now; down the old 'funeral road', the way that was used to carry the coffins shoulder-high to the horse-drawn hearse waiting at the foot, or along the track to the old crofting settlement where only one house still stands.

This is surely one of the most superb walks in all of the Highlands. Originally a footpath, it was engineered by succeeding generations of crofters into a track now navigable by tractors and vehicles with four-wheel drive. Mercifully not many of these use it, so that it's a haven for horse-riders and walkers. Over the edging of conifer and birch there is a wide view to the hills beyond the big loch. The big loch itself lies there below, so near that you can count the ripples on the surface, yet as remote as ever. Along the road the green verges are studded with flowers in spring and summer—primroses, tiny violets, wind-flowers, saxifrage, tormentil—and in the turf down the middle the wild thyme grows. In autumn there are berries—raspberries, juniper and mountain cranberry.

Half an hour of leisurely walking takes us to the house. Tucked into the shelter of a dip in the ground, it's a substantial one and a half storey structure of the type built about the turn of the century, with a roomy steading—byre, barn and stable. The old single storey house remains, used as extra accommodation for hens and stores. Bits of the old timbers and partitioning can still be seen, though the thatch has long since disappeared. This place, we are told, is one of the few which were not discovered when Cumberland's men were harrying the glens after Culloden. My companion is an artist and has been painting the remaining old houses of the neighbourhood. I'm hoping this one will be her next.

At one time, perhaps 150 years ago, there were five crofts here, five houses, five families. One field is still known as the 'Tailor's Park'—park denoting a field of grass. Perhaps he kept a number of sheep, his wife would spin, he would weave and then make up the cloth. This was surely a sensible procedure, when the town with its tailors was a good day's journey away and they would be charging hefty prices.

There were several shoemakers in the area, too, some practising their trade to within living memory. With the one surname being widely held, people were often known by the name of their occupation or the place where they lived. Thus Elizabeth Fraser became Lizzy Balbeg, Mary Fraser became Mary Tailor if her father plied this trade, William Fraser might become Willy Balagreusaichan if he was a shoemaker.

We linger a while about the house, imagining, sadly, how full of life it must have been at one time: long summer days of work, winter evenings of ceilidh when neighbours would be made so gladly welcome and might be snow-bound for days. The last member of the family struggled on here on her own, with her cattle and sheep, some hens and her devoted collies, till ill-health forced her to leave. The blackcurrant bushes in the old garden still bear quite luscious fruit.

We wander on, then sit for a while on the moss-covered rocks by the waterfall. The little fields sloping down to the trees above the loch are still unbelievably green. Sheep are grazing contentedly. I spend a moment wishing someone would press a time-switch to take me back to this day, say, a hundred years ago. I could see one man spreading dung, another making a start at the ploughing. A boy would be herding cattle up the hill. I could hear him whistling for sheer joy at being out on this bright day. I could hear children playing by the door, a woman calling, dogs barking. A thin plume of blue smoke is rising straight up from the chimney. There is the welcoming smell of peat. I wake reluctantly from my day-dream. The sky is still almost cloudless, only puffs of dazzling white gliding slowly in from the west, like ships in a heavenly regatta. There's a hint of warmth in the sun. It really is a magic day!

I can understand how people living in these idyllic places, living at a measured pace, dependent on things beyond their control—gale, snow, flood—could well imagine that there were creatures around which were also beyond their control, beyond their ken. A man from these parts, who became a minister of the church and served abroad as an army chaplain, told me not long ago that, as a young boy sent to herd the cattle in a green place not far below the house, he encountered a small group of 'fairy folk'. He took the cattle home and went excitedly to tell his mother what he had seen. She promptly gave him a skelping for telling lies. He firmly believed, for the rest of his days, in what he had seen.

About the same time, in another place, an old couple had 'brownies' living in their outhouse. Every evening they would put a dish of milk out in a hollow stone for their small guests. Every morning it was gone and they were well pleased, for the brownies had to be looked after if they were to be helpful.

In the island of Gigha a local brownie who was a most useful helper in the big house—bringing in peats for the fire, washing the dishes and so on—had a pew to himself in the parish church.

Until quite recently the people of the crofts often brought up orphan children along with their own. Fostering had been widely practised in the old days. The chief's son would often be reared in quite humble homes, thus forging the link between members of the clan. I was thinking of these orphans as we walked back along the track. To the children of the crofts every tree and boulder, every corrie and burn was familiar and most often a source of delight. To a child straight from the streets of a city, as most of the 'boarded-out' orphans were, it must have been a terrifying experience to walk this way to school, especially in the winter. I remember once meeting a little fellow on the road, his face a white mask of fear. He had got himself completely lost. I set him on his way. He went on, looking back only once. A few months later I met this same boy with his pals. A wide, cheery grin of recognition lit up his weather-beaten face. His footsteps were sure and confident. Some sort of magic was working for him. He'll be back, as so many like him have been, in later years, to look up his old

a swarm landed on a sturdy plant

haunts and his guardians, or their families, and to tell his own children how it all was.

We reach home as the light is beginning to fade. Tea at the fire rounds off this lovely Bride's day to perfection. Bride herself would have enjoyed it, I feel sure.

February 2nd

> Candlemas day, gin thou be fair
> The hauf o' winter's to come and mair.
> Candlemas day, gin thou be foul
> The warst o' winter's ower at Youl.

An elderly neighbour of mine used to quote that to me every year. He firmly believed the dictum and it did, indeed, very often tell the truth.

The very name of the month—February—seems to have connotations of new beginnings, almost of growth, as the hours of daylight continue to increase. Then we remember that other saying about the cold strengthening. It has many germs of truth, too. So we study our Candlemas day with the utmost care.

This year it looks like being just as glorious a day as yesterday. There is the same lift in the air, the same feeling of time stealing a march on spring. I'm out early again to check on wind and sky. There's no movement of cloud, just a clear expanse of pale blue, waiting for the old sun to rise to his full height and suffuse everything in his kingdom below with light and colour. So we accept this day as another godsend, but warily, remembering that old sayings have come down through the generations, accumulating layers of truth.

Chores completed as quickly as conscience allows, I emerge for another check on the weather. There's still no sign of a change. The bees are out, the birds are chattering, there's even a small dance of midges in a sheltered corner of the green. This is a day for positive action. That pile of good-sized stones, which has been growing over the years, has the makings of a rock garden, there, at the turn of the big border. Alpine strawberries are growing there happily already. A patch of wild plants that flourish among rocks would be ideal! I survey the area, then look at the stones again. Many bring back memories of summer expeditions here and there—a piece of white Skye marble, green shiny rock from a north-east beach, sturdy, wave-smoothed stones from the west, whinstone and rose-red granite from the garden itself. Thyme and saxifrage and some little yellow rock-roses would nestle quite contentedly among these stones, I reckon, settling to the task.

The day wheels on overhead. I warm, literally, to the work, oblivious of everything but the placing, and spacing, of the stones. The garden robin keeps me company, flitting from bush to tree, to wall, alighting sometimes on the next stone to be moved, as though signalling encouragement and approval. When hunger drives me in for a bite and sup I suddenly realise that the day is passing, has almost passed, with no drop of rain, no blast of wind. It is fading, now, gracefully, into shades of pale gold, pale pink, with a hint of green where the sun is sinking. So we shall have to brace ourselves for the 'hauf o' winter to come, and mair'. The stones look well. It has been a good day, come what may.

February 6th

The snowdrop month came in with much chirping of finches, 'sawing' of great tits and general commotion among the budding branches of rowan and birch. The blackbird had been singing his 'inward' song for several weeks and was tuning up for his full-throated version to come. Fresh snowdrops were opening daily and a blue primula was venturing into flower in the shelter of the ivy-covered wall. There was warmth enough for the bees to fly down looking for their beloved crocuses. They were not disappointed. They seem to favour the yellows. To see them walking into the opened flower, in a dazzle of sunlight, makes it seem summer's happening tomorrow. Of course, experience tells us otherwise, but we cling to the illusion for a few magic hours. Discarding jackets and with sleeves rolled well above the elbow, we tackle even the most laborious garden jobs with gusto. Collecting dead grass, branches and raspberry canes for a spring bonfire, digging the plot left unturned in the autumn, any job is a pleasure when the first whiff of warming earth is rising.

When friends arrive out of the blue I spread a rug on the short, dry grass and entertain them out of doors. To go inside would be unthinkable. It's a day for the first picnic of the year. Soup and sandwiches, taken under a sky of speedwell blue, in the company of singing birds and happy bees, taste better than any imagined caviar and champagne. We know this cannot last. There are gales to come and blizzards and floods. But a February day of sun and calm makes the most memorable *entr'acte* in the drama of winter.

Sure enough, within twenty-four hours our capricious weather system brings cloud and a west wind with an edge to it. A good time for work in the lee of the west wall, tidying, weeding among the plants in the rock garden. Dead leaves, twigs, even branches are everywhere. It's the penalty paid for having so many trees around. We're glad enough of the shelter they provide, but the debris is great. Rhones and gutters everywhere have to be continually cleared. But at least there is ample provision for bonfires and an endless supply of leaf mould. Weeding at this time of year is not a hard chore. Even the old perennials are easily dragged out, though there's the occasional 'snap' as a stem is severed and I have to probe deeper for the last of the root. The compost heaps grow higher and higher. Straightening up between emptying loads I look up the length and breadth of the garden, imagining how it might be altered. The trees planted for shelter have grown leggy. I have had one or two cut down, one or two have crashed in gales, more will have to go. They take up a lot of moisture and cast too much shade. I spend my rest-pause in contemplation.

Will my dream-garden ever materialise? I go back to the job in hand. Soon it will be the time of garden openings. That's a happy thought, though seeing other gardens sometimes makes one despair of one's own!

We're lucky enough to have several nursery gardens within reasonable reach of us here. My favourite is the one I can walk down to, taking a short cut through the old oaks and hazels, right down to the shore of Loch Ness. There, among the rock and heather, the rowan and birch, these neighbours have created a garden of tremendous character and charm. Overworked words, perhaps, but ringing absolutely true in this case. The amount of energy that must have gone into the making of terraces, paths, plots, can only be guessed at. The result is sheer joy. You walk up into the wood, go round a bend and there is a planting of rhododendron, azalea, among the wild growth of primrose and dwarf willow. It's ideal territory for rock plants. They spread and cascade, obviously happy to be where they are. There's a place for everything herbaceous as well. Shelter from the north wind and from the prevailing westerlies makes it an early place. Only occasionally does a vicious easterly come whipping across the loch, and then not at a time to blacken blossom.

February 14th

My valentine arrives in the form of a burst of song from the top of the tallest cypress opposite the window. The blackbird! His practising is over. It's now the full-throated song. I stand absolutely still, gazing up, fearful of disturbing the singing. I can see the movement of his throat as the notes emerge. It's a moment of magic. I know, of course, that it's not a question of artistry, but a challenge he's uttering, a challenge to any others of his tribe who may feel like contesting his right to this particular territory. I back him to the hilt, for he is my particular blackbird.

I remember others—the one who fed his first brood so competently with scraps scattered on the grass, while his mate was brooding their second lot. One wintered in the byre years ago and would sing his quiet, inward song whenever the milk started to spurt into the pail.

This morning the singing is confident and clear, a kind of signal that, from his vantage point, all's well. Then, suddenly, the singer takes flight, straight as an arrow, towards the plantation up the road. He has to be about his business. I shall be hearing him again at dusk.

Meanwhile, I stay a moment gazing up at the empty tree. It's a huge, solid structure, taken so much for granted because looked upon every day, yet really worthy of wonder. That great trunk, tapering as it rises, the strong, supple branches and the delicate fronds, the colossal roots hugging the ground, all this has grown from a minute brown seed. In growing, the tree has scattered further seed, at random, so that saplings can be given to neighbours desperate for shelter for their plants.

I look beyond the garden wall, across the fields to the planting on the opposite hill. Larch, birch and pine make the most beautiful winter patterning of colour, which I never tire of admiring. Will it be allowed to remain beautiful for at least a little while? I hardly dare to hope so when so much is changing hands, being altered or destroyed. I have an artist friend who prefers to paint these trees in winter, when the structure and colour of stems and branch is clearly apparent, without the distraction of leaves.

What of the rain forests? Only now, as destruction goes on, are we beginning to realise what is being lost—people, wild creatures, plants. And the forests of India? Their loss means soil erosion, villages emptied, people starving for the sake of making fine furniture for the houses of the rich. Isn't this absurd?

In our own country it has taken us a long time to accept what our forebears knew generations ago—that native plants, including trees, may provide cures for even the worst of human afflictions. The bark of the willow, long known to contain healing powers, is now being studied as a possible cure for cancer. The willow is said to have been sacred to the Moon goddess. Thousands of years ago arrow-heads, shaped after the leaf-pattern of the willow leaf, were found in burial places.

Sallow, or salley as in Yeats's poem, was another name for the tree:

> Down by the salley gardens my love and I did meet

Then, at parting, we would 'wear the green willow', one for the other. The old craft of basket-making, still practised today, depended on the small osier willows growing by the burn. The bees get their first cargoes of pollen from the pussy-willow flowers.

I turn away to walk up the garden, for a look at my own willow-tree. There is the sound of bees! They can't be sensing nectar yet. No, they're having a cleansing flight and making for a row of white washing on the line! I don't grudge it to them as a staging-post. It's good to see them lively and celebrating a fine day!

I wander on and come to my rowans. The rowan is an amazing tree. I've seen one growing out of a tiny crevice in a rock-face, flourishing quite happily. It's a tree with magic properties. I had a neighbour not long since, who would never burn wood from a fallen rowan on her fire, though she would use it outside to heat food for her hens. Every house had a rowan by the door and a small branch would be fixed over the lintel of the byre and the stable to ensure protection for the beasts against evil. The berries, too, had magic in them and were used in divination rites. Still today children make rowan-berry necklaces which remain attractive even when dried out. Sometimes I have hidden a tin of berries in the ground and dug them up at Christmas to decorate the house. They certainly make a wonderful wine, with a touch of magic in it, and a good red jelly. They can also provide a sweetener, I'm told, suitable for diabetics. The brown and grey bark of my rowan is covered in lichen, so that the limbs look more grey than brown. This lichen means, of course, that the air is pure, for lichen cannot survive where there is much air pollution. Fingering it gently I give a small signal of thanks that 'my lines are set in pleasant places'.

I look on this old garden with new eyes

Over the west wall of the garden I look onto an area of heather, moss and natural tree growth. At one time this was part of the common grazing but, as sheep are kept now mostly in fields which no longer grow crops and are fed, in winter, on silage or concentrates, the grazings are abandoned as such and are planted with trees or 'developed' for housing. I climb the wall and look, while I still may, at the self-sown silver birches. Along with the rowan, the birch is one of the hardiest of trees. Its graceful outline, the shine of the bark and the delicate colour of its bare winter branches and of its leaves in spring and autumn, make it a refreshment to the eyes and the spirit at any time of year. Babies' cradles were made of birch and the sap is extracted to make a potent wine.

Dwarf alder grow among the birches on this stretch of moor. The wood of the alder has the unusual property of turning black and hard when submerged in water and was therefore used in the building of bridges and the making of containers for liquid such as milk. The green wood was used to make whistles and pipes. The leaves can soothe burns. Most people rush to find a docken leaf to soothe a nettle-sting. I wonder if anyone looks for an alder leaf to apply to a burn.

Next, in my tree-walk, I come to the hazel. In Celtic legend the nuts of the hazel tree contained all knowledge. It was said that the salmon in the pool ate the nuts that fell from the hazel and so became the 'salmon of wisdom', having eaten the 'hazel nuts of knowledge'. To divine water the hazel-twig was always considered the most appropriate.

I wander on, thinking of all these magical properties of trees and beasts and wishing we still relied on them, for they would tie up many of the loose ends of our lives today. They must surely have helped our forebears to make sense of the world about them. They were surely more worthy of belief by humanity than the stories conveyed by those tottering little figures on the video screen.

The mosses underfoot make wedges of carpet between the heather clumps. They are marvellous plants, growing in soft, smooth hummocks of greenery, some sporting little bright red and yellow flowers, perfectly adapted to their environment, keeping low below the wind, thriving on the peaty damp. A friend who lives not far away has inherited the old knowledge about mosses and lichens, making wonderful dyes for her hand-spun wool. People come out from town, sometimes, to cut swathes of the sphagnum moss. This is probably for flower arrangements, but the moss has antiseptic properties and was widely used in dressings during wars.

Coming back by the road to the garden I pass the hawthorn hedge. It has grown tall and thick and gnarled. Bulky lorry-loads sometimes take a swathe off it when passing by. It's a good shelter from that cold south wind and a welcome roosting-place for many small birds. Its thorns are a good deterrent to erring sheep. On the lower ground hedges such as these were torn out and replaced by fences. What wire fence can give shelter, protection and a tasty bite to grazing animals? The tasty bite is good for humans too. On many a summer walk I've pulled a handful of fresh green leaves and chewed on them for my 'bread and cheese'. An infusion of the berries is said to be helpful in problems of blood pressure, high or low. Everywhere about us plants are there, ready to make us healthy: maybe not wealthy, but hopefully a little wiser than before.

February 18th

Showers of sleet today and a wind rising to gale force 8 or 9. The longing for a greenhouse is strong. But I water the trays of seedlings on the bedroom window-sill and visualise the hoped-for result. The bedroom marigolds did well last year and the sweet william should flower this summer. The dianthus have made healthy growth as edging everywhere.

As the sleet begins to whirl in horizontal patterns and the wind howls among the slates, I tire of watching the tree's pre-carious bending, turn from the window and pick up a gardening magazine sent by a friend. It makes fascinating reading, but its world seems totally unreal. Asparagus beds, pagodas, outdoor peppers and tomatoes . . . would any of these survive in a hill-top garden, in a climate full of wild uncertainty?

I suppose some of them would, with adequate shelter and sources of labour. Certainly there have been gardens in Scotland, and in the higher reaches of the country, for many hundreds of years. I think of the Queen Mother's garden at the Castle of Mey in Caithness. You can't get a place more exposed than that. Mary, our Queen, had a tiny garden made for her on the island in the Lake of Menteith, where she played as a child for a short while, before being sent to France in 1548.

There was a famous Physic Garden in Edinburgh, originally at Holyrood House, from 1670. James Sutherland had 'care of the garden' and later became 'professor of Bottany in the Collidge of Edinburgh'.

John Reid, gardener to Mackenzie of Rosehaugh in Ross-shire, wrote a book *The Scots Gard'ner*, first published in 1683. It went through several editions at the time, reappeared in 1907 and is still available in a reprint made in 1987. In the preface he says 'because the many books on gard'ning are for other countries and other climates, and many things in them more speculative than practical, this ensuing treatise the rather be acceptable'. He was clearly a gardener for us today. Scots gardeners are, of course, renowned practically the world over. Even to children they are famous, since the appearance in Beatrix Potter's tale of Mr McGregor.

Perhaps the most famous Highland garden is the one at Inverewe, on the northwest coast, where the Gulf Stream brings a whiff of tropical air, allowing some exotic plants to grow happily. There are many native species, too, and a good feeling of wildness persists. Gerard Manley Hopkins, in his poem 'Inversnaid', says:

> What would the world be, once bereft
> Of wet and of wilderness? Let them be left,
> Oh let them be left, wildness and wet;
> Long live the weeds and the wilderness yet.

That poem has given me comfort many a time when I contemplate my own patch!

February 24th

Persistent cold winds, driving flurries of snow, mean that outside work is held up, though the lengthening days tempt everyone to get on with it. I can remember late February days like the one we experienced earlier this month, so mild that the midges were dancing. Coming down the garden in late afternoon, sleeves rolled high above the elbows, you stopped to watch a lark swing into the sky above the trees, scattering his song, and there, beyond the big loch, the hills had put on their Italianate air, mauve shadows filling the hollows. To the north the high tops still held a glisten of snow, but that might well be there till mid-summer or beyond. It's good to have the mind stocked with memories like these, as good has having a library, shelves well filled with books and documents which can be consulted at will, when you're coping with the present or planning for the future.

This particular day, jacket sleeves well fastened and a scarf tied round the ears, I walk up to one of the wild corners of the garden. Here, more than a dozen years ago, when clearing a patch for planting, I had built some turf sods into a wall to give shelter to young plants. This wall still stands, firmer than ever, welded together with tough grass roots.

I often think of how the little houses of the Highlands were built in prehistoric times. Low walls of stone, traces of which can still be seen just beyond the garden, had long roofs of heather thatch, supported on poles and tapered to a central pitch, in the manner of an American Indian tepee. Later the walls were built of sods and raised higher, the roof supports sunk into the ground. Later still, and to well within living memory, the walls of stone were doubled, with an infill of rubble for greater warmth. In the islands the ends of the houses were rounded to defeat the wind, and the roofs were low and battened down with hanging stones. Hens roosted on the rafters; cows and horses found shelter under the same roof, at a slightly lower level, in an adjoining part of the structure. Humans and animals shared body heats quite happily. These living units were ecologically quite perfect, built with renewable resources, made to fit the environment of hill, glen or shore and adapted to prevailing weather conditions—gale, rain, snow.

Many times I've dreamt of retreating to a small, a really small, fairly remote house, with chickens and a garden patch, with a nearby well, a peat fire and an oil lamp or two. To have no frozen pipes, no electric meter ticking away, no thought of road conditions—would that be paradise? As long as a neighbour's light would wink out at dusk, there was the sound of children calling, a dog barking now and then.

These are late winter dreams, when far horizons always loom! Soon we'll be back in port again, with more practical thoughts!

MARCH

Waking to what looks, from the window, like a reasonable day, reminding myself that this really is March and we should be heading for spring, I hurry through a watered-down version of essential indoor jobs and make for the garden. I work it on what are, I hope, essentially 'green' principles. Scanning it today I smile ruefully as I look in vain for a rewarding sign of anything green. Dead growth I leave on the perennials as protection against frost. This growth now lies in sodden brown masses, covering the entire border and the path. Drifts of wet fallen leaves lie on ground cleared of crops in the autumn. The bare grey branches of rowan and bird-cherry overhang the prostrate brown stalks of the willowherb.

This is the time when, every year, I wonder if I'll ever get things to grow again in any sort of order, yet, somehow, it is achieved. Once or twice I've had the idea I'd like to put part of the garden to 'fostering'. This came about when, some years ago, a young man who had no garden asked if he could use the greenhouse here to grow on some plants. I said 'with pleasure' and supplied him with putty to replace some missing glass. But it didn't happen. He left the place soon after. However, I'm glad to say he then became a gardener and I hope is gardening still.

I very much hope, too, that some of the young people who live here now may get the gardening fever. It has to be a fever, I think, and an incurable one at that, a passion, a lifelong passion, that not even a wheelchair can dampen. The thing must start early in life. I'm always thankful I used to try handling a hoe when I could only just stagger after my father on his way to the vegetable plot. Children today have so many after-school ploys and distractions and maybe haven't the patience to wait for seeds to sprout, though they do grow cress on the windowsill.

I survey the whole depressingly brown scene again. There is one sign of life—the mole-hills in the grass. These I have no objection to. They supply beautiful earth for potting up plants, or can simply be dispersed with a blow of the spade. Moles do sometimes disturb seedlings, but they also aerate and drain the ground. My only fear is that too many of them may destroy too many worms, those much-prized underground workers. So highly valued is the contribution worms make to the conditioning of the soil that they are actually being farmed these days.

Perhaps I really should do something to reduce the area under crop, I reflect. Perhaps sow one plot to mustard or field lupins? They are said to make excellent green manure when dug in in the autumn. Then, weed control really should be tackled. Old carpets are the answer, I believe. I do have some stacked away in the loft, probably making nests for mice. In the garden they smother weeds at birth and eventually rot down to build humus. They can be covered with peat or chipped bark to avoid visual offence. These are things I really should try. Perhaps . . . next year?

A vicious little wind is rising, flinging small, icy darts of rain against my face. It's not such a good day after all. With a shiver in my shoulders I turn away from thoughts of next year. Here and now I must try to warm up at least one small plot, one bed for salad things. The means are to hand, in the shed—tattered strips of black plastic bin-liners, kept from last year. I stretch them out, weighing them down with sturdy stones. If they warm the ground only a little perhaps the lettuces, radishes, spring onions will get away a little quicker than the weeds. I'll soak the seeds, split them, scarify them, do anything that will let them avoid being smothered by that all-pervasive chickweed and its companions.

The rain really has an edge to it now, coming almost horizontally, in wind-chilled bursts. My morning thoughts and hopes of spring are dashed. Of course, our seasons don't go by the calendar, but by whatever is brewing somewhere up about Siberia. I have to acknowledge this was a false start. There will be more to come. Still, I've made a gesture, just a small one, to boost the warming-up process we all depend on.

I retreat reluctantly indoors, make a cup of tea and sip it in the kitchen. My kitchen is the despair of family and friends, most of them. Some are discouraged from even entering. There's a cooker and a sink and a small larder, the usual kitchen equipment. In actual fact this is the engine-room of recycling activities. In every corner, on every shelf, there are plastic containers of all sizes for seed-growing, plastic food-wrappers for making mini-greenhouses, plastic bottles ready for decapitation as cloches for fragile plants. These are at least some beneficial uses to which plastic can be put and I'm grateful for them.

On impulse, I fill a margarine container from a bag of seed compost, which has also found its way into the kitchen, and push in some parsley seeds. Maybe it's just another, devious way to steal a march on spring!

March 7th

At last a day of calm, when to get up and go straight outside is sheer indulgence. There's the smell of earth crumbling from the frost. The blackbird's song is so loud it's almost a call, as he hits one particularly high note. I whistle him back my nearest imitation, which he seems to enjoy. He's perched on the topmost branch of the cypress. We pursue our duet for a minute or two, then, looking down, I stop in my tracks to wonder at the first primrose to flower. It must be spring, though officially it's still two weeks away.

What to do first is the only problem. A neighbour arrives to give a hand at gathering material for the bonfire. Loading and carting goes so much more easily and quickly with two. Everything has been well dried by a day of east wind, so the burning will be easy. One schoolmaster of old had great faith in the value of wood ash, when 'artificials' were almost unheard of. He would get the scholars to collect branches from the wood and great fires would rage for days. Mine is a more modest affair, but the result will be invaluable. At one time a kind neighbour who burned only wood and peat on his domestic hearth used to bring me pailfuls of ash for the strawberries.

When the fire is safely smouldering I make a start at clearing the big border. Dead growth is mostly left till spring as protection against frost. Now it comes away in chunks and goes straight to the burning. Soon it will be time to divide up blue geranium, lupins, marguerites, which quickly overgrow in the shelter of the west wall. Even my most precious astrantia, given to me by a friend years ago, spreads happily. It's good to be able to share these plants with people starting gardens from scratch. Scratch it really is, up here. The first year must be spent digging up heather, rushes, all the moorland scrub, before applying a good dose of lime. Black plastic is spread and at last some sort of tilth emerges. But all this work goes for nothing if the garden ground is not protected from the invasion of rabbits, hares, roe deer, sheep. John Reid said in the seventeenth century 'As there is no country can have more need of planting than this, so non more needful of Inclosing, for we well know how vain it is to plant unless we Inclose'.

One neighbour has planted a hedge of briar rose. The thorns do seem to prevent invasion by sheep, the flowers, of course, are lovely and the hips are the size of tomatoes and can be made into all sorts of preserves. A New Zealander tells me that they make hedges of whin (gorse). That should keep everything out! There is certainly plenty of whin here. In early summer it brightens the whole landscape. At one time growth was encouraged, as whin was used as fodder for the horses when winter supplies were finished. Every place had a 'knocking stone', a hollowed-out stone in which the plants were pounded into a mealy substance. In some parts there were 'whin mills' specially made for the crushing of whins. Broom, too, makes great splashes of yellow, of a much warmer shade than that of the oilseed rape favoured by the low ground folk. *Ach buidhe*, the yellow field, is a common place-name in the heights.

March 17th

St Patrick's Day! It's good that we should set aside certain days to commemorate the lives of people who left their mark on time. St Patrick, of all the saints, would have felt at home in these hills, I think. So today's a day for the 'wearing of the green' and for hoping that that lovely island of his will find its way again.

Two great men of comparatively recent times were Columba of Iona and Francis of Assisi. Both were men of the world, with inner visions of how good life could be. Both built their citadels in places apart, for both wanted close contact with the natural world, with the cycle of sun and moon, of life and death. Both loved their fellow creatures, animals, plants, all created life. Francis, in particular, called animals and birds his 'brother' or his 'sister'. In Columba's case the love of animals—I'm thinking of his beloved white horse—may have stemmed from very old Celtic beliefs about reincarnation, which have parallels with Hindu beliefs, showing the Indo-European origins of the Celtic peoples.

For the Celts cattle were the mainstay of life. The bull was practically deified, its great strength and energy making it appear kin to the great god Beli, the father of all life. The cow was regarded as the provider of earthly bounty—fertility, nourishment, clothing. There would appear to be an Indo-European link here, as the cow is the most sacred animal of India.

Cattle were also the mainstay of later Highland people, until the coming of the 'big sheep' towards the end of the eighteenth century. Previously, two or three sheep would have been kept, like pets, perhaps along with a goat or two, to provide wool, meat and milk if the house cow was dry. The cow gave milk, butter, cheese and even, in the hardest times, blood to be mixed with meal for an emergency diet. The country is criss-crossed with drove roads used to take the cattle to far-off markets and many tales are told of the experiences of the drovers.

The last of the cattle have gone now from our hills here, cattle that kept the land in good heart, trampling rough growth, yet eating their fill and manuring copiously. Only the sheep remain, leaving the ground bald with their constant over-grazing. The cows and their followers became almost an extension to the family, having names and recognisable individualities. In very old times, on cold winter nights, when the sound of their munching could be heard through the partition wall, there must have been a close bond between man and beast. Our fields are sad now, rushes and bracken choking the bright grass. The hills where the sheep used to be are now only home to the hare. On the lower slopes roe deer and pine marten find shelter among the scattered rocks and pine. The fox still roams unhindered and the odd half-wild 'moggy' ventures into chicken runs.

It's good to know these creatures are all about us, though we only catch glimpses of them as they flee. Snow-tracks bring pictures of them to mind—the hare, with his great powerful back legs out-pacing the two at the fore-end—the fox, with his delicate tread, leaving a small trail of footprints as he sleuths his prey. Up at the loch I've seen the imprint of the fox crossing those of the otter on the snow-covered ice. I've wondered what happened when fox and otter met!

Then there are the tiny footprints of mice and voles, left as they venture out looking for provender in some known cranny. Small waves of wisdom emanate from all forms of life. The deer, the song-bird, the leaf, the flower, they all accept life as it comes and death as it comes. Immortality is a very old human concept, though the Christian form of it is comparatively modern. To the ancient Celts, with beliefs, as it seems, perhaps more akin to those of the Indo-Europeans, it appeared that we all passed through various life-forms during our time on earth, from 'a wave on the sea to a mighty oak', as I've heard it put. We therefore share kinship with every form of life and have much to learn from our fellows. The American Indians had this feeling for life and would ask forgiveness of a tree which had to be felled.

The sad feature of modern times is that urban life cuts people off from the life-forces, even of night and day, of sun and moon. In town the stars are invisible, snow melts fast, there is shelter from wind and rain. Dependency on man-made devices for survival becomes the norm for daily living.

Nevertheless, people are looking, I think, for contact with other forms of life. Perhaps the only manageable animal companion for the townsman is a dog. Many seem happy today with a dog, often a large, very active dog, sharing their life.

To the Celtic people the hound was an indispensable ally in the struggle for life, guarding the house, fighting off enemies, helping in the hunt. The sheepdog of today has the same capacity for loyal service, his hunting instincts curbed and transformed into one for herding. Many place-names commemorate the importance of hounds in daily life. Just up the road here there is a hillock, *Tom Choin*, 'the hounds'.

There are also many areas of hill-ground known as *Caiplich*, the place of horses. The horse was another great companion-animal for man. In older times he was endowed with magical qualities and could carry his rider to *Tir nan Og*, the Land of Youth. He could also, in the form of a water-horse, or kelpie, drag him down below the dark waters of a loch. In Ireland the cult of the horse remains, his power of speed being paramount and leading to the breeding of fine racing animals. In the Western Isles, too, there were famous horse-races during the festivities of Michaelmas.

The red deer stag perhaps reigns supreme in the animal world for the Highlander. Huge, powerful and horned, he epitomises the wild natural force that has inspired the generations. He and his hinds lived in the forests in older times, when the forests were of native pine growing in natural spacing, not in thick-set plantations grown commercially. They were said to be the cattle of the fairy folk, supplying them with milk.

The salmon who ate the hazelnuts of knowledge as they fell into the pool was another symbolic creature for the men of the hills. As they watched the great fish in its tragic struggle to swim upstream to the spawning ground, only to die when its task was accomplished, they saw that this represented the goal of all wisdom, the acceptance of death as the gateway to new life.

The birds of the air must often have caused the people to feel envy as they watched the great wings outspread and the creatures soaring away, seeming to rise above all earthly troubles and cares. Probably in spirit, they journeyed miles with the eagle and the hawk. Certain birds inspired fear. A neighbour of mine still dreads seeing a heron fly near her house. Its slow, sombre wing-beats carry, for her, a premonition of death.

March 28th

Official spring came in a week ago and today it's 'summer time', so we should be feeling like a gambol with the early lambs in the field over the road. But March is the month of hard graft. My diary entries certainly record this. Shifting barrow-loads of dung, still digging and forking out recalcitrant weeds, doing all the donkey-work in preparation for the great days of sowing and planting. This year the work has gone ahead fairly smoothly. Times of snow and gale have been only intermittent and short-lived. One sunny morning a wagtail appeared, running happily along the ridge of the roof. The flowering currant began to blossom in the hedge. Then, the clearest signal of spring—a curlew calling. It's a sad, lonely, quivering call, but it means that these incomparable birds are back. They've left their wintering on the coast and are here to nest and make increase. That's enough to lift the day.

We can cherish our garden birds—clearing snow, breaking ice, to keep them fed and watered. But the birds of hill and moor have to survive in their own way. Sadly, there are fewer of them every year. When spring was a time for ploughing and the work turned up worms and grubs and attracted insects all birds made bonanza. Now the ground is left to insipid pasture with encroachment of rushes, nettles, thistles, every kind of weed. The nettles do help the butterflies and the thistles would delight goldcrests, but these are now so few. And no larks sing here now.

We have one thing to be grateful for, as we look out on our changing landscape. Foresters are abandoning the planting of dense stretches of conifer. 'Bring back the birch' is a welcome slogan today. The birch—from the winter outline of its mauve branches to the May-time greening and the autumn gold, and the year-long shine of the silver bark, it's an incomparable tree. And to think, as a friend said lately, that we used to be told to dispose of the seedlings as weeds! Now it is recognised that, as timber, birch wood is a useful product. Bunches of twig still make good garden besoms, though they're no longer used to punish small boys!

Already, there are several 'amenity' plantings in the neighbourhood, small enclaves of native trees—gean and rowan, with their beautiful blossom and fruit; hazel, with its catkins and nuts. Willow still grows in the damp places, though it's no longer used for making baskets and creels. Larch, not really a native, but a welcome incomer, makes a good protective border and oak flourishes further down the hill. Bird cherry is everywhere, with its lovely blossom and its profusion of fruit, which is edible, but, alas, has too bitter a taste.

APRIL

April 9th

The curlew's call now accompanies all the garden work. There is a feeling of companionship about it. The pair of them must be as hard-worked, over there, in the rushes by the burn, looking for a nest-site, building, warding off rivals, as I am digging, clearing, preparing the way for the year's growth.

Perennial things are moving, but slowly, cautiously, on account of the persistent easterly winds. A breeze from the south-east, for a few days, is welcome, for it normally brings clear skies and some sunshine. But a continuous stream of cold air from the east or north-east is a real deterrent to growth. The early bite of spring grass can be vital at lambing-time. Where are our westerlies, we wonder. They must be blowing somewhere, blowing softly, bringing the small rain. T. S. Eliot said,

> April is the cruellest month
> Bringing lilacs out of the dead land . . .

'The cruellest month' . . . I wonder if he really knew how right he was. The vegetable plots are ready now and I'm tempted to sow and plant. But the whisper of experience is there, close to my ear. There's frost to come and lashing rain and all the other enemies of tender plant and burgeoning seed. I know, I know, though it's difficult to believe, when the blackbirds are singing non-stop and the sun is warm on the hands. We must wait a month yet and try for a waxing moon, so it's on with the eternal weeding. Nothing holds back the weeds—chickweed, shepherd's purse, couch grass and sorrel. A farming friend from the low-ground is ridding her fields of corn marigolds, one of my best-loved flowers. We transplanted some last year and I'm fervently hoping they will have seeded.

Meanwhile, the laborious task of clearing is often relieved by the unearthing of strange things. Many times small, discarded, and mostly broken, toys have appeared, the remains of dumps made by former tenants who did not work the garden. These, and bits of broken china and glass, have mostly been disposed of now, over the years. At one time I was gathering pailfuls of burnable cinders, thrown out with the ashes when coal was cheap. They made a grand glowing winter fire!

An interesting find one day was a Lovat Scout badge, perhaps fallen from the lapel of a digger of years ago! My collection of prehistoric scrapers is growing all the time!

April 16th

Easter is past and no tatties are in the ground. But, as Easter is a moveable feast, so, too, is the time for the planting of tatties. They must wait till the ground is ready and, as the weather is often good in autumn, they can be left to mature fairly late.

This is still the time of preparation for all future growth, the time for the most arduous effort of all the year. Diary entries are terse as time and energy are fully expended outdoors. But this is a day which must be recorded, as it was one which really lifted the spirit. The smell of fresh earth, the curlew calling, bees flying free, these things not only lift the spirit but bring a surge of energy to limbs and back. Work goes on overtime, till late sunset.

Working alone, one yet has a sense of companionship, as all life is busy at renewal, bees foraging, birds nesting, trees budding into leaf, early flowers blooming. There's also the knowledge that gardeners everywhere are at the same tasks, the same muscles aching, the same satisfaction in the smile at the end of the day.

I look up as the sound of tractor-work, far off, draws the ear. Over there, across the big loch, in the distance, small white puffs of cloud are appearing over the brown fields. Someone is spreading lime. This is great news, for it means that one field, at least, has not been 'set aside'. Will it be an experiment with oil-seed rape? This is being grown extensively in some places, the oil being made into a source of energy. Lately, a bee-keeper has brought his hives up here to get them away from fields of this crop, as the honey the bees make from it is almost inedible.

The quest for sources of energy is what is destroying the planet. If we must go on for ever moving over land and sea and into far-off space, if we must have machines to take over all the hard labour, then it's imperative that we harness the energy already existing. At almost any time of the year, on the coast or in the islands you will see and hear energy rushing at you at a speed of knots. Those waves crashing to death against the rocks, urged there by a wind roaring that it has nowhere to go, this is energy in the raw that has been expending itself since the beginning of time.

There are hopeful signs that heed is being taken. In Benbecula, in the Hebrides, a giant windmill helps to power a magnificent new school complex. On Loch Ness I've seen small 'ducks' bobbing about, measuring wave power. Much more could surely be done.

I stretch up, easing those back muscles, then hunker down again, nose near to the weeding. There's quite a comfort about this position, all one's person in close contact with the earth, no head-in-air remoteness. They do say some of our modern ills have come about since we started walking upright!

Inspired by the sight and sound of that far-off tractor-work, I slit open a bag of lime and scatter the contents on the brassica plot. Most of this ground can do with sweetening, even the tattie plot, especially after heavy winter rains have leached it.

In a spell of good weather such as this the work builds up into what seems an indestructible pile. Will one ever demolish it before the next onslaught of gale, late snow or frost comes in to the attack? It's a question, of course, of sorting out priorities. The lime is spread. Ground not tackled in autumn or winter must now be cleared and manured. The weeding of perennials is a job that's with us always. As long as the more ferocious

Drawing back the curtain
I looked out at the morning in disbelief

weeds are got out before their roots really bite, the lesser ones must be left for the time being. Dividing of plants, too, and giving portions to friends is a pleasurable activity, but not one of great urgency at the moment. All strength must be concentrated on getting that ground ready for the seed. A spring day generates its own energy. As normal tea-time approaches, I shake the lime from hands and sleeves, go into the house to wash and make a cup of tea. I take it out to drink as I wander round for a listen to evening bird-song.

A slight breeze is rising. I'll spread no more lime today. Then I catch a whiff of something . . . something pleasant, but something that strikes fear, too, at this time, in this weather—the smell of wood-smoke. Again I look to the distance. There, on the moor ground, to the west, smoke is rising and billowing slightly, billowing this way and that, as the breeze takes it. Surely no one would be starting a heath fire at this time of day? It might be a picnic fire. People are tempted out on fine evenings, in early spring, for a picnic supper.

The first drying winds of the year soon make the heather and the dead grass tinder-dry. An innocent disposing of weeds and rubbish, even in an incinerator, can cause havoc if a spark is carried on the wind into a plantation. This happened here some years ago. I have been very wary of wood-smoke ever since. That afternoon I smelt and saw the flames coming steadily nearer the edge of the planting just beyond the field adjoining the house. Probably the bare ground would halt it, I thought. But I wasn't taking any chances. There were no telephones in the houses then. I alerted a neighbour, who went on his bike to the nearest kiosk and within half an hour a squad of firemen were at work. Forestry workers soon joined them and for hours they hosed and battered the flames. Such fires can smoulder for days when they get a hold of the underlying peat. The ground is then pleasantly warm to the feet, but there's always the fear that fire may break out again. The exhausted firemen stood by all night, refreshed in relays by tea and sandwiches. At last, when daylight came, we all got some rest.

'Muir-burn', that is, the burning of the heather, inadequately supervised and outwith certain times in the year, is an offence, punishable by law. This fire, though purely accidental, did a great deal of damage and caused much distress to the people responsible. The memory keeps me on the alert.

I sniff the air. The smoke smell is still discernible, though the actual grey cloud has disappeared. Not quite reassured, I walk up the road to investigate. Nearing the plantation, beyond the heather, by the loch, I hear talking and laughter. Two cars are parked in the lay-by. As I thought, it's a picnic party and the fire is now down to a red glow. There are young people, older people, children, quite a crowd. There must be a safe pair of hands there, I decide.

The walk is rewarding. I find coltsfoot flowering along the roadside ditch and a woodland blackbird is at his evening choir practice. Tomorrow I must have a garden bonfire, a small one, started early and strictly supervised. The ash is so good for all growing things.

April 30th

Today, in the early morning time, with light around the curtains, I heard it. Or was it part of a dream? With opened eyes, I listened hard. It came again, unmistakably, the sound of the cuckoo. It's a reassuring sound. These parts must still be his haven for summer, no matter what the season brings. He's here! Neighbours come on the phone. You heard him? I did. So all's well! Sometimes we see him, too, Like a small hawk, he looks. And we know about his selfish habits. But still he's our welcome guest.

The swallows are the worry. Up till two years ago we had them nesting in a disused shed. All summer they would be flying happily in and out. Later on, a row of fledglings would perch precariously on the electric cable, parents stuffing the small beaks with food and dive-bombing any human venturing past.

Now we look anxiously, hopefully, for them coming, but to no avail. We think of those ghastly Kuwaiti battlefields in the desert. Did the birds mistake pools of oil for pools of water? Did they succumb to sand-storm, wind-storm, hail-storm? How they manage the flight at all has always been a mystery. We miss them sorely.

The starlings don't nest under the eaves now, either. That's something we don't regret, for the young usually found their way into the loft and would often die of starvation. The starling is not my favourite bird. He's noisy and brash and on occasion has had me running into the house to answer a phantom 'phone'! A flock of starlings, one year, caused a blackout, when they perched, tight-packed, on an electric cable up the road.

Another noisy bird is the black-headed gull, but we're so glad to have them back nesting on the island in the loch, when for ten years or so they were absent. Now they rise in a white, screeching cloud when they're frightened. In the evening they fly silently down to the lower fields to feed and later, eerily, in the dusk, they fly back. It's good to have them, for it means there's returning life on the loch. The tufted duck are busy there, too.

MAY

May 1st

I'm up early, not to wash in the dew, but to listen to the cuckoo, to watch for the swallows, to smell the warming earth. Beltane! 'Beil-teine'—the fire of Belus, an ancient god—this was the name of the day in older times. It was the first day of summer and called for a special celebration, after the suffering and uncertainties of winter and spring.

This was a day for positive activity. Great fires were lit on the hill-tops and the cattle driven through them to ensure good health for the year. All the hearth fires were extinguished and re-kindled with a torch from the purifying flame. Sometimes the young men would leap through the flames to show their daring. A great Beltane bannock would be baked and, in some places, a batter of eggs, butter, oatmeal and milk would be cooked on the Beltane fire and some of it spilled on the ground as a libation.

Bannocks would be baked, too, on St Bride's day, February 1st, the first day of spring, at Lammas, August 1st, for the first day of autumn, and at Hallowmas, the first of November, for the first day of winter. These small ceremonials gave a shape to life which was dearly prized.

There will be no Beltane fires today. The hills have to be made to conform to other patterns, when their main function may well be to provide good hunting and shooting. The cattle are no longer taken up to the heights for the summer grazing. Those must have been happy days when the women and young people would stay up in the shieling huts, herding the cattle and making butter and cheese, while the menfolk watched the growing field-crops and re-thatched the roofs of the houses.

The cutting of peats was another happy May-time occasion, when more distant neighbours, some of whom had perhaps not met for months, would join forces to make light of the work, exchanging news and much banter over a dram at the days' end. Many of the peat-banks are now swallowed up in trees, though the old grazings enjoyed the right to 'graze sheep, cut peats and bleach linen'.

Again in May the custom was to visit a healing well. It was firmly believed that these wells had the power to cure and give protection from diseases of many kinds. In the hills not far from here there is the 'red' well, with water which must surely have contained iron. Offerings of coloured threads and scraps of garments were hung on the trees and bushes round about, as propitiation. These can be seen in several places today.

Thinking of these things and with the feel of May in the air I skip non-essential jobs and walk out to a place I remember. It is hidden in a plantation now. Quite blatantly, I trespass, climbing the fence and following a narrow track through the jumble of trees. Disoriented at first by the changed land-pattern, I come to a gap and look round with recognition. Here, once, a stone-age dwelling stood, the outline of the foundation still clearly visible. Here, before the trees were planted, I had come on arrow-heads and a scraping tool on the fresh-turned furrows.

I find my bearings at once and, a few paces further on, I reach what I'm seeking—a small well, half hidden now in over-growth. Pulling aside the ferns and rushes, I gaze into the water. It's still dark and clear. There's no sign of the small fish reputed to be there, keeping the water pure. But it's pure enough for me. I scoop up a handful and drink it slowly, relishing every drop. I gaze into the water again and put up a small plea, not for healing or protection for myself, but, perhaps, for the earth, for the whole earth which is in more danger than any of us.

I imagine a man of the flints, tired and thirsty from the hunt, coming for a drink of the water, the water that meant life as surely as fire did. As he stooped over the smooth surface and saw his face reflected there, did he stop for a moment to wonder where he came from, where he might be going? I think he did, for he spent so much of his strength hauling those enormous stones and standing them upright, pointing to the sun, moon and stars. That labour did not profit him or his family in any material sense, but it must have given him immense satisfaction.

A curlew rises from the wet slope below the well. My flint man must have heard the marvellous music of its call and watched the perfect pattern of its flight many times, as I listen and watch now. Nothing can really separate us from the past.

So I've had my May morning. I leave no propitiating rags at the well, only a small whisper of thanks, and wander back, deeply refreshed. On the doorstep I find two people waiting. They are young. They look a little weary under the burden of their heavy back-packs. Hesitantly, for the language is not their own, they ask for water for their flasks.

'Of course!' I say 'come and sit on the green while I fill them.' They accept gladly. I tell them of my well and bring them two brimming glasses of water. 'This is from a well, too. My well is away up in the hill there.' 'You are lucky', they say. Then, over copious drinks and a plateful of rock cakes we talk—of the Highlands, the weather, of Austria their homeland and many other things. They will send me a plant for the garden, some edelweiss, they say. I mark on their map the tracks they can take through the hills and wave them off at the gate to the wilderness places they love.

I often remember an old Gaelic rune:

> I saw a stranger yestreen;
> I put food in the eating place,
> Drink in the drinking place
> And, in the sacred name of the Triune
> He blessed myself and my house,
> My cattle and my dear ones,
> And the lark said in her song,
> Often, often, often
> Goes the Christ in the stranger's guise;
> Often, often, often
> Goes the Christ in the stranger's guise.

*they will fashion most
beautiful wreaths and garlands*

May 3rd

An invitation to join a family outing to the west is always irresistible. This year the May holiday did not bring the weather one would have wished, but it was pleasant to down tools, pack a picnic and set off. There's always a feeling of growth in the west and of kindness, kindness in the air and in the people. Frost and snow don't linger. The prevailing wind is soft and brings welcome rain. The dry east wind is half spent before it arrives and usually brings the sun. And, of course, there's the Gulf Stream. This time we didn't make for the gardens of worldwide renown at Inverewe, but drew into a quiet, unknown place on the shore of Loch Broom and into the shelter of a huge garden wall. This is a Victorian garden which has passed to various owners over the years. For 45 years, from 1940, it lay unattended. It is now being restored. There was no one about. We found an honesty box for our donations, a leaflet and a map. We followed the path and pushed open an enormous door. It was like entering the realm of the secret garden of childhood days. The lilac was in bloom. There were rhododendrons of colours that took the breath away, trees that had overgrown into the most fantastic shapes and small, unexpected patches of plants among the rocks. Paths led in all directions. We followed one to the shore, lured by the scent of salt water and seaweed, then back by mysterious ways to the vegetable plots. Here seaweed was mulching strawberries! I grew the tatties, one year, on a bed of seaweed. They throve magnificently! Then we came on a real surprise—asparagus! The balm of the west was at work.

There was no tea in the house here, no plant stall, not even a gardener to be seen, but the tortuous little paths, the sudden glimpses of colour, the smell of the sea, the happy entanglement of wild and cultivated growth gave it a feel of mystery and magic which many spruced-up places lack.

Next day, at home, I look on this old garden with new eyes. It's a Victorian garden, too, in its way, with its laurel hedge, its ferns and rhododendrons and statuesque lilies. And it has passed through many hands. For me, it has that touch of mystery which overgrowth and the intrusion of the wilderness brings. I take a wander and a muse and try not to be too busy for a while.

I watch the birds as they fly off with beakfuls of tasty scraps for mates and nestlings. The daffodils will be out any day and the strawberries are beginning to flower.

John Reid, our Scots Gard'ner, tells us, in April, to 'Sow all your annual flowers . . .' and to 'Open the Doors off your bee-hives now they hatch'. But I think, maybe, we've had some climatic change since the 1600s. We're into May now and we'll still leave our sowing yet a little while. I'll take his other advice and 'Fall to your mowing and weeding.'

The grass got its first cutting today!

May 8th

A few days of warm showers and the ground feels really ready for the seed. When you can pick up a handful of earth and let it trickle through your fingers and there's a whiff of damp about, that means it's a day John Reid would have approved of for planting. These days I feel he's often at my back with his couthy comments and advice. But I have to remind him that this is not a laird's garden with labourers to hand.

It's certainly time the tatties were a-bed, so in they go, into a good mixture of manure, with a blessing on their heads. They are Kerr's pinks. I've never found one I like better. Sometimes I wonder who this Kerr was and how he grew his pink potato. With the tatties in, in go the onions. There's the potential making of a good pot of soup. These are two crops which risk little from the garden predators. Only that big cock pheasant has been known to gouge a tatty out of the ground with his large greedy beak.

Cabbage whites and tortoiseshells are on the wing among the dandelions, and the first swallow swoops out of a grey sky high above the roof-top. Will he be back to build? There's the hope. Then, something that really gives a lift to the day—the sound of a peewit. I stop to listen. It comes again. Could it really be a pair prospecting for a nest site, as they used to do? Again, there's a hope.

With a great renewal of energy I work on till dusk, sowing the first rows of salad seeds—lettuce, radish, spring onion, carrot. Tomorrow the turnips, then the annual flowers—nasturtium, cornflower, love-in-a-mist. I'll find room for them all somewhere. This year I shall make companion plantings—marigolds among the carrots.

Wandering back to the house I see the grass is shooting up. At this time of the year if you turn your back on one bit of the garden for five minutes or more it gets completely out of hand. You wonder if there will ever be a time when you can walk round appreciating everything without seeing something—an outcrop of weeds, an unpruned bush—that urgently needs doing.

The grass—the word 'lawn' is not really in my garden vocabulary, I prefer to call it the 'green'—I am always reluctant to cut. Let it grow and it's a meadow, a dampish meadow with lots of moss, wild flowers—eyebright, lady's smock, lady's mantle, self-heal, speedwell, stitchwort, hawkbit, bird's foot trefoil, buttercups and daisies. And mushrooms in season, even chanterelles. Over the years it has given so much to the life of the house—picnics, nights out in a 'bivvy' to catch the early sights and sounds, sunbathing and football games. This year I shall cut a good patch in the middle for the ball games and leave wide swathes round the edges for the flowers.

May 15th

Today, drawing back the curtains, I looked out at the morning in disbelief. I thought it was a dream. I rubbed my eyes and looked again. It was reality. There was a white garden out there, a spring garden lying under snow, quietly accepting its fate. And the day before I had enjoyed the first real leisurely outdoor tea-break of the year. I clear a path to the gate. By mid-morning the wind is rising and more snow falling, heavily. The blackbird is singing his heart out in the blizzard. I bless him for his brave reassurance. But the snow is still falling, sleety at times, then in heavy flakes again. With night there will be frost. Stories are circulating—of folk snowed up, of cars stuck on the hill. There is great discussion about climatic change, global warming, a new ice age. Then we remember—only a few years ago there was a snowfall in early June! So it's just our eccentric weather at its tricks again.

The blossom on the bird cherry is miserably bedraggled, the daffodils that cheer the high places are flattened, only the low-growing plants and herbs stay happy under their strange covering. Then the wind veers to the east. It brings no clear skies, but cloud and a chill mist, so growth in everything is halted. And the east wind goes on blowing.

May 19th

If April is the cruellest month, May, so far this year, is not much kinder. Still, the tatties and the first sowings of vegetables are in the ground, though they'll be wise enough to bide their time before emerging. Curlew and peewit are calling down the wind, their flight patterns hidden in the mist. It's a day for feeling restless, perhaps for a foray down the road, instead of up, to see what signs of growth are on the way.

The birches are greening and in the hollow by the burn there's the gleam of celandine. Chaffinches are singing non-stop and a thrush is shouting from the top of the highest pine. Lambs are leaving their mothers's sides to gang up with their siblings and try out their skills at racing and butting. There's life enough to defy whatever the weather can devise.

I turn off the road and wander through what was once a busy settlement. The houses are fewer now, for they are bigger, the people in them not depending on their surroundings for a living. But some of the little abandoned gardens can still be seen. The little old houses would have had a few flowers growing near the door, but the word 'garden' would have meant a small plot, walled with stone for protection from the wind and predators, on the edge of the ground cultivated for the main crops of the croft—oats, hay, turnips, potatoes. In the garden would be grown ingredients for the soup-pot—carrots and kale and some soft fruit for puddings and preserves.

Some years ago, when there was no one living in these parts, I came on one such garden, a long, narrow stretch beside the burn. Rhubarb plants had grown to the size of small trees, there were blackcurrant bushes drastically overgrown, but alive, and gooseberries still bearing yellow fruit. I took cuttings of these and now have half a dozen good bushes fruiting happily. Gooseberries and blackcurrants were always part of the summer diet and made valued winter preserves. Raspberries were gathered wild, for puddings also and for jam. Wild mint and wild garlic were everywhere. This little garden must have had a really devoted gardener, for in one corner was a lilac and in another a gean.

I wandered on down the track to inspect a certain hollow tree, a very ancient, gnarled hawthorn, for here, I was told, a colony of honey bees, a lost swarm, had been nesting for years. Had they survived this long period of cold and wet, I wondered. There was no sight or sound of them. I drew closer and looked into the hollow. There was wax, untidy wax, and some bee corpses, but, alas, no sign of living bees. Perhaps, I hoped, they had moved elsewhere last summer. A nearby landowner once sold some ground to a neighbour on condition that he agreed never to cut down a certain tree in which bees had been nesting for two hundred years. Would that conditions like that were laid down more often! I thought of my pampered bees, fed icing-sugar and covered with strips of old blanket. Perhaps these things act as sops to my conscience for robbing them every year of their surplus stores!

A young hare springs from almost under my feet. He wouldn't have found much joy in this old garden today, but his forebears would have had many a tasty treat. Before the days of wire fencing total protection of crops was well-nigh impossible.

A leap or a scramble could take predators of all kinds over a wall, unless it were six feet high. Thinking of this, my thoughts went out and back, through the years, to the crofter's wife who cherished this plot.

Little walled plots like it are everywhere, turfed over now, beside ruined croft houses. One such, up the road and past the loch, where a single tree now stands sentinel, took the laird's prize for the best-kept garden on the estate. Now that new people are in the old houses, little sheltered plots are most often swept away, in favour of landscaped areas, planted with flowering trees and shrubs. These are very pleasant places, too, reflecting new ways of living and working.

I wander back to my own portion of earth, I mean the bit I have on loan from the planet, refreshed by this foray into the past. I'm glad of the links with former times. I can see the look of distress that clouded and wrinkled that woman's face, when she went out to gather kale for the soup and found it lying in shreds on the wet ground. I've found devastation like that. But to give up growing for the kitchen would be unthinkable. No supermarket greenstuff can ever compare with what you gather on a bright morning from your own plot. Tatties dug and boiled within the hour make a feast for any epicure.

In the evening, warmed by thoughts of the past, I switch thoughts to the future. Tomorrow, weather willing, will be the time to confront the problems of this reluctant spring.

May 23rd

The wind is still in the east and there have been spells of drizzle, but the ground is drying out a little. Lettuce, radish and onions are through the ground and the peas look healthy, so there must have been a dearth of the wee mice that sometimes decimate the crop. One year I tried everything—black pepper, sprigs of furze, anything to deter the hungry little rascals, as I re-sowed and re-sowed the peas. The rest of the vegetable seeds, turnip, beetroot, American land cress, will have to take their chance of being washed out of the ground by sudden onslaught of rain from the north-east. Chinese cabbage is best sown late, to prevent it shooting. The wildflower seeds should surely be hardy. They went in in a waxing moon.

One great pleasure to be relied on every year, come any kind of weather, is the appearance of the garden's own secret flowering. During our first year here we let the garden have its own say. We knew there would be flowering currant and raspberries. We were not disappointed. And yellow raspberries? They were all appreciated, with dollops of cream. But the flowers—they were to surprise us. Aquilegia, granny's bonnets, have seeded everywhere and in the most beautiful range of colours—mauve, deep purple, pink, blue. Neighbours come to look at them with envy! Then there are the Welsh poppies, bright splashes of yellow after the daffodils have gone; periwinkle, that even risks the winter cold; London pride (a favourite of Gertrude Jekyll) and woodruff, making a delicate ground-cover in the half-shade under the trees. Forget-me-nots are cherished, and honesty, with its promise of autumn silver. Foxglove flowers everywhere, in quiet corners and in the herbaceous border. Sweet cecily, of course, rampages, valiantly resisting any attempt at cut-backs.

Now, over the last few years, there have been some really astonishing surprises. The sudden appearance of poppies, enormous poppies, in great profusion, and of all shades of mauve and pink, brought neighbours to admire and to beg for seed. How they came is a mystery. We accept their presence with great joy. Every year they appear, even among the brassicas or the onions. This year they are in the salad bed. I weed carefully to keep as many as possible. Another mysterious arrival is a most beautiful clump of eryngium, blue-stemmed and blue-headed, the envy of dried-flower arrangers. I have no recollection of having planted them.

Beyond the garden wall, in the grass-grown yard, is a very special flower—the purple orchid. The old walls themselves carry their own small flowerings. In the secret crevices stonecrop grows happily along with toadflax and bright mosses.

Even with vicious east winds and cold mist May is still the season of forward-looking days. Everything will right itself in the end, we feel. The weeds are certainly never inhibited by the worst the weather can bring. Shepherd's purse and sorrel are growing apace, many small seedlings showing up among the rows of vegetables. Every year I vow to hoe before any new weed grows big enough to be absorbing the nutrients meant for food crops. I never quite achieve this, but I try! I remember Robert Louis Stevenson's lines 'To a Gardener':

> Friend, in my mountain-side demesne
> My plain-beholding, rosy, green
> And linnet-haunted garden-ground
> Let still the esculents abound.

I had to consult a dictionary for 'esculents'. It means food plants. I hope my esculents are happy!

JUNE

June 1st

A dry day, but a cold one. The siskins are still coming to the nuts at the window. I should really wean them off, in case they give up looking for their natural food. They are so attractive to watch. Perhaps I'm being selfish.

A morning walk up the garden shows me the tatties are through the ground. A reason to celebrate! The failure of the potato crop often meant near starvation in the old Highlands. Their progress is still closely watched, with a touch of anxiety, even today. People still living remember when a pot of tatties, turned out straight on to the scrubbed kitchen table and eaten with the fingers, with a knob of butter when the cow was in milk, was a sumptuous midday meal. I look forward to my first dish of tatties, dry and crumbly, the 'apples of the earth'.

The grass is growing fast now. Soon I must take the mower to the green again, though I'm always reluctant to cut back those first bright shoots and the incipient stalks of wild flowers. I wander up to the strawberry patch. An orange-tip is there before me, flitting from flower to flower. That seems like another good omen.

This is a time of waxing moon, a propitious time for planting. Older Highland people still watch the moon closely, in all its phases, for weather predictions, days appropriate for certain activities and so on. The waning moon is good for ploughing and peat-cutting, for the 'sap' is going, leaving everything dry. An old lady will still walk clockwise three times round the house at the first appearance of the new moon. People don't like to see the half moon 'lying on her back'. This is a bad omen. Looking up at 'Paddy's lantern' on a winter's night one wonders just how clever they could be?

The waxing moon being a good time for setting out on a journey, I go down to give a gardening hand to a friend who is crippled by arthritis. Between us we clear the small plots along the front of the house, where nettles and creeping buttercup are threatening his roses. These roses, pale pink and deep red, are a delight later on and the envy of his neighbours. At one time climbers covered the whole wall. I also envy him his blue irises and the mass of crocuses and primulas which he grows for his beloved bees. The weeds eradicated, we put pansies from our local nursery in every available space. There will be colour against the grey stone wall till well into the autumn.

Down the south-east-facing slope below the house there is a vegetable garden which would have provided everything for the soup pot when the family was growing—carrot, cabbage, swede, kale—and blackcurrants and raspberries for jam. Still the rhubarb is healthy and the old trees sport apples and damsons when they feel like it. Now this small plot looks a little like the 'Gudeman's Croft', a small piece of land dedicated to the 'Gudeman', a kind of earth spirit, which was sacrosanct and not to be touched by plough or spade. There are one or two such spots up my way! I call it Permaculture!

A quick cup of tea and I'm back home to catch an hour or two of waxing moon for a planting. I usually indulge in the purchase of a few brassica plants from our nursery in case the seedlings already in the ground should fail. In go some cabbage and purple-sprouting broccoli. The cabbage is often wrongly maligned, I think. Raw, in a winter salad, or lightly cooked and eaten with a sprinkling of pepper and a dash of butter, it is supremely good. The broccoli, of course, lasts the winter through and is as good a stand-by as kale. Now it's good to see a row of 'greens' looking so sturdy at this time of year, even though there was a slight cheating involved.

After supper, with the urge to plant still strong, I go out, in the quiet evening, to sow another row of calendula between the lines of carrot seedlings. Companionship certainly won't do any harm, though the flowering may be late.

A leisurely stroll back through the herb plots is always a pleasure, especially in the evening, when there's the scent of lavender and

a white foxglove stands,
tall and straight

balm. Stooping to pick a leaf of sage I look round with care. Weeds are appearing. Couch grass is shooting up even in the middle of that clump of lemon-scented thyme. I dug it up last year, cleared it of weeds, as I thought, divided and replanted it. A truce is out of the question with weeds. It has to be war. Buttercups are creeping, clover too, and even that dreaded horse-tail here and there.

Normally there's not much worry with the herbs. They spread and grow close so that there's little room for intruders. But it's when most of your time is spent sowing or planting in other parts that they sneak in. Sometimes I think of the Zen garden I saw once, in Glasgow, at the St Mungo centre. Stones of varying shapes and sizes are interspersed with finely raked white gravel. Not a weed is to be seen, not a flower either. There is nothing to distract eye or ear. It is purely a place for contemplation, meditation. As such it has much to offer in times of noise and stress. But . . . a garden?

Did God establish that first one 'east in Eden' ? It had an apple tree. To enter the world of Tir nan Og, the Land of Youth, the heaven of the Celts, one carried a branch of the apple tree, laden with blossom or fruit. I know the magic of my own old apple tree, when the blossom shines against the summer sky.

June 8th

A June day at last! This year they have to be counted in ones, or, at the most, twos. With the warmth, of course, out come the midges. Scratching the bites being impossible, with dirt-filled fingernails, much time is wasted going indoors to wash and apply layers of lotion. Even this is not totally effective. Gardening friends have invested in masks which, though expensive, do seem to keep the creatures at bay, I have tried my bee-veil, but the mesh is not fine enough for the midge.

Whatever the weather, nothing, not even the threat of snow on the high hills, can deter the weeds. Shepherd's purse is the main offender this year. The tantalising little white flowers stick up in the rows of carrot and beetroot and have to be removed singly, by hand. Whatever happened to that beautiful bare brown ground of sowing time, you wonder. Gardening magazines and the television screen show pictures of lovely weedless earth. Is there a magic we have missed?

This is the time of year when the whole garden seems to take over and resists all attempts to tame it. As one row of seedlings is cleared of shepherd's purse another begins to disappear in clumps of chickweed. Clover creeps into the strawberry bed and sorrel clutters damp patches everywhere. Nettles and dockens do confine themselves to the edges, but something akin to a machete is needed to clear a path up to the orchard.

Everything is late in flowering this year, but the blue geranium never fails to cheer and this day the first of the oriental poppies burst into flame.

June 9th

Thursday, St Columba's day, said to be the best day for making a start at anything—that's today! A cowherd in South Uist gave Alexander Carmichael, the great collector of Celtic lore, a poem about this. It runs:

> Thursday of Columba benign,
> Day to send sheep on prosperity,
> Day to send cow on calf,
> Day to put the web in the warp.
>
> Day to put coracle on the brine,
> Day to place the staff to the flag,
> Day to bear, day to die,
> Day to hunt the heights.
>
> Day to put horses in harness,
> Day to send herds to pasture,
> Day to make prayer efficacious,
> Day of my beloved, the Thursday,
> Day of my beloved, the Thursday.

I can't let the day go by without a salute to St Columba. He passed this way some 1,400 years ago and has left his mark in the remains of his settlement down by the big loch. The sanctified ground extended well beyond the initial boundaries. At one time the whole area was considered a sanctuary, though it is not marked out, as it was in Applecross. A sanctuary meant safety in a place beyond the reach of the law or the sword. It is said that in this place some MacDonalds sought refuge after the massacre in Glencoe. It is certain that the name MacdDonald is still the oldest here and it was that borne by the bard, Thomas, and by many skilled masons of his family, who worked the granite and whinstone of the area.

Columba's island, Iona, is a magic place even today. He came from Ireland and soon settled to become an islander, though he and his followers made many forays overseas. I understand his love of the place, for an island gives one a sense of wholeness, of circumscription. One is held by the surrounding sea, but not limited by it. It bathes one round in reassurance, yet it beckons, too. It carries pictures, visions, of boundless, unnamed possibilities, not outwith one's grasp. I think that's how St Columba and his followers must have felt.

It is sometimes difficult to remain whole on the mainland. I try to visit an island every summer. I come home wearing what my friends call my 'island smile'. I think it means I've had a taste of honeydew and maybe a sip of that 'milk of paradise'. Hardy knew about this. He put it this way:

> When I came back from Lyonnesse
> With magic in my eyes . . .

I certainly have in my mind's eye the sight of those flowers on the machair and I still hear the sounds of the birds and the seals.

Now back to today, St Columba's day, and for me it's going to be a 'day to find plants for healing', for healing and for health. Within walking distance, I'm sure, there are wild plants here for treating all the common ailments and most of the more serious ones, and also for promoting health in general.

I take the road up to the hill loch, always a favourite summer walk. Here, in late spring, the little 'wind flowers' always delight us with their surprise appearance. As they fade, the primroses arrive. Some forty or fifty years ago, when the scholars went on foot to school, often barefoot in the summer to 'get the feel of the ground', they would while away the walking time sucking the primrose stems. 'As good as sweeties', they would say. They are still blooming, in this early summer time, tucked away in damp, cool spots between the road and the trees. They can certainly cure a child's longing for sweet things.

Coming to the shelter of the trees, we find the delicate wood sorrel still in bloom. This sensitive small plant loves shade. The clear green leaves, very like those of the shamrock, will close up if touched, as will the flowers, at night. An infusion of the plant can be used as a gargle and it's said that, externally, it helps to cure scabies.

As we reach the loch the scent of bog myrtle is rising from the damp ground. It grows in such profusion that I can happily gather a bunch. In a jar on the kitchen windowsill it acts as a deterrent to flies and wasps. Next I look for that supreme provider of cures—the meadowsweet. It's there, in its accustomed place, stems and leaves appearing. It will flower later in the summer. It deserves its name 'queen of the meadows', for its properties are many. Its fragrance made it a 'strewing herb' in older times. About a hundred years ago, it was used in the formulation of a drug to control fevers which was called aspirin, after the plant's botanical name 'spirea'. It has anti-inflammatory properties, so is helpful to sufferers of rheumatism. Its tannin content can cure cases of diarrhoea. It has an antiseptic action and also contains vitamin C. It really is a miniature 'pharmacopeia'.

The usual formula for most herbal remedies is one large handful of the dried plant to two cups of water, simmered for a few minutes, then allowed to steep, preferably overnight. Many herbs can be eaten fresh and raw, which is probably what nature intended, or they can be chopped finely and steeped in cold milk, a tablespoonful to a cup. Often, as I walk around the garden, going from job to job, I pick a handful of feverfew, leaf and flower, to chew on, though I'm lucky enough not to suffer from bad headaches. Thinking about it now, perhaps this habit is the reason why!

Coming home by the path that snakes through the moor ground, I find another great cure-provider—the tormentil. It is good for assuaging toothache, the great 'torment'. Also, the root is astringent and was used at one time in tanning.

I reach the garden and think again of Columba and his followers as I bend to the weeding. They had weeds to contend with, I'm sure, for everything would flourish in that small island. It is windswept but seldom frost-bitten, and the machair ground is rich in calcium. In my patch the never-ending battle is with couch grass, shepherd's purse and chickweed, yet even these can be beneficial. Cats and dogs eat grass to cleanse their systems. In humans the roots of couch grass, those long, white, fleshy roots we love to hate, can be used to treat gall-stones, kidney and bladder infections. A tablespoonful of small pieces to one and a half cups of water is simmered briefly, then allowed to steep and taken with honey, one cup in the morning, one at night. Shepherd's purse can be used as a first-aid treatment to check bleeding. A cloth soaked in a brew (a dessertspoonful to a cup of water) of the whole plant can be applied to a wound. Chickweed cures many ailments, internal and external. Eat a handful raw twice a day to make a healing agent for inflammation of the whole of the digestive system. Apply the herb fresh, after washing, to sores on the skin and it will draw out impurities.

Even a small understanding of the properties of all these plants helps us to look more kindly even on those which invade our 'cultivated' crops.

There are so many more—the rose, the raspberry, ladies' mantle, eyebright, the list is almost endless. We have our ancestors to thank for the patient experimenting they must have undertaken before discovering the cures they needed. It's good that we are now rediscovering them and appreciating the wisdom of former ways.

June 15th

Another summer day to celebrate! A cool wind from the east brings a cloudless sky and bright sun. It's not quite warm enough for breakfast on the green, but the afternoon tea-break will surely be taken there.

The bees are out early. Every day I walk up through the willowherb, now grown tall and sturdy, with flower-spikes beginning to colour, to inspect the hive. Every day I hope to find the happy, busy flying of bees in and out. There are bees flying, but not in the numbers expected at this time. They won't be swarming, that's one thing sure. A swarm in June is 'worth a silver spoon', the old saying goes. Some years ago I had several hives and could happily give swarms to neighbours. Today the important thing is to keep my few precious bees alive. I remember the time when they died, unbelievably, in early summer. To work about the garden with no humming of bees brought such a sense of unreality and loss that I scoured the countryside looking for someone's surplus hive, begging for a swarm. Eventually I found a beekeeper with a nucleus for sale. I brought it home in triumph in the back of a friend's car and got a hearty stinging as I fitted the newcomers into my old hive. They've adapted and built themselves into a reasonable colony now and are a most precious asset. I'll slip another chunk of last year's honey into the hive to make sure they don't starve. It seems absurd to be feeding bees in the summer, but the weather has been so unpredictable—snow in May and gales and heavy bursts of rain—that the good has been largely washed out of the flowers. The late flowering plants may have escaped and the heather is still to come. So we still hope there may be a little surplus honey for our winter toast.

Feeling that this may be our one and only summer's day I decide to celebrate with the bees. No weeding today! Instead,

I go in search of birch twigs for the peas to climb. Already the little delicate tendrils are groping for support. There's no lack of branches, for so many were brought down by the winter gales. And they're easily trimmed. I sharpen the ends slightly and slip them gently into the ground between the row of mange-tout and the row of green peas. It's good to be doing a positive job.

The next salute to summer is to take a slow walk round the whole garden, into each small secret, hidden corner, looking into a flower here, into the incredible structure of an aquilegia, for instance, stooping for the scent of the pinks by the gate, standing to watch the bees going from bloom to bloom in the blue geranium.

This is a day, if ever there was one, for the garden to be enjoyed. I stretch out on the green, hands clasped behind my head, gaze up and send a small canticle of thanks into the blue.

June 21st

The longest day—midsummer! I'm promised a touch of happy madness in the day today, for it's the day of the Garden Party. There will be no cucumber sandwiches, grey toppers or flow-ered gowns. In the afternoon some young people will arrive, wearing jeans, strong boots and coloured tops. They will dis-perse, across the moor, into the wood, up the road and soon reappear carrying birch twigs, flowers and grasses. On the patch of rough meadow between the garden and the yard they will set up a pole, fixed firmly into the ground. Then, with birch twigs interlaced with flowers they will fashion most beautiful wreaths and garlands and hang them from a cross-bar near the top of the pole. The whole structure will be festooned in all its length. There will be much laughter and talking in various tongues. This is to be a Scandinavian celebration of summer.

I go up to take the workers a cooling drink. The day is not brilliant but at least it's dry and calm. 'Just like Sweden!' they say. I stand back to admire their handiwork. It really is amazing. I look up and understand. This is surely the christianised version of the maypole. I remember how wise the early christianisers were to take over pre-christian customs—the veneration of wells, for instance—and this, the acknowledgement of the power of the sun to bring out life in everything on earth—humans, animals, plants. In northern lands in particular the warmth and light of the sun are valued above all else. In Sweden, at the approach of the winter solstice in December, a young girl, wearing a head-dress of lighted candles, will walk through all the rooms of the house, bringing light into every corner. This festival is dedicated to St Lucy, Lucia, the saint of light.

Now, six months from the winter solstice, the light is at its zenith. In the Scottish Highlands the sun was venerated well into Christian times. It is said that, even barely a hundred years ago, old men in the Islands would uncover their heads when they first saw the sun in the morning. In the evening, at sunset, they would again remove their head-covering and bow their heads to the ground, and say a prayer—

> I am in hope, in its proper time,
> That the great and gracious God
> Will not put out for me the light of grace
> Even as thou dost leave me this night.

This was recorded by Alexander Carmichael in the middle of the last century. The sun is not showing its brilliance this day, but we have the assurance that there, beyond the cloud cover, is warmth enough to keep things growing.

In early evening, the work-day over, more people arrive, parents and children. They set up a charcoal burner and soon a barbecue is under way. When appetites are satisfied and all greetings and news exchanged, the real celebration begins. To the music of fiddle and pipe we dance round the garlanded pole, holding hands and singing. The words may be Swedish or Danish, Norwegian or Scots. We all follow the gist and the tune. Some of the children do an action song. The words may be strange to most of us, but the meaning is plain. Song after song and dance after dance we do, till the sky miraculously clears and the sun gives us a farewell gleam, almost as though on cue. The western sky will scarcely have faded when the east will begin to shine. There's not much rest for the sun, the eye of the great God, at this time. We send him a small salute of thanks as we say our good-nights and goodbyes till next year.

I leave the pole, with its garlands, till the flowers fade. When, eventually, the time comes to discard them and put the pole away, the feel of that evening comes back, clear and fresh. I see a farmstead in Norway, small mixed woodlands surrounding the fields, orchards with blossom and fruit flourishing in the shelter. Perhaps, one day, we shall have native trees in the Highlands again—birch, hazel, rowan, alder, gean. We could do with another Norse invasion, a friendly one this time, from those friendly Norse cousins of ours—an invasion of ideas!

June 23rd

A day of humdrum jobs—weeding, staking drooping plants, watering seedlings—and any gardener would surely begin to wonder—is this drudgery? Where's the magic now? It will surely be back tomorrow, after a good night's sleep. But . . . when supper's done I go outside. Shall I gather the rhubarb for jam? Even the thought of that succulence on a winter scone seems to lack relish. The midges are not biting. The sky is fading to a duck-egg green. Not even the palest star is to be seen. Of course, we're just past midsummer and . . . this is the eve of St John. Surely a time for celebration. The good saint gave his name to so many healing plants. And he was a wandering man, leaving his footprints in the hot, red desert sand.

I look around. Over the garden wall, among the heather and the seedling birch, a white foxglove stands, tall and straight. A garden escape. It's like a signal. I scale the wall and make across the moor ground to the remains of what was known as the witch's house. Here, in a single room with a leaking roof of thatch, lived an old lady, perhaps eccentric in her ways, but with much goodness in her heart and patience with the young. I salute her memory and walk on.

Crossing the burn, I make back to the road. In the plantations the trees grow too close for access. I remember sometimes, somewhat sadly, the great broadleaved forests in France, where birds sing and flowers grow in the glades. These serried ranks of conifers are gloomy. Even the fire-breaks grow only the rankest grass. But they are a refuge for some forms of wildlife. There is shelter from wind and rain and some warmth in the dry pine-needles. Once, in full daylight, I caught a glimpse of a pine marten crossing the road before disappearing among the dark pine-trunks.

I wander on, all sense of time forgotten, tiredness gone. The night air is scented with bog myrtle. Suddenly, there's the sound so seldom heard these days—the vibrating sound of snipe rising. I catch sight of one in zig-zag flight, silhouetted against the fading sky. It brings back memories of the days when all this ground was alive with birds—with nesting curlew and plover, with redshank, mallard and oyster-catcher and all the small summer birds. Now the pattern of cultivation has changed so drastically we are deprived of these lives.

I reach the woodland by the loch. Here the trees are less dense. I move cautiously. Footfalls are noiseless on the thick carpet of pine-needles. This is the time for wildlife to be on the move, when their world is their own and they can go about their business as they will. Foxes are hereabouts, I know. There is the snapping of a twig. Looking up into the thickness of the wood I glimpse a slender brown form disappearing through the trees. The grace of movement is unmistakable. A roe hind. She may have a young one near. Have I deprived her of a drink? I move on slowly. She'll be back.

Reaching a dry spot near the water's edge, I sit down in a natural hide of fallen branches. The water is calm, reflecting the last tinges of yesterday's sunlight, as today's moves imperceptibly round by the north, hardly fading in its slow course. I gaze across the water. Mallard, tufted duck, coot, little grebe

A sleek, dark body scrambles ashore

will be safely nesting in the rushes on the far shore. There is a certain eeriness about the water, lying there so still in the half light. Could this be the calm before a storm? I remember how certain of the older folk were reluctant to pass by the loch after nightfall. Was there a kelpie lurking there in the peaty depths? On this particular night the supernatural seems incredibly real.

I lean back, eyes half closed. A ripple on the surface of the water is spreading into a wider and wider ring. Have I missed the surge of a kelpie? There is no creature to be seen. It would have been a fish lured to jump by a passing cloud of night flies. Something flickers against my face. Not a bird, surely? It comes again. Of course, a bat, several bats. Feeling happily absorbed into the night life of the loch shore, I draw a deep breath and close my eyes.

When I open them again the whole sky is suffused with pale pink light. The water is still dark and smooth but, close at hand, a ripple is emerging. Moments later a small dark head appears. A miniature kelpie? Of course not. A sleek, dark body scrambles ashore and makes for the sandy patch where a burn enters the loch. Totally unaware of me, the otter searches about for his breakfast, uttering soft whickering sounds, as though calling to his family. None appears and he moves swiftly off and disappears into the deep water. Wild swans I had seen many times on the loch and once, unbelievably, a storm-strayed cormorant. This is my first glimpse of an otter on shore, going about his business.

A small flotilla of mallards comes nosing out of the rushes on the far side. A heron flies in with great slow wing-beats, and stands, an elegant grey statue, eyeing the shallows. A fox will be standing somewhere, bright-eyed, too, though I can't see him. This is the time to be about, I think, as, reluctantly, I slip out of my hide. Walking slowly back by the road I hear a faint squeaking from the tumble of stones by the dyke. As I stop to watch, a mother stoat emerges, carrying a minute young one in her mouth. She will be shifting her family to safer quarters, obeying her own sure instincts. I wish her luck and pass on.

As I reach the house the sun is climbing steadily into a sky that changes almost imperceptibly from pink to pale green, to deeper and deeper blue. I look at the clock. In human time it is still only a quarter past five. Completely refreshed by my outdoor sleep, but exceedingly hungry, I make tea and a plateful of egg on toast and go out to my deserted garden. The flowers are incredibly lovely in the early light. There are long, low shadows across the green. Things should always be seen in a new perspective from time to time. Swallows are chattering overhead, in busy flight. The magic is back!

The weeds are still there, of course, among the growing esculents, as Stevenson calls the food plants. I'm useless with a hoe, knocking out almost as many seedlings as weeds. So it's down on my knees with a hand-fork and a will for a long day's work! This is St John's Day now. Any aches or pains will surely vanish when I remember the flowers of his plant, steeped in olive oil, made a cure much prized by the Crusaders.

Bed, that evening, seems a very stuffy place to be. I shift uneasily, tossing off cumbersome covers. I remember the time in the shelter beside the loch, the timeless time, when night and day merged in one smooth continuum. Is that what is meant by eternity? To have no clocks or watches, no signals of any kind breaking time up into neat segments, this is an enormous relief. The old sun knows what he's doing as he roams around the north sky, waiting to reappear in the east. The animals, flowers, trees, all of life responds to him. It's good to get out of our human capsule and to take a look at what our other earthly neighbours are up to.

As I drift into sleep I resolve to have the children up, to share in a night-time outing—to let them hear the owls' cry and to watch the smooth, dark gliding of wings out of the shadows. At first light fox, pine marten or roe deer may well cross our path. At the loch fish will jump and, with luck, an otter may emerge.

The children will instinctively learn to move in silence, to look, to listen, to be on constant alert, as the animals are. Awareness will grow. On the way back they'll stop to watch the fuzzy caterpillar make his sure way to safety on the grass verge, to see how the daisy—the 'day's eye'—slowly opens its petals to the light.

Reaching home, they'll eat ravenously and by afternoon a sleep on the green will seem like bliss. Waking, with all their energy restored, I think they'll agree that summer nights are too good to waste in bed.

JULY

July 1st

A glorious morning leads in the month, when, surely, the esculents must abound. Radishes, lettuce thinnings, spring onions, land cress, chives and parsley make a memorable first salad of the summer. Soon there will be strawberries for dessert. The plants are full of leaf this year so that the fruit is quite well hidden from the family of blackbirds which have neighboured me all year. If they're deprived of fruit I compensate by throwing out crumbs for them, even though it's (supposedly) summer.

Singling lettuces is a pernickety job, but I fill any available space with the tiny plants in the hope that they'll provide late salads. Strangely enough, I usually find them slow to develop and often have to use several at a time. Kale is a crop that never fails. I'm always glad to be able to give thinnings to a neighbour. He also takes turnip thinnings from me and, to everyone's amazement, they grow and thrive. Kale is delicious, lightly steamed and served with butter. Young turnip, thinly sliced, is good to eat raw and, of course, is the making of a stew or summer soup.

We're lucky, here, to be well out of the way of garden thieves, indeed, to have nothing with commercial appeal, not a gnome in sight! I did, once, from the bedroom window, hear the ecstatic comments of a lady helping herself to an armful of honeysuckle from plants trailing over the wall. As she sped off in her shiny car I smiled and wished her happy smelling. Perhaps she took cuttings that grew. I hope so.

Now that the tatties are 'filling the drills', earthed up and looking promising, the peas are staked and the greens singled, it feels almost as though the esculents are winning. But, of course, we know that there's no off season for chickweed and shepherd's purse is endlessly productive.

The carrots are slow this year, though the marigolds and spring onions I sowed as guard crops are doing well. The beetroot is suffering from the proximity of those glamorous poppies which I'm always tempted to keep growing. Friends come specially to admire them and to ask for seed, attaching labels to the heads they most admire.

One wild flowering I'm missing this year is the white, silky heads of the bog cotton in the damp ground by the loch. Some years it's like a huge drift of snow. A bunch kept in a waterless vase will last two winters through. In older times the heads were used as stuffing for pillows.

July 8th

An evening so cold that the windows were 'steamed', as though with frost! The wind is in the east now, which means a chance of clearer skies and even some sun. The bees are encouraged, though warily. They have a feel for the weather more accurate than that recorded by all the technology down south, and a solid instinct for survival. This means that they're having to consume most of what they make in order to stay alive. There may not be much surplus this year, I'm afraid.

The 'green' is sporting its crop of wild flowers—bird's eye, bedstraw, bird's foot trefoil, hawkweed, lady's mantle. I'm tempted to let them all grow on and have a meadow. But space is needed for ball games when the children come, so the mower must be applied whenever a dry spell allows. I like what Hudson said: 'I am not a lover of lawns, rather would I see daisies in their thousands, ground ivy, hawkweed and even the hated plantain with tall stems, and dandelions with splendid flowers and fairy down, than the too well-tended lawn'.

Wild flowers, I suppose through years of adaptation, seem to do well whatever the weather brings. This summer, in particular, the yellow bedstraw is thriving along the roadside as never before. It's a particularly delicate shade of yellow and so feathery a structure. I'd love to have seen Laurie Lee's mother's garden which he describes so well in *Cider with Rosie*:

Our terraced strip of garden was Mother's monument, and she worked it headstrong, without plan. She would never clear or control this ground, merely cherish whatever was there; and she was as impartial in her encouragement to all that grew as a spell of sweet, sunny weather. She would force nothing, graft nothing, nor set things in rows; she welcomed self-seeders, let each have its head, and was the enemy of very few weeds.

July 20th

An early phone call carries an invitation to an evening visit to a friend's garden. It's one I have seen evolving over the years, from the slope of an overgrown field, edged with thistles and bracken, to a place of colour and enchantment. It has superb surrounding features—massive slabs of rock, a waterfall in the adjoining gully, overhung with huge oaks, a birch glade and a view down the loch to near and distant hills.

Quite clearly this was a place for a garden on the heroic scale and luckily it found the gardener it needed. The approach to the house carries a hint of mystery. Leaving the road, you cross a cattle-grid, with its hedgehog-escape, and enter what has become almost a tunnel, as the bordering shrubs and trees encroach. This evening, as I emerge from the tunnel, I turn to look at the flowering on the natural rock face by the granite slab. Patches of alyssum, rock roses, tormentil, ground ivy, stonecrop, wild and cultivated plants are growing happily together.

The scent of thyme rises in the still air. My hosts appear. We stay for a moment watching the buzzard glide by, high overhead, then we wander down to the sheltered terrace below the house for a long summer drink. The midges, miraculously, are not on the rampage. Their biting would have been the one thing to drive us indoors. In summer, houses are only for shelter from rain or midge, or for a night's sleep.

We sit quiet, watching a wagtail strut and bob about the turf, happily snatching at whatever insects are near for his supper. We reflect on the amazing balance nature has perfected. The frog, the ladybird, the bee, so many creatures are benefactors in a garden, working away quietly, minding their own business.

'Any hedgehogs about?' I ask.

'Haven't seen one lately, but we're always hoping.'

'Mmm . . . So am I.'

'Come and see the new strawberry bed. It's looking promising.'

Strawberries always do well hereabouts. Some years ago a Cornishman grew them by the acre, along with raspberries and daffodils. He has gone but the daffodils survive, to cheer every spring. We wander past the Himalayan poppies, the Peruvian lilies, yellow loosestrife and blue geranium, which I recognise as old friends from my border, to a path of bark chippings, edged by the most glorious massed deep pink dianthus.

'You grew them from seed?'

'I did.'

A quiet smile of satisfaction is allowed, for the nursing of plants such as these does give one a sense of satisfaction. In the border flowers of all kinds grow happily together—sea-holly, soapwort, goldenrod, Jacob's ladder, along with corn marigolds, poppies, corncockle,

cranesbill and many more. My friends are keen collectors, always with eyes open for attractive plants. It's good that we have several growing gardens in the neighbourhood now, so that much exchanging of ideas and plants can go on. They are all tended by busy people with limited gardening time. This means they are all the more dearly cherished.

We ignore one another's weeds. Nettles make marvellous soup, we remind any critical strangers, and they are a haven for butterflies. Dandelions bring out the bees and the roots make a very acceptable substitute for coffee. The strangers listen, in half-belief. We reach the strawberry bed. This has been newly made on a patch of field previously sown to a small crop of corn, so it is well manured and protected by a deer fence. The plants look vigorous and happy. There should be much succulent fruit next year.

'The vegetables are doing quite well this year. We'll lead the way.'

I follow on, past the terrace again, to a sheltered corner near the ravine. Vegetables? I can't see any. My host bends down, pulls out and holds up for inspection the most beautiful carrot, clean, straight, tapered to perfection. I look down. There, among an almost jungle-like proliferation of weeds—chickweed, shepherd's purse, sorrel—are rows of superb carrots, beet, swedes, onions—and beyond, holding their heads high or hidden, Brussels sprouts, cauliflower, broccoli, cabbage.

'Good ground-cover!' says my host, a touch ruefully, gouging out a huge handful of chickweed. 'The root crops we can store, but the greens will need more protection before the winter.'

'You mean . . . ?'

'From the four-footed ones'.

'Oh, of course.'

I gaze into the ravine. The water foams white as it falls into smooth, dark pools. The giant oaks overhang it with mystery. Druids must have been here. Today otters travel up this way to the hill-loch, fox and pine marten have their territories mapped. None of these would threaten crops. But this is a garden where a roe-deer may appear at the window in early morning, having breakfasted off lettuce or spinach.

It's a garden after my own heart, full of sap and vigour, a haven for wild plants as well as wild creatures, with hidden corners and sudden, unexpected flowerings of shrubs and trees—lilac, bird cherry, rowan . . .

I walk home slowly, breathing in the cool, dusk air. A few late swallows are flying high, forecasting another bright day.

July 26th

There are strange cars around these days. Tents appear in odd corners. Occasionally a caravan ventures up. This is the holiday month, of course. This morning I am not surprised to see two people, unknown to me, walking up from the garden gate. They are not young, they are walking slowly, stopping now and again to look round, this way and that. I wait on the doorstep till they come close, then hold out a hand in greeting. They are brother and sister, they tell me, James and Peggy to name. They were at school here fifty-odd years ago.

'We wouldn't have been walking so slowly in those days! My, how those trees have grown', James says, gazing up at the cypresses. 'And the hedge.'

'I remember there were bushes right up to the door,' Peggy says, turning to look back.

'Bushes?'

'Yes. Laurel, I think. Or rhododendron. I'm not sure.'

'And there was a big tree. Too near the house, I thought it was.' James is looking round.

'That must be the stump there.' I point it out.

'That will be it,' he agrees. 'You have a nice green now. When we were at school the war was on and the grass was dug to grow tatties. We all did a lot of work in the garden.'

'And I remember we had to come in the summer holidays to weed the carrots and the peas,' Peggy says, laughing.

'Aye. I remember that all right. But we got some to eat sometimes. That was good. We were always hungry.'

'Were you a big family?'

'No, just the two of us. But we were boarded with a big family. Four of them and two of us, that took some feeding.'

'I'm sure it did. Come on up the garden now.'

They follow me slowly. Clearly their minds are full of memories. What will they make of the enormous compost-heap, the stands of willowherb and sweet cecily? Such things wouldn't have been allowed in their day. They make no comments. Nearing the top of the garden James turns, his face grown young with the glint of his smile.

'I see the old apple-tree is still standing. I remember . . .'

'Aye. And I remember the sore stomachs we had, eating yon green apples!'

Peggy's smile is wry with memory.

'Come this way,' I say. 'Here's something sweeter.' I pick a huge strawberry for each of them.

'My! That's good. I wish we'd had some of them long ago.'

'We'll have some more when you're ready.'

I take them to see the old schoolrooms. They are quite overcome with memories. Peggy disappears into the 'infants' room'.

'It's still there', she calls in disbelief.

'What, Peggy?'

'The hole in the floorboard where I dropped my slate-pencil. Come and see.'

Sure enough, there is a hole in the floor, in the corner, by the window.

'My! What a row I got! I can feel it yet.'

We laugh. Memories are strange things, sometimes so precise, sometimes misleading. Every summer people come, looking about them with bemused expressions, remembering this, forgetting that, sometimes contradicting each other when memories don't coincide. Their coming is always welcome. So much has changed since they were young here, yet they still see what they want to see—the green apples, the hole in the floorboard, the patch of blaeberries on the roadside bank, the hollow on the hill-side where they fetched sand for scrubbing the kitchen table, the short-cut through the wood that took them down to the grocer's van on a Saturday night. All these memories make the place live for us who are here now.

I settle James and Peggy in chairs on the green. Between us we devour a huge bowl of strawberries, with sugar and cream. I make tea and offer oatcakes and crowdie. They eat with great delight, savouring each mouthful. The noon sun shines on their faces and hands. The meadow-scent rises from the warmed grass. Suddenly a curlew swings into the air, above the moorland opposite. Peggy gasps, stifling a cry.

'A curlew. Oh, I'm sorry, it makes me . . .'

'Now, now, Peggy. You're O.K.'

She recovers at once. James looks at me in apology.

'It's so . . . bonny here. She . . .'

'Don't worry. I know how she feels. Have you a garden at home?'

'A garden? No. We're in Dundee. That's where we came from.'

Peggy looks up.

'We have a wee back court. I wonder . . . could I . . . take a wee cutting, maybe, for a pot?'

'Of course. What would you like?'

'Well, I could smell it when we came down from the garden. In among the rocks there. It minds me of walking in summer, in our bare feet, along the road to Corro . . .'

'I know. You mean thyme!'

'Aye. That's it.'

'Of course you shall have some. I've walked that Corro road."

I dig up a plant for her, carefully, and ease it into a pot. She smiles her thanks, keeping her smile bravely. I often wonder how that little thyme is doing in the wee back court. I'm sure I shall hear one day.

AUGUST

August 2nd

A good summer day and I commit the unforgivable sin of setting off for a two-week spell, leaving the garden on its own. Kind neighbours will check that the gates are kept shut against wandering sheep. The roe deer are well up the hill at this time. But rabbits are reappearing perilously near and a pair of pheasants go scuttering over the wall when I go up to collect some strawberries. One year I found a whole family of them in the long grass under the apple trees. The cat will be on patrol, of course, and I've seen her catch a young hare as big as herself. Young hares, poor souls, are rather stupid and tend to lie crouched too long, imagining themselves invisible. Then their legs are still clumsy and can't match the speed of a practised feline.

So . . . I'm off to the station in a kind friend's car. There's time for a browse at the bookstall and to indulge in buying one of the glossiest of gardening magazines. Gardening colour photography has now reached such a peak of quality that the images one gazes at seem totally unreal. Could one really have a herb garden where the plants grew to such perfection, in rows interspersed with neat box hedges and weedless paths? Could cabbage, cauliflower, carrot, beet reach such sublime form as to appear almost too good to eat? I sigh involuntarily, thinking of my garden on the rampage, weeds choking nascent late sowings, predators lurking in every corner and emerging undeterred. Then I close the glossy pages and gaze at the changing scene outside the carriage window.

Leaving the hill spaces and the wooded glens the train passes through one set of suburbs after another. I glimpse small patches of garden, a shed here, a greenhouse there, a row of begonia, a bed of roses, and imagine the pleasure these small plots must give. But I'm thankful for my own old flowering wilderness and begin to think about taking the first train back to it. Sense prevails, however, and I disembark at Glasgow, my stopover for a few days.

Next morning my first call is to the Botanic Gardens. A deep breath of grass-scented air and a chat with friendly gardeners and the chaos of the streets is distanced. The great glass-houses with their displays of exotic plants are really not for me, but I find quite fascinating a bed showing the dates, back to the sixteenth century, when various flowers were introduced to this country.

Glasgow, the 'dear, green place', has many little unexpected oases of greenery. A patch of grass, some flowering shrubs, a seat where, perhaps, a house had stood. Even the derelict buildings sprout ferns and happy-looking buddleias. The gardens of Kelvingrove, with the river running through, the pond, the glorious trees and the grass and the huge herbaceous borders make a place to spend at least one summer's day.

August 7th

Today brings the start of the second part of my holiday. A bus journey from Glasgow to the West, to the coast of Kintyre, and a brief ferry crossing to the small green island of Gigha. Here I enjoy hospitality in a building which once housed a school and part of which is now a post office. It proves to be a home from home. In Gigha Sir James Horlick, fifty years ago, created the famous Achamore (Big Field) Gardens, to which I make instant pilgrimage. His greatest passion was for rhododendrons. These and other flowering shrubs are, of course, best seen in spring, when people from all over the world come to visit. Thanks to the drift of the Gulf Stream and the shelter of mature trees many plants of all kinds grow happily here.

Once again shunning the exotica, I linger in the walled gardens; take shelter from the rain, with a friendly tabby, in a little old greenhouse. When the sky clears I climb up to the viewpoint, where the hills of Islay and Jura and even the coastline of Ireland stand out miraculously blue across the blue water. A memorable moment!

Back down the steeply winding path, where I hear busy bees foraging, I explore the named parts of the gardens—the Hospital Garden, not, as I first thought, a place for growing medicinal herbs, but a place where sickly plants are cared for, in the shelter of cypress hedges; the Fragrant Garden, which explains itself; Hugh's Border (who was Hugh?); and the Malcolm Allen garden, named after the Head Gardener who worked here for fifty years. These are gardens which have to be visited many times.

Feeling almost overwhelmed with the sight and the scent of so many plantings, I wander back to my pleasant lodging. All along the roadside and the bordering fields nature has done her own sowing. Meadowsweet and purple loosestrife grow in profusion everywhere, beyond hedges of fuchsia and little white and pink roses. The delicate forms of harebell and yellow bedstraw edge the roadside banks. Corn marigolds brighten the fields of barley and oats.

Visitors from the towns and from country places that are drenched in chemicals can only marvel at this flowering. And here we have the late summer picture. Early summer is the time to come, when the machair is carpeted with primroses, gentian, thyme, flowers of every form and colour. It's good that such places are holding their own and producing a valuable surplus to boot. Big herds of dairy cattle and goats mean a daily export of milk to the mainland and cheeses which go all over the world.

Gigha . . . the name, they say, means 'God's Island'. I think God keeps an eye on all these islands in the west. Let's hope they can continue as part of the first patterning of things.

August 14th

With eyes fresh from looking at long distances of sea and far-off hill, I walk up my old garden again. Weeds, weeds, weeds, of course, have been having things their own way. However much you try to accept that they are to be lived with, sometimes you wish they were a little less exuberant. Chickweed and shepherd's purse among the salad crops are easily pulled out, but those wretched old horse-tails have been invading the herbs again. There are still late strawberries and raspberries. The peas, both plain and mange-tout, are standing proud, all weeds well smothered, pods shining with health.

I gather the makings of a good summer surplus of salad and fruit, then, before reckoning up the jobs that must be done, take a wander round the flowers. The willowherb is full of the sound of foraging bees. The annuals, always late in developing here, are putting on their show for me—cornflowers of every colour that only they can produce, scarlet flax, marigold. In the wildflower corner, to my delight, corn marigolds and scabious are out. The robin gives me a short burst of song—a lovely sound, but with a tinge of sadness, for it signifies the turning of the year. Butterflies are everywhere still—white cabbage, tortoiseshell, Scotch argus, small blue—and moths which I can't put a name to. It's good to be back with my familiars.

Ripe apples will not fall about my head this year, nor will I stumble on one of Andrew Marvell's lovely melons, though I did once grow a passable pumpkin on a compost heap. There are no plums to speak of, either. These two harvests will be sadly missed. Many a
succulent pudding, many a jar of jam or jelly will just not be there. The early summer frost and snow must be the cause of the dearth. No doubt next year the trees will produce a bounty, after a season's retreat.

Reaching the top of the garden I look up. Something else is missing. The rowans are green-leaved and fresh, but there is no shine of scarlet berries. No rowan jelly, no rowan wine? It's unthinkable. I'll have to forage further afield, perhaps on the lower ground. I remember last year, when the boughs were weighted to the ground with fruit. The 'snow-birds' will be disappointed when they fly in from the cold.

I, too, feel bereft of this grand blaze of colour and promise of succulence, but there, just over the garden wall, is the flowering we can always depend on—the heather, in great sheets of colour,

"you have orchids growing in the yard!"

from pale to deepest purple, the honey-scent of it riding on the light summer wind.

Drawn irresistibly, I leave the garden and follow the old footpath, nearly overgrown now, by the hut circles and clearance mounds, towards the high croft lands. Footpaths through the heather, linking neighbour with neighbour, are rare enough today. Wide access roads to plantations of trees or houses are needed now, for the carrying of wheeled and motorised traffic.

Walking on, I remember what the heather must have meant to our ancient forebears—nourishment, warmth, shelter. It still means sustenance to grouse and bees, but it's not looked after as it was in former times, when planned burning of the old plants meant the subsequent growth of fresh, tasty shoots. I stop to watch my honey bees taking their fill, then wander back, still reluctant to pull out a weed, remove a dead flower head, stake up a rambling plant. The garden has got on quite well without me, I reflect. It has had its own quiet little riot of growing and flowering. Tomorrow will be time enough for some taming, for thinning of carrots, for tying of peas, for gathering of late rasps.

Feeling like the lady of old who had only to 'go down the garden smiling' I stretch out a hand to gather some flowers for a neighbour, some marguerites and yellow larkspur which proliferate. Suddenly, the sight of that hand amazes me. It is smooth and clean, with dazzling white finger nails—a holiday hand! It's high time to get some dirt into those crevices and under those nails, I say, almost aloud, to the bees in the flower heads and a passing butterfly!

August 19th

With the garden spruced up after my holiday desertion I find myself dogged by an almost irresistible longing for a sight of the sea again. Childhood memories may have something to do with it. I can so clearly remember rushing barefoot across firm yellow sand and straight into the water. How can I justify asking a kind friend to take me the short trip by car to the nearest stretch of sea? I have it! We could bring back seaweed for next year's crops! The sky is blue today, there's a slight breeze, so the water will be dazzling. I lift the phone.

'You're right. Seaweed is grand manure. Have you plastic bags?'

'I have.'

'Good. I'll be up at one.'

Agreement is very satisfactory. We stuff bags into the capacious boot and set off happily.

It's not the open sea we are making for, but a firth, a long inlet off the north sea, where wintering geese, ducks and swans find shelter and food and which is often graced by the presence of dolphins. We go round by the head of the firth and emerge onto the road which runs close to the shore. I open the window wide to get a whiff of the salt air. It sets the blood racing!

The tide is out. There is no firm yellow sand here, only stretches of pale mud, but the smell of the seaweed is authentic and irresistible. We draw in to a layby and take a long look. The water out there is a dazzle of blue, with the white flecks of small waves riding in from the east. A pair of swans is riding in, too, with a small flotilla of young ones in their wake. They must have nested happily. There are mallard in good numbers and family groups of shelduck busy feeding at the tide-line. They nest here, too, along the shore. To see the dolphins leap would be asking too much of our luck, but we scan the water carefully, nevertheless. We remember other times, when we've seen these fabulous creatures suddenly emerge, in formation, disappear, then emerge again, as though tantalising us with play. Joyful and carefree as they appear, we know that their existence is a miracle, with all the dangers that lurk in the seas these days.

The upper reaches of this firth are, in fact, mercifully free of pollution, with no heavy shipping penetrating this far. Birds that normally live far out at sea sometimes seek refuge here from storm and starvation. The seaweed is uncontaminated.

We unearth the wellingtons, a couple of heughs and the plastic bags and set out to cut our crop of bladderwrack. It's a pleasant task on such a day and soon accomplished when there are only half a dozen bags to fill.

My thoughts go back to the days of the 'kelping'. In the middle of the eighteenth century it was discovered that the cal-cinated ash of the seaweed known as 'tangle' was rich in alkali, which was used for bleaching linen, an important crop at the time, and in the manufacture of glass and soap. The burning of the seaweed became an important industry for a time. People were offered the inducement of small, enclosed holdings, known as 'crofts', to supplement their incomes, if they would work at the kelping. This was, in fact, the start of what became known as the 'crofting' system of land-holding, as opposed to the old way of working the ground in 'rigs', or long, unenclosed strips. Many people were attracted by this arrangement and came to work the kelp. It was extremely hard work and led to much suf-fering—rheumatism and pneumonia brought on by exposure to the cold and wet. After the end of the Napoleonic wars cheaper sources of alkali were imported from Spain and the kelp indus-try collapsed. Latterly, in some of the islands, Alginate Industries have been reviving the processing of seaweed and it is still used there, of course, for fertilising the fields.

'We could do with a trailer-load of this stuff', I say, coming out of my thoughts.

'We certainly could. Maybe we'll come again another day.'

With this happy mutual assurance we make tracks back to the car. The seaweed will be stacked, for digging in next winter. I'll chop some up to make activator for the compost heaps. If I had more I'd burn some, as the kelpers did, to make a marvellous fertilizing agent. It can also be liquidised and can be used as a mulch. With all this in mind I find that another trip to the beach is essential. This one has been wonderful.

The tide is on the turn now, long, smooth ripples sweeping in towards the shore. Looking up to the tall hills at the head of the firth, feeling the movement of the water and smelling the sun-warmed seaweed, it can seem almost as though we are in the west. The flowers are here too—sea-pink and silverweed and the little white roses. Later on there will be brambles. I hope the water level never rises to drown this lovely shore.

Out there, nearly covered now by the rising tide, is the outline of a crannog, a little man-made island where people once lived in happy retreat from the dangers of the world. They probably ate the seaweed, fresh or dried, as the kelpers did, and as people still do in Wales and in the Far East. I must try a dish of it myself. What's so good for the garden must be good for the gardener, too.

The sky is clouding, the wind rising, with the sting of rain on the cheek. A kelper's day, after all! But we've had the magic of it, too. We travel home happily, determined to return.

August 23rd

The rain is still falling relentlessly. The backlog of jobs is piling high. In theory the wearing of rubber boots and plastic garments should make one impervious to weather conditions, at least in summer. But is this summer? Sometimes one wonders. It becomes a case of watching ceaselessly for a break in the cloud cover, rushing out to finish the task abandoned when the last downpour came along, say, the thinning of the carrots. The late raspberries have perished, sadly, on the stalk. There will be a lack of jam this year. Of course, one can weed in the rain, but the work doesn't prosper. Too much earth is taken up with the roots. As you scrabble about to get done before the next pelting of hailstones or raindrops, the weeds you missed start to thrive maliciously in their new-found, roomy, damp beds.

The old people had a song to help them through every kind of monotonous labour—rowing a boat, harvesting, spinning, churning, milking. The cows became so used to the milking song that they wouldn't let down their milk without it. Waulking the cloth, that is, shrinking it by handling, was a long, monotonous process. A dozen women would gather at one place, sitting in rows along a makeshift table, working the cloth with their hands. The songs they sang were often composed extempore and were mostly satirical, poking fun at menfolk of their acquaintance. This must have been a therapeutic exercise! I feel almost inspired to compose something, something satirical, at least about the weather!

The rain eases, thinning to drizzle. I empty another pailful of weeds onto the compost heap and turn to a more positive job, and one done standing upright—fixing extra stakes for the peas. This is a crop that never fails. The pods swell whatever the weather. Shelling them always reminds me of childhood summers. This was a Saturday morning chore. It's sad that so many of today's children see peas only as something coming out of a can, as they see milk only in a bottle. The discarded pods always made a delicacy for Bridget the goat. Nowadays I give them to my neighbour for her chickens. I pick a couple of pods of mange-tout for instant consumption. They're best eaten raw.

The beans, too, are looking sturdy. They'll provide many a good supper dish, with a thick cheese sauce and some salad. Absorbed in the task of staking and indulging in memories, I suddenly realise that no moisture is falling from above. I look up. Unbelievably, the sky has cleared to a pale greenish yellow in the west. A watery sky, this, but at least something is trying to shine, somewhere. Positive thoughts come thronging in, thoughts about the future. It's always next year in a garden and soon it will be planting time, planting for next year. Then I remember—I have a garden centre token, a present from those who understand my way of living.

The nearest garden centre in the town is a vast emporium. I most often feel as bewildered and disoriented there as I do in one of the bigger supermarkets. That seemingly endless array of seed packets, from all the different merchants, the flowers so temptingly depicted, dazzles the mind. I know I shall succumb to their appeal, though sense tries to tell me they'll never succeed in my small battered plots. Bulbs are a better proposition. Most of them survive and flourish here, though a few fall foul of that old pheasant's beak. I'll probably opt for small, low-growing things—crocus (for the bees), dwarf iris, snowdrops, aconite.

Different brands of fertilizer and weed-killer take up what seems like acres of space. Sometimes I shudder at the thought of all those chemicals being scattered over so many gardens everywhere. They may help in the production of cabbages like footballs, carrots as thick as your arm and some dazzling blooms fit for the flower show. But . . . I close my eyes and think of the island machair—those little tight crops of barley, corn marigolds happily flowering among it, tiny wild pansies bordering the bounds . . . Seaweed is what the ground loves here. There are loads and loads of it to hand.

For a time, two hundred years ago, when the lairds found there was money to be made in burning the seaweed to produce kelp, the crofters were forbidden to use it as manure. Now they are being actively encouraged to ignore 'artificials' and go back to the old methods. The thought of those few faraway acres being tended as they should be is an inspiration which helps in periods of despondency and gloom when reminders rush in, reminders of the damage being done to this lovely planet of ours.

So I shall turn away from the displays of chemical products to gaze incredulously at the rows of garden machinery—strimmers, angled hedge-trimmers, shiny spades, two-way hoes. And lawn-mowers almost the size of a small car. Anything powered would be sure to break down with me. I shall choose my bulbs and opt for a useful-looking gadget—a hand-held device for planting bulbs in wild places, for naturalising, under trees. Then I shall wander round the outside section, looking quite longingly at flowering shrubs priced a long way out of my reach, consoling myself with the thought that they probably wouldn't like the move anyway, repair to the café for a hot drink and come home loaded with catalogues to browse through and discard.

August 28th

I'm up early today, for a check on the weather. It looks promising—puffs of high white cloud with sheets of blue between.

I scan the whole spectrum, hoping the magic will hold. I'm almost sure it will. I can remember only very few wet days for the Games. This is Games Day in the glen. People come, now, from many parts to compete and to watch. In years gone by it was a time, between harvesting the hay and cutting the corn, when folk could meet, engage in feats of skill and endurance, sing, dance, exchange greetings and news. It's still like that, though a certain element of entertainment and perhaps of over-competitiveness has crept in.

In the morning, heats are run off for the various races. By early afternoon the crowds are arriving. From all over the world they come, tourists and holidaymakers, some wearing exotic clothing, speaking in excited, unrecognisable tongues. There is track racing, high and long jumping, a cycle race, then the entry of exhausted marathon runners from the town.

Some of the special things go almost unnoticed—small girls in their beautiful Highland garb, dancing their hearts out on a tiny platform; young men, in quiet corners, playing pibroch to a steady tread in front of the judges' shelter.

Time goes quickly as friends meet friends not seen since the last Games. Wise people take a picnic snack to share, as the tea-tent and the ice-cream stall always sport queues. There's talk, inevitably, of the weather over the year, of sheep and cattle prices, of 'set-aside' and much speculation about what the government may be up to next. Fatalism usually surfaces and there's always time for a good joke and a laugh, as the men toss back a nip from a proferred bottle. The Games are to be celebrated, come what may!

The pipe band marches by, players resplendent in kilt and bonnet, giving a mighty lift to the occasion. Then we settle to watching the 'real' events of the day. We scan the nearby hillside for a sight of the hill-race runners as they emerge above the tree-line, a gap showing, now, between the fast and the slow. With glasses and telescopes we watch the progress of the pack. This race recalls the time when news had to be carried by runners from glen to glen; by hill tracks, in every kind of weather.

The 'heavy' events have their origins in everyday doings of former times. 'Tossing the caber' is a feat demanding unimaginable strength and skill, when something like a telegraph pole has to be lifted and flung so that it goes up and over in as straight a line as possible. This, at one time, was found to be a way of getting felled trees clear of the wood, when they were needed for building or other purposes.

Weight-throwing was said to be a pastime enjoyed by men waiting at the blacksmith's for jobs to be completed at the anvil. Testing your skill and strength against another's has always been attractive to the young.

The hill-runners come back to the arena with applause for each one of them. The winner looks almost as fresh as when he set out, the tailenders are almost at the point of exhaustion, but they come in, one and all. Modern living has not ruined as many constitutions as was feared.

At last the final event of the day looms large—the tug-o'-war. This is when the 'heavies' really show their worth. Muscles bulge, chests heave, as the opposing teams dig in their heels and amass their will-power. Spectators suffer with them as they egg on their favoured side. When the final collapse comes there is much good humour and handshakes as winners and losers take their leave.

After long applause people begin to disperse, slowly, happily. There's the nostalgic sound of old fairground music, the smell of chips and hot doughnuts. The children have a last go on the 'dodgems', a last lick of iced-lollies and it's home, five, ten, twenty, fifty miles away or more, maybe to some lonely place in the hills, where gatherings such as today's are highly prized.

'It was a good Games,' one friend says. 'The best,' says another. 'See you next year,' says a third. I smile in agreement to them all. Then it's back to 'auld claes and parritch'. The garden has had peace without me. I'll be back there on Monday, tearing out weeds, cutting back bushes, digging out compost, with renewed energy and drive.

SEPTEMBER

September 2nd

One glorious day this week raised hopes of an Indian summer. It was not to be. Nevertheless for eight beautiful hours the sun, our old 'hay-maker', dazzled us from a sky of ultramarine, as if to reassure us that he is still hereabouts. We stretched out on the grass—skin troubles, headaches, the very thought of them dismissed, as we revelled in the luxury of a brief spell of heat.

Now we are back to reality, with grey skies, a north wind, misty mornings and drizzle. Misty mornings can give moments of sheer delight, when the sun breaks through to light up the thousands of delicate cobwebs linking the wayside grasses and flowers. Perhaps one of those mornings is still to come.

Meantime it's a question of sorting out priorities in the line of jobs. I heard somewhere that 'good gardeners garden in the autumn'. Inspired by this timely thought I set out to work. It certainly is autumn. The birches on the hill over the road are slowly changing colour. Leaves from the garden rowans crinkle against my face, as the soft wind comes from the west.

It's difficult, this year, to accept the fact that summer has gone, for it seems as though it never really came. Yet things have grown. Some have outgrown their strength, grown sappy. Indeed, over the last two or three years everything seems to have had an explosion of growth. Trees, the birches and rowans, the hawthorn hedge, weeds, of course, all seem to have grown greatly taller, as though they were groping for the sun. Foxgloves, six feet high, stand sentinel above the garden wall. Whether this is part of global warming or not, people disagree. The facts remain. I read of a farmer in Aberdeenshire who cropped a field of sunflowers, though he counted only four days of sun. He harvested them for the oil, and florists, he said, had customers avid for the flower heads. I remember, nostalgically, the fields in Slovakia. We spent a memorable holiday, once, in Slovakia. There, in vast fields, the sunflowers stand, turning their heads, majestically, to the sun. *'Tourne-sol'* the French call them. Perhaps I could try some, next year . . . ?

Autumn is the time for planning. I make a start at re-shaping the bed below the sitting-room window. The clematis I planted two years ago, and had almost given up for dead, is thrusting nicely up into the ivy in the corner by the porch. I decide to cut back other climbers, put in more spring bulbs—crocus, scylla, miniature iris—and low-growing plants—thyme, alyssum, aubretia, campanula, all well-loved flowers with manageable roots.

It's good to get the spade into the ground again and to be planning and planting. When work has to stop for a heavy shower I plant the indoor bulbs—hyacinths and crocuses, yellow ones to bring sunlight a little nearer in the dark days. A neighbour has a most attractive rock garden, with limited space and exuberant plantings, so that I am lucky enough to be able to offer a home to plants clamouring for *lebensraum*.

In my turn I look for homes in the burgeoning gardens of new residents for my exuberant growths of blue geraniums, larkspur, marguerites, Peruvian lilies, herbs of all kinds, which were given to me when I started planting. Two days of scrabbling about among the plants, clearing weeds and stones, and my hands are recognisable again. I never feel happy in gloves, except for gathering nettles or pruning roses.

The flower border under the west wall needs a drastic cutting back. Every year I say this and every year I do give away boxes of roots, yet every year there's overcrowding. Perhaps the plants are too well sheltered, when they spread so happily. The deep pink flowers of astrantia have been thrusting through the orange Peruvian lilies, making their own most attractive colour patterning. Now, with autumn, Michaelmas daisies are every-where. The real signal of the turning of the year is the flowering of montbretia. For most of the summer it keeps itself to itself, but then it makes a real show—though a slightly sad one, the last till next year.

Going in to supper as the light begins to fade, I notice honey fungus on the logs edging the small raised beds beside the holly tree. I'm glad it has its brief spell of growth, for it has a strange beauty, though it flourishes in decay.

That evening I hear a light thudding against the uncurtained window, where the moths flit. Bats are on the move! A cheering thought, when so much wildlife is in peril.

September 14th

Wildlife of a more terrestrial kind is on the move today. I had heard that rabbits were reappearing not far away. Now one is lolloping happily across the green. Frowning almost in the style of Mr McGregor in the Beatrix Potter story, I watch from the window. I remember bygone days when each small cabbage plant had to grow in the protection of a plastic jar. Cloches were expensive and could be burrowed under or overturned in a gale. Will these days come back? I scrutinise the esculents. No damage is apparent yet. I think of people with gardens almost impossible to fence who had to give up growing everything but root crops on account of rabbits, hares or roe deer. Hares and the very occasional roe I have here, but rabbits . . . ! I come, momentarily, to a full stop.

Root crops have been meagre this year, carrots poorly, though I grew marigolds and spring onions for protection. Beetroot, which I depend on for winter salads, is also very sketchy. Only summer turnips are really plentiful. The onions are reasonably sound, if on the small side. It's good to see, and smell, them, lifted and drying in the sun and wind.

With a few square yards of bare ground visible, at last I settle to some autumn digging. Has anyone, I sometimes wonder, got ground like mine, with wriggles of old tree-roots, rogue raspberry shoots, never-ending stones? Pictures from those glossy, and even not so glossy, gardening magazines flash through the mind. I think of the television programmes watched avidly and, it must be admitted, enviously. Other people's ground always appears so smooth and clean, almost in its pristine state. Perhaps such perfection might pall. There is certainly great satisfaction in actually clearing a piece of ground, making it ready to receive seed or seedling.

Forgetting rabbits, their staggering rate of increase and the havoc they threaten for next spring, I take a weekend walk up the road. Panacea can always be found somewhere there!

A Highland autumn has a special, fragile feel. Spring is often disappointing, late, long-awaited and chilling. Autumn lingers precariously, as though reluctant to give in. There is usually a fresh green bite for sheep and cattle till well into November.

This day the roadside is bright with late summer flowering. Scabious! There should be a colour known as scabious, for it's a shade of blue of its own amazing intensity. Thistles of all sizes, yarrow, tansy, add their special forms and colours. Further up, where large loads of earth had been dumped as in-fill at a widening point, bright yellow mustard has shot up, above a covering of delicate fumitory. Further on again, deep ditching had been done and here, incredibly, patches of red poppies and ox-eye daisies have appeared. Red poppies have not been seen for years. The seed, I believe, can stay in the ground for long periods and the plants emerge when conditions are right.

So these are colourful days indeed. Soon, as the heather fades, the bracken will be turning gold and brown. The only colour sadly lacking is that brilliant red of the rowan berries. I must take time for a walk down to the low ground. The hazel nuts look promising. I had a Swedish friend who would gather them green, for pickling. I tend to wait till they're on the ground. The brambles are still hardly out of the flowering stage, so that's another harvest which must wait. I gather three big brown boletus from the roadside and wander home for tea.

House martens are darting and swooping in the high air, gearing up for that incredible journey to their winter quarters. We shall miss them.

Back in the garden I try to take a long detached look, to see the prospect as a whole. It is, after all, only a portion taken from the wild, from the heather and scrub, from self-sown conifers and birches. The wild would so gladly take it back and let its native creatures have their fill. Even now parts of it are developing a will of their own, and in a way of singular beauty. That willowherb, those grasses, ferns and ground-ivy in the wall, mosses on the stones, who could devise anything so innately appropriate? I think of the advocates of Permaculture, who favour letting things grow in harmony and find living space happily together. Not for me trim lawns, neat parterres, knot gardens or topiary. I found a somewhat disappointing passage in Victoria Sackville-West's *The Garden Book*:

> Then there are dead-nettles. You have to be a very highbrow gardener indeed to like dead-nettles. Personally I prefer every nettle of every kind dead and eradicated, but then I must confess to a preference for keeping my garden weedless and tidy.

Perhaps she never knew the taste of nettle soup! Feeling suddenly hungry at the thought, I put a fork to the first of the year's potatoes. The tubers come up dry and clean. New-dug potatoes for supper, with eggs, a dish of peas and a green salad! That's something the ancient inhabitants of this ground never had. There's a lot to be said for a certain amount of draining, digging, weeding, all that cultivation involves. But the wild growth must have its say.

Some years ago, when I started the reclamation work, I kept half a dozen chickens and a goat. Supper for Bridget, the goat, consisted of a huge armful of nettles, dockens, willow-herb, chickweed, ground ivy, almost any weed available. And she produced a quota of creamy milk after a breakfast of concentrates in the morning. The chickens, too, gave a surplus of huge brown eggs, though the extent of their original free range sometimes meant precious seed was scratched up and they had eventually to be confined to their own corner, with large amounts of green stuff thrown over their fence.

I kept white doves, with a dovecote made from scraps of wood and slate by a neighbour. They roosted mostly on the high rhones of the house. It was a great joy to have them flying down to a call in the morning, their wings translucent in the early sun. They nested and had young, but there was no way of protecting them from the hungry sparrow-hawks which haunted the plantation up the road. Risking their lives daily, the doves gave us many hours of delight. They were greatly missed.

So there it is—a garden on the wild side, a garden which must co-exist with all the forms of life surrounding it, a garden which has taught its gardener many things. There is much to marvel at—a plant thrusting through the smallest gap between heavy stone slabs and producing the most exquisite flower; delicate ferns with roots in the heart of a tree-stump or a dry-stone wall; wild orchids. As one visitor exclaimed, 'you have orchids growing in the yard!'

The introduced food crops may vary in yield from year to year. This autumn the failure of the beetroot is sad and spinach and broccoli have bolted. There's a lesson in that. They should have, and could have, had food and water at appropriate times. Natural growth will seldom fail. It's thanks largely to it—willowherb, heather and many roadside flowers—that the bees are now well and active and may have made some surplus. I'm waiting till the last flowers fade before opening the hive.

September 24th

This is a time to gather seeded heads—of astrantia, of poppies, both oriental and glamorous. Those wonderful deep shades of brown mean mellow fruitfulness just as do ripe plums and apples. I'm not a flower-arranger. Any flowers I gather go straight into a big jug and arrange themselves. But a few dried leaves or flowers will last all winter and foretell seed-time again.

There is still some late flowering about. At this height annuals always bide their time. Nasturtiums are only now making signals, and welcome they are. Michaelmas daisies, of course, keep time with their namesake, he of the flaming sword. Their range of colour is as beautiful as any, fending off winter valiantly. I believe Gertrude Jekyll had a whole border given over to them. And there's a succulence in the tiny Alpine strawberries, which will fruit till the first hard frosts. They have seeded everywhere since I first sowed them years ago. So the garden dies graciously, being certain of rebirth.

Warmed by this feeling of faith in the future which contact with the garden gives, I decide to take one more wander abroad before the impending equinoctial gales, floods, storms of any kind. I take a track through woodlands a few miles from home, a wide track, made for the planting and ultimate extraction of timber. The conifers grow gloomily together. There is little sign of bird or animal life. A few flowers grow limply along the edge of the plantations. A disused double track, probably now serving as a fire-break, takes off through the trees. I follow it, clambering over wind-blown branches, skirting boggy holes. This was once a cart-track through croft land. Among the conifers, on higher ground, to the left, are the tumbled walls of small houses and steadings. To the right is a small glade, grass still growing lush and bright, holding its own, where once there would have been small harvests of oats and hay. Here and there a native tree shines in the gloom, a silver birch, a rowan, a gean. The conifers are sadly dull.

With a sense of relief I reach the higher ground, above the tree-line and on to the open slopes. Here, unbelievably, a late lark is startled into song. Small paths go snaking through the heather, linking the vanished settlements. Neighbours would have walked them many times, carrying news, a bottle of milk from a freshly calved cow, a broody hen to sit on a clutch of eggs, happy exchanges of many kinds.

The wide sky, the glimpses of far-off hills and lochs, would have inspired many a young mind to go travelling, exploring. Some of the greatest plant-hunters must have been born in places like this. China, India, South America took them away, as sailors, missionaries, traders. They would have found ways

It will always be June

and means of bringing home pocketfuls of seeds, dried plants, plants in pigs' bladders. I like to think my Peruvian lilies came from a Highland horseman's saddle-bag and thence to his native heath. They grow naturalised in many places hereabouts.

Plants introduced like this found their way mostly into the gardens of big estates, which were modelled on those of the south. Working crofters and farmers had little time to make gardens, though the women grew kale and carrots and herbs for the broth-pot. Wayside flowers were plentiful and fields were bright with poppies, cornflowers and marigolds. Daffodils began to appear at one time, probably in imitation of the garden at the Big House. Now, even at the sites of long-deserted croft-houses, they flourish and spread, undeterred by the attentions of sheep, rabbits, hares, roes or other inquisitive predators.

Where it was possible to fence a small plot round the house and to provide shelter with a hedge of hawthorn or broom, then little pink roses would climb the walls and pansies and forget-me-nots grew happily by the door. Foxgloves would seed and spread, giving height, and, if there was a green for the washing, where the children could play, it would soon become a meadow, full of native flowers of every kind. So a Highland garden was just a small part of the surrounding wild.

Whoever comes after me to this garden will make many changes, I'm sure. Many are needed. Trees have grown too big, making too much shade, and will have to be felled. The hawthorn hedge, which shelters many birds in winter, is trespassing, protruding over the road, where large vehicles brush against it noisily. Several hidden corners, deep in dead leaves, where I always hoped the hedgehog would settle, will probably have to be cleared. The gigantic compost heap, where rogue potatoes flourish and where nettles and comfrey, cut down in autumn, produce a natural store of plant food, is a legacy of a kind.

A garden is so much more than a piece of ground growing things to order. I remember clearly, as a child of nine, looking in amazement at the tiny plants which had sprung, almost over-night, from the packet of 'cottage garden' seeds I had bought with my pocket money. I came in late for tea, fingers caked in earth after weeding my tiny plot meticulously, with a firm determination to be a gardener. Later, I still considered this seriously, but felt I hadn't enough background in science to become a professional. I've had the good fortune to be always a happy amateur and to have had somewhere, just outside the door, to wander or to work in. Days of stress, sadness or disappointment in any facet of life can be smoothed out as you look at the perfect structure of a flower. You stop and remember that root, stem and leaf have survived frost, snow, gale, every kind of storm or weather. You walk on, gather a sun-warmed strawberry, and realise that growing things give and give.

After this garden? I can think of no other. Indoor plants don't do well for me. I shall have to rely on memory. This store is well-stocked already and capable of total, or almost total, recall. There are few, very few, black spots—the decimation of greens by rabbits or caterpillars, the uprooting of bulbs by the neighbourhood pheasant, a late frost—these will soon be obliterated. All the other images will have the freshness and colour of a morning in June. The scents and sound, too—clover in the early sun, the cuckoo calling from the hill-side birches, the swish of swallows' wings round and round the eaves. It will always be June.

A SCHOOL IN THE HILLS

PREFACE

Schooling, in the literate sense, has been going on in these hills just beyond the Great Glen for close on 1,500 years. In earlier times the children would have been taught the basic skills for survival. The coming of Columba and his followers to the west in the year 563 brought the beginning of book learning, of the acquisition of the alphabet, of reading and of writing.

The Great Glen forms part of the long diagonal split which opened a gateway from the west. It has been called 'the valley of the Saints', for many holy men, including Saint Moluag from Applecross, travelled it in their mission to the northern Picts. Columba came this way on his journey to Inverness to parley with King Brude. It was not an easy journey, made in frail craft which had to be carried overland between the lochs. There were mishaps and encounters with unfriendly people. But at last, some ten miles short of their objective, the 'palace' of King Brude, they stopped on a green shelf by the shore of Loch Ness. It was a good place, looking into the morning sun, with fresh water cascading over rocky pools. Here, as the years passed, a settlement grew and teaching flourished.

Though the records are blank during the turbulent times of invasions and civil war, there is no doubt that learning went on in the precincts of nearby Priories and Abbeys, till the emergence of schools and the appointment of scholarly men as teachers in the fourteenth century. It is more than likely that boys from these hills would have attended institutions such as the 'schule' in Beauly and later on the grammar school in Inverness. A distance of ten miles was not considered an impediment. And they would have spread their learning among their friends.

From the late eighteenth century there are records enough, of teachers, their salaries, the numbers of scholars, the joys and problems of the whole drama of education as it was played out in many parts of the Highlands. The people of this particular region have been fortunate in having had access to learning from the earliest times. There have been many periods of darkness, but the lamp has never been extinguished: it still shines out through the generations of pupils of the last school at Abriachan, who have gone on to work as teachers, doctors, ministers, engineers and lawyers in many parts of the world.

The school has closed its doors now and today's children must go elsewhere to be taught. Yet there is still the aura of learning about the place, not only of book learning, but of learning, as Columba's scholars learnt, about bird and beast, rock, tree and flower, how to cherish and respect them and so learn to keep the planet alive.

In this, the 300th year since the passing of the great Act 'for the Settlement of Schools', I thought it might be interesting to see how the provisions of this Act worked out in the Highlands generally and in the area of Abriachan, by Loch Ness, in particular. I looked at the state of education prior to the Act and the measures that stemmed from it and gradually a wider view began to emerge.

In the telling of the story of learning in these hills I have found help in many sources: the archives of the Highland Council, the Scottish Record Office in Edinburgh and the Educational Resource Centre in Inverness; the *Transactions* of the Gaelic Society of Inverness, those of the Inverness Field Club and of other learned societies in the Inverness Library. The recollections of many former teachers, pupils and other people connected with schooling have been invaluable. I should like to thank the Highland Council for permission to include extracts from the Log Book of Abriachan School. My special thanks go to Mr Steward, archivist for the Highland Council, for his ever-friendly help and encouragement. And, of course, to Tom Johnstone of the Mercat Press, who has nurtured the story from the start.

DEDICATION

Remembering Hilda and Richard, my mother and father
and my first teachers, who showed me flowers and birds,
an island and the sea, pictures and books and
the pattern of the stars

ONE

When we arrived in the Highlands to work a croft, a number of years ago, the schooling of a small daughter, then just three years old, was not an immediate topic of discussion, though the subject was always alive at the back of our minds. We knew there were schools in the neighbourhood, good primary schools, staffed by good Highland teachers. We assumed there always would be.

It was November. The priorities were to have some basic alterations to the house finished, to get the water in, to assess what needed to be done outside – fencing, draining and so on – so that real work could begin in the spring. We had an early fall of snow. We trailed a sledge to collect eggs from a kindly neighbour. We learned to stock the larder to tide us over the days, or weeks, when the grocer's van couldn't get through the drifts. We were all learning, all the time.

Neighbouring children, orphans brought up on the crofts, came, shyly at first, to play. Play was a treat when there was so often a job to be done – collecting sticks, fetching water, bringing in the cow. They soon became good friends. Their guardians, our crofter neighbours, became good friends, too, and by new year we were visiting their homes and enjoying many a ceilidh.

In the winter months that followed, the short daylight hours were mostly filled with basic outdoor chores – clearing snow, collecting and cutting firewood. But there was always time for the radio. 'Music and Movement' made us think there were at least twenty children capering round the kitchen. 'Science and the Community' and many other schools programmes might bewilder slightly, but could certainly stretch keen young minds. Teatime on Saturdays meant a capering by all of us to the sounds of Scottish dance music. There were regular reading-aloud sessions from colourful books, print and picture easily followed by finger and eye, and within the year Helen had learnt to read on her own.

I remembered my own childhood and its early learning. My father, a history and English master, was teaching in a remote part of the country. There was no primary school within miles, but the house was full of books and my brother and I would scrabble about among them on wet days, when our main preoccupations out-of-doors were curtailed. My mother was a linguist and occasionally she and my father would hold brief conversations in what was to us a strange and mysterious tongue. Gradually the words 'pas devant les enfants' and the sudden cessation of an interchange in English gave us the delicious sensation of having been on the verge of some revelation about one of the intriguing things of our world. Thereafter my mother taught us many fascinating phrases which was the start of a continuing absorption of everything Gallic – language, and culture in the widest sense.

These memories helped me in my new role as educator. There were books always to hand, pencils and paints. Cardboard boxes were an endless source of pleasure. The big ones made boats and houses, the small ones could be shaped and coloured and made into an enormous variety of artefacts.

With our third winter under way, life on the croft settling down, we came to a decision about schooling. It happened that, geographically, we were within the catchment area of two schools – one in Abriachan, one in the neighbouring parish at Glenconvinth. At that particular time the pupils in Abriachan numbered only six – five boys and a girl. Prospects of companionship for Helen did not seem good. Bertha, who was fostered by our good neighbours the Macleans, went to Glenconvinth. She had already told us a lot about the school, the teachers, the girls, the games they played. It seemed there would be an easy entrée there for a very new girl.

One afternoon in late January, when winter was wearing on, the light was strengthening and new beginnings were in the air, we set off, the three of us, to see the school over the hill, and, we hoped, to meet the couple who ran it. We took the way that Helen would take – along the edge of the lower field, down the heather slope to the burn, over the clear brown water on stepping-stones, past the Macleans' house, where Bertha would meet her, and up another heathery slope to the stile and the road. For half a mile along this road our eyes never left the sky to the west, where hill after hill, still streaked with snow, was etched against the blue. A solitary buzzard came planing high overhead. The good day would have brought him out prospecting. Nearer hand the little scattered houses lay snugly in the pattern of their fields, thin plumes of smoke rising from the chimneys. To sense this landscape as a child would surely mean a lifelong love of stillness and space, we thought. Then it was down to the shelter of roadside birch and alder and the sight of the school building, with the branches of a great oak tapping on its window.

We stood there together for a few moments, listening. There was the sound of an adult voice, a firm but friendly tone, then young voices in turn, confident and calm, responding. It sounded like a good learning atmosphere. Minutes later, a door opened and children of Helen's age emerged, giving us shy smiles as they scampered off to their nearby homes. When she had helped the last one on with coat and school-bag, a lady appeared. She was smiling, too. 'This is Helen?' she said. 'Bertha has told me about her. Come on in. My wee ones are off home now. I'll get my husband to speak to you.' She disappeared into the 'big' room to supervise while her husband came to greet us. His voice, like his wife's, had all the welcoming and sensitive cadences of the West. No child could be in better hands than these, we felt. Would it be in order for Helen to come to his school, we queried, when Abriachan school was actually nearer? He smiled. 'You come to school tomorrow, Helen' he said.

So that was happily settled. It was arranged that she would start as soon as the worst of winter was over and would come three days a week until Easter. We made our way home as the sky was fading and a handful of pale stars was starting to shine. A hare streaked across the road ahead, a roe deer was barking excitedly, in alarm, among the pines. Hills, trees, roe deer, a great silent bird – surely vital elements in education, to supplement the three Rs, we thought. Reaching the stile, we caught sight of our home again, another small stone house in its pattern of fields. Soon we'd have the smoke rising from the chimney and cups of hot tea on the table. We would be able to see Helen coming home in winter dusks. The link between home and school was forged.

TWO

Next day Bertha appeared with a book from the school library, lent by the teacher. This thoughtful gesture of welcome was much appreciated by us all.

The spell of bright, calm weather and the lengthening of the light raised our spirits to the point of imagining spring wafting in on a westerly from somewhere beyond Strathconon. But of course we knew this was only a dream, a chuckle in the face of the unknown. Sure enough, within a week the wind was roaring out of the north, not the west, bearing the mark of Siberia. The numbing ferocity of this wind was such that to venture outside meant progressing with the utmost wariness, one step at a time, half bent, holding on to fence posts, till the steading was reached. Peering from the shelter of the byre we checked the damage – one huge old rowan down, the roof off the hen-house, scattered debris everywhere.

During the days of storm that followed there was nothing for it but to stay indoors, once the essential outside chores were done. It was a time for reading, writing, inventing fascinating ploys. The shrieking of the wind under the slates, the moaning in the chimney, became as much a part of life as the bubbling up of the porridge-pot for breakfast in the morning, the discovery of a forgotten book to absorb the mind or the sound of a hen happily announcing the laying of an egg in the comfort of her new nest in the stable.

There would have been no school for children in the past on days such as these. The teachers in Highland schools could assess the risks involved for children travelling even comparatively short distances from their homes and were given leave by the desk-bound authorities to close school early or to close it altogether on the worst days. The parents knew this and reacted accordingly.

At last, however, winter slackened its grip. The air had a whiff of fresh earth and the time for journeying had come. On

Helen on the way to her first school

a morning filled with early lark-song we set off, Helen and I, on the way to school. Her bag held only an apple and a pencil or two, but it was a much-prized piece of equipment. Bertha met us at the burn and we walked on cheerfully together. Half-way along the top road, at a junction with another smaller one, we stopped.

'See that stone' Bertha said, pointing to a flat boulder by the wayside. 'If the kids from along there have passed already they'll have put three small stones on the top of it. They haven't, so we'll put our two to show we've passed.' This was an intriguing idea and added a touch of excitement to the journey.

As we came in sight of the school three small girls came running to meet us – sisters, obviously, for they were as like as three apples on a tree. Smiling happily, they took charge of the new pupil and shepherded her inside. There was hardly time to wave goodbye. The feeling of calm confidence was very satisfactory. I remembered my own sickening trepidation on the first ever day of school and was very glad there was to be none of that. I waited a short while, had a welcome cup of tea with Mrs

Maclean's daughter, who lived near the school, then set off to retrace my route.

It was a route we were to get to know well, in all kinds of weather. I thought of yesterday's children who had gone this way, many of them barefoot and without weather-proof coats. The rest of the day passed quickly and by late afternoon we began looking for the wandering scholars. The spring sky was beginning to fade when we glimpsed the two figures jumping the stepping-stones. A mutual wave of the hand and they moved their separate ways. The smaller figure seemed minute in the vast landscape, but she was coming steadily and surely home.

'How was school?'

'Fine.'

'Hungry?'

'A wee bit. Mrs Maclean gave me a scone.'

That was the first of many journeys made pleasurable by the kindly friendship and support of our neighbours. Mrs Maclean's always cheerful greeting and her farewell 'haste ye back' as she waved goodbye from the doorstep had made our day many a time. Often, in winter, she would have us in to sit at the fire burning in her old black range. Over tea and a scone straight from the oven, after making sure we were warm and dry, she would gaze through the bars at the glowing peats. With a small, contented half-smile she would say: 'Aye, we have much to be thankful for.' Then, a reminiscence, perhaps about the installation of the range and how it was a great advance on the days of the open fire, when the pot hung down the chimney and was used for baking 'oven'scones. Oatcakes were made on the girdle, then toasted in front of the fire.

In summer there would be crowdie and blackcurrant jam on the oatcake or scone and we would join Mrs Maclean on her little seat at the end of the house, where she could gaze up to the hills and the path to the 'glen', as Glen Urquhart was always known. This was the way the women of the glen took when they went to the battlefield at Culloden to look for their men. Still just discernible, in a fold of the high ground, is the remains of a croft house. 'That was the home of my dearest friend' she tells us. 'I mind when she had her first baby up there and the doctor came over on his horse from the glen.'

There was no question of loneliness in those days. No place, however remote, was beyond the reach of neighbours. You looked for the smoke rising from the chimney in the morning, the glow of the lamp in the window at night, and knew all was well. She was still remembering. 'There were shielings up there, so they had good company in the summer. That's when they took the cattle up to the high places to graze. The women and the girls stayed up there in wee huts and made butter and cheese when there was plenty milk. The men and boys stayed at home to watch the crops and maybe to put a new thatch on the roof of the house.

'What about school? Well, no book-learning, maybe, but I think they learned a lot . . . about animals and birds and flowers . . . You see that wee island in the burn there? It's called the 'island of the cheeses' because one day a sudden summer storm came up and washed the cheeses downstream, till they stuck there.'

Mrs Maclean

The whole picture of summer life came clearly before our eyes. Many times we listened, enthralled, to these tales of the not-too-distant past. Most were happy, some had, perforce, to touch on the macabre, like the fact that, in a desperate attempt to cure epilepsy in a much-loved child, recourse was had to the burying of a live cockerel under the doorstep of the house. This was oral history in a very real sense. Remembering, now, I often wish we had had a tape-recorder in those days, though we might not have had the opportunity to use it much, as our time was mostly taken up with work of one kind or another. Listening to our neighbour was the happiest form of relaxation.

Mrs Maclean's husband was a skilled slater. He had roofed many houses in the neighbourhood, including our own, as thatch and corrugated iron gave way to slate. He was a reader, too, and was often to be found with a tome from the library. And he was a piper. It's said he liked to have a blow sitting astride a roof he had just finished slating! He kept the local Home Guard on the march during the war. It's sad indeed when folk like these neighbours of ours are no more. They taught us so much.

Helen's schooling went happily ahead. School was really an extension of home. With a teacher who was herself the mother of four growing children and whose classes numbered only a handful of pupils, it could hardly be otherwise. Each child was known as an individual and his or her background understood, so that needs could be met. There were many homely customs. On days of rain, wet shoes or coats would be put to dry by the glowing stove, which would be opened up for a few minutes so that numbed fingers could be warmed.

School for the junior classes finished at three. Any little ones living in the Caiplich area were allowed to wait in the school-house till the big ones had finished, so that they could share a lift on the school bus which took the pupils from the nearby Junior Secondary up the road as far as the stile. Sometimes, on a day of sudden storm, by tea-time the burn, which had been easily crossed in the morning, was quite impassable. Then, our two would have to go up-country to the point where the road-bridge crossed the water. We'd watch for them, tracing their way along the moor, then we'd go to meet them so that Bertha could make for home. Our torches, in the dusk, would reveal two laughing faces, gleaming in the rain, with no hint of distress. On evenings in early summer they would take their time on the homeward way, looking for tiny trout in the clear brown water, watching the baby mallard ducklings trailing their mother through the rushes. These adventures were part of the school day.

Time spent in school was an adventure, too. Some of the younger pupils, having had their lesson and finished the task set them by the teacher, would listen in to the older ones' lesson. Information thus acquired surreptitiously had the gloss of magic about it, so that even the choice between 'should' and 'would' or the correct placing of the apostrophe seemed more like an intriguing puzzle than a dismal obligation.

The education in these small Highland schools at the time laid great emphasis on plain learning. It recognised the fact that most young minds are ready and eager to be stretched, to receive knowledge, to cope with facts, to find them fascinating. The patient guidance of dedicated teachers was always at hand, with quiet encouragement. Of course, there were problem children. They were coped with and accepted as they were at home, in their own family circle. And there were the fostered ones. Fostering had always been a part of Highland life. In older times the chief would foster a son in the home of a clansman, so that he grew up as part of the clan, in its widest sense as an extended family.

From very early centuries respect for learning had been widespread among the people. It was recognised that knowledge could have a direct bearing on the quality of daily living. Years of quiet observation by thoughtful men and women had led to the acquisition of knowledge about the value of plants as food sources or healing agents, about the ways of animals and insects, about the portents of wind or cloud. Those who had access to this continually increasing stock of knowledge would share what they knew with those around them and so became the first highly regarded teachers. They also had the status that doctors of medicine were later to enjoy, as their healing powers were recognised.

Spiritual needs were also catered for, as the stone monuments and burial mounds testify. So the three mainstays of Highland life – the teacher, the doctor and the minister of religion – had been established since the earliest times. We were fortunate in our first days here to have the dedicated teachers of the two local schools, a doctor in the next glen – son of the doctor who would take a short cut to see his patients, coming on horseback through the hills – and a minister of religion from the Islands who could conduct a service in the village hall and converse with his parishioners in Gaelic or English, as required.

Though plain learning was the order of the day in school – the 'Three Rs' had always been the basis of what was really a 'national curriculum' – importance was attached to the development of many skills. Singing had always been a part of Highland life. There were songs to go with every kind of work, love songs, dirges, lullabies. Singing came naturally to the children and was easily adapted into choral modes. Bible study and the learning of psalms and the catechism made a normal part of class work. The minister visited regularly. In older times, of course, the Presbytery ran the schools and kept a close eye on them. Religion was not for Sundays only, an attitude which surely made sense. There were lessons in drawing. The girls did needlework. Each had her own 'lap-bag', to keep her sewing or knitting in. These crafts, learnt at an early age, stood many of them in good stead in later life. The boys did many kinds of handicraft, skills which they could turn to good account later when they grew up to be 'do-it-yourself' men.

A kindly district nurse visited the school regularly and the services of doctor or dentist could be called on when needed. In this way the children soon lost their fear of medical examination. And what of playtime? The morning interval was short but the 'dinner-play' was longer. These times were filled with energetic ball games, skipping games, round games, using the old traditional words with their meaning lost in time:

> The wind and the wind and the wind blows high,
> We are all maidens and we must all die . . .

This was sung quite calmly, with happily tripping steps. It is recognised today that these 'round' games represented a kind of therapy, curbing agressive instincts and encouraging co-operation. They have none of the over-competitiveness of many modern games and sporting activities. Even a 'counting-out' game – 'ittle, ottle, blue bottle, ittle, ottle, out . . .' had its significance, leading to acceptance of the fact that chance has a hand in determining one's place in the order of things.

For the boys it was mostly a question of shinty practice. This was a game engaged in by players and spectators with as much enthusiasm, even passion, as football is today. The big, round ball was kicked about too, but it was the wee fellow, bashed by those wicked sticks, that took skill and strength to put between the posts, that was the favourite. In quieter moments the boys manipulated the 'bools'. Several of these, made of light brown clay, not as glamorous as their modern equivalents, I have retrieved from corners of the playground. Breaks in the school day, those short spells of play, were avidly enjoyed, especially because, before and after school, chores would be waiting.

So the summer term went by, with its easy walks to school, lessons in the garden on really warm days, long evenings outdoors at home, ball games and skipping games learnt with friends, running and jumping practice for Sports Day and at the end a book gifted to acknowledge progress.

THREE

On the worst days of rainstorm we would start up the old Hillman, an appropriate name for our ramshackle car, and go the long way round to school, picking up the other children on the way. This journey was usually made to the accompaniment of song, anything from opera to pop, from 'The Volga Boatmen', to 'Puppet on a String'. We were sure the kindly bus driver would take our two round to the bridge on the way home, knowing that the burn would be impassable.

Occasionally, snow, piled into drifts on the top stretch, would make the journey impossible. The bus driver would attempt it. Failing, he would report back to both schools, so that there was no concern for the children.

Then it was back to indoor pursuits again, to reading and to radio. The radio programmes for schools were quite invaluable. The act of listening could, in itself, lead to a lifelong ability to concentrate. It also built up the power of the imagination, as pictures in the mind grow out of the words and sound in the air waves. There was no question of leaving the radio on, to churn out an endless session of 'pop'. Weather forecasts, of course, were vitally important and were listened to in strict silence. News bulletins, too, were treated with respect. Though we lived at a remove from most of the events recorded, we had no wish to exclude the reality of happenings elsewhere. Atomic warfare, talk of the 'ultimate weapon', the exploration of outer space, mention of these and many other things came out of the air. It all had to be considered, since it could not be ignored, though it sometimes sounded like a nightmare from which we struggled to wake. Was reality, we wondered, not actually here, in our days of tending cattle and sheep, ducks and chickens and our beloved horse, of watching things grow and ripen, of battling with storms, of relishing sun and gentle rain? We believed it was. And we cherished the company of neighbours whose outlook was like ours. 'What will they come up with next?' was a common rhetorical question as we gathered for a ceilidh, after hearing of the latest invention for exterminating half, at least, of the human race. Our agricultural experts were urging us to use chemical fertilisers on our 'marginal' fields. But these 'artificials', as they were known to our neighbours, were only grudgingly accepted as essential to the growing of good crops. As long as there were cattle, housed in winter, there was dung, and nothing, they reckoned, could beat dung for the production of full-bodied oats and tatties the size of neeps. How right they were, and how famished the land is without the sustenance of dung. Today, some kinds of dung can be bought, sanitised, in plastic bags. 'Back to basics' has become a slogan.

Coming home from one of these ceilidhs, on a calm winter evening, when frost had settled on the snowfields, we were quite overwhelmed by the crowding of the stars. They were enormous and seemingly so near you could stretch out a hand and pull one down to earth. Slowly, we picked out their names – Orion, the Seven Sisters, Venus, Jupiter, the Pole Star. We remembered the stories the old shepherds had invented for these stars, as they lay out in the desert watching their flocks. We concocted a home-made telescope. Many evenings after that we ventured out, muffled to the ears, to scan the Milky Way, to watch for shooting stars. Helen was enthralled. The world up there was mapped for our delight, adding another magic element to life. We composed a letter to the Astronomer Royal and got a most courteous reply, appreciating our interest and telling us what phenomena to look out for in our particular part of the country. Lately, a keen amateur astronomer has said he would dearly like to see an observatory set up here for the study of the skies.

With the coming of spring and regular days of schooling, evenings were spent mostly outside, watching the young stock: day-old chicks that had travelled miles from their place of birth and were to be installed beside their brooder-lamp, twin kids that their half-wild mother allowed us to glimpse from a safe distance and, of course, black-faced lambs everywhere. Helen, who had long been used to bringing in the cow for milking, was now promoted to feeding her calf from a pail, a job she enjoyed. She also had collie pups to feed and a pet lamb on a bottle, the little creature becoming importunate in its constant demand for sustenance, following us all over the house, sometimes bleating piteously from the landing upstairs.

It was a busy time but in the few spare hours we could carve out Helen was inspired to make herself a garden – just small plantings in a little patch of rock and heather, a natural rock garden. The sheep tended to ignore it as long as there was succulence for them elsewhere and it flourished quite happily. Meanwhile I was tending vegetables in a small plot fenced off in a corner of the near field. In older times every croft had a garden, just a patch guarded from marauding beasts by a solid, dry-stone wall. This wall sheltered the crops as no wire can. Kale, cabbage, carrots and onions would flourish happily, also blackcurrants and gooseberries. Turnips and potatoes would be grown on a field scale. Latterly, with the coming of the weekly food van, there was less incentive to grow the ingredients for broth, expecially when, some years, the crops were devastated by hungry roe-deer, which could leap five feet in the air! These little plots are still to be seen and they made excellent cover for ewes at lambing-time. Some crofters' wives, not to be outdone, grew little strips of pansies and wallflowers near the house, protected by some precious netting. Geraniums, of course, blazed in every window.

Summer came and holidays from school. When the peats were cut and drying and if the hay was in or safely standing and long before the corn was ready, we would think – 'could we get away, just for a weekend?' Billy, from our neighbour's house, would come quite willingly to look after things for a short while.

Where to go was never questioned, or how. We simply packed a box of provisions, sleeping bags, a pot and a kettle and made for the west coast in the old Hillman. We slept in the van, cooked on the beach and revelled in the sea and on the sand. Many crofts in the west were still being worked at that time. Holiday homes were few and traffic was very light. The roads were narrow and twisting, with grass growing in the middle. We loved it that way! There were birds everywhere, different birds, and different kinds of flowers – yellow irises and purple loosestrife along the roadside, corn marigolds in the little fields of oats. The working of the land in the traditional way was more environmentally friendly than it is with modern methods. Seaweed was the main source of fertiliser and the crops were harvested from the edges inwards, instead of across. In this way creatures were safeguarded. Nowadays, crofters in the west are being encouraged and subsidised to revert to these traditional ways in order to save endangered species, such as the corncrake. When spending a few days in North Uist recently I saw fields fertilised and cropped in this way. Oats and barley were flourishing and there was room for the marigolds and tiny wild pansies. I heard – and even saw (an unusual event!) – a corncrake. We would return after a few days inspired and refreshed and ready to tackle the main harvests of the year – the oats and the tatties.

Before the days closed in, and whenever croft work allowed, Helen and I would go down, on a Saturday afternoon, to the village hall, where there was an ancient piano. We would get the key from the caretaker and I would show her what I knew of piano-playing, a few simple exercises and scales and how to read music. Then we would find a friend who lived nearby ready to regale us with tea, milk from her tiny Dexter cow, and all the news from her end of the parish, and we would swop magazines and newspapers. This outing put a highlight on the week.

Neighbourly visits were a much-prized facet of life. A child was greeted with as much grave courtesy as an adult, a gesture which inspired responsible behaviour. To know that you were assured of a welcome at any time was a great source of reassurance. No matter how busy your neighbour might be, work would be put aside till you were welcomed, news exchanged, and problems discussed, over a cup of tea or a dram. As lives were lived mostly to the same pattern difficulties were easily understood and could often be anticipated or even solved. Today, of course, neighbours live lives that differ outwardly, and though the fundamentals remain the same, problems cannot be shared or removed to the same extent.

FOUR

We were now reaching a sort of turning-point in our life on the croft. So far there was little return on our capital outlay in stock, implements and so on. Like so many crofters before us we realised that we would have to seek supplementary sources of income. Jim could get temporary work, but it would mean absence from home for certain spells. I could cope with the day-to-day running of the place as long as he was there at ploughing and harvest. We knew we could always rely on the help of neighbours in any time of crisis. We drew up a plan of campaign and discussed all the issues. One serious problem was the daily walk to school. With only myself on hand it would mean a chunk taken out of the morning hours. I had the cattle to see to, the horse and the poultry. The sheep could be left mostly to their own devices.

It was decided that, from the start of the next session, Helen would go to the Abriachan school, which was easier of access. There were few pupils, still mostly boys, but Helen was now well used to school and undaunted by the idea of change. We went to see the teacher. She belonged to Abriachan, and was an ex-pupil of the school and had taught in it from an early age. Her sister was an accomplished cook whose school dinners were famous. They both made us very welcome in the schoolhouse and said they would be happy to have Helen in school. We sat at the fire in the cosy kitchen, drank tea and ate fresh scones. They showed us how they, too, were making a rockery and gave us plants for Helen's garden.

Their friendly approach reassured us. Again, there was the feeling that school was just an extension of home, not an alien environment. It was good, we felt, to have a teacher whose family had been part of the community for generations. Her particular branch of it came from a croft not far from our own, on the high ground up the road. She and her sisters had been brought up to crofting life, so knew at first hand what problems the children had to face – doing jobs before and after school, getting out on days of storm, having to work long hours at harvest times, when home lessons should have been learnt.

One day in the summer holidays, before the change of school, when the first weeks of freedom and play had passed, I found Helen scrabbling about among the books, as I remembered doing at her age. There were many of my favourite French authors among them, some of my old French textbooks. These she found intriguing and an inspiration to learn the language. I thought of my mother and how she had set me off on my way to Paris, Grenoble, Provence. On our next trip to town I managed to unearth, from the bowels of our excellent bookshop, an attractive first book for very young beginners in the learning of French. Thereafter I made a good forty minutes available, every morning between early chores and midday mealtime, for explaining the elements of the language. Soon we were able to enjoy it, with songs and rhymes and little phrases, just as I had done those years ago.

Helen was well used to being set tasks to do on her own by the teacher in school and was quite happy for me to leave her with some simple exercises to work out. One day, when she had been a long time up in the bedroom where we worked, I went back to find her valiantly struggling to translate a story into English, looking up each word in a dictionary she'd found. We had to get a move on after that! She loved to pass on the songs and poems she'd learnt to friends who'd come to play. She had also acquired a smattering of Gaelic from Mrs Maclean, so the concept of language was one she could easily grasp.

'Ça va?' – 'Ciamar a tha thu?'

The sounds went echoing happily round the house.

'Très bien, merci' – 'Tha gu math tapadh leibh'.

It was sad to see the 'Language of Eden' dying out all around. In the houses of our neighbours middle-aged parents and foster-parents would communicate with each other in Gaelic, while the young generation spoke and understood, apart from a few phrases, only English. With the best of intentions the elders discouraged the use of the native tongue, knowing that work in the wider world where the young would have to go demanded the use of English. Teaching in the schools had long been conducted, compulsorily, in the official language of the State. In former times the use of Gaelic, or 'Erse', as it was known, identified the speaker as one of what was looked on as an alien people, a wild people who indulged in idolatry and even witchcraft.

Various attempts had been made to stamp out the use of this language. In 1609 some of the most powerful Highland clan chiefs were 'kidnapped' by the forces of the Crown, taken to the island of Iona and made to sign what became known as the 'Statutes of Iona'. They had to swear allegiance to the Crown, of course, and one of the Statutes, to which they had to put their name, stated that: 'Every gentleman or yeoman within the said Islandis or anyone having thriescor kye sall put at leist thair eldest sone, or having no children maill their eldest docter to the scuilles in the lowlnd and bring them up thair until they be found sufficientlie to speik, reid and write Inglishe.' This whole affair, was, of course, really an attempt to destroy the power of the Highland chiefs by destroying their culture, and was the start of a long process.

A hundred years later the Scottish Society for the Propagation of Christian Knowledge sought to enforce the use of English in the teaching in schools for the whole populace. In a school in the 'Glen' any pupil caught using the vernacular was punished severely. It is recorded that the master would hand a small piece of wood, called a 'tessera', to the first miscreant, who would then pass it on to the next and so on till the end of the day, when the punishments would be meted out. These were mostly devices to humiliate, the sinner being spat upon, put in a corner of the room or made to wear a collar of thorns.

Later, the prohibition of the vernacular was modified, as the children, who spoke only Gaelic at home, had become completely confused and were merely repeating sounds heard in school without any understanding. Today, strenuous efforts are being made to reinstate the Gaelic language, with the main

Abriachan School and Schoolhouse

teaching in some schools being in that language. New literature is being created, poetry and prose of the finest quality. Some jobs in the Western Isles now demand a knowledge of Gaelic as part of the applicant's qualifications. Changed days!

When the new term began, in mid-August, Helen set off quite confidently on the new road to the new school. It was an easy way – up the field, over another stile, through the patch of felled woodland and the road was reached. Then it was a saunter or a race, with two or three others from a nearby house, down to the school, half a mile away.

Fears for safety on this road were few. It was a very little school now. The teacher herself must have felt it strange to be teaching a handful of children in one of the smaller rooms, when she had been one of nearly a hundred and taught by the master in the 'big' room. Many were the tales of his authoritarian rule! She had survived it and become a pupil-teacher before eventually returning as assistant and then head.

With so few children in front of her she was able to give them individual attention and tuition. Her sister saw to it that they were well fed, with good hot meals prepared in a kitchen which had been specially built a few years previously. An extra classroom had been built on as well, with facilities for the teaching of technical subjects for the boys and domestic science – now 'Home Economics' – for the girls. The purpose was to make the school into what was then known as a 'Junior Secondary', so that the children would not have to travel to Inverness to complete their education. But the school roll had been falling. This was due mostly to the fact that, as potential foster-parents were ageing, there were fewer and fewer fostered children in the area. It was they who had kept the intake of pupils to a reasonable level. Local children had grown up, and gone to raise families elsewhere. The croft could not support more than, perhaps, two, the older of whom would expect to inherit the tenancy or the freehold.

Schooling for Helen went on well enough, though the small numbers limited certain activities and the scope for play was also restricted. One memorable winter the children were at home almost as many days as they were in school, though they had only a short distance to go and most of it on a surfaced road. This was the winter of the 'big snow', when drifts froze into gigantic mounds of all shapes and sizes that nothing could shift. Blizzards blew up out of every airt. For weeks on end no wheeled vehicle could reach us. We learned to survive on eggs and tatties and oaten scones. Oatmeal sustains the brain, as is being rediscovered today. We certainly kept ours alive, with pencil and paper ploys, reading and the never-failing radio. Talks, music, drama, everything that came out of that small box of tricks added to the fabric of life and kept us in touch with worlds everywhere. It was certainly not a winter of discontent.

It was followed by an equally memorable summer. Eventually, of course, this meant a water shortage. The well dried almost to vanishing point. I took the washing to the burn. We even managed to bath in a pool still deep enough to sit in and well screened by bushes and dwarf alder! A swim in the loch, followed by a picnic tea among the meadowsweet and bog myrtle was a treat indulged in several times a week. We were always reluctant to leave the water. Dragonflies shimmered over the smooth surface.

Swifts circled and screamed in the bright air overhead. Was this a taste of paradise?

We would go wading in again, watching the small fish darting in the shallows. This glorious warmth, after the long weeks of intense cold, had made us acutely aware of our dependence on the elements. Earth, air, fire, water – we saluted them as old friends, old friends to be treated with respect and a touch of awe. We felt linked, too, to the long-vanished people who had lived their lives out here, in the same landscape, thrilled, as we were, to hear the first lark in spring, happy with the wild harvests of autumn, biding their time in the cold months, keeping to the shelter of home. It is thought that the small island in the loch, where the black-headed gulls now nest, was originally a crannog, a man-made island, built as a safe dwelling-place for people and their livestock. So far, this has not been proven.

When at last the rain came, the well overflowed again and the water-butts were brimming. That was a signal for celebration, as we splashed about the steading in plastic macs and hats and wellingtons. Eyes shone out of bronzed faces as we licked the drops trickling from cheeks and brows!

FIVE

Almost every Sunday, most of the year, we would go walking to explore different parts of our surroundings. Quite often we would go across a nearby slope of moorland, on our way to a higher point, where there was a wide encompassing view in all directions. One spring this heather-covered slope was burned, as part of a 'muir-burn' operation. This particular burning got out of hand and was excessively heavy. It uncovered what looked like the outlines of an old settlement. In the long beams of evening sunlight the shapes of hut circles and of small stone walls were clearly delineated, as on a three-dimensional map. Many times, after that, we walked it, always discovering new things – signs of terracing, of a larger, almost rectangular enclosure. Surely not a school! We dubbed it the village hall.

We visualised the children who must have lived there. Education, for them, would have meant learning the skills necessary for survival. We had often unearthed evidence of the long past efforts to keep fed and warm. Flint arrowheads, meticulously shaped, still lie at a spade's depth below the ground, though the wooden shafts have long since perished. Many a small boy must have watched, in fascination, as his father worked at the shaping. Soon he would have learnt the craft for himself, been on the alert to fit arrow to bow and take aim. Prey would have been plentiful – roe-deer, boar, wolf, grouse and waterfowl on the loch. The girls would have learnt to use another of the tools in my growing collection – the flint scraper. The skins of the animals brought in from the hunt would have been cleared of adhering body tissue before being dried, stretched and made into warm clothing.

Having learnt the techniques for survival from an early age, the children would have been proud to be part of the family work force, using their skills, as their counterparts do in Africa today. They would have had time and freedom for fun, too, time to wander up the hills, to paddle in the burns, to guddle small trout, to gather nuts and berries and honey from wild bees. Their imaginations would have been fired by the tales of heroes, of heroic beasts and of heroic men. Each tree and flower would have had a significance as healer or as food and a story telling of its origin and power. The world must have seemed a fairly magical place in spite of the hardships of daily life. Only now are we trying to get our children of today back in touch with the realities of physical hardship, of hunger and cold, as we send them off on 'adventure' trips and they struggle to find their way through storms and darkness on forays into the hills. And we're telling them stories again, great powerful stories of yesterday and today. Held in the spell of the story-teller's voice, their minds create the images they see.

The more we explored 'our' settlement the more determined we became to have it recognised by some acknowledged expert in the field of archaeology. We invited several likely people up to walk it with us – a retired schoolmaster, a countryside Ranger – till finally some experts from Edinburgh heard about it and it was duly and officially recognised as a settlement of late bronze or early iron age. It is now scheduled and known as the 'Loch Laide Settlement' or an early iron age farming settlement.

A photograph of the site is on display now, in the Inverness museum. Children have come to look at it as part of a summer activity known as 'Landscape Detection'. People walked it lately on an 'Archaeology Week' outing. The place was part of a For-estry Commission holding and has recently been sold to a private owner. He is, I'm glad to say, happy to have it identified, with a small plaque on a piece of natural stone. This will replace the sign put up some years ago by the Field Club, which had fallen into disrepair under the onslaught of weather. We hope that one day some of the hut sites may be excavated, so that more precise dating of the likely occupation can be established.

Meantime, it's good to know that people have lived here over so long a period of time, most leaving little trace – a few scattered stones, some patches of bright green among the heather, here and there a well, the outline of a hearth. It's a place that would have been attractive to settlers, even temporary ones, in nomadic times, then to their farming descendants. Not far away there is a cup-marked stone, mysterious sign, perhaps, of awareness of powers beyond their ken, perhaps of a signal to those powers. Who knows? It's good that they've left us with a mystery, in our world where we insist on explanations.

Living here, at 800 feet above sea level, with no dense afforestation such as that in lower regions, they would have had little likelihood of attack by predators, bear or wolf. Any human enemy could be spotted from afar. The nearby loch would have been a source of food, along with small game, nuts and berries. There were scattered stands of birch, willow and alder, heather, scrub and stone, everything needed for the spare and daunted lives that were lived here over the millenia.

There were several deaths of elderly people in the neighbourhood about this time. We were privileged to help at some sad funerals, sad because they marked the end of an era. We went, later, to some displenishing sales and acquired, also sadly enough, some tools and plenishings – a peat spade, a cheese press, an iron pot – things which symbolised a way of life which was passing away, as the men and women who had lived it were passing away. This was a natural enough form of depopulation, but it meant that, as the younger family members had mostly moved away there was little chance of more children finding foster-homes in the neighbourhood. As the remaining boys in the school went on to secondary education, just two girls were left. This meant they got individual tuition and made good enough progress. But clearly there were limitations, a certain lack of stimulation and scope for practising social skills.

Then, one day in early spring, I glimpsed someone coming down through the felled woodland. It was a man, wearing a town suit and carrying a briefcase. He climbed the stile and made his way down the field. Who could it be? The house was in a mess. We had been at spring work in the fields, my hands were mud-stained, my skirt and jumper holed and crumpled. There was no time for repairs. Approaching the door, the visitor smiled

A selection of crofting tools: home-made turnip chopper, flail and potato basket

and held out a hand in greeting. I grasped it, apologising for the mud. He laughed.

'Don't worry' he said, ' I know it's a busy time. I'm from the education department. I've come to tell you . . . we shall have to close the school. You'll understand . . . with two pupils . . . it's a question of economics.'

'Yes, of course, I understand. I thought, perhaps, as they're so near finishing their primary days . . . ?'

'We might have delayed the closure another year or two. Alas, I'm afraid not.'

'So where . . .'

'. . . will the two girls go?'

'Yes.'

'They'll go to the primary department of the school over the back. In Kiltarlity. There will be transport. The bus will come to a point at the end of your place. To the west.'

This was near the bridge, where the driver used to drop them on days of storm, when they came home from Glenconvinth.

'I see. And this will start . . . '

'Next session. In August.'

'I see. Well . . . Thank you for letting us know.'

'It's a good school. And I daresay the girls will enjoy being among more children.'

'Well . . . will you . . . have a cup of tea?'

'Thank you. But I won't stop. I have to see the foster-parents of the other pupil. You will want time to think this over. Be sure to let me know if you have any queries. Now, I'll say goodbye.'

'Goodbye.'

I watched him go. I was thankful, in a way, that he didn't stay for the customary cup of tea. The kitchen was in a mess and it would have taken many minutes to get the dirt from under my fingernails. Besides, I needed time, as he had said, to think the situation through. The closing was inevitable, of course, and we must have known, even subconsciously, that it was coming.

To close a school . . . that must be a hard decision to have to make. In the case of Abriachan school there was clearly no alternative. With only two pupils on the roll it was costing as much to educate them as to send a boy to Eton or Harrow, so it was reckoned! But the closing of a school seems almost like sounding the death-knell of a district. A flourishing school brings people flocking in. And the name 'Abriachan', as we will see later, had for years been synonymous with song, with Gaelic music and Gaelic song. That may be only a memory now, but good memories linger. They spread like the ripples on loch water in the wake of a delicate bird, till the singing rises again, in distant places, even on distant shores.

A few years after this the school at Glenconvinth was discontinued also. Some thirty years on there would be close on twenty children of primary school age in this area, a whole schoolful, with more to follow. It could not, of course, really have been foreseen that the place would become a favoured area for commuters, with their own transport, to live and bring up families. So transport was the answer for the few remaining scholars. School buses and mini-buses are everywhere, now. Their use, in some places, means early-morning departures and late home-comings, hard to endure in winter conditions of snow, frost or fog. Some

THE LAST LESSON . . .

THE small country school at Glenconvinth, near Beauly, Inverness-shire,
closes down tomorrow.

The 12 pupils are being transferred to
Tomnacross School, two miles away. And
headmaster Mr. Peter Macaskill (64) is
retiring after 41 years in the Highlands.

He has been in the one-teacher school
for 15 years. Before that he was headmaster at Dalwhinnie and at Northton,
Harris.

"It is a sad moment for me," he said
yesterday, "not only my retirement, but
the closing of the school.

"When I arrived here there were about
60 pupils, but as people moved to the towns
the number of children dwindled."

At the end of lessons tomorrow parents
will climb the steep hill to the tree-
shadowed school to say a thank you and
farewell to the school and the schoolmaster.

The last day of teaching at Clenconvinth School, as described in the local paper. This was Helen's first school and the picture shows her first headmaster, Mr Peter Macaskill

children have home-sickness and bullying to contend with, also. Clearly, as the standard of facilities and equipment deemed essential in schools today is continually rising it would not be possible to bring all the old schools into line, so centralisation has to occur. There is the upkeep of the old buildings to be considered, too, the salaries of teachers, the provision of meals, and so on. Schooling is an essential social service. Yet it is a miss, in a community, not to see, and hear, the small bands of children on their way to and from school. It's a miss for the children, too, not walking the road, with a saunter and a last-minute rush to beat the bell in the morning and a great capering of freedom on the way home.

The girls took the news of their move to a new school quite calmly. The adaptability of the young has always amazed me. I think, as long as they have the security of a stable background, the outside world can wobble as it likes.

SIX

It may have wobbled a little for these two in their first days at this much bigger school, but I think children grow a light covering of protective skin, a sort of bullet-proof vest, strong enough to withstand the impact of any slight shafts that might be coming their way. There was now diversity of lessons and pupils and teachers, which was intriguing but not overwhelming. Everyone made our two from the wilds most welcome. New friendships were formed. One in particular, for Helen, was to be of real and lasting value. There were better facilities for the practice of more formal sporting activities. Hop-scotch and skipping were still enjoyed but now there was really competitive jumping and even hurdling.

In no time at all, it seemed, the famous '11 Plus' was over and a place at the Royal Academy in Inverness assured. This was a school renowned throughout the country. I remembered from my own student days in Edinburgh how highly regarded were the people from Inverness. Kingwall and Kingussie schools also produced students of the highest calibre, many of them coming from the Islands and the far west.

So, after a care-free summer – swimming, camping, reading sprawled on the grass – there was the first day at school number four and another big first – the first day as a weekly boarder at the school hostel in Inverness. This is a situation which many children in the Highlands, and especially the Islands, have to cope with. In some places – Benbecula, for instance, and Castlebay in Barra – big new schools have been built, offering a full secondary education and many community facilities – swimming-pool, library, restaurant and so on. Here the move is less drastic. Children have to board from Monday to Friday, but to come from, say, Eriskay to Benbecula is not too traumatic. Those coming from the small, close-knit communities of the small isles to Dingwall, Inverness, even Kingussie, were often lonely and homesick for quite a time. And there were, of course, the sometimes doubtful distractions of town life for the uninitiated.

We had no car at this time and the daily walk to and from the bus on the main road would have been too much, even in summer. But this further adaptation to living with strangers during the week was accomplished easily enough. We met the bus in late afternoon on Friday and would walk down again on Sunday evening. The new subjects – maths and science – were again intriguing, though a little intimidating. Latin was a bit of a conundrum, with words that seemed to go their own strange ways. As we walked down to the bus in the autumn dusk I would rack my brains to remember case endings and declensions and we'd end up intoning '*rosa, rosa, rosam*' or '*amo, amas, amat*', as the roe-deer barked in greeting and an owl hooted encouragement. The house seemed empty and cheerless during the week, but we filled the days with work and relished the weekends.

I spent a good many hours trying to made a contribution to our supplementary income in the only way I knew – by writing. I had always, since childhood, had paper and pencil handy, for writing a diary, editing a junior magazine and so on. Poems, too, I had secreted at the back of a drawer. Now I settled down to writing about what I knew best – Highland life, Highland history. I had submitted a piece about a Highland Christmas to the BBC people in Aberdeen. To my amazement I got word from them that, as they would like me to read it myself, would I please give them a call on the telephone so that they could judge the suitability of my voice. We had no telephone. I walked down the road to the phone box and dialled the number indicated. Then – what to say? 'Anything at all', someone said at the other end. In a panic, I intoned: 'Mary had a little lamb, Its fleece was . . . '

A giggle came down the line. 'That's fine' the voice said. 'Can you be here at ten o'clock next Tuesday morning?'

'I . . . I think so. Yes. All right.'

'Good. See you then.'

So, somehow, the journey was arranged and accomplished. A lift to the station, train to Aberdeen, an overnight stay at the home of an old student friend and by 10 am the next morning I was in the studio. A warm welcome was reassuring, then came 'rehearsal', watching for the green light in the producer's loft, reading what seemed to sound like sheer nonsense from one's script, fitted in with other much more sensible-sounding items. Then – dispersal, with the injunction to be back in good time for the 'real thing', at 2 o'clock. I wandered the streets, desperately hoping for a huge hole to open, swallow me up and spare me the coming ordeal. But, alas, no cataclysm occurred. On the precise dot the green light came on and I was 'on the air'. After the first moments the panic, mercifully, subsided. I got to the end of my piece.

Then the journey back to normality. On arrival home the family outcry was 'Oh, what a pity . . . you were too nervous . . . you didn't read it!' 'What?' I screamed. 'Of course I read it. What do you mean?'

It transpired that my voice, over the air, had been unrecognisable to my nearest and dearest! The follow-up to the broadcast was quite gratifying. There were letters from Army wives in Germany and one I particularly treasured from Alasdair Alpin MacGregor, of Western Isles fame.

After that I did several short stories and documentaries for schools for the BBC. The stories – 'Morning Stories' – were read from London by James McKechnie. With his Highland background he seemed really to enjoy what he was reading and he made an excellent job of the broadcasts. The producer, James Langham, showed great empathy and this collaboration went on for a number of years. For the documentaries I found another very co-operative producer, Marinell Ash, a history graduate of St Andrews. We worked happily together until her untimely death some years later. I was also contributing short pieces about crofting life to the *Scotsman* publications and a book about our own life on a croft had been accepted by Oliver and Boyd, the highly regarded Edinburgh firm. The stories and the pieces in the old *Weekly Scotsman* brought us letters and pen-friendships from many parts of the world, particularly America and Australia. The feel for the 'old' country dies hard.

This was satisfactory and rewarding but still the gap in income was not really filled. We had to decide, reluctantly, to give up working the croft, to sell the stock and to let the land for grazing. Finally, it was remembered that I had a degree in French, there was a demand for teachers and a Special Recruitment Scheme had been set up to encourage older people to go into teaching. Small grants were available to help with costs. So – Helen went to stay in a school friend's house, Jim found a lodging near his work and I went off to Aberdeen to take a six-month training course in the art and craft of teaching.

I adapted to the life of a 'mature' student more readily than I could have thought possible. After years of working on the croft – harvesting, lambing, butter-making, peat-cutting – it was certainly strange, first of all, just to be sitting down, listening to lectures, reading. The 'Master of Method' was a big, amazing man, a poet, whose endearing Aberdeenshire voice told of his country origins. He made a link with home. Strangely enough, he had read my newly-published book and liked it to the extent that he put ten copies of it into the College library. This gave me a real lift.

My fellow students, mostly just graduated from the University, were inclined not to take the training too seriously. For me it was essential. I had been out of touch for so long with scholastic matters. We had lectures in Method, psychology and some from a medical man who showed us how to recognise symptoms of epilepsy, dyslexia and other conditions. The only thing they couldn't really teach us was how to handle a class of reluctant pupils who were only waiting for the bell to ring. We did go out to schools and got a certain amount of practice, but we knew this was not exactly for 'real'.

My first assignment, after only a few weeks in the College, was to a Primary School. I was lucky to find there an excellent young teacher who made me very welcome and initiated me into the ways of marking the register, learning to fit names to faces, how to spread questions round the class, and so on. My College tutor came to 'hear' my first lesson. There was no French taught, so

I had to take the class in history, on the subject of the battle of Bannockburn. The story of that battle has stayed in my mind ever since! Eventually I was sent to a secondary school and duly took a lesson in French in front of a Chief Inspector who happened to be visiting! By that time I was beginning to feel my way and did not find the occasion as much of an ordeal as I had feared.

I lodged in a small bed-sitting room, in a pleasant house, near the outskirts of the town, with kind and very understanding landladies. Most evenings I spent reading or writing the innumerable set essays, trying to shut out thoughts of life as I knew it. I treasured the regular hospitality of my friend from student days. The weekends, mostly, were the dreariest times. I would walk out into the flat countryside, visualising the hills and the wide sweeps of moorland that formed the usual background to my days. We kept in touch, the three of us, with many letters and phone calls. An occasional celebration brought us together for a Friday to Monday break, when the good ladies of the house provided accommodation. Christmas came and holidays. We opened up the house and had a brief good spell together. After that, with the daylight soon lengthening, time raced ahead. I passed the necessary exams, had an interview with the Director of Education for Inverness-shire, and found I had a job teaching French in the High School of Inverness.

We rented a small flat in the town and put our furniture, books, pictures, all our precious things, in store. Then, one day in late summer, I set off for school. It was a glorious morning. My mind, still on automatic pilot, registered that it would be a great day for ripening the crops. I came back to earth. A great day for marking the register, assembling the class and getting into some sort of a stride. So it went on. I had the good fortune to have a genial and understanding headmaster and a head of department who quickly became a friend. Many people in other departments were most supportive, too.

Looking at the sea of young faces confronting me – in those days we had 40 plus in some classes – I wondered how I would ever get to know even their names, let alone what sort of people they were, how best to approach each one in the learning process. Sometimes I imagined how it must have been in the schoolroom at Abriachan – 70 pupils facing you in tiered rows, all at different stages and many of them still thinking in Gaelic!

Eventually I found it much easier than I would have thought possible to attach names to faces. To fathom what went on in the heads behind the faces was a much more difficult task. Perhaps my biggest problem was learning to cope with a huge class of 'less able' boys who came to my room for 'Bible'. We were all expected to take classes in scripture, though few of us were qualified to do so. Eventually I learned a few tricks and found even the toughest customers quite liked listening to a Bible story, preferably one of the more bloodthirsty ones, and then, perhaps, drawing an illustration to it, in colour. With older boys I sometimes read stories of the missionaries in Africa or China and found they could relate to them. With all the classes I learned many tactics and often found surprising elements of kindly goodwill in the most unlikely sources. Any human predicament, which many of the children probably quite often experienced, always evoked a sympathetic response. Once, for instance, when I had to apologise for not having the homework corrected as my husband had had an accident and had to go into hospital, there were expressions of gloom on the faces and little moans of sympathy. Then, after the interval, the scruffiest little girl in the class slipped a tube of fruit drops on to my table as she passed. What did the correct agreement of the past participle really matter compared to these glimpses of humanity?

It was when starting work with a second year class that I encountered a real problem. We had got past the stage of naming objects, of repeating attractive little phrases, of reading and even writing some simple stories, of singing French folk songs and of learning something about France. Now, with pupils who would be expected to write a fairly well turned-out piece of prose in a couple of years' time, I was up against the fact that the teaching of grammar was fast disappearing from lessons in the English language. I remembered my early days in an old-established

'Grammar' school near Edinburgh, the only secondary school in place. It was so old that the classrooms were tiered and the blackboard stood on an easel. There, in our early teens, we read Virgil and Shakespeare and the *Canterbury Tales* and were introduced to Euclid. 'Grammar', by comparison, was almost a relaxing exercise, like solving a crossword puzzle. I remember analysis and parsing, parts of speech, subordinate clauses, figures of speech with their marvellous names, derivations and so on. We had some wonderful teachers and a lot of fun, addressing each other in Chaucerian English, with much ribald laughter. Now, with my 13-year-olds, the problem was how to explain the notion of tenses, of subject and object, of direct and indirect object, let alone of participles, to young minds devoid of any points of reference. To make the past participle agree with a preceding direct object is imperative when it comes to writing a letter to one's pen-pal with a description of holiday adventures. I didn't dare admit that sometimes the French themselves get this wrong! Slowly, with the discreet application of carrot (or meringue) and stick (very gentle) I would manage to get a few notions of grammar across. Some of the girls actually came to enjoy getting things right. But some boys decided that French was not for them, despite the fact it would come in handy for holidays abroad.

In those early teaching days I would come home at half past four, utterly exhausted, but with some small sense of achievement, and after a short stretch relaxing on the sofa and a family supper, I would tackle correcting a pile of jotters and be ready for next day. At the end of the month that pay cheque was certainly a welcome sight. The money was essential for our daily living. But as time went by the teaching itself, and the learning how to teach, became absorbing and more and more deeply rewarding.

I had been teaching for about a year when the gods flashed a smile at us. We were told that the schoolhouse, attached to the school at Abriachan, was available to rent, as the occupant, a teacher in Inverness, was leaving to take up another post. His wife had worked the Post Office from the front porch. We applied immediately for the tenancy. There was not a great demand for it as to many people Abriachan was a remote, almost inaccessible small spot on the map. For us, it was home. In actual fact, it is only ten miles from Inverness. The access road is steep, but there are several passing places and latterly crash barriers have been erected. It didn't daunt us. We knew it well. The rental of the house was minimal. Jim would do the Post Office.

But – I had to learn to drive. Being over-anxious to succeed, I failed the test several times. Then, at last, I managed to discard the 'L' plates and could sail quite happily up and down the hill, though reversing on the steeper gradients could be quite perilous in times of frost or snow. We had bought a small Austin van with collapsible rear seats. A normal, cushion-seated car was still not quite our style. The van had possibilities for picnicking and camping, as well as for the transport of equipment and goods. It proved all its possibilities over the years, taking us on camping holidays in many parts.

SEVEN

We settled gradually into our new life in the Schoolhouse. Helen was preparing for exams at the Academy, I was acquiring some skill in the art of teaching, Jim was learning to deal with daily customers and the handling of stamps, postal orders, pensions and so on. Learning is a continuous process, we are told, a lifelong process, and so it was proving with us. Teachers of old, we had heard, quite often acted as Postmasters, in return for a small welcome addition to their pay. Deliveries were infrequent, perhaps twice a week in summer, seldom in winter. The bearer would come on foot or on horseback. Some lost their lives in flood or blizzard. In Abriachan, in later days, the steamer brought the mail from Inverness, the postie collecting it at the pier. Many a crofter receiving a letter, perhaps from a relative emigrated to America, would seek the schoolmaster's help in reading it and in composing a reply. This custom prevailed until quite recent times, not so much for the actual reading of the missive and writing the reply, but in the explaining of Government directives and the filling up of forms. This was a task we ourselves were to be glad to perform over the years.

Our first entry into the Schoolhouse, with a large key to the front door, was a memorable occasion. We had long known it from the outside, of course, having passed by many times, walking or on our way to town. It had often seemed to us like a minor mansion, standing in its own grounds, in the shelter of its huge cypresses and pines and hawthorn hedge. There were rhododendrons, too, the hallmark of the Highland estate. Was this really going to be our home? The sitting room faced south, big sash windows looking across grass and hedge to a hillside of heather and scattered trees. The bedroom above was an equally pleasant room. There were two further bedrooms, kitchen, scullery and bathroom. It was a typically Victorian house, with high ceilings, panelled doors each with brass handle and keyed lock, picture rails, moulded skirtings and fireplaces to match. It would have been built soon after the Education Act of 1872.

We visualised the various headmasters who had lived there, and their families. Some were remembered happily, we knew, others with feelings mixed with trepidation or awe. All had left their mark on the community. We were to learn much more about them in later days. For the time being we were spending the Easter holiday getting our furniture out of store, unpacking cherished books and pictures, settling in. It was a real spring. Bulbs were pushing through along the verges – snowdrops, crocuses, daffodils. Soon many self-sown early flowers were to appear. We explored the garden to the back. Here, the plots were largely over-grown. The short-term tenants who had latterly occupied the house had had young families and not the time to tackle the required cultivation. This task would have to wait till we ourselves had the opportunity to get round to it.

Meantime, we had finally and reluctantly decided we would have to sell the croft. A neighbouring crofter had for long been keen to acquire it. He worked it well, bringing in more rough ground, and it is still being worked, for which we are thankful. Our 'croft' now consisted of, perhaps, a quarter of an acre of ground, some of it tidy, some of it a wilderness. The tidy part was the typical Victorian frontage of grass, hedge, laurel, trees and one flower border. The walls of house and school were ivy-covered. The wilderness was at the back. Here, the ground sloped up to the heather-covered moor beyond and had been terraced into plots to be used for teaching gardening. Willowherb had taken over an area at the top, raspberries were growing wild, a few blackcurrant bushes had survived.

We heard stories of one headmaster who would have great fires of brushwood in the garden, to provide fertiliser for the vegetables. We liked this good organic thinking. He had certainly made a start at creating a garden out of a plot of ground and had got 'gardening' firmly on the curriculum. Another headmaster had installed stone drains and another, in later years, took the garden into another league, making a rockery, a herbaceous border, a lawn. This had subsequently to be planted with potatoes in the 'dig for victory' campaign during the Second World War. He also kept goats, chickens and bees and set a great example of self-sufficiency.

One spring, we decided it was time to make a start at bringing the place under control. With the lengthening daylight I would come home as early and as fast as possible so as to get in a couple of hours battling before supper. 'Battling' was really an appropriate verb. As well as the willowherb which was beginning to appear in its first delicate shoots, which look deceptively like asparagus, there were also chunky shoots of what turned out to be sweet cicely. A little of this would be a good thing, I knew, but the quantity of shoots that were appearing was quite overwhelming. I tried in vain to eradicate the roots. They were brown and enormous and seemed to go down to the centre of the earth. The hollow stems made excellent pea-shooters, we were told, and always brought back memories of schooldays to old pupils. I reminded myself that the flowers of this plant could be used as a sweetener when stewing fruit, and the old monks, God rest their souls, would concoct a liqueur from it. I now give a small plant to interested friends, with dire warnings to keep the thing in check.

We hired a rotavator and rough-cleared half of the plots in one day. The rest were to wait another year. Here and there we came on the stone drains that had been so carefully constructed long before the coming of mechanical cultivation. We tried desperately to avoid them and to repair any that had been damaged. We lit huge bonfires of burnable material and piled much debris into what became vast compost heaps. One or two boys in the neighbourhood, keen to earn a little pocket-money, gave a hand on a Saturday. We unearthed small stone paths, where the plots had been terraced. We cleared small rubbish dumps of broken glass and discarded plastic toys.

Against the wall at the top was a large mound covered in nettles, ground elder, thistles, dockens, growth of every kind. Nettles usually mean a dump of non-plastic interest. One day I stuck a spade in. It clashed against some obstruction. Another dig and I unearthed a small pile of old school slates. They must have been abandoned the day the jotters came in! Thereafter my helper and I dug and dug. We found some china inkwells and a cream jar, among many broken pieces of pottery and glass. The pottery fragments themselves, bits of old porridge bowls and plates, are very decorative. I use them to make small mosaic patterns among rock plants or in bowls of bulbs. They are beautifully coloured reminders of the old way of life. We eventually cleared almost the whole dump but found nothing more of real interest. People everywhere, at that time, were laboriously working over old rubbish dumps in the hope of finding treasure. The surrounds of one or two ruined mansions in the neighbourhood seemed promising, but must have been explored long since, for we found nothing but broken wine bottles. Our happiest hunting-ground was a village dump, not far away, where we came on a box of books, a huge earthenware crock and, unbelievably, a silver spoon!

About this time, we got permission from the Education Authority to house the small collection of crofting implements and artefacts we had brought with us in the outside classroom at the top of the playground. We whitewashed the walls and cleaned up the objects for display – the peat-spade, the hay-rake, the pitchfork, the scythe – things we had handled so many times when working the croft and which were rapidly going out of use. There were domestic artefacts to clean, too – a girdle, an iron kettle, a cheese press, a butter churn. We began to make a catalogue of the items, with short notes on their provenance and use. We would welcome anyone who cared to handle and examine them. To some people they were strange, almost unknown objects, to others they brought back memories and engendered fascinating tales of former times. This was our reward – to see the look on the face of the old man as he picked up the peat-spade, put his foot on the bracket and remembered the far-off days of May-time at the peats. There was the granny, too, who brought a grandchild to show her, in clear words, exactly how you made the butter, the cheese, the oatcakes and the scones.

Early days at the Crofting Museum

The school itself, with its three classrooms and small cloakroom at the back, was still unknown territory to us. It had a quite separate front and back door, though it shared a roof with the house. It was being used by the Education Authority as a store to house surplus desks and benches and other school equipment. Occasionally a lorry would arrive to discharge a load or to take one away. The cooker was removed from the outside kitchen, leaving a very derelict small building.

One day in early summer I looked up from weeding the flower border I was making at the front of the house as I heard a strange sound I couldn't easily identify. It stopped. It came again. It was coming from the school, a gentle thudding against the inside of the window. I looked closely. Young starlings were trapped in there, trying desperately to make for the light, the air and freedom. Their parents had nested under the eaves and the young birds must have found their way into the loft and down through a ventilator into the schoolroom. We rang the Authorities asking for someone to open the place so as to release the birds. Next day an official travelled the ten miles, at our request, and thereafter we were given a key to the premises for keeps! We thanked the starlings!

So, at last, we were able to venture in on our own and take a long look at this ancient seat of learning. Its use as a store was to be discontinued, we were told. We were glad of that. It seemed an ignominious use for such a venerable old building.

The 'big' room, where the headmaster taught the senior classes, had originally been bigger than it is today, accommodating over a hundred children. One end had been partitioned off in later years to make a room for juniors, when an extra member of staff was appointed. There was a third room, known as the 'infants'. The big room had been tiered, so that the pupils at the back could see, and be seen by, the teacher. He would stand with his back to the open fire, keeping most of the heat from the children. Those at the top of the room spent many winter days with frozen fingers. There was an open fire in the infants' room, too. Here there would have been less 'talk and chalk', a little more movement allowed and better circulation of warmth! In the partitioned room, the only one used in later days, a stove had been installed, with an iron flue projecting through the wall. The desks used by the last pupils had gone, but the cupboard still held books – readers, history and geography and arithmetic books – and a box full of green and white shorts for wear on Sports Day. These things, evidently, were considered so far out of date as to be worthless. To us, they brought glimpses of the generation of children who had come here, some willingly, some unwillingly, to school.

We went into the big room again. A schoolroom empty of children is indeed a sad place. Looking closely round, we could visualise the rows of faces, the hands shooting up to please the teacher, with tentative proffered answers to his peremptory questioning, the undercover smirking that must have occurred when a harsh teacher was in command and his back was momentarily turned. We could hear the drone of repeated 'tables' and of the long drawn-out spelling of complicated words. The Shorter Catechism, question and answer, would be intoned.

There would be singing, too, and sometimes in Gaelic, with a Gaelic-speaking teacher, and that would have been welcome, though knuckles would have been rapped if anyone hit a wrong note. Tales were often told of the standard of singing in the 1920s which had earned the school a reputation as almost a 'Sang' school, when cups and prizes were won in competitions and at the Mod.

On the wall by the door is a marker-board for recording the children's heights. The little orphans from Glasgow would have had a long way to go till they caught up with the crofters' children. We could see their small, startled faces on their first day in school, when they were weighed and measured and given their new identity.

Outside there are two playgrounds and a shelter divided in two – a girls' and a boys'. This shelter was built in the mid-twenties when the parents of children living two or three miles away petitioned for them to be allowed to use the classroom at dinner-time on stormy days. Many scrawled initials are clearly visible. J. McD. must surely have been a John Macdonald, or a James; D. C. could have been a Duncan Chisholm; D. F. for Donald Fraser . . . ? The girls seem to have been less keen to leave a record of their presence.

Up at the top of the playground is a row of small 'privies', known in the older records as the 'offices', small closets with slats in the doors. Town children who see them today are scared to use them in case someone peers in! In their day they were a great advance on the old pail and spade!

I have the great good fortune to have as a neighbour a former pupil whose schooldays began in 1913. He remembers them well, happy times with a patient lady in the Infants' Room, times of trepidation in the 'big' room, where discipline had to be strict when 70 or more children, seated in 'galleries', as the tiered benches were known, had to be taught by the one teacher. The headmaster at that time was the first non-Gaelic speaker to be appointed. There were good times working the garden, good games of shinty and football in the playground or in the field

*An ex-pupil of the 'new' school (in 1913-18) standing by the
remains of the 'old', Mr Lachlan's, school*

over the road. And there were the holidays, with swimming in
the loch in summer, and ferreting and going down to the pier
to meet the steamer. In winter there was sledging, very precariously, on sheets of corrugated iron.

My neighbour's mother was among the early intake of pupils
into this new post-1872 school and had happy memories of her
days with a Highland master. She emerged as one of the few who
could read and write Gaelic, as well as use it in daily conversation. She also wrote verse, in the bardic tradition.

His father had been a pupil in the last days of the 'old' school,
with a schoolmaster whose Gaelic was more fluent than his English. Both these Highland schoolmasters are remembered with
affection. Sadly, my neighbour and his brothers and sisters were
not encouraged to use their native tongue. English was needed in

the wider world where job prospects were better. But the words of the old songs and the place-names of fields and hills and lochs are firmly rooted in their memories. Their great-uncle, who was descended from Helen McLachlan, daughter of an eighteenth-century schoolmaster, was known as the 'Bard', his poetic gift no doubt bequeathed by 'Mr Lachlan'.

As time went by we found ourselves wandering often into the school, admiring the workmanship of the building, the great blocks of red sandstone, the lofty ceilings, the window built high up the walls so that young minds were not distracted by the sight of the outside world. The sandstone for the window surrounds was brought from a quarry down by Loch Ness. The walls are of local whinstone and granite, as so many of the houses are, built by masons who could hew and shape the stone as well as build it. The roof timbers would have been supplied by the estate and the slates would have come from Ballachulish. In the plans it is described as a 'school for 100 pupils'. It became almost as much part of our lives as the adjoining house we lived in.

EIGHT

Abriachan is a surprising place. Less than ten miles after leaving Inverness, on a good tarmac road to the west, you turn off, rise quickly to 800 feet or so and are in a country of old croft land, heather and pine. Most of the heather has now been covered in rows of planted conifer, but those years ago, when the moors stretched for miles, it was the sweeps of heather which brought us a most interesting and inspiring summer.

One lovely morning a young man called Peter Watkins came to the door to tell us he was about to make a film of the battle of Culloden. 'Come in!' we said, opening the door wide in welcome. This sounded like something after our own hearts. He went on to explain that the actual site of the battle was not suitable for filming as trees had largely taken over the ground. (It has since been de-forested and restored to its former state.) He had got permission from the landowner to film on the Abriachan moors and the Education Authority had authorised the use of the old school as a base. He spoke with great clarity and enthusiasm and had obviously done much serious research. We assured him of our whole-hearted support.

Next day we stood wide-eyed on the doorstep to watch the arrival of actors and crew. They were to come out in buses, on a daily basis, already rigged out as Highlanders or Redcoats, to the delight and amazement of passing motorists and walkers. Rations were provided by a restaurant in Inverness. Cameras, microphones, all the filming gear and huge baskets of props were unloaded into the schoolroom, a cannon was parked in the playground shelter. Ponies from a nearby riding school had been hired. A band of 'extras', mostly young men from Inverness, was despatched up the hill to build the famous dry-stane dyke, which figured largely in the battle. This wall was to stand for many years, providing welcome shelter for sheep!

Then, it came time for the battle to start. One morning I went up to the moor. A group of young Highlanders was standing at the ready, broadswords swirling, targes held firm, obviously desperate to have a go at the line of Redcoats in the distance, well marshalled and equipped, standing in an orderly squad. Peter shouted 'Hold on! Remember you're dead beat. You've done a long march and had no sleep. You're starving. You've had no food for days. Some of you aren't sure what all this is about. I want to see all that in your faces. In the way you move. Right?'

Gradually Peter got across to the people in the film the reality of what they had to portray. They had to learn something of the background and the intricacies of the situation. There were split loyalties among the clans, jealousies and disagreements between the commanders of the Highland forces, the Prince obstinately refusing to allow his most able general, Lord George Murray, to make the most important decisions on the course of the fighting. The stark fact was that defeat for the Highland force was inevitable since the Government army consisted of 9,000 fighting men, well equipped and provisioned, with adequate cavalry and cannon, while the Highlanders numbered 5,000, all desperately ill-prepared and obliged to operate on ground unsuited to their traditional way of fighting.

We went up to watch the encounters on the moor, marvelling at the skill of the cameraman as no one was injured in the bursts of violent activity he had to capture on film. One day, in late afternoon, a dishevelled Redcoat appeared at the door, in a state of near collapse. We took him in, slipped off his tunic, administered a wee dram, then a cup of hot tea and some oatcake. 'Thanks' he murmured, smiling apologetically. 'Sorry about this. I died three times up there in the rain before I got it right.' We laughed. Peter was concerned. But there had to be perfection. That was the making of the film.

With the fighting ended we glimpsed the Prince, weary and unkempt, leaving the battlefield and the dead, making for the hills, followed by a few exhausted Highlanders. This is, I think, a fair picture of the man. He had shown courage when things were going his way, but vanity and obstinacy betrayed him in times of stress.

This film is a documentary, a film for our time. In the aftermath of the battle we find the real meaning of the whole suppression of the Jacobite cause. After two weeks filming on the moor, scenes were shot in the old streets of Inverness and in the dungeons of Fort George, showing the atrocious treatment of prisoners. Then, in the hills of Glencoe, the continuing barbarity of pillage, rape, the burning of houses, the butchering of whole families, the whole desperate effort to wipe out an ancient race, was portrayed. The aftermath was eventually to include the banning of traditional garb, the kilt, the tartan, the playing of the pipes, the carrying of weapons. Today we call this ethnic cleansing.

All this comes out in the film. Made on the tightest of budgets, with integrity, energy and imagination backed by careful research, as an indictment of war and barbarity it is superb.

As I write, this year, I have had the great pleasure of attending a reunion of people involved in the making of this great film. Thirty years on, Peter Watkins has still the look of youth which I remember. The cameraman is as active as ever. We watched a screening of the film, spell-bound. Then we talked and talked. Next day they came out to Abriachan, walked the battlefield and went into the old schoolroom. At once, more memories came back. 'That was where I changed my boots', 'The tea-urn steamed over there', 'Mmm . . . I remember . . . '

I hope this film will be seen and seen again. Will we ever learn? A showing once a year might help.

Our next encounter with film-makers was a few summers later when a truck-load of young students from a London Film School drew up in the playground. They had heard about the museum collection from a colleague in Inverness and wanted to borrow some items for a film they were making about the 'Seven Men of Glenmoriston' who hid the Prince, after Culloden, in a cave in the wilds of Glenmoriston. Though suffering great hardship and with their lives at risk, they steadfastly refused to accept the price that was on the royal head. Strangely enough, as we told the students, a descendent of one of the 'Men' had lived at one time in Abriachan.

We lent them a creel, a whisky jar, some items of clothing and wished them well. Our two granddaughters, then small girls, on holiday here at the time, were invited to take part in the film as extras. After a long day they came home, with blackened faces, exhausted and not too thrilled with film-making! The museum items were eventually returned, a little the worse for wear, and we never heard what success the film achieved.

On another summer day, of the wet and windy kind, I looked up from some indoor chores to find a young woman nearing the door.

'We're making a film. We'd like some shots of open moor ground. We thought there would be some here. Could you tell us where we might go? Perhaps . . . some open moor and . . . some rough stone walling . . . '

'Yes. I think you could find that. Perhaps further up the road. I could show you . . . '

'Thanks. We're just going to have lunch. Then we'll follow your guidance.'

'Right.'

I went with her to the gate. A small fleet of vehicles was parked along the verge, among them a snack-bar. People of all shapes and ages, dressed in '20s country-worker style, were queuing for soup and pies. They were windblown and wet. I opened up the school to let them eat in comfort. They were making a film based on a story by Jessie Kesson.

'She lived here for a while, as a young girl. A few old people remember her. There's the house . . . up on the hill.'

They were interested, but busy eating and discussing film technique. I gave them directions to the moor ground and waved them off. Some years later I saw two or three seconds' worth of the moor ground in the film *Another Time, Another Place*, which won great acclaim.

Looking back on these encounters I think we must have been, unwittingly, pioneering the current trend of locating films in the Highland area. None of the recent ones have come up to the standard set by our early ones here!

As word got round that the school premises here were available to accommodate groups such as our film-makers on a daily basis, particularly during the summer holiday period, contact was made by the Inverness Art Society. They came out on several occasions over the years and were always gladly welcomed. There was something here, they found, to catch the eye of every kind of artist – croft houses, the Mill, ruins, hills, trees, burns, loch water. They would spread out over a wide area and could work all day undisturbed. Some would come back the following day to finish off drawings or paintings. If the weather broke they could find shelter in the big schoolroom. A picnic lunch could be taken by the fire. Many were intrigued by the feel of the old place, the aura of the drama of school life which had been played out there – the rewards and punishments, the bickerings and laughter, summer sun streaming through the big windows on the south side, winter storms raging outside to the north. Some people would make sketches of the old furniture in the room. One architect member did a most remarkable study of the less conspicuous back part of the building. To my great joy, one summer I found a picture called 'Mrs Stewart's Garden' in the Society's annual exhibition.

NINE

Over the next few years we had little time to work on things about the house. We didn't want to make many changes, anyway. We preferred to look and listen, to make the place speak out on its own. It rapidly began to make itself heard. Its Victorian aura was everywhere – in the high-mantled fireplaces in every room, in the low-slung, back-breaking sink with its brass taps in the scullery, in the porch with its double outer door, and inner door with panelled glass. Here and there were signs of former tenants of modern times – the red-painted floor boards in the kitchen, the draught excluders round door-jambs and window-frames. We had long learned to live with draughts. Sometimes we felt an old Victorian draught-screen would have been an asset, when sitting in the Victorian-style room of an evening in winter. In the bedroom we mostly favoured the fresh cool air on the brow, as long as the covers didn't slip off the bed. By day we wore several layers of wool, as we had done in our croft house. This way we managed to avoid most of the colds which seemed to afflict friends from town who came to visit. Their homes, of course, were so well insulated and double-glazed that they expected to live in shirt-sleeves indoors. Somehow or other we kept the frost away, with old-fashioned methods – bales of straw at the water inlet and outlet, small lamps at vulnerable places inside. Old nylons, we found, made good insulation for pipes at risk. When time allowed, we papered one bedroom afresh, and touched up the paintwork in the kitchen and scullery.

As each spring came round it was the garden that absorbed our energies. Every year we came on something new – little clusters of snowdrops emerging from under piles of leaves, woodruff carpeting the ground beneath the huge birches, a rock garden almost completely overgrown with bishop weed and couch grass. Each discovery was hailed with jubilation. We knew the work would be endless, but that didn't matter, for each bit accomplished was a satisfaction in itself. As a plot was cleared in the shelter of the west wall, friends with established gardens would give us great clumps of perennials – lupins, blue geranium, marguerites, lysimachia, scarlet poppies and my all-time favourite – pink astrantia. We constructed a makeshift cold frame out of old windows we found on a scrap-heap and grew wallflower, sweet william, marigolds, all the old-fashioned flowers, from seed. Meantime, tatties, onions, roots and salad crops were flourishing in some well-manured plots of their own.

I had been teaching in Inverness for several years when it was decided that the High School should have an Outdoor Centre. Many schools in the area were establishing such centres. And where better to set one up than in the old school at Abriachan? On first hearing the news we were slightly perturbed. Would the peace and quiet we prized so highly be shattered by the shouting and skirmishing of hordes of the young let loose from the bonds of the classroom? We dwelt on the prospect at length, as we singled the carrots and staked the peas up at the top of the garden. The apples would go, that was one sure thing. The branches of the old tree overhung the playground. Its fruit had always disappeared in days gone by. The children would grab the apples long before they were ripe and discard most of them, half eaten, along the roadside. After a while we began to think, well, it would be good to have the children about the place again. It had been built for such as them. There was plenty of space in the old playground and there were the hills . . .

That first summer small groups came out in the mini-bus. An art class would spend a day sketching. A gym class would go orienteering. Then the woodwork class got busy making bunk-beds so that people could stay overnight or for a weekend. The accommodation was primitive – cold water in the cloakroom, outside loos, cooking on Calor gas in the 'Home Economics' room. The hill country, with its remaining croft lands, was a revelation to many of the children. Living only ten miles away, in the small town of Inverness, many of them had never ventured further than the local football ground or the canal banks.

Some of them were apprehensive at first, as the orphans from Glasgow often were, looking at the vast spaces of hill and sky around them, afraid of getting lost, of a wild fox leaping from the gloom of the trees, even of ants and spiders in the heather. Going to the outside loos after dusk was a dreaded venture. More than once a small boy crashed from his top bunk on to the hard wooden floor. But after several outings fears generally subsided and the days spent in the hills were relished. To come on a young roe-deer, a tiny calf, almost hidden in the bracken or heather and to be told 'Don't touch her. Her mother will be back. She won't like the smell of human hands on her calf' – this was learning in a real sense, learning at first hand how animals live, how they respond to humans, how to respect them, not look on them as prey. Then there was the day the boys out orienteering almost stumbled on a nest of young hen-harriers and had to dodge the irate mother's beak. And the time they stood to watch blackcock 'on the lek' and the unbelievably fierce battle the birds engaged in when the females arrived. To this day men and women appear in the playground or come to the door, their families in tow, recounting to their children the exploits of their youth.

About the time the Field Centre was set up all secondary schools in the Highlands were notified of a scheme sponsored by the Crofters' Commission, the Civic Trust and the Education Department whereby pupils might 'initiate and carry out projects for the improvement of the appearance of a village' in their area. The scheme was to be completed by 1970, which was to be European Conservation Year. The High School submitted a plan for a project in the area of Abriachan. Villages are not the norm in crofting places. This was evidently understood and the plan was approved. It consisted of four parts – the tidying up of the old burial ground of Kilianan, at the foot of the hill, the cleaning, repairing and painting of the Community Hall, which had been unused for a considerable time, the reconditioning of a former croft house up the road, at Druim, and the establishing of a small croft museum. Trees and flowers were to be planted

Planting trees at the Hall

at the three sites. A small sum of money was to be granted by a Highland landowner to finance the plan.

Two years of steady work lay ahead if all this was to be accomplished in time. A start was made in the autumn – the cutting of weeds, repairing of fences and so on. Then, with the spring, parties of volunteers began coming out at weekends. A woodwork class would stay for a week, or longer, getting practical experience of renewing joists and rafters as they laboured at the croft house. A science class would botanise as they identified flowers and herbs that used to grow there. One day, working at the plot, I heard a voice at my shoulder. I looked up. A big, tough-looking lad was standing there.

'What's that plant you're putting in? I've seen my gran put it in the soup.'

'That's parsley.'

'Parsley? And you get it here?'

'You do.'

He was genuinely interested and amazed and didn't have the growing of drugs in mind, only what went into his gran's soup!

Work at the Hall involved parties of girls in doing a thorough cleaning. The dust of years lay everywhere. The windows were encrusted with dirt. In a cupboard ancient encyclopaedias and other books were testimony to the efforts of bygone teachers to provide some sort of 'further education' for interested people. Under the stage was packed away some of the equipment for badminton and other indoor games. There was an ancient piano, complete with candle-holders, and old paraffin heater and a tea-urn. The Hall had been built by public subscription in the early 1930s. Much hard work was put in on a voluntary basis – the digging of foundations, the erecting of walls and roof – by people in their spare time. It was to be used for social gatherings and also for religious meetings. There was some heated objection to this combined usage by those who thought that no minister should preach in a building which was also used for secular amusement, in particular card-playing. The custom of gambling at cards was still regarded as pernicious, for much ruin had been brought on families over this in the past. However, things settled down eventually, draughts, chess and badminton were played with relish and many concerts and dances enjoyed.

The Second World War brought changes, as it did in most parts. The black-out, the scarcity of heating oil, the absence of many in the Forces, all these things and other factors meant less and less use of the Hall. The Home Guard met there from time to time. There would be an occasional whist drive in an effort to raise funds. The minister would take a Sunday service in summer. But gradually, when most of the trustees died and after the school closed, the Hall became disused. It was good to see it coming back, now, to some sort of life. Woodwork teachers supervised senior boys in the replacing of some roof tiles, the clearing of rhones and down-pipes. Outside painting and the repairing of the door was done when weather permitted. The tumble-down fence round the building was replaced, a job at which the country boys excelled. At one time the surrounds had been used as a 'fank' to house tups awaiting release among the ewes! Gean, rowan, sloe and broom were planted there, in the well-manured ground. A few enthusiasts tried their hand at dry-stane dyking in a effort to repair the wall along the roadside.

It was a happy time. New and different relationships between teachers and pupils, and between the pupils themselves, were established as they worked together, on thought-provoking, yet practical tasks. There was time to talk, to laugh, to be amazed. The realities of country living in older times were a source of endless fascination to the town children. The girls couldn't believe that water had to be fetched from the well before you could fill the kettle, and that a fire had to be lit before it would boil. Also, that your hands came quite clean washed in cold water and a rub with docken leaves took the sting out of a nettle bite! The discoveries were endless.

We came to realise more and more clearly that this was education in a very real sense. Working as a team, each member contributing a portion of the effort, with no time for slacking, seemed to bring out unrealised potential. The 'maths genius' could measure and calculate and work out the number of tiles needed to repair the roof, but equally important was the effort of the 'less able' boy who climbed the ladder and sat fearlessly astride the apex to fix them.

Today we speak of 'work experience' and 'job satisfaction'. In their time here the pupils got a taste of both. To work with no financial incentive, no pay-packet in view, but the sense of achievement as they stood back to look at the mended roof, the fresh-painted walls, the planted garden plot, this seemed to fill a gap in their lives. They seemed to grow with the job, finding a surprising value in themselves, building a fresh identity. For the over-nighters there was a further sense of community, as they gathered round the fire in the old schoolroom after tea, comparing notes on jobs, laughing about mistakes, bantering, attending to cuts and bruises, planning next day's work.

'The stairway up at the croft house . . . '

'Yon's no' a stairway. Yon's a ladder!'

'That's what you'd think. But it was used. The kids slept up there, in the loft. Bob broke two steps and . . . '

'No wonder wi' his big feet.'

'Well, we'll need to replace it in the morning. There's work to do up there.'

'Right.'

The croft house had, unbelievably, been used to house hens in deep litter by people running a poultry farm at Leault, the old school croft. We knew this, but until we opened the door and went inside we had little realisation of what it actually entailed. There were two rooms on the ground floor, the 'kitchen' and the 'room', with a small bedroom off the kitchen. Above, there were two rooms with skylights, in the loft. Every inch of floor-space throughout the house was deep in litter – of sawdust, chopped straw, paper and, of course, droppings. This was grand manure for the garden, but the barrowing . . . ! And for years small shovelfuls of litter would fall from behind the upper floor-boards, from under window ledges and other hidden spots.

By the end of the first year's work, with some week-long stays and week-end shifts, things began to take shape. As the momentum increased people were quite happy to come out on a Saturday, when transport could be arranged. The girls would marvel at the amount of sheer hard work their grandmothers must have put in to keep a shine on their pots and to clean their wooden milk churns when water had to be carried from the well and boiled on the fire. As for trampling blankets in a huge tub, well . . . they reckoned that might be quite pleasant on a good summer day!

At last, with new joists and floorboards, fireplaces renovated and curtains at the windows, the croft house was ready to be furnished. We had gathered odds and ends from every available

Early days working at Druim Croft

source – a table and chairs found abandoned in an old house on ground taken over for forestry, a dresser dumped as being too old-fashioned when shiny plastic came in, a cradle that had been used as a nesting-box when the place had housed hens. Then our own growing collection of plenishings was moved in. It was good to see it in the setting it was made for – the girdle and the kettle by the kitchen fire, the cheese-press and the butter-churn in the cool of the 'room', a Gaelic Bible on the dresser. The peat-spade, the scythe, the pitch-fork and the hay-rake found a place in the steading.

As time went by other items were found, some on dumps, some discarded in overgrown fields. Once we had to check an enthusiastic boy who brought in a scuffler from a nearby croft, an implement which might still have been in use! During the long holidays we would go far afield in the old van collecting what was deemed 'rubbish' by many. A nettle patch by a ruined house was always an area worth searching. If girdles, kettles, iron pots, smoothing irons had been thrown among the nettles, which thrived on them, we reckoned they could be retrieved from their ultimate fate of oblivion, and no harm done. To remove anything found in the vicinity of a living place we always asked permission. Almost invariably it was a case of 'good riddance' or 'glad to get it out of the road'. I remembered from our days on the croft how neighbours were happy to discard work tools when new ones, involving less labour, became available. Heavy iron pots and kettles were replaced by light enamel or aluminium pans. Nothing could really replace the girdle, but plastic eventually did away with cumbersome pails. In the fields new ways of harvesting were introduced. All the labour of the travelling mill and the building of stacks vanished. Only in the smallest places where the huge machinery could not operate did the old methods survive, with the use of scythes to cut the edges, of hay-rakes and pitch-forks as the stacks were built. So it was that many of these old muscle-building tools were discarded and came our way, and we managed to give them some sort of new life as their uses were explained and demonstrated to interested people.

It soon became apparent that in this small house and steading we were going to run out of space to accommodate the growing collection. The Community Hall was now tidied up. In fact, standing there by the roadside, neatly fenced, with the surrounds planted, it looked like the asset it was always meant to be. It was not actually in demand by the community, whose interests lay mainly outwith the area, since communication had become so much easier with access by car to other parts. We approached the one remaining trustee of the hall for permission to house in it the overflow of interesting objects, with historical documents relating to the area, photographs and so on, on the understanding that everything would be removed should people wish the place to revert to its original purpose. This was agreed. A busy programme of preparation then began. Pots were freshly blackleaded, cheese-presses scoured, chairs polished, tools oiled. Photographs were arranged in albums and a label made for every item, with fine lettering produced by the High School's art department. A card index was started to take over the information from the original catalogue. These activities involved many people and increased interest in the project as a whole. The history and geography people began to wonder what they could contribute. A map was made showing walks to places of interest, including sites of prehistoric settlements. The science department sent some seniors out to look at the life of the loch. There were water-birds of many kinds, different species coming and going at different times of year, trout and many smaller fry. Botanists studied the special flora of the area, thrilled to find orchids, sundew and butterwort, lovely flowers growing even in the school playground.

Meantime, work at the old graveyard at Kilianan had been going on quite steadily. Weeds had been dug out and overgrown bushes cut back. We planted a gean, a willow, a laburnum and many daffodils. Snowdrops, primroses and wild hyacinths were there already. There are several inscribed headstones with quite recent dates and many blocks of granite marking the resting-places of the unnamed. One day, a great discovery was made. The clearing-up in a small railed-off enclosure revealed an ancient carved grave-slab. There is a rosette at the head and at the foot a shears. The shears are said to represent the burial-place of a woman. Local tradition has it that this stone marks the grave of a 'Norwegian Princess'. Could she have been a descendant of the Norse people who farmed in nearby Glen Urquhart? According to legend she was beloved by the native families. This would seem to bear out the belief that many Viking invaders eventually settled down peaceably and adopted the Christian faith. The grave is recorded in the annals of the Society of Antiquaries. The moss had covered it.

This burial ground was part of a settlement of the early Celtic church, probably founded by followers of Columba after his journey up the Great Glen, from Iona to Inverness, to confront King Brude in the sixth century. The first attempts at schooling would have been made here. The monks would have taught some likely boys to read and write, to measure and weigh, the first elements of metal and stone-work, probably some Latin and a little

Greek, so that they could follow acts of worship and praise, as well as the craft of growing plants for food and healing. In later years ambitious boys would attend the school run by the monks at Beauly Priory, some ten miles away. Education, sometimes known as the 'handmaid of religion', was to remain under the aegis of the church for many centuries.

TEN

When the two years for work on the project were nearly up excitement grew as the 'Day of Judgement' approached. There was a final skirmish of tidying-up, litter was cleared from roadside lay-bys. It was hoped the project really had 'improved the appearance' of the area. Certainly, a derelict croft house, latterly used to accommodate hens, had been restored to something of its former dignity, the Community Hall had been repaired as far as funds would allow, the old graveyard had been cleared and planted, a collection of artefacts and documents relating to the district had been put on display. The adjudicators arrived on a beautiful morning in June. The Crofters Commission, the Scottish Civic Trust and the Education Department were all represented. The headmaster of the High School, several members of staff, the ever-helpful janitor and many of the pupils were there, too, to act as guides at the various sites.

It was a day to lift the heart – a turquoise sky, the birches in fresh leaf, larks rising and falling in ecstatic song. Our visitors must have been glad to leave their desks and paper-work behind and to feel the reality of this hill-land. So many had come to love it as they worked and walked about and looked at things with new sight. Something of its spirit had rubbed off on them, I think. It showed in the quiet, bright smiles, in the quick response to questioning, the touch of pride when comments of praise were made.

When everything had been inspected our visitors were entertained to tea and scones in the outside classroom, now known as the canteen. There was good talk and much laughter as we told the story of our two years' work – how some of the boys had made firm resolves to become joiners or stone-masons or even gardeners, girls had ideas about museum work or even of marrying a crofter! Few had found it hard or boring. There were no speeches made and the project was duly awarded an inscribed plaque.

In the croft house at Druim

After the goodbyes, when our visitors had set off for Inverness, Edinburgh or beyond and their congratulations were ringing in our ears, we three – the heads of geography and building and myself – who had been largely responsible for organising the project, sat down to consider the situation. We knew this was not the end, but only the beginning of the planned operation. We had created something which would have to be maintained, developed, allowed to grow.

Meantime, our thoughts went, as they often did, to the people whose families had lived and worked here for generations and of whom so few remained *in situ*. Many were scattered in far-off places, but some were probably within reach. Would it be possible, we wondered, to have a reunion? We put a notice in the Inverness paper. Transport could be arranged for a ceilidh in the old school on an evening in September. Come early and stay late, we said. The news spread like wildfire, a happy version of the Fiery Cross! So, on a glorious autumn afternoon, they came, from Perthshire, from England, from Dundee, from the West, as well as from Inverness. We met at the school, then, before the afternoon faded, we made our way up to the croft house at Druim. Not for years had we seen so many walking the road and talking and talking! Some smiles were a little sad, most were wide and happy as the women gathered round the open fire, picking up the huge black kettle, the girdle, the old iron pot and reminiscing about the food they got in their youth. The men were examining the implements in the steading – the ploughs and harrows, scythes and pitch-forks and peat-spades – and remembering the hard labour that had given them mighty appetites and muscles of iron.

The collection in the Hall intrigued them all, too, There, they could see photographs of themselves in school groups. There was much eager identifying of friends and erstwhile enemies. The teachers came in for some caustic comments, though many were remembered happily and there was laughter all round as anecdotes were recounted and happenings recalled. Memories were astonishingly clear. Schooldays must have been tolerable when the thought of them had not been banished from these minds. Then it was into the old schoolroom and more memories evoked. One woman drew a deep breath as she came through the door.

'Ah . . . ' she said, with a smile in her half-closed eyes, 'that's it! It's that smell I remember – the old damp woodwork and the smoke from the fire. That's school on a winter day. We were glad to get in, out of the cold, though the teacher might be glaring at our muddy boots. We didn't care. We'd take what came. We were part of the crowd. It was great!'

So many had come to the reunion that there was no room for a sit-down supper at tables. People were too busy talking, anyway, and happy to be moving about. Soup was taken on the hoof, with sandwiches, sausage-rolls and cakes, baked in the High School kitchen. This was a ceilidh in the real sense of the word, a meeting of folk to exchange news and views and then, when the spirit took them, to sing a song from the heart, to play a tune for the tapping of feet and the forgetting of all worry and care. We made up the fire, somehow we got everyone seated, on chairs, benches or footstools, and a hush came as a woman's voice rose softly. The Gaelic words were strange to some, but many remembered and the chorus was joined with growing confidence and pleasure. Then it was song after song, a spontaneous succession of songs, some sad, some funny, in Gaelic and English and even in Scots. We had a piper, too, and a fiddler and a man to tell tall tales. At last, as some had long journeys to go, there had to be farewells. But first, somehow, a space was cleared and an eightsome danced with all the verve of long-ago schooldays. We joined hands to sing 'Auld Lang Syne'. We couldn't believe this was an ending. Already, on the doorstep, there was talk of the next time.

ELEVEN

In 1971, a year after the completion of the Highland Village Project, the scheme went into a second phase, 'Highland Village 1973', initiated by the Crofters Commission, to be financed by the Highlands and Islands Development Board and the Countryside Commission. This led to the development of parts of the original project – electrical installations for lighting at the croft house and the further planting of the garden there and the publication of a small booklet on the area, with illustrations by pupils of Inverness High School Art Department. The preparation of the booklet involved a fair amount of research into the history of the district. We were lucky enough to have friends whose families came from Abriachan and were only too willing to give us any information they had. The few remaining native inhabitants had for long been telling us of happenings and beliefs, signs and wonders that made the place come as intensely alive for us as it had for them. The transactions of the Gaelic Society of Inverness and of the Inverness Field Club supplied us with the facts of history and of science.

Originally, to primitive people, a site in bare uplands, about 800 feet above sea level, would have been an attractive place to settle. No dense forests meant no hiding place for fierce beasts. Birch, alder, gean, rowan and scrub grew in sheltered hollows to provide timber and firing. Game, berries and nuts were in abundance. In the nearby loch were fish and waterfowl for the taking. Life could have been quite pleasant. Enemies would have been spotted from afar and warned off promptly.

As time went by these early settlers gradually ceased to depend entirely on hunting and gathering for sustenance and began to cultivate small patches of cleared ground. Signs of this activity can be seen in several places today. Probably a primitive form of barley would have been grown, to provide meal. In the early part of the Christian era news of the teaching of the monks at

Kilianan would doubtless have reached the uplands. The arts of husbandry would be learnt and practised, with much benefit to the community.

The first mention of Abriachan in written history occurs about the beginning of the thirteenth century, when it is described as being in the possession of the Byssets of Lovat. These Byssets, great benefactors of the church, founded Beauly Priory. The power of the church grew steadily and among the lands gifted to it at about this time was the Barony of Kinmylies – 'including Easter and Wester Abriachan'. In 1334 John, Bishop of Moray, gave to Sir Robert Lauder, Governor of Urquhart Castle – 'for his manifold services to our said church' – 'a half davoch of land at Abriachy' upon payment of an annual feu of '4 merks sterling'. Sir Robert's successors resigned the lands and they were then granted to Alexander, brother of King Robert III, known as the 'Wolf of Badenoch', on 3rd February 1386. We have often wondered if the 'Wolf' roamed about the hills here and whether he pillaged the remains of the little settlement at Kilianan. By 1451 the lands had been returned to the church. Then, in 1544, Bishop Hepburn granted a charter to Hugh Fraser, Lord Lovat. A hundred years later they were sold to Colonel Hugh Fraser of Kinnaries, whose son resold them to Ludovic Grant. In 1704 they were put under wadset (mortgage) for 10,000 merks to James and Alexander of Reelig, who conveyed the wadset in 1730 to Evan Baillie of Dochfour, a great friend of Lovat of the '45. This wadset was redeemed by Sir J. Grant, and Abriachan became part of the Seafield Estates. In 1946 it was split up and sold to tenants and others.

This is the story of buying and selling recorded in the musty old charters. The lives of the people went on year in, year out, no matter to whom they owed allegiance or paid rent. They had to fight for survival against the forces of nature, against invaders in the Wars of Independence, in their allegiance to their chiefs in inter-clan battles, in the harrying after Culloden. The two great civilising factors in their lives were their attachment to the church, from its beginnings at Kilianan, and, later, their belief in the value of education.

Records show that, in 1589, Maclellans and Mackillroys were the dominant people. These names, however, died out later when Frasers, Macdonalds, Grants, Chisholms, Mackenzies and Macleans became the most numerous families. Some of the Macdonalds are said to be descendants of those who sought refuge in the fastnesses of Abriachan after the massacre of Glencoe. Abiding by the old Highland custom of hospitality, the people seldom denied welcome to the landless and the outcast which the old feuding clan system threw up. Abriachan had always been looked upon as a sanctuary. After the massacre of Culloden it is likely that Government troops carried out atrocities in the area, as they did much harrying in the Great Glen. Tradition has it that one part – Corryfoyness, where there was a settlement of five families – escaped the pillage. It was, and still is, comparatively inaccessible. The going would have tried those men in their cumbersome uniforms, carrying their cumbersome guns.

Today, even Frasers and Macdonalds are few and far between. But the sanctuary element remains, as incomers from many parts seek to establish roots in the quiet of hill and moor and native wood.

Abriachan had always been a self-contained community. Its geographical position, above the fault known as the Great Glen, on a green shelf smoothed out as the ice slid down, gives it a certain inaccessibility. The people had, perforce, to become skilled in the arts and crafts of daily living. The skills of the chase came instinctively and there was plenty of prey. Materials for the building of small houses were to hand – granite and whinstone for walls, timber and heather thatch for roofing. In later years many young men developed their skills in building while waiting to inherit the family croft. In this way the community was blessed with many full-fledged craftsmen – joiners and especially masons, as the abundance of superb stone inspired their work. There were shoe-makers, too, working in hide, and tailors. Tailoring would have developed, naturally enough, from the craft of weaving. Women, also, were skilled weavers and spinners. Blacksmiths plied their trade. Young women often went to the harvesting on big farms in the south and men to the shepherding, to earn something of a wage. And, of course, there was always sale for a drop or two from the hidden 'still'.

Wedding gatherings were held in the garnished barn, with a white flag flying from the house chimney. Funerals, too, were conducted in the house of the bereaved family and were occasions of companionship in sorrow, the coffin carried on friendly shoulders to the burial ground. The young found ways of enjoying time out of school after work. In summer there was dancing at the crossroads by the bridge, with music on the mouth-organ or the 'box', and fishing in the small lochs hidden high in the hills, and swimming. Winter was for shinty to get the circulation going and ceilidhs in the long evenings. There was plenty to do within the bounds of home.

There was no church after the decay of the early chapel at Kilianan, but there was always a prayer meeting on Sundays, either in the school or out-of-doors. At one time, in the 1920s, Evangelists would put up a marquee on a piece of spare ground, hold services and visit houses.

The corn-mill was often a centre of activity, with comings of loads of oats and goings of freshly-ground meal. Sometimes volunteers were needed to turn the water on or off at the sluice up at the loch.

Until comparatively recently the community had all the familiars of so many places in the Highlands, first and foremost a bard. He was Thomas Macdonald (1822-86), son of John Macdonald and Helen Maclachlan, daughter of an early schoolmaster. He composed many poems and songs, some in a sarcastic vein, which he may have learnt from his father-in-law, who often used satire as a way of upbraiding people for wrongdoings. He also wrote, in the old bardic way, praise poems for people deemed worthy of praise – one for Major Grant of the local laird's family and one for Baillie W. G. Stuart. A song in praise of Glen Urquhart has also survived, but poems of his are difficult to find, as, on his death-bed, he is said to have asked for them to be destroyed. Religious teaching at the time perhaps considered the writing of verse an ungodly pursuit and he wanted to be right with his Maker. I think the compositions probably came to him as naturally as music and song always came to the Gaels.

Also in the community were several women who had the 'second sight'. One, in particular, often wished this faculty had escaped her, for her 'sightings' were always of sad things, forebodings of illness or death, which weighed heavily on her spirit. Another woman, remembered still by one or two of the oldest people, was reputed to be a witch. I think she was really a slightly eccentric old lady, who lived alone in a one-room house, the walls of which still stand, built for her as a 'granny-house'. When the thatch gave way one night of storm she stayed quite happily in the shelter of a huge black umbrella till a repairer arrived. If she was a witch I think she must have been a white witch, for she was always good to children, giving them a scone if they passed nearby, nursing them through whooping-cough or measles.

As the last of the old folk go, so the belief in magic will go with them – the faculty of seeing the 'wee folk' in a grassy hollow under the crags, those fairy folk who took the milk you put out for them so that they wouldn't harm your cattle. There will be no more fear of the 'evil eye' that could put a curse on man or beast, or of the kelpie that might lure you to ride on its back into black depths of the loch. Equally, there will be no more faith in the beneficence of the rowan tree that guards your door. And who will walk widdershins three times around the house, then bow to the new moon in her slim splendour?

These things added poetry to the prose of everyday life. The children of today have other sources of magic, I know. I just wish they would come dancing off the screen and be there – on the grass, among the trees, by the loch shore, in the wind and snow. Outer space is where the dreams are now. But inner space needs the young, with their energy and drive, to salvage it from exploitation and distress.

Back in the seventies, when Environmental Studies became popular, students began coming out to look at what the area had to offer. Geologically and botanically it was interesting, they reckoned. It is known as a 'hanging valley', left behind as the ice-floes sank into the Great Glen. Rose-red granite, smoothed to the shine of marble, had long been quarried on the slope. It was used for gravestones as well as for building. There is blue clay, and here and there the glitter of pegmatite. One specific mineral – blue 'Abriachanite' – is found in places among the granite. As there has been a minimal use of artificial fertilisers over the years, there is quite a profusion of wild plants, in particular those which thrive in the damp acidity. Gean and bird cherry blossom in spring. In autumn there is the splendour of birch leaves, bracken and heather. A photographic record of the flora was made at this time, using a telescopic lens. It is hoped the flowers will continue to bloom, in spite of acid rain, nuclear fall-out and all the perils of today. In some years fungi are plentiful – boletus along the roadside, chanterelle in favoured spots among the birches. Wildlife is comparatively undisturbed. Fox, badger, pine marten, roe and red deer and a few red squirrel live in reasonable peace, along with buzzard, grouse, kestrel, heron, waterfowl and many summer birds. Peewits, the long looked-for heralds of spring, are scarce now and there is a sad lack of larks, as traditional methods of cultivation have all but disappeared.

For the students there was always the question of land use. Large tracts were being planted with conifers. Was this a good thing or a bad thing, they queried, as they trudged around with binoculars, cameras and notebooks. Still today, this is a question which hangs in the air. But at least native trees are holding their own. Birch still stand among the pines, rowan and gean thrust their colours through the everlasting green. Hazel and alder appear unbidden wherever their seed falls easy. The plantings had to be fenced, of course, to keep out marauding animals, and deer-fenced at that, which meant that access for orienteering, or even for walkers, bird-watchers or botanists, was limited. Camping was not allowed as there was the fear of fire. Today, now that the trees are established, limited access is possible, there are stiles here and there, but still the lack of freedom to roam is felt. The old people remember when the hills were the common grazing ground for sheep, cattle in summer and horses – not the fine riding horses that graze the fields now, but the sturdy garrons that did the work of the crofts all week and had their Sundays to rest in the sweet hill grass.

Eventually, of course, trees have to be felled or sold, or both. It is hoped, however, that one small area which was designated an 'amenity planting' and is very attractive, can be saved and become an asset for the community.

Meanwhile the school was still in use as a Field Centre for the High School. Over the next years it was made available to parties of Scouts, Boys Brigaders and others for weekend or week-long use. Some of these parties came from more distant towns and did not know the area at all. Some came armed with air guns and fearsome-looking knives, obviously hoping to go hunting. Shots sometimes whistled perilously near anyone working in the garden! We had some moments of trepidation, too, when the more adventurous wandered off into the mud flats on the far side of the loch. And we had to keep a close watch when sparks were streaking from the old schoolhouse chimney as they dried their clothes in the course of the night. But we, and the old school, survived! It was nice, too, to be surprised by the appearance of flowers or a wee bottle of Scotch on the doorstep on the morning of an early departure!

As work on the project became gradually less demanding we were able to indulge our wish for some of the old self-sufficiency we had had on the croft. We acquired Bridget, a loveable white nanny-goat with amber eyes, who gave us ample milk on a diet of docken, willow-herb, nettles and grass, with a supplement of mash in the morning; half-a-dozen chickens, and five hives of bees. The chickens settled in quickly and soon produced a surplus of eggs. The bees, also, made more honey then we or our friends could eat and we were able to sell some to eager customers in the town. In older times the schoolmaster always had what amounted almost to a croft – a garden, the 'keep' of a cow and a share in the hill grazing. So we were carrying on the tradition!

Over the next few years the character of Abriachan began to change. Whereas when we arrived, some 25 years previously, it had been considered a somewhat wild and remote place, it was now, with the car, or two-car family, being reckoned a very desirable place to live. Commuting to work in Inverness was quite possible, since the road had been up-graded, with adequate passing-places. There were even litter-bins at likely picnic spots. Houses were being renovated and new ones built.

At the same time the school was in less demand as a Field Centre, as other, better-equipped places were opening up in different parts. Outside 'loos' and cold water washing facilities were considered too primitive for modern, town-bred youth. In summer an art class would come out for a day's sketching, gymnasts would do some 'jogging'. A party of boys with a 'technical' teacher would carry out a repair job at the croft house or paint the roof of the playground shelter.

As staff changes in the High School occurred, interest in the maintenance of the project naturally dwindled. The newcomers to the place had, of course, little knowledge of what had been going on. Slowly, as more people arrived in Abriachan, a demand grew for some sort of meeting-place for the occasional gathering. The school was there, it had electric lighting and at least an open fire for warmth, so gradually it reverted to one of its original roles, that of a place for religious assembly. The schoolmasters of old had always been expected to act as catechist for the whole community, to take a Sunday school for adults as well as for children and sometimes to preach a sermon. In older times the 'big' room was filled with desks, into which men and women of all shapes and sizes would cram themselves when they came on a Sabbath evening to hear the sermon. Very attentive they would be and often very critical of the prowess of the preacher. There would be serious discussion of the contents of his discourse in many homes later on. A minister from one of the nearby parishes would come at regular intervals to take the service. This custom was now revived, with the congregation accommodated more comfortably than hitherto, on chairs, and warmed by portable gas heaters as well as the fire. It was good to hear the old hallowed words sounding round the room again and the voices rising and falling in the long-familiar psalms and hymns. These had always been church lands, as we have seen. The old Sanctuary stone still stands. Now one could feel the serenity of the past echoing clearly into the future. A cup of tea, a practical offering of which the monks of old would surely have approved, was served before the minister took his sometimes, in winter, precarious journey home. Then, all the little bickerings and arguments, inevitable in any small community, set aside, people would gather round the fire to exchange news and arrange lifts back to the more outlying places.

The next custom to be revived was that of holding a party for the children at Christmas. I remembered those held when the school was still open and the thrill of coming out of an evening of fierce frost into the light and warmth of a blazing fire, the huge, dark green tree in the corner, with its shiny tinsel making it magic and the aroma of steaming tea and hot pastry. There would be a gigantic hammering on the door and an enormous 'Santa' would appear, his sack brimming with small, gleefully awaited presents. There were round games like 'I sent a letter to my love and on the way I dropped it' – this always engendered a tingle of excitement – other singing games, musical chairs and 'pass the parcel', all played equally enthusiastically by children and adults.

As plans were made for the renewal of festivities we had to cater for the children of today. Christmas never fails. The tree was there and the fire and the party food. Some of the old games were played as happily as ever, and there was music for eightsomes and Strip-the-Willow. The Dashing White Sergeant pranced around. Mothers slow-waltzed with toddlers or babes-in-arms. Granddads sat it out, reminiscing quietly. We had songs from our one native Gaelic singer and music from a brother and sister on the pipes.

As the Christmas party became an established tradition again many talents were uncovered. Plays were written and performed with great acclaim. More instruments were played – the guitar, the whistle, the clarsach. So music was there again, as it had been some fifty years before, when the Abriachan School Choir was famous for winning prizes at the Mod and in all the local competitions. Until recently the old people remembered the occasion when the bus driver, joining in the excitement of a big win at Oban, missed the turning at Spean Bridge on the way home and had to make the journey the long way round, while anxious parents waited all night at the foot of the hill with pony and trap to take the tired children home!

New Year was, and still is, celebrated in houses. One house in particular, that of our oldest native of Abriachan, had become the 'ceilidh' house at this time, crammed to the door, with twenty or thirty people queuing for the warm room and a seat at the fire. He entertains us with the Gaelic songs of his youth. We join the choruses and the young musicians of today keep the music going on instrument after instrument. Drams circulate and companionship is enjoyed. Later, tea is brewed and by then the New Year is well on its way in. Not long since the oldest people here would recall the days the 'old' New Year was celebrated, before the calendar was changed. This meant that festivities could go on till, and after, January 12th!

TWELVE

As I lived practically next door to the two main parts of the project – the collection in the Hall and the croft house up the road – I was naturally made key-holder and custodian of these places, a charge which I accepted gladly enough. It entailed, of course, opening up and explaining things to interested visitors, as we had already been doing, on a much smaller scale, with our collection in the out-building. My husband helped out with this on many occasions, when I had to be elsewhere. Sadly, some of the older girls who had been really interested in the collection, who had industriously cleaned black pots and been willing to come out on a Saturday to act as guides, were due to leave school. Some came during the holidays, when transport could be arranged. We encouraged a few from more junior classes to learn the job, but not many were as interested as those who had worked throughout the two years. There was a revival of interest in the Art Department which produced some beautifully lettered information sheets, as well as labels for the increasing number of objects. A couple of talented teachers in the Department spent part of their summer holiday in a caravan arranging things in attractive settings. We had been noting down the provenance of the various items as they were acquired and now began drawing up a rather more ambitious catalogue. It fell short of being really professional but served its purpose adequately for a number of years.

We clearly had none of the expertise of museum curators. In fact, I avoided as far as possible using the term 'museum', as it still resonated, for me, with the sounds of being marshalled with a group of young contemporaries into enormous buildings full of enormous stuffed animals and innumerable objects in glass cases, when I would much rather have been out on a hill-walk or a day at the sea! I still prefer to use the word 'collection', and all the things in the collection, or nearly all, can be handled, examined and some can be made to work. Of course, care has to be taken that heavy or sharp objects are treated with discretion.

Judging from the comments in the Visitors' Books over the years most people appreciate this way of presentation. We have had visitors from all parts of the world and have enjoyed their entries in the column headed 'Remarks'. One Indian lady said of the implements and tools they were 'just like India today'. A lady from Mexico was thrilled to see the old cooking-pots. 'My mother has one of those' she exclaimed delightedly. Could a Highland emigrant family have settled in her village, or did the foundry export its pots, we wondered? The French most often recorded their appreciation in their own language – 'Petit musée plein de choses interéssantes'. 'Ce musée m'a aidé à comprendre l'Écosse'. These entries and the many conversations we had with visitors were a great encouragement and made us feel the work was really worthwhile. Even small contacts made with other parts seem to diminish the gulf that can divide.

The happiness of the reunion of former residents of Abriachan inspired us to have a gathering of local people at Hallowe'en. We remembered so clearly the Hallowe'en of our first year on the croft. Then , when treats were fewer and further between, the children would prepare well ahead for a real night out, incognito, when they could get away with all sorts of tricks and harmless enough mischief. Two or three came to our door wearing unimaginably weird disguises. Only a laugh or a giggle could disclose a slight clue to identity. We left them to the anonymity they wanted, admired their amazing turnip lanterns, heard a verse of song and thrust sweets and apples into eager, grimy hands. They played no tricks on us but we heard tales of bygone days when a divot would be thrown down a lum to made the fire smoke, the pony would be loused from the stable and sent careering down the brae, tatties would be thrown at the roof to make the slates clatter. It could all be blamed on the evil spirits abroad that night!

The party we planned was to be a tame affair compared to the doings of earlier days, but the children brought turnip lanterns and the best one won a prize. They dooked for apples and snatched at hanging treacle scones. There was tea and cakes and a ceilidh. Three Abriachan brothers entertained us with their wonderful fiddle playing. A piper gave us a pibroch that took our thoughts to Skye, and beyond. The schoolroom, with its high ceiling, was acoustically good. We asked for more music, and more . . . Then we had songs and stories that made us laugh. So the evil spirits were kept at bay and in the morning we welcomed the saintly ones.

THIRTEEN

The year 1972 marked the centenary of the famous Act which brought education under the aegis of the State and out of the direct control of the church. Religion still had a part to play with morning prayers and hymns, Bible classes and School Chaplains. Today, of course, there is less observance of these remaining traditions. School Boards were set up, comprising elected members, mostly professional people, with powers to promote the building of large new schools and to enforce strict attendance by the pupils. Board members could, and often did, visit the schools, although they were not regarded as official Inspectors. Sometimes they fell out with teachers.

Schooling, in the terms of this Act, was made compulsory between the ages of 5 and 13. Twenty years later fees were abolished. In the towns, large numbers of children, whose families had migrated from the country, were taken off the streets. For those still living in the country there was now a chance to take advantage of a sound primary education, in adequate surroundings, with adequate facilities, and the possibility of obtaining a scholarship for further study and entry to the professions. Among the new, fine schools built at this time was the one in Abriachan.

In the towns, many Victorian school buildings are disappearing. Glasgow, in particular, has a wealth of magnificent schools. It is to be hoped that some, at least, can be saved to serve acceptable purposes. One which I visited in the old town ten years ago had a special interest as the Alma Mater of several members of the family. It was in use as a Community Centre. When I next went to see and photograph it, as a keepsake, it had gone, along with a neighbouring sandstone tenement. One outer wall remained, where the words 'Girls', 'Boys', and 'Infants' could still be read, carved into the stone. Probably on my next visit I shall find a huge uninspiring office block rearing up on the site.

School buildings similar to the one in Abriachan are to be found all over the Highlands. Mostly they stand serene, though deprived of the life they were intended for. Many have been converted to a variety of purposes – as dwelling-houses, as social centres, as craft shops. The one we first knew, those years ago, where Helen was a pupil and the learning and the playing went on quietly, noisily, happily, is now a residence of note. Through the high windows of the 'big' room one can catch a glimpse of pictures on the walls, of tall indoor plants, of ornaments on the ledges, things of beauty, all of them, but where is that feel of contained vibrancy, of young energy waiting to burst forth into life? It has taken itself off, of course, to other parts, with the children. The playground is there, the shelter, even the old toilets, but there is an emptiness all around. The children who would have gone to these schools find themselves bussed to bigger places, cut off from their roots, ill-adapted to the different life-style of their new companions.

Recalling the importance of the great Education Act of 1872, we decided to celebrate its centenary by mounting a display in the museum showing the history of the school here. We already had a list of head teachers and some accounts of visits by Inspectors in times prior to 1872. We had been given copies of photographs of school groups and we had access to the school Log Books, kept in the archives of the Highland Council in Inverness. I remembered consulting these when doing a paper during my training in Aberdeen. We now had recourse to them again and found them a fascinating source of information.

The keeping of a weekly record of progress and attendance in school was made compulsory by the new Act. It was stipulated that the book should be 'stoutly bound', consisting of not less than 500 pages and that no entries of a personal or critical nature should be made.

From the entries, particularly the early ones, a picture emerges, not only of what went on in school, but of the life and times of the community as a whole. There is mention of storms, of illness, of deaths and funerals, of outings to celebrate events in the wider world, of the visits of Attendance Officers, of the arrival of orphan children, of the problems of bilingualism and of the need for children to help with work about the crofts. The entries also reflect the nature of the headmaster making them. Some later ones are frankly tedious to read, repetitious and dull. Many show a lively interest and compassion for the families as well as the children. Some contain hints of rebellion against authorities reluctant to meet demands such as an improved water supply, drainage of the playground and so on.

The first entry in the Abriachan School Log Book, made by headmaster Alexander Maclean in February 1875, when there were 70 children on the roll, states that attendance was irregular owing to storms and sickness and that by the end of April of that year children were being kept at home to help with potato-planting. The summer vacation, or 'harvest play', was from 20th August to 2nd October, which would cover the hay and corn harvests. They were still lifting potatoes till the middle of November. These absences were understandable in a crofting area, where the gathering-in of supplies was of prime importance, but the situation must have been frustrating for a young, keen schoolmaster like Maclean.

On December 25th, attendance was good and on January 1st it was 'very good'. On January 8th there were 'New Year holidays'. They must have been keeping the 'old' new year and probably ignoring Christmas.

The first Inspector's report under the new regime, issued on 25th July 1876, states that '[this school] is taught with great ability and very good results, most creditable in the circumstances'. It goes on: 'all should have slates and a quantity should belong to the school for occasional use and slate racks and pen-holders in desks should be provided'. His report on the subjects taught went thus: 'Dictation – good. Arithmetic – good. Notation – good. Industrial work – good'. Then he notes 'arrangements should be made for having music taught'.

School Inspectors had been going their rounds since 1840. Initially they were supposed to visit five schools a week. This was

Summary of Inspector's Report.

25 July 1876.

This school was examined for the first time. It is taught with good ability and very good results most creditable in circumstances. Children tidy. Order very good. Class movements unusually good & smart. Tone good. Work very smart. Intelligence well cultivated. School neatly adorned. Reading distinct & very fluent. Matter of lessons very well known. Meaning of words good. Books too advanced. Grammar good. History and Geography very well begun with large number. Writing good and clear on slates. Copies good & clean in the second, very good in the third Standard. Figuring very good. All should have Slates; a quantity should belong to the school for occasional use. Dictation good. Arithmetic very good. Notation good. Industrial work good. Arrangements should be made for having music taught. Very good premises have been erected. Slate backs and penholders in desks should be provided

Inspector's report on Abriachan School in 1876

quite clearly impossible in the Highlands, where they sometimes had to travel on horseback, were often held up by bad weather at ferries, and so on. Many good stories have been told of their adventures. Though the going was hard they were most often accommodated in comfort in manse or inn, when they could not reach the schoolhouse. They found headmasters of many diverse kinds and were presented with many and diverse problems, but it was an interesting life for men of the right calibre.

Most often their visits were anticipated. Some headmasters would post a boy as look-out to warn of their imminent arrival. Occasionally they would make a surprise visit so as to obviate over-preparation, when pupils would learn passages by heart and be unable to answer questions on the content!

In 1864 a 'Revised Code' for education had been issued, in which 'payment by result' made grants available for proficiency in various subjects. The standards required were prescribed by the authorities, in what amounted almost to a national curriculum. For instance, in the Three Rs:

Junior pupils
Reading: Monosyllables
Writing: Capital and small letters
Arithmetic: Figures to 20, oral addition and subtraction to 10

Senior pupils
Reading: A news paragraph
Writing: A news paragraph
Arithmetic: Practice and bills

In 1950 the system of 'payment by result' was discontinued. Inspectors today work in an advisory capacity, with less fault-finding. In Mr Maclean's day their visits were in the nature of an ordeal for teachers and pupils. Most often a day, or several days, of holiday came after the inspection.

In his report of August 1877 the Inspector states 'This school continues to be taught with the same vigour and sweep'. This phrase brings a picture of the master and of the Inspector, I think! He describes the children as 'tidy, earnest and thorough and very willing'. The discipline, he says, is 'good, but might be more genial' and says ' the books are still too advanced'. He is evidently pleased so see that 'music was begun this year.' He is worried about attendance and says 'this should receive the Board's attention' and goes on: 'the need of a monitor should be considered by the Board'.

Abriachan since ten years.

Abriachan 20ᵗ Feb. 1882.

Dear Sir,

there is no doubt that Abriachan has greatly improved since the last ten years. Perhaps the most important of these improvements is the new road which was constructed several years ago. This road is a great benediction to the place; and serves for the purpose of carrying on traffic. A few years ago a new school-house was erected, where daily instructions are given. We have a new mill also built, which saves considerable trouble from going elsewhere to grind our meal. There was a wood planted three or four years ago, above Balmore, and we hope when old enough it will supply us partially with fire, &c, as well as protect us from the severe northern winds laden with keen frost from the Polar regions.

I am, Dear Sir, yours truly
John Fraser.

Extract from an Abriachan student's notebook

Schools were often closed from a Thursday to the following Monday for 'Communion week'. This was an important time in the Free Church calendar when people came from far and wide to attend services, often held in the open air in summer, when congregations could meet at a sheltered spot on a hillside. This happened in August of the year 1878, and again in November. On October 12th, Mr McGillivray, Mr Maclean's predecessor, who still lived in the former schoolhouse, had called in to the school and had 'urged upon the children the necessity of attending school as the Board was determined to prosecute all defaulters'.

During the following winter severe weather kept attendance down, but in his summer report the Inspector says 'Very good results notwithstanding the severe winter. Arithmetic: Very good indeed. Fingers should not be used'. Perhaps fingers were a better form of calculator! Mental arithmetic certainly kept young wits active in those days!

Mr Maclean clearly had problems to overcome in the running of his school, but he must have had pupils in whose progress he could rejoice. In a notebook kept by John Fraser, of Abriachan, in 1878, we find, beautifully written, a Latin vocabulary, parsing of the sentence, 'How do you do?' and an essay on the 'Life of Cromwell', marked '9 v.g.' and a letter to an imaginary recipient which reads: 'Abriachan has greatly improved since the last ten years' and goes on to mention a new road, the new school, a new mill and the planting of a wood. Less tidily written, perhaps added much later, after he left school, are the words of songs such as 'Wae's me for Prince Charlie', 'The Last Rose of Summer'. 'A Man's a Man for a' that'. There are also some in Gaelic. At the end, in pencil, are a few shorthand symbols. Along with the notebook is a tattered copy of Thomson's *Seasons*. One wonders what he made of that . . .

Mr Maclean stayed only five years in the school. His successor was Mr Evan Munro who arrived on 27th October 1880, when very few children were in attendance. Probably they were at the potato harvest. The following January and February saw extremely severe weather but on the 19th February we read that 'the Latin class is making considerable progress' and on the 26th there is recorded a 'great improvement in the reading of Gaelic'. So things were moving along, and from these entries we see that there is some flexibility in the teaching of Gaelic and of Latin. In April children were kept at home 'in planting a wood at Caiplich'. This would have been work for the laird and presumably there would have been some payment made to the parents.

The summer report says 'the school has made a very good start under the new teacher . . . very creditable after the severe winter. Music somewhat rough. The grant for geography and history is allowed with some hesitation'. In the period 1881-82 snow-storms are reported in October and in April. Attendance was badly affected. Some of the children had to walk considerably more than two miles and waterproof clothing was really non-existent. In April 1883 we have the first report of infectious illness – measles – afflicting the children. It amounted to an epidemic and in May the school was closed for disinfection. Brought up in the pure hill air the children did not build up immunity to infectious illnesses and many such diseases became killers. Young men joining the army often succumbed to measles and its complications in camps in the south.

On June 16th 1883 we read 'Lessons not so well prepared as most of the children required to herd before and after school'. With crops growing apace in the unfenced fields it was, of course, essential to keep the cows and sheep at bay. The children must have spent many happy hours tending the beasts and cheerfully forgetting most of their book-learning! Then, on November 3rd the entry reads 'There being only ten present school was dismissed at 1pm. The Default Officer went through the district on Thursday and Friday. The people, however, will not send their children to school until the potatoes are lifted'.

A report dated January 12th 1884 states: 'with 95 pupils on the roll this school has an average attendance of 40. These figures require no comment. The work is remarkably well done . . . and the discipline is all that could be required'. With a smaller number of children the teacher no doubt found it easier to maintain higher standards of work and discipline. But the absentees must have suffered.

In April of the year 1884 the Earl of Seafield died. His forebears had encouraged education, providing help in the building of the old school and schoolhouse. The school was closed on the day of his funeral.

That autumn Mr Munro, perhaps discouraged by the poor attendance at school, took his teaching elsewhere and on the 6th November Mr Donald Mackay arrived. He was a man who really understood the people better than his predecessors and he was to stay at the school for 22 years. He is still remembered with affection by descendants of the pupils he cared for. On December 26th he notes 'the children coming from Caiplich are very backward – the want of English and irregular attendance account for this'. Next year, on February 3rd, Donald Fraser, from Caiplich, was appointed Monitor during the winter months. Soon afterwards he got a job in Caithness as clerk in the Highland Railway, the great new enterprise that was opening up the country. On April 10th, Catherine Macdonald from Bracklish was admitted. She 'comes a distance of between 3 and 4 miles'. Ten days later he notes: 'Admitted Cath Ann and Emily Fraser, 7 years of age, from Inverness Poor House and lodged with a family in Caiplich'. This is the first mention of 'boarded-out' children. On June 12th we read 'Admitted Cath and Mary Ann Fraser from Corifoines. These girls have been taught to read by their father and they can speak English which is a very great advantage'. On December 11th the entry reads 'Attendance very good. Almost all the children have come back to school now, but those who have been away since the end of spring forgot a great deal of what they acquired previously'. It is clear that the rule of compulsion to make the children attend school could not really be made to apply in the Highlands, in spite of the work of the Defaulting Officers.

1886 was an exceedingly cold winter. On March 19th the record states: 'Most elderly persons do not recollect such a continuation of stormy weather'. On April 16th this, by way of compensation: 'This evening the children and also many of their parents and friends had a social entertainment of tea etc. in the school room. There were about 200 present. Mr McIver, Inverness, showed a great variety of views by the Magic Lantern, which interested the children immensely. A most enjoyable evening was spent. We had no school today'.

On May 21st this extract shows another side of the attendance problem: 'Attendance fair . . . above Standard III irregular, just day about, when one is at school another must stay at home, but that is a much better plan than to keep one child away altogether'.

So the year went on until in December: 'the drift was so blinding on Thursday that the children from Caiplich and others far away did not venture to come and it may be noted that these children are exceedingly hardy and brave to face a stormy day'. These were the conditions prevailing in the winter of 1955 when Helen could not reach school from Caiplich for several weeks.

This year 1886 is memorable, of course, as the year of the passing of the Act assuring security of tenure for crofters on their holdings. After months of deliberation and the recording of reams of evidence it was deemed that justice must prevail in this regard. It certainly gave the people much encouragement to improve the land they held, with the knowledge that they could pass it on unhindered to their descendants. They still did not have enough land and there were still restrictions. Poaching a rabbit for the pot was still a punishable offence. But hope was in the air.

The following February, in 1887, a six-year-old boy died of diphtheria. In March there was 'hooping cough' and 'what is called German measles'. The parents dreaded infectious illness and there would have been more sterilising of the premises with sulphur candles.

1887 was, of course, a celebration year nation-wide – the Jubilee of Queen Victoria. It was not forgotten in Abriachan! On October 1st a treat is recorded thus: 'The School Board having granted a Jubilee gift of £5 to the school, the scholars, along with some of the parents and friends, on Thursday of this week had a trip by steamer to Fort Augustus, which they enjoyed immensely. School was kept today Saturday for Thursday'. Soon after this, on the 21st of the month, we read: 'The School Board Officer called on the most of the parents this week and told them distinctly that the Board was determined to prosecute all those who did not keep their children at school'. There were certainly instances of parents being fined for the children's absences. The teacher was doing his best to help. In September of the following year he says: 'opened school today at the request of some of the parents, as the harvest is so very late this year . . . better to give a fortnight or so again when the harvest comes on'. The parents are having their say and pointing out their priorities and the teacher is trying to co-operate.

January 25th 1889 has an important entry. It reads: 'Opened a night school on Monday of this week for grown-up boys and girls. The attendance is good and they are very diligent at their work, which is reading, writing, arithmetic, singing by the notes at the close. Hours from 7 till 9'. This report makes one wonder what the boys and girls did in their younger days at school! It was good that they had a chance to make up for lost time and that they ended their evening with song. This was typical of the teacher, Mr Mackay.

The entry for February 1st states 'D. Mackenzie, John Shaw, Monitor, and John Macdonald understand Euclid wonderfully well' yet on February 22nd an Inspector reports 'If better results are not produced by next inspection a reduction of grant may be made. It should be noted that special allowance has been made for the peculiar circumstances of the district'. Could it have been that the 'lads o' pairts' were outshining their less able contemporaries?

May 3rd brings a sad note – 'Catherine Macmillan died from diphtheria this week and as the house is so close to the road from Caiplich the children from that district are afraid to come to school'. The peoples' great fear of infection probably originated in the time, not long past for them, when cholera reached epidemic proportions and caused many deaths. Families evicted from their homes all over the Highlands would congregate in villages and towns, hoping for shelter and perhaps work, and living in appalling conditions of squalor. They succumbed to diseases of many kinds and the contamination spread.

On June 2nd of that year Mr McGillivray, teacher in Abriachan for many years, died. His widow lived on in the old schoolhouse for a considerable time, bringing up orphan children. One of them was still there in our early days in Caiplich. He had the croft, had married a neighbour's daughter and brought up a fine family of his own. There were books in the house, he played the fiddle and one of his daughters was a pianist. It was a sad day when they all left the place and this old link with the school was gone. We went to the displenishing sale, bought a peat spade which I like to think was probably used by Mr McGillivray himself, and joined the neighbours in farewells.

In 1890, on March 21st, it is recorded: 'Mary Anne Macrae is still absent and the reason given is want of boots. She lives at a very high and cold place in the direction of Glen Urquhart'. When the weather warmed up she would have come barefoot, in any case. Attendance continued to worry the authorities. On May 22nd next year 'Mr Cameron, Default Officer, visited the school and told the children, in both languages, that the Board are determined to summons defaulting parents at their next meeting'. Is there a lesson here for parents of today?

In 1892 an important step was taken in the direction of looking on education as an essential social service. The payment of school fees was abolished. On 8th July there was a visit by the School Board members, 'a very pleasant one to the children and parents, a number of the latter having been present all the time'. In November we hear 'Wednesday, Thursday and Friday have been given for the lifting of the potatoes, by order of the school Board'. From these two entries it would appear that parents and Board are trying to co-operate. On December 30th 'Attendance was good, except today when some of them were sent to Inverness for the New Year messages'.

In 1893 on February 24th, 'By order of the County Council Dr McFadyen, Inverness, vaccinated 30 of the scholars today'.

Here we have more evidence of social concern for the health and welfare of the children as well as the training of their minds. In that summer 'Three handsome books are to be given as prizes to three most deserving pupils by London, Inverness, Ross and Tain Association'. Next year was received 'A copy of scheme for Gaelic as a specific subject which is filed in the Portfolio'. One hoped it didn't stay in there too long! In April of the next year: 'The Hon. Mrs Baillie of Dochfour visited the school. She started a knitting class of grown-up girls, herself supplying all the materials to make stockings for the Highland Industries Society. The girls are very interested in the work'. This was part of an attempt to provide some small means of employment for the women. In May and June the 'Feeing Market' in Inverness and Parliamentary Polling Day meant no school. The following March brought outbreaks of whooping cough and scarlet fever. The school had to be closed until it had been 'thoroughly disinfected, whitewashed and the wood all varnished'.

On the Queen's Jubilee day in 1897 the children were 'taken to Inverness in four carriages. They enjoyed the day immensely and were all home about 8pm. They also each received a commemorative cup'. That same year the Inspector's report states, sadly, 'A higher grant cannot be recommended until the habit of inaudible answering in the senior room is eradicated'. Next January Jessie Mackay, the teacher's daughter, took charge of the Infants' Department. From then on there was always a woman to see to the youngest children.

That the school kept in touch with many events of importance is shown in the entry of June 8th 1900: 'On Friday school from 10am-2pm. The children were then taken to the top of Benlie [a nearby hill] to celebrate the fall of Pretoria, which they all enjoyed very much'. In February 1901 we read: 'For the last three months the children were supplied with soup between 1 and 2pm, greatly appreciated'. Times were evidently not getting any easier and the authorities were reacting to circumstances. A few years later a member of the School Board was supplying the children with warm cocoa, which was also much appreciated.

The entry for October 4th reads: 'The children take a special interest in the free-arm drawing on the walls of the schoolroom which have been specially painted for this purpose'. Next we read: 'Corporal David Whitelaw of the 78th, an old pupil of the school and who is on furlough for a few weeks, is giving the boys drill in which they are most interested'. The interest of the pupils seems to have been always uppermost in this teacher's mind. In 1906 the much-loved Mr Mackay retired. He was given a pension of £48 6s. Thereafter the entries in the Log Book are of a different kind, strictly factual, giving less of the picture of the community.

Mr Peter Campbell was the new teacher. He stayed seven years, then moved to a low-ground school, where perhaps he had fewer problems with attendance, Gaelic-speaking and so on. His two sons distinguished themselves academically, one becoming Medical Officer of Health for the county, the other a lecturer in Classics at Edinburgh University, whose classes I was privileged to attend. His Highland voice reading Horace I shall always remember. Little did I think I would come to live in the house where he grew up!

In 1907 a Mr Buchanan of the Band of Hope in Glasgow gave a lecture to the children on Alcohol, its Nature and Use. Their enjoyment of this meeting is not recorded! The following year the Government, continuing in its role as good provider, made medical inspection and the serving of meals to poorer children compulsory.

In 1909 the Log Book reports: 'For the further development of Nature Study, practical School Gardening is to be introduced forthwith'. This was to be the start of many years of work under-taken with varying degrees of enthusiasm by different teachers over the years. After the first three years, when the school roll was 116, with many hands to lighten the work, the garden was inspected by an official of the College of Agriculture. One wonders what he made of this plot carved out of the moor.

In 1913 the first non-Highland and non-Gaelic speaking head-master was appointed. His salary was £125, plus £5 for cleaning the 'offices' and £5 for superannuation. He had the house and

The girls of Mr Campbell's school, about 1910. Notice the bare feet!

garden with rates and taxes paid. He was from Glasgow and had been teaching for a short time in the Western Isles. He at once started lessons in Phonetics, as he found 'reading and writing very unsatisfactory'. By the following year he was getting homework done in jotters. He also had all the children weighed and measured.

There is little record of the impact of the Great War on the school. Teachers' posts were to be kept open and their salaries safeguarded. Not till near the end is there mention of any 'war effort' by the children. In September 1918 a letter from Mr Morrison, the Inspector, urges the importance of bramble-gathering. Very soon 35 lbs were duly dispatched. Sphagnum moss was also gathered. It was used in dressings for wounds. That same year School Boards were ended, their function taken over by Education Authorities. This meant a great loss of personal touch in the supervision of the schools and was regretted by many.

The Inspector's Report of 17th March 1920 says, quite simply, 'Singing is of exceptional merit in all respects'. This is the first indication of the particular achievement of this particular teacher, the superb training of the children in choral singing. He provided the accompaniment, with only a tuning fork, and his Highland assistant would see that the Gaelic wording was correct. The headmaster clearly recognised that the natural,

Abriachan School Gaelic Choir

inherited talent of the children had only to be discovered and a golden sound would emanate. And so it did. On September 24th of that year we read: 'Headmaster off duty on Tuesday, Wednesday, Thursday and Friday of this week attending the Mod in Oban with a junior choir'. In June 1928 the School Choir won the Craigmonie Trophy offered to Gaelic Junior Choirs and stood second among the Rural English Choirs at the Festival. In September they went to Fort William and got first prize for Choral Singing. Later that year they gave a concert in the Town Hall in Inverness, but were disqualified in one Trophy competition 'because the percentage of Gaelic speakers was below requirements'. This seems strange indeed, but shows how English was permeating the children's lives. Also, there were probably several 'boarded-out' children in the choir who had no Gaelic. Thereafter, we read that 'the timetable was to be re-arranged to allow 2 periods of Gaelic of $^3/_4$ hour each in the Senior Division. Other periods amounting to 2 hours to be spent with junior classes'. This meant a welcome revival of Gaelic. The following year the choir attended the Music Festival in Inverness and retained the Craigmonie Trophy for the third time. Eventually, they were to keep it six times and to secure the highest marks among sixteen school choirs. Their fame spread far and wide, and is remembered today.

In 1929 a shelter in the playground, for which parents of children who could not get home at dinner-time had been asking for several years, was at last completed. In January of the following year a dramatic entry records the 'sinking of the gallery in the classroom'. The result of this is left to the imagination! At that same time two boys reported their caps missing from the pegs in the cloakroom. Work had been going on at the water pipes and the cesspool. Eventually the caps were found – in the cesspool! Thereafter the headmaster demanded a fence round this unsavoury area.

In March 1932 there is the first record of a visit by Nurse Cran. Over the following years her visits became frequent and welcome. The state was continuing its job of providing welfare and the headmaster of the time certainly kept it and its agents on their toes! He was an innovator, and by dint of quite a bit of blustering he got things done. By pointing out the health risks of having 100 children using dry closets (which he objected to having to empty!) he persuaded the authorities to install flush cisterns. He agitated for the introduction of the telephone. On November 25th 1925 it was recorded: 'the local telephone office opened today and one of the children engaged the Town Clerk in conversation'. He insisted on better measures to prevent marauding sheep and roe deer from damaging vegetable crops in the garden. This meant putting up wire netting along the top of the wall. Some of it is still there. He got an extra classroom by partitioning the main room and got an extra teacher appointed.

In his personal life there were innovations, too. He had a bathroom installed in the house and he was the first person in the area to acquire a motor car. Many a time he sent the children scattering as he motored up the hill in his old Morris. Driving tests were not required at that time and red flags had gone out! The acquisition of the car meant that the pony which had pulled the trap to take his wife the ten miles to town could be put out to grass and a boy was no longer needed to walk at its head!

In 1932, on September 21st, the Log Book records: 'The centenary of Sir Walter Scott was observed by closing the school for one afternoon. Lessons were given appropriate to the occasion'. This shows, I think, the calibre of this teacher, who was, about this time, attending meetings of the Educational Institute of Scotland in Edinburgh.

After his retiral in 1935 and the death of his wife, he lived as a recluse in an isolated house on the hill road to Glenconvinth. The young people from Mrs Maclean's were in the habit of getting groceries for him from the van. He was still here when we came to live in the area. We were reluctant to visit him as we thought he would not welcome intrusion by strangers. Then, when we were on the point of venturing to make his acquaintance, we heard that he had died. His only daughter, also a teacher, made the arrangements for his burial in the nearby ground at Glenconvinth, where many Abriachan people lie. She took away all she wanted from the house and died herself a few years later. A family moved into the house and set about clearing the rooms. Bonfire flames were soon leaping into the evening sky. Knowing our interest in books they asked if we would care to save some of them from the flames. We were over at the double! It was then that we realised what must have been the quality of the man's mind. There was a piano. There were books on every kind of subject – literature, the classics, art, music, crafts. We filled pillow-cases and staggered home under the weight of the tomes. Only then did we realise what his life must have been, isolated as he was, intellectually as well as physically.

The next headmaster was a very keen gardener. Two years after his appointment the Inspector's report goes like this: 'the headmaster here has transformed the garden into something very pleasing and deserves very great credit. With the help of the pupils the following improvements have been carried out: flower-plots, herbaceous border, lawn, rockery, crazy paving, hedges, rustic frame with roses, all carefully planned and neatly executed. The productive side is also included and the education aspect kept in view'. Alas, in subsequent years many of the attractive features created by this teacher were neglected as short-term tenants came and went. We have tried to rescue some of them.

In September 1939, as the Second World War was beginning, the school was closed for ten days. It was thought evacuated children might be coming, but this was not the case. In December the school won a Challenge Cup for gardening. The headmaster arranged lectures on bee-keeping for the boys. He kept goats and chickens and set a great example to others trying to help the war effort. Eventually he went to a bigger school not far away.

The school roll had fallen to about 45 when the next teacher took charge. The following year, as the war ended, an Act was passed which aimed to give children an education 'appropriate to the age, ability and aptitude' of the pupils. It also aimed to widen the scale of its provision of social welfare. The school leaving age was raised to 15. In Abriachan a canteen was opened for the service of school meals and over the following years, in spite of the decrease in the number of pupils, plans went ahead to erect

Abriachan children at the 'Tattie Howking', 1943

a new building at the top of the playground so as to make the school into a Junior Secondary establishment. But nothing could stop the decline in the number of pupils.

By 1950 the school was reduced to one-teacher level, with its first headmistress in charge. There were 15 pupils on the roll. The idea of conversion to Junior Secondary status was given up. The equipment was removed from the classroom. In spite of a still falling number in school, electricity, which was coming to the whole area, was installed in the schoolhouse and the classrooms. Finally, in 1958, the school closed, as we have seen. It must have been a sad day for Miss Fraser to see the school close, the school where she had been a pupil, a pupil-teacher, then head. Her sister, too, had been a fellow-pupil and her forebears had attended the old school over the road. She continued teaching in other schools, before retiring and settling in Inverness. She came out many times to see us, always ready to help with our researches into the story of Abriachan, giving us many photographs and answering our many queries.

FOURTEEN

The display of the Log Book extracts, together with a list of teachers, records of pupils and photographs of school groups taken at various times proved to be of great interest, especially to former residents of the area. In due course the improvements at the croft house, the publication of the booklet and the display of artefacts in the hall earned a further accolade from the authorities and an ornamental shield.

As news of the collection spread many interested people would come to visit. We had to restrict the opening hours and days so as to be able to cope with the situation. My husband was intensely interested in all aspects of the project and would often talk to the boys about old methods of construction and point out to them the remains of an old cruck-framed roof in a ruined building nearby, where the beams were held together with wooden pegs. Sometimes he would have to rush from the hall to the Post Office as a small queue of pensioners began to form at the schoolhouse door!

Our visitors were all people after our own hearts – people who would pick up a horn spoon or a chisel, turn it over and over, close to the face, smile, perhaps sigh a little and say, 'Aye, many's the time I've used that. I must bring you an adze. I have one out in the shed, I'm sure. I'll be along, maybe next week'. So it was that the collection slowly grew and grew. The things brought in were lovingly restored and labelled. Some were simple gifts, some on loan. Always it was understood that they would be returned if their owner so wished. Occasionally we managed to go to farm or croft sales to buy what we could afford. We still wandered round abandoned places and ruined the underparts of the van transporting cart wheels and, once, a stone roller!

One summer a party of French scouts arrived, without warning, pitching their tents in the field over the road. A thunderstorm, with torrential rain, greeted their arrival. We opened up the school, lit a fire in the grate and let them stay there till they were warm and dry. They were amazed to be welcomed in French and so thankful for the hospitality that they asked to be allowed to help in some way. The offer was gladly accepted and they put in a good day's work cutting weeds at the old grave-yard at Kilianan. We became firm friends and they returned the following year to help again. On their last evening, they sang and played for us. It was good to hear the old schoolroom filled with the sound of French music and song. They had all heard of 'Marie Stuart' and her sad life. We told them of the affinity of the Highlands with France, of the many Jacobites who had fled there, of the clan chiefs who sent their sons to be schooled there and of the Auld Alliance which went back hundreds of years. They proudly displayed the tartan 'bunnets' they bought on their next day off, in Inverness!

Another year some Swiss scouts arrived. In return for permis-sion to camp they, too, insisted on helping and did some good work in the garden of the croft house. The enthusiasm of both French and Swiss scouts was quite an inspiration and continued contact with them gave us a real link with Europe.

Very soon word got round the schools in Inverness and be-yond that the Museum and the croft house were ready to receive visitors. Their educational potential was being recognised and assessed. Teachers would come out to look round, then, back in school, they would prepare the way for the children, perhaps make out sheets with basic questions for quickly pencilled an-swers. The children would certainly make a day of it, thrilled with everything they saw – except the loos in the playground! A picnic lunch and a walk, if there was time, would follow. Next day there would be a follow-up in class and the writing of a thank-you letter, saying what they had most enjoyed and why.

We enjoyed these visits. The children had a natural friendliness, we found. It seemed to shine out of them, especially on a fine summer day. They were mostly town children, the country an almost undiscovered wonderland. I would sometimes accompany them a little way up to the road to where the wild raspberries grew.

'Can you eat yon, Miss?'

One was always 'Miss', no matter what one's age or marital status.

'You can. You try.'

'Mmm . . . they're good.'

A friend comes up.

'I wouldn't. There's a spider on mine.'

She would only have seen nice clean rasps in tidy punnets! We sometimes wondered what the children really made of coming from their shiny houses, their shiny school, in their big shiny bus to see these old tools and cooking pots and implements that belonged to what must have seemed like another age. They liked the fact that nothing was out of reach, in a glass case. Everything could be inspected at close quarters, handled, picked up. And, amazingly, nothing got broken!

I remember one small boy, a quiet little fellow, picking up a small plane from among the joiners' tools. His face suddenly lit up.

'I mind – my grand-dad had one of those. He used to make . . . '

Suddenly overcome with shyness, he put it carefully back. As he moved on I could detect a touch of pride, of new assurance, in his walk. Was he thinking, 'Grandad's tools . . . in a museum? He must have been someone. Maybe . . . I'm someone?' Could he have got out of his visit something that formal education can't seem to give – a sense of his own identity? I think it's possible. He might have. I hope so.

Many of the children who came out in groups had read, in school, the story of 'The Kelpie's Pearls'. This is set in Abriachan. The author, Molly Hunter, lived here for a while. I remember her coming up, with her young son, to visit us, when we would discuss writing projects and ideas. She has since, of course, written many highly-regarded books and the 'Kelpie' has become a classic. After a close look, with the children, at the pots, the girdle, the kettle, the flat irons which old Morag of the story would have used I would point out the place where her house had been, the pool where the kelpie lived, the way down to the big loch and the one over the hill to Kiltarlity. Their eyes would widen as the story came so very much alive for them.

Members of various societies came to visit, too. Field Clubs, the National Trust. These learned visitors all contributed their valued share of knowledge and expertise, for which we were always grateful. The Inverness Field Club had been founded in 1875 after a memorable visit to Abriachan to study the geology of the area. Professor Young, of Glasgow University, had given three lectures on the geology of Scotland in Inverness. Thereafter, as recorded in the first volume of the Transactions of the Field Club, on 6th November 1875, a 'small party of seven, including Dr Young, set out in an omnibus – four inside and three perched on the box, to survey as much of the country as the mist left exposed to view'. At Abriachan the party examined the granite quarry, which 'yields a fine reddish stone, now frequently used for monuments'.

On their return home the interested parties resolved to constitute a society which would organise lectures in the winter months and outings in the summer, to 'seek and reveal' things of interest. A lively interest in Abriachan has been maintained through the years and several further visits made. Careful research and preparation are always undertaken by the leader of the group. Local people are always asked to contribute their knowledge and experience and many happy contacts have been established.

One year a visit was made to Craig-na-Uamh (the rock of the caves), which is $16\frac{1}{2}$ feet high and $31\frac{1}{2}$ feet long. Outside is a large boulder called Clach-na-Fion (stone of the Fingalians). Place-names give so many clues to history. It is said that Deirdre and her lover stayed for a time on a hill on the opposite side of Loch Ness at Dun Deardl. The cave at Craig-na-Uamh was said to be of a size to 'shelter forty sheep or goats on a stormy night'. Smugglers hid their bags of malt here. There were many cunning smugglers, who devised many cunning ways to outwit the gaugers, who were forever on their trail, sometimes sailing up and down the loch looking for tell-tale smoke from the distillers' fires. But some bothies were hidden underground and distilling could be carried on in broad daylight with fires of burnt heather or juniper, which give a smokeless fuel.

On 5th June 1886, during an outing to the area, there was much discussion about the derivation of the name Abriachan. Many theories have been put forward. It seems that the most likely origin is: Aber-riach-an – that is, the confluence of the speckled stream. The water from the hill burns meets the waters of Loch Ness after a series of magnificent waterfalls which are 'speckled' when the sun shines on the underlying granite and whinstone.

More stories about the big cave had been collected by the leader of the expedition, one concerning a notorious cattle-lifter, one Samuel Cameron, who sought shelter there when under threat of death. Out hunting one day, the Sheriff of Inverness came on him in the cave. Cameron at once threatened the intruder with his pistol, and, on learning who he was, shouted, 'Declare me a free man at the Cross of Inverness or I shoot you dead.' In this way he obtained his pardon and went on to live a sober life and to raise a large family.

On the loch shore below this famous 'Robber's Cave' were caves containing stalactites and stalagmites, which are still marked on some tourist maps. Sadly, they were demolished during road-widening operations in the 1930s. Children on their way to church at Bona, along the loch shore, would have had their first lessons in geology sheltering in these magical places. Travelling people – the 'summer walkers' as they were known – would shelter there too.

These 'summer walkers' of last century were mostly honest people living hard lives with quite strict codes of behaviour. Even forty years ago I remember a group of Stewarts who would camp at the roadside every year in Maytime. They were tin-smiths and the pans I bought from them lasted for years. One evening we would hear the scrape of a fiddle and next morning they would be gone. Many were descendants of those who had taken to the heather after Culloden and had never gone back to a settled life.

Mostly they were made welcome during their brief stays. They brought news of other places, other happenings, in the days before radio and the easy circulation of newspapers. Sometimes a lone walker would appear, on his way over hill-tracks known to few to the west coast or the islands. He would get his bowl of brose or porridge and oatcakes for his pocket and be sent on his way with 'See you next year!' and a parting wave.

These people had a life-style and a culture all their own. 'Living off the land' came naturally to them, when there were fish to be 'guddled' in the burns, rabbit and hare to be despatched swiftly with a well-aimed stone, berries and nuts in season and all the summer plants to flavour the stew. Thyme made a healthy infusion and heather saw to many needs. It made a springy bed, a sparky fire, a quick hot drink and a long, cool, delicately flavoured thirst-quencher as ale. It figured in their crafts, too – small, tightly-bound sprigs of dried stalks making excellent pot-scrubbers. Clothes pegs of split birch twigs, baskets and creels of willow-wands – these would have won design awards for useful, environmentally friendly objects in today's age! Such skills are lost now as plastic and mass production take over the world of manufacture. Seasonal work can hardly be obtained these days, for machines cut out the need for 'hands'.

Story-telling, the singing of traditional songs and ballads, which was the customary way of passing the evenings and the winter days, these are going, as the radio blares out entertainment at all hours.

'The children get more schooling now,' I said to one traveller who has been calling at the door for years, selling mats, towels, needles and thread these days, in the style of the 'colporteurs'.

'Aye, they can read the paper and write their name and . . . '

'And add up the money at the end o' the day,' her husband chips in – 'but they canna tell a horse fae a pony, nor light a fire at the roadside, nor find gulls' eggs for their breakfast. See me? I canna read nor write, but I can live the way I want. And they could, if they would learn.'

'I know what you mean.'

I think of the songs and stories being lost, too, as this old form of native education goes. We share a cup of morning tea and I wish them well 'till next year'. The children are at the gate, bright-eyed and sunburnt, on their summer trek. I wonder about school and those 'shades of the prison-house' . . .

The Inverness Field Club outings to Abriachan brought the place alive for many people. In 1975, to mark the centenary of the founding of the club, I was privileged to give a talk, illustrated with slides, on the history of the area, from the earliest times. This was followed by an outing, one September day, to look at the various places of interest. We walked over the site of the prehistoric settlement on the hillside, went to see a smuggling bothy on the far shore of the little loch and looked at the cruck beams in one of the earliest houses. The flora and fauna were studied, too. A heron was fishing the loch. Buzzards were calling overhead, roe scampering through the birches. On the way home plastic bags were filled with brambles and various kinds of delectable mushroom.

On another occasion the graveyard at Kilianan was explored. It was not difficult to see, in the mind's eye, the early Columban settlement, the monks busy at their tasks and the boys coming to follow their teachings.

As time went by friends contributed many items of interest to our museum. One, a geologist, made up a collection of local minerals. Another, an artist, mounted a display board showing how lichens made different coloured dyes for wool. This interest we found most helpful and inspiring.

One day, in summer, a young scientist from Aberdeen University turned up at the door.

'I heard of the Museum here. May I see it?'

'Of course.'

She looked at everything with intense interest.

'I'm so pleased to be here. You see . . . my great, great, great, I forget how many greats, grandfather was headmaster in the school here.'

'He was? What was his name?'

'Lachlan Maclachlan. You've heard of him?'

'I have. Indeed I have. He was very well known. In fact, he was remembered, or his name was, until quite recently, by the old people.'

'That's good. I'd like to give something in his memory. I'll leave the money with you. Let me know what you decide to get.'

'That's a wonderful idea.'

'Lachlan Maclachlan' – the name had always had magical connotations. We had read about the man. He had become much more than a ghost-like figure. We had heard about his descendants and now we had met one. He had come here in 1776, somewhat reluctantly, as he had heard that the people were wild and addicted to smuggling. The making of the illicit dram was a common practice in many parts of the Highlands. It was a particularly strong brew and much favoured by many. Some of it was sold in order to pay the ever-increasing rents. Some of it was, inevitably, consumed locally. The Abriachan area was exceptionally suitable for the enterprise. The water was plentiful and pure, there were many hiding-places on the steep slopes, access by the gaugers was not easy and there was juniper, which gave a smokeless fire. The people became very clever at outwitting anyone who tried to curb their activities. Some of them also indulged in gambling at cards, a game perhaps learned through service at the 'Big House', where such things took place. The main sport was shinty. Their love of the game was such that matches often took place on the Sabbath.

Lachlan Maclachlan, whose duties as schoolmaster included catechising and sometimes preaching, as well as teaching, went warily about his mission among the people. He even agreed to join in their Sabbath game if they would agree to play fair and to come to his religious meeting afterwards. I think he was well ahead of his time in many respects. The people agreed with his proposal and kept their word, so real contact was made.

Lachlan was a poet, too. He used this gift to write satires on gambling, drunkenness and other vices. The people appreciated this and responded in large measure. Soon he became highly regarded and was known as 'Mr Lachlan'. Descendants of his were famed Gaelic scholars and ministers of religion in Edinburgh and elsewhere. So . . . how to keep his memory alive?

We decided to buy a seat which people could rest on as they looked across to the fields and hills that Lachlan must have looked at so often. The remnants of his little school remain, just a tumble of stones now, some of them made into a wayside dyke. But the building served its purpose until 1875, when the big school was put up. Mr Lachlan would have had to make do with a very primitive schoolroom, about 36 feet by 16, with an earth floor, small windows, a thatched roof, often leaking, and a fire in the middle, for which the children brought peats. For furnishings – a table for himself and forms for the pupils, but no desks and few books. This school had been established by the Scottish Society for the Propagation of Christian Knowledge. In the records, against Mr Maclachan's name, the comment 'wants books' occurs regularly. One can imagine the scholarly man's frustration at the lack of this basic work tool. Perhaps things have not changed much 200 years on! As for his house, it probably consisted of not more than two rooms, of primitive structure, attached to the school.

We bought a teak seat and a plaque for Mr Maclachlan's name. In order to get the dates of his schoolmastering accurate, we wrote to the Church of Scotland Offices in Edinburgh. They referred us to the Scottish Record Office, where the records of the S.S.P.C.K. are kept. The people there we found most cooperative. They sent us, not only Mr Lachlan's dates, but the dates of all the other schoolmasters of the Society who had served in Abriachan and also accounts of visits by Inspectors over several years, from the early nineteenth century. These we found of great interest. They give a picture of schooling as part of the life of the community. We hear of times of hardship and illness, of catechising and religious meetings, of the children who have learnt to read reading the scriptures to their parents in their homes, especially during the winter when they could seldom go to the Parish Church, which was ten miles distant.

The memorial plaque for Lachlan Maclachlan

Mr Lachlan's wife taught sewing and knitting to women and girls, in an evening class. It is not recorded whether she was paid. Her husband's salary was £10 a year. This was more or less the equivalent of a labourer's pay. He would also have received a small sum from the Heritors, small emoluments for acting as Catechist, perhaps as Registrar and so on, and fees paid by the parents. These varied from place to place. The year was divided into four quarters – Lammas, Hallowmas, Candlemas, and Beltane. Fees were paid by the quarter, typically:

1s 6d a quarter for reading
2s 6d a quarter for reading and writing
2s 6d a quarter for the 3 Rs
2s 6d a quarter extra for Latin

Some parents could only afford to send their children to school a quarter at a time.

In most places the master's salary was augmented by a charge for cock-fighting, which took place in the schoolroom. There

432

is no record of fights in Abriachan but they probably took place. They were held on Shrove Tuesday. Parents and very often the minister would attend. Defeated birds became the perquisites of the schoolmaster and were no doubt a welcome addition to his larder. Hugh Miller, in his book *My Schools and Schoolmasters*, gives an account of the fights in his day. He says:

The school . . . had its yearly cockfight, preceded by two holidays and a half during which the boys occupied themselves in collecting and bringing up their cocks and such always was the array of fighting birds mustered on the occasion that the day of the festival, from morning till night, used to be spent in fighting out the battle. For weeks after it had passed the school floor would continue to retain its deeply stained blotches of blood . . . the yearly fight was a relic of a barbarous age. Every boy had to pay the master two pence per head for leave to bring his birds to the fight.

Miller goes on to say that he never attended a fight. This is perhaps an interesting glimpse of his true nature. He was writing of what took place in the early years of the nineteenth century. He describes his school thus: 'The building in which we met was a low, long straw-thatched cottage, open from gable to gable with a mud floor below and an unlathed roof above'. This sounds very like Mr Maclachlan's school.

The teaching in schools run by the S.S.P.C.K. was supposed to be in English, but many times Gaelic had to be used as the children really understood no other language and would be repeating words with no understanding of their meaning. The hours of attendance were long – from February to October the school was open every weekday from 7 to 11 am and 1 to 5 pm. For the rest of the year the hours were 8 to 12 am and 1 to 3 or 4 pm. In late summer there were three weeks of holiday (the 'harvest play'). Christmas or New Year breaks were very short and Easter was barely recognised.

The children's lives were thus filled with long hours of school-ing, largely dispensed in an alien tongue, with alien ideas having to predominate. Mr Maclachlan would surely have tried his utmost to keep things in some sort of proportion, but his efforts would have been restricted by his commitment to the Society. It must have been galling for a man of his intellectual calibre and with so close an affinity with his charges, to have to witness the slow erosion of their culture, in what must surely have been the start of a kind of ethnic cleansing. His daughter Helen, as we have seen, married a local Macdonald; another daughter, Janet, married a later teacher in Abriachan and their son became a teacher in the area. A grandson was the Rev. Dr Thomas Mclachlan (1816-86), one of the foremost Gaelic scholars of his time and a Moderator of the Free Church. The struggle to preserve the old Highland heritage would have gone on valiantly in hands such as these.

FIFTEEN

About this time I began to wonder whether I could risk giving up my 'day job' so as to be able to be full time 'at home'. Home was the centre of much activity, people coming and going to the Post Office, the Project sites, naturalists, archaeologists passing by, young friends, old friends, relatives turning up to stay. This activity we enjoyed immensely, of course. But it did demand a toll. After days and evenings of discussion it was decided that I would take what we now call 'early retirement' and retreat to the home front. I found myself, of course, busier than ever! Breakfast was a snatched cup of tea taken standing at the toaster, lunch a sandwich munched walking round the garden, looking at the jobs to be done. But the evenings were relaxed, with no papers to correct, mark sheets to add up, reports to be written or lessons prepared. I missed the daily contact with the school. I remembered my father's saying: 'Being with the young keeps you young'. Gradually things settled down. I taught an evening class at the College for several winters and very much enjoyed working with a group of interested adults. I was also doing scripts for schools radio and – there was the garden. We grew most of the vegetables we needed by dint of ingenious methods of protecting seedlings, including jam jars and plastic bottles. We had Bridget the goat, our chickens and five hives of bees. So basic sustenance was assured.

Helen, after getting her degree and teaching English abroad for a year, had married and was living on a small farm, almost a croft, some twenty miles away. She was milking a Jersey cow, tending calves and chickens and growing vegetables of a size we never managed to achieve in the heights. In due course, two small girls arrived. They did much to lighten the next few years, when Jim's health was failing, and at five and six years old they smoothed the way for him to the Elysian fields.

I knew where he would like to be remembered. In the little burying-ground at Kilianan we had worked together so often, cutting weeds, planting bulbs. We had come to feel we would recognise the people lying there. A few had carved and inscribed memorial head-stones showing lineage and identity. For most there was a rough-hewn piece of granite, decorated only with moss and lichen.

It is said there was a chapel there long after the monks had gone, and latterly it had been a preaching-site. St Columba's font remains and the sanctuary stone still stands. Not far away, in the shelter of a stand of tall pines, is the place where a small tinker child was buried, her parents not seeking the comfort of a Christian burial. Though the nearby road is busy, now, with traffic, there is still the aura of peace about the place.

For weeks I searched for a stone, along the loch shore, among the crags, up in the hill-top quarry which had yielded building material. To find a piece of the right size and shape and then to think out means of transport, these were the problems. At last I found it – a beautiful piece of rose-red granite, lying on the ground at the entrance to an old steading. It had evidently formed the lintel of the doorway. And it would have come from the hill-top quarry, as this was one of the high crofts. The owner of the property more than kindly allowed me to have it and another neighbour, who was working with a digger in the area, transported it willingly to a sculptor for inscription. It was arranged that it could be placed in a quiet corner of the graveyard, where the snowdrops come, even in the snow. We scattered the ashes round the foot of the stone, some round the sanctuary stone, and planted bulbs of all the companion flowers of spring. We knew Jim would have been happy in the company of the crofters, the stone-mason, the shoemaker, the Norwegian princess, all the others who share his resting place.

It was decided, then, that I would keep on working the Post Office, as otherwise, they said, it would be closed. It is a very small office, some say about the smallest in the country, and not a very busy one, as the commuters tend to buy stamps or Postal Orders when out shopping at lunch-time in the town. It still has a purpose, though, as the one focal point, now when there is no school, no church and no shop. The Postman can report any illness or accident he may have encountered on his round and prompt action can be taken, neighbours alerted, help summoned on the phone. There is also a small branch of the Public Library squeezed into an old bookcase in the porch, beside the office equipment, the scales, the leaflets and so on. This collection of books is prized by the few remaining readers, especially when snow or ice make the journey to town hazardous.

My duties in the Post Office kept me tied to the house every morning and for a short spell in late afternoon. This meant that escorting people to the Museum had to be fitted in between afternoon hours in the garden. Somehow, it was managed. Parties coming by appointment could be coped with reasonably easily. When a small, eager group arrived, just as I had started to single lettuces on a glorious summer afternoon, I had to struggle a welcoming smile as I kicked off my wellies, washed my hands at the water-butt, smoothed my hair, found the keys and began my 'spiel'. The interest and appreciation in the faces and voices of the folk as they packed into their cars for 'off' was certainly rewarding.

There were many happy occasions, too, when I would hear a creak as the garden gate swung open, approaching footsteps, a murmur of voices and would look up to find two or three people 'of a certain age' gazing at the house, at the school, obviously re-orienting themselves after a long absence.

'We were at school here' one of them would say. 'I remember yon high windows. We could never see out. But the ivy would come in!'

'As it does today' I say, looking up. 'I have a grandson who's better than I am at climbing ladders now. He'll be here one day soon to cut it back. Would you like to see inside the school?'

'Oh yes, please.'

They wander round, looking into every corner, in silence. Then the real remembering starts.

'That was the infants' room' the oldest visitor says. 'That's where I started. I mind it like yesterday. And the teacher was

Miss Fraser and the pupils of the school in 1952

good to us. She would take us out on a summer's day for a walk down the road and a lesson sitting under the bushes.'

'Aye. And on the Sabbath she would have us to her house to sing hymns and give us sweeties afterwards . . . ' her friend remembers.

'But the master. In the big room. That was a different kettle o' fish.' The man in the party has his own memories.

'Well, he had to keep you laddies in order.'

'He did that. And it must have been some job when there were near a hundred o' us. We knew fine when to expect the worst – the days he came into school wi' his hat on. That was a bad sign. We'd try to hide the strap on those days, if ever his back was turned.'

'And he was daft about singing. I can see him now, wi' his tuning fork. And the skelp you got if you sang a wrong note.'

'But he made a good job of the choir.'

'He did. And all the prizes it won made the school famous.'

'And some boys got Latin and geometry. They were the brains.'

They were all reminiscing now, thoughtfully. I imagine a small, barefoot boy, a last-minute rip in his kilt held together by a safety-pin, trudging along the track from one of the high places, puzzling over the square on the hypotenuse or the use of the ablative case in a subordinate clause, as he swings his small bundle of tattered books to the rhythm of his stride. He would have been heading straight for a job in a bank or on the Highland Railway, so his parents hoped.

'And out of all those pupils, have you kept in touch with some?'

'With some, yes. But many went away to the war. Highlanders always did that, of course. There were doctors and teachers and engineers, aye, and ministers, too, among them. Education went into most of them, one way or another.'

'Your families belonged to Abriachan?'

'No. We were orphans. But we were all lodged with good people in good homes. So this is real home to us still.'

They were reluctant to leave the school premises.

'D'you mind if we take a wee walk round outside?'

'Of course not.'

'The shelter's there. I bet my initials are on the wall yet.'

'And the loos . . . ' with a giggle, 'I hated having to go, with yon wee slats on the door!'

'But we'd sometimes find some fallen apples off the tree up yonder. They were soor!'

'Come in for a cup of tea before you go . . . '

They wander off. Reminiscences such as these brought the place so vividly alive that sometimes I wondered if I was living in yesterday or today. Some days people would come from overseas, looking for the home of their ancestors. We could perhaps trace it from the name, then have to announce, sadly, that it was now no more than a heap of stones. Sometimes the information was so scant that it was impossible to recommend a visit to the library in Inverness, where there is a resident genealogist and much material on computer.

Interesting documents and photographs continued to arrive from people who seemed as glad to find a home for them as we were to provide that home. Photographs were always copied so that the originals could be returned to their owners, if they so wished. I particularly treasured the school groups and only wished the camera had been invented in the time of Lachlan Maclachlan and his scholars.

Glimpses of schooling in the not-too-distant past led me to try to reach back into the very earliest times. The people in these parts must have been among the most fortunate in the Highlands. They had the centre of learning established as early as the sixth century by Columba's missionaries at Kilianan, just down the road. Here, as we have seen, able boys would have been taught the elements of Latin grammar, some Greek and also to read and write in their native tongue, which was akin to Columba's own. They would have learnt husbandry, too, and some basic technical skills in the working of wood and metal. Another craft – the illumination of manuscripts – they would have learnt readily enough. From their Pictish ancestry they would have inherited the gift for working in stone. Embellishing parchment would have seemed a logical transfer of skill. Music and storytelling would have fed their imagination. Columba himself was a writer of no mean ability. He is said to have composed many 'lays', or tales of heroes. Wandering minstrels, too, would have provided history lessons in a very attractive form.

Sadly, many of these civilising influences would have been lost over succeeding centuries when Viking invasions and civil wars dominated peoples' lives. But as Christianity re-asserted itself and priories and abbeys were founded, notably one at Beauly, only some ten miles distant, teaching would have been available again for young men wishing to enter the church. Some less ambitious scholars were catered for also. They were known as 'scolacs' and earned their keep by doing manual work in addition to studying. Some well-known scholars taught in the Priory at Beauly and at the Abbey at Kinloss, a few miles down the coast.

Sculptured grave slab from Kilianan

As time went on and the value of education was recognised more and more fully, schools were established in towns such as Inverness, a place reasonably accessible to boys from Abriachan and to which all the secondary pupils of today go. There were also the 'Sang Schules', in which singing was of prime importance, this to ensure choral excellence at church services. The main schools, too, were church-oriented. They were known as 'Grammar' schools, the grammar being Latin grammar, as Latin was the language of the church and also an international language, used in teaching all over Europe. Scholars could wander happily from one University to another and often did. The Scots of Leyden, Paris and Rome may well have included young men from Abriachan.

By an Act of 1496, James IV made it incumbent on barons to send their sons to the Grammar Schools. He was keen to build up a body of educated men to run the establishment. This was the first Act of its kind – an Education Act – to be passed in Europe. In the Miscellany of the Spalding Club there is a reprint of the Rules and Statutes of the Ancient Grammar School of the city of Aberdeen. These would have applied in most of the pre-Reformation schools of the time. Life was not easy. The day started with prayers and at 7 the 'prescribed task' was begun. Those who failed in this would be punished 'by word or lash' by the preceptor. Thereafter lectures went on with an interval for breakfast and one for dinner at 12. From 2 to 4 there were more lectures and from 5 to 6 'disputations', followed by prayers. Pupils were able to speak in Latin, Greek, Hebrew, French or Irish (Gaelic), never in the 'common' tongue. Presumably this common tongue would have been a dialect form of English. This is interesting in view of later developments regarding the use of language. No gambling or dice-playing was allowed. There were many punishable offences, including 'wasting time when allowed to leave the room'. One can imagine boys from the hills, encouraged to attend a school such as this one, finding the going difficult. Yet many Highland chiefs sent their sons to the Grammar Schools.

With the Reformation came a renewed interest in the spread of learning, possibly partly as a means of propagating the new ideas in religion. Looking at this period, I find John Knox appearing in a new light. He and his coterie, known as the 'Six Johns', in 1560 drew up a treatise called the 'First Book of Discipline'. These Johns were really men of vision, who regarded education as the right of all children, girls as well as boys. The rich were to be compelled to send their children to school and 'the children of the poore most be supportit and sustenit on the charge of the Churche till tryell be taken whether the spirit of docilitie be fund in them or not', docilitie meaning the ability to undergo instruction. Knox must surely not have been without a (perhaps unconscious) sense of humour when he declares, somewhere in the treatise, 'God hath determined that his Church shall be taught, not be angellis but by men' and 'now cessaith to illuminat men miraculaslie'.

Knox would have wished to see a school in every parish. The parishes, of course, were enormous, some of them the size of a whole county of today. Many schools would have been needed to cater for even half the children. It was not until nearly a hundred years after Knox's time that a start was made, with an Act for the Founding of Schools. These early Parish Schools were set up in any available building, even a church, a barn or an inn. The masters, though poorly paid, were mostly men of sound learning, many hoping to become ministers of religion. The Heritors, as the landowners were known, were supposed to see to the setting-up of the schools. In some parts they complied in a satisfactory way, in others they did not. There is no record of a Parish School in Abriachan, though there were several in nearby Glen Urquhart. School life was hard for teachers and pupils alike, with long hours, few holidays and, for the master, scant reward. But there were times of enjoyment. At New Year great day-long shinty games were played, with few restrictions on the number of players or the size of the field of play. Sometimes the ball would land in the next parish and half the players with it. On Candlemas Day – 2nd February – each pupil was supposed to bring a gift for the master, a kind of late Christmas present. The biggest event of the year, as we have seen, the cock-fight, was held on Shrove Tuesday. This somewhat barbaric activity was continued over the next some three hundred years.

Throughout the seventeenth century the Assembly of the Church made valiant attempts to ensure the establishment of schools, but without the cooperation of the Heritors this was an uphill task. Times were hard, there was much poverty and unrest, with Civil War raging in many parts. The Heritors themselves were not wealthy. The provision of proper buildings and the master's pay would have taxed their resources. It is likely that, in some cases, they were not too keen on having an educated tenantry. The illiterate were, perhaps, easier to control. The days of the clan as an extended family, under the patronage of the Chief, were beginning to disappear. The clan lands, becoming known as 'estates', had to be made to produce some sort of profit. As communication with the south was opening the Highland Heritors saw their counterparts there enjoying lives of comparative luxury, which they resolved to emulate.

SIXTEEN

The year 1696 marked a watershed in the story of education in the country. Two hundred years after James IV's Act, an Act of Parliament – 'The Act of Settling Schools' – finally established the Parochial System, making it obligatory for Heritors to erect a school and provide for a teacher, with a threat of penalty for non-compliance. For many years, in the majority of Highland parishes, the Act was ignored. The chiefs sent their sons to the grammar schools of Inverness and other places. The sons of some true Jacobites were sent to school in France. In some cases the better-off hired a teacher to instruct their children privately. For the children of the poor there was no provision made.

The master was to have a salary, fees and 'perquisites'. The salary was 100 - 200 merks (£5 - £10). The minister had twenty times more. The fees were fixed by the Heritors, e.g. 5 shillings a quarter. The buildings were everywhere inadequate. One 'school' is described as consisting of one room, the master teaching at one end, his wife cooking at the other.

The running of the schools was to be undertaken by the Church Presbyteries. Some Heritors saw this kind of schooling, where the teaching was to be in English, as an assault on their native culture and an attempt to lessen their hereditary power.

Travellers from the south were beginning, at this time, to make their way into the more remote regions of the Highlands and to report back on the conditions in which they found the people living. Some of these reports no doubt spread fear and alarm among the citizens in the south. The thought of increasing numbers of uneducated and probably undisciplined young gave rise to feelings of unease.

Then, in 1701, in Edinburgh, a few private gentlemen met to institute a society for 'further promoting of Christian knowledge and the increase of piety and virtue within Scotland, especially in the Highlands and islands and remote corners thereof'. Members were to be Protestant. Teachers were forbidden to teach in Latin (the language of the Catholic Church) or Gaelic, all instruction to be in plain English. One of the first schools of this Society, now known as the Scottish Society for the Propagation of Christian Knowledge, was set up in St Kilda in 1711, when there were 28 scholars. Some Society teachers ventured to America, to work among the 'Indians'. Their first Highland school, in the village now known as Fort Augustus, was a failure. The style of teaching, in English, for children whose language and cultural background was entirely Gaelic, was so disliked by the people that the establishment had to close after 18 months. Later, the Society relaxed its attitude to the prohibition of Gaelic in the schools. In 1767 a Gaelic translation of the New Testament was introduced.

There is no record of a school building in Abriachan, but the name of James Rhind appears in the annals of the Society as teacher there in 1766, at a salary of £6 a year. There were 9 girls and 25 boys on the register. Ten years later, when Lachlan Maclachlan was appointed, there were some 40 scholars on the roll. He had been teaching in other parts of the parish and had to be persuaded, by means of a 'peremptory letter', to take up the post in Abriachan. Once settled there, he made, as we have seen, a solid success of his time among the people. It was not an easy time in the country as a whole. Families were being evicted from their homes, to make way for sheep and sheep farmers, in what became known as the Clearances, when the Heritors were making 'improvements' on their estates. It is interesting to note that during Mr Lachlan's time Burns was writing valiantly and the French Revolution was taking place. News of these happenings would surely have reached his ears.

Schooling continued in Abriachan for close on two hundred years. During those years the names of 16 head teachers are recorded. Some stayed only three or four years. These were most likely men hoping for a more lucrative appointment, perhaps overseas, in India or wherever opportunities were opening up. Most stayed some ten or twelve years, the longest spells being those of Lachlan Maclachlan's 21 years and Donald Mackay's 22.

These were people who clearly understood the way of life of a Highland community and, because of this, they received the affection and support of the people.

In some places the Parish Schools continued to exist along with those established by the S.S.P.C.K. Elsewhere, the establishment of a Society school gave the Heritor an excuse not to provide a Parish School. There were some disagreements between the two types of school over the methods of religious instruction. The Heritors, ever reluctant to heed directives from the south, allowed things to drift. In 1803, soon after Lachlan Maclachlan had ceased teaching and when John Fraser was headmaster, an Act was passed 'for making better provision for the Parochial schoolmasters and for making further regulations for the better government of the Parish schools'. The master's salary was to be raised, he was to have a house of at least two rooms, with a garden of at least $1/_4$ acre Scots. This valiant attempt to improve standards in education was prompted, at least in part, by the Napoleonic Wars, when it was feared that the soldiers were not sufficiently educated to meet the demands of modern warfare. In places where the Parish school was inadequate to provide education for the growing number of pupils, 'side' schools were set up, small establishments, often poorly housed, with unqualified teachers, to take the overflow.

During the early years of the nineteenth century Gaelic Societies were established, their aim being to support schools in the Highlands and Islands in which teaching would be in Gaelic, so that the children would be able to read the Bible in their native language. The teacher's salary would be modest as he took no fees, but he could rely on the people to provide his material needs of shelter and food. Sometimes a student was appointed who taught during his summer holidays and spent the winter studying.

No mention of any of these agencies to promote education occurs in the annals of Abriachan. After Mr Maclachlan's departure in 1797 the names of Lachlan Fraser and John Fraser appear in the records. They remained in charge for three years and thereafter John Fraser stayed in the post for a number of years.

A report dated 1803 states that the number of scholars was 41 and that they were competent in reading the Bible in English and in Gaelic and also in repeating the Lord's Prayer, the Creed and the Ten Commandments and in answering the questions of the Shorter Catechism. So the Gaelic was clearly surviving here. The schoolmaster's wife had a 'thriving school of industry' going, teaching the girls spinning, sewing and knitting.

In the more remote areas of the Highlands, where there seemed little likelihood of a school of any kind being set up, families would join together to employ a student to teach their children, independently of any organisation. It is interesting to note that Robert Burns' father employed a tutor to teach his son Latin and Greek and a smattering of French, to supplement the teaching he must have had in school.

The population, at this time, was increasing, in spite of emigration, and there was a growing realisation that many children were receiving little or no education. In Inverness a 'Society for educating the poor in the Highlands' was started. In 1825 it sent out to every parish minister a questionnaire which he was to distribute to all the families asking the numbers who could read, whether they understood English or Gaelic best and the distance they were from the nearest school. The investigation found that half the inhabitants were unable to read and one third lived more than two miles from school. Many thousands lived more than five miles from school.

One day, during John Fraser's time in the school, a Mr Thomas Fraser, along with an elder, a tenant and some parents was visiting the school in this 'detached and isolated place' and was struck by the scarcity of books, particularly of Bibles and other religious books. He therefore wrote to the heritor, Sir James Grant, requesting him to obtain the necessary books from the Society so that the children could read the scriptures, at home, to their parents, who were mostly illiterate. It is likely this request was granted as Sir James was not an illiberal heritor.

In 1824, when 55 scholars are in attendance during winter an Inspector finds the master confined to bed and his son taking the lessons. The people express to him their concern over the master's illness, as they value his religious instruction, given with the approval of the parish minister (which was not always the case) as well as his teaching of their children. They also value his encouragement in their learning to read the Bible in Gaelic which they much prefer, as they hardly understand any other language. Teaching methods were clearly becoming more relaxed.

This report contains the first mention of a school in the neighbouring area of Caiplich, which it described as being one mile distant but separated by a hill 'impassable in winter'. In later years this school is described as being 'four miles distant'. In actual fact it is probably somewhere between the two, unless you're a crow! There were 40 scholars there at the time, with a young schoolmaster 'of apparently serious disposition'.

The next mention of this school is in a report of 1867, when Mr Lewis Robertson is named as teacher, with 25 pupils on the roll. Religious knowledge was very good and the Shorter Catechism excellent, the report says. Gaelic was often used in teaching, as the children did not understand English. There is no mention of a schoolhouse. Very likely the teacher, if he was a young man, would lodge with a family. From 1870 to 1873 Mr Archibald Maclean's name is on the register. He is still remembered as a legendary character by the few remaining native people of the area. After this it seems that the school may have been discontinued for a time, perhaps after the provision of the new school in Abriachan. It is next mentioned in the minutes of the School Board of the 11th April 1902 thus: 'The inhabitants of Caiplich . . . wanted a school as they are 4 miles from Abriachan school'. On 6th May of that year the minutes record: 'It is to be built. It is to have two rooms'. The parents were evidently making themselves heard and heeded. I can find no reference to the closing of this school. One wall still stands, tall and firm, though much of the stone has been removed from other parts, probably to repair dykes or houses. The perimeter of the playground is still visible and the well still flows. Legend has it that the sound of children singing can be clearly heard on a still day. One of Mr Robertson's hymns or of Mr Maclean's songs? A happy haunting, anyway.

In 1825 Mr Neil Maclean, a married man of 30, arrived to teach school in Abriachan. The population then was 300 and the language exclusively Gaelic. 84 scholars attended during the winter months. A new schoolhouse was built at this time, but Mr Maclean stayed only seven years, then went to teach in Lewis.

In 1833 Mr Donald Tolmie is in charge. He is well spoken of by the Inspector and by the people. On the day of inspection the scholars had been competing with four other schools for prizes given by the Celtic Society and had carried off the greater number of awards. Two years later, in 1835, another visit of inspection took place. Mr Tolmie was away at a funeral. They examined 'such of the classes as understood English' and were quite satisfied with what they found.

Mrs Fraser, widow of John Fraser, the teacher, who died in 1825, was still in charge of the 'female school' and was in the habit of making one girl read while the others were sewing or knitting. This was considered 'an exceedingly good plan' and was much approved of. Mr Tolmie eventually seceded to the Free Church after the disruption of 1843, and from 1846 to 1859 the register of teachers is blank. The people petitioned for his return, but the Society had strict rules. Seceders were considered to have disruptive tendencies. The school was probably taught by students or other volunteers, but there is no record of their names. The Free Church authorities were setting up schools of their own.

In 1838 another Act had been passed, in a further effort to 'Facilitate the Foundation and Endowment of additional schools in Scotland'. Under the terms of this Act the Government would provide the teacher's salary, while the heritors continued to maintain the school and schoolhouse. Still there was an ever-increasing demand for educational facilities. There were 'adventure' schools, small schools set up by private persons for their own benefit. These were often held in cramped conditions and taught by an elderly woman, the children sitting, along with her own family, round the fire. In one case it is recorded that a shoe-maker taught

The 'School Croft'

a group of boys to read, while plying his own trade. Doubtless they learnt to make shoes as well as to read!

For one year, 1859-60, a Mr Duncan Ferguson's name appears in the record of teachers in Abriachan. Then, in 1861, things are back to normal with the appointment of Mr Angus McGillivray, who was to remain at his post for 13 years. He had 45 pupils on the roll and was to be the last man to teach in the old building. It is described by an Inspector as 'sound but very rough'. Mrs McGillivray taught sewing in the same room used by her husband for his classes. In these cramped conditions reading and spelling yet achieved the comment 'good', though geography and arithmetic were only 'fair'. Copybooks are described as 'clean and carefully written'. Of singing there was none. Discipline was good and the school was considered a definite asset in the community. In a later report reading is described as 'fluent and careful' but 'the Gaelic accent which is marked renders it less intelligible than it might otherwise be'. Writing and arithmetic are pronounced only 'fair', though 'dictation and slate writing' are very good.

The school accommodations were by now in a 'state of great dilapidation'. Mr McGillivray must have had strange thoughts as he watched the great new school being built just over the road. He was no doubt glad to be retiring, to be escaping all the new rules and regulations coming in after the 1872 Education Act and to be retreating to his cosy house and his 'school croft'. All this – house, garden, croft and grazing – is still in existence today, the place being still known as the School Croft. It is, appropriately, occupied by a schoolmaster, a man genuinely interested in education, and his family.

During Mr McGillivray's time, in 1864, the Argyll Commission (named after its chairman) had been set up to investigate and report on the state of education over the whole country. It recommended an education rate, rigorous inspection, grants for much needed new buildings and a superannuation scheme to relieve teachers of worry over security in old age. These recommendations were reflected in the provisions of the 1872 Act.

SEVENTEEN

Many fruitful hours and days were spent delving into records, listening to stories, studying photographs till the tale of schooling in these hills became as real to us as the doings of day-to-day life. We could see the children coming down the high tracks, in summer sun and winter blizzard, hear the bell clanging to gather them into the playground, hear the buzz of learning and reciting lessons, the shouts and laughter at the dinner-play, the gruff tones of an over-wrought headmaster.

Meantime the present-day function of the school was changing with changing times. Over the next few years new burdens in the shape of massive amounts of paper-work, record-keeping, the design of teaching modules and so on, with changes in the patterns of the curriculum, weighed heavily on teachers everywhere. Less and less time was available for peripheral activities and eventually outings to Abriachan ceased altogether. Only in times of real crisis could help be called on from the 'technical' staff.

One such occurred one morning in May when a neighbour, making a call from the telephone box up the road, reported that the door of the croft house at Druim had been broken. I hurried to investigate. Sure enough, the old double door had been forced and part of it shattered. I went in. The bed had obviously been slept in, but nothing had been taken. It had obviously been a case of bed and no breakfast. I rang the High School and explained the urgency of getting a repair done. We couldn't afford a string of benighted tourists sleeping in the old box bed. The response was swift. Hammer and nails and some planks of wood restored the door.

Strangely enough, almost exactly a year later, on a beautiful morning in May, we found the same thing had happened again. The door was forced, the bed slept in, nothing was taken. I imagine the same wee man must have come wandering this way again, knowing he could depend on a good night's sleep in the house at Druim. Perhaps he or his forebears had lived there once? It was intriguing. But repairs were needed again. This time a local man, a skilled joiner, was available to help. He worked with care and concern and we drew breath once more. After that, I felt obliged to remove some of the things that future guests might one day feel like removing – the porridge bowls and horn spoons from the kitchen table, the tea-pot and the Gaelic Bible from the dresser. The following May I kept as strict a watch as possible on the house, but no traveller arrived.

Our next intruders were of a very different ilk. The bottom part of the side of the double door which had not been forced, and so not repaired, had been rotting. We knew it would have to be replaced eventually, but reckoned it would do for a time, as long as the lock was fast. For our intruders it opened the way to exciting possibilities. On my next visit to the house I noticed

The pine marten.

that the rotting portion at the foot of the door had been enlarged. Intrigued, I went inside. There was a scuffling and the sound of a hurried scamper up the ladder-like stairway to the loft. I crept up cautiously and managed to glimpse a pair of very bright eyes staring, or rather glaring, with more than a touch of menace. A small brown body, with a flicker of orange, vanished into a dark corner and all was quiet. Unmistakably a pine marten. I had seen one before, with a baleful look in the same bright eyes, as it was forced to abandon a marauding attack on a bevy of hens. Beautiful creatures they are, but fearless, with a vicious touch to their natures. I went down. There was no further sound. In the two main rooms there was no sign of occupation or damage, but in the small closet off the kitchen a rug had been torn to shreds and was clearly the makings of a nest. Pine martens, I had heard, were tending to come out of the wild, to feed from litter-bins and even to occupy uninhabited houses. Druim was evidently much to the liking of a pair settling into domesticity. It was sad. They would have to be caught.

I wondered what the 'old lady' of Druim, as she was known, would have made of this intrusion. Such a thing would never have occurred in her day, of course. All the little houses contained their families of humans. She and her husband had worked the croft land adjoining the house. Many times she had walked the path to the little well, where a minute fish lived and kept the water pure. She had tended herbs for the soup in her tiny garden plot. A strict Sabbatarian, she would admonish a boy for whistling on a Sunday. The people of Abriachan, in keeping with their character, had mostly gone over to the Free Church at the Disruption. This had meant many a long walk to a church service of their liking, sometimes the outing taking up the whole day, with hunger driving the boys to chew on raw turnips from the fields on the way home. But a strict regime does build character. The 'old lady' and her husband spoke only Gaelic but they knew all about the intrusion of the English and what it meant. Often, on a summer afternoon, they would sit on a bench at the end of their house, beside the road. As the children came up on their way from school, they would ask to be shown the reading books and to be helped to say and understand the words.

She was a story-teller, the old lady, and her granddaughter, Eona Macnicol, has inherited the gift. In English she tells her tales, and beautiful they are. One, called 'A Window Westward', tells how, after her grandmother died, her grandfather, in his old age, came to live with her family in Inverness. He had every care, but was restless and disturbed. Only when they made a window in the west wall of their town house so that he could look in the direction of his beloved bit of country did he settle. His granddaughter has given us many precious things for the Abriachan collection – many photographs, a porridge bowl, books, a hand-woven blanket, the real things of life.

In her imaginative book of short stories, all centred on Abri-achan, called *The Hallowe'en Hero*, she talks of her grandfather like this:

But grandpa must follow the course of the Tallurach burn, far up till it winds free of bushes and comes out thin, clear on the open moor. It is a bare landscape, quintessential, austere. There is a hill face, veiling itself at times with mist like some holy mountain. There is a small reed-fringed lochan where waterfowl cry. And there is the moor, with a cold sweet air blowing over its bog myrtle and heather. Hill, lochan and moor. The three. And that is all.

There grandpa's solitary croft lies. His forefathers wrested it from the moor. They scratched out little squares and lifted off the heather and went through the soil beneath, sifting out by hand every individual stone! Thin oats for food and thin barley for drink grew as best they could against the wind. There were potatoes and turnips and a little grassland forever being encroached upon by heather and bulrushes.

Above the croft the cottage stands, twin rowan trees growing by the gable and one wild rose bush. A path of flat stones lead through the swampy land down to the well. The well has three stones for walls, a fourth stone for its roof, with fern sprouting between them. And in it lives a fish, a tiny priestess keeping the water clear.

This is his world, his universe: he has no identity apart from it.

The story of Druim was set to continue. The man who had bought it along with the old schoolmaster's house and who was happy for it to continue to be part of the museum project died quite suddenly in England. His son was not inclined to continue the connection with the Highlands and the place was sold.

Reconstruction is the name of the game, of course. If only it were done in the style appropriate to the environment. The old stone houses with roofs of thatch or slate fitted perfectly into the landscape. But too often they are turned into what could pass for suburban dwellings, complete with mock facade and patio.

At Druim the old steading remains. The path to the well is overgrown with plantings of conifer. The plenishings from the house – the table, the chairs, pots, crockery, beds and bedding

Mr Donald Fraser, Eona Macnicol's grandfather, at Druim

– and the implements from the steading, all had to be removed and put in store. When the builders moved in, the little garden, which we had replanted with herbs and flowers, those the old people remembered seeing there, all disappeared under loads of rubble. I managed to rescue some feverfew, which seeds all over the schoolhouse garden now and which I can happily pass on to friends. I often think of the old lady of Druim curing a headache as she chewed on a handful of the aromatic leaves. I missed my walks up to the place, to tidy the house or tend the garden or to take round a party of visitors eager for a glimpse of the old way of life, to assess its value, to compare it with life today.

But the old way has, of course, to change as the new way moves in. People who had come to live in the area now had children of school age. A mini-bus was coming to collect them in the morning to take them to a school down on the main road, a country school still, with about 20 pupils. There, they have all the equipment that modern technology can provide. They meet children from a near-urban area, they exchange ideas with them, compare notes on life-styles. Inevitably, contacts with the roots of the home environment are minimal. Summer evenings and times of holiday may be spent nearby, but the car makes access to the town Sports Centre an easy 15-minute drive away. Even the shinty-pitch needs 15 minutes car-time, in the other direction, westward towards the glen. Orienteering, too, is organised elsewhere. Kite-flying, bike-riding in summer, sledging or skiing in a winter snow-spell can be enjoyed right from the doorstep. But the idea that the fields and hills surrounding them were once the providers of the means of living is an alien one to most of the children. Bread and oatcakes come package-wrapped from the supermarket, milk is delivered in bottles in the early hours. Heather and rushes are over-taking the fields, the hills grow rows of conifers. Some sheep are grazed, though they lack access to the healthy hill-ground. A few children take part in a family activity of gathering and feeding the flock, even helping at the dipping and clipping. But there are now no cattle-beasts, no milk cows and so no calves to feed, no dairying to learn. The milling of oats, the making of butter and cheese, is something to read about in a Project book.

It's sad to see the old work ethic go, along with early rising, hard-backed chairs, home-made food, neighbourly ceilidhs. With machines taking over the work-place – the office, the factory, the farm – it is clearly becoming unreasonable to expect full-time employment for all the children when they reach maturity. Hence, I suppose, the building of so many leisure complexes, aquadomes, sports centres, theme parks and so on. School, at least the classroom, is perhaps the one place where it can still be considered 'fun' to work at something till you get it right – say, to calculate the cost of building a garden pool, to draw an accurate map of the way to a favoured picnic spot, to write a description of something of interest seen on an outing, to translate a letter from a pen-pal in another country. The relevance of learning to living can put a shine on school work.

I think some notion of the simplicity of the old way of life may rub off on today's children, particularly if they have the opportunity of talking and listening to some of the older native people. Work was hard, but a lot of it was shared. There was always time for a hearty laugh. Welfare was assured on a neighbourly basis. Officialdom was largely mistrusted. One's door was never locked, for someone might need shelter. There was nothing to tempt a thief, in any case. The only recorded instance of a stranger having to knock and be refused instant entry occurred, not so very long ago, in a remote part of the north, when a soldier, strayed on manoeuvres, came to the house of an elderly woman. 'A soldier?' she said, doubtfully. 'Well, I'm sorry. The last time they were here, I'm told they wore red coats and they did a lot of harm. Wait you there.' Moments later she handed him a dram and an oatcake, through the half-opened door, and set him on his way. So memory dies hard.

Contemporary in-fighting in many parts of the world, as seen on our television screen, bears a clear resemblance to the Jacobite days, with their many battles. The political aftermath has many similarities, too, with repression, confiscation and other drastic measures carried out in the bid to rule. *Plus ça change* . . . Jacobites and Redcoats made a better game than Cowboys and Indians for the children of these parts. How could it be otherwise, when in one of the oldest and more inaccessible places lived a descendant of one of the seven men of Glenmoriston, those seven men who sheltered the Prince in a cave high in the hills, risking their lives daily, and steadfastly refusing to accept the ransom money placed upon his head. There is ample scope for a history lesson at a stone's throw from our doors here. Let's hope compilers of curricula will allow flexibility and scope to include variations in approach, so that matters studied may be relevant to the childrens' situations. The swotting-up of innumerable Acts of Parliament, even learning the story of the American Civil War, for instance, would seem to have little bearing on life in the Highlands yesterday or today. Tell a child the story of his own country and he begins to understand who he is. This is family history in an extended sense. Let him hear the myths and legends as well as the stark facts. That was what helped the children of long-past ages to grow in stature. Let them absorb the reality of their surroundings, too. Show them a flower, a rowan growing out of the rock, a stag as he roars defiance at the world, an eagle soaring, a canopy of stars.

So many times I saw that look of stark wonder on the faces of the children who came out here from the town. To find that things grow and die and grow again, that a bee-sting can be easily cured and that you don't harm a creature that gives you honey, that foxes have to live, though the loss of a lamb is hard: these discoveries and many more led, I think, to an inkling of what the world is about, to the tentative beginnings of wisdom.

There are signs here, now, of a revival of interest in some of the traditional pursuits of Highland people. Children are playing shinty, many are learning to play traditional music on clarsach, fiddle, accordion, recorder and penny whistle, to sing the old songs and to dance the old reels and dances. All this is done, of course, in the context of today, of telecommunication, of video, of electronic and computer technique. So much, nowadays, is recorded, filed away in tidy packaging. There is no recording of the bruises on the shinty-player's legs as he's carried away in triumph from the field, of the sweat on the brow of the fiddler as he plays his heart out at the ceilidh! These must be experienced in the raw.

Song and dance have always been a natural part of people's lives the world over. They reflect the underlying realities of hope, fear, conflict, love, endeavour, loss. This context is the one that children may glimpse if they grow to it from their early years.

More importantly, there is, here, a continuing of the traditional sense of community. Work cannot be shared as it was in former times, as peoples' lives now vary greatly, but the old ways of helping life along are there and the children are encouraged to take part in them. There is a sharing of care for the old and alone, for the very young and vulnerable, a ready hand at the cutting of firewood, the weeding of a garden plot, the feeding of cats, dogs and chickens. There is still the assurance that help is there should it be needed.

As more people moved into the area, some from more populous places where social life was active, a movement to re-establish the village hall as a centre for gatherings gradually emerged. It had always been understood that the collection housed there would be removed should there be a demand for the place to revert to its original status. So, one December day, a party of volunteers arrived, with wagons and trailers, and all the well-loved objects, with documents, photographs and tools, were put in store.

Grants were obtained for the refurbishing of the hall. Toilets, electricity and hot water were installed. Much hard work was put in on a voluntary basis – painting, repairing windows and woodwork, partitioning and so on. Meetings are held there now, a recently formed youth group pursues various activities, there is some country dancing. A winter ceilidh and a summer barbecue are popular. At ceilidhs we sing the old songs, listen to the old music, dance a reel or two. For those of us who remember the fireside ceilidhs of older times, when you met on a winter's night, happy to see half a dozen neighbours, to exchange news and views, to enjoy a dram and a cup of tea, to sing a song if the spirit took you, maybe to tell an old story heard many times before, while the women knitted, the men smoked, and the children dozed off in a corner, for us few the public ceilidh has more the feel and structure of a concert or entertainment. As a social occasion it is enjoyable and people do like to get together in numbers, but it lacks the intimacy of the fireside gatherings. Perhaps we came nearest to that when we met round the open fire in the old schoolroom.

EIGHTEEN

I began then to dream, to think seriously even, about the possibility of re-instating the school as a centre of learning, in a new form. I could visualise one room as the schoolroom of 1875 . . . On the first of February of that year Alexander Maclean, a young man of twenty-five, was appointed headmaster in the new school. What do we know of him? He had trained for a year at the College in Moray House in Edinburgh and taught for four years at nearby Glenconvinth School. There were about seventy pupils on the roll. His salary was £85 a year. He had an assistant who was paid £20 a year. Fees paid by the parents were 1s 6d to 3s 6d per quarter. There is no record of the subjects taught, but it is likely they were similar to those taught by his predecessor in the old school, Mr McGillivray.

These were (for 85 pupils) –

Reading: 85
Writing: 50
Arithmetic: 50
Grammar: 24
Geography: 20
Sewing: 20

There were 40 in the Sabbath school and 26 were taught Gaelic.

How the Gaelic teaching fitted into the curriculum is not clear. Children of today, coming to visit, might come to understand and appreciate the difficulties their forebears, perhaps their own grandparents, had in acquiring knowledge. No flickering computer screens brought them fascinating glimpses of things in far-off parts, but they did learn how to deal with the things that immediately concerned them – getting to school on a day of drifting snow, in leaking boots, for a start. Then, on the way home, in summer, they learned which plants were sweet to chew on and how to guddle small trout from under stones in the burn to take home for tea. There would have been jobs to cope with before and after school – bringing in the cow for milking or washing tatties in the ice-cold water of the burn. Holidays were not long and punishments could be harsh. Taking the strap on fingers reddened with chilblains in winter must have been an agony of pain. But lessons had to be learnt. The well-being of the school and of the master depended on scholarly achievement in the days of 'payment by results'. Truancy was penalised, parents being fined or even imprisoned when a grant for good attendance was at stake.

The children, looking round the old classroom and comparing it with their own brightly-lit, well-furnished premises, would shudder at the thought of being educated there, though when the 'new' school was completed and Mr Maclean arrived, it was regarded as a palace.

Today's children could have a lesson in the old style, sit at desks, copy some magnificent writing from the blackboard, do 'spellings', recite the multiplication table, add, subtract, divide 'mentally' (no fingers to be used!). Books being in short supply, they would listen to stories and poems the master read to them. Stories, tales of 'olden times', when their forebears lived and died, would make their history lesson. The poems they would have to write down and learn 'by heart'. Singing, with the master and his magic tuning fork, would be a relaxation, but a disciplined one, with no excuse for wrong notes or giggles. A dunce's cap or a flick of the tawse were always to be dreaded, but a glint of approval in the master's eye was something to be prized.

After a while the children might well be surprised at the extent to which they'd been 'stretched', pleased with their achievement or eager to do better. It could be more than 'play-acting'. It could be an eye-opener to those watching and those taking part.

For the adult visitors there could be talks and discussions on the story of education yesterday and today. There would be a special welcome for people from rural schools abroad, who could exchange experiences with teachers in these parts. In the old 'Infants' Room' a small library could be used for private study.

How to get children to fulfil their potential, to live life to the full, to adapt, to communicate, isn't that what it's all about? When we think back to the appalling conditions in which schoolmasters lived in the days of the Parish Schools and the early days of those of the S.S.P.C.K., while yet managing to produce many 'lads o' pairts' who contributed much to the world, the problems of today's educationists do seem less significant. Books and equipment were hard to come by then. Even as late as the 1920s there were many practical difficulties to be overcome in the running of the school here. The building itself, a product of the Victorian age, was made to withstand the onslaught of storm – rain, gale, snow – unlike some modern schools, with roofs that blow off or leak. But there were other problems. The water supply, which comes from a spring high in the hill, was often giving out, owing to choked or damaged pipes. Many times the Log Book records the summoning of plumbers. The dry closets had to be emptied and cleaned by the headmaster, for an additional £6 a year. Not till 1928 was water installed, after the unsanitary conditions were reported to the health authorities.

Over the years, education in Scotland, from the days of the Church administration, has tended to be academically inclined. Early schoolmasters were often 'stickit ministers', or even part-time students for the ministry. Gifted children were favoured and often scant attention paid to the less able. This is not so today. Pendulums swing high. But recent investigations into teaching have shown that a return to more formal methods is needed. Children taught in the old-fashioned way, sitting at desks, in rows, pay more attention to the spoken word, learn more, retain more, than those sitting at tables, moving round the room and talking a good deal. In this school of thought education is, perhaps less child-centred, more teacher-centred. In fact, the most important person is the teacher. When this is acknowledged the children benefit.

Today, education is very much in the political arena. To a certain extent it always was. In our age we need skilled operatives to ensure success in the ever-more competitive market-places of the world. To help increase the speed of economic growth would appear to be the aim in educational reform. We must hope that there are teachers perceptive enough to ensure that the well-trained, industrious people coming out of the schools of the future will also have had their minds stretched to include the appreciation of poetry, music and drama, and have acquired the ability to discriminate between the good, the bad and the indifferent in the arts as well as in modes of behaviour.

Education and its problems is now an everyday topic of conversation, as it is becoming apparent that more and more children are leaving school unable to read, write or count. The size of classes is often discussed. In the old school in Abriachan, in the 1920s, the number of pupils in the 'big' room was 70. Today, classes of 30 are anathema. In 1866 members of the Argyll Commission, investigating the state of education at the time, wrote 'a good master is quite able to interest and teach 80 or 100 boys in the earlier years of their course'.

In my experience, it is the ability of the teacher to teach that matters. Children will listen to someone who clearly knows and likes what he is talking about and can communicate his enthusiasm. All the equipment really needed is a blackboard and some chalk. Yes, chalk and talk again! Books for follow-up work at home, are, of course, essential. There must be respite from those hours of television. This, supplemented by time spent outside the classroom, looking at things, doing things, perhaps digging a garden, planting trees, clearing rubbish, would keep them in touch with true reality, which is so much more satisfying than the virtual kind. Computers are a necessary part of modern equipment, maybe, but still they are only machines. They can calculate, if properly fed, can inform and compare, but they can't discuss things with you, answer your unexpected questions, crack a joke with you, give you a dressing-down if you need one.

Our old school in the hills here, with its high windows and its dusty floors, its outside toilets and its stone-strewn playground would obviously fall far below the standard deemed essential to meet the needs of the modern child. Yet it still retains the feel of the children, of the headmasters, of dedicated assistant teachers and anxious parents, of Inspectors, Attendance Officers, visiting ministers and landlords, of all the human beings who frequented it over the years. And there are no ghosts, no unhappy hauntings, only, I hope, a prospect of its future as the interpreter of its past.

THE POST IN THE HILLS

To celebrate the work of all those bearers of great tidings –
from the runners of old to the Post Bus drivers of today

FOREWORD

For over thirty-five years now we have been involved, as a family, with one of the smallest Post Offices in the Highlands. Small and down-to-earth as it is, it has forged for me a strong sense of linkage with the early days of the postal service. Times of snow and storm have meant delivery of mail on foot, as in the days of the 'runners'. With the breakdown of telephone communications urgent messages have been taken round by word of mouth.

The office is the natural centre for the dissemination of news affecting the area, where the activities of the Community Council, of the School Board, of the Village Hall Committee can all be scrutinised and discussed, as in former times the newspapers would be perused, the Postmaster charging a small fee for reading them aloud!

There is a linkage with the future, too, now that computerisation has reached even the smallest outposts. But that is another story. The past, the present and the future of the postal service, this great effort in communication, all hold fast to the watchword of service. We've come a long way since the first recorded 'runner', bringing news of victory in battle, died after accomplishing his mission. But I reckon he considered himself privileged to have been given the task, as, in a small way, we feel a certain sense of privilege in being, by stamping and dating and processing the mail, the bearers of news to people in many parts of the world.

From the bushman putting his ear to the ground to the advent of the silicon chip, between the foot-post and the sender of electronic mail there is a vast gap in the story of communication. The bridging of this gap has been accomplished by the ingenuity and energy of many people. Science has performed miracles beyond the reach of the imagination. But in our small corner we have been able to keep in close touch with the human side of things, the look in the eye, the touch of the hand, as news, good or bad, is communicated. In the record of day-to-day doings in the story of the postal service we can almost feel the weariness in the bones of the 'runners', hear the hoof-beats of the Surveyor's horse, the sound of the mail-coach horn. Here, in the Highlands, we can still follow the foot-post's track, the coaching inns where the horses were changed are still there, as are the little toll-houses, where the gates were flung wide for the passage of the mail-coach. 'Acceleration' is a key word in most facets of life today. But I'm glad to have been involved in the service of the Post Office when speed was not necessarily of the essence, when time still seemed as limitless as space and there was enough to spare for the exchange of greetings, for a blessing here, a good wish there, a sharing of whatever the day held, as the simple routine of work went on.

I should like to thank many people for help in the preparation of this book – Mr Steward and his staff at Highland Archives, where a box of old letters set me on a trail, Miss Mackenzie at Inverness Museum who dug out old photographs, Dr James Mackay, whose handbook on the postal history of the Islands and other publications provide an invaluable source of information, Mr and Mrs J.A. Mackintosh who lent me many of these books, Mr Martin Cummins and Mr Alistair Ramsay of the Scottish Post Office Board in Edinburgh and Mr Adam Borwick of the Royal Mail (Scotland and Northern Ireland) for generous help with illustrations and encouragement, the staffs of Royal Mail and Post Office Counters, Inverness, and of the Post Office Archives in London and, of course, Tom Johnstone of the Mercat Press for his ever-ready guidance.

I
LETTERS FROM THE HIGHLANDS

When we inherited the charge of running the small Post Office, along with the tenancy of the old schoolhouse, in the hills above Loch Ness, some 35 years ago, we had little inkling of how the systems of communication had evolved over the centuries, or, indeed, how they were to develop during the ensuing decades.

To us, as to many people, the Post Office was, in our early years, the place where you could buy stamps and postal orders, cash orders, make deposits in a Savings Bank, post a parcel, send a telegram. Everything was weighed and calculated, often from behind slightly intimidating metal bars, by slightly intimidating, often elderly, personnel. Letters were delivered by postmen who were most often unseen when they came in the early hours and pushed the envelopes through a slit in the front door. We remembered the arrival of the telegram boy, wearing his little round, chin-strapped hat, who handed in his little yellow envelope and waited to see if a reply was needed. He was greeted with trepidation, followed most often, mercifully, by relief.

We had collected stamps, of course, in our young days, and postcards, but it had never really occurred to us to wonder how the perilous journey of a fragile piece of paper from, say, one of the more remote small islands of the Hebrides to our doorstep was accomplished successfully for our delight. Now, with a book of stamps to hand, scales, weights, a date-stamp, forms of all kinds, we began to think about how the whole business of communication world-wide was managed.

For a start, we looked back to our first days in the hill land where we had come to live and work. Our post arrived in early afternoon. We saw its bearer from a distance as he came down through a patch of felled woodland from the road where he had left his motor-bike. He was one of our nearest neighbours – Bill-the-Post – and his coming was always welcomed with a blether, an exchange of news, sometimes a cup of tea, even when his delivery consisted of small buff envelopes containing bills or forms. On days of storm he would battle his way through waist-high drifts of snow to deliver the mail. Many times, when his round was done and his own well-tended croft was not demanding attention, he would give us a hand at whatever job we were at – getting a crop in before the weather broke, seeing to a sick cow or finishing some fencing to keep the roe out of the turnips.

In older times, before the luxury of a delivery to the door had been introduced, a letter would have to be collected from the nearest receiving office, probably the one in Inverness, ten miles away. Here, the postmaster would stand in the market place on market day, and call out the names of any persons from the country for whom letters had arrived, perhaps from relatives who had emigrated to the towns in the south or to countries overseas.

From the late 1700s, when a school had been established here by the Scottish Society for the Propagation of Christian Knowledge, it is probable that the schoolmaster would have kept for collection letters sent by a 'runner' from the town. He would have also seen to the despatch of mail by the same means. And he would, on request, have read the letters to recipients who had never attended school and also write answers at their bidding. In some places, letter-writers earned a small fee performing this task. Even in our day, fingers roughened by years of toil took badly to the handling of pen on paper.

With all the facilities we have for the writing of letters today it's sad that so few are written. Telephonic messages are essentially ephemeral. There is poetry in speaking to a beloved in a far-off place while walking in the garden, an instrument tucked close to ear and mouth. But where is the relic, to be read over, thought about, cherished and put away for future reference? Luckily, in the Highlands, we have had letter-writers of great talent who have left us priceless records of the times they wrote in. Mrs Grant of Laggan, wife of the local minister, wrote letters to many friends, over a period of years, which were eventually published in London in 1809, in three volumes, entitled *Letters from the*

Letters from the Highlands

Mountains, being the real correspondence of a lady between the years 1773 and 1807. She travelled quite extensively round the country and in her letters discusses many topics, social and political, as well as personal and domestic matters, illness, bereavement and so on. A picture of the times certainly emerges. The publication was well received and went into four editions.

Captain Burt, an officer of engineers, was sent into Scotland about 1730 as a 'contractor'. After his return he published, in 1754, his *Letters from a Gentleman in the North of Scotland to his Friend in London*. There was a strict injunction that they were to be shown to no one but one nameless friend, but this was clearly disregarded when they appeared in book form. One can understand his fear of possible lynching when reading his description of a 'Capital Town in that Northern Country' – obviously Inverness. He talks of the squalor of the 'Huts' and streets, the filth of the inhabitants and their strange ways. Fortunately for him these hapless people had no contact with him or his writings. There must have been many places furth of the border where similar conditions prevailed. His descriptions of other parts of the country, where his engineering skills would have given him a different outlook, are, however, valuable. He talks of roads, bridges, ferries and so on. There is a definite impression that he has an eye on methods of 'civilising' the ignorant peasantry. Could he have been a Government spy?

Our great writers, too, have found time to send letters to fellow-writers which give us fascinating insights into the world of literature and of literary criticism and also glimpses of the personal lives of the writers. Fortunately many of these letters have been preserved in book form. The original copies are in the National Library in Edinburgh. Neil Gunn, Naomi Mitchison, Hugh MacDiarmid have left us letters which show how their minds worked, what influences they accepted and bestowed, how they reacted to criticism, what were their relations with the world at large. Their problems in matters of finance, ill-health and domestic arrangements are also touched on, giving us a rounded picture of the human being pushing the pen.

Today the air-waves must be resounding with like messages, but where are they? Lost among the clouds or stars? Perhaps recorded in the minds of recipients, but ephemeral as life itself.

The writing of diaries or journals, not meant originally for publication, has also been largely abandoned. The one I keep myself I find invaluable, not for the re-reading of any profound reflections inscribed therein, but as an *aide-mémoire*, reminding me of when certain things took place – a meeting, a visit to friends, the posting of an important letter.

Dorothy Wordsworth's *Journal* of a tour she and her famous brother made of parts of the Highlands gives us glimpses of the conditions of the time, descriptions of the houses, of the inns, of the food provided. William's poem about the 'solitary Highland lass' does show some empathy with the people.

Queen Victoria was an indefatigable diary writer and no mean artist. Her sketches of Highland people and places are full of life. She writes mainly, of course, about the daily doings of herself and her entourage, but she also describes meetings with the real people of the country. She went to watch the sheep-dipping, which she called 'juicing the sheep' and 'salmon leistering', catching the salmon driven into nets or speared, attended the Games and a christening and visited many elderly women, of whom she became really fond. Between these entries there are references to events in the outside world such as the death of the Duke of Wellington, the fall of Sevastopol. The *Leaves from the Journal of our Life in the Highlands 1848-1861* was published in London in 1868; *More Leaves 1862-82* was published in 1884.

The Memoirs of a Highland Lady, the Autobiography of Elizabeth Grant of Rothiemurchus 1797-1830 is another delightful book, recording the daily life of a family of the minor Highland aristocracy. There are accounts of hardship and happiness, rising at six on winter mornings and breaking the ice in the jug to wash, picnics in the hills, boating on the river, dancing and singing. The outside world is always there, in the background. When Napoleon threatens to invade the south there is talk of raising a body of hardy volunteers from among the local people. Is anyone today, I wonder, recording life in this charming and authentic way, so that future generations can appreciate the truth of the past?

II
EARLY DAYS

As time went by old houses were being renovated and more telephones installed. There were more cars around. People could commute to town for work, post letters and buy stamps there. But did they, we wondered, have time to write letters anyway? Telephone communication was fast and to the point, but what was it doing to the language? Was everything to be abbreviated, reduced to the monosyllable or to capital letters? Already, in our relations with what we then called the 'Head Office' in town and which have always been most cordial and helpful, we were having to get used to referring to official forms by acronyms. Sometimes, in confusion, when consulting on the phone, we would have to invent an urgent customer at the door so as hurriedly to look up the real name of the form referred to.

Letter-writing was not really dead. At Christmas, from friends in far-off places, letters would come recounting the events of a whole year in their lives. These were welcome, though they lacked the intimacy of a personal letter, for we knew that they went out to a host of other people who were strangers to us. Only a short note at the end and the signature were really directed at ourselves. What joy it was to find, among the drab little scraps of official paper, an envelope addressed by a known hand and inside at least two whole pages in the same hand, detailing events and thoughts expressly for our delight!

Letter-writing has been an important form of communication since the earliest times. Writing itself originated as far back as 3,000 B.C. in the country we now call Iraq, which has been known as the cradle of civilisation. It was pictographic, that is, consisted of pictures of familiar objects used as signs. This developed into cuneiform (wedge-shaped) writing, which reduced the pictures to simpler signs, representing syllables. Gradually the number of signs was reduced to about 300. The early scripts soon

A cuneiform letter from Ur, written between 2100 and 2000 B.C.

spread from Babylon to neighbouring peoples and then to the Greeks, the Etruscans and the Romans, who later developed their own styles. In the sixth century A.D. a form of writing known as Ogham had spread to Scotland from southern Ireland. It is based on a form of 'finger' language, with strokes in a series of five, and is found on the stone monuments erected by the Picts.

How did they write? About 2,000 years B.C. the Assyrians and the Egyptians were composing messages inscribed on tablets of baked clay. Messenger services, of course, have been in existence since the earliest times, when the strongest and fastest young runners would be chosen for the task. There is the famous story of the runner from Marathon, in 490 B.C., who fell dead on arrival with the news of victory. When writing was discovered runners would carry a message written on their shaven skulls. Their hair grew on the journey and on arrival at their destination their heads were shaved again to reveal the message.

The Pharaohs had a system of express messengers who delivered the tablets travelling on small punts in the network of canals in the valley of the Nile. About 500 years B.C. the Persian king, as Herodotus relates, set up a relay service of mounted messengers. There was also a service across the desert, linking the oases.

The Greeks had a courier system, messages being written on the skins of animals. News was also sent from island to island by means of lighted torches. The Romans developed a sophisticated, well-regulated postal service with relays of mounted couriers and light, two-wheeled vehicles drawn by two horses, which could cover distances easily over the network of well-maintained roads. The first mail-coaches! They wrote on wax tablets with a stylus.

In the Bible (*Esther* chapters 3, 4, and 8) we hear of 'the king's scribes' writing letters, sealed with the king's seal, to be sent to the provincial governors and of letters 'sent by posts on horseback' and riders on 'mules, camels and young dromedaries.' In the New Testament we read that Paul's first epistle to the Romans was 'written to the Romans from Corinthus and sent by Phebe, servant of the church at Cenchrea.'

As time went by developments progressed. The Egyptians began to use papyrus, a rush grown in the delta of the Nile, as writing material. Gradually, about the sixth century A.D., it was superseded by parchment, which was made from calf skin or the tanned hides of sheep or goats. Eventually, paper, made from cotton fibres, came from China. Later, it was made from rags and wood pulp and it is still the main material used for writing, to the detriment of many valuable forests. In India palm leaves, tied with pieces of kelp, were used for writing up to the ninetheenth century and were accepted by the British postal authorities. Sharpened reeds were used for writing on paper. Then a bird's feather, known now as a quill, was found to be effective. The word pen comes from the Latin for a feather and the French word *plume* means both feather and pen.

I have in my possession a goose quill and a bottle of 'ink', made by soaking a rusty nail in water, both of which were in use last century by a man from the hills. Until the nineteenth century letters were folded and sealed with wax. My grandfather wore a wide gold 'signet' ring, with his initials emblazoned on it, which he used for sealing his letters, even after the introduction of envelopes. I well remember the delicious smell of hot sealing wax! And I remember my grandmother receiving 'crossed' letters, letters written both down and across the page. This was to save paper and to save weight in the post and so to save the cost of postage. Some were difficult to decipher!

As time went by we heard of the different places in the area still known as the 'Old Post Office', where postal business had been done. One house is a rickle of stones now, but others have been maintained and modernised. In the days when Loch Ness was an important thoroughfare through the great glen, the postie would go down to the pier to collect the mails, take them to the 'office' (his kitchen) to be sorted, then set out to deliver them. A bicycle was provided, but many places could only be reached on foot, and on days of winter snow and storm his hours of duty extended well into the night. Many of these far-away places are now, sadly, uninhabited.

In our early days Bill-the-Post still followed this procedure, taking the out-going mail, not to the steamer but to the bus, and collecting the in-coming for sorting. His motor-bike he ran at his own expense, being allowed only a pedal cycle by the authorities. Often in winter no other form of transport was of any help, with frost and snow lying on the steep hill road, which rises to 800 feet in a mile and a half. Many times, in spring, summer, autumn and winter, it must have been irksome to have his day taken up with the post, when his crops and beasts were needing attention. But his sense of duty was strict and he never failed to deliver.

He took a spell of leave, at appropriate times, of course, usually coinciding with an important time in the crofting year, sowing or harvest. Then a temporary substitute would do the round. There was always someone local ready to do the job. There was a time when what were known as 'soap coupons' – the junk mail of the day – were bulking up the mail-bag. One substitute postie, fretting at having to carry these scraps of paper, which would be discarded as soon as delivered, to the high and outlying places, stuffed a bundle of them into a whin-bush. That night a gale blew up and the coupons were scattered far and wide. Some

Collecting the post from a roadside letter-box near Callander
(The Post Office)

were gathered up by excited children, hoping for a reward, some were used to kindle fires.

Our postie, being a native of the place, was known to every household. At that time there were few incomers. He could keep his peers acquainted with the ongoings of the neighbourhood – the home-comings, the departures, illness or death. His arrival was a high-point of the day. Even the soap coupons, the vet's bill, or the latest form from the Department of Agriculture, commonly known as the 'Board', any or all of these were accepted gladly when they brought the chance of a 'news' with the post.

Some people may have envied him his job, for it did provide him with a small but steady income. Others pitied him for having to devote so much time to it when he might have been tending a sick ewe or rushing the hay in before a sudden summer storm. When his retiral day came we met in the schoolhouse for a ceilidh. By removing all the furniture except the chairs and a small table we managed to squeeze a good crowd into the sitting-room. An official came out from the town to make the presentation of a gold watch. Bill, a little reluctantly, made a short but happy speech. We had Gaelic songs, stories in the old style and many a goodnight dram.

Thereafter things were organised differently. The mail came out, ready sorted, in a smart red van, driven by a postman from the town. We were to be only part of a wider round. Was there an increase in efficiency? I doubt it. There was certainly a decrease in the involvement of the postmaster with the mail. It arrived in neat bundles, packed away in the van. 'Himself' handled only the official communications and his own personal letters. There was no more puzzling over and re-writing of scarcely legible addresses, sometimes with the Gaelic spelling. Those letters would have to take their chance or be 'returned to sender'. We were lucky enough to have an official 'town' postman who was really a countryman by nature and even had his own small croft not far away. He made his official tea-break at Bill-the-Post's house, so keeping contact going between the old ways and the new.

After his retirement Bill was able to devote all his time to the work of his croft. The older sister who had kept house for him had died long since, the two young men who had 'boarded' with them had been sent to other places. He had everything to do, but still his place was a model of good agricultural practice. One day, eager to get going with the ploughing when the weather was ideal, he went out early to start up the tractor, an old tractor with the starting handle at the front, forgetting that he had left it in gear. It darted forward, knocking him to the ground, where he lay in agony till a neighbour spotted him some time later. Shock and some cracked bones and bruises didn't keep him laid up for long.

When at last he was compelled to take things more easily I would visit him on a Sunday afternoon, giving him a hand to formulate his right to cut peats on the hill which was about to be planted with conifers. He won that one! Then he was anxious to make sure of his boundary by the loch. He was a fighter to the end. After a talk he always insisted on making tea and providing cakes. Happily he did not have long to suffer in hospital and friends and neighbours thronged his bedside over his last days. His place is safely in the hands of a relative now and a neighbour's cattle graze the fields. When, in his turn, Bill's successor, Kenny Chisholm, reached retiring age we wondered who our next postie would be.

John Kay had acted as substitute on several occasions and he now stepped into the breach quite happily. He was familiar with the round, had coped with it in all weathers, knew the exact spot on the hill where the wheels would start spinning in the frost, the boggy bits to avoid on the way to the isolated crofts. He had covered rounds in various places in his day and was very much a countryman, with a special love of gardening. Many times we discussed plants, their likes and dislikes. In summer he never passed the border without stopping to admire a bloom and to breathe in its scent. He entered into all our enthusiasms and many times he brought small things he had come across on his journeys to add to the museum collection. His family had had connections with the postal service for over 200 years. He has in his possession a whistle which a forebear would blow to summon people to collect their letters at the Receiving Office.

However, he was not to be our new permanent 'man of letters'. This was to be Willy Urquhart, who also knew the round well and was also a born countryman. As I write he is still faithfully working his round, doing many acts of kindness and always with unfailing cheerfulness. A smile and a joke will always carry the day. He brightens many a community ceilidh and has displayed a hidden talent as a raconteur.

III
SHARED NEWS

We soon came to realise that running the Post Office was something more than having a 'job'. We were on a modest pay-roll, we had hours of work – 9 to 1 in the morning, 4 to 5.30 in the late afternoon. We had records to keep, forms to fill in, stamps to sell, queries to answer, but we also had human beings to deal with. The three hours of freedom in the afternoon were invaluable for working in the garden or doing repair jobs on the house. But crofting people are not used to keeping set hours, so if someone turned up in mid-afternoon to cash a postal order or send off a parcel we would attend to them quite willingly. We would also attend to other needs they might have – an ear to listen to an item of good news or bad. We had a bell fixed to an outside wall in case the phone rang when we were pruning the blackcurrants. For a caller there would be a seat at the fire in winter or on a bench in the garden in summer and a cup of tea and a scone. Perhaps a son or daughter had just graduated from University. This was news that had to be shared, rejoiced in, though it was divulged shyly, so as not to appear a boast. We remembered how it always was – you never praised a child, for this was tempting providence to diminish the gifts bestowed. In very old times it was thought that the fairies might steal a sturdy baby. In actual fact it might well have been taken to build up the strength of a rival tribe.

So news of family achievement was kept in a low key, but news of loss or bereavement was something to be warmly shared. The idea of mortality was ever present in the minds of the older members of the community. When a death occurred the intimation spread over a wide area amazingly quickly. With few telephones and a reluctance on the part of most people to put pen to paper the news travelled speedily by word of mouth. This 'bush telegraph' worked almost as well as the telephonic methods of today. Sometimes the postie was asked to carry word to the more outlying places if he had mail to deliver.

Funerals were, and still are, occasions of great significance. It is important to be buried close to one's forebears and to be interred with dignity and respect, close relatives and friends helping to lower the coffin into the earth. I think this feeling dates back to the days when ancestors were 'worshipped', or at least highly regarded as the progenitors of the race. So dark clothes were taken out of cupboards for an airing. Food was prepared for those coming from a distance. Greetings and reminiscences were exchanged as people began to wend their way from the graveyard. Then it was quite in order to eat and drink, for life must go on.

These gatherings, along with those connected with work on the crofts – sheep-shearing, peat-cutting and so on – were valuable means of keeping people together in a shared acceptance of the facts of living and dying.

Most of our Post Office 'customers' had known us in our crofting days and were happy to have a 'news', knowing that we would appreciate the birth of a heifer calf or the loss of lambs in a sudden spring storm, the depredations of roe deer into the root crops or the need for repairs to the road. These exchanges over a cup of tea or a dram at New Year brought back all the feel of the time before we went into the worlds of teaching and 'posting'. As in our crofting years we had become deeply interested in the history of land use and tenure over the ages, so now we were drawn to look into the history of the 'post'.

Here we were, selling a stamp for one neighbour to send a letter to a relative ten miles away, to another to send one four hundred miles, at the same price. The postman might be delivering a packet from a town on the other side of the world to a small croft in the remote uplands. Looked at dispassionately these things do seem to have a touch of the miraculous. Not as miraculous, perhaps, as African drum-beats or the Kalahari Bushman with his ear to the ground. But – how had they come about?

We had vague recollections, from stamp-collecting days, of the 'Penny Post', of someone called Rowland Hill, of mail-coaches and 'Wells Fargo', of highwaymen and Auden's marvellous poem about the Night Mail. It all began to take shape. How had it started?

The beginnings of the service in our area we had heard about from the recollections of the neighbours. The very earliest forms of communication we had learnt about in our reading. When we had more time, we promised ourselves, we would delve into records and find out how this service, which had become indispensible world-wide, had grown and developed over the centuries.

IV
SMALL POST OFFICES

Meanwhile I was teaching in Inverness, sharing the Post Office duty at holiday-time. We had the garden to see to and I was also involved in a project undertaken by my school which meant helping in, among other things, setting up and looking after a small museum near the house. Our time was very fully, and happily, occupied. Helen, our daughter, did a stint, one year, as extra-postie, helping to deliver the Christmas mail. There was a good covering of snow at the time, so the going was hard, but it cleared the lungs of the student from Auld Reekie. The family involvement continued when, one winter, Jim had an accident, slipping on the ice and crashing into a stone wall, which landed him in hospital for several days. And I was laid up with a stomach bug! Helen, on holiday from the University, stepped quite naturally into the Postmaster's tackety boots, dealing cheerfully with customers and responding to messages of sympathy.

Days off were looked forward to and planned for weeks ahead. The occasional Monday 'public holiday', which coincided with a school long weekend, in summer, meant that we could get away sharp mid-day Saturday and be back late Monday evening. We would pack the van with camping gear, as we had always done, and make, as we had always done, for the west . . .

There, for close on 48 hours, we would be back in the world of the working crofts, with the scent of new-cut hay and wild flowers in June, the corn in the stook and peats in the stack if it was September, glossy black cattle on the machair, everywhere a feel of positive fruition. We'd set up camp in the dunes and wash the ink-stains from our fingers and our minds in the clear green water. The hill birds of home are fine – the buzzard with its high-planing reach and the curlew's sweet, sad call. But the white sailing of gulls over the depths of blue carries the human spirit into unknown spaces.

Melvich, a little post office in the far north of the Highlands
(The Post Office)

The taking of a longer spell of leave involved quite complicated arrangements. Whoever did the post office had to have access to the house, to understand its workings, to cope with a possible failure of the water supply, to keep the mice at bay, to remember to shut the garden gate against marauding sheep and the occasional roe-deer. There were also the many questions from passing walkers or motorists to be answered, questions about fishing rights on the loch, camp sites, rights of way, houses for sale, homes of long-lost forebears, where to get milk or drinking-water or a cup of tea, bed-and-breakfast places or even the way to an almost illegible address on a crumpled scrap of paper. There would be bona fide 'travelling people' to be welcomed and salesmen in smart cars to be sent away empty-handed.

My sister-in-law solved our problem for us. She was active and competent, having coped with several jobs during her life and now retired. She came up with a friend, took instructions from her brother, became quickly confident and ended up thoroughly enjoying her spell as sub-postmistress. The Head Office was used to dealing with situations like this and the customers treated her with their normal Highland courtesy.

So we were able to set off on longer travels – once through France to Venice where we saw Helen off to work in a kibbutz in Israel. But nothing could quite compare with our spells in the west – Morar, Arisaig, Oldshoremore (where we got milk from John Gunn whose cow was a direct descendent of the one they brought on eviction from Kildonan) – the names are like a litany.

We visited many small Post Offices in the course of our journeys, noting with interest how they managed things. Some were housed in very unsubstantial premises, small buildings with walls of corrugated iron, small sheds at some distance from a dwelling. Security, when they were established, was not the problem it has become. Then, it was still a time for the house door to be left unlocked, in case a stranger needed shelter. There was little to steal, even in a small *Oifis a'Phuist*.

We had been in our own small office for a few years, had become accustomed to regular visits from the 'Accounts' to check our balance, to supervision from a most friendly 'Surveyor' who left us a set of impeccably hand-written instructions on procedure and who entertained us, when his work was done, on a one-stringed fiddle, when news reached us that there were to be discussions about the closure of small Post Offices. Ours was certainly small. In fact, it had acquired the tag of being the smallest one in Scotland.

We began to look at it with new eyes. There it was – the stone-floored porch, a table to hold the scales and weights, the leaflets, a drawer for odds and ends, a chair for a tired customer – that was about it. But – it was also a way into a house where further welcome was assured. It was also a focal point for the area, since there was no longer a school, no church, no shop. We carried on as usual, ignoring the rumours.

V

THE POST IN ALL WEATHERS

That small Post Offices were to be closed was rumoured several times over the years after that. But always second thoughts prevailed. One reason, we were told, for the maintenance of the office in Abriachan was the fact of our comparative inaccessibility, which could prevent people getting to other offices five miles away on the low ground by Loch Ness. Nowadays, with tractors, Land Rovers, cars with four-wheel drive, it takes an exceptional storm to cut us off completely.

We have had them, of course. One winter the sheer volume and weight of snow on the trees, power and telephone lines was so great that the whole landscape was transformed. The birches flanking the road that rises steeply from the loch shore were bowed down on either side, completely blocking the way. Even our intrepid postie had to leave his vehicle at the foot of the hill and walk up through the drifts with his heavy bag. A neighbour and I then divided the mail between us and delivered it by hand, like the 'runners' of old, to the places we could reach, while he went to the outlying houses. Luckily there were no obviously urgent missives for the furthest away places. Those we could contact by other means were asked to collect their mail at the office, as was the custom in former times, before delivery was guaranteed.

This particular storm lasted for days. Soon telephone lines were down and the power failed. Modern households with their stand-by portable gas lamps and solid fuel cookers suffer little at such times. We were all confident that help would be forthcoming should a real emergency occur. Strong arms could clear a way for stretcher-bearers or a landing-space for the hospital helicopter. We ourselves had few devices to sustain us. We had kept to our crofting ways! But we had plenty of logs for the fire, a camping spirit stove for a quick cup of tea, coffee or soup and candles.

How the 'hydro-men' manage to restore the power in the driving snow and bitter frost is beyond belief. One evening a group of them came to the door to see if we were alright.

'We saw your candle in the window.'

'Yes. Thanks. We're fine. Come in.'

Leaving their cumbersome outer gear in the porch, they approached the fire, stretching their hands to the welcoming glow. In the light from the row of candles on the mantelpiece we could see the strain on their faces. It eased as they drank cups of steaming tea, before setting off again on their all-night task.

We found a certain satisfaction in being cut off from the world, our only callers these hydro-men, who, in their strange garb, seemed almost like visitors from outer space. We had no livestock to be fed and cared for. Our cat was lying snug on the hearthrug. Everything outside was stilled, becalmed, in its great mantle of snow. The beauty of the sculpted drifts and the brilliance of the icicles was indescribable. Inside, we had books to hand and music on the radio. We could even write some letters! At night the stars were huge. It was a time apart.

We thought, of course, of neighbours who had sheep buried in the drifts. Digging them out and getting hay to them would be a task for heroes. We remembered, too, the days of the 'runners' and the mail-coaches stuck in the snow and the drivers and guards risking their lives to get the mail delivered.

We changed the date-stamp every morning, signed the daily despatch form, cleared a path from the gate and waited to see how each day would develop. During the fair, windless daylight hours the telephone men got busy and soon the bell was ringing and our isolation was over. Most places were connected to the line. It was good to be able to let people know if letters had arrived for them. We only hoped nothing urgent would come for the really far-away places which didn't have the phone.

Soon the blessed silence of the snowbound world was broken by the sound of amateur snow-plough drivers urging their machines through the drifts on the side-roads. Tractors did a useful job but diggers were apt to go too deep and lift quite a

Fighting through deep snow to deliver the post
(Aberdeen Journals Photography)

lot of the underlying surface. The official snow-plough was busy clearing the main routes down below. Our hill-road had to wait. I remembered an old neighbour of ours who had knocked up a snow-plough, just a triangular concoction of wood, which he pulled with his horse. This worked successfully when the snow was soft, but after a hard night it would freeze into concrete.

Snow-clearing efforts brought the community alive. Cups of tea were proffered to the drivers. There were exchanges of food, fuel, medicine, anything that might be needed. The young cleared paths for the old. The school children prayed the bus would get stuck on the brae, while they sledged and ski-ed and skated. One year the loch froze so firm that a bonspiel – curling match – was organised. After the road was cleared people came from far and wide, curling-stones were unearthed from cubby-holes and a great day's sport was enjoyed.

Delivering the letters by hand and on foot had given us an inkling, a very small one, of what the 'runners' must have experienced. Post-boys, or in some cases post-girls, rode horses in southern parts, where roads, or at least paths, existed. Beyond Inverness the country was more or less trackless, with bridgeless rivers. 'Runners', who worked for a pittance, were expected to cover up to 30 miles a day, in all weathers, often denied shelter or rest. When one man, weak from hunger and exhaustion, stayed for a few hours overnight in a barn, he was harshly penalised. The runners were often at risk from attack, as it was known that they carried the money paid by recipients of letters which they had to remit to the sending office. Yet it was a job men were glad to take at a time when many were being dispossessed of their land and their livelihood. The path on the north shore of Loch Maree which the runners used to carry mail from the west to Dingwall and thence to Inverness can still be made out and walked.

During the eighteenth century the bags of mail grew excessively heavy as more and more official correspondence and newspapers had to be carried. In 1778 one John Ross, a runner in Inverness, failed to deliver a letter (express) to Thurso, as directed by the postmaster in Edinburgh. Robert Warrand, the postmaster in Inverness at the time, gave orders to 'apprehend and incarcerate his person within the Tolbooth of Inverness and therein to remain until there is advice that the said letter addressed to the postmaster at Thurso is received, to the deterring of others from committing the like in time coming according to Justice.' It turned out that Ross, detained at a ferry, gave the letter to the Tain runner in order to expedite it. After a night in prison, Ross, pleading ill-health in the damp and cold, was released on a 'Bond of Caution' for six months, Dr John Alves, physician, agreeing to pay £100 of any further penalty incurred. He must have been a valuable runner!

It's in times of storm that the value of the one focal point which the Post Office represents is fully realised. As soon as a path is trodden through the snow the postie will be on his normal rounds again, calling at every house he can possibly reach. Should he find illness or accident or other suffering in any of the houses he can pass word on to the Post Office, where it can be relayed by phone as soon as the line is restored, or by word of mouth to people beating the snow to collect mail or to cash allowances or buy stamps. Hardship does make for solidarity in any community.

One day, in a time of thaw, after a long spell of frost and snow, a young postie from the town, who was standing in for a sick colleague, found water seeping from under the roof of a house on his route. He knocked. There was no reply. Not wanting to push the letter through the pool of water, he tried the door. It opened easily. To his horror he found a woman lying on the floor. A burst pipe was flooding the kitchen. Being young and nervous, he panicked, and came rushing back to the Post Office. My husband went down. The woman, who lived alone, had collapsed and died. The doctor was called, the police and relatives were contacted.

On another occasion the regular postie, calling on another old person who lived alone, and getting no answer to his knock or shout, tried to push the door open, as he had a parcel to deliver. The door half opened, then stuck. To his amazement, looking down, he found a body lying across the threshold. He closed the door and came at once to the Post Office. We telephoned the doctor. He came quickly, broke a small downstairs window, climbed in and found the woman had had a stroke, but had survived. Arrangements were immediately made, an ambulance summoned and she was soon in hospital. There she was devotedly nursed for some considerable time, but died before she could return home.

Neither of these old people were native to the place. Had they even been returned wanderers there would have been relatives not far away who would have given them shelter or at least have seen regularly to their welfare. There are always those who prefer their independence to soft living, but the going of these two left a sadness in the community. We missed having them come up to collect their pensions, walking in all weathers – rain, frost, fog, all but the heaviest of snow-falls, refusing to take an offered lift, sometimes even a cup of tea. Life, after all, held more for them than one could imagine. Realising this was a sort of inspiration for us all.

VI
A POST OFFICE LIBRARY?

With death comes change, inevitably. Houses are sold, newcomers arrive. Would we have young people coming to the office, with family allowances to cash? Would they be commuters, doing business during lunch hour in the town? We could only await developments. Meantime other houses were being modernised, building plots advertised, holiday 'lets' being arranged. Friends were beginning to suggest that we should open a small shop to run in conjunction with the Post Office. But we were reluctant to involve ourselves with the inevitable curtailment of free time, the extra paperwork and so on. I did ask a friend to produce some really good photographs of the area which could be sold as postcards, but the complications of reproduction and the cost were prohibitive.

Close on a hundred years ago there were several 'shops' in the neighbourhood. These consisted of small stocks of dry goods – tea, sugar, flour, salt – kept in the kitchen by a crofter's wife, who made a little profit out of selling them on to neighbours. One place, a little further away, was known as a 'butcher's' because they kept some fresh meat, probably mutton, and no doubt a cut or two of venison. These small stores were of value to the community, especially when the horse-drawn grocer's van from the town was held up by snow and ice in winter. With improvements in communication and better roads they were no longer needed.

'What about a little café?' other friends suggested. Many a time summer tourists, arriving at the door soaked to the skin or exhausted by the heat on their long trek up the hill, have asked desperately where to find a 'tea-room'. In most countries in Europe, they tell us, you can never climb to such a height without finding somewhere to get a drink. 'Sorry' we say 'but come in' to the wet ones, or 'Do sit on the grass' to the hot ones. 'Would you like tea or coffee, or perhaps a glass of cider or orange juice?' In this way we have made many happy friendships, including one with a Frenchwoman who was so surprised at our French and our glass of cider on the green that she invited us to dinner in her flat in the Île St Louis when we went, some years later, on holiday to Paris.

People from many parts of the world would reach our door. We would see them, from the window, drop their heavy packs and scrutinise the name on the letter-box by the road to find out where they had arrived. From the garden we would hear their valiant attempts to pronounce the word 'Abriachan'. The sound of 'ch' stumps even visitors from England! Most often they would then make their way to the door and ask to have their water-bottles filled. I suppose the days have really gone when you could scoop up water in your two hands from a hill burn and drink your fill. Weed-killers and fertilisers, sometimes sprayed from the air, are liable to be wind-borne far away from the plantations they are aimed at and so pollute the most innocent sources of water. Water – that magic element that life depends on – we hand it to them with a smile. They smile back. There is mutual understanding of the significance of this gift.

Those with a little English, looking round, will sometimes exclaim, in disbelief, 'This is a Post Office?'

'It is.'

'But it is . . . so small.'

'It is. Some people say it's the smallest in the country'.

They laugh. 'So . . . you have stamps?'

'We have.'

The stamp-book is produced and they look eagerly through it. The pictorial stamps, produced regularly these days, are a great attraction. They buy what they can afford and wave goodbye from the gate.

In the eyes of young Germans, easily recognisable by their accent, we sometimes detect a glint of unease as they identify us as members of a war-time generation. 'We are from Germany' they say. We instantly put them at ease, appreciating their love of wild country, pointing out hill-tracks, lochs for a swim, birds to look out for. These contacts often generate ripples of understanding. One year another group of young Germans arrived, telling us that the hill tracks we had told the first group about are now on a hill-walker's map in Germany!

In these long busy days of summer, with visitors, campers, walkers calling at the door to be attended to, the thought of the office closing is far from our minds. But there is bound to be uncertainty. The place is in a state of transition. Some older people have died, young ones have gone away, to College or University or to find jobs. The houses being built or modernised are clearly for the well-to-do people who will commute to work if they are young or, if they are retired, will certainly have transport and will probably do their postal business, along with their shopping, in the town.

Then, one autumn day, when the summer people were vanishing, we were asked if we would care to accommodate a small branch of the Public Library in the Post Office. We responded with enthusiasm. There would be no kind of salary attached, we were told. No, no, that's all right. There was just room for an ancient book-case of ours in the porch. Soon we were eagerly awaiting the first delivery of books. Our friends were amazed, as the house was already brimming with books which we lent out gladly. But we were as keen as children to have our own official lending library, with tickets fitted into slots and each borrower having an official ticket to his or her name. These books were to be exchanged by the Council librarians at regular intervals – every three months – and over the years they have sent out a very satisfactory selection of books, fiction, non-fiction and books of all kinds for children.

Each time a delivery was due we would be contacted on the telephone and asked the preferences of our borrowers. Often requests for specific books would be granted, to the delight of the borrowers. We ourselves were privileged to browse through many fascinating volumes. To have them under our roof, close at hand, not scattered over many shelves in a huge building, was a great source of pleasure. I remembered how Alain-Fournier, who wrote the classic *Le Grand Meaulnes*, used to revel, as a child, in the books which his schoolmaster father received for the school library. In our case, the children, in particular, enjoyed being able to help themselves, with no demands for silence! They soon learned how the system worked and became adept at sticking the tickets into their individual cards.

Among the adults we discovered one avid borrower of 'Westerns' and another of 'whodunnits', but few aficionados of Mills and Boon. Most popular was the wonderful selection of books on wildlife, gardening and crafts and biographies. There was no time limit on the borrowing, no 'overdue' fines as long as books were returned before the new lot arrived.

One day, in summer-time again, hearing the door open but no sound of the customer's little hand-bell being rung, I went towards the office to investigate. A man was standing there, staring at the 'library'. He was a stranger, a rather scruffy-looking stranger. A book-lover in disguise, I wondered? As I watched he opened the glass-fronted door of the book-case, examining it as he did so. I realised, then, that it was not the books he was interested in, but the book-case. Catching sight of me, he smiled. 'That's a grand book-case you have there, lady' he said. I recognised the accent – Galway . . . or Killarney?

'Would you think about selling it? I'd give you a hundred pounds . . .' His hand was in his pocket.

'I'm sorry. We need it. For the books.'

'You do? And that's some fine books you have there, too.'

'Yes. They belong to the library.'

'Oh, well . . .' He was looking over my shoulder. 'What about that grandfather clock in the hallway?'

'No, no, that belongs to the family.'

'So you're not needing money? I can give you a good price.'

'I can't reckon these things in money. They're . . .'

He wasn't listening. His eyes were everywhere, on a vase full of marguerites, on the chair for weary customers. 'The straw chair?' he queried, his voice now with a touch of desperation.

'No, I'm sorry. Why don't you try the place over the hill? There's a village there. More houses. More people.'

Reluctantly, he turned towards the door. 'Goodbye then, lady.'

'Goodbye.'

Feeling slightly guilty at sending him off, maybe to other unsuspecting householders, I watched him get into the van in the yard, where two other men were waiting. These Irish dealers come over every summer trying to buy old furniture and furnishings still to be found in the remaining croft houses. What they manage to buy they sell on at a handsome profit, most often to other dealers overseas. We have never encountered actual dishonesty in their dealings. They give what is agreed upon, in sound money, and do not steal. But the profit is theirs. And they are very persistent.

Sure enough, a week or two later, coming in from the garden, I again find someone gazing at the 'library'. 'Give you two hundred for your bookcase, lady.' The price had doubled! And word must have spread to other members of the group.

'I'm sorry. I'm not selling it.'

'You'll not get a better offer.'

'Maybe not. But I'm not selling.'

'Och, well. We'll be away next week, mind. See you next year then.' The Irish good humour seldom fails. But I'm thankful to see them go.

I take a closer look at the old bookcase. We had bought it for ten pounds at a house sale some twenty years before, I remembered. It was of oak, glass-fronted at the top four shelves, cupboard-doored below. I resolved to give the glass a clean-up. Was that a trace of woodworm on the middle shelf? I hunted out the bottle of remedy and applied some hurriedly. Then I stood back to have a good look. It certainly was a handsome enough bookcase, though it had never been one of my favourite belongings. Thank goodness, I thought, the dealers hadn't set eyes on my father's knee-hole writing desk or the small mahogany bookcase I really liked.

VII
THE POST GOES ON STRIKE

We had been working the Post Office quite happily for some ten years, had grown accustomed to the form-filling, to dealing with customers, to coping with visitors from a' the airts, when we became aware, through the press and broadcasts, that there was growing unease among postal workers in many places. There had been a few 'go-slow' days, of which we had been scarcely aware, the pace of our life not being over-fast at any time.

We ourselves had always felt at one remove from the hurly-burly of the main Post Office life, though we glimpsed it on our occasional visits to Head Office. In our relatively isolated premises, where we were sometimes cut off, in reality, by storm or technical breakdown, we sometimes wondered whether we were actually part of this enormous organisation, with its world-wide ramifications. We wore no uniform. The only official identification of the office was a sign which had become almost illegible from the wear and tear of wind and weather. We liked it thus. As long as our local people knew the way that was all that mattered.

When visiting Head Office we would wonder at the smart appearance of the cashiers in their bright uniform outfits and at their brisk and confident manner in dealing with customers' often complicated requests. Then we remembered those other small, landward offices, where the postmaster had sometimes to be summoned by bells, or a whistle, to come in after office hours to attend to an urgent matter. He would arrive, scrape the dirt from his muddy boots, wipe his hands on a damp towel and leaf through the files to find the official form required. Then, perhaps after a phone call to headquarters to confirm his decision, and a cup of tea in the kitchen, the customer would depart satisfied. We ourselves came into that category of postmastership.

'Unsocial hours' had hardly been heard of in those days. Postal workers of all grades carried on their work largely unsung. Early rising, shift working, overtime was all part of the business. But over the years the demands on the system were getting heavier and heavier. The loads in the postmens' bags were getting heavier, too, clogged up with junk mail of every description. When a chance to work overtime was eagerly seized, that was surely a sign that wages were not adequate to meet the expected standards of life. The hectic rush entailed in coping with the Christmas mail, which was growing greater every year, led to a lowering of morale, bouts of sickness and even absenteeism. So the unease grew and signs of it reached our small outpost.

With our ever-friendly and supportive rapport with Head-quarters, our ever-cheerful and indefatigable postie, it seemed unlikely that anything would occur to change the way of things for us. But occur it did – the decision, on 20 January 1971 – that there was to be a postal strike. A strike? We knew about them, of course – picket-lines, jeering shouts of 'scab', hardship for the families of those involved. We could do without the arrival and despatch of letters and parcels for a while, but what about funds for our pensioners? There were always enough difficulties for the elderly in the middle of winter.

The first days passed in an eerie calm. With no postman to look out for, the mornings seemed long. There was no exchange of news, no delivery of forms or leaflets, no re-addressing of letters. The stamp book was locked away. The date-stamp remained unchanged. It was as though we were in a time-warp. Was it really possible, we wondered, that all these letters, parcels, docu-ments, newspapers, forms, were no longer circulating round the country, that communication of this kind was at a standstill? It seemed almost like a page of science fiction.

Then the phone calls began. People in outlying places were the first to miss the arrival of the postman, with his bits of news, a daily paper, perhaps a letter. Even a Government form was better than nothing.

'You're not on strike, are you?'

'I'm afraid we are.'

'But . . .'

The Post Goes on Strike

The situation seemed totally unreal to him, as it did to us. The Post Office door closed? Surely not.

With the passing days we became almost accustomed to the lack of letters. The telephone was there though the thought of the mounting bill made you stay your hand unless the message was really urgent. Unfortunately, it was not a time for working in the garden. The ground had the ring of frost. Some tidying up left over from the autumn was about all that could be done. Repair jobs, of course, were always with us. Fences, walls, sheds, were in a constant state of disrepair. This uninspiring but necessary work filled many daylight hours.

Always at the back of our minds was the fate of the pensioners. One who rarely listened to news bulletins and didn't have a paper delivered, was the first to arrive. The door was open. It was our own front door.

'I've not seen the post,' our pensioner said. 'Is he ill?'

'No. I think he's all right. But . . . ' We explained the situation. He looked round then and saw that the scales, the array of leaflets, the handbell, everything that identified this small space as a branch of the Post Office was shrouded in a thick grey blanket that covered the table. He drew himself up. He had walked a long way on frozen roads. His frailty was apparent, though he would never admit to tiredness. We knew what must have been in his mind and we understood his reluctance to express it.

'Come away in' I said, 'the kettle's on the boil.'

Over a cup of tea I reassured him. We could pay out pensions at least as long as funds remained. Ater that . . . the future was uncertain. 'Perhaps it won't last much longer. Next week – maybe . . .'

'A strike!' he said, shaking his head, slowly, in disbelief. 'Well, well, I never heard the like . . .'

'It is an exhausting job for many of the postal workers.'

'Exhausting?'

'M'm. Up early, 4 a.m., all the year round for the posties, and the sorting office people hard-pressed, maybe with out-of-date equipment and the shift-work and the pay . . .'

He was smiling ruefully. I guessed he was thinking of his own early risings, seeing to calving cows or lambing sheep, his long days ploughing, long summer evenings struggling to get a harvest in and then, maybe, everything lost to a storm. 'Well, well . . . I suppose that's so. Yes. Well, many thanks. I'll be away.'

'See you next week.'

He managed a smile. 'Just so . . .'

Our unreal situation continued. We could no longer contact Headquarters on the telephone for information or guidance. The lines were dead. Several more pensioners arrived and we honoured their claims until funds ran out. Then, on a visit to town, I discovered, to my delight, that there were members of staff in the accounts department who were not members of the striking union and who could dispense cash, by hand, to sub-offices. In trepidation, I entered the building, after passing through many security devices and check-points. Things were getting unreal again! I handed over the counterfoils from my pensioners' books and received the corresponding amount of cash. This was a great relief. Funding was assured for at least another week.

As time dragged on I made several more visits to the cash department and so managed to keep the pensioners happy. The owner of the grocer's van, who had known the community over the years, would have allowed them to run up bills, we knew. But that was not the way they liked business to be done. Tea and sugar in exchange for eggs, potatoes, or maybe a chicken, was one thing, but for flour, tobacco, a tin of syrup or treacle, for these they liked to pay cash.

Then, one February morning, we had a sudden visitation by several keen stamp collectors from town. The currency had just been converted. The time-honoured old £.s.d. had gone. We were all to think in terms of our fingers. Decimalisation had arrived. The old system – 12 pence to a shilling, 20 shillings to a pound – it might have been illogical and tricky for people from other countries to grasp, but it was our own and thus beloved, with all its idiosyncracy. Even the letters – L and s and d – were somehow attractive. Could the amount of shillings to the pound – twenty – have been a recollection of the old Celtic way of counting in scores? Sheep are certainly counted like this still today.

Well, our stamp collectors had acquired First-day Covers for the big day of conversion and would like them date-stamped, please. What could we do? The collectors were people known to ourselves, upright citizens of Inverness. So, quite openly and without a glance over his shoulder, the postmaster changed the date-stamp, gave it a lick and a polish and brought it down firmly on the First-day Covers! That historic date-stamp must still be there, in someone's collection.

Over the years we have built up a stock of first-day covers of our own. Every time a new set of pictorial stamps appears we simply stick them on an envelope and date-stamp them. Most of these stamps are extremely attractive, so attractive indeed that we found it inadvisable to put them on parcels going to certain places abroad as they would be detached by avid collectors and the parcels would be 'undelivered' as 'underpaid'. I often wonder at, and silently applaud, the overall honesty and goodwill of the vast majority of those in the postal service in this country. Occasional cases of blatant dishonesty do occur, of course, but are quickly detected and firmly dealt with.

At last, just over six weeks after it started, the strike came to an end. There was little rejoicing. Our postmen, the foot-soldiers of the service, were hardly better off. The service as a whole was possibly weakened somewhat as firms had to seek alternative means to get their vital correspondence delivered. During the strike the Minister of Posts had waived the Post Office monopoly and had permitted private carriers to handle letters, postcards and parcels, providing they had authorisation from the local Head Postmaster. In this way 300 local services sprang up. Telegraphic communication is useful, but there are always certain documents that have to be studied, forms that have to be signed. In the towns foot carriers took round letters marked 'by hand'. But so much had been missing – the assurance of the safe delivery of even the most valuable of documents or goods, the prompt and assured payment of allowances of all kinds, of postal and money orders, let alone receiving the news of family and friends in far-off places. To live in a time-capsule for a short while can be relaxing, even invigorating, but then comes the urge to break out into reality.

It was early March, the snowdrops were whitening, the black-bird was proclaiming spring from the top of the huge cypress, there was the crying of curlew on the moor, when we heard that things were back to normal. Quickly, we unearthed the stamp-book. Things were perhaps somewhat too normal for our postie. He found himself little better off for the strike efforts, but there he was, smiling as ever. He dumped a huge packet of mail on the table. 'There you are, then. Sorry I'm late. I hope it's all good news. And how are you all keeping?'

'Fine. And you?'

'I'm all right. But you should see the backlog in the office!' He seemed positively glad to be back on the job, whatever the outcome of his absence. That's how it is in a service, which is so much more than a business.

VIII
THE FIRST POSTAL SERVICES

During the days of the strike, when alternative methods of delivering mail were being devised, we thought to take a look back at how the idea of a 'service' to do the job had originated. Like other forms of service, for instance education, which had at first been mostly for the aristocracy, the delivery of letters, documents and so on, had been the prerequisite of the favoured. The unfavoured, of course, could not write or read. The old universities developed means of communication by courier with their counterparts in Europe from the time of their formation in the fifteenth century. The Church, too, had its emissaries Europe-wide and beyond from very early times.

The idea of a regular postal service originated in England in Tudor times with the practice of employing royal couriers for the conveyance of the monarch's mail. Along the more important roads out of London, or wherever the court happened to be, were lines of posts, known as the Royal Posts, marking the way. An official of the royal household, known as 'Master of the Posts' supervised the service. Postmasters were appointed for each stage of the route. They were usually inn-keepers. They were responsible for forwarding the royal mail and for providing horses for the couriers. Post-boys travelled with the couriers, brought back the horses for each stage and served as guides along the tracks.

The first record we have of a royal courier reaching Scotland is that of the arrival of Sir Richard Carey, on Saturday 28 March 1603. Three days earlier, in the small hours, he had left the royal palace near Richmond in Surrey and had galloped north, changing horses at Post-houses every 20 miles or so, to ride into the courtyard of the Palace of Holyrood in Edinburgh and there, on bended knee, to present to King James VI of Scotland the news that his cousin, Queen Elizabeth I of England, was dead.

The sending of letters by private couriers did occur but was not encouraged for fear of plotting against the monarchy. Then, in 1635, Charles I threw the Royal Mail open to the general public. This was the first of the great public services. It was also a way of raising revenue. Strict postal rates were levied and paid by the addressee on delivery, the postage assessed by the number of pages written and the number of miles the missive was to be carried.

Letter rates were as follows:

Single letter:	under 80 miles	2d.
	80-100 miles	4d.
	over 100 miles	6d.
	to Scotland	8d.

Eight pence was a considerable sum at that time.

The carriers of these letters rode their horses at a regulation speed of 7 miles per hour in summer and 5 miles per hour in winter.

Links between Scotland and England increased after the union of the crowns. The need for an extended network of communication, like that in the south, resulted in the establishment of a foot-post between Edinburgh and Inverness in 1669. It operated 'wind and weather serving'. The Receiver of Posts in Inverness was a Mr William Trent. Then, with a growing demand for a better service, at last, in 1695, a fully equipped Post Office was opened in the Scottish capital and soon letters were being carried regularly from there to Aberdeen and then, on three days a week, to Inverness.

Beyond Inverness, as roads were at best no more than tracks, or non-existent, 'runners' were employed to deliver mail. They worked for a pittance and were expected to cover up to 30 miles a day, over trackless country, in all weathers, often denied, as we have seen, shelter or rest.

During the time of the rebellions in the Highlands little progress could be made in the expediting of mail. Sometimes letters arrived, weeks after posting, marked 'Opened by Rebells'. In England things were improving. With the establishment of Turnpike Trusts

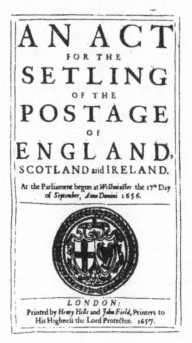

AN ACT
FOR THE
SETLING
OF THE
POSTAGE
OF
ENGLAND,
SCOTLAND and IRELAND.

At the Parliament begun at *Westminster* the 17ᵗʰ Day
of *September, Anno Domini* 1656.

LONDON:
Printed by *Henry Hills* and *John Field*, Printers to
His Highness the Lord Protector. 1657.

Act of Parliament of 1656 establishing the postal system

to help pay for the upkeep of roads made by statute labour, it was possible for wheeled vehicles to run between major towns, and in 1786 the first mail coach ran from Edinburgh to Aberdeen at an average speed of 7–8 miles an hour in summer and about 5 miles an hour in winter.

A Post Office guard travelled with the coach. Often an ex-soldier, 'accustomed to the discharge of firearms', was employed. The guard was responsible for the safe delivery of the letter-bags. He was equipped with a cutlass, a brace of pistols, a blunderbuss, for use if necessary, and a time-piece for recording the time of arrival and departure at each stage of the journey. There was to be no dallying at the inns! He also carried a horn, used to warn other road-users that the Royal Mail had right of way on the King's highway. The horn was blown, too, when approaching inns, to warn the horse-keepers to bring out fresh horses, which were changed every 10 miles, and when nearing a toll-gate so that the keeper would open up quickly and not hinder the passage of the coach, which was exempt from the payment of toll. Sometimes the mail-bags would be slung over to the inn-keeper without the coach stopping, only slowing slightly. On occasions, the guard, who sat alone at the back of the coach, would be thrown off by the roughness of the road and would blow his horn to draw attention to his predicament!

Many hazardous journeys were undertaken by the old mail-coach drivers. There were hazards for the passengers, too. They were expected to walk up some of the steeper hills, to act as brakes on the downward slopes and to endure all the hardships encountered on the way. Bands of highwaymen would ambush the coaches by blocking the roads with tree-trunks and even ploughs taken from the fields, to cripple the horses. Sometimes ropes would be slung between trees to topple the drivers. The greatest losses were usually incurred by thefts from mail-boxes during the changing of horses. There were other perils – bridges breaking under the weight of the vehicles, runaway horses breaking free of the shafts and, in winter, the ever-recurring threat of snowstorms.

In February 1831 the Edinburgh mail-coach became snowbound at Moffat. The driver sent one man back to get help for the passengers, then he and the guard mounted the horses and, with the two post-boys, set off towards the next stage. The drifts were too deep for the horses and they had to be sent back. The two men set off alone, carrying the mail-bags. Next day these bags were found, lashed to the post beside the road. The men's bodies were dug out of a snow-drift many days later. They had honoured the watch-word of the Royal Mail – the post must get through. Many similar incidents occurred.

In 1808 the 'Caledonian' coach was running regularly from Inverness to Perth. At stops in Perthshire Neil Gow, the famous fiddler, would entertain the passengers while mail-bags were unloaded. Business was booming and in 1809 a mail-coach was running from Inverness to Aberdeen and the Town Council subsidised the 'Duchess of Gordon' for a twice-weekly run from Inverness to Edinburgh. After about 1819 small, light mail-gigs were venturing further north.

In all these early years of the story of postal communication there had never been an instance of workers in revolt. There had always been a certain prestige attached to the holding of the position of Receiver of Posts. There had been complaints of low rates of pay, but no stage-managed protests. The deliverers of mail were mostly men or boys who were glad of a job, though they worked often in perilous circumstances.

The days of the strike and the introduction of alternative means of distribution of mail had made us think back to these early times. The alternative couriers of today would have little hardship to undergo. They would be well motorised. Their problem would be to find their way through unfamiliar country and to strange doors in far-away places. We ourselves preferred the orthodox service and refrained from writing all but a minimum of essential letters during the time of the strike. Meanwhile, our forays into the early history of the postal service made us keen to follow these up with the study of later developments.

IX

MAIL BUSES – A VITAL LINK

After the long period of strike-led stagnation, the Post Office authorities got busy with an idea which must have been in the pipeline for quite some time – the launching of a fleet of Mail buses. The small red vans with the emblazoned gold crown on the side had always had room for even fairly bulky parcels, even for the old collie dog found straying and to be returned home, even for a ewe spotted injured at the roadside, its mark recognised, to be handed over to its owner for care. These things are part of the day's work for a postman in the hills. Now the new type of vehicle was to accommodate 6 to 8 passengers, on comfortable seats, as well as provide room for parcels, bags of groceries, bread and medical prescriptions in areas where access to shops was very difficult.

The first Highland Mail Bus took the road from Broadford to Elgol, in Skye, in the summer of 1972. It still operates there and has been of tremendous value to the people of those isolated parts, where few other buses run. Its drivers are remembered with gratitude and affection for all their small acts of kindness and help, which often went far beyond the actual scope of duty, giving reassurance to the lonely and the sick as well as practical help to the active and their families. Again, the idea of service predominates. There is a small charge for the ride, but no tipping or extras.

My experience of using Mail Buses has been happy in the extreme. One year I set out for a short holiday in North Uist, having arranged to stay in a small place near a nature reserve, to look at the flowers and birds. Arriving in the evening after a longish sea journey I stayed overnight in Lochmaddy, the first port of call. I was to take a service bus in the morning to my destination. My landlady told me there was a Mail Bus which would take me there if I wasn't in a hurry. If I wasn't in a hurry? One is never in a hurry in the islands!

The first minibus mail service, at Innerwick in the Borders, was started in 1968 (The Post Office)

So, at ten o'clock the following morning I was glad to take my seat beside the driver of the shiny red Mail Bus. 'You're not in a hurry.' It was not really a question. The lilt in the voice meant, I knew, that the idea of time being recorded in hours was meaningless! My destination was to the south, but we went north, through a strange land of moor and bog, with little lochs and, here and there, croft land in bright green patches. We turned off down tracks to isolated houses, waited for a while where a small sign indicated a Post Office and made a stop at the terminal for the ferry to Bernera, Prince Charles's favoured island. All along the way the driver pointed out places of special interest – a crannog on a small loch, the township that was cleared a hundred years ago, where the people still remember the tales of unbelievable hardship suffered at losing their homes and their land, the unspeakable conditions on board the ships that took them away and on the land the survivors found on disembarking. These memories die hard.

'Visitors today – they have their own cars. They come for the fishing or the yachting. They don't know what happened not so long ago.'

'I know. Were some of your people evicted?'

'They were.'

A curlew is gliding overhead. Its flight is beautiful. Its call is sad. Pre-history, recent history, the curlew will have been there through it all.

We pull in to the side as a huge lorry approaches. My driver gives the lorry driver a cheerful wave and we manoeuvre to safety. Coming to a cross-roads, we slow to a halt beside a small red letter-box fixed to a post. A sign on it reads 'out of use'. As I look, a small bird flies out of the opening. My driver smiles. 'It's out of use till the wee bird has reared its young ones.' I smile back. 'You see, there's not many bushes for the wee birds to nest in. The big ones nest on the ground.'

'Yes, I see. That's wonderful.'

'You may wonder about the letters. They're not great letter-writers about here, but if they have one for the post they put a sign at the box and I can call and collect it.'

'So you never know how long your round will take?'

'I have a good enough idea. As long as I reach the airport before the plane takes off. In winter weather I may be held up, but so is the plane!'

From crannogs to airplanes, the island encompasses it all. By the time I reach my destination I feel almost I am no longer a stranger. I risk a thank-you in my halting Gaelic and am rewarded with a far finer turn of phrase and a cheerful wave.

Several times after that I rode in the Post Bus to different and busier parts of the island. Here we picked up many passengers, housewives with bursting bags of groceries, workers from the fish-farm round the coast, campers with enormous rucksacks. Somehow they were all accommodated with much good humour. Their history has left little bitterness in the island people. There's a trace of sadness in some of the old, lined faces, but the eyes soon light up and the hand is outstretched. They positively

Mail Buses – a Vital Link

A modern mail bus near Lochinver (The Post Office)

welcome people from other parts of the world, amazed at the love and concern we feel for their strange land.

'And you have the Gaelic?' they say, wonderingly, as I manage a greeting and a comment on the weather in the 'language of Eden'. I smile. 'Just a little. I wish I had more.'

'Well, well . . . '

Somehow a Gaelic equivalent to 'Well' has never been devised. The older generation regarded the acquisition of English as essential for their young. The teaching in school was in English. English meant jobs, a better standard of living. Gaelic in the home was strongly discouraged. Only now are some of the present generation regretting this. Affluence can sometimes pall. Gaelic meant the homeland, the freedom to put your own rhythm on the day.

In parts of Canada, where so many island people were landed and left to cope as best they could, the Gaelic language survives, along with the music, the story-telling, the song, the dance. These things must have been essential to their way of life, more essential than their acquisition of 'the English'.

About the middle of the nineteenth century large ocean steamboats started taking mail to many parts of the world. Though there were still many among those who were left at home and among those who went, or were sent, overseas who were not fluent in reading or writing, some form of communication between the two worlds could then be started. As the settlements became established, teachers or ministers of religion could be asked to act as letter-writers for a whole community and their letters despatched to the nearest sea-port. This was a tedious practice but at least it kept families in some sort of touch.

At about that time some islanders, nearer home, were feeling their isolation acutely. In St Kilda, in September 1855, after the crops were ruined by storms, Alexander Gillies, in desperation, despatched several 'mail-boats', with messages telling of the islanders' plight. These 'boats' were hollowed-out pieces of driftwood, attached to an inflated sheep's bladder as a buoy. News of the situation did actually reach the mainland and a rescue operation was mounted. Many of these 'mail-boats', made of canisters, bottles, any type of container that came to hand, were launched over the years. Carried by the North Atlantic drift and the prevailing westerly wind, they sometimes landed in places as far away as Orkney and Norway.

Today, of course, with instant communication by telegraph and telephone, with the whole world connected up by wire, cable and, now, the internet, news of births, deaths and marriages can be transmitted promptly. But these innovations, which were bound to come, have meant that the writing of letters is largely dying out. What a joy it is, rarely experienced now, to come across a bundle of old letters, hidden away in the back of a drawer, carefully tied with a shiny ribbon. There they are, on thin paper, envelopes clearly addressed and bearing the stamps of many countries: Canada, Australia, South Africa, India, New Zealand. Highland people, of course, have found their way to most parts of the world. One hesitates to pry, even at a distance of years, but, at a glance, one can marvel at the delicate handwriting in the delicate prose, the circumlocutions, the whole style of a more leisurely age.

Handwriting, now, has deteriorated to the point of becoming an indecipherable scrawl. I have heard of University students failing exams on account of the illegibility of their papers. The sheer beauty of 'copper-plate' handwriting of Victorian times should make it a recognised art-form. The calligraphy in the illuminated texts of the old books of the monasteries and other sacred texts, dating back 1400 years, is still a wonder today.

I have a neighbour, a lady of 97, who writes the most beautiful hand. She was schooled in the days when such things were important and has practised the art ever since.

X
VISITORS FROM AFAR

Over the years we became accustomed to the arrival of strange customers of different kinds, particularly in the summer-time. Most of them were pleasant people, on holiday or passing through, making the buying of a stamp or two an excuse for asking the way. Some of them, particularly those from the U.S.A., would appear quite disorientated in this seemingly wild hill country. They would come slowly from the gate to the door. Then, looking wonderingly round, they would say: 'This is a Post Office, a real Post Office?'

'It is.'

'We saw a kind of a sign. We weren't sure.'

'I know what you mean. It's different!'

Our usual interchange again! We all laugh. It was good, they would say, not to have to stand 'in line', to have time to study the stamps. Often, in the end, they would buy a whole set, stick some on postcards they had bought, but not yet written, and get them date-stamped.

The business done, they settle to discuss the real reason for their visit.

'We're looking for a place called Kirkhill. I guess that means the church on the hill.'

'It certainly does.' I give them a description of Kirkhill and how to reach it.

'Thanks a lot. Gee, I sure am glad we called in to your place. We'll remember it back home. You see, my great grandfather came from Kirkhill. He was a shoe-maker. I guess he made good shoes. We still have a pair he made after he landed in the States. Brogues, we call them. Is that right?'

'It is.'

'He was a Chisholm. So am I.'

I explain about Chisholm country, Chisholms we know and

how to look up family records in the archives in Inverness. Contact firmly established, we exchange waves as their car moves off. Some months later a card arrives from Vermont. They found Kirkhill and some Chisholms, though no sign of a shoe-maker.

A hundred years ago there were several shoe-makers in our area. *Greusaiche* was one of the first Gaelic words we had to puzzle over after taking on the Post Office. A letter arrived one day addressed to '*Bail na greusaichean*', difficult to pronounce, but a lovely sound once you acquire the skill. It means the township of the shoe-makers and, sure enough, we were told, there were several men who plied their trade in that part over the years. Good shoes they turned out, too, of hide, strongly sewn and made to measure. Lined with hay for warmth, they would carry you safely over the roughest ground and keep out the worst of the cold and wet.

There was a tailor, too, whose trade is recorded in the name of one of his fields, '*Parc an Taillear*'. He made fine suits of tweed. The story of an area can so often be read in the place-names that linger. The shoe-makers have gone, like the tailor and those who spun and wove to make warm garments, but they have left traces that can still be followed. Someone known as the *breabadair*, the weaver, has never woven a thread in his life, but his father wove before him and is not forgotten.

Weavers, tailors, shoe-makers, they all worked their crofts as well as following their trade. One shoe-maker even found time to work as postman. In the early nineteenth century there was a foot-post from Inverness on alternate days by the north and the south side of Loch Ness to Fort Augustus and thence to Fort William. Letters for Abriachan would have been left at the inn not far from the foot of the hill. After 1840 a mail-cart was tried for a short time, then a daily horse-post, until, in 1876, a steam-boat came daily up the loch. It was at that time that a postman was appointed in Abriachan to collect the mail at the jetty, sort it in his kitchen and distribute it round the area. All this he accomplished on foot. In winter sometimes his tour of duty took him till far into the night, when waist-high drifts of snow barred his way into the outlying places. One such postman was our shoe-maker. He could only ply his trade when the mail was light, the weather good or in the long summer evenings. Sometimes he got in an hour or two while waiting for the arrival of the steamer down at the waterside, where he had a little shed. The tumble of stones that was his house is still referred to by the few remaining native people as 'the shoe-maker's place', rather than the 'postman's place.'

Perhaps because their trade was a sedentary, indoor occupation, shoe-makers often rendered service to the community as teachers of the young. They would gather a small group of boys about them, hear their reading and their mental arithmetic, tell them the old stories of the clans, and teach them the songs and proverbs handed down through the generations. They would probably hand on a few tips about the making of shoes as well!

It must have been good to see the old paddle steamers sailing up and down the loch, carrying people going about their business, goods, potatoes, many other things besides the mail and calling in at various points for loading and unloading. At one time juniper berries from the south side of the loch were taken aboard and exported to Holland for use in the making of gin. The loch was busy, with real purpose. Now the jetties have rotted away. A few trawlers go through, fulfilling the original purpose of the great canal-builders – to make a safe passage from east to west. There is an anchorage for pleasure-boats and some noisy water-skiing goes on on the south side of the loch. There is a fish-farm there and, of course, hordes of motorists in the parking places along the loch shore, looking for the mysterious creature that lives in the deep.

The daily steamer carried the mails till well into the twentieth century, then the last one, the *Gondolier* of happy memory, was put to rest as part of the Churchill barrier in Orkney. The great Caledonian Canal, of which Loch Ness is a part, is in dire need of repairs now. We hope, desperately, that funds will be found to keep it working. The building of it by Telford in the early 1800s was an engineering feat of the first order. The work involved, by men delving with pick and shovel and carting earth and stones in barrows, is unimaginable. They were accommodated in wretched huts, but they earned a little money which was welcome. Sometimes they had to be severely dealt with when they walked off the job at harvest or sowing-time to attend to matters on their crofts. Their superiors lived in good stone houses which still stand. The children go swimming, now, and dive off the broken jetty in the bay where the steamer used to call.

One question our summer customers inevitably ask, after their drive up from the loch shore, is have we seen the 'monster'? Though I travelled that road twice a day, five days a week, to my work as a teacher, I had never seen any sign of an unusual creature in the water. I had long ago come to hate the use of the term 'monster', which seemed to designate something not only huge, but ugly, forbidding, in fact, monstrous. People we know who have, without doubt, seen a creature in the loch, describe it as sinuous, long-necked, graceful even, as it occasionally emerges and submerges. One young woman I met, minutes after a 'sighting', the wonder of it still in her eyes, described the head of the creature as like that of a Cheviot sheep. It had been as real to her as the sheep on the croft where she lived. Another sighting was described to me by a man on a place close to the loch shore. He had just climbed on to his tractor and started up the engine when, looking up, he glimpsed something long and black and sinuous disappearing below the surface. Clearly, the noise had disturbed the creature. He stopped the engine and waited till the small waves of the wash broke gently on the pebbled shore. Neither of these sightings were revealed to the press.

One stormy day in autumn, towards late afternoon, a customer arrived who was not going to ask about any strange creature we might, or might not, have seen, but to tell us about strange things that, he reckoned, had been going on in our area for countless years.

'This is the Post Office?' he wondered.

'It is.'

He made no attempt to buy a stamp. 'You've been here quite a long time? You know the area quite well?' It was more as though he were telling us these things, not asking.

'Yes . . . we've been here getting on for thirty years. That's nothing, of course. You count in hundreds here.'

'Hundreds? Millions, I should say.'

I laughed. 'You're right, if you count the rocks.'

'I do. Tell me, do people living here have a reputation for longevity?'

I thought of the hearty nonagenarians who worked their ground. 'I believe they have.'

Some sort of rapport with this strange customer was beginning to emerge. I looked at him more closely. He was dishevelled, with a scruffy beard, a mud-stained jacket hanging loose on a thin frame. Glancing over his shoulder I could see, in the lay-by, an old van, bashed on the side, an untidy pile of equipment sprawled on the roof.

'Have you a map of these parts – ?'

'Yes. Will you come in? My husband will show you what we have.' He knocked the worst of the mud off his boots and followed me into the sitting-room. 'A cup of tea? . . . or coffee?'

'Thanks. Tea, please.'

I poured a big cupful and handed him a scone. A full dinner was what he really needed, by the look of him. But hunger was clearly unimportant to him, as long as his mind was satisfied. He took a long drink, then, taking out a small magnifying glass, he began to pore over the map.

'You know . . . there's a big stone, just up there, at the cross-roads, with markings on it?'

'Yes, I know it.' I passed that stone almost every day and had often looked at the markings. 'The marks are not cup-marks, I think.'

'No, no. Cup-marks were made by humans. These go way back in what we call time. Now, look. Here, on a map of today we can read things about the past. See the line of the stream, the contours of the hills. They tell us something of what has been going on below the surface. All this pre-dates the existence of humans. But they followed, the early ones, they followed instinctively, the ways they felt were right.'

'So that stone was a marker?'

'I believe it was. And this house . . . it stands very nearly on the line pointed out. That's why I had to come. And your garden, up there. There are marks all over your garden.'

'Really?'

'Really. These old ancestors of ours had a good inkling of what the world was all about. We've lost so much of what they learnt. We've covered everything, almost everything, in concrete. True, we've built palaces and towers, but take one flower, one autumn crocus I saw by your gate, and – you remember – Solomon in all his glory . . . '

For the first time he was smiling. He folded the map and stood up. 'I must go. Thanks for the tea.'

'Are you camping?'

He laughed. 'I just doss down in the van.'

I saw him to the gate. The sky was clearing to make way for the first stars. He looked up.

'You know, I think a day may come when this old earth re-asserts itself, maybe joins forces with the planets and sends us all tumbling into space. Let's wonder at it all for a while, anyway.'

'Yes, indeed.'

I watch as his rickety vehicle lurches up the road. We never saw him again, but what he said haunted our minds for long. Working the garden ground in spring I felt a strange sense of awe as I thought of the origins of that substance which we'd tamed to serve our needs. We were clever at taming, but there were forces we'd never overcome. Had we invented our gods out of fear, setting up palaces for our kings, placating our overlords with offerings we could ill afford? Perhaps our 'customer' was right to go around the world in poverty, looking for signs and wonders, telling of them to those who'd listen.

In summer, walking the moor ground where we always looked for the hut circles that told of human habitation, realisation came to us of the vast underlying sources of energy we could feel in our bones. Of course, we said to our inner selves, this is why we feel so well. We can partake of this energy. It's better than any meal. We thought of our 'customer', his thin frame and his immense vitality. 'More things in heaven and earth', perhaps? We were glad the Post Office had brought him to our door.

XI
CHANGES, AND THE VOTING SYSTEM

We had been in the schoolhouse/Post Office for rather more than ten years when Jim's health began to give us cause for concern. He was so strong, wiry, resilient, always so cheerfully ready to tackle anything, had never had a day's illness in years, his worst pain an attack of lumbago a long time before, so that to think of him as incapacitated in any way was almost impossible. But even the hardiest frame has to give way some time. He developed osteo-arthritis. Pain-killers did nothing to alleviate the suffering. He was taken into hospital for a general 'assessment' of his condition. Hospital in the beautiful days of June was anathema to him. I was trying to make arrangements to get him home, with or without 'assessment', when he had a stroke and did not recover.

I was glad that his last years had been busily happy. I had taken early retirement from teaching so that we could share fully the work of the Post Office and looking after the house and garden and 'curating' the museum which we had been involved in over the years. Our daughter had married and two small granddaughters had been trotting in and out of the house and playing in the garden, to his great delight. His going left a great blank in many lives, not least in those of the community of which he had been a part and where his nature had been fully appreciated. He had always made time for people, time to talk, time to listen, time to have a joke, to help where he could. The young people who came about working on projects liked his sense of humour, the very old appreciated his kind approach.

In due time the Head Postmaster came to see me. In those days we had a Head Postmaster and he came quite often to visit. Now we have an Area Manager. He is probably snowed-under with paperwork, as all administrators are today. Contact is less frequent, but we have regular visits from other supervisors.

On this occasion the Head Postmaster had time to sit down, to talk quietly and to ask me whether I wished to take over the Post Office duties officially. If I did not, he said, it would be quite understandable, but it would probably mean the office would be closed. Closed? Surely not! I thought of the shoe-maker, cobbling away while he waited for the steamer, sorting the mail on his kitchen table, taking it round on foot, in all weathers. I remembered the five other houses, some still known as 'the old Post Office', where letters had been posted, stamps sold, orders cashed, news exchanged. No Post Office? I thought of the men, and one woman, who had carried the mails in our time – close on thirty years. They were all crofters with places of their own to see to – crops, sheep, cattle – people who could turn their hand to many jobs. Now we were modernised, the mail arriving at our door ready sorted, in a shiny red van, but surely not modernised to the extent of shutting the Post Office, the only focal point for the area, since the school had been closed for nearly twenty years and no-one now ran a shop.

I looked at the Head Postmaster sitting there, with the power in his kindly hands to mark the end of an era. I had an idea he was aware of that and was quite glad when I said I thought I would like to keep the Post Office going. He got up with a smile and said: 'Well, now, think it over and let me know in a day or two what you decide'.

He had always been more of a father-figure in our lives, rather than a boss, someone we liked and respected and did not need to fear. He had always been interested in our books, our museum activities and forays into local history.

It didn't take me long to make up my mind. I had been initiated by Jim into the ways of filling in returns, working out the balance, ordering stock and so on. The Post Office must stay. The place must retain its identity. Abriachan was known in song and story since the days of Columba's settlement at Kilianan, down on the shore of Loch Ness. It had been church land, had provided sanctuary for the persecuted. Part of it had once belonged to the far-famed Wolf of Badenoch. Its inaccessibility had allowed for the concealment of stills and the production of sellable drams, when money had to be found to meet the rising cost of rents. In the 1920s its children had made the name Abriachan synonymous with excellence in Gaelic singing.

It is no longer inaccessible, but it retains much of its special character. Large areas of moorland have been afforested but some native trees remain – birch, rowan, hazel, alder – and on the lower slopes, oak, holly, hawthorn. There are still enough patches of heather and bracken to gladden the eye in autumn with the glory of purple and gold. The rocks still shine, the granite and whinstone that built the first solid houses of stone. The water still cascades into the big loch down below, forming deep brown pools and providing power to run a dynamo for the nursery garden on the shore. The name Abriachan is said to mean the confluence of the speckled burn with the water of the loch.

Montrose's troops had passed through the Caiplich area, just to the north of the Post Office, on their way to make camp near Beauly. They had made themselves unpopular, as soldiers do, by carrying off cattle on their way. Skirmishes took place. The 'battlefield' can still be made out. No doubt the troops dined well that night, but the quiet people would have lost a large part of their livelihood. War always overides normality. Andrew de Moray, the great Scottish patriot, was here, too. He and his men ambushed the governor of Urquhart Castle on his way from Inverness and inflicted damage on his cavalcade. Wounded men from Culloden had passed this way, too, limping back to their homes in Glen Urquhart. These things were often in my mind as I walked in Caiplich, where our crofting days were spent.

Next morning I was up early, gave the date-stamp a thorough cleaning and brought it down vigorously on the daily despatch form – ABRIACHAN. We were lucky, I knew, to have our own named stamp. Most small offices in the area came under the umbrella stamp of Inverness. Old-fashioned our equipment might be, but we liked it that way. The stamp-book was held together by the good workmanship that must have gone into the making of it.

In the back flap were labels of amazing antiquity. There was a set of delicate bronze weights for the delicate bronze letter-weighing scale. I was surprised, one day, to see in the Inverness Museum a parcel scale, the exact replica of the one we had in everyday use. It serves its purpose very adequately and no one is in the greatest of hurries here. The weights go on and off and on again till the exact figure is worked out.

Our nursery gardeners from the loch shore who often have a number of parcels of plants for despatch and scales of their own, have everything ready-weighed so that we only have to check them and work out the cost. This is a great saving of time and the plants get away fresh. So . . . this morning – it was a bright blue summer morning – I looked round the little office, at the clear word Abriachan on the despatch note, at the old stamp-book still holding together, at the sturdy old scales, at the books on the library shelves. I looked round again. Then I went to the phone and spoke to the Head Postmaster. 'I'd like to stay on' I said. He was happy with my decision and I duly signed the Official Secrets Act – what official secrets would come my way, I wondered? – and was sworn in.

Some time previously I had been co-opted on to the Community Council and it was to be my privilege to serve on it for a number of years. We met, originally, in a very small hall, known as the 'hut', some 5 or 6 miles nearer to Inverness. In winter we wore our heaviest clothes as the heating was minimal. Getting home, when frost had turned the snow to concrete, could be tricky. But it was good to be able to discuss the problems affecting different areas – road maintenance, rights of way, water supplies, facilities for children and pensioners.

Latterly, meetings took place in a big, warm room at a nearby school, which was more congenial but lacked something of the intimacy of the early days. It was always difficult to make the general public aware of the importance of having a Council near to them, anxious to hear of their grievances, to do things to help. Attendance at open meetings was always poor. However, with the re-organization of local government, the Community

Councils are, I think, coming into their own as a valid link between people and power.

One of my duties as a Council member was to organise the election of members which was to take place at regular intervals should more than the requisite ten put forward their names. In fact, this rarely happened. My appointment to this duty came about because it was known that my husband and I had always organised the voting for elections of other kinds – local, parliamentary, even, once, a referendum. This voting took place in the big schoolroom, just through the wall from the house and the Post Office. Elections always seem to happen on a Thursday, which was half-day in the Office, so little disturbance was caused. I would put a notice on the house door, telling customers to use the school door. Then I would take the necessary equipment for the morning duty through to the schoolroom.

Some time before Polling Day I had swept and garnished the place, fixed the polling booth, filled the coal scuttle, brought in some vases of flowers. Then I went to town to fetch the ballot box and all the necessary equipment. Over the preceding days party workers had been busy, sticking notices on telegraph poles, bushes, trees, in valiant efforts to get the voters to the poll.

On Polling Day I was up by half past five and into the schoolroom to light the fire, back to snatch a quick breakfast and to fill flasks of tea and coffee. Then the Post Office equipment was taken in and when by seven o'clock my assistant, the polling clerk, had arrived the fire was burning brightly and we were ready for our first voter. The sealing of the ballot box was an incredibly old-fashioned process. We fumbled about with red tape, wax spills and sealing wax till it was secured to our satisfaction.

With only about 80 voters on the register we knew that we would not be rushed, but the long day did loom ahead of us. Over the years different people have been sent as assistant to the Presiding Officer, the title I rejoiced in. All have been congenial companions and have helped to make the day pass pleasantly. The first people in to vote were always the commuters on their way to work in town. Some were joggers who came extra early, trying us out to make sure we hadn't overslept, they would say, with broad healthy smiles! There would be a lull, then, till after nine, when the local bobby would look in, just to make sure everything was in working order and running smoothly. We assured him we had no problems, offered a cup of tea and saw him off with a 'see you later' smile.

The postie would arrive at his usual time, well briefed about the slight change of location of the Post Office. The routine office work was soon accomplished.

'I've been reminding them all about the voting. It's a good day. They've no excuse!' With his usual cheery wave he'd be off, to jog more memories on his way.

By mid-morning we were ready for a coffee-break. If we were lucky there'd be just time to quaff a mugful between voters. A few people found it convenient to buy a few stamps after voting. I knew all our voters by sight so when a strange head appeared round the door we realised it was a party worker or an election agent, just sounding out the ground, reckoning up the turnout. There was no exit-polling with us. We would just smile at the anxious faces and make a polite comment about the weather. We had always been lucky with our electorate. There were no problem voters, no handicapped or blind people, just the occasional proxy voter.

By late morning another lull would set in. The Post Office closed and the apparatus was locked away. I brightened up the fire. Even in summer there's a chill in the old schoolroom. I turned on the radio to hear news of polling over the country as a whole. Munching our sandwiches we listened intently as word came over the air of the numbers who had voted. I did a quick count of ours.

'We've had 35 so far!'

'But remember, that's nearly half the electorate!'

'You're right. The percentage is quite good!'

In early afternoon another bobby would arrive to make sure we had no rioting. Rioting? We asssured him all was quiet!

'Not too quiet, I hope?'

'No, no. Just normal. How are they doing down the way?'

'They're quiet, too, they say.'

'We've had nearly 50 per cent in so far.'

'You're doing fine, then. See you later.'

As the next hour or so passes we begin to feel slightly drowsy, the early start to the day beginning to tell. I brew some good strong coffee in an old pan on the fire and we revive. Then what amounts almost to a 'rush' occurs. Some older people arrive, driven in neighbours' cars, a young mother with a child in a push-chair; another bringing an older child, just home from school, to let him see how voting works. I remember how, in our early days here, we went to some of the most outlandish places in the area to fetch people to the polls in our old ramshackle vehicle.

Things brighten up fast. Tea-time brings returning commuters, some we haven't seen for long enough, as they tend to buy stamps in town. Greetings are warm, news is exchanged, they meet up with people they also haven't seen much with the busy lives they lead.

'It's almost a party!' one exclaims. 'Why don't we do this more often?'

The laughter and the cheer revive us. The pile of voters' cards on the table is rising. We check the number again. We listen to the 6 o'clock news. The evening is long. Another bobby arrives, a sergeant this time.

'Any problems?' His smile is wide, his presence welcome.

'None at all, thanks.'

'You'll get the box back to town all right?'

'We will.'

We're secure in the knowledge that, should there be a breakdown in our arrangements he will see to transport. Contact with the police, our Highland police, is always reassuring. They are there, always, to help. Strong, courteous, always totally reliable, if they have to make arrests, that too, is a help. Many of them are from the croft lands in the west, some are Gaelic speakers, all of them understand the people, the country and its ways. You find them in the big cities, too. Along with engineers, doctors, vets, they carry their own special brand of integrity.

After a supper snack we begin to look out the numerous forms which have to be filled in before the box is despatched. Nine o'clock comes. Another news bulletin. The sound of a tractor outside just drowns the reader's voice. I switch off.

'Sorry I'm late. The cow was calving'.

It's a neighbour from the heights. Apologising for his grubby hands he wastes no time in making his cross and slipping his paper into the box.

'It went well?'

'Aye. A bonny wee heifer.'

'That's good.'

There are more important things, even, than voting. A last-minuter arrives, with no excuse, only a dash and a wave and a closing door. Ten o'clock and the poll is over. Before fatigue clouds our brains we do the last calculations together, checking each other's results, complete the forms, I sign everything, we close the hole in the box, with sealing wax and red tape again, parcel up all the stationery and equipment which can be used next time and we're ready for the road.

The counting-house is a lively place – bright lights and bright people at the long tables, eager to begin their task. Our box is checked in and we retreat. The result of the count in our widely scattered area will be long in coming. Reaching home I switch on the television, watch for a few minutes and fall fast asleep. The cat wakes me, jumping on my knee. I stagger up to bed, listen to the radio for another few minutes and have to give in. The Post Office must be open in a few hours time.

XII
MORE VISITORS

The little museum next door with which I was involved brought people of many different types, some of whom came to the Post Office to buy stamps and to linger for a chat. Most of them were genuinely interested in the old artefacts and the glimpses of a former way of life which they gave. Many were knowledgeable and contributed a lot to our own understanding. Some of the elderly men of crofting background, for instance, were able to explain to us exactly how a horse-driven mill was worked, something we had never seen. Some visitors were a little strange.

One large, portly gentlemen, with an unmistakable German accent, asked me:

'Please, can you tell me, where is Elgin?'

'Elgin? Well, it's quite a long way from here. Have you a map?'

'Yes, I'll get it from the car. You see, I am a geologist. I want to see those Elgin marbles.'

I try to suppress a smile.

'But . . . they are not in Elgin. They're in London. In the British Museum.'

'Oh! How is that?'

I try to explain about Lord Elgin and Greece and . . . .it's difficult. He goes away, not totally convinced, I feel. But then neither am I.

Another day, a young couple, mid-European this time, I judge, looking perplexed, ask: 'Where is castle, please?'

Mid-Europeans often leave out the definite article. 'A castle?'

'Yes. We see picture of it in Tourist Office. Where Queen comes. Here, on my map. I show you.'

It's a map of the area. I look. Underlined, in pencil, is the word 'Balmore'. I smile.

'Oh, that's a common place-name. It's from the Gaelic, turned into English – "bal", a collection of houses, and "more", meaning big. We have Balbeg, too. That means a small collection of houses.'

They listen intently, their faces falling.

'Oh . . . so Balmoral not here.'

'No. It's a long way away. In Aberdeenshire.'

'Oh, and what is here, please?'

'Well, here we have just the hills and the trees. People don't work the small fields much now. But . . . '

The listeners' eyes brighten.

'Oh, that is good, isn't? So you have not much what is it? Pesticides?'

'You're right. That is good. We still have birds. Not as many as long ago. But still . . . '

'And flowers. We see them by the road.'

'Yes. A good lot of flowers.' I begin to feel we can really compete with Balmoral. Then comes the inevitable question.

'And have you seen monster?'

'No. I . . . '

'But it's so near, big lake. You can see it almost from your door!'

'That's true. But we have a small lake here. Just up the road. We call it a loch.'

After several valiant attempts they achieve a remarkably good pronunciation of the word.

'You mean there is also monster?'

'No, but . . . ' I embark on the story of the kelpie, the water-horse of legend. It's difficult with their limited understanding of the language, but gestures help, and their co-operation, their willingness to understand.

'Oh, we go there, then. And we see birds. And flowers. Thank you. Thank you.'

I point out the road and wish them well. No castles here, but birds and flowers. I scan the sky. Not a golden eagle, maybe, but buzzards and curlew, swifts and wheatear and at the loch there will be sandpipers, maybe dragonflies skimming the water, and the scent of myrtle and meadowsweet and the little white rose. I envy them their walk. Their memories will be happy.

People from the U.S.A. are often amazed at some of our postal arrangements. One large gentleman, wearing a large Panama hat, and a very large smile, came slowly up from the gate.

'My, you have a pretty garden. And is this really the Post Office?'

'It is.'

'I thought so. We saw the letter-box over the road. But there's not much of a sign.'

'No. But people know.'

He laughs. 'They have second sight maybe?'

'Some of them have!'

'And I guess your mail-man would have to have it to find some of the places he has mail for. Some are way off the road. In the States we have a box at the end of the side-road, even at the end of the garden path, at the gate, for the letters to be deposited. And a place for parcels, too. The folk can collect them at leisure. That saves a lot of time and wear and tear on the delivery vehicle, I reckon.'

'I'm sure it does, but here people like to have a visit from their postie. Especially those who live alone. And they mostly don't have mail every day.'

He smiles. 'You folk like a touch of feeling in your services, I guess.'

'Well, yes, if you like.'

I venture into a homily of my own.

'About a hundred years ago it was decreed by Queen Victoria, no less, that every household in the country should have a free delivery of mail. It was to celebrate her Jubilee.' His eyes are wide.

'What d'you know? Well, well. The old lady did you proud.'

'She did. Before that you had to collect your mail at the nearest office or pay to have it delivered, sometimes by people of doubtful honesty. But, of course, this nation-wide delivery did mean problems in the Highlands and particularly the islands.'

'You can say that again. Imagine taking a letter to some place in the Isle of Skye when the ferry couldn't operate on account of a storm. And there was no bridge, like now, and no airplanes. Oh, my!'

'And there were places much more remote than Skye. All the Outer Isles. And the islands of Orkney and Shetland. Now, of course, everything goes by air.'

As I speak a deafening noise from overhead makes my visitor cower.

It subsides. He straightens up.

'Sorry about that,' he apologises, 'it reminds me . . . well, never mind.'

Probably Vietnam, I think.

'Well now, I've enjoyed our talk so much. I guess I'll buy a stamp or two.'

I produce the stamp book and leaf through it.

'Your stamps are so pretty. I like them all. But I guess some are a bit big for my postcards home. I write such a lot on them about your lovely country. There's no room for big stamps.' After much careful choosing he makes his purchases and pays up, with a satisfied smile.

'You like it here. Have you, perhaps, forebears from the Highlands?'

'I haven't but my wife has. She's back in the States. So I reckon our kids are half Highland, bless them. No, my folk came from Austria. They had to get out. I've heard about Highland people having to get out, too. 200 or so years ago. Is that right?'

'It is. A lot of them were forced out of their places to make way for sheep. The clan chiefs had become more like landlords than father-figures and wanted to make money out of their estates.'

'Yes. That's what I heard. It was known as the Clearances, I believe.'

'It was. That's how there are so many people of Highland descent in Canada, Australia, New Zealand and . . . '

'And the States!'

'That's right. Some of them did leave voluntarily. Things were bad at home and they hoped for something better elsewhere. But it took them a while to find it.'

'And now? How are things now?'

'Getting better slowly, I think. But the huge numbers of sheep that were imported and then the red deer that were allowed to breed unhindered for the hunting fraternity, have done so much damage to the natural environment. It will take years to recover.'

'I can imagine.'

'But we have people working on it, here and there.'

'More of your pioneering spirits! That's good to hear. I'll be telling the folks back home where to come when they're in Scotland. I guess for the price of a stamp or two I got good measure. Now, goodbye. God bless!'

There's the trace of a jaunt in his step as he goes back to the car he left in the lay-by.

Another time, a bright summer day, brought us a family from Canada. Three children came racing up the path, bright eyes dancing in sunburnt faces. They reach the door and burst in.

'This is a Post Office?' It's the disbelieving tone we're used to.

'It is. Would you like a stamp?'

'We have no money. We'll have to wait for Dad.'

'He made us walk up. He's coming in the car.'

'Told us he's walked the road so many times. He was at school here.'

'He was?' I get a word in. 'Would you like to see inside the school?'

'Oh yes!'

I fetch the key and open up the schoolroom. They look round wonderingly.

'Did Dad really study here?'

'You can't see out the windows.' The small girl shivers.

'It's kinda spooky.'

'I know what you mean. That's because it's been empty for a good while. When there was a fire in the grate and lots of children at their desks it was fine.'

'Dad must have learnt something. He's an accountant now.'

'A very good one.'

'I'm sure he learnt a lot. He'd certainly know his tables. And he'd have no calculator to do his sums for him.'

'Tables? What do you mean?'

'Maybe you don't call them that. It's . . . multiplying in your head.'

They laugh. 'That's funny – multiplying in your head!'

' "9 9s are 81, 9 10s are 90"! We were always so glad when we got to the tens. That was safe ground. And we weren't allowed to use fingers for adding!'

We turn. Their father is standing in the doorway, smiling, savouring the atmosphere.

'Can you still multiply in your head, Dad?'

'I can. And I can add without using fingers. And . . .' almost talking to himself, 'I can say poems. "Young Lochinvar, he came out of the west". It's handy when you're on your own, on a journey. It brightens up your thoughts . . .' He comes back to earth. 'It's great to see the old place again.'

'Where was your Sports Field, Dad?'

'Sports Field? We had the playground. And we played football in a field over the road. And shinty.'

'Shinty?'

'Yes. I guess I've a lot of explaining to do. Now let's say thank you to this lady.'

'And can we buy some stamps?'

'Of course.' I get back behind the counter and open the stamp-book.

'These are lovely ones. Can I have a set, please, Dad, for my collection?'

Dad obligingly opens his wallet. My stock diminishes alarmingly. I make a rapid note of re-stocking needs.

'Come on, kids. We've got a long way to go yet.'

'It's only a flying visit?'

'Afraid so. But we'll be back.'

'I'd like to stay . . .' the small girl looks sad.

I make up a bundle of Post Office leaflets and put them in her hand.

'Would you like these to remember the Post Office?'

She smiles.

'Yes thanks. My friends at home would like some too.'

'Good.'

'Goodbye' comes in chorus as they turn towards the gate.

'Goodbye' I call, and 'haste ye back.'

'What does that mean?'

'Your Dad will tell you.'

'I sure will.'

The car roars up the road. '9 9s are 81' and 'Young Lochinvar' . . . I'm glad they've survived those long years and miles.

XIII
SUPERVISORS AND SURVEYORS

During our twenty years in the Post Office we had had comparatively few visitations by officials from the Head Office. The accounts people had kept a check on the books, of course. A young man would appear at the door, briefcase in one hand, his identity card in the other. In the sitting-room I would clear a space on the cluttered table, bring in the cashbox and stamp-book, make up the fire if it was wintertime and settle down discreetly in a corner while he did his adding up, on his calculator. On one occasion when the result came out, alarmingly, with quite a large cash shortage, it was decided to do a recount. To my great relief it was discovered that one of the small dockets from a pension-book had attached itself to another. It was unstuck and the sum was duly rectified. When everything was checked and checked again we exchanged smiles of satisfaction and I went to make coffee.

Subsequent re-organisation of the postal hierarchy has meant that we have quite regular visits from an area supervisor who comes, not to check our business, or our ways of conducting business, but to see to any needs we may have, to listen to suggestions. This attitude is very welcome. The people at Headquarters have always been there, of course, helping out with problems of all kinds, sending emergency supplies of cash or stamps following some unexpected demand, explaining the filling-up of new, unfamiliar forms, their friendly voices on the phone always reassuring, though we never met. Now an actual personal contact was established we felt less isolated. Once, when the lock on the cash-box jammed and pensions were due a locksmith was sent 'post-haste' from the town to sort the problem out.

In older times a most important position in the Post Office was that of Surveyor. In 1789 Francis Ronaldson was appointed Joint Surveyor for the whole of Scotland. The work involved was

A Post-boy riding at full gallop in about 1800 (The Post Office)

arduous in the extreme. Covering hundreds of miles, mostly on horse-back, sometimes by coach, over unmade roads, in all kinds of weather, would have tested the stamina of the strongest man. Ronaldson was of small stature, but a great personality, with a strong sense of humour. As a member of the Royal Edinburgh Volunteers during the Napoleonic wars, he almost disappeared when on parade among his taller comrades. He had a specially light musket made for him! The salary, on appointment, was not high – £150 a year, plus a subsistence allowance when travelling of ten shillings a day. Later, salary and allowances were increased owing to the special circumstances of travel in Scotland, the Highlands in particular. Scarcity of mail-coaches meant that private vehicles or horses had to be hired and inn-keepers charged their highest rates to Government officials.

Surveyors were expected to keep a full record of all their journeys, commenting on the standards in the various offices they visited. Their accounts also served to justify the amount claimed for subsistence and travel allowance. Ronaldson's journal from 1786 to 1814 has survived, giving a valuable picture of the working of the Post Office and of the abuses by serving officers and by the public which it was his duty to uncover and remedy.

The Surveyor, who represented the 'eyes and ears' of the Post Office, often found himself unfairly blamed for lack of vigilance when things went wrong. Things did quite often go wrong. Many postmasters, who were also inn-keepers, were sometimes busy attending to customers and indulging in drink, with their postal duties handed over to illiterate servants. Occasionally they practised deliberate fraud, forging 'dead' or mis-directed letters, postage on which could be deducted from the sum they had to remit to the head office. The low rate of pay accorded to the postmasters was the main reason for their yielding to the temptation of the many opportunities for dishonesty with which they were presented.

The actual carriage of the mail was arranged by the postmaster, with a mileage rate allowed, and delegated to runners or riders – 'Post-boys' – who received five shillings a week, the postmaster keeping the surplus. Thefts of mail inevitably occurred when boys of 14, ill-clad and underpaid, had to cover distances far beyond their strength. Punishments in those days were severe in the extreme. Erring Post-boys could be imprisoned or deported. In 1796 the postmaster in Kirkwall was executed for the theft of £9 from letters.

The public, too, indulged in dishonest practices. When the custom was for postage to be paid by the recipient, the actual arrival of a letter would be enough information for the addressee, who would refuse to take delivery and thus avoid paying the postage.

Franking – the free carriage of letters through the post – was another custom which could lead to abuse. It had long been the privilege of M.P.s, the Commissioners of Supply and certain other public servants to use this service. In the nineteenth century several poets and novelists, whose work entailed a fair amount of correspondence and whose financial situation could be precarious, made good use of the franking system. Shelley is known to have profited by it and Sir Walter Scott, in a letter preserved for posterity, refers to 'Mr. Freeling, G.P.O., who gives me the privilege of his unlimited frank in favour of literature'. Francis Freeling was the Secretary of the Post Office.

All these things, and more, made the Surveyor's task a difficult and, in some cases, a distressing one. Francis Ronaldson must have seen many facets of human life as he travelled the country – the whole of the mainland and as far north as Orkney. This wide travelling enabled him to perform another important part of his duties – the seeking of alternative and improved routes for the carrying of the mail. There were problems. Freeling, the Post Office supremo, knew nothing of the geography of Scotland, or of the climactic conditions found there, the severity of storms, blizzards and ensuing floods. The landowners, particularly in the Highlands, still maintained a feudal authority and, with the increasing volume of mail which they despatched and received, were insistent that the delivery should be routed to suit their convenience. Only by constant pressure on the authorities in the south, headed by Freeling, did the Surveyors for the north, Ronaldson and, later, James Shearer, manage to get some sort of justice for the Post Office servants – the postmasters, the post-boys, runners and riders and the operators of the mail-coaches.

There were other problems. In 1832 a serious outbreak of cholera affected the whole of Scotland. Runners were refused entry into many places for fear that they carried infection. Mail bags had to be fumigated and routes altered.

Anthony Trollope, who worked for over 39 years as a postal Surveyor in the south, wrote, later in the century, about his life's work: 'You have married no wife, keep no hunters, go to no parties, read no books, but have become a machine for grinding and polishing Post Office apparatus. This is not good enough for any man, though there are worse ways of spending life.'

Freeling had written of the Surveyors: 'The Surveyors must be of respectable description, high character and unexceptionable integrity and of good education. The salary and allowances are not equal to the constant duty, trusts and responsibility and expense.'

Anthony Trollope is, perhaps, the Post Office figure best known to posterity. In a Minute to the Postmaster General dated 4th November 1834 Freeling, the Secretary to the Post Office, wrote: 'I beg to submit . . . the name of A. Trollope as a junior clerk in the Secretary's Office. Mr Trollope has been well educated and will be subject to the usual probation as to competency.' Many years later, in his autobiography, he described how he entered Post Office service and worked out his probation. As a handwriting test he copied a page of Gibbon which was never inspected: a threatened arithmetic test was never applied. During seven years at Post Office Headquarters he was underpaid, neglected and largely ignored. He felt morally degraded and a professional failure.

A chance vacancy for a junior official in the west of Ireland, for which he applied in despair, was to prove his salvation. Subsequently, during his long years as a Surveyor, with the sensitivity of the artist, he observed and sympathised with the hardships of the postal workers. Accompanying a Glasgow postman on his delivery round, climbing tenement stairs, he recorded that this was the hardest day's work he had done in his life. He also pointed out that 16 miles a day should be the greatest distance required of a foot-post. Trollope was also a keen advocate of the idea of a free delivery of letters to every house, which did eventually materialise. He fulfilled his Post Office duties with energy and drive and at the same time managed to pursue a successful career as a writer. His mother had written novels. This may have spurred his ambition. His travels up and down the country, his meetings with people of all kinds would have provided a rich source of ideas which he was able to develop while he rode or rested at inns. He was a prolific writer and his books are read by many thinking people today.

Nowadays, with smooth roads through the glens and routes mapped in the skies, the Surveyor's job is quite different. He, or his equivalent official, can reach the furthest outposts of the business in a matter of hours. He has few travelling problems to contend with, but still complaints have to be heard, complaints by postmasters about lack of funds, complaints handed on by customers about the occasional lost, delayed or damaged letter.

When he, or she, appears out of the blue, we greet him, or her, no longer with apprehension (did we fill in that new form incorrectly?) but with relief, knowing that he, or she, will listen sympathetically to our request for a new cash-box or a rack to display the ever-increasing number of leaflets for distribution to customers. With my concern for the rain-forests of the world I'm always pleading for a reduction in the supply of these leaflets, but it seems there is a standard quota for each office. At least I hope the recycling unit is in good working order. Our Surveyors of today are certainly good listeners and do understand the problems of postmasters working in the comparative isolation of a country office.

XIV
READ ALL ABOUT IT – IN
THE POST OFFICE

When the grandchildren came to stay at holiday time the place became lively indeed. A toy Post Office, in a box with fake stamps and postal orders, was no use to them. They had the real thing. When 'Postman Pat's' shiny red van was glimpsed from the window there would be a stampede to the door and out to watch him empty the roadside letter box. 'Steady on, now' I would call. They were sure of a cheery greeting from our friendly postie, which they reciprocated energetically. Then, quietening down, they would watch with bated breath to see what was in the delivery. Bills, receipts, advertising material, anything at all was exciting when it came straight from the hands of their uniformed postman. When he had letters collected on his route, for posting, their privilege was to lick the stamps for him. The date-stamp was the greatest thrill. In off-duty hours they were allowed to practise using it, on odd scraps of paper.

On a visit to town they would wander round the big Post Office shop, with its somewhat forbidding grilles and uniformed staff. With holiday money to spend they were spoilt for choice in the bright array of things on show. The Post Office does look after the interests of its young and future customers. Models of Postman Pat were of no special attraction to these particular young customers who had a real one to hand, but bright postcards, colouring books and letter-writing outfits were well worth spending pennies on. This needed no encouragement from me. After their return home I was always thrilled to find small envelopes in the post, stamps carefully fixed, the address in best handwriting, with small items of news on the paper inside.

The Post Office encourages letter writing by organising a competition with quite valuable prizes for school children in various age groups. I always hope that competitions like this may do away with that ghastly comment 'boring' – applied by so many young people to so many activities such as letter-writing. The grand-daughter who enjoyed our little post office the most, who once date-stamped her own hand, which must have been extremely painful, has developed, I'm very glad to say, into a writer of most attractive letters. Like her mother before her, she spent quite a lot of time abroad, as a student, and, again like her mother, found time to write at some length and in distinguished handwriting, letters of real interest. These I keep tied, not in ribbon, but in stout rubber bands. She also liked to receive letters, thus encouraging others to try their hand at this art. I firmly believe letter-writing can be considered an art-form. What is it but the spontaneous expression of thoughts and feelings committed to paper at a certain time, in a certain place, thoughts and feelings about people and events as well as thoughts and feelings directed to the recipient of the letter? Isn't this what the painter does in his picture, showing us what he thinks and feels about his world as he fills his canvas? The poet, too, baring mind and heart in the lines he writes, hopes we will catch a glimpse of his meaning. Letters, pictures, poems are surely all means of communication. And calligraphy is certainly a form of art.

The Post Office also sponsors events of literary significance. Every summer, at the Edinburgh Book Festival, a huge tent, in the gardens of Charlotte Square, hosts lecturers and writers of distinction who speak about their work and inspire many apprentice writers. The function of the Post Office has always been more than that of carrying letters. Today, as we have seen, it is a focal point for small communities where neighbours can meet and local news is exchanged.

During the eighteenth and nineteenth centuries, when the whole country was desperately anxious to hear about the events taking place, not in their locality, but on the continent – the French Revolution, the Napoleonic Wars – the Post Office became a place for the reading of newspapers. These were sent to the postmaster ready franked, that is, without payment on receipt, and he was able to make a small profit by charging customers for reading the paper. As many people were unable to read it is likely that a literate member of the community, probably the schoolmaster, would read the news aloud to the assembled company. In the days of the mail-coaches people would gather at points along the route shouting for news from the guard or other out-riders. These would shout back and this verbal exchange would sometimes lead to distortions of the actual news. In case the distortion might lead to panic or disaffection the authorities in London and in Edinburgh thought it prudent to issue, from time to time, hand-bills giving a correct account of events, sending them to postmasters with instructions to distribute them in their towns or villages.

For example, one such issued in London on 10 February 1817 ran thus:

> The statement in the morning papers that several persons have been arrested by warrants from the Secretary of State is true. The meeting was held this morning in Spa Fields, but the arrests which have taken place and the precautions adopted by Government caused everything to end peace-ably and the town is perfectly quiet.

Today, we have no mob-quietening devices in the sub-post offices – we leave that to the police! – but we do act as information-gathering centres. A small fee is paid by the local government for the display of planning applications for houses or buildings in the vicinity. The Register of Electors for the area is held in the office and many notices on a variety of subjects – accounts of Community Council and School Board meetings, lectures, sales of work, meetings of all kinds – are pinned up on the notice board.

XV
LOVE LETTERS AND THE PENNY POST

All during the eighties I kept the Post Office going, juggling my duties there with hours spent curating the small museum next door, seeing to the chickens, the goat, the bees and the garden. It was a busy life, but it never palled.

New and very attractive stamps were appearing at regular intervals along with corresponding postcards. My pile of home-made first day covers was growing steadily, as was my collection of cards. These I found too attractive to send away. Some day they must go into an album. The artists employed in the designing of these stamps and cards are of high calibre.

The Post Office first thought of issuing cards in the late 1880s. Later they were issued commercially and after that there was a deluge. Some people were slightly apprehensive about messages going out unsealed, to be read by all through whose hands they passed. Mostly, the cards bore only short greetings. Today, they are sold in large quantities in holiday resorts, but are not in everyday use. Those produced in the Highlands at the present time, depicting landscapes and wildlife, are of exceptionally high quality. An album collection of them could well be made to delight the eyes of future generations, when perhaps most greetings, holiday or otherwise, may well be transmitted electronically.

Meantime, the profusion of greeting cards for every occasion – birthday, wedding, retirement, illness, sitting of and result of exams and so on and so on, and of course, Christmas – augurs well for the sale of stamps. As I marvel at the design and colour of each new issue I think back to those in my old childhood collection, still lingering somewhere in a cupboard, for the grandchildren to inherit. How dull most of those stamps are, compared to today's, though they did teach us a little about the world, at least how to recognise the native names of countries – Helvetia meant Switzerland, Suomi was Finland, Magyar stood for Hungary and so

Sir Rowland Hill, the great pioneer of the Penny Post

on. My most longed for stamp – which I never acquired – was, of course, the Penny Black. Some Penny Reds I did inherit later.

Hunting out that old album and studying its contents made me curious about the origins of those old Penny Blacks, with the gracious silhouette of the young Queen Victoria. She was a great letter writer and keeper of journals, I knew. I dug out the story.

In 1836, one year before Victoria came to the throne as a girl of 18, a schoolmaster's son named Rowland Hill happened to spend a holiday in a village in the north of Scotland. (He was a member of a Society for Popular Education and had much sympathy for the poor.) There he witnessed a scene which touched him deeply. A letter from London arrived for a village girl. The postal charge was great and she refused to take delivery of it, though she knew it was from her fiancé who was working in London. The couple had devised a system of signs and marks on the cover of the letters he sent which let her know that he was well and that he loved her.

Profoundly disturbed by this story Hill gave much thought to the matter. He concluded that the vicious circle – in which high postal charges caused a diminution in the number of letters carried and this then forced the rate up in order to make a profit – must be broken. In 1837 he published a pamphlet, *Postal Reform*, in which he explained his proposals and also pointed out the enormous social advantages which even the poorest would enjoy. He proposed 'small stamped labels' to be sold in advance and attached to the letter by the sender. A committee was formed and more than four million signatures were collected in support of the project. Hill made great efforts to influence public opinion. The Post Master General, the Earl of Lichfield, opposed the plan vigorously.

However, in September 1839 Hill was given a temporary appointment at the Treasury, where he could supervise the introduction of his reforms. He managed to get the support of the progressive elements in Parliament. A letter from his brother at that time says: 'That a stranger should be bold enough to attempt to penetrate the mysteries of our postal service was something which those who had the professional charge found disagreeable, but that he should be so successful was even worse!'

Hill's committee, which consisted of twelve London businessmen, published numerous pamphlets. One they called *Examples of Postal Charges in 1839, to be preserved as Curiosities in Museums*. There is no doubt that postal charges in the years after the end of the Napoleonic wars were excessively high, being looked on as a form of taxation. Ways of avoiding them grew more and more ingenious.

The committee issued posters, as political parties do today. One proclaimed:

Mothers and fathers who wish to have news of your absent children: Friends who are separated and wish to write to each other: Emigrants who do not want to forget your motherland: Farmers who want to know the best places to sell your produce: Workers and labourers who want to know or find the best work and the highest wages – support the Report of the House of Commons by your petitions in favour of the Uniform Penny Post.

TO ALL POSTMASTERS
AND
SUB-POSTMASTERS.

GENERAL POST OFFICE,
25th April, 1840.

IT has been decided that Postage Stamps are to be brought into use forthwith, and as it will be necessary that every such Stamp should be cancelled at the Post Office or Sub-Post Office where the Letter bearing the same may be posted, I herewith forward, for your use, an *Obliterating Stamp*, with which you will efface the Postage Stamp upon every Letter despatched from your Office. *Red Composition* must be used for this purpose, and I annex directions for making it, with an Impression of the Stamp.

As the Stamps will come into operation by the *6th of May*, I must desire you will not fail to provide yourself with the necessary supply of Red Composition by that time.

By Command,

W. L. MABERLY,
SECRETARY.

The announcement of the new stamped postage

Eventually, the Prime Minister, Lord Melbourne, put it to the vote, the proposal was carried and on 10 January 1840 the Penny Post was established. The huge cut in postal charges resulted, of course, in massive bottle-necks of mail at the post office counters.

A competition was held, the public being invited to submit designs for the proposed stamps and envelopes. The winning envelope depicted Britannia sending winged messengers to all parts of her vast empire. This design was subsequently ridiculed and withdrawn. The stamps, however, were a great success. They bore the effigy of the young Queen Victoria, her crowned head facing left. The penny stamp pre-paid postage to any part of the United Kingdom on a letter weighing up to half an ounce.

A grateful nation raised a subscription to Hill amounting to over £15,000, Parliament granted him a gratuity of £20,000 and he was eventually made a Knight Commander of the Bath.

He died at the age of 84. On his statue outside the G.P.O. in London are the words 'He created a Uniform Penny Post 1840.' Hill could never have envisaged the world-wide spread and development of the stamp he had created. One hopes that the young couple in the north of Scotland who helped to inspire his work took advantage of the new rates and were eventually re-united.

XVI
THE ACCELERATION OF THE MAIL

The Post Office, like any large organisation designed to be of service to the public, has, of course, to be subject to many changes over the years. In our small outpost we saw those changes, as it were, at one remove. We were aware of what was going on and were kept well informed by documents emanating from headquarters at regular intervals, but we saw comparatively few of the changes in action, since our customers were not numerous and their needs did not vary much. As long as they got the stamps they needed (and most were not great letter-writers), the occasional postal order, the occasional parcel posted (though both these items had become increasingly expensive), and pensions and giros cashed, they were happy. Telephone, Hydro-electric and, later, community charge bills they were glad to settle locally, thus avoiding queues in the busy offices in town.

We were aware that Royal Mail and Post Office Counters had separated, but this might have happened on the moon for all the difference it made, in reality, to us. Our postie still arrived in his smart red van – red the colour of royalty – with the golden lettering and the golden crown on the side, wearing his smart navy uniform. We were conscious, perhaps, of our own dowdy appearance, as we stood behind our 'counter' – wearing normal working clothes, using our tattered stamp-book and clumsy scales. We were quite happy that way, preferring old, well-made equipment to modern, more flashy devices. We resented a demand for the obsolete brass letter-weights to be sent to a postal museum somewhere in the south. We treasured our museum pieces, especially our own named date-stamp. When the old roadside letter-box went the same way, replaced by a modern version, we began to fear for the old red phone-box up the road. So far it is still with us. When it was our duty to empty it I would sweep and dust it regularly and hang bunches of myrtle to keep away the flies. Phone-boxes in the wilds hold happy memories for me, of shelter from rain-storms and blizzards, even of somewhere to cook sausages on a spirit stove, out of the wind, on camping holidays! The care of the box is now in the hands of other workers.

The Post Office is always striving to improve the quality of its service, with independent research companies monitoring the mail delivery performance over the country. A customer service is in operation to deal with enquiries or complaints and question-naires are often sent out inviting comments. Increases in the cost of services is announced well beforehand. A Post Office Users' Council is ready to take up really serious complaints regarding delay or loss of mail, though the Recorded Delivery, Registered and Registered Plus services should obviate most complaints.

A vast amount of effort has gone, and goes, into ensuring the satisfaction of users by assuring the safety and increasing the speed of delivery of items posted. This has been going on for many years. On 14 December 1758 a letter from the post office in Edinburgh acknowledges receipt of a letter about the 'slow progress of riding the mail between Aberdeen and Inverness' and the 'great remissness of duty in the several postmasters entrusted with the execution of that service.' On 13 March 1710, in a let-ter to Alexander Duffy, Provost of Inverness, about complaints against Alexander Cumming, Deputy Postmaster at Inverness, it was said that there had been 'intercepting, delaying, opening several letters sent in the bags of Inverness to the great prejudice of Correspondence and the diminution of this branch of her Majesty's Revenue.' Several gentlemen of Inverness were to enquire into the problem.

There were problems too, with the safe carriage of goods. In September 1747 Mr Thomas Wedderburn of Inverness wrote three times to the storekeeper at the Excise Office stating that there had been 'this long time complaints that our stores were much spoilt in the carriage'. Thereafter they were to be sent otherwise, that is, by Alexander Calder, Carrier, who is to go eight times a year from Inverness to Edinburgh at £16 a year'

Mail coach handing over mail bags to a postmaster in the 1840s
(The Post Office)

and 'he is to get two boxes with locks and a wax cloath to lye over them: so we expect to have none of them spoilt as before was often the case.' The temptation must have been great to have a taste of the cargo on the long journey south!

In 1798 a mail coach from Edinburgh to Aberdeen at last started running, though Francis Freeling, the then newly appointed Secretary to the Post Office, considered that, on the surveyor's report, 'the state of the roads is highly unfavourable for the passage of coaches.' There were worries, also, about the crossing at Queensferry, particularly in the winter months.

That same year the 'Memorialists', that is people writing 'memorials' or memoranda to the authorities, were complaining bitterly that 'letters from the south and west and their foreign correspondence are detained eight hours daily in Edinburgh, whereas the official duty necessary for forwarding them does not require a detention there of more than two hours.' Apparently business was done at a leisurely pace in Edinburgh, with the fashionable hours for dining strictly adhered to.

The Acceleration of the Mail

The previous year Alexander Allardyce, M.P., had written that 'the mortifying neglect with which their applications and remonstrations . . . have been treated by the Post Office have . . . resolved, as their ultimate resource, to bring the matter before Parliament.' Francis Freeling, based in London and ever anxious about the profits of the Post Office, had perforce to listen to his Surveyors in the north who knew the country well.

In 1803 work was started on the construction of the Caledonian Canal. The improvement of Highland roads and bridges also went on apace and this naturally facilitated the running of the mail coaches. The north was coming to be recognised as a region of importance to the economy of the country as a whole. Yet in 1822 there were still cries for the Acceleration of the Mail. William Blackwood, in Edinburgh, printed a 'Plan for expediting the Mail London to Edinburgh' so that 'It shall arrive at 10 o'clock on the 2nd day (and eventually earlier), proceed immediately for the NORTH OF SCOTLAND and cross at the Queensferry all the year in Daylight'.

When the coach was scheduled at seven miles an hour the coachmen often stopped at the ale houses and loitered, then drove too fast. Accidents occurred. With the improvements in the roads they could do nine miles an hour. To save time they would hand over the mail-bags without stopping, merely slowing to an adequate speed.

Much debate went on about the best route between London and Edinburgh. Telford, the great engineer, was asked to advise. Finally, in 1823, a committee was appointed to obtain an 'Acceleration of the Northern Mails'. Through the 1830s, 1840s and 50s the efforts to expedite the delivery of mails continued. With industrialisation in the south, the development of the fisheries in the north and so on, there was urgent need for an efficient postal service.

At last, in February 1864, the Provost of Inverness received a letter from the G.P.O. saying that mail would be carried by rail as soon as the necessary preparations were completed. In 1866, when the Highland Railway was in operation, 'memorials' of complaint were still flying about. One, from the Town Council of Inverness, on the old topic of 'acceleration', now referred to the 'Acceleration of Mail Trains' and was to 'receive consideration'.

Ten years later a speed-up was still being demanded. From Inverness to Aberdeen the train ran at 19½ miles per hour, whereas from London to Perth the speed was 39¼ miles per hour. In 1881 a letter from Alan Cameron, Provost of Elgin, to Provost Fraser of Inverness stated: 'Train service between Inverness and Aberdeen disgraceful: 20-30 minutes wasted at Forres and Keith: takes nearly six hours to travel a hundred miles'. Could there have been specially welcoming refreshment rooms at Forres and Keith? Perish the thought! It must have been a question of dilatory loading and unloading.

The Railway Company was clearly eager for trade but it had a lot to learn in the operation of its service. Drivers had to be taught to handle machinery and to keep to strict standards of discipline. Once, at Christmas time, on the Inverness to Nairn line, the driver and fireman were both drunk and quarrelsome and were dismissed on the spot.

The transition from mail coach to train took time. Initially, the whole coach, with mail-bags on board, was transferred to the train, along with the guard. The problems of travel were not over. Even sturdy engines, with sparks flying and smoke belching from the funnel could, and did, get stuck in snow, which banked up on the line. And there were no 'post-boys' to stagger ahead through the drifts with the bags of mail. The 'Acceleration' was well and truly hampered on those occasions.

It was still not adequate for people in the north even in normal circumstances. In 1881 a deputation of fifteen landowners, most of them M.P.s, led by the Duke of Sutherland, went to London to meet the Postmaster General, Mr Fawcett, to urge the necessity of an improved mail service to the north of Scotland. They pointed out that Aberdeen had 'the advantage of a special mail-bag engine from Perth to take forward the London mails at a high rate of speed'. They wished to have the same for Inverness, Wick and Thurso. Mr Fawcett agreed that an improved service was highly desirable, but made it clear that cost was the important factor and asked these worthy gentlemen to use their influence in getting the Railway Company 'to meet the department in a liberal spirit'. The ball was neatly back in their own court!

XVII
SERVANTS OF THE PUBLIC

Today the Post Office is firmly resisting attempts at privatisation. It is still essentially a service, though, of course, it must find the means to pay its way, as its great eighteenth century Secretary, Freeling, did. Even he heeded the advice of his Surveyors, men of great humanity, who knew the country well and were able to stand up to the fierce demands of economy in practice coming from the south. They knew only too well the frustrations of the grossly underpaid servants of the Post Office. The postmaster's job, in particular, seemed to be in many ways an unenviable one, having great responsibility attached, for little pay and the threat of heavy punishment for misdemeanor. Yet the position of postmaster was still attractive to many. It gave the holder a certain standing in the community and kept him well-informed about events in the country at large. It seems to have counted in its ranks mostly people of basic integrity and worth.

These days we have a chance to meet our counterparts from a fairly wide area at conferences in Inverness. Transport is arranged for those who don't run cars and we meet in a comfortable room in the hotel built on the site of the old inn which used to see off the 'Caledonian' coach with the mail to Edinburgh. After the initial greetings and exchanges of news our sense of isolation disappears. We realise afresh that the folk gathered here have the same hopes and fears as ourselves – hopes that the business in our small offices can be maintained, fears that our identity may be lost as we are, perhaps, swallowed up in amalgamation with bigger places. Small country schools are closing. To modernise and equip them all with the new tools of technology would be too costly. To modernise and equip our little offices – would that be impossible? Probably. But I think our customers don't really notice the state of our equipment as long as we're there when they need us and have the supplies they're looking for.

Our 'passing' customers, tourists and holiday people, positively appreciate, I suspect, our lack of sophistication and the fact that we have time to pass more than the time of day. Computerisation may be in the air, but I put the thought of it to the back of my mind. Our supervisor has not, so far, hinted that it is imminent.

Modern devices are certainly to the fore at our meetings, clip-boards much in evidence, of course, and screens flashing up information at the touch of a button. But the talk is on an informal level and we are all encouraged to give our views on proposed developments as well as to air criticisms and complaints. Even the 'airing' is salutary, though we know that most grievances must go, if not unheeded, at least unresolved. On the whole we do not complain overmuch. We know the rules. We are, by nature, inclined to respect them. Our work is not stressful. We can soldier on till well past normal retiring age if we feel so inclined, knowing that we are not keeping anyone younger out of a job, for the work is home-based and devoid of glamour. In a neighbouring glen two sisters ran the Post Office from their croft house, one at the counter and the other taking the mail round on her bicycle, till they were both in their nineties. In another, a postmistress of 87 has just had a presentation in recognition of her sixty years in the job and has no thought of retiring.

Looking round the company at these meetings, I see men and women of widely differing ages. Some will be running their offices in conjunction with a shop. Some will have taken over after the death of a spouse. They all seem to have the same sense that what we are engaged in is a form of service. We have rules to stick to, but we can, sometimes, go out of our way to help. When a young man walks straight through to the kitchen, where I'm making jam, at seven in the evening, demanding one first class stamp, I turn down the heat, wash my hands and unlock the cupboard. 'It's an application for a job' he says. 'That's fine. Good luck to it!' A smile lights my jam-smudged face.

Our local imbiber has been known to arrive home in a hired car, stumble up to the door at night and demand a 'sub' on his pension to pay the driver. This was in my husband's time. 'I can't do that, man,' he had to say. Then he would delve into his own pocket. 'You can pay me back on Thursday.' These small acts help to humanise the great institution that does depend so utterly on the integrity of its servants.

The faces I see at our meetings reflect that sense of loyalty. There's humour in them, too, love of a good joke as well as the appreciation of the stark realities of life. Contact with people at large certainly makes us all aware of the wider world out there. The relief on the face of a young mother, her husband unemployed, as she cashes the family allowance and the money goes straight into her own hand – that is a look to treasure. Pensioners, too, show relief as they pocket some actual cash, though some of them still appear slightly diffident, as if to accept the money, however well-earned, is like admitting to poverty. This was a thing abhorred by Highland people. Poverty was hidden till relieved by the shared generosity of one's own kind, generosity which could be repaid when another's need arose.

So, the business of the meeting ended, we exchange experiences and comments and find much strength in the renewed sense of solidarity among ourselves and with the powers-that-be, at least the local ones, in this huge organisation.

XVIII
WILLIAM DOCHWRA AND
'INDIAN PETER'

The postal service has thrown up, in one way or another, some characters of amazing strength and originality. During the eighteenth century, when, with standards of education rising, and more people able to read and write, the demand for communication facilities was growing, a Londoner, William Dochwra, organised a system of delivery of mail which he called a 'penny post'. This was a form of protest against the high rates of postage charged by the official authorities.

In several hundred taverns, coffee-houses or stationer's shops, the public could leave letters and packets to be collected and sorted. 'Penny Post' messengers would then deliver them, five times daily in the suburbs and fifteen times daily in the city. This 'Penny Post' soon became so popular that it posed a serious threat to the monopoly of the official post office. After a legal action brought against him, Dochwra was fined a hundred pounds and ordered to cease operation. Eventually, his idea was taken over by the Post Master General and he was awarded an annual pension of five hundred pounds for ten years.

At about this time Peter Williamson, a remarkable Scotsman, came on the scene in Edinburgh. His story is as remarkable as himself and is worth the telling. He was born in Aberdeenshire in 1729 and was sent by his parents to an aunt in Aberdeen, where he went to school. In those days there was a busy trade in African negro slaves, supplemented by a more discreet enterprise – the kidnapping of young children to be shipped to the plantations in America, supposedly as apprentices. Peter was playing along the quayside in Aberdeen one day when he was decoyed on board a ship, then seized and pushed into the hold with about fifty other children. On the voyage they suffered indescribable

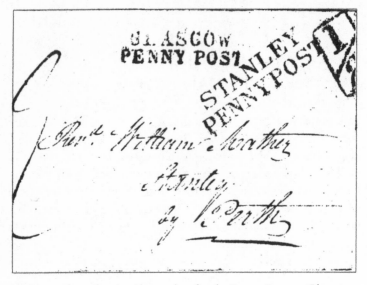

An envelope showing the marks of early Penny Posts – Glasgow and Stanley in this case

hardship. Arriving in the teeth of a gale, the ship grounded in Delaware Bay, the captain and crew taking to the boats, leaving the children to their fate. Next morning, the storm abated, they returned to the ship to salvage the cargo and found the children had survived.

Peter was sold for £16 to a Scottish farmer in Philadelphia, who had himself been kidnapped as a boy. This farmer treated Peter well during the seven years they worked together. When he died he left the boy £150, his best horse and other goods. This enabled Peter to marry and acquire a strip of land. But in an attack by Indians, who sided with the French, his wife was murdered, his farm burnt and he himself carried off as a prisoner. Eventually escaping, he enlisted in the British army, was wounded and imprisoned in Quebec. When finally released he returned to England, landing with six shillings in his pocket.

All this he wrote down. On his way north, stopping at York, he met a kindly gentleman who gladly undertook to have this account of his adventures printed and circulated 'for his benefit'. With the small profit made from selling his book and from impersonations of Indians on the war-path, he was able to complete his journey to Aberdeen. On arrival there he lost no time in accusing one of the City fathers of being responsible for his kidnapping and that of other boys and was soon arrested, fined and turned out of the City as a vagrant.

Now nick-named 'Indian Peter' he made his way to Edinburgh, where he opened a tavern known as 'Indian Peter's Coffee House', in the hall of Parliament House. He next moved an action against Aberdeen Corporation and was awarded £100 compensation and costs. While his luck was riding high he opened another tavern – 'Peter's Tavern' – in Old Parliament Close, which did so well that he was able to open a bookshop and printing house in the Luckenbooths, near St Giles.

Here, in 1774, he printed an *Edinburgh Directory* in which he stated:

> The Publisher takes this opportunity to acquaint the Public that he will always make it his study to dispatch all letters and parcels, not exceeding three pounds in weight, to any Place within an English mile to the East, South and North Leith every hour through the day, for one penny each letter or bundle.

The letter-carriers were called 'caddies' and wore hats with the words 'Penny Post' on them. Letters were postmarked to show whether the postage had been paid by the sender or was to be collected on delivery. The business flourished and Peter was able to marry again and bring up a family. He later divorced his wife, she declaring that he had left her destitute.

'Indian Peter's' Penny Post, although a challenge to the monopoly of the official organisation, was allowed to continue for close on twenty years. Thereafter it was taken over by the Edinburgh Post Office and Peter was paid a pension of £25 a year as compensation for the loss of his business. 'If you can't beat them, join them'!

In the following years local Penny Posts were established in many parts of the country. They worked smoothly and were fast and inexpensive. Their success was no doubt an inspiration to Rowland Hill in his work in establishing the official Penny Post in 1840 and in the regularisation of the costs of postage from which we all benefit today. So 'Indian Peter', with his colourful life, has earned a niche in the story of the postal service and in the social history of the country as a whole.

XIX
ABRIACHAN IN THE NEWS

Our post office is small, there is no doubt about that. In fact, it seems to grow smaller as time goes by and the piles of leaflets and official documents, some in large plastic folders, grow ever larger. I am often guilty, too, of cluttering the corner by the door with the odd garden tool as I come in in a hurry after a spell of digging or weeding. As I sweep out the stone floor and polish the old brass door handle I often realise how much I treasure it as it is, warts and all.

But just how small it is and how it must strike other people sometimes was brought home to me one morning when a reporter from the town, looking for a story, arrived at the door. He stood there, gazing round, scrutinising everything as news reporters do, his facial expression growing into amazement. I waited. Then he said: 'I reckon you must be the smallest post office in the Highlands.'

'You think so?'

'Well, I don't know how they can get any smaller!' Very soon he was into superlatives of all kinds. I began to think this must be the smallest post office in the country, if not in the world! 'I'd like to do a piece on it. D'you mind if I send out a photographer?'

'Well, I don't . . . '

'It won't take a minute. The photographing, I mean.'

'Well, I . . . ' I seemed to have no defences handy.

Next morning, sharp at nine, the photographer arrived. Taking in the set-up in a couple of glances he quickly re-arranged all the movables, turning the table round to catch the light, piling the weights on the scales. 'Have you a parcel anywhere? It could look as if you're weighing it.'

Feeling completely out of my element and into something phoney, I obey his instructions like an automaton. When all is posed to his liking a young assistant appears with a huge reflector which he holds at an angle to the picture. The feel of unreality grows. At last, the eye of the camera is glaring at me. Panic strikes, but I hold firm, as though trying to outwit an enemy.

'That's great!' There's reassurance in the tone. Then: 'Just a minute. A little bit this way. And again. Now we'll just try once more. To make sure.'The clicking goes on and on. I look up. Two people are waiting outside. They smile.

'I didn't know you were in films!' one said.

'Neither did I!'

We hurriedly put the post office together again. I deal with the customers, the photographer packs up his equipment and life gets back to normal.

The piece did appear in the paper. It was quite well done and the photograph was passable. But this was not the end. Stories are picked up here and there all over the world of journalism, I suppose. It was not long before another photographer was sent out by a well-known Sunday newspaper and our little place became part of a feature on rural post offices all over the country.

Some time after that I was able to breathe a sigh of relief when I heard that someone in a village over on the other side of the loch had opened a post office in her broom cupboard. Her *broom cupboard*? That must make hers smaller than ours, I reckoned. And so it proved. Hers featured in a television broadcast and in a magazine in Canada, so we were let off further reportage.

Nevertheless reporters continued to come out from time to time. Knowing our long-standing interest in the history of the place, they would come looking for 'stories'.

'Any illicit stills about these days? Any poaching? Sheep-stealing? Come on, you must know!'

They seemed to have a total disregard for the effect any disclosures might have on the people involved in unusual activities of any kind. It's only when you live in a small community that you understand the great value of discretion.

We knew of no stills in action, though we had friends who made many a bottle of first-rate wine – rowan, elderberry, birch-sap. We knew where the remains of the old bothies were. We had heard many a good story about the ingenious ways the gaugers had been outwitted. That was history.

Poaching? Well, if you heard the echo of a shot coming through the still air over the hill on a spring evening you might think to yourself 'that'll be one for the pot'. But it could just as easily be a keeper from the Forestry Commission out to kill some roes or getting a fox before he got the lambs. As for the fishes in the small loch up the road, well, you can take them from the bank and no one can stop you, but sadly there are so few fish since the surrounding hill was planted with conifers, the fertilisers have washed down and the water now sprouts greenery of various kinds.

Sheep-stealing? Now, that's a thing that can only go on at night, surely. We do sometimes hear heavy vehicles in the small hours, but most often we just turn over and go back to sleep. Only our vigilant police will have an idea about a crime as serious as that – one which was punished by hanging not so long ago – and they will exercise all the discretion their job demands.

Our communities' peccadilloes are as nothing by comparison. A dog allowed to roam the countryside may be impounded, a neighbour's sheep are hounded out of garden crops, but certain codes are strictly kept. Gates have always to be shut, fences not climbed for fear of damage, no lighted matches dropped, sheep, cattle or horses found straying are rounded up and herded to safety. Adherence to rules such as these keeps the community going along happily, but they don't make headlines. Most often our visiting reporters have to be turned away, after a cup of tea.

One story which might well have been a scorer I kept under wraps with the utmost vigilance. Quite often someone would come to the door asking for eggs, or milk, or other country produce, thinking the houses were farms. One slightly dishevelled young man appeared one morning with such a request. He was living in a shelter he had made from pine branches just up the hill, he said. Invisible neighbours like him are welcome. I gave him what I could and wished him well. He loved the solitude, he said, in impeccable English. A poet? I hoped so. What a wonderful way to spend a summer, I thought – walking all day, having the time to look at things, at birds and mosses and butterflies – lying on a bed of heather at night, with a pale star or two glinting through the shelter of the branches.

Another day a couple came to the door asking for potatoes. From their accent I knew that they were French.

'Des pommes de terre. Je regrette . . .'

Amazement lit their faces. 'You speak French? Up here?'

I laughed. 'Oh, yes. We're quite civilised!'

We lapsed into good-humoured French. They were camping in the wood down near the bottom of the hill, they said. They had been there for several days and were running short of supplies. If there were no farms, was there, perhaps, a shop? I had to say sorry on both counts, then had them in to tea and ransacked the larder for something to keep them going. I filled a bag with oatmeal and a jar with honey and told them how to make brose.

'Just hot water stirred into the oatmeal? No cooking?'

'That's right. You get all the goodness, the vitamins and minerals and you can add anything you like – a little salt, honey, whisky! It'll keep you going all day!'

They laughed. 'That's wonderful!'

'It is. It's what has kept the Highland people fit and strong.'

'You don't grow oats, but you have bees?'

'Yes.'

'May we, perhaps, see them, another time?'

'Of course.'

We parted on friendly terms. I was sure they would be back. They were: many times over that summer they would appear, saying everything was fine, they had made a shelter in the wood, had a good fire for cooking and warmth, a pool in the burn for washing, in fact, they could stay happily there for ever. They knew how to live off the land, gathering wild raspberries, strawberries, blaeberries and fungi, guddling for trout, snaring rabbits. It was great, they said, to discard all the trappings of urban life and they were grateful that no one turned them away in disapproval. They offered to give me a hand with jobs about the garden, an offer I was glad to accept. There was never a hint of scrounging.

It turned out that he was from Corsica, had joined the Foreign Legion, as many young Corsicans did and was sent on some sort of mission to South America. There, he witnessed the inhumane treatment of the native peoples and was so revolted by it that he joined up with an Indian tribe and lived as one of them for a year. Did that mean he went A.W.O.L.? We never enquired.

One day he came up on his own, carrying a long, slender piece of wood.

'This is how the Indians hunt. I'll show you.'

He inserted something into the end of the wooden shaft, put the other end to his mouth and blew.

'Of course. A blow-pipe.'

'That's it. With a small poisoned arrow you can kill many kinds of game. You have to, when you're hungry!'

I drew back, hoping there was no poisoned arrow in this particular pipe. He smiled.

'Don't worry. There are no poisons here!'

Sadly, as autumn came and just when their wood was bearing a wonderful harvest of hazel-nuts, brambles, rose-hips and all kinds of fungi, they decided they would have to move. He had been making many beautiful things out of material he found to hand – wood, bone, stone – and had hoped to make a small income from selling them. Innately an artist, he never got round to the marketing side. Before moving on, he left us a gift – a most marvellously carved ceremonial machete, as made by the Indians he loved. I treasure it. I had lent him a copy of a book I had written about our life in the crofting community before we came to the schoolhouse. He said it would improve his English. As we said our goodbyes he asked: 'May I translate your book into French? I like it. May I?'

'Of course. That would be good.' And he did. We kept in touch and some months later the French version arrived. So far no French publisher has been found.

During the months that they were living in the wood their privacy was respected, no one intruded. Then, one day, after they had gone, a stray walker, taking a short cut up the hill, came on their encampment. An excited young man arrived at the door.

'What's going on down there, in the wood?' He was glaring at me, as though I were involved in something unspeakable.

'What do you mean?'

'You don't know? Look.'

He produced some instant photographs, holding them high for inspection. 'There's something very strange happening there. I don't know. It looks like witchcraft to me.'

'*Witchcraft*?'

I looked at the photographs. I had never been near their place, the Corsican's place, not wanting to intrude, but I realised these were pictures of their encampment. They had clearly left the branches of the shelter, knowing they would rot away naturally. In the bushes were some animal bones, the skull of a sheep he had found dead at the roadside, I remembered. These were the materials of his trade, his art. There was a pattern of stones beside the fireplace and an old iron pot full of water. An Indian tradition, I remembered he had told me, was to leave shelter, water and firing for whoever might pass by. Surely a Highland tradition, the tradition of hospitality. I smiled and tried to explain something of this to the excited young man. He was unconvinced.

'I think there's more to it than that. Have you heard of any practices of witchcraft in the neighbourhood?'

'I have not.'

'Well . . . I'm going to show these to someone who'll be interested. A journalist. He'll send a professional photographer out.'

'Please don't do that.'

'It'll make a good story.'

'An entirely false one.'

He named a paper which might be interested in the story, sufficiently to pursue it.

'May I use your phone?' He was determined to have his say.

'I'm sorry. I have some calls to make. There's a phone box up the road.' It was seldom we refused to help.

'Right. Cheers.'

Cheers? There were none from me! I spent the rest of the day making phone calls to the paper he mentioned, getting doubtful answers all along the line. Witchcraft? The word seemed to have irresistibly magic connotations. From people at various stages up the editorial ladder there were unsatisfactory responses, each one reluctant to let go of such an exciting item. At last I reached the editor himself, explaining that I had known the people involved personally, that a story of witchcraft would bring many unwelcome visitors, maybe even practitioners of the black arts, to the area, that the folk who lived here would naturally be upset and angry. Eventually, after a long conversation, he agreed that the 'story' should not be written up.

All this did not detract from the value of the legacy which visitors such as the loner in his shelter on the hill and the Corsicans in the wood left with us. They bought few stamps, letter-writing was not their business, though they sent a card home from time to time. But what they left could not be counted in monetary terms. It was rather a sense of perspective, of seeing oneself as part of the huge structure of rock and sky, of river and loch, woodland with its bright-eyed creatures, and moors with flowering moss. Living in this perspective meant working along with the natural forces, with wind and storm, along with the heat of the sun, the light of the stars, accepting them all as beneficent. Perhaps, with time and talent, things of surprising beauty can be made out of the natural things lying about, with the simplest of tools. We learnt this, too. I often look at the Indian-style machete, run my hand over the smooth wood, study the intricate design of the stones and the delicate, carved images of eagle and deer.

XX

THE POST IN THE ISLANDS

Latterly, when my husband had not been well, we rarely went away for a holiday. There was always the problem of finding a substitute postmaster and the upheaval was quite great. But after I had been working on my own for a time I thought a break would be a good idea and, to my great delight, a young neighbour was more than pleased to act as holiday relief. She had been a good customer herself and quickly picked up the idea of working from the other side of the counter. Knowing that things were in capable hands I could set off confidently for a couple of weeks. Inevitably, I made for the west and the islands of the west. On arrival in each island I went to over the years I would make for the post office and have an interesting discussion about procedures, problems and so on. In my first island, Barra, I found the office in Castlebay had its notice above the door in Gaelic. It was good to see the native language take precedence. It was run in conjunction with a shop and was a very busy place in the summer.

The first post office in Barra was established in 1855. As the average number of letters posted per week at that time was only 67, bringing in four pounds, ten shillings and fourpence, and the estimated cost of operating was £18 (£3 salary for the postmaster and £15 for the ferry to South Uist) the business was run at a loss. The first postmaster was Dr MacGilivray, who was also the medical doctor and factor for the estate. He lived in the mansion house at Eoligarry which had been built by the MacNeils. The newly established Fishery Company was pressing for a better postal service and in 1875 the office at Castlebay, where the steamers came in, was opened. The postmaster also acted as 'runner', delivering the mail on foot.

In later years Compton Mackenzie had a house on Barra. During the Second World War the postmaster had to transmit by Morse code a series of telegrams to Compton Mackenzie's publishers in London, postal services being often subject to delay. These turned out to be the outlines of his famous book *Whisky Galore*! Sailing packets kept the mails going between all the islands. Now, of course, Barra has its own special air-mail delivery, when the Post Bus meets the plane coming in to land on the famous cockle beach.

In Iona English was used in the name of the office. There was even a board announcing 'Telegraph Office' with an arrowed sign. There were no postal facilities on the island before the mid-nineteenth century. People had to make their own arrangements to collect their mail at Bunessan in Mull. In 1851 a runner was appointed to take letters to Fionnphort and thence across the sound to Iona by open-decked ferry boat. He did this for three shillings a week, out of which he had to pay sixpence as ferry charge. A small receiving office was set up in Iona.

As the tourist trade to Iona increased greatly during the nineteenth century special mail runs were made from Tobermory during the summer and there were extra deliveries from Bunessan, where mounted postmen had taken over from the runners. Many thousands of postcards have been sent from Iona over the years, yet the same hand-stamp was used for nearly half a century. The postmaster – or mistress – today must have to answer many queries expressed in broken English regarding rates of postage to many parts of the world, as visitors from overseas eagerly throng the island. Day-trippers, too, want their cards date-stamped 'Iona' and have no time to queue as their steamer awaits. Much patience must be needed in that small office!

For centuries the islands have felt themselves to be isolated, their language, customs, whole way of life different from that of most parts of the mainland. By the eighteenth century, however, they were gradually being drawn into the web of the modern world. The clan chiefs had lost their status as fathers of the clans and were becoming landlords anxious to make their vast clan lands, their estates, pay dividends. The kelp industry – the burning of sea-weed to produce potash – was flourishing, there was development in the fishing business and large numbers of sheep were being imported to provide wool for the factories in the south. Later, there would be the letting of the shooting and fishing to wealthy patrons from all parts. All these developments demanded contacts with the mainland and the only means of communication was by written message, that is, by the post. The native people wrote few letters, their language having a largely oral tradition. Writing things down was said to damage the memory! But the landlords – the Campbells, the Mackenzies, the Macdonalds, the Macleans, were all English-speaking and literate. They made their words heard! So desperate were they to get postal services established that they sometimes ran them at their own expense and even persuaded their tenants (as the clansmen had become) to take a share in the cost. They did take on the responsibility of providing guarantors should some schemes fail disastrously.

Another of my much-loved islands is Coll. In the principal village of Arinagour there is now a flourishing small post office, which also sells postcards, small booklets and other items of interest to visitors. In 1829 the landlords and tenants of Coll, along with those of Tiree, had to petition the Post Office to provide a regular, costed service by sailing packet. Hitherto they had had to provide it at their own expense. Freeling, the man at the top, regarded their request sympathetically and, as the amount of correspondence was estimated at only £15 a year, it was granted, experimentally, for twelve months. It was not successful, but was continued for a further year, on condition that the proprietors guaranteed revenue against loss. The distribution of letters within the island was another matter. There was no attempt to deliver mail locally for another fifty years, though by 1903 it was agreed that purely local mail could be delivered on days when the steamer failed to call, which could be quite often during the times of winter storms.

One drawback to the arrival of mail in Coll was the fact that large steamers could not anchor in the harbour and had to be unloaded off-shore and passengers, cargo and mail to be ferried

The post office on the island of Coll (The Post Office)

ashore in a rowing-boat. Since then a great new pier has been built and there are now roll-on, roll-off facilities for motorists!

Raasay was an island I had for long wanted to visit. We had often heard and read about its owner, the famous Dr 'No', a medical man from the south of England who had steadfastly refused to allow a car-ferry from Sconser, on the neighbouring island of Skye, to operate. Iron ore had been discovered in 1896 and a Lanarkshire Company – Bairds – had built a railway line from the mine to the pier. The bed of this line can still be followed and makes a pleasant walk. During the First World War German prisoners had worked the mine. A mail-cart was used to convey letters and parcels, twice a week, from the post office to the pier. The presence of the prisoners had greatly increased the volume of mail. But the working of the mine was not a viable enterprise and the rusting machinery was eventually sold as scrap.

In the eighteenth century a ferry-boat operated weekly between Sconser and Raasay. It is reported that Dr Johnson, who stayed in the big house during his famous tour, wrote a letter to Boswell dated 10 April 1775 which only reached its recipient in London on 6 May. One wonders through how many hands and how many ferries and mail-bags it passed! A receiving office was established in Raasay in 1803, with a salary of £2 for the receiver. Later a sub-office was opened at Torran, in the north of the island, and a postal service extended over the strait to Rona, for the lighthouse there.

In 1904 Miss Mary Macmillan was postmistress in Raasay. Her predecessor and 'Deliverer', that is the person who delivered the letters, according to a memorandum dated 12 March 1907, are 'both in the employ of Mrs Wood [wife of the owner of the island], the Renter of the private bag, and although both are aware that they were entitled to payment, preferred to accept presents, usually at Christmas. Articles of clothing were given to the Deliverer, but he also received perquisites in the form of game, etc.' This is surely an example of the paternalism, or maternalism, prevailing at the time.

When old age pensions were introduced in 1909 – at five shillings a week – the people on Rona got their money from the local postman, who received a penny for every pension he paid out. He was a travelling post office! The office at Torran was closed at the start of the First World War and the mails for that area were delivered by a mounted postman from the south of the island. Rona, however, could only be served by a foot-post. Mary Macleod, the 17-year-old daughter of the former postmaster at Torran, carried the mail-bag along a perilous coastal foot-path to the tidal island of Fladday.

The north of the island became famous for the work of John Macleod who, working with pick, shovel and barrow, hacked out a road to link his community with the south. I travelled this road and was entertained happily to tea in his house by his grandchildren. The post office in Raasay is now a busy and popular place, part of the general store in the village of Clachan.

Raasay, to me, meant, of course, Hallaig and the wonderful poem of that name by Sorley Maclean. I walked there, on a perfect summer day. The sadness of the little ruined houses in their stretch of bright green sward was intense, but even over the desolation the beauty of the poem and the promise of it rose, like a shaft of light.

Eigg is another island, one of the many, which has suffered from absent landowners who have neglected it and used it as a plaything. As I write, it is at last enjoying the right to be itself, in the hands of dedicated Trustees. When I visited the post office was running as part of the one shop, in the middle of the island. It is such a little place, six miles long, four miles wide. On arrival by small ferry-boat from the big steamer I found I had missed any kind of transport to anywhere. I found a phone, booked myself into a farmhouse and walked there happily on a traffic-free road.

It was in 1874 that a post and telegraph office was opened on the island. In 1897 a foot-post to Cleadale, in the north-west, was instituted and, later, another to the south coast. A weekly ferry by sailing-boat to the small island of Muck took mail for the people there, who had no post office of their own. The steamer from Greenock to Stornoway delivered mail twice a week in summer and once in winter, which had to be trans-shipped by rowing-boat to the landing quay. On her way south the steamer called again, the postmaster at Portree telegraphing the sub-postmaster in Eigg to tell him the time of departure from Skye, so that the boatman at Eigg could be standing by. This was to prevent undue delay in MacBrayne's schedule.

MacBrayne's certainly ruled the waves round the Western Isles then, as they do today. I wonder who composed this scurrilous, well-known verse:

> The earth belongs unto the Lord
> And all that it contains
> Except the Western Islands, they
> Belong unto MacBraynes.
> *(To be sung in the manner of a metrical Psalm)*

Today, of course, the isolation of the islands is very much less than it was. Occupation by the land and air forces, use of the deep waters by submariners, all these developments, still much in evidence in spite of the ending of the Cold War, have meant a vast proliferation of facilities for rapid communication with the centres of power. The native people benefit from these facilities to a certain extent, but the change in tempo does not suit them all. There are signs of reaction which bode well, I think, for a healthy readjustment between old and new.

In Gigha – God's island – I stayed in the actual post office. It's part of the busy shop in the village of Ardminish. This shop is on the ground floor of a substantial house which was at one time the school and the schoolmaster's residence. On the upper floor are rooms let to summer visitors. A motor launch from Tayinloan serves the island. A receiving house was first established in 1859. After many ups and downs in the establishment of house-to-house delivery of mail, with interceptions by landowners and M.P.s, order now reigns. The problem in Gigha, as in so many of the islands, was the small number of letters posted, the revenue in postage not meeting the cost of running the service. Today, with increasing numbers of visitors and some stabilising of resident populations, the losses are less.

Another island which I had visited briefly once before and which I had long hoped to see again, was Lismore. It is so easy of access – ten minutes in a ferry-boat from Port Appin. In older times the ferry was summoned by a blast on the horn. St Moluag founded a monastery on Lismore, which eventually housed the cathedral of Argyll and the Isles. Many famous clerics served the parish. In the *New Statistical Account* of 1841 the Reverend Gregor MacGregor says:

> There is a great improvement in the Post Office since the old statistical account . . . at that time the mail came only three times a week from Inverary: but now there is a daily post contributing greatly to the improvement of the parish: and there is a penny post at Lismore, to which there is a runner twice a week from Appin . . . so easy and expeditious is now the communication with the south that a newspaper

that is published in Glasgow in the morning is in Appin that night and may be, and often is, in Lismore next morning.

A post office had been established in Appin as early as 1788 and by 1831 an onward delivery to Lismore was in operation, with a receiving house at the northern end of the island, which was later removed to Clachan. One Lismore family, the MacColls, served the posts through Lismore for six generations. Today the post office is situated in a shop at a central spot, convenient for people from all parts of the island. Protests and petitions and interventions by clerics and M.P.s have meant that the receipt and delivery of the mail by ferry and van is adequate. And there is a Post Bus on which I travelled happily on several occasions.

Colonsay I visited during that week in June 1995 when the temperature rose to unbelievable, hitherto unrecorded, heights. The post office is in a well-stocked store near the landing-stage. A friendly postman runs the post bus on which passengers can take the slightly hair-raising passage across the tidal sands to Oronsay. Lord Colonsay – Duncan MacNeil, the lawyer – managed to get a postal service for the island in 1871, with a receiving office at Scalasaig and a twice-weekly service to other parts. There were the usual problems with the cost of the service proving uneconomic and vicissitudes in the provision of steamer sailings. But eventually things evened out, communication being vastly improved by the introduction of telegraph cables and, later, telephone links. While glad to remain isolated as a retreat from the hurly-burly of life on the mainland, Colonsay is nevertheless happily confident that contact can be established at will. The need for this is especially great today as a publishing house, dealing largely with Scottish books, has been established and is run in conjunction with an excellent bookshop at the hotel.

An unusual way of improving communication with some of the islands was tried out in 1934 with a possible link between Harris and the small island of Scarp – by rocket. Gerhard Zucker, a German inventor, whose speciality was rocket propulsion, had the idea of firing mail-carrying rockets from the island to Harris.

Sadly, this was not a success. The rocket exploded on detonation and the letters were scattered far and wide. Some were salvaged, charred or scorched. Zucker was later involved in war-time rocket experiments in Germany.

XXI
ELECTRONIC MAIL

On arrival home from one of my islands I always feel a renewed sense of solidarity with all the servants of the Post Office. Those I have met on my travels have all taught me something. Observing their ways, comparing notes, listening to their experiences and problems is an inspiration for work in one's own sphere . . .

In many ways our own small place, though it is only ten miles from the capital of the Highlands, has less contact with the wider world than some of those in the off-shore islands – Iona with its thousands of visitors, Benbecula with its army of occupation and its busy airfield. Soon, however, it was to take itself onto the modern map, with the arrival of the new technology.

On a walk up the road one autumn afternoon I found a large white van drawn into a lay-by and two men delving into the ground. The van door was open. Glancing inside, I saw the most marvellous collection of multi-coloured wires coiled in a dazzling pattern.

'Looks like the end of the rainbow!' I said, in amazement.

They smiled. 'Aye. I don't know if it's the end. Maybe it's just the beginning.'

As they worked away, smoothing out the wires, putting them in place, they explained that this was part of a vast plan for linking the Highlands with the world-wide network of communication. Network? Web? Internet? Where had I heard those words? I looked up at the sky. It was pale green as the light was fading. There was a streak of rose-red at the horizon.

'You mean . . . all these messages are coming through the air. And what are they telling us?' I was talking to myself, really, but the men were happy to make it a conversation.

'Aye. I sometimes wonder about that. The telly's enough for me. And there's good stuff on the radio. But what's in those wires, that doesn't bother me.'

The other man laughed. 'I get plenty blether from the wife. And I like time to think a bit, too.'

Were these two kindred spirits? I watched them working away with such precision, deftly, the coloured wires passing smooth and straight through their hands. It was clear they knew exactly what they were doing. They were part of this great conglomeration, this great structure, should I say, of the world of information technology, yet they were still human, apart, not overwhelmed. Information? About what? Did I want to know exactly what the price of sugar shares was that day, who was likely to start an offensive in the troubles in Indonesia? Surely these things are of great importance to some people, but, having got the answer you were, perhaps, looking for, would there not be a temptation to go on pressing buttons, turning switches, quizzing the ether, till you found yourself engulfed in a mass of facts and figures impossible to digest? I remembered those flickering screens I'd seen in shop windows. Headaches and eye-strain must afflict the devotees, I thought.

I said goodbye to the engineers and walked on. The information I was seeking was the whereabouts of the wild swans on the loch up the road. They had just arrived. Were they in the rushes on the far bank or near the outlet which was hidden by the trees? My own two eyes would give me the answer.

Since that day and the coming of the magic wires, 'tele-cottages' have arrived in the area. Their operators patronise the post office, buying quite large quantities of stamps, sending off packets and so on. This is, of course, very welcome. The whole idea of doing office-type work from home is a good one. It cuts down on the use of cars, those perpetrators of the sin against the ozone layer. It allows time for the development of small subsidiary enterprises, such as organic gardening and the tending of live-stock, so keeping a small acreage in production and making for a balanced life-style, with the flow of 'information' kept in check.

Our 'tele-cottages' are Aladdin's caves, full of wonders. Wires, screens, recorders, computers, word-processors, shine from every corner. But the two with which I'm familiar boast, also, I'm glad to say, bevies of chickens in the garden ground, one has a few sheep scavenging the hens' food, another keeps bees and ducks.

There will never be an end, of course, to the inventiveness of people everywhere and to the general speeding-up of every process of manufacture, transportation, communication. We are now in the era of electronic mail. This service can only be used by those who have the necessary devices for the transmission and reception of the messages. As a means of keeping in touch, at short notice, with friends or relatives in far-off parts of the world it is greatly valued by those who have the equipment. As private individuals they must be few in number.

I think back, again, to the bundles of letters from my daughter and grand-daughter, kept tucked away and re-read for the feel of youth and energy they contain and for the elegance of the hand-writing. Is the time for the writing of letters slipping away altogether? When I look at some of the scribbles of the very young and the odd spellings . . . I wonder. The stationers' shops are full of attractive packages of letter-writing equipment – coloured or decorated paper and envelopes, pens of all kinds – even the old fountain pen coming back into circulation. These make quite acceptable presents at Christmas-time, but are mostly, I suspect, put away at the back of a drawer, or passed on, unopened, to an unsuspecting relative or friend.

What about the production of books, I often wonder. Students still wander around with two or three under their arm. The library has a queue of readers waiting to check books in or out. At the occasional charity book sale scores of buyers hunt for bargains, and find them. Hardbacks £1, paperbacks 50p. In discarding the rubbish, treasures can be found. People must be reading.

Could we, perhaps, tire of the race to be first with the news? What news? The newness of events all over the world? I re-member our tele-cottages when they were croft houses, places where you went visiting on a winter evening when work for the day was done. You would smell the peat reek as you came near the door and would know there was a good fire on. You'd enter, pushing the door, without knocking. Through the pipe smoke friendly eyes would peer from behind the pages of the newspaper. No virtual reality here, but a cup of tea, or a dram, then some drastic criticism of the Government's many failures – a Government that can't even control the weather! – maybe a tune on the accordion if the mood was swinging that way, and home again, warmed and cheered.

The tele people in occupation now have swept away all the cobwebs, letting in light and air. There's not a warm, dusky corner to be found. Muddy boots must be left at the door. Should we, we wonder, perhaps have a shower before coming in? They are good people, I'm sure, but it's difficult to make real contact when they seem to spend so much of their time on the telephone, even when they're feeding the hens outside, or transfixed by the dazzle of the messages they've called up, or scrutinising the words as they appear on the computer screen. When, one wonders, do they switch everything off and relax?

Highland people have for long been accustomed to welcoming the stranger in their midst. We knew this when we first arrived and found ready help to erect a larch pole with a small engine and rotary blades attached which was to make electricity to light the house. The neighbours must have thought it was a pretty daft idea, but their code of manners would never let them say so and they were generously happy when they found it did work. So the tele people will, I'm sure, find their place as they settle down with all their magic wires in place. Maybe we shall manage, in time, to learn enough of the new language of technology to be able to carry on a discussion on the merits of the new communication systems.

One thing I think I shall never accept is the electronic pet. What's wrong with a good old moggy if you haven't time to walk a dog? She'll keep down the mice which might chew your cabling to shreds in the winter cold. You can stroke her and listen to her purr and she'll warm your chair on a chilly evening. There must be something beyond the surfing of the web. What about those glorious beaches on the island of Tiree?

XXII
FROM BISHOP MARK TO POSTMARK

We had always been proud of the fact that our office had its own hand-stamper, brass with a wooden handle, clearly marked with its own name along with the date. Most other small offices came under the umbrella of Inverness. Quite often we would receive a request from a collector of postmarks to date-stamp a couple of stamped envelopes he enclosed. We were happy to oblige.

In the early days of stamp-collecting it was considered best to have new specimens in mint condition in one's collection. Latterly, clearly postmarked stamps, still adhering to the paper, were preferred. The postmark as we know it today, a circular mark on the envelope, obliterating the postage stamp and showing clearly the name of the office where it was posted and the date of posting, this postmark owes its origin to the fact that, in England, in the seventeenth century, there were many complaints about delays in the delivery of letters. Often, on an urgent letter, people would write the words 'Haste, post, haste!' with a little sketch of a gallows with a post-boy hanging. The addresses were often extremely imprecise. For instance, an Ebenezer Halcrow might be addressed as 'living near the bridge' with the name of the town or village added.

There was a complaint that mail-bags going from London to Edinburgh were being opened on the way, on the excuse that they were not properly labelled. Colonel Henry Bishop, who was running the Post Office at the time, ordered that, to prevent this 'breaking open the Scotch Baggs' every bag was to be securely sealed with a brass tag, each postmaster who handled it to certify that the seal was unbroken. As complaints about the delays continued Bishop declared that 'a stamp is invented that is putt upon every letter shewing the day of the moneth that every letter comes to the office, so that no Letter Carrier may dare detayne a letter from post to post, which before was usual.' These marks were known as Bishop marks and their use continued, with certain changes in size and shape, until the early nineteenth century.

In the days of the mail-coach, in the eighteenth century, the postmarks showed a figure representing the number of miles between the destination of the letter and London. This was a help for postmasters in calculating the postage charge which then depended on the distance travelled. Thus the mileage mark for Dumfries was the number 341, inscribed in a box below the name of the town.

After the introduction of the adhesive stamp the type of post-mark which we know today came into use—this to prevent the re-use of the stamp. One type of postmark was known as the 'killer' as it totally obliterated the stamp.

A strange story concerning postmarks is that of their impor-tance in the trial for murder of Madeleine Smith, in Glasgow, in 1857. Charged with the murder by arsenical poisoning of her lover Emile L'Angelier, proof of her guilt was dependent on the postmark of a letter sent by her to L'Angelier in which she referred to a meeting, after which he became ill. The postmark had been struck carelessly and was illegible. The controller of the sorting office in Glasgow, called to give evidence, admitted that he found the mark difficult to decipher. Addressing the jury the judge said: 'I trust that this will be the last occasion on which the postmarks are so carelessly impressed as they have been. It is a very important matter for the ends of civil and criminal justice that the postmark should be properly stamped.' So, for lack of evidence, the verdict was Not Proven, by a majority. This sensational trial and its outcome is still a matter for discussion. Madeleine Smith married twice and lived out a long life in America. The Glasgow postmarks of the time were withdrawn soon after the end of the trial. To the lucky philatelist who possesses a few of them they are known as 'the Madeleine Smiths.' The moral of this story, for all postmasters, is surely—'Watch your date-stamp, keep it cleaned and use it carefully.' I try to do this, but fail quite often, I admit.

The slogan postmark is one we know well today. It was another of Colonel Bishop's innovations back in the late seventeenth century. Eager to promote the use of the official postal services and to outdo rivals who were causing loss of revenue, he advertised the daily posts to the south with a slogan 'the post for all Kent goes every night from the Round House in Love Lane and comes every morning'. The practice then lapsed for two and a half centuries till, during the First World War, the Post Office introduced a slogan—'Buy National War Bonds'. As a publicity measure the imposing of slogans was soon seen to be important. 'Post early in the day', 'Say it by telephone' were used during World War Two. 'Dig for Victory' was a winner. The 'Empire exhibition Glasgow May–October 1938' was the first specifically Scottish postmark. It had a lion rampant incorporated in the design.

After 1956 the G.P.O. allowed postmarks to be used, not only for Government-sponsored campaigns, but to mark anniversaries or events of a more local type. For instance 'National Bible Society of Scotland 1809–1959'. Later, tourist publicity was allowed. 'Inverness the Highland Capital' was used between 1963 and 1965. The use of postmarks as an inexpensive form of publicity gradually became widespread. The proliferation of so many divers types has created a wide field for collectors to explore. Most have had to restrict themselves to amassing those of a certain type, or relating to a certain theme or location. Most often the slogan is cut from the envelope, with the date-stamp and the postage stamp intact. Sometimes the whole envelope is collected.

Today we take slogans on envelopes so much for granted that we tend to ignore them. In front of me, as I write, I have an attractive example—'Scottish Wildlife Trust' in capital letters, 'Working for wildlife' in script and a pattern of lines in an oval frame. Alongside is the Edinburgh date-stamp, very clearly registered and the postage paid. This is a first-class example, clear and uncluttered, which could well grace a collector's album.

XXIII
TRAVELLING POST OFFICES

Often, in my young days, when it was great adventure to have a 'pen-pal', especially one who lived in a far-off country, I used to wonder how this fragile piece of paper, with my name inscribed on it, had reached me safely across the miles of mountain and sea. I would scan the postmark and the date of posting and marvel again at the speed of its delivery. The stamps, too, were a joy, most often of Canadian origin, for there were relatives there and I was an avid reader of Jack London. Later, I was to have correspondence with people in many places – Europe and the Far East – and it was always a thrill to read their letters. The handwriting, even the paper, was different, inviting, calling up a picture of the writer. Thoughts and feelings, accounts of activities, descriptions of place, all these things, even clumsily expressed, if read with sympathetic understanding, do make for a real sense of communication. Letter-writing is going out now, I know. Attractive 'notelets' tempt one to write only short notes. Everything speeds on, regardless.

The postal authorities have always been aware of the need for speed, since the days of the post-boys who could be deported for 'dallying'. In the mid-nineteenth century, the heyday of Victorian Britain, when everything was on the move, including the railways, the Post Office, feeling 'bound to keep pace with the wonderful improvements with which the present age abounds', decided to make use of this latest form of transport.

The first bags of mail were taken over from the coaches, sometimes including the coaches themselves and the guard. There were fears for the safety of the mail on the first railroads in England. The track had to be lit the whole way at night. One Superintendent of Mail Coaches reported to London, 'Conceive an engine and five or six large carriages in its train rushing along at 20 miles an hour . . . the constant care of the

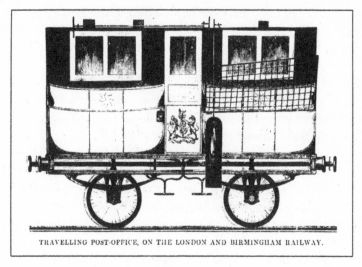

TRAVELLING POST-OFFICE, ON THE LONDON AND BIRMINGHAM RAILWAY.

The first Travelling Post Office, put into service in 1838
(The Post Office)

Road Engineers may prevent all accident but it has a frightful appearance.'

In order to speed the mail even further, in 1838 the first Travelling Post Office, a converted horse-box, was put into service. It was a great success as it made possible the sorting and exchange of mail en route. As in the days of the mail coaches the mail-bags could be thrown out at certain points, as the train slowed, and the in-coming bag could be taken on board by means of a pole stretched towards a worker in the office.

Working conditions in the early Travelling Post Offices were atrocious. The carriages were fitted with counters, desks and pigeon-holes, but there was poor ventilation and no seating or sanitary provision. Many workers travelled as many as forty nights consecutively in order to make up their pitiful allowance. Between 1860 and 1867 there were 28 accidents in which post office men were killed or badly injured. Fumes given out by the oil lamps and the wax used for sealing the bags caused nausea and even affected the brain. Some workers were forced to retire at an early age, even in their mid-thirties, with paralysis or mental debility. Slowly, conditions improved. The railway network was spreading fast. In June 1862 an express train left King's Cross station in London at 10 a.m. every morning bound for the Waverley station in Edinburgh, 393 miles away. This was the *Flying Scotsman*. As the main-line railways reached Scotland, the railway post offices soon followed, the first, the *Caledonian*, running from Carlisle to Glasgow in 1848.

An outstanding example of Post Office efficiency occurred in the aftermath of the Tay Bridge disaster of Sunday 28 December 1879. The bridge carried the main railway line from Edinburgh to Aberdeen. As a north-bound slow train, carrying 6 bags of mail and 78 passengers, approached the bridge in the evening a gale of alarming ferocity was blowing. The train proceeded but the centre section of the bridge collapsed. The whole train and all the people on it disappeared into the waters of the Tay.

That same evening two mail bags were recovered from the beach at Broughty Ferry, four miles downstream. The letters were sent to Dundee and dried out. They were delivered the next day. Only seven of the recovered letters have been traced.

In 1885 came the first of the special Mail Trains which were not intended to carry passengers and were used only for the work of the Post Office. With the ever-increasing volume of mail, particularly business items, newspapers and Government circulars as well as personal letters, this was a necessary move. Soon fifty men were working in about a dozen coaches. Crewe became the 'night mail capital of the United Kingdom'. The Night Mail train stirred the emotions of the people as the old mail coaches had done many years before. W.H.Auden caught the mood of the time in a wonderful poem he wrote as part of the commentary to the film *Night Mail* which John Grierson produced in 1936 for the G.P.O. Film Unit. In it you can hear all the nostalgia of the railway age, as well as the sound and rhythm of the train. It's so good I can't resist quoting its opening lines:

The Post in the Hills

This is the night mail crossing the border,
Bringing the cheque and the postal order,
Letters for the rich, letters for the poor,
The shop at the corner and the girl next door.
Pulling up Beattock, a steady climb –
The gradient's against her but she's on time.

XXIV
THE POST AT SEA

Those letters I used to get from relatives and 'pen-pals' in Canada and Australia and elsewhere had travelled, I realised, at least half the way from their place of origin, not overland, but over the water. Throughout the years, messages, despatches, letters of love must all have been moving over calm waters, through storm and shipwreck, attack by pirates and enemies, through days and nights many times more perilous than those passed on land. Being an island has great advantages – no fear of invasion by land, perhaps, but there are drawbacks. In the days before the conquest of the air there was the sea in constant contention.

In England, as far back as the reign of Henry VIII, a vessel carrying despatches ran from Dover to the continent. Aptly named the *Post Horse*, it was a small sailing ship with a crew of six to eight and could carry a dozen passengers. These vessels were known as Packet Boats or Packets. Hence the French word *Paquebot*.

During the ups and downs of the relationship with Ireland in the sixteenth and seventeenth centuries it was essential to keep a postal service going across the North Channel for military as well as commercial purposes. Queen Anne's Act of 1711 combined the English and Scottish Post Offices and a regular service of packet boats to Ireland was established.

This packet service was greatly extended over the years. The vessels, built for speed rather than security and unarmed except in time of war, flew a special flag as identification – the 'Post-boy Jack', showing a rider blowing a post-horn. During the Napoleonic wars the packet boats encountered many dangers. The working conditions were appalling and the pay poor yet the crews performed amazing acts of bravery in the protection of the Royal Mail, fighting off French pirates and, in one case, actually boarding and capturing a privateer.

The Falmouth Packet, 1822 (The Post Office)

After a small quantity of tea and tobacco was smuggled ashore and seized by the Customs at Falmouth in 1810 the packet men mutinied, demanding better pay. The Riot Act was read and thereafter the Admiralty took control of the packet stations.

Without the stimulus of military necessity, as in the case of Ireland, postal services for the Scottish islands lagged far behind those for other overseas destinations. However, soon after the Rebellion of 1745, a link between Lewis and the mainland was organised, mainly through the enterprise of local lairds and merchants. There were many hazards – bad weather, long distances and poor roads, as well as the obstinacy and parsimony of the postal officials in London, who had no idea of the conditions prevailing in the Islands and often paid little heed to the reports of their Surveyors. The Islands, as well as the mainland area of the Highlands, were awakening to the possibilities of trade, particularly in the fishing industry, the manufacture of seaweed products and so on and were no longer to be looked on as wild and remote. So, at last, it was agreed that a sailing packet would take mail from Stornoway to Poolewe whence it could go by foot-post to Dingwall and thence to Inverness. The Post Office made a contribution to the cost of the service, but the Earl of Seaforth, proprietor of Lewis, paid most of the balance.

The difficulties encountered by the letter-carriers of the time are graphically described in a memorandum sent to the Postmaster General for Scotland in 1798 by Lord Macdonald, Macleod of Macleod, Clanranald and other landowners in Skye and the Uists:

> The Posts from Dunvegan to Inverness, who go alternately, week about have an allowance each of 5s. for every time they go to Inverness, a journey going and returning of fully 226 miles including six ferries. This sum of 5s., it is evident, cannot be an inducement for any man to take such a journey and the Post of necessity has been and is still the Carrier for the whole country, and from being overloaded with commissions he very frequently is detained beyond his usual time, and he generally takes a small boat at loch Carron whereby his own life as well as the mail is in imminent danger of being lost.

Just as roads were being made and improved in the early nineteenth century, so waterways were also being developed. The Crinal Canal in 1801 and the Caledonian Canal 22 years later allowed traffic to pass from Glasgow to Inverness. Small paddle steamers were plying along the west coast and by 1851 the famous red and black funnels of MacBraynes's steamships were to be seen. Two of the best-known steamers were the *Columba* and the *Iona*, on which the Post Office installed travelling post offices.

For letters to Orkney and Shetland the Post Office agreed, after much persuasion, to make a payment of twopence for each item to the captain of the vessel carrying them. They were known as 'ship letters'. This amount was charged over and above the normal postage. Such a system of payment to the captains of ships was used by the Post Office for the world-wide transport of mails.

In the early 1800s steam was being developed as a great source of power. It could provide energy to drive engines to pull trains on land and energy to move paddles to progress the movement of ships on the water. So the great challenge arose – the crossing of the wide gulf of the Atlantic to foster communication with the increasing number of immigrants to America and with the enterprises that were developing there.

In April 1838 the Great Sea Race took place, the contestants being the *Great Western*, a ship designed by Brunel, and the *Sirius*, both carrying passengers and mail. The *Sirius* made the crossing from Cork in 18 days, and at the end had just 20 tons of coal left in her bunkers. The *Great Western* steamed into New York four days later, to be greeted by crowds of excited New Yorkers, having made the crossing in 15 days. Samuel Cunard, a ship-owner from Nova Scotia, was one of the first to realise the potential of steamship communication across the Atlantic. With ever-decreasing times for the voyage and several competing companies engaged in the business, the famous Blue Riband was awarded for record-breaking Atlantic crossings.

Mail services to India, Australia, New Zealand and South Africa, all parts of the world where British people were settled, had many problems to contend with. Conveyance, combined with overland carriage, was a long and cumbersome business. The invention of the screw propellor, which ousted the old paddle wheels, did help to make these long voyages feasible. In 1858 the Marine Mail Service set up sorting offices on the steam packets in order to accelerate the delivery of letters once port was reached. The sorters were obliged to provide themselves, at their own expense, with a distinctive uniform – a blue frock coat with Post Office buttons, dark 'pepper and salt' trousers and a forage cap with a gold band.

Later, a Sea Post Office, staffed jointly by British and American Post Office sorters, was set up. The ill-fated *Titanic* carried five such sorters, two British and three American, when she set off from Southampton on her maiden voyage in April 1912. The obituary of the sorters recorded how 'all five completely disregarded their own safety when the vessel sank, and began to carry the 200 sacks of the registered mail to the upper deck . . . As the situation became more desperate they appealed to the stewards to help them and continued their work to the last'. The vain attempt to save the Royal Mail showed the same spirit of dedicated service as that of the crews who fought the privateers a century earlier.

The deliverers of mail today do not have privateers or highwaymen to contend with, but they have problems of different kinds and they cope with them in the same spirit. Motorised vehicles don't mean the end of all troubles on the road. With black ice on the hill it's safer to sling a bag on your back and let your legs carry you and the mail. Our postie arrived one winter morning having survived a minor crash on the main road, his vehicle still usable but his head with a nasty bruise. 'Ach, it's nothing. I'll see the doctor later. Maybe.' It turned out he had a crack on the skull bone, but that only meant a couple of days' rest and he was back on the job.

XXV
KEEPING IN TOUCH AGAINST
THE ODDS

My earliest non-contact with the Post Office service was when, in the early stages of the Second World War, I decided against applying for a job in the Censorship Office, which was based in Inverness. The idea of living and working in the Highlands was certainly a most attractive one, but the thought of reading letters from stranger to stranger, endlessly, day after day, looking for possible indiscretions regarding the war effort, or hints that might lower morale, was not appealing. There were many 'prohibited areas' in the Highlands during the war, as people planning holidays knew only too well. Training areas for the troops, deep-water anchorages for convoys, these and many other war-time 'facilities' were situated in the far north. Today these places are still looked on as 'facilities', that is, possible dumping-places for the waste products of the modern age.

In any war discretion is, of course, vital. Hence the 'secret service'. In peace-time, too, the utmost care must be taken in the dissemination of news of national importance. Hence the 'diplomatic bag'. In the Censorship Office, during the two world wars, letters from sensitive areas were officially opened and read, anything considered dangerous obliterated, and they were then resealed and marked. One of the earliest examples of censorship is that used during the Jacobite rebellion of 1745-46, when letters from Edinburgh to London were intercepted by the Highlanders, marked 'opened by the Rebels', then sent on to their destination.

In war-time the postal authorities had to adapt to many different situations. During World War Two various issues of stamps had to be made for the use of governments in exile in Britain. Poland, Yugoslavia, Holland and Norway issued stamps for use in the army camps, these stamps often being used in the countries concerned after liberation.

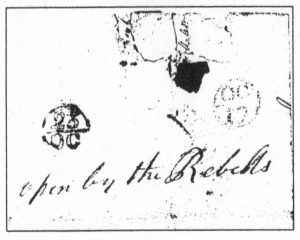

Cover of a letter sent during the 1745 uprising, marked 'open by the Rebells' after being intercepted by the Highlanders

Wars inevitably bring disturbances of kinds other than the actual fighting. Prisoners-of-war in their thousands are kept in camps. Civilians are interned. For all these people some form of communication with the outside world has to be provided, on humanitarian grounds. The Red Cross issued forms which the 'displaced' could fill up to let their families know that they were alive, without giving away any information as to where they were, or indeed any other factual matter.

For soldiers on active service contact with home is an essential factor in keeping up morale. The transmission of letters to and from the field appears incredibly difficult. Yet it was accomplished. The numbers involved were enormous. There was also the problem of the movement of troops from one field of battle to another. And the movements had to be kept secret. During the First World War the British army operated a mail train, manned by the Royal Engineers, for the delivery of letters. Servicemen could also post letters on board and special postmarks were used – F.P.O., Field Post Office.

The transmission of military orders and information required, of course, the utmost secrecy. Speed was always essential. At one time relays of skilled horsemen carried despatches hidden on their person, sometimes committed to memory. In later days despatch riders used motor-cycles, risking their lives on every journey.

During the Boer War Baden-Powell, who later founded the Boy Scout movement, organized scouts to undertake liaison work during the siege of Mafeking. A postal service was established, with stamps depicting a scout with a haversack, on his bicycle. During the Second World War, in Poland, boy scouts were involved in carrying mail, in secrecy, at great personal risk.

Postal authorities have had to deal with many contingencies other than war. Before the use of vaccines serious epidemics ravaged many countries. Plague, leprosy, smallpox, cholera and other diseases broke out, causing millions of deaths. As these diseases were highly infectious and more or less incurable, all that could be done was to protect towns by isolating them. Ships carrying infected passengers were to remain offshore, usually for a period of eighty days. Travellers reaching ports were to remain in quarantine, confined in special quarters, which were then fumigated. Goods were to be exposed to the air and ships treated with lime. Letters were considered high risk carriers of infection. They were fumigated at the quarantine stations and sometimes were specially postmarked. They could be split 'to let out the pestilential air', held over a sulphurous flame or sprinkled with vinegar, which was considered a disinfectant. Letters bearing the marks of these forms of purification can still be found. Vehicles carrying mail were equipped with sulphurous sprays to disinfect the boxes where letters were left.

Another emergency with which the postal authorities have to deal is industrial action by postal workers. Three times in quick succession – 1962, 1964 and 1971 – there were delays and breakdowns in the service in Britain. In 1962 the letter-mail was held up, but only for a few days. On this occasion the People's League for the Defence of Freedom organized a temporary service, until they were ordered to desist by the Post Master General as their effort constituted an infringement of Government monopoly. In 1964 the dispute amounted only to a 'go-slow', though some chaos ensued. In 1971, when a lengthy struggle was anticipated, the authorities, as we have seen, waived the Post Office monopoly, allowing many services to take over the work of handling the mail.

Before the coming of the railway, the carrying of mail posed problems enough in this country, with the hazards already described encountered by 'runners', post-boys and the mail-coach men. In other parts of the world the problems were greater and the means of overcoming them were ingenious in the extreme. Postal authorities everywhere have recognised the need that people have to communicate and also that that need is greatest in the most isolated areas. The more I learn about the measures taken to ensure that communication was maintained the more I marvel at the enterprise of the authorities concerned and at the courage and endurance of those who carried out the feats of daring which made a reality of the enterprise.

In North America there were deserts, unfriendly native tribes and high mountains to be encountered. The Pony Express company, subsequently part of 'Wells Fargo', operated a route with 600 hardy ponies, staging posts and, if needed, a small escort of cavalry. The isolated trading posts in Canada and Alaska communicated with the outside world by means of sledges drawn by dogs or reindeer.

Along the roads in the flat country of northern France and Belgium dogs were also used to pull small, two-wheeled mail carts. In the Nordic countries, where snow lies for months, the postmen travelled on skis. They were the cross-country skiers of their time and covered enormous distances. In remote mountainous country, where no motorised vehicle can venture, a sure-footed ass or a mule is still used to carry mail. In the marshy districts of south-west France, where stilts are commonly used for getting around, the postmen walked this way, covering the ground in great strides, the recipients of letters having to tread warily and stretch long arms to reach their mail.

It's clear that, since the earliest times, people the world over have had this strong desire to keep in touch and that organisations have been created to meet this desire, overcoming what seemed insuperable difficulties all along the line. Now, with air-mail, e-mail, fax machines, telecommunications of all kinds, it would seem that the problems are vanishing 'into thin air'. But are they, perhaps, only beginning, the problems? Are we casting aside the reality of a piece of paper, held in the hand, the texture felt, the individuality of the writing clearly recognised, are we casting this aside in favour of a few words on a crackling line, a flickering image, perhaps, on a dimly-lit screen, words on a long scroll turned out by a machine? Will all this dependence on mechanical devices not inhibit the true transmission of ideas and feelings which can really only be faithfully expressed in the intimate contact of pen with paper, made in quietness of mind? Will our correspondents become akin to all the other figures we see daily on our television screens, figures of virtual reality? There is still nothing comparable to the pleasure of receiving an envelope straight from the postman's hand, recognising the handwriting, admiring the stamp, slitting the seal, unfolding the paper and reading the lines.

The look of the handwriting is a joy in itself. The long loops, the leaning uprights, the rounded vowels, the scratchy middle consonants, the whole aspect of the sheet brings the writer to life. A science has evolved from the study of handwriting. I don't need that to help me identify the character of my friends. I love the spidery scrawl of the busy, lively minds, the more graceful, easy flow of the warm-hearted. I can still visualise my father's style, his slightly withdrawn, cramped script, with Greek 'e's and no flourishes. My mother's had a more rounded, less ethereal feel. They both wrote a lot but never used a typewriter.

Formal script can be learnt and has a beauty of its own, but I truly appreciate the individual quirks and talent of my letter-writers. Long may they fill the postie's bag and let the junk-mail be discarded on the internet!

XXVI
PROBLEMS WITH PARCELS

We do not often have parcels to despatch from our office. The cost has risen alarmingly lately, making tokens an easier option to send as gifts. Nevertheless, in the weeks before Christmas we do have busy times, with the old scales and weights brought into operation, much looking-up of unfamiliar destinations and the postal rates thereto, the filling-up of Customs declarations, certificates of posting, checking information on insurance costs and rates of compensation in case of loss. This, we realise, is the kind of work done on a daily basis in the bigger offices. We are quite glad to be stretched in this way from time to time. It brings home to us, too, the fact that the postal services in some other countries are perhaps less strictly supervised than ours. When sending mail to one central European country I was advised not to put on attractive pictorial stamps as these were very often detached by collectors and the letter or packet remained undelivered as unstamped. Parcels to this particular country also most often disappeared en route.

These busy times bring people to our door who normally do their postal business in the town to which they commute daily. With us they dodge the queues. 'We must do this more often!' they say, as they heap their parcels on to every available space, ready for the postie to load them into his van in the morning. 'Why not?' we reply, thinking that such a volume of mail might justify an increase in our meagre pay!

The establishment of a Parcel Post lagged far behind that of the Government-controlled letter post. A reduced rate had been introduced for the sending of books through the letter-post, a special Book Post, which continued for many years. By the mid-1800s the railway companies had cornered most of the parcel business, though in the country districts carriers operated, with horse-drawn carts. These are remembered still, with affection, in many places.

Problems with Parcels

After years of thoughtful discussion, research, visits abroad to inspect other ways of delivering parcels, the working out of practical details such as the building of depots and other problems in the actual handling of the goods, eventually, in August 1883, the Post Office was authorised to introduce the Parcel Post. Problems were soon encountered. Circulars were rushed out to postmasters everywhere. Damage to parcels due to insecure packing was a headache. One circular stated: 'Damage is occasioned to Parcels by the insecure packing of fruit. As a rule, fruit and butter should be sent in tins, even rather than in wooden boxes, as fruit (strawberries, raspberries, etc.) is reduced to a pulp by jolting in the trains and then exudes from the cracks of the Boxes.'

This reminds me of one instance when an untidy package, inadequately addressed, arrived in the post office at New Year time. The postie delivered it to what he took to be the right place. Two days later it reappeared with us. It was a case of 'Return to Sender', but by this time the contents was revealing itself as a very 'high' duck, too far gone for anyone's dinner, which had to be dumped. None of this damage would have occurred in the days of the old carriers.

The question of registration of parcels had not been worked out when the Rev. Charles L. Dodgson (alias Lewis Carroll) complained that he was unable to register valuable packets of drawings etc., which were too big for the letter-post. One hopes they were not any of the lovely 'Alice' ones that might have gone astray.

The problem of the delivery of parcels to their final destinations then came to a head. When the Royal Mail consisted of letters and perhaps newspapers it had been carried on foot, on horse-back, by Mail Cart and, for long distances, by coach, as we have seen. The carriage of parcels would require some other means of transport. 'Velocipedes' and tricycles were tried out and also a contraption known as 'the hen and chickens', which had a large wheel in the centre and smaller ones at each end, with big baskets attached. Resort was made to the use, once again, of coaches on some of the busy roads out of London. This was done under contract with

A fine flock of 'Hens and Chickens' during the 1880s
(The Post Office)

a Post Office employee as guard, armed with a sword-bayonet and a revolver. These parcel mail coaches carried no passengers and travelled at night. The coachmen and guard were known as the 'pilgrims of the night'. They brought back nostalgic memories to the older people of the days of the mail coaches. The guard worked away all night, sorting the mails, blowing his post-horn to alert other night-time drivers of wagons of the Mail's approach and chatting with his own driver to keep him awake.

Royal Mail letter-carriers, now known for the first time, officially, as Postmen, were under great pressure, being expected to cope with the sudden influx of additional mail. It was not long before a poem appeared in *Punch* (29 September 1883) describing the plight of the rural carrier. I quote the first part:

An Old Postman's Story

Tis true, your honour, I'm fair dead beat, so I'll snatch a
    rest on this country stile.
For I've trudged and tramped with loaded back from
    county town 'tis many a mile
Up at the hour when the cock's awake and shuffling
    home when the bat's on wing,

A-calling here and a-calling there, with a wait for a
    knock and again for a ring:
A pleasant life do you call it, Sir? to skirt the hedges and
    brush the dew,
Well it's all very well for the folks in town, who come
    down here just to take their rest:
But with chaps like me when my labour's done and I
    long for leisure, then bed's the best.
It wasn't so bad in the days gone by, with letters tied up
    in a handy pack,
A stick, a satchel, a pair of legs, a sense of duty, a big,
    broad back:
But now it's different, quite, look here, when the grave is
    ready and sexton host
Let them bury me quiet, and put on the stone, 'His back
    it was broke by the Parcels Post'.

The authorities took this poem quite seriously, knowing that *Punch* was read by influential people, many of them country dwellers. But reaction soon set in. 'The rate of wage for rural letter-carriers, say, 16s. a week all the year round for 16 single miles, six days a week has not yet failed to get good men . . . We now . . . only allow our men to carry 30 or 35 lbs . . . they say nothing about uniform, Xmas boxes and other advantages and little sources of income.' And the hours worked – from about 5.45 a.m. to 9.30 a.m. and from 3 p.m. to 7 p.m. gave postmen a nice long rest in between, enabling them to 'find some occupation for which they receive pay or food'. Was that official connivance at 'moonlighting'?

By the end of the century motorisation was on its way. In 1897 the Post Office was experimenting with motor vans driven by steam, electricity and oil, with a variety of extraordinary vehicles. In 1899 a Daimler motor mail van took to the road, to great acclaim. During the 1914–18 war, when rubber for tyres was scarce, postmen on pedal cycles often had to ride on the rims. Then, after the war, with things beginning to get back to normal, the Post Office built a fleet of thousands of vehicles. In the country motor cycles and 'combinations' were in use. Though horses were still on the move in certain areas, such as the Highlands, by the 1950s the day of the horse as the faithful carrier of the mails was over.

Today, we have a stock of the most splendid vehicles, from the modest rural delivery vans to the enormous long-distance lorry, all resplendent in shiny red paint, with golden crown and lettering operating under the Parcel Force organisation of the Post Office.

There are certain rival operators, too, with alluring names and symbols, the word 'Express' much used and arrows and pigeons, perhaps standing for speed and direct delivery. The Post Office does not have a monopoly of parcel delivery. In my experience the standards of these alternative schemes do not match those of the official service. Their arrival time is not known, and parcels are left in odd places if one is out, with a note sometimes, not always, pushed into the keyhole or under the door. The drivers are mostly strangers to the area and frequently lose their way, get stuck down side-roads and have to be pulled out by tractor. Some refuse to tackle farm roads and leave goods 'to be collected' at the post office.

XXVII
THE POST TAKES TO THE AIR

I shall always remember my astonishment one Sunday evening, in Skye, looking from the window and seeing people wandering past, Sunday newspapers tucked under their arms. Sunday newspapers on Sunday in Skye? It seemed incredible. Then, of course, I remembered. From Inverness by air Skye is the merest hop. This was long before the days of the bridge, when you travelled by train or car, waited for the ferry and had all the thrill of that crossing by sea which, short though it was, gave you the feel of going abroad, to a different country. I realised that though the Skye people could get Sunday papers on Sunday many would not read them till Monday. That was the custom.

Nowadays I have only to look up at the sky as I hear the sound of a plane, to think 'there goes my card. She'll get it in time for her birthday'. 'She' lives in London and her birthday begins in the morning, but I can be sure the greeting will be there in time. Acceleration of the mail must surely have reached an all-time high! Only once has this service to the south come to grief. One winter night of fog and rain, the plane crashed into a hillside quite soon after take-off. Luckily the pilot escaped death. The mail was scattered, but much of it was retrieved in daylight and returned, as far as practicable, to sender or sent on to the addressee, the Post Office always taking its duty seriously.

Have we really conquered the air? Man has been preoccupied with the idea of flight since the earliest times, his experiments often resulting in disaster. But he has persisted.

Long ago the Persians and the Arabs used homing pigeons for sending messages. This ensured an easy passage over enemy territory. It is said that swallows were used at one time in the East.

It is well known that pigeons played an important part in maintaining communications during the siege of Paris in 1870-71, when the Government had moved to Tours, in the south. The

611

birds were transported, two or three at a time, in baskets attached to balloons. Official despatches were written by hand in minute letters, on tissue paper. The paper was rolled up and placed in a tiny tube which was tied either to the pigeon's leg or to one of its tail feathers. A waxed silk thread was used to minimise weight.

Micro-photography had been invented at this time. This allowed long messages to be sent in very small bulk. The pigeons had snow and frost to contend with. Many of them never reached their journey's end. Their services were highly valued during the long months of occupation.

Pigeons were used in peace-time, too, carrying messages between Auckland and the off-shore islands of New Zealand, until the extension of the telegraph service came along. The micro-filming of mail was used again during the Second World War by Britain and America, these letters being known as 'airgraphs.'

Another important factor in the development of aerial communication was the use of the balloon. During the siege of Paris, which lasted from mid-September 1870 until the end of January 1871 and was causing much misery and starvation, many balloons were able to leave the city in comparative safety, sailing over the heads of the Germans, anti-aircraft artillery not having been invented then. Some flights were nevertheless extremely hazardous and some ended fatally. Most of them carried mail, official and unofficial. Balloons had been invented at the end of the eighteenth century, hot-air balloons being superseded by those filled with inflammable gas. Ballooning became a craze in Europe and America. Some deliveries of mail were made by the early pioneers, but the unreliability of the balloon, which only needed a change of wind to go off course, precluded the setting-up of an official balloon mail service. During World War One the dirigible balloon, known as the 'Zeppelin', after its inventor, was used in bombing raids. Later, during the twenties and thirties Zeppelins did carry mail.

Meanwhile, much progress was being made in the development of flight by winged aircraft, both in Europe and America. The Post Office, always anxious to use new means of expediting

An Imperial Airways mail-plane in 1935. An airmail van stands ready to transfer mail (The Post Office)

the delivery of mail, was soon involved in the testing of these machines. The first flights were hazardous. Inevitably bad weather, engine trouble, forced landings in unknown territory – these were some of the hazards that had to be faced.

France had always been particularly keen to develop aviation. One famous pilot – Antoine de St Exupéry – flew the mails over the North African desert. He was so passionately devoted to flying that he could not live happily for any length of time on the ground. Several times he crashed in the desert and was rescued by Bedouin tribesmen. Even after suffering severe injuries he kept on flying. Eventually, he set off one day and did not return. No sign of him or his aircraft was ever found. He left us two marvellous books – *Terre des Hommes* and *Night Flight* in which he tries to tell something of what it meant to him to fly, his vision of the world below. He also wrote a story – *The Little Prince* – which can be read on the philosophical level of an adult or a child, as an allegory set among the stars.

The first airmail service in Britain was that between Inverness and Kirkwall, in Orkney. It was inaugurated on 29 May 1934, the plane piloted by Captain Eric Fresson, a great pioneer of aviation, whose statue now stands at the airport at Dalcross. After a frantic clearing of sheep off the runway at Kirkwall the plane landed safely, marking the start of a regular service.

Mails have been carried by glider, by radio-controlled pilot-less plane and have been dropped from the air by parachute, in canisters with a 'chute which opens only when it nears the ground, thus ensuring a soft landing. Helicopters are widely used to carry mail and, as we have seen, there have been experiments with rockets. In 1969 the Apollo XI crew took a letter to the moon and stamped and franked it there. What would St Exupéry have given to have been there!

There is no doubt that this conquest of the air and the development of aerial transportation have been greatly helped by aid and subsidies from postal administrations in many countries. Next stop the interplanetary mail!

XXVIII
SCARLET COATS AND RAGGED TROUSERS

Sometimes, on visits to the Head Office in town I would look wonderingly at the smart attire of the ladies at the counters – flowered blouses and well-cut skirts – the men in regulation shirt and trousers. Their bright appearance certainly did give one a feeling of confidence in their ability to ensure the safe expedition of one's mail to the trickiest corner of the planet, if not (yet!) to outer space. They were friendly, too, even though contact was minimal, just a smile from behind the grille and a glimpse of well-manicured fingers as they pushed your stamps and your change through the hollow below the bars. It must be a little like that when you visit someone in prison, I would think.

There was never a question of a uniform issue for the postmaster /mistress. Were we supposed to be a cut above the counter clerks and therefore able to dress as we liked, at our own expense? A flowered blouse and a well-cut skirt would seem a little out of place behind our old deal table, I thought, remembering the many times when I would hastily remove a kitchen or a garden apron as I hurried to answer a summons by the bell.

We were, however, issued with name badges in the late eighties, this at a time when personal identification had become imperative. They are certainly useful at meetings and conferences, but in my small sphere not strictly necessary for everyday use. I've been known to most of my customers for a good many years. Sometimes the badge is forgotten.

So – no uniform dress for me, but our postie sports his regulation navy outfit, with the scarlet piping at the pocket. For a while a light grey suit was tried out, but soon the navy blue was re-adopted. I often envy him his wet-weather coat of yellow oilskin, guaranteed to keep out the wildest downpour.

Our young relief posties, once clear of the town, can adapt their uniform to suit themselves, or the weather. In summertime it's good to see them relaxed, shirt open at the neck, sleeves rolled high, clearly enjoying the round. One manages to pursue his hobby of photography, taking shots during his tea or lunch break. It's good to see these young men clearly finding pleasure in their day, with no fear of being assaulted or robbed, as their forerunners in the old times might have been. There was no question of an issue of clothing for the foot-posts. Many times they must have been soaked to the skin on the outward way with no time to dry off before the return. The mounted postboys did have headgear of a sort and big boots.

The earliest reference to postal clothing dates from 1590 when the Council of Aberdeen ordered for William Taylor, known as the 'Post', a livery of blue cloth, with the armorial bearings of the town worked in silver on his right sleeve. This was before the days of the state Postal Service and was purely a local organisation. Later, every letter-carrier was supposed to 'wear a brass ticket upon the most visible part of his clothing, with the king's arms upon the same'. I doubt whether this injunction was strictly obeyed everywhere.

When the mail coach service started in 1784, the Guards were provided with an official uniform – a scarlet coat with gold lapels and gold braid and a black hat with a gold band. The driver wore the same. Red was the royal colour and also the colour of the soldiers' uniforms. A military image was useful as a deterrent to the highwaymen who were always on the lookout for easy prey.

Letter-carriers in London were provided with uniforms in 1793. The men objected to this as it would mark them out as people carrying large sums of money and therefore make them liable to be attacked and robbed. However, they were over-ruled. One reason for the introduction of a uniform was the ragged condition of the letter-carriers' own clothes. So they were issued with a beaver hat, with gold band and cockade, scarlet coat (cut-away style) with blue lapels and cuffs, with brass buttons on which the wearer's number was inscribed and a blue cloth waistcoat. The uniform was to be renewed every year. They must have been a resplendent sight! But . . . they were still required to provide their own trousers, so that 'It is recorded that the splendid coats and hats presented a strange contrast above the ragged cloaths of trousers which seem to have been not uncommon with the Letter Carriers of those days.' Some forty years later there was a suggestion that the letter-carriers should be supplied with waterproof capes as well to be attached to the coats as protection in bad weather, or that the coats should be made of waterproofed material. Both these ideas were turned down. Expense was probably the reason for the rejection of the ideas as there were by that time nearly 2,000 employees in several cities, including Edinburgh and Dublin, all issued with uniforms.

In 1855, at last, trousers were made part of the issue and waterproof capes, with scarlet frock coats, were provided. This must have been a welcome move. Not so welcome, however, was the adoption of the glazed tall hat as worn by the postmen of Paris. *Punch* got another word in on the subject, saying 'we hear that the new hat weighs very heavily on the heads of the Department on whose behalf we seriously suggest the removal of an invention which gives both heaviness and headache to a very meritorious class of public officers.' Sure enough, four years later it was superseded by a hard felt hat and then by a peaked cap.

The same issue of *Punch* had more to say regarding postmen's attire. Under the heading 'The Post Office in a Blaze' it said:

> We lately had our eyes dazzled by the sight of the Postmen in a glaring red uniform, more fitted to the Fire Brigade than for a peaceful body of men connected with the department of *literae humaniores*, as the couriers of letters. We cannot comprehend the taste which has pinned a large pair of scarlet skirts to the coat of the Postman, and caused us to mistake him for a sentinel off his post, by his resemblance to a Foot Guardsman in one of the new regulation wrappers. Considering there is a Reward payable for the apprehension of a Deserter, we wonder that half the Postmen in London are not taken into

custody every night on suspicion. We can see no necessity whatever for the military aspect of these men: and indeed in these war times it is enough to alarm half the old women of London to have their portals thundered at every hour of the day by men of military aspect. We recommend the immediate abolition of this very martial attire, by elevating the Postman into a very formidable rival to the Policeman, in those little flirtations with our female servants, which have often kept a sentimental Constable grunting hoarse nothings into our housemaid's ear, while some burglarious gentleman has been emptying our neighbour's plate-chest. The Post Office is in every respect a Model Department, and the new costume has probably not originated from its heads, which are too much occupied with improving our means of communication to be able to bestow much time on the cut and colour of the Postman's attire.

Punch also fabricated a petition from the wives of Postmen regarding the non-issue of trousers to their husbands. Thus:

To her Gracious Majesty the Queen: the humble petition of the Wives of the Postmen – Madam, May it please your gracious goodness to look with a smiling eye upon the husbands of your Petitioners. Your gracious goodness supplies to 'em from the Crown a coat, a waistcoat, a hat with a band which only the illiterate multitude take for gold. Your Petitioners pray that the Crown would not leave off at the waistcoat, but continue its bounty in the way of trousers and end it with shoes . . . Your Petitioners humbly appeal to your Majesty's sympathies as a wife. What would be your Majesty's feelings to see Prince Albert in the fine laced coat of a General, with shabby trousers and boots not fit for any painter to take him in?

One wonders if copies of *Punch* ever reached the tea-table at the Palace or Balmoral? Gradually the issue of uniforms was extended to the Provinces, the Surveyor of Manchester pointing out that 'it is important to the safety of correspondence posted in the pillar boxes (these were proliferating) that anyone seen opening a pillar should at once be recognised by the public as our servant'. Thereafter all Post Office employees were provided with uniforms.

Soon the London letter-carriers were getting two pairs of trousers and a new hat each year, also two coats a year, and waistcoats and capes every two years. The provinces did less well. There was still no mention of trousers, only one hat and two coats a year and a cape biennially. Then, in 1861,

as it had been found that the scarlet uniforms of the Letter Carriers very quickly became soiled, this colour was discarded, in favour of: A blue coat with scarlet collar and cuffs and scarlet piping – the letters G.P.O. above the wearer's number being embroidered in white on each side of the collar. A blue vest similarly piped with scarlet. Blue winter trousers, with a broad scarlet stripe. The summer trousers, in grey, with a scarlet cord stripe.

A few years later the frock-coat was replaced by a tunic of military pattern. In Edinburgh and London a tunic with tails was adopted, as the letter-carriers were required to do so much stair-climbing that it was often inconvenient for them to wear their greatcoats and the tail-coat gave them the necessary protection from the cold.

In 1870 the Telegraph companies were taken over by the Post Office and the boy messengers were supplied with uniforms. Soon the rural letter-carriers were equipped with standard dress. During the 1914-18 war many women joined the Post Office Department. They were issued with a blue cap and blue straw hat, blue serge skirt and cape and boots.

Some day, I promise myself, I will take a trip to the Post Office Museum in London to see some of these marvellous uniforms of the past. Looking at our postie of today, well-equipped in his neat, blue outfit, with boots and a waterproof coat as protection against any kind of weather, I think of the days of the ragged trousers topped by the scarlet frock-coats with the top hats and wonder how his predecessors ever managed their rounds in such theatrical garb.

XXIX
MORE HIGHLAND POST OFFICES

One summer, staying for a few nights in a Bed and Breakfast establishment, in one of the islands, I met a couple who were 'collecting' small Highland Post Offices. This meant photographing them and showing them to friends as mementoes of their holiday. The town-dweller of today is accustomed to find the local post office a place one goes to for the carrying-out of somewhat boring, business-like transactions. Coming across a small tin shack on the edge of the beach in one of the islands with the familiar label, in the familiar design, 'Post Office' stuck above the door, or perhaps the Gaelic '*Offis a'Phuist*', he is amazed.

We have had encounters of this kind ourselves. Pushing open the door, we look round. There is a counter, some rather tattered posters and notices on the walls, no sign of an official. A child comes in.

'Sorry. Gran will be here in a minute' she says, with a shy smile.

A moment or two later an elderly woman appears, wiping her hands on her apron. 'You've not been waiting long, I hope. Morag said she saw you coming across the sands. I was just chasing a cow from the garden.'

'No. That's all right. We've only just arrived.'

'And are you on holiday?'

'Yes. We're staying a few days.'

'You like it here?' She gives us a quizzical look. 'It can be fearful wild sometimes.'

'We like it. Tell me . . . What's the name of the castle over there, at the head of the bay?'

She smiles, almost apologetically. 'Ach, that's just a ruin. The MacLeods had it long ago. It's called Castle Leod, for them. Are you quite comfortable where you are staying?' The present day is clearly of more importance to her than the past, with its memories of betrayal.

An islander collecting his pension in the Isle of Coll post office
(The Post Office)

'Yes, we're very happy.'

'That's good, then.' By now she is composed, smiling and at her place behind the counter. Morag was regarding us with half-concealed curiosity.

'Has Morag far to go to school?' We could see no sign of a building looking like a school, only a few scattered houses, no shop, no church.

'About twelve miles. There's a mini-bus to take the children. But she has had the toothache and her not sleeping.'

'Oh, dear. That's sore.' Morag gives a half smile. Here we were, in the middle of someone's day, with a cow in the garden and a child's sore tooth. The transacting of business seemed relatively unimportant. But we did need stamps.

'Och, yes. Now wait a minute. I've some nice new ones. They came the other day.'

She hunts in a drawer and we exclaim with delight at the beauty of the fresh issue. 'You like them? I have others.' She turns the pages of the old stamp-book. It is a replica of our own. Feeling guilty at not disclosing the fact that we, too, run a post office, but not wishing to embarrass her, we pick out several attractive pictorials.

'We don't sell so many of them. Folk here seem to like the plain ones better.'

'Are you kept fairly busy?'

'Not what you'd really call busy, I suppose. Not like I've seen them in Fort William when I was there one day. But the pensioners need an office here. They could never travel twelve miles to collect their pensions. And they often get big parcels. They buy from the catalogues. And there's the phone here. And they like a wee blether.'

'Of course. Are there many?'

'Quite a few. They like to stay on in their old homes, even though the young couples move in to keep the ground worked. They like their independence. And . . . they love the place.'

'I can understand that.' We gather up our stamps and settle the bill, amazed at how quickly the postmistress adds up the amount. 'That was fast work!'

She smiles. 'We did lots of arithmetic in our heads. I've never forgotten.'

'Were you at school here?'

'I was. It was just a wee school. Called a side school. It took a kind of overflow from the bigger one where Morag goes now. In fact . . . it was in this very building.'

'Goodness!'

'It was. There was just about a dozen of us. We had desks and slates and some books. Sometimes the rain came in the roof, but we had a wonderful teacher.'

'Well, that's . . . '

'Excuse me now. I see the post coming. He'll be ready for his tea. He has the nurse with him. She'll be going to see Mrs Mackinnon and she'll get a lift back with him when he's finished.' Sure enough, on the nearby road the small red van has drawn up and the post is making his way down, a large bundle of packages on his back. The catalogue buys, we reckon.

'Thanks then. And goodbye. All the best.'

'Goodbye. Haste ye back!' Morag smiles again, confidently now.

We leave reluctantly, greeting the postie as we pass. Gazing round at the sea, with the small waves breaking on the dazzling sand, at the distant curve of hills and breathing in the scent of the machair and its flowers, we're glad there are those clinging to the place they love and making room for the young to follow. We remember, as they do, all those others who had to leave. We're thankful there's a place, a small focal point, where their needs are understood and can be seen to cheerfully, a tiny post office, in a tin hut by the beach.

If you want to get the feel of a place this is where to come, to the small post office, the smaller the better. It is nearly always run by somebody local who has lived there all his, or her, life. The hotel, if there is one, is most often run by an incomer or an employee of a big group. He'll give you the statistics – the height of the hill, the state of the tides, where to get your fishing permit and so on, but he'll speak with the accent of Glasgow or Leeds and his bright young assistants will be from Australia or New Zealand and will be gone by the end of summer.

These small post offices were only set up with a struggle. In the early nineteenth century, when contact with the south and its commercial enterprises was increasing rapidly the need for postal services was also increasing. The lairds, as we have seen, were active in promoting the development of these services, since it was greatly to their benefit to do so. Postal services were to mean more than the provision of a runner, or letter-carrier from the nearest town.

One of the earliest offices to be established in the north was at Balbair, in Easter Ross, in October 1843. It was a Receiving Office, and Andrew Ross, the Receiver, along with the villagers, guaranteed to meet any expenses incurred by the Post Office. The office remained in the same building for many years. A Mrs Ross, sub-postmistress in 1966, reckoned that the premises she worked in were the very ones in which the original office had been set up. This Balbair sub-office was renamed Edderton in 1879 and in that same year, during the night of the Tay Bridge disaster, its original thatched roof was blown off. The Post Office was subsequently moved into the village shop and later it was taken into the hotel where it is worked on a part-time basis.

At Crathie, near Balmoral in Aberdeenshire, a Receiving Office was established in September 1842, a Mr Anderson as guarantor of the Post Office expenses of £5 a year. The first Receiver was Charles Thomson, head forester on the Balmoral estate. Realising that the introduction of the Universal Penny Post of 1840 would mean a large increase in the volume of mail, he had set about building a post office, combined with a house. It was of the usual traditional style of cottage and barely furnished, a wooden dresser having a special drawer for the post office equipment. Charles Thomson carried on the business here for 45 years, until his death in 1887. Queen Victoria, who was an inveterate letter-writer, visited the post office regularly. She refrained from using the royal prerogative of franking, that is, non-payment of postage, though some of her letters were sent by royal couriers. After Charles Thomson died she wanted his son Albert to take over the office, but Albert was following a successful career in London. The queen, not to be outdone, undertook personally to make up any deficiency in income which the change of job might bring and he was duly installed as postmaster by royal request! Later, she saw to it that two rooms were added to the building and the post office moved to the new wing.

After 43 years service Albert died and his widow took over the office until her eldest son, another Albert – a favourite name at the time! – was appointed postmaster in 1947. He and his brother Gordon carried on the business for many years in the same building which had been the family home for over a century. The thousands of tourists who flock to Crathie every summer have certainly made good use of the postal facilities there. It is often the case, as recorded in the Post Office Archives, that a rural office remains in the hands of the same family for several generations and often in the same building.

In our own area there are several houses which are known, or were known – two have been demolished – as the 'old' post office. I can count four before it came to the schoolhouse, where it has been for close on fifty years, with postmasters of the same family for close on forty. Records show that Abriachan had a date stamp in 1904, so it has been in the annals for nearly one hundred years.

As regards the 'Head' post office for the area, the office in Inverness, it had a chequered history, too. A Miss Helen McCulloch is in the records as having the title Postmistress in Inverness in 1737 and was said to be responsible for all letters despatched north of the Firth of Forth. Mr Penrose Hay, postmaster, who published in 1885 a short book called *Post Office Recollections*, says:

> in and prior to 1790 the head Post Office of the town was situated at what is now 32 Castle Street, when the whole business was easily disposed of in a room 14 feet by 9 feet 6 ins. The aperture for the letter-box was in the old window shutter and, as there was no coach beyond Inverness, neither was there any bridge, the mails to and from Dingwall, Caithness and Skye were conveyed on a pony ridden by old William Smith, afterwards Bellman and Shoremaster. The ponies used for the purpose were stabled in rear of his premises in Castle Street.

The townspeople would call at the Receiving Office to collect their letters. On market day the names of people from the country for whom a letter had arrived would be called out.

About 1810 the post office was moved to a more central place, near the 'Exchange'. Ten years later it was moved again, to a house in Church Street, on the corner with Bank Lane. The office covered about 110 square feet. The letter-box measured exactly 4 inches by ¼-inch. Letters of that time were of a single sheet so the aperture was adequate. We are fortunate in having a sketch of this old post office and of the letter-box, done by Pierre Delavault, who was art master at the Academy and made

Inverness Post Office, by Pierre Delavault (courtesy of
Inverness Courier)

sketches of many of the old buildings of Inverness, most of which
have now, sadly, been demolished.

The staff in this old post office consisted of the postmaster and
one letter-carrier. Business was not brisk. Mr Hay says: 'I recollect
distinctly of the postmaster going away in that year (1829) for a
twelve hours holiday, leaving the whole department in charge
of the one old letter carrier, who discharged the whole duties
of the day most satisfactorily'. This is certainly extraordinary as
the letter-carriers were Gaelic speakers and mostly more or less
illiterate. How the letters reached their destinations has always
been a mystery.

In 1841, the year after the Universal Penny Post came in, the
post office was transferred to Baron Taylor's Lane. There were
then four postmen. A few years later it went to a substantial building in the High Street, where a Victorian letter-box in the wall
is still in use. Post office business was increasing rapidly and the

staff soon rose to sixty-three. By 1890 premises in Queensgate had been specially built to accomodate the post office, with a staff of one hundred. The present building, modernised and equipped to a high standard, is on the site of this Victorian model. This is the place whose portals we enter from time to time, to marvel at its weighing and stamping devices, at its safety measures, at its orderly queue, at its tidily uniformed staff. We return to our own small corner with a slight sigh of relief.

Next morning I give the floor an extra careful sweep, polish the brasses till they gleam, tidy the piles of leaflets, put some flowers on the window ledge. Standards must be seen to.

XXX
POST OFFICE CATS

An essential member of any country household is a cat. Two is an even more desirable number and can usually be quite quickly achieved. Country mice, which usually take up their abode in warm corners of the house by late autumn, can do an amazing amount of damage. One winter we had a plague of rats, when a neighbour found water coming through his kitchen ceiling, the hungry rodents having chewed through the plastic piping in the loft. Mice can attack electric wiring, too. That particular year we had to call in the Pest Officer.

Normally our cat, who is a great hunter, often catching young hares bigger than herself, is sufficient deterrent. Sometimes, alas, she kills birds and once or twice, with a puzzled expression in her eyes, she has dumped a small lizard at my feet. Her main job is to keep the mice in subjection and that she does work hard to achieve. They love paper, these small rodents, and can eat their way through plastic containers, too. With the multiplicity of forms coming into the office, cramming the drawers where they are lodged, I have to think of ways to protect them from possible onslaught. Tin boxes are the only mouse-proof containers and they are hard to come by.

In older times post office equipment was more vulnerable to attack than its modern type. Mail-bags were of canvas and made quite a tasty bite for a hungry rat. Even leather travelling cases were not immune. Leave the catch half open and the mice would be in, nesting cosily among the letters. The authorities were quick to see that measures must be taken to protect valuable documents of all kinds from attack by destructive rodents.

The Post Office Archives have a most evocative account of the introduction of cats onto the premises as a means of controlling vermin. By courtesy of these Archives I am tempted to quote at some length from their Information Sheet called 'Cats on the Payroll.'

In September 1868 the Controller of the Money Order Office in London asked the Secretary of the Post Office for authority to pay two shillings per week for the maintenance of three cats. The Secretary's reply reads: 'Three cats may be allowed on probation – they must undergo a test examination and should, I think, be females. It is important that the cats be not overfed and I cannot allow more than one shilling per week for their support – they must depend on the mice for the remainder of their emoluments and if the mice be not reduced in number in six months a further portion of the allowance must be stopped.

A further minute to the Secretary, later in the month, reads:

These directions have been communicated to Tye [the Resident Porter] who will no doubt find means to inform the cats upon what terms they are to be employed and what is expected of them . . . it is hoped that the cat movement will be successful.

On 5 May 1869 the Secretary, having called for a report on the cats, was told

whether influenced by the Secretary's caution that they would under certain contingencies have diminished rations or by a laudable zeal for the service and their own character, cannot clearly be made out, but it is certain that the Cat System has answered exceedingly well, and that the cats have done their duty very efficiently, except as respects one point of the Secretary's order which implied a probable increase to that portion of the Establishment.'

The following suggestion was put to the Secretary:

. . . in the event of a Committee of Inspection being appointed I would suggest that Tye's evidence should be taken as to the test examination. I understand he can explain the reason why the cats have not acted up to orders in the matter of increasing the Establishment.

In 1873 the postmaster at Southampton was refused an allowance of one shilling and ninepence per week for a cat. He protested, saying:

Mr. Wadman, the Guard . . . argues that such a sum would be quite insufficient. He says no nourishment can be derived from rats which reside in the Post Office store-room: that picking such rats, fed as they are upon nothing but Mail Bags, is no better than picking Oakum . . .

He (Mr Wadman) also complains about 'the loss of dignity in carrying the cats' food through the streets in her Majesty's uniform' and demands compensation for this. But no increase was granted.

In 1877 several cat allowances were granted, in Nottingham, Deptford and in the Post Office Headquarters in London. In February 1919 a Report from the Accountant General's Department, Telephone House, London reads:

a few telegrams have been eaten away by mice to such an extent as to be useless. Beyond the inconvenience caused by the mutilation of forms, etc. I have no particular objections but some of the ladies are rather perturbed. How about instituting an office cat?

Later, he appealed: 'at least two cats seem to be necessary . . . '

Questions in the House 1953

On 18th. March 1953 the Assistant Postmaster General was asked, during question time in the House of Commons, 'when the allowance payable for the maintenance of cats in his Department was last raised, what is the total amount involved: what is the present rate per cat in Northern Ireland: and how this compares with the rate in London?' He replied: 'There is, I am afraid, a certain amount of industrial chaos in the Post Office cat world. Allowances vary in different places, possibly according to the alleged efficiency of the animal and other factors. It has proved impossible to organise any scheme for payment by results or output bonus. These servants of the state are, moreover, frequently unreliable, capricious in their duties and liable to prolonged absenteeism . . . There are no post office cats in Northern Ireland. Except for cats at Post Office Headquarters who got the special allowance a few years ago, presumably for prestige reasons, there has been a general wage freeze since July 1918, but there have been no complaints!' The member then asked: 'How does my honourable friend account for the fact that no allowances are payable for cats in Northern Ireland? Is it because the post offices there are more sanitary, and will he say what happens if a cat has kittens? Is there a family allowance payment?' The Assistant Post Master General replied: 'There are no cats in Northern Ireland, I presume, because there are no mice in post office buildings. With regard to the children's allowances I'm afraid there is none. But the Head Postmasters have full discretion to give a maternity grant . . . ' He was then asked by a lady member whether 'this is one of the occasions on which equal pay prevails?' to which he replied 'Equal pay has been accepted both in principle and in practice.'

Celebrity Cats

In December 1964, to the distress of the staff, Tibs, the giant official cat of the Post Office Headquarters Building, who weighed 23 lbs., died, after 14 years' service. His wages had been 2/6d. a week and his office was in the old St. Martin's Refreshment Club in the basement. He had his photograph in the book 'Cockney Cats'.

Famous among Post Office cats of 1968 were Persil, who protected Dial House in Manchester, and Chippy, who looked after the Supplies Department in Bridgwater. Persil sometimes took only two hours to patrol his huge building, but when, in 1968, he had attained 13 years of age, he did take the lift between floors. Chippy's only fault was that he frequently got into one of the railway vans bound for the neighbouring town of Taunton, when his keeper had to go and bring him back.

In April 1971 a strange, obviously lady cat, was observed wandering along the basement corridors and rooms of Post Office Headquarters building, trying to find a suitable place to call 'home'. She was provided with food and milk and very soon produced a litter of five sturdy kittens. One of the male kittens, black and white in colour, was kept for duty at Headquarters. The new post office employee was given the name Blackie and taught to catch mice by his adept mother. Over the years that followed Blackie did a magnificent job in keeping Headquarters mouse-free . . . In June 1983 the Personnel Manager for Post Office Head-quarters, John Roxby, pleaded to the Post Office Pay Group for an increase in Blackie's pay, the Cats' Official Allowance having stood at £1 a week, unreviewed, since 1967. Top level pay talks were quickly held and a pay award of 100% awarded to Blackie and all post office cats.

These extracts show, I think, that the postal authorities were basically humane and certainly had a good sense of humour! The story of Post Office cats, an illustrated history, has been told in a book by Russell Ash – *Dear Cats: The Post Office Letters*.

XXXI
THE RED LETTER-BOX

Looking from the door at the bright red letter-box firmly attached to a solid wooden post at the roadside, I often think what a useful purpose it serves. Every morning postie opens it and deposits the contents on the counter. 'Not much today' he'll say, or 'someone's been busy!' as a whole lot with addresses in the same hand appears. I tie the letters into a bundle and put them into his safe grip. Sometimes I wonder what he's carrying off on the first stage of their journey to . . . Aberdeen, London, Canada, Australia – what news, accounts of events, messages of hope, perhaps of despair. That small letter-box has carried them all in its day. It sits there, so accessible, subject to the ravages of the west wind, the rain, snow and frost. From time to time it gets a much-needed coat of fresh paint.

I remember the letter-boxes in the islands where the birds are allowed to make their home at nesting-time and where benighted travellers stop to read the name of the location and to find they are at least on the map. That happens with our letter-box, too. Young walkers, in the summer, tired from their trek up the hill road, slip off their gigantic packs, peer at the name on the box and slump down for a rest among the flowers on the bank. 'A-b-r-i-a-c-h-a-n' they chant, putting the wrong accent on the wrong syllable and defeated by the sound of 'ch'.

'That must be somewhere.'

'Maybe it's on the map.'

'We'll see later. I'm for a drink.'

'There's not much water left.'

'There's a house in there, behind the hedge.'

'A house?'

'M'm . . .'

Next moment I'm filling water-bottles and pointing out camping-places and receiving thanks with friendly smiles. The letter-box has done its little trick again!

A Victorian rectangular letter-box

In older times letters were often left at inns or other meeting places known to be frequented by the recipient, a sort of unofficial *poste restante* system. I have seen a letter written soon after the battle of Culloden and addressed to its recipient at the Laigh Coffee House, Edinburgh.

After the introduction of the Penny Post there was, of course, a tremendous number of letters written. People had already been asked to provide slots in their front doors to speed the delivery of incoming mail. Now, Post Office officials set about installing boxes for the outward despatch of letters in the streets of the towns and at places on the roadside in the country. France provided the example for this facility. In 1851 Anthony Trollope, then a mere Surveyor's clerk, proposed that the scheme operating in France should be tried out in Jersey. It was. Next year the postmaster in St Helier reported that 'the Roadside letter-boxes work satisfactorily', and in England 'they must be introduced liberally and energetically . . .' In St Peter Port, Guernsey, a hexagonal pillar box 4 feet 8 inches high, erected in 1853, is still in use today.

The first one to appear on the mainland, in that same year, was at Carlisle. Two years later the first boxes were installed in London. They were sturdy, rectangular boxes, about 5 feet in height. After public complaints about the ugly appearance of these boxes an official invitation to submit an improved design was issued to the Department of Science and Art. The result was some very ornate specimens, with intertwined leaves and the Royal Cipher prominently displayed.

Pillar boxes in the county towns, which were emptied less frequently than those in London, were soon found to be inadequate for the ever-increasing amount of mail. A larger size had to be introduced. All these boxes were dark green in colour. In 1874 red was adopted. This made the boxes easily distinguishable. Over the next ten years boxes everywhere were painted red. In France yellow is the preferred colour, in Ireland bright green. Red, as noted earlier, has always been the royal colour in Britain.

As there were many complaints of letters being caught up in the internal structure of the hexagonal boxes and so delayed, the cylindrical, or pillar, shape was re-introduced. Still there were complaints that larger letters and newspapers became lodged in the tops of these new boxes, as garments become lodged in washing-machines today. The posting aperture was thereafter placed a few inches lower in the body of the box. Strangely, it was not until eight years after their introduction that it was realised the boxes did not bear the Royal Cipher nor any indication that they were Post Office property. Thereafter the letters V.R. and the words 'Post Office' were incorporated in the design.

In 1912 the Postmaster General observed that pillar boxes were 'unsightly objects and that in these days of Town Planning and Municipal Aesthetics we ought to show better examples of art applied to postal uses.' Students of the Royal College of Art were invited to submit designs, but the First World War broke out and adoption of any of the designs chosen had to be suspended.

Today our town pillar boxes look very similar to those of close on a hundred years ago, with the addition of a plaque showing the times of collection and, in some cases, a machine

The Author with the letter-box at Abriachan
(John H. Paul Photography)

for buying stamps. In Inverness there are several letter boxes of a different type – set into solid stone walls and bearing the Royal Cipher – V.R. for Victoria. Aberdeen has two Edward VIII pillar boxes. In the Inverness Museum are two old letter-boxes. One, called a Lamp letter-box, has a socket for a lamp attached to the side of the depository for letters. There are other old Post Office artefacts in the Museum – a post horn used on the mail coach, old scales, a hand cart. The interest in all aspects of the history of postal services is such that study groups have been set up covering various facets. One of these is the Letter Box Study Group which keeps updated information and listing of interesting boxes of which there must be many up and down the country. Letter-boxes, like other street furniture – seats, litter bins and so on – are prominent features of a townscape. It's important that their design strikes easy on the eye.

XXXII
COMPUTERS DON'T BITE

As the advent of the millenium drew nearer and nearer, with the brilliance of technology growing brighter and brighter, I began to think seriously about my place in the great scheme of things. I fingered my identity badge. Did this small piece of plastic add anything to my stature? Not really. Most often I forgot to put it on. Postal instructions continued to pour in, their plastic folders cluttering every available shelf and drawer. I perused them before filing them away, but they really contained little relevance to the situations encountered here. The insuring of certain packages to a country in the Middle East was something seldom, if ever, asked for in this particular office.

A video was circulated among the small offices. The sight and sound of all those highly efficient people working away among the forms and documents with which they appeared so alarmingly at ease, only added to one's feeling of inadequacy. Then I remembered – probably these people never had to deal with lost travellers, with road accidents or sudden death, or even with sad folk in need of a listening ear. A reading of the Postmaster's Contract made one realise how fastidiously correct the rules of employment had to be. The rate of compensation for the loss of half a finger, compared to that for the loss of a thumb, in the course of one's work, how could it be calculated? Attendance at meetings of other rural postmasters/mistresses was useful. We could discuss somewhat similar problems, though none of them were quite as rural as us. Most of them had a small shop attached and were familiar with the workings of V.A.T., advertising, consumer protection and other quantities unknown to me. Some friendly conversation over a meal was cheering. Then I got back to my corner, to be greeted by my cat and to change the date-stamp in readiness for the morning.

Passengers on board the Post Bus (The Post Office)

The arrival of Willy-the-Post was always a bright occasion. His never-failing cheerfulness put a smile on the day, as it did for every house he visited on his round. Sometimes he would have a younger man with him, a trainee learning the routine work for future employment as a holiday relief. It's good to know that some younger people are coming into the business. A country round in the Highlands must surely be an attractive proposition. It means early rising, as many jobs do. Once you're away in your little red van, out of the town and up the hill road into the sweet air, the day is yours. You can be sure of a welcome in every house you call at, a laugh and a crack, a hot drink in winter, a cool one in summer, a tractor to pull you out of a snowdrift or a pool of mud. Then you're finished for a long evening of freedom. You may not make a monetary fortune, but who can count the price of glimpsing a pine marten as he flashes into the wood, a fox standing bright-eyed by the road, roe-deer in Tom Fraser's turnips, these are the early morning sightings to be enjoyed at no other time. Later, the buzzards will be on the move, gliding serenely above their prey, and, if it's a lucky day, there may be whoopers on the loch, or heron, or a little grebe.

There are the personal encounters, too, apart from those on the doorstep. The lone bird-watcher whose bike has sprung a puncture may flag the post bus for a lift. A foreign tourist, always forgetting which side to drive on, may well collide with a truck emerging from a croft road. The post bus comes in handy for a pull to clear the way and perhaps the loan of tools from its well-stocked bag. It's all part of the service!

One day our trainee met a couple from Poland who stopped him to ask the way. Their English was halting. He made his explanations as clearly as he could and was for moving on. They wouldn't let him go. They walked round the van, their eyes shining with admiration. The woman pointed to the lettering and ran her fingers round the golden crown. 'Please, what it means, "Royal Mail"? You have letters from the Queen?' That made a good story for his mates!

The days passed happily into summer that year. The children came to borrow books from the library. The holidays brought the usual influx of visitors from far and wide. Avid stamp collectors would stand goggle-eyed as I turned the pages of the stamp book for them.

'You have some of those? What luck! I just need two to complete another set.'

The Scottish standard issue, with the special little lion rampant, was much sought after. And the pound notes were prized.

'We don't see many of them now,' a southerner would say. I began to feel Scotland was 'abroad' to them! People came, as always, looking for their roots. Standing at the gate, they would gaze around at the small tumbled ruins, at the re-built houses, at the modern designs, at the barren fields.

'I guess folks today think maybe more about their houses than about the ground they live on,' one Canadian visitor said, with sadness in his voice. 'I've heard the stories my grandad told, of how it was a handful of earth they took with them across the Atlantic. That was the most precious thing to them, their land.

They could build a house most anywhere. That's what they had to do on arrival, build a house, not out of stone, but out of the trees they had to cut down.'

'Yes. I know what you mean.'

We're gazing now, both of us, at the little fields over the road, with the tumble-down fences, rushes and heather encroaching, where oats and potatoes, roots and pasture would have kept life going along quite happily a century ago. I remembered how one elderly visitor from Ireland, gazing at it a few years ago, had said, with infinite sadness in his voice, 'Oh the lovely valley that's in it!' That's what it was – a 'hanging valley', left behind when the ice slid down into the big hollow below. Alas, now, it was uneconomic to put money into small agricultural units that would each only serve the needs of one family.

I came out of my day-dream. The Canadian was still lost in his. Then – 'Tell me about those clearances' he said. I told him what I knew. It would be a long time in the telling, the whole story.

'But this is not a place that was cleared. This is a place people came to after they were cleared from the fertile glens.'

'So they had to start all over again, from scratch?'

'They did. They carved those fields out of the heather. They worked hard to provide for the next generation.'

'And then the young ones left?'

'They did well. There was always a good school here. And they took jobs in the town or emigrated voluntarily.'

'So now you have a new kind of Highlander.'

'You could say that. We're lucky here. Only two or three of the old families remain, but the newcomers are understanding. They look to the future for their children's sake but they don't ignore the past.'

He is still deep in thought, then he turns to shake my hand.

'My, am I glad you had time to talk to me about all this. I'll be telling them back home. Goodbye now and God speed.' The post office bell rings. Someone had come in by the side gate.

'Goodbye to you. God bless.' I hurry back to the office. A family allowance is due. And there are parcels. A car comes into the yard, reverses, turns, parks. It is not one I recognise. A small lady emerges and stands quietly by the door, as though forming the start of a queue. I finish stamping the parcels and see my customer off. The lady comes in. I know her now. My 'guardian angel' I call her, the person I can call on in any emergency, who can be 'paged' and contacted wherever she may be.

'You're busy' she says, with a warm smile.

So she hasn't come with news of office closures, not with a smile like that. Has she? Or could she be going to discuss the possibility of our becoming a Community Office? I didn't want that. I knew my customers would never remember which days and at what times the office was open. Community offices are open only on certain days and at certain times. What about the retired academic who lived at the top of the hill and came every day to collect his mail, on skis in the winter? There was a road of sorts to his place, but he came down every day. He liked it that way. And our geologist who used to tell people it took him a couple of hours to buy a stamp. How's that, they would say, there must be a long queue! No, no, but by the time I've had a cup of coffee and read the papers the time's up! he'd grin. So – no community office here.

'I was just passing' my lady says 'so I came in to see if there was anything you were needing.'

'Thanks. No, I think everything's all right.'

'You will have heard about the computerisation?'

Computerisation? Dreaded word.

'Er . . . no, not really.'

'Every office is to be on the system. Soon.'

'Oh? Even this one? How soon?'

She smiles again. 'Quite soon, I think. It's not exactly certain yet. They're marvellous machines. Make everything so quick and simple.'

'Quick and simple'. That's it, I thought. That's what machines do. But do we really want everything to be quick and simple? What about the hours, days, months, years those monks on Iona spent on their daily job of producing illuminated manuscripts which are now priceless treasures? One day the machines will produce works of art? And we shall sit back and watch? I come back to the conversation in hand.

'I'm not very handy with machines' I apologise.

'Don't worry. There's nothing to it. You'll see. Goodbye, now. I'm off to the islands today.'

'To the islands? Which ones?'

'To the small ones. Raasay first.' Raasay my well-loved island!

'And they will be computerised?'

'Eventually, yes. Remember the slogan – "computers don't bite"!'

'I'm sure they don't. But I believe they can make mistakes!'

'That's not really their fault. You'll see. Don't worry. See you soon.'

With a wave and a smile she slips into her car and is off. So the millennium and its technology is on the way. But there has been no mention of office closures. Perhaps we can survive!

XXXIII
LINKS WITH THE FUTURE

The imminent arrival of computerisation to the office made me realise that I must forge links with the future. The present had always seemed good enough for me, especially on a warm, blue day in summer, even on an ice-cold one in winter, on every kind of day really. The past held a special kind of fascination for me, as I saw it here, before my eyes, and held it in my hand in the shape of our venerable date-stamp or an old iron griddle on its way to the museum collection.

The future I was leaving in the capable hands of my grand-children. They were all, even the youngest, computer experts, I knew. E-mail, fax machines, the web, the internet, held no mystery or terror for them. They were fluent in the new language of technology, too. Language is another of my loves, but this one holds little attraction. Nevertheless, I began to feel it was incumbent on me to learn the rudiments. Did it have a grammar? Not really, I reckoned, just a plethora of strange words—nouns and verbs made out of them. Thus—to computerise.

At least I could gather some statistics to find out which way the Post Office was going. I had seen signs of competing structures—fleets of vans named 'Northern Express', 'Highland Delivery', 'Pegasus Express', even one calling itself a 'Courier'. I knew the Post Office held no monopoly for parcel delivery. These vehicles were quite impressive but not as smart as our own Parcel Force vans.

The Post Office Archives in London have provided me with much very valuable information about all aspects of the history of the postal service. For the picture of modern times in Scotland I turned to the Scottish Post Office Board in Edinburgh. The Board covers the four branches—Royal Mail, Post Office Counters, Parcel Force and Subscription Services (telemarketing). In a foreword to its information brochure it states: 'The

Links with the Future

Post Office . . . has a long tradition of strong social commitment, particularly to rural areas.' That statement cheered me at once. Then I read that 'over 92% of first class letters posted for delivery in Scotland are delivered next day. There are over 2,000 post offices in the country, with 3.5 million customers a week. Parcel Force handles 140 million parcels a year, its world-wide network covering 239 countries. In 1995-96 Royal Mail handled 17.5 billion items of mail'. The mind shivers!

The technology used in processing the mail is now of the highest order. Looking ahead the report says: 'In the not-too-distant future delivery postmen will be able to come to work and find their mail already sorted, house by house, into correct walk sequence.'

The Post Office Act of 1969 changed the status of the Post Office from that of a Government Department to that of a Public Corporation, and a Post Office Users' National Council was set up as an independent watch-dog. There are Post Office Advisory Councils so that customers' complaints and advice can be heeded. Consultation with these bodies always precedes changes in prices or service. Consumer protection is clearly a priority in the management of the Post Office, the Royal Mail Customer Service always at hand.

What cheered me most in the Board's report was the account of the efforts made to oversee environmental issues. Investment projects are required to include a detailed environmental impact statement. There are trials on ways of reducing the impact of road vehicles by using fuel oil made from rape seed, low sulphur diesel, electric-powered vans and the VW Ecomatic vehicle, designed to minimise noise and exhaust gases. Parcel Force has fitted excessive-speed limiters on its large trucks to save fuel.

In 1995 a collection and recycling scheme for Christmas cards run by the Post Office resulted in the equivalent of over 5,000 trees being planted. The reduction in landfill costs meant that savings were used to plant 2,760 trees in community forests throughout the United Kingdom.

Post Office Counters conducted environmental surveys with suppliers to identify their level of commitment to care of the environment. They also continued to identify ways of reducing waste and minimising harmful environmental effects in the production of its stationery and leaflets. I was particularly glad to read this as I had always thought small offices such as ours would benefit from a reduction in the number of leaflets received. The rain-forests of the world would benefit, too.

Parcel Force has developed a new type of label to replace the current four-part document, thus reducing by 80% the amount of paper used per year. Paper from well-managed forests is used, forests which have three trees replanted for every one felled.

The Post Office Community Involvement Programme has given major financial support to the Groundwork Trust's 'Bright-site' which seeks to improve the built environment in marginal areas. The Post Office staff secondment programme has provided skilled professional support to the National Trust and the British Trust for Conservation. The Post Office was also a founding corporate partner of 'Forum for the Future', a new charity set up by leading environmentalists.

All this information heartened me greatly. I had always been aware that I was part, even though a very small part, of an organisation which had always considered itself to be a service. This meant that its primary objective was a commitment to its users. Now I could more fully appreciate the extent of this commitment. I could appreciate even more fully its involvement in the over-riding consideration of reducing harm to the environment.

Its support of the arts I had always admired. So often one sees the words 'Post Office' in the list of sponsors for festivals, such as the Edinburgh Book Festival, when well-known writers are engaged to talk about their work. Books, too, have been supported, and the Post Office film unit has produced valued documentaries. In the children's Letter-writing Competition this year, on the theme 'Applying for my dream job', a record 500,000 young people, of whom 34,000 were from Scotland, responded. As one newspaper report said 'Despite hi-tech advances in communications, it appears that the art of letter-writing is alive and well.'

Links with the Future

Artists have been encouraged to submit designs for new issues of pictorial stamps and over the years a collection of work of real merit has appeared. Posters, too, have been designed by artists of distinction. In these many, largely unsung, ways the Post Office has contributed to the cultural well-being of the country.

I am glad to have been involved with it, as part of a family concern, for close on forty years. And it's good to know that there are family members in the wings who have been part of the scene, too—a daughter who first stepped into the breach when the postmaster and his wife were temporarily laid low, to deliver the Christmas mails, and a grandaughter, now also a student, who date-stamped her own hands as a five-year-old and is now adept at date-stamping forms and dealing happily with customers as a holiday relief. That's how it goes in rural post offices.

It's really quite a unique position, that of a country postmaster. New types of job are being created now, in our age of telecommunication, but this one goes back for close on three hundred years, to the days of the Post-boys, the runners, then the mail coaches, now the steamer, the train, the plane. In all these times there was a Receiver and a Distributer of mail, a man at the centre, who saw, as we do today, beyond the paper-work, the customers, the human beings and their need to communicate. There's a good feeling of solidarity being part of a long tradition of service. The outcry is loud when a small office in a remote area is threatened with closure. That's surely proof, if one were needed, that the service is greatly valued.

SOURCES OF INFORMATION

Jean Farrugia and Tony Gammons, *Carrying British Mails* (1980), from which the pictures on pp. 543, 558, 593, 597 and 608 are taken.

Dimitry Kandaouroff, *Collecting Postal History*.

Dr James Mackay, *Islands Postal History* and other publications.

Information Sheets from Post Office Archives, Freeling House, London.

The Post Office, Scottish Post Office Board.

Penrose Hay, *Post Office Recollections, Inverness 1885*.

C.W. Hill, *Scotland in Stamps*.

A.R.B. Haldane, *Three Centuries of Scottish Posts*.